Contemporary Religious Ideas

Contemporary Religious Ideas

Bibliographic Essays

G. Edward Lundin
Anne H. Lundin

1996
LIBRARIES UNLIMITED, INC.
Englewood, Colorado

Libraries Unlimited, Inc.
P.O. Box 6633
Englewood, CO 80155-6633
1-800-237-6124

Project Editor: Kevin W. Perizzolo
Copy Editor: Tama J. Serfoss
Proofreader: Jason Cook
Interior Design and Layout: Pamela J. Getchell
Indexer: Nancy Fulton

Library of Congress Cataloging-in-Publication Data

Contemporary religious ideas : bibliographic essays / G. Edward Lundin
    and Anne H. Lundin [editors].
    xxxiv, 538 p. 17x25 cm.
    Includes bibliographical references and indexes.
    ISBN 0-87287-679-9
    1. Religions.   2. Religions--Bibliography.   3. Religions--Study
and teaching.   I. Lundin, G. Edward.   II. Lundin, Anne H., 1944- .
BL80.2..C596   1995
016.291--dc20   95-24234
                                                                CIP

Contents

Part 2
The Literature of Liberation

6 Twenty-Five Years of African American Religious Literature

7 Latin American Liberation Theology

Part 3
The Literature of Teaching the Faiths

Foreword

The Rev. G. Edward Lundin and his twelve contributors to *Contemporary Religious Ideas* know how to do theology; and, even more important, they know what theology does for us. This book is one of the most ecumenical studies I've seen in my nearly thirty years of ministry. *Contemporary Religious Ideas* fulfills as it exemplifies the dynamics of ministry—imparting the knowledge of the Word to the world. The authors do this by understanding so well and communicating so clearly the missions of the global village church, synagogue, mosque, or ashram. No other book or books, including the magisterial *Encyclopedia of Religion* have done a better job of introducing the history and practice of world religions and assessing the literature that defines and articulates them.

I wish I would have had this book on my desk years ago when I assumed command of, and responsibility for, the Navy Chaplain Training Program. I shall strongly recommend that the one hundred or so Navy chaplains under my command be given a copy. These chaplains are called to minister to servicemen and women coming from a variety of faith traditions, the glorious diversity of the world's religions. *Contemporary Religious Ideas* provides essential (I am tempted to say invaluable) information about the world's religions—Christianity (Protestant and Roman Catholic), Judaism, Islam, Buddhism, Taoism, and Hinduism—through these carefully edited and clearly written essays. Each essay gives readers the benefits of the experience and evaluations of a leading authority about her or his subject.

My chaplains' needs for information for their sea-going congregations are no different from the needs of their counterparts in worshipping communities who serve land-bound congregations. *Contemporary Religious Ideas* breaks down any notion of a religious enclave. Too often we fail to recognize or resist acknowledging how one religious system relates to another. These essays dispel that fog.

Each essay includes a wealth of information and commentary you will look for in vain in any other single work. *Contemporary Religious Ideas* is an invaluable reference book and an equally worthy history of and commentary on the human search for Divine Being. The richness of worship, which re-enacts and manifests theological insights, shines through these individual essays. The contributing authors comprehensively review the major tenets and texts of the world religions against a carefully articulated historical and liturgical background. If they had stopped there, it would easily be worth the price of admission. But each essay takes us further by also identifying and analyzing the major critical studies that spread the zeal and hope of the faith traditions they comment on.

Contemporary Religious Ideas belongs in every church, synagogue, seminary and community library, and certainly every college and university library should include this volume in their reference collection. In using *Contemporary Religious Ideas*, readers will enter the vast universe of religious beliefs and practices throughout the world. This collection is a testament of faith in the power of inspiration to understand and to express the most profound beliefs about faith and spirit, praxis and polity, time and eternity, creation and Creator.

Enjoy your voyage!

Benny J. Hornsby
Captain, Chaplain Corps
The United States Navy

Director of Domestic and International
Chaplain Training

Preface

Contemporary Religious Ideas is designed to help church/synagogue librarians as well as public/college librarians assist readers in identifying, locating, and assessing books, tapes, films, and articles on religion. Charged with the responsibility of ministering to, and addressing the needs of, their clients, librarians will find *Contemporary Religious Ideas* an essential resource in their professional library reference collection. *Contemporary Religious Ideas* includes twelve chapters devoted to the world's leading religious and related issues and problems—from classic Christian devotions to the theology of ecosystems. *Contemporary Religious Ideas* was designed to meet the needs of two groups of readers: first, library and information specialists who guide users to the most helpful resources on a given subject, and, second, the individual reader who may want or require further information on a specific subject (such as Islam or Liberation Theology) when a church or synagogue librarian is unavailable. Each chapter will give librarians and their patrons a comprehensive, up-to-date evaluation of these and a host of other subjects. Each chapter is a handy, user-friendly guide to the vast body of materials, print, on a particular religion, belief system, or religious topic.

Contemporary Religious Ideas is divided into three sections, reflecting the ecumenical ethos which informs and inspires this collection. The first section, "The Literature of Knowing the Faiths," begins appropriately with the major faith traditions of the world. In "World Religions," Edward Hughes, in the first essay in this section, provides an historical and bibliographic survey emphasizing both western and nonwestern faith communities. Moving from the foundations that Hughes supplies, Rabbi Peter Haas then turns to the major tenets of Judaism, pre- and post-Holocaust theologies. Under five rubrics, Haas evaluates leading texts and themes giving readers an essential introduction to Jewish heritage, thought, and practice. Exploring the rich Judeo-Christian backgrounds of Roman Catholicism, Father Michael Tracey takes readers on a guided tour of the most essential sources, print and non-print alike, of contemporary Roman Catholic spirituality. Then Professors Aminul Islam and Gorden Welty survey reference materials, critical books, articles, and media central to a knowledge of Islam. Given the growing importance of Islam worldwide, Islam and Welty's historical and bibliographic survey will be of great value to librarians in locating information for their patrons.

The second section, "The Literature of Liberation," contains four essays that define and identify key movements, audiences, and beliefs that have dynamically evolved from the traditions surveyed in section one. Starting with a crucial topic in liberation theology, the Reverend Shelley Davis Finson specifically focuses on gender issues in her "Resources for Doing Feminist Liberation Theology." Davis Finson assesses an engagingly wide range of sources that recognize and restore women's centrality in faith traditions and rituals, church leadership, ethics and spirituality. Expanding still further the concept of liberation, Father Cyprian Davis, O.S.B., describes the origins and achievements of the Black church in America, including the thought and practice of early Black church leaders and the estimable contributions of Dr. Martin Luther King Jr. In his essay on "The Literature of Liberation," Phillip Berryman analyzes the liberation theology that has revolutionized the church in Latin America, paying careful attention to the major texts and contexts behind the religious roots of rebellion. In the final essay on liberation themes, Kathleen O'Gorman investigates those religious issues that support human stewardship and responsibility for our world—the environment (or eco-system) and God's original blessing in Creation. In "Eco-theology: Religion's Recovery of Ecological Perspective," O'Gorman explores those topics and the resources on them (books, articles, audiovisuals) that shape and enlarge our understanding of the covenantal role we have with Creation.

The third section of *Contemporary Religious Ideas* is "The Literature of Teaching the Faith." In the four essays included, contributors address the problem of communicating and incorporating the values of the preceding chapters by focusing particularly on education, special ministries, devotional resources, and church libraries. In "Religious Education," Kathleen O'Gorman stresses the importance of religious education and its invaluable place in the faith development of the worshipping community. Logically following O'Gorman's discussion, the Reverend Elaine Tiller supplies critical information on an issue which, by the grace of Divine Being, affects us all in "The Gift of Long Life." Her chapter persuasively advocates that we pursue a caring ministry to older members of congregations who oftentimes were the lifeblood and leaders of the church in which they worship today; Tiller's evaluation of numerous resources will help any church or synagogue to recognize and promote the contributions of senior members. In his essay titled, "Devotional Classics for Church Libraries," the Reverend William Yount provides an enormous educational service to readers of *Contemporary Religious Ideas* by paraphrasing and summarizing ten classics of Christian devotion, such as St. Augustine's *Confessions*, Bunyan's *Pilgrim's Progress* and *The Institutes* of John Calvin. He identifies and assesses an essential group of resources for accessing these historical/classical testaments that should be indispensable to all students of spirituality. In the final chapter of this section, Joyce White, the eminent former President of the Church and Synagogue Library Association, identifies the materials needed to establish and organize a church or synagogue library. White articulates and evaluates procedures for constructing the right learning environment, administering library collections, incorporating those library resources into the total program of the church or synagogue, and promoting reading as a source of wisdom and insight for all seekers—young and old, men and women, teachers and students, clergy and laypersons—in the community of faith.

The main contribution of *Contemporary Religious Ideas,* then, is to meet the needs of a diverse group of readers. I hope that librarians entrusted with religious literature will find much of value here in guiding their congregations into a deeper and more mature knowledge of their own and others' faith traditions. Further, I hope that library information specialists will find this collection valuable in answering the wide variety of questions their patrons may ask on religious topics. But my ultimate hope is that *Contemporary Religious Ideas* will significantly contribute to the spirit of ecumenism that unites us all as male and female, Christian and Muslim and Jew, believers of Eastern faiths and followers of Western traditions. Through ecumenism we can all appreciate that what unites us, what characterizes our humanity, is far more important than what divides us; our life in the faith, our journey on the pilgrim's way, brings us all closer to Divine Being. Whatever our faith traditions, whatever our church-synagogue-mosque affiliation, whatever sacred or inspired text we study, we read to find Divine Presence. I pray that *Contemporary Religious Ideas* will faithfully and happily accompany readers on their journey.

G. E. L.

Acknowledgments

I wish to thank all those friends and colleagues who encouraged me in the origin and development of this anthology of essays on religious issues and topics called *Contemporary Religious Ideas.*

Dr. Philip C. Kolin, Professor of English, the University of Southern Mississippi; Mr. William Griffin, Former Religion Editor of *Publishers Weekly*; Dr. John Hutchison, Danforth Professor of Philosophy of Religion (Emeritus) at Claremont Graduate Schools; Dr. Rosemary Radford Reuther, Professor of Theology at Garrett Evangelical Theological Seminary; Dr. David G. Buttrick, Professor of Theology and Homiletics at Vanderbilt University; and, Mr. William Gentz, Former President of the Church and Synagogue Library Association.

I wish to thank all of you for your recommendations, suggestions, and gracious endorsement of our labors. The original vision which I hoped this book would fulfill was made manifest through the encouragement, counsel, and guidance of these individuals. Through their imprimaturs and recommendations I was able to secure the rewarding contributions that are offered for your greater knowledge and understanding. I am grateful to God for my friendship with Philip C. Kolin whose wit and wisdom inspired and sustained me throughout this project.

I want to thank Dr. Anne H. Lundin of the Graduate School of Library and Information Science at the University of Wisconsin for the research and energy she contributed to this volume during its earliest stages.

My heartfelt gratitude goes to the congregation I serve, St. Elizabeth's Episcopal Church in Collins, Mississippi for their prayers, love, and encouragement. I have experienced the Household of God in their fellowship and their love has sustained me. I will be eternally grateful.

I express my thanks to the Bishop of the Episcopal Diocese of Mississippi, the Right Reverend Alfred Marble Jr., for his encouragement and support. His vision for the Church and for the People of God is expansive and inclusive. We are called, in his words, "to respect the dignity of every person and to work for social justice." I have attempted to build on his spirit of ecumenism in this book.

Additionally, I am indebted to the administrators of the University of Southern Mississippi for encouraging me in my research and writing over the course of this volume's completion. In particular, I wish to thank Dr. Gloria Slick, Director of Field Experiences; Dr. James Schnur, Dean of the College of Education and Psychology; Dr. G. David Huffman, Vice President for Academic Affairs; and Dr. Aubrey K. Lucas, President of the University of Southern Mississippi.

I am grateful to my editor, Mr. Kevin W. Perizzolo, for his guidance and patience, which were so necessary to the completion and enhancement of this book. I am also grateful to Pamela J. Getchell, my typesetter, and all the other staff at Libraries Unlimited for their help and encouragement.

Finally, I want to acknowledge my belief in God's grace and favor, which have sustained me through the years, but particularly in the preparation of this book. Without God, nothing of value endures; with God, all things are possible, even *Contemporary Religious Ideas*. Thank you, God, for everything.

Enjoy,

G. Edward Lundin

An Introduction to Contemporary Religious Ideas by The Rev. G. Edward Lundin

"In the beginning was the Word" (John 1:1). Perhaps no other Scriptural pronouncement reverberates with more meaning than this for today's world. Whether we follow Christ, Mohammed, Moses, or Confucius, we begin with the Word, for truth, for guidance, for consolation, and for learning. *Contemporary Religious Ideas* rests upon the Word, the most elementary yet quintessential unit of meaning and message in our society. The Word has profound significance to members of all religious communities/organizations, for it is the Word that is the basis of the words that teach and inspire followers.

The central office in charge of getting the words out, so to speak, is the church, synagogue, or mosque library. The library is the repository of official texts for studying, and ultimately leading, a religious life. The church or synagogue library is teacher, mentor, counselor, reference guide, and clearinghouse, helping readers understand the Word, the written collection of beliefs that each of us holds central to the perfection of our faith.

Each of the bibliographic essays in this collection values the Word as a means of spiritual enlightenment. Ultimately, the Word, and the study of the Word, function in teaching and promoting faith—through homilies and exhortations, critical and philosophical studies, histories, guides, biographies, articles, and monographs. The essays provide a guide to the Word in a variety of religious/cultural contexts. Starting with the primacy of the Word, each essay takes readers on a journey to the words of people (the works of art, bibliographies, histories, articles, and theological studies) that stimulate further growth and extended religious enlightenment. In sum, church and synagogue librarians function today in a special kind of discipleship. Their task is to gather, evaluate, discern, and disseminate the messages in, through, and about the Word. In so doing, each bibliographic essay here acknowledges the crucial job of church librarians and assists them in accomplishing their goals for their congregations.

Part one, "The Literature of Knowing the Faiths," discusses major world religions in four separate essays. The lead essay is, appropriately, "World Religions" by Edward Hughes, a scholar of comparative religions. Hughes addresses one of the most fundamental questions posed by students of religion: Why should we explore religious belief systems that, by definition, are alien to our experience and potentially critical of our own religion? Often, individuals from a Western faith tradition feel a primary need to be more committed to or more knowledgeable about the doctrines, practices, and history of their own faith.

However, it is foolhardy, in light of the religious-cultural upheavals of this last decade of the twentieth century, to say we cannot afford the time or energy to explore another's faith. Knowledge of another's religious traditions is a matter of undeniable urgency. We may try to renounce that urgency and retreat behind the cloistered walls of our own faith traditions, but insularity dulls or prejudices the mind and leaves unanswered questions that believers need to confront—questions that those outside our faith traditions want to learn more about. And, paradoxically, asking questions about someone else's belief system can shed light on our own.

The two worst responses a true believer can offer to someone who asks "why?" are (a) you wouldn't understand, and (b) unless you believe my way, you are doomed to wander in ignorance to the peril of your eternal soul. Professor Hughes urges all believers to inquire objectively into other religious traditions in a "new cosmopolitan spirit," a spirit that is brave enough to assert one's faith without defensiveness and is genuinely respectful of other traditions, to study and discuss those beliefs without condescension or censure. He emphasizes that scholarship in comparative religions has moved beyond the smugness of eighteenth- and nineteenth-century scholars who investigated other cultures and faiths. These scholars judged all other religions as inferior to Christianity because their cultural expression was different from, hence less than, Christianity's. Such arrogant parochialism and sectarianism only diminished the value that these faith traditions could have for other cultures.

Theological imperialism has been challenged and, we hope, unseated. Religious exclusivism is both bankrupt and self-defeating. Faithful study of religion, however, can give meaning and power to people in their daily lives as well as in the larger context of existence; there can be no eschaton without the quotidian. Ultimately, knowledge of world religions is a necessary part of our own firmly held beliefs in a divinely-sanctioned moral order. What is needed among students of religion, therefore, is the ability to identify and put aside one's own religious and cultural biases, and the ability to empathize with—to describe and step inside—other cultures and faith expressions.

Hughes's essay provides a rationale for the study of world religions and an extensive survey of appropriate works to study in these topics. As a scholar and bibliographer of world religions, Hughes provides an invaluable guide—a *vade mecum*—to major faith traditions and the resources available to understand these traditions. His survey helpfully describes and reviews these works, separating them into those essential for initial study and those that provide a more in-depth and comprehensive assessment. His essay on world religions sets the tone for *Contemporary Religious Ideas*, because while belief is universal, understanding must come from studying "particular beliefs, at particular times, in particular places." Hughes challenges us to explore other faith traditions, to expand our knowledge, and to free ourselves through the power and consolation of learning how another believer confronts self, the world, and the eternal.

Following Hughes's essay on world religions is Rabbi Peter Haas's careful survey of resources on Judaism, one of the world's oldest religions. In "Contemporary Jewish Literature," Haas explores a complex and diverse faith tradition in highly readable, informative and comprehensive terms. Employing the same rigorous standards of evaluation as Hughes, Haas encourages us to step inside the traditions and practice of Judaism to appreciate the dominant themes, dynamics, and tensions of the faith of the Hebrew testament.

Of central significance is Haas's discussion of the most horrific fact in Jewish existence—the Holocaust. Haas discusses, from a theological perspective, the impact of war on families and on politics. According to Haas, the Holocaust solidified and energized disparate and diverse movements in the Jewish community, enabling the formation of the Jewish nation of Israel. While Zionists had been working to establish a Jewish state for some time, it was the horrors of World War II that provided the catalyst for creating Israel, which was founded in 1947 when the British departed from Turkish Palestine. Haas explains the relationship between the formation of the nation of Israel and the evolution and assertion of Jewish identity. He provides helpful background information on the question of residency: Can one live in dispersed regions such as the U.S.A. and be a faithful Jew, or does fidelity require physical residence in Israel?

Including significant sources on the Jewish experience in America, Haas demonstrates how the values of culture often pull against avowed beliefs and practices. Resources explaining the roots of this conflict are divided into two sections, "Jews by Choice" and "Spirituality." In "Jews by Choice," Haas discusses conversion to Judaism, which is an increasingly important subject because of the growing number of marriages between Jews and non-Jews. Haas estimates that fully one-half of all Jewish weddings in the United States are between Jews and non-Jews. Because the Jewish faith is realized through ritual observance in the home, the incompatibility between faithful practitioner and nonfaithful nonpractitioner is evident. The books, articles, and other bibliographic materials Haas evaluates offer church and synagogue librarians a vital starting point for investigating these issues.

In "Jews by Choice," Haas presents the case for conversion and an appreciation of the complexity inherent in integrating different faith traditions. In "Spirituality," Haas delineates the differences between mainstream Christian and Jewish spirituality. Finally, Haas investigates how Judaism comes to terms with both the aspirations and official recognition of women. While Jewish women are central to the daily practice and ritual observance of Jewish law and customs, Judaism's patriarchal culture has in the past restricted the full leadership potential of women in the rabbinate. Haas offers a learned yet readable introduction to leading issues in Judaism today and a review of the resources necessary to explore all of these issues in depth.

In chapter 3, "Catholic Spirituality for 'Everyperson,'" Father Michael Tracey, who directs the Newman Center of the University of Southern Mississippi, surveys the major topics and resources of Catholic spirituality. According to Tracey, Catholics see society as a "sacrament" of God, a set of ordered relationships, governed by both justice and love, that reveal, however imperfectly, the presence of God. The Catholic experience is filled with images of a loving God, the importance of community, institutional hierarchy, devout ritual and ceremony, and devotion to and reverence for those who have been part of their rich tradition. Tracey then defines and describes that tradition through clear and effective examples and describes the resources that reflect the diverse richness of the Catholic imagination as it relates to spirituality. Without either simplifying or complicating Catholic spirituality, Tracey isolates the various factors contributing to this diversity: the growth of lay movements, small Christian communities, the expanding role of Scripture, diverse forms of prayer styles, the impact of behavioral sciences, social consciousness, evolving marriage and family lifestyles, movement from a Fall-Redemption perspective to a Creation-centered motif, and expanded ministries for the laity. These beliefs and practices help make Catholic spirituality a diverse and rich faith tradition.

Catholic spirituality is as diverse and unique as each person's journey to God. This diverse spirituality includes lay ministry, psychology and religion, contemplation and action, feminine and masculine liberation, and the use of journey, story, and small-group methods of worship and instruction.

Completing a bibliographic troika of the world's most populous religions surveyed in *Contemporary Religions Ideas* is Gordon Welty and Aminul Islam's essay, "Islam," which provides an historical review of the development of Islam and a clear view of its present tenets. Welty and Islam, professors of sociology and anthropology, are keen observers of comparative religion. Unlike Judaism or Catholicism, Islam is inadequately understood as one of the world's great religions. Welty and Islam describe—through example and precept—the Five Pillars of Islam, the core of Islamic devotion and the common bond of faith and practice among the wide-ranging followers of Islam in Asia, India, the Middle East, and Africa. Evaluating pertinent histories and guides, Welty and Islam trace shifts of power within Islam, Islamic influence on art and architecture, Islam's wars with the Crusaders and the Mongol hordes of Genghis Khan, and the development of the Ottoman Empire. Receiving special attention is Islam's influence on Europe and the Indian subcontinent and the background behind the clash between Sunni (orthodox) and Shi'ite (partisans or opposers of orthodoxy) branches of Islam.

Of great interest, too, is Welty and Islam's discussion of Sufism in this chapter. If Islam is little understood in the West, Sufism is even less well known or understood; moreover, it is not often included in discussions of Islam. The authors explain with clarity and authority Sufi mysticism, thought, art, poetry, and wisdom. In their chapter, Welty and Islam also investigate materials about the two heresies of Islam: (1) renunciation of faith, or (2) conversion to another faith, and the movements within the Islamic world embodying these heresies, the Ahmadiyya Movement and the Baha'i Movement.

The *Shari'a* (Islamic Law) holds that there are two ways a Muslim can renounce the faith: *Ridda*, converting from Islam to another religion, and *Irtidad*, falling from Islam into unbelief. Either of these forms of apostasy is considered to be a very serious matter by Muslims. (p. 153)

The Ahmadiyya and the Baha'i movements combine elements of unbelief and conversion to another religion. Labeled as apostates by Islamic law and devout Muslims, followers of these movements are persecuted and frequently put to death.

In every part of this essay, whether presenting history, form, influence or struggle, Welty and Islam offer ample direction, through references to histories and other guides, to illuminate a religion whose passion demands an understanding in today's world.

Part two, "The Literature of Liberation," offers three essays, focusing on various contemporary belief systems devoted to this key theological concept, religious topic, or issue. In "Feminist Liberation Theology," the Reverend Shelly Davis Finson, a professor of theology at the Atlantic School of Theology in Halifax, Nova Scotia, analyzes titles in an extensive bibliographic overview of the feminist liberation literature from the last twenty years. Finson defines feminist liberation theology as an attempt to challenge the foundations of Western religion and theology. Its basis reflects the masculine experience as well as the feminine. Claiming that the trend is revolutionary because it exposes and challenges the patriarchal bias of Western faith traditions, Finson explores such issues as sexism in the church, feminist re-readings of the Bible and liturgical texts, inclusive language, sexual ethics, marriage and divorce, and sex and power. In addition, Finson devotes several sections of her essay to ways of teaching theology to meet the needs of the growing number of women seminarians; creative ways of perceiving spirituality based on women's experiences; the debate over the ordination of women; writing women back into religious history; the contribution of women to homiletics; and pastoral care by women for women.

Finson's research spans many denominations, including Judaism and such non-Christian beliefs as witchcraft. She also emphasizes the importance and relevance of feminist liberation theory to all minority groups, including women of color and gay and lesbian believers. Indeed, while much liberation literature of the last twenty years has been written by white, Western women, Finson has not neglected materials pertaining to women of the Third World. She usefully includes a wide variety of print and audiovisual materials.

Liberation, of course, is not the exclusive concern of women. People of color have also professed the theological urgency to include liberation and identity. Explaining these topics, Fr. Cyprian Davis, a Benedictine monk and expert on black Roman Catholic spirituality, provides an in-depth view of African American spirituality in his "African American Religious Literature." Davis's essay invites comparison with those by Father Michael Tracey and Shelly Davis Finson for the light they shed on various reflections of Roman Catholicism. Davis admirably meets his own stated goal of accounting for the significance of African American spirituality by providing "ample evidence that the black church is still one of the most potent elements in the African American community." Davis also cogently argues that the influence of the African American church is both widespread and fruitful.

What first concerns Davis is documenting, summarizing, and evaluating the wealth of different (and conflicting) materials—books, articles, monographs, and primary documents—dealing with the heritage, the roots of black spirituality. He turns next to the political and social implications of black spirituality and so sketches in the history of blacks in Protestant and Roman Catholic faith communities. Interweaving artful summaries of the chief biographies of leading black clergy in his discussion, Davis helps readers to learn about and understand the individuals responsible for the achievements of faith in the black community. One of Davis's many strengths is that he does not simplify the cultural context of black spirituality; instead, he lucidly introduces the dynamic and diverse forces shaping black religion.

Critical to any study of black spirituality are the accomplishments of Dr. Martin Luther King Jr. Appropriately, therefore, one of Fr. Davis's most significant sections is "The Legacy of Dr. Martin Luther King Jr." Succinctly yet thoroughly, Davis reviews the biographies, bibliographies, and critical literature on Dr. King. So extensive is the literature on this black churchman that David Garrow has already assembled eighteen volumes of commentary on King's accomplishments. Dr. King's genius, his faith and witness, and his martyrdom influenced race relations and civil rights in contemporary American society as no other black churchman had ever done. Fr. Davis presents literature that amplifies the social and political legacy left by Dr. King, and he restores the emphasis on Dr. King as a man of deep and life-giving faith in God. Davis concludes his chapter with a survey of research on black muslims and blacks of other faiths.

In "Latin American Liberation Theology," Phillip Berryman surveys the recent political, religious, and military movements in which this theology most fervently took root. Mr. Berryman is an author and translator who writes about Central and South America based upon his experience as a missionary in those regions. His brief historical sketch shows how the concerns of Central and South American citizens have generated a theological movement that brings the life of God and the mission of the Church into daily life. Latin American liberation theology emerged from the pastoral concerns priests were hearing about and witnessing in some of the poorest regions of the world. The combination of poverty and military repression created a climate in which people cried out for redemption, for deliverance, and for liberation.

Priests schooled in theology written from a Third-World perspective saw an opportunity to communicate the reality of God's love and the possibility of spiritual empowerment to the disenfranchised and dispirited peasants and workers of Central and South America. Vatican II, with its emphasis on expanding roles for laypersons in the life of the Church seemed to provide encouragement for ministry to the poor and disenfranchised. Because of the strong commitment of liberation theology to the plight of the poor, detractors characterize it as thinly-veiled

Marxism. In fact, some apologists for liberation theology use the language of class struggle to dramatize the suffering of the disenfranchised and their repression by the powerful.

Berryman presents the current tensions and polarities that liberation theology confronts: rich vs. poor; the theology of developed peoples vs. that of "nondeveloped" peoples; hierarchy vs. community; orthodoxy vs. heterodoxy; the Vatican hierarchy vs. worker-priests; Church doctrine vs. grassroots experiences; passivity vs. activity; formal debate vs. praxis (theology informed by reflection on experience); neutrality toward the powerful vs. advocacy for the poor; faith for dying vs. faith for living; institutions vs. people. Drawing on his ten years as a missionary in Central and South America, Berryman witnessed the tensions about which he writes; he has interviewed or worked with many of the writers and theologians he cites. His essay supplies the historical context for understanding the development of this grassroots theology; he also evaluates the extensive resources enabling readers to appreciate the contributions and impact of liberation theology.

The essays in the third section, "Teaching the Faiths," logically follow from those on liberation, for it is only when we are free to think and to act that we can successfully impart that religious wisdom to others. Religious wisdom and spiritual truths emerge from the rich soil of human experience; they are grounded in personal understanding and a perception of divine action in our lives. We can't teach what we haven't experienced. Witness to truth has greater impact than knowledge of subject matter.

The essay, "Eco-theology: Religion's Recovery of Ecological Perspective" by Kathleen O'Gorman, a professor of Christian education and religious studies at Loyola University of New Orleans, explores yet another manifestation of theology, "eco-theology," or freeing nature as part of God's creation. In brief, O'Gorman's thesis is that a growing number of specialists within the scientific community are initiating collaboration with theologians in order to more fully understand and describe the natural world. Conversely, more and more theologians are recognizing the importance of scientific literacy in rendering credible and inclusive interpretations of their religious traditions. The chapter introduces literature coming out of the scientific enterprise that allows for discussions of divine presence. It then presents the work of theologians who seek to incorporate ecological perspectives in their reflections and research. In brief, the chapter represents the beginnings of a resolution in the centuries-old rift between sacred and scientific research. The chapter is animated by a theological vision that recognizes the spiritual dimension (at least, potentially) of the scientific enterprise, as it simultaneously asserts the primacy of the natural world in any theological reflection. O'Gorman raises the central question of her essay: How can modern believers restore balance and harmony to our relations with the natural order? Drawing upon the resources of contemporary science, O'Gorman describes two kinds of bridge-building that are taking place: first, science and theology are one in their attempts to present the Divine Source of Creation. The language of science suggests the *mysterium tremendum* (the Divine Presence) and the language of theology employs the metaphors of science. Second, the insights of science are causing theologians and other believers to see humanity as part of a matrix of creation rather than the premier link in the great chain of being. As O'Gorman points out, devastation and profit-oriented development in one area affects natural systems in all areas of God's created world.

O'Gorman's insights exhort us to question our stewardship of creation and to suspect the morality of any short-term gain that compromises long-term devotion to environmental well-being. The challenge is for believers to re-visit God's Church and to profess and commit to reverence for all of Creation. If we see all of Creation as God's House, should we not proclaim boldly with the psalmist, "Zeal for God's house has consumed me"?

O'Gorman evaluates numerous resources—both print and film media—available to young adult and adult study groups. These guides present the problems created by contemporary lifestyles—lifestyles that deplete limited natural resources. But beyond presentation of the problem, these educational materials suggest constructive ways to respond to the environmental calamities of our era. In other words, the books and films that O'Gorman cites not only lead the student into but also out from the wilderness. Wisely, O'Gorman's chapter suggests a means of leaving the polluted forest and arriving at a place that respects and promotes the connectedness of all creation.

Kathleen O'Gorman (who also contributed the preceding essay on "Eco-theology") contributes another essay titled, "Religious Education: Contemporary Theory and Practice." O'Gorman reviews the literature that both reflects and shapes contemporary theory and practice of religious education within a Christian framework. She begins with a set of texts animated by Enlightenment and Protestant traditions, which assigned a spiritual and moral dimension to formal education, and moves from this generalized discussion to a survey of the field in its explicit modes of practice within various Catholic and Protestant contexts. A primary emphasis in the works selected relates to the interplay of education sponsored by religious institutions and education practiced in various cultural settings—an interaction in which each form functions as critic and resource for the other. Overall, the chapter sketches the dynamics and dimensions of a profession and a field that is dynamic in its evolution and plays an increasingly important role in our world today.

O'Gorman has gathered, organized, and evaluated extensive resources on the theory and practice of religious education in parochial settings. Her work presents some provocative possibilities for inquiry, intellectual growth, faith development, and creative expression through religious education. O'Gorman's essay should be required reading for anyone involved in Christian education programs. She provides invaluable assistance to individuals who need to establish or coordinate such programs. But the audience for O'Gorman's essay is even farther-reaching than Christian educators alone, for she shows how faith is affirmed or lost through interactions in the religious environment. Ushers, church janitors, and members of the finance committee are teachers, too.

The Reverend Elaine Tiller's essay on aging, "The Gift of Long Life," presents materials and approaches of inestimable use to church librarians and pastors who must meet the needs of an aging congregation. Tiller directs the Community Ministries Program of Baptist Senior Adult Ministries in Washington, D.C. She challenges readers to question attitudes toward aging found in our culture and its youth-oriented image of the good life, which promotes denial of the aging process. Rather, Tiller encourages a healthy acceptance of a stage of life that we will all, by God's grace, experience. Moreover, by citing pastors, writers, and scholars, Tiller offers resources for seeing aging and its attendant qualities as a period of growth and opportunity, not stagnation and despair.

Her essay treats several aspects of the issue of aging: understanding aging issues, spiritual growth and aging, caregiving and aging, memories and remembering, how-to books for creating senior adult ministry, and future issues in aging. Tiller draws upon her experience as a denominational leader in senior adult ministries to counter attitudes that diminish the importance of senior adults in the life of the congregation, attitudes that place congregational priorities attracting young families to the church, rather than on ministering to faithful older individuals who are already present in the pews. Tiller has also provided a subject index, an author index of books and pamphlets, a title index of books and pamphlets, and a title index of videos, films, and slide shows. While secular organizations and agencies address the social and health concerns of the aging, the religious community is in a unique position to contribute to the spiritual vitality of an older person. Tiller evaluates resources for understanding spiritual attributes of the older person and for celebrating the gifts of this age. One of these gifts is the rich resource of stories and memories a person stores up through life experiences. The importance of telling one's life through stories, notes Tiller, will help congregations through reminiscence and active listening.

Finally, Tiller delineates some of the ethical issues paramount in the health care industry, in religious communities, and in society-at-large. Clearly, she argues, the only way to move beyond vexatious questions about allocation of resources (time, money, energy) is to engage people of goodwill through dialogue and prayer. She concludes with this hope-inspiring topic. Her work, then, is both a call to concern for a significant portion of our membership and a call to action through prayer, study, and advocacy.

Complementing O'Gorman's bibliographic essay on curriculum theory and educational design is Rev. Bill Yount's "Devotional Classics for Church Libraries." A professor of religion and philosophy and former seminary librarian, Yount reviews the bibliographical and interpretative resources on classical Christian devotional literature. Classics are defined as those works that possess universal or historically significant religious or theological value, the religious equivalent of Dr. Samuel Johnson's definition of a classic as "what pleased long and

pleases many." Yount surveys scholarly books and articles that interpret the most significant classical Christian literature. Also valuable
are Yount's assessments of collections, anthologies, devotional books
in series, and bibliographical guides.

In the second part of his essay, Yount surveys ten of the most
significant works of classical Christian devotion—the works included
are based on an informed analysis of the literature, and these are the
books included in almost every listing of the best examples of this
literary genre. For each work, Yount gives a biographical sketch of the
author, the historical setting of the devotional work, a concise survey
of its general content, structure, literary style, and topics. In his third
section, Yount turns to recent (since 1950) books and articles on the
use of the Christian Classics for devotional reading, and a second
bibliography of recent bibliographies of devotional classics is included.
Yount pinpoints those essential resources that assist readers wanting
to expand their horizons by studying the classics.

Contemporary Religious Ideas appropriately concludes with Joyce
White's chapter, "Church Libraries: Their History, Organization, and
Development." She is library director at St. Thomas Theological Seminary
in Denver, Colorado, and one of the founders of the Church and
Synagogue Library Association. White presents strategies and organizational concerns to address the information explosion that confronts
churches, synagogues, and other religious communities. As stewards
of educational resources, librarians know the importance of anticipating
and responding to new perspectives on our faith traditions. Librarians
play a vital role in creating communities of faith that are knowledgeable about, and responsive to, the challenges and opportunities presented by the "global village" to our culture, our faith traditions, and
our religious experiences. How does the local congregation open its
mind and heart to information and experience from around the world?
Similarly, how does the local congregation stimulate members to learn
more about the movement of Divine Being in other faith traditions,
religious groups, and spiritualities?

White shows how the church librarian can build collections, expedite
circulation of resources, and provide the foundation for a church's or
synagogue's religious education program. A vigorous, imaginative and
highly engaging program of adult religious education is essential if the
person in the pews is to understand the faith issues presented by other
peoples and their faiths.

Church libraries are, in many ways, still in a growth phase. Major
denominations and faiths have developed libraries over the past twenty
to thirty years, and there is an abundance of literature explaining the
rationale for church or synagogue libraries and the procedures for
establishing, maintaining, and promoting them. Whether for the smallest rural congregation or the largest urban church or synagogue, the
principles for organizing and promoting libraries are similar. White
articulates these principles and specific steps to take in administering
the library as part of a total educational effort. She also provides an
extensive bibliography of resources that will assist everyone—from

beginners to advanced practitioners—in the administration of library services.

As the preceding summaries indicate, *Contemporary Religious Ideas* surveys a host of accomplishments and programs. I have tried to follow the teaching of Ecclesiastes in compiling and editing this volume. I hope that my twelve contributors and I will have inspired your heart, enlightened your mind, encouraged your soul, and not wearied your flesh. The last word about the Word can be none other than

> Yours, O Lord, is the greatness, the power, the glory, the victory, and the majesty. For everything in heaven and on earth is yours. Yours, O Lord, is the kingdom, and you are exalted as head over all. (1 Chronicles 29:11)
>
> Amen.

The Rev. G. Edward Lundin

Contributing Authors

Phillip Berryman
Commercial translator from Spanish and Portuguese
Published Latin American Liberation theology texts
Catholic priest in Panama and Guatemala (1965-1980)

Rev. Cyprian Davis, O.S.B., Ph. D.
Professor of Church History in the St. Meinrad School of Theology, St.
Meinrad, Indiana

Rev. Shelley Davis Finson, Ph. D.
Professor of Pastoral Theology at the Atlantic School of Theology,
Halifax, Nova Scotia, Canada

Rabbi Peter Haas, Ph. D.
Professor of Religious Studies at Vanderbilt University

Dr. Edward Hughes
Associate Professor of Religious Studies at California State University
at Long Beach

Dr. A. K. M. Aminul Islam
Professor of Anthropology at Wright State University, Dayton, Ohio
Speciality in Anthropology of Religion

Dr. Kathleen O'Gorman
Loyola Institute of Ministry, Loyola University, New Orleans, Louisiana

Dr. Anne H. Lundin
Assistant Professor at School of Library and Information Studies at
University of Wisconsin-Madison

Rev. G. Edward Lundin, Ph. D.
Vicar, St. Elizabeth's Episcopal Church, Collins, Mississippi
Assistant Professor of Education, University of Southern Mississippi

Rev. Dora Elaine Tiller
Director of Community Ministries Program at the Baptist Senior Adult
Ministries in Washington, D.C.

Fr. Michael Tracy
Director of Campus Ministry for the Diocese of Biloxi, Mississippi
Newman Chaplain at the University of Southern Mississippi, Hattiesburg

xxxiii

Dr. Gordon Welty
Sociology Department at Wright State University, Dayton, Ohio

Joyce White
Master of Arts in Religion
Master of Science in Library Science
Librarian Director of Saint Thomas Theological Seminary, Denver, Colorado
President of Chuch and Synagogue Library Association

Rev. William Yount
Assistant Professor of Philosophy, Jackson State University, Jackson, Mississippi
Master of Science in Library Science

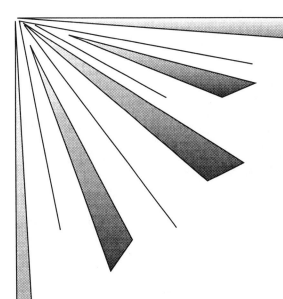

Part 1

The Literature of Knowing the Faiths

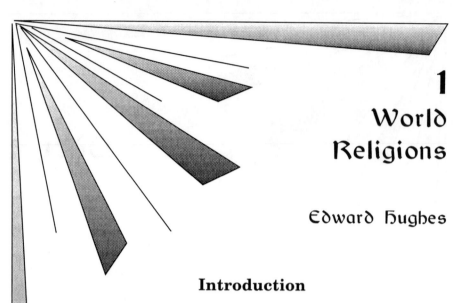

1
Worlд
Religions

Edwarд Hughes

Introduction

The discipline that studies world religions is normally
called "history of religions" or "comparative religion." Comparative religion is the older label and is still widely used in Great
Britain and the British Commonwealth, while history of religions is preferred in the United States and North America. The
labels of this discipline, however, are not as significant as its
content and common domain.

The academic study of world religions is usually understood to have begun in earnest in Germany with the writings
of Max Müller (1823–1900). Its origin is part of the nineteenth
century's grand project of developing an accurate, scientific
historical account of the earth's civilizations, an account free
from theological interference.

Scholars prior to Müller had, of course, been concerned
with understanding the interesting reports of "alien" religions
that continued to flow into Europe during the time of exploration and colonialism in the New World. However, the information received was often based on incomplete and biased
travelers' reports or missionary observations. Although some
observations were sympathetic and objective, they were token
efforts that most often showed little understanding of the world
from the other culture's perspective. Frequently, such reports
demonstrated a range of prejudices (theological, mercantile,
cultural, or imperialist) with the express purpose of proving
how non-Christian civilizations were inferior, or establishing
how other religious traditions were savage in comparison with a
gentleman's idea of a contemporary, civilized, post-Enlightenment
religion. Still, it was not always the case that Christianity fared
best in the comparison. Leaders of the French Enlightenment,
such as Voltaire, found Confucianism to be a humanistic, non-
dogmatic philosophy superior to Christianity. More commonly,

though, Christian and humanist polemics hindered the understanding of foreign religions.

One of the extraordinary achievements of the nineteenth century was a vast compilation of information about the religions of the world. Prior to this period, Europeans did not know that Buddhism was a separate religion from Hinduism, and the rest of the world knew little or nothing about Christianity. The acquisition of accurate information, including efforts to translate the sacred books of the East, continued into the twentieth century. For the first time in human history, global access to the world's scriptures was becoming available.

Other developments in archaeology and comparative linguistics led to radical conclusions that contradicted beliefs held by various religions (including Judaism and Christianity) as to the age of scriptures, the dating of temples, and the authenticity of legends. Frequently, it was found that religious traditions had not adequately distinguished between myth and fact and had surrounded holy persons and sacred writings with an aura of antiquity that could not be substantiated. Certain Hindu, Buddhist, Zoroastrian, Shinto, and Sikh traditions were found to be in error. In studies of Judaism and Christianity, Moses was dethroned as the author of the Pentateuch (first five books of the Old Testament), David was shown not to be the sole author of the Psalms, and obscure authors were believed to have written much material in the Old and New Testaments. In studies of Islam, *Hadith* (sayings by or about the Prophet—a major source of orthodox law) were found to be spurious.

The ability of scholarship to challenge tradition successfully was one of the ingredients in the split between fundamentalists and liberals in early-twentieth-century Protestantism in the United States. While conservatives were anxious to preserve the uniqueness of Christian revelation against comparisons with other religions, liberals were eager to show that the Divine had revealed Himself more universally, thus escaping the doctrine of Christian exclusivism.

The discipline of comparative religion entered a new phase in the late twentieth century. The efforts of the earlier period had led to a new sophistication in understanding the complex and changing nature of all religions. Today, rather than ask what a particular religion believes, scholars inquire as to the beliefs in each century, each country, each social strata. A religion is seen as a shifting network of beliefs and behaviors, with certain core themes remaining at the heart of the tradition throughout change, such as the centrality of Christ, or the Qur'an, or Amida Buddha.

The world religions have nurtured most of the elevated values of history, and have supplied people with hope in the midst of death and meaning in the midst of seemingly arbitrary fate. Religions have supplied human beings with answers to universal questions about the nature of existence: Why does life seem unfair? Why do the unjust prosper? Is life chaotic, or is there a meaningful thread that gives it rhyme and reason? Is death the end? Are values human-made or are they grounded in something or someone that transcends the human?

From a numerical perspective, religion has had the most success when responding to such existential questions.

In an age of shrinking economic, geographic, and communication barriers, misunderstanding between persons of different religious traditions may be the last wall to fall. Mistrust and misunderstanding between religions have engendered in war, colonialism, fear, and apathy; people from one culture have seemed unable to comprehend what is held dear by others. Because a religion cannot be understood unless one goes beyond a superficial presentation of facts and sees it from within, it has become the task of many scholars to show what the facts of a given religion mean to those within the faith, to show how a particular religious vision of life offers believers personal meaning.

When discussing Hindus or Christians, it is no longer sufficient to say that the one believes in the divinity of Christ and the other in the perfect law of reincarnation (*karma samsara*). Such bald statements reveal little about how these beliefs affect the life of the believer, or why an intelligent person from either tradition would derive intellectual or emotional satisfaction from such tenets.

The ability to see the world from another's perspective requires that the other be present to correct us when we misrepresent his or her beliefs. It is therefore no longer appropriate to write articles about Buddhist or Muslim belief or practice without input from that group. Fortunately, the discipline of comparative religion is now international—there exists a global community of scholars who respond to articles written by members of one faith about members of a different faith.

Although the discipline of comparative religion was a European invention, such scholarship is no longer an exclusively Western activity. In the study of comparative religion, humanity is beginning to understand its age-long religious heritage. Such understanding has practical implications for businesspersons interacting with other cultures, for students who wish to understand other faiths, for churches wanting to correct centuries of misunderstanding, and for governments wishing to understand the motivations of other cultures.

As comparative religion developed in Europe and in the United States, it interacted with such other newly formed disciplines as anthropology, sociology, psychology, art history (iconography), and economics. From its inception, researchers have drawn upon history, philosophy, and linguistics. The breadth and complexity of the subject at hand—the religious life of humankind—requires a complexity of approaches. It is therefore generally agreed that a balanced approach to world religions is polymethodic, and that all methods reveal something of importance to understanding the phenomenon of religion.

A growing consensus suggests, as Ninian Smart (1983) has argued in his book *Worldviews*, that the most fundamental object that comparative religion can study is the religious worldview of a people, its basic life-orientation. This is especially true in the case of traditional societies that are not as secularized as the West. Many in the West think of religion as a separate, distinct part of life, whereas in most societies, religion is the unifying vision of reality that binds all facets of life together into a meaningful whole. Even in the secular West, this point is understood by believers who bring the totality of their activities under the guidance of religious values.

The study of any religion requires recognition that religion is a multifaceted affair. Several important components of a religion include: beliefs, myths, scriptures, ethics, spiritual discipline and religious experience, polity (types of organization), rituals, and art. Each of these aspects interrelate in complex ways that continuously change. Sometimes this change is dramatic, as when Martin Luther interpreted the Scripture to mean that all Christians were priests, changing the nature of ministry, the content of belief, the performance of ritual, and the understanding of ethics. Sometimes the change is imperceptible. In either case, change in any part of the system involves shifts in meaning throughout the religion.

When analyzing comparative religion, myriad combinations emerge. One can compare aspects within the history of the same tradition or compare aspects of one tradition with another. For example, one might wish to study Christian prayer (a subset of spiritual discipline) in the first century and compare it with prayer in the thirteenth century, or contrast the way prayer is understood in the Christian tradition with the understanding of prayer in Hinduism or Buddhism. The comparison can be carried through the entire history of a religion, through a particular period, or through a single movement (or individual).

Comparative religion also studies ideologies, such as communism, capitalism, and fascism. These are worldviews that often take on a pseudo-religious quality in their rituals, myths, and beliefs. The prefix *pseudo* indicates that, to many scholars, such an ideology does not constitute a religion *per se* because its beliefs do not point to an ultimate reality, but instead to a finite god: the state, the *volk*, the will of the people, the evolutionary process, success, and so on. Other scholars argue that, if an ideology functions like a religion it should be considered a religion. Ultimately, this debate is between substantivists and functionalists. The former says that a religion points to an ultimate, sacred, transcendent reality. The latter (usually social scientists) say little about concepts of the ultimate, but prefer to analyze the way religions and ideologies affect human personal and collective behavior.

Both approaches have made significant contributions to understanding religious life because human beings are what they believe in as well as what they do. Note that neither approach is theological or philosophical in a normative sense; that is, neither approach makes statements about truth or falsity, nor about the rightness or wrongness of religious beliefs and behaviors. The purpose of both the substantivist and the functionalist is to understand rather than evaluate. Even substantivists, who hold that a religion must have a transcendent dimension, do not argue for the actual existence of an ultimate reality. Their statement is descriptive and simply asserts that, universally, people believe in and experience what seems to be a sacred reality that transcends the normal world of space and time. Once an historian of religions makes a statement about the truth or falsity of the religion under study, he or she becomes a philosopher or theologian.

The theologian reflects on the sphere of faith based on revelation; the philosopher reflects on the sphere of faith based on reason and the ability to discern the truth. The two disciplines are related in that both evaluate truth and falsity, right and wrong. Some theologians, such as Thomas Aquinas or Augustine of Hippo, are also philosophers, depending on whether they are speaking from faith in God or faith in reason. Their writings are used in both disciplines, but their writings are unlike comparative religion, which is a nonnormative discipline and doesn't seek the truth. This is evidenced in Roger Schmidt's definition of religion given in *Exploring Religion* (1988), which says that religion is "a human seeking and responding to what is experienced as holy." Note that the "holy" is not prejudged to be a single personal God, or a pantheon of deities, or an impersonal cosmic spirit or law. The definition does not profess that any one of these "holy" experiences exists in reality, or that one concept is superior to the other.

Although the demands of objectivity are central to the pursuit of comparative religion, the scholar will in many instances use his or her own religious sensitivity to discern the role that religion plays in another tradition. A person of prayer understands something about prayer that may transfer to the study of the spiritual disciplines of other traditions. Sympathetic understanding need not lead to a lack of objectivity, but rather to increased objectivity—if the goal is to understand the religious life of others.

Introducing the Study of Religion

Judging the quality of introductory texts is an important prerequisite for teaching religious studies. The function of an introductory text is to allow the reader to grasp the technical terms and the methodologies that the study of religion requires. Introductory texts should be polymethodic in character and should acquaint the student with the variety of ways of being religious. Such texts are not about the history of a particular religion but rather are about the study of religion in general, and are an invaluable aid for comprehension of the issues raised in the study of world religions and in the study of contemporary theology.

Introductory Textbooks

Ellwood, Robert S., Jr. *Introducing Religion: From Inside and Outside.* 2d ed. New York: Prentice Hall Press, 1983. ISBN 0-13-477497-3.

Although this is a shorter work than Schmidt's *Exploring Religion*, 2d ed., its seven chapters cover many of the same themes. Chapter 1 enables the student to arrive at an inclusive definition of religion and introduces important concepts of transcendence, the sacred and the profane, and the relationship between one's religious beliefs and character formation. Chapter 2 deals with the origin of religion and its many forms, from prehistoric to contemporary times. It discusses the founders of the larger world religions and offers summaries of the positions of major interpreters of religion, including Schleiermacher, Hegel, Kierkegaard, Otto, Barth, and others. Chapter 3 is a helpful introduction to the psychology of religion. It discusses a plurality of religious experience and recounts the theories of Freud, Jung, and Maslow that concern the role of religion in the psyche. There is also an interesting presentation of the type of religion appropriate for the different stages of life, from infancy to old age.

Beginning in chapter 4, Ellwood offers a lucid presentation of the nature of religious symbols and how they function in ritual, myth, and doctrine. Chapter 5 introduces issues from the sociology of religion: types of religious groups; great and small traditions; dominant and emerging religions; and different types of religious personalities such as mystic, priest, and reformer. Chapter 6 analyzes the importance of conceptual truth, or belief in religion, and discusses differences between traditionalist, liberal, and fundamentalist styles of belief. It also describes the various ideas of the divine and examines the different criteria used in evaluating truth in religion, such as reason, authority, and experience. Chapter 7 discusses the future of religion in relation to developments in science (space flight and genetic engineering), the growing role of women in organized religion, and the continuing tension between the process of secularization and religious existence.

Introducing Religion: From Inside and Outside is an excellent teaching tool; it has a useful summary and glossary at the end of each chapter and aids the student in developing a sense of objectivity in exploring religious issues. Though not as intellectually challenging as Schmidt's *Exploring Religion*, it raises issues that could readily be used in small-group education in churches and temples.

Schmidt, Roger. *Exploring Religion.* 2d ed. Belmont, CA: Wadsworth, 1988. ISBN 0-534-08874-0.

This is one of the most thorough introductions to the contemporary study of religion. Schmidt's sixteen chapters combine an aspectual approach to world religions with a phenomenological (descriptive) approach. Part 1 excellently summarizes the problems of adequately defining religion, concisely portrays attempts to discern the earliest form of religion, and describes the nature of the holy. Part 2 focuses on the conceptual dimension of religion and has significant chapters on the nature of religious symbolism, religion's use of language, the nature of sacred story, and the meaning of scripture in different cultures. This section also clarifies the differences between the disciplines of theology, philosophy, and religious studies. Part 3 presents the social dimension of religion and analyzes types of religious communities, varieties of religious experience, concepts of salvation, and the nature and types of holy rites.

Exploring Religion also features an excellent glossary of technical terms and a helpful bibliography for each topic covered. The coverage is well informed and presents a range of theories with examples, giving the work a balance of abstraction and concrete illustration useful for beginning students. Recommended for people with some college education.

Streng, Frederick J. *Understanding Religious Life*. 3d ed. Belmont, CA: Wadsworth, 1985. ISBN 0-534-03699-6.

This advanced introduction offers a sensitive and complex understanding of the nature of religious life and is ideal for those who have already done some college work in religious studies. Unlike Schmidt or Ellwood, who offer a broad sample of the ways in which religious studies can be approached, Streng begins with a phenomenological analysis; that is, he offers the reader categories that illustrate the various ways people experience the world through religion. His concern is not primarily factual or social scientific; rather, Streng is convinced that the heart of religion is religious experience, and his concern is to show how people with different types of religious experience evaluate the world, themselves, and others.

Streng's book has fifteen chapters. Chapter 1 deals with the nature of the study of religion and the problem of defining religion broadly enough so as to include all its manifestations. Chapters 2–10 analyze in detail the following ways of being religious: personal apprehension of a holy presence; creation of community through shared sacred symbols; harmony with cosmic law; mystical freedom through spiritual discipline; humanistic fulfillment of mature human relationships; the religious dimension of social political action; the commitment to reason as a religious act; art as a means of ultimate transformation; and science and technology as religious ultimates. Each religious position is defined in terms of the way it views ultimate reality, the manner in which it understands the primary problem of being human (whether it is sin, ignorance, neurosis, etc.), the means for solving the human problem, and the way the religious position is expressed socially and personally. Streng's treatment orders the many ways of being religious with striking clarity.

Chapter 11 evaluates theories of the origin of religion, while chapter 12 explains and evaluates the psychological and sociological study of religion. Chapter 13 discusses comparative religion from both historical and phenomenological (analyzing types of religious experience) points of view. Streng's examination of these two methods are central to understanding the major approaches used in comparing two or more religious traditions. Chapter 14 gives an important and often neglected look into the nature of interreligious dialogue, and chapter 15 explores the consequences of understanding religious variety in a pluralistic society. The tone throughout is learned and cosmopolitan.

Understanding Religious Life has a companion reader, *Ways of Being Religious*, and the two texts together provide a thorough introduction to the study of religion.

——. *Ways of Being Religious: Readings for a New Approach to Religion*. New York: Prentice Hall Press, 1973. ISBN 0-13-946277-5.

Although this is a companion volume to Streng's *Understanding Religious Life*, this work stands on its own as a rich collection of abbreviated essays (most under seven pages in length) that illustrate each individual author's perspective on the basic ways of being religious. The introductory section answers the question: What is religion?

Sections 1–8 give examples, interpretations, and criticisms of each way of being religious. The essays are drawn from Christian, Jewish, Islamic, Buddhist, Hindu, preliterate, and secular sources. This is the largest and most diversified collection of significant essays available in English. Further, each section contains articles regarding the "pros and cons" of each religious position. The range of articles will refresh the beginner and the professional. This is an invaluable book that no library should be without.

Studying World Religions

After a student has covered introductory material concerning contemporary approaches to the study of religion, he or she will wish to learn about the world religions themselves. This makes the quality of the introductory text crucial. The authors must not only decide what is important to communicate about a given tradition, but they must do so in short compass. Each text will represent a somewhat different approach. Some will emphasize doctrine; others will emphasize geographical and cultural factors. Some will focus on the nature of a specific tradition's religious experience, while others will speak of the development of the tradition as a response to external and internal political and military pressures.

Because the emphasis should be on understanding, all major texts should avoid normative approaches and refrain from criticism of the tradition, either in its customs or beliefs. If, however, a certain custom or belief has been altered under the duress of criticism, or is in a debated situation within the tradition, a major text might address the issue. The Hindu custom of *sati* (widow burning), for example, was criticized by Western-influenced intellectuals, who noted that the practice was not part of early Hindu custom, and that it should be viewed as a degeneration of the tradition. The Christian doctrine of exclusive salvation through Christ is a teaching currently being debated within the church, and an historian of religion treating the unfolding of Christianity might well address the various positions of the debate. However, if an historian was to interject his or her own theological reading on this issue, then the position would become normative and inappropriate for one introducing world religions.

One difficulty in developing a suitable text is the problem of objectivity. It is always difficult to attain objectivity regarding issues in one's own culture, and objectivity is even more difficult to maintain when studying foreign traditions. Nonetheless, it is possible to approximate an unbiased telling of the story of religion by heeding the criticisms that arise within academic debate, and by listening especially to the criticisms of those within the culture one is writing about. This will unearth the majority of assumptions that might distort accurate reporting.

It is a matter of record that a number of writers on world religions have received acclamations for their objectivity from intellectuals of the particular faith under discussion. For example, Muslim scholars have for decades praised the dispassionate and insightful quality of scholarship in H. A. R. Gibb's *Mohammedanism*, published in 1948 (even while objecting to the title that implies that Gibb is not a Muslim). Frederick Denny's more recent *An Introduction to Islam* (1985) has received similar praise and applause.

Reportorial objectivity, though essential, is not sufficient alone for crafting a complete introductory text to world religions. One of the finest presentations of the facts about world religions can be found in *A History of the World's Religions* by John and David Noss. In many ways, this work is the fruition of the past 100 years of scholarship. Its only defect is one that most texts suffer from: it does not present the material in such a way that the reader understands why an intelligent, sensitive person would be a member of the religion discussed, or why he or she would take pride in the tradition. *A History of the World's Religions* misses the sense of what it means to see the world from within the tradition.

The first adequate general text to depict a sense of the excitement of being within a different faith is Huston Smith's *The World's Religions* (originally titled *The Religions of Man*). Readers from several different faiths can find their own enthusiasm for their religious vision of the world presented in Smith's superb prose and remarkable perception.

In a field as wide as the religions of the world, every selection must necessarily entail some omissions, as one cannot present the entirety of information that has been gathered in the past 100 years. An author must not only choose a methodology, but also must decide what aspects of the world religions are most essential to communicate. Some choices are based on whether to include material on dead religions, such as pre-Christian Scandinavian or Mesopotamian traditions, or whether to emphasize contemporary religions. When discussing live religions, one must also determine whether to give greater emphasis to a religion's earlier aspects or to its modern phase.

Because the science of religious studies is a recent Western achievement, textbooks written by Westerners have the impress of their culture's concerns. For example, Noss includes an interesting chapter on bygone religions that have left their mark on the West. This is appropriate for a Western audience, and Noss incorporates material on the Celts (Druids) and the Teutons (ancient Germanic people). If the author was instead writing for a Japanese audience, these factors should be excluded and material related to the archaic phase of Japanese culture, including data on Polynesian civilization, incorporated. However, Noss inserts data on Mesopotamian and early Greek religion, which have so significantly influenced the religious cultures of the world that a scholar should most likely include such data, regardless of audience.

Although preliterate traditions are often given sketchy attention in introductions to world religions, some ambiguity exists in their treatment. This is because anthropology more often deals with smaller preliterate traditions, while the study of world religions grew out of linguistic concern with classical manuscripts, and is therefore more concerned with literate traditions. However, with the growing emphasis on writing about contemporary religion as opposed to classical, the divide between anthropology and world religions as guides to preliterate traditions is breaking down. Certain authors, such as Mary Douglas and Robert Bellah, influence both disciplines. An emphasis on the importance of fieldwork and personal observation for students now pertains to both world religions and anthropology, and has further broken down barriers between them.

Different aspects of religion have received more attention at different periods. The nineteenth century paid fervid attention to ancient scriptures and the development of comparative linguistics. At present, three areas are receiving more notice: the role of women in religion, the role of ritual in religion, and the nature of a living religion. Scholars agree that the role of women in world religions has not been given sufficient attention. With the development of feminist scholarship, and with the entrance of more female scholars into the field, this lacuna is being addressed. One notices that standard texts such as *A History of the World's Religions* are using inclusive language in new editions. In *Paths of Faith*, John A. Hutchison has upgraded the bibliographies to address women's concerns. Denise Carmody's *Women and World Religion* is a challenging work that is both accurate in its factual material and normative in its criticism of male dominance in each of the world religions.

Another issue at hand is the role of ritual in religious life, an area that, many argue, has been neglected in standard presentations. Still another concern may be found in the recent focus on the meaning that a living religion holds for its adherents today. This corrects the classical manner of writing introductory texts in which one presents the history of a religion but does not give a sense of the meaning that contemporary followers find in their faith. Mary Pat Fisher and Robert Luyster's *Living Religions* admirably corrects this problem.

Though all approaches to the study of world religions enrich our understanding of their complexity, sometimes popular culture and political factors influence the direction such study takes. In the 1960s, a popular concern with meditational techniques inspired works dealing with religion and consciousness; works on Hinduism were quite popular. More recently, with the religiously-motivated Iranian revolution, Western culture has become interested in Islam, especially its fundamentalist expression and Shi'ite branch. Changes within public consciousness also affect the type of material that is published. For example, as sensitivity increases to the growing Asian population in the United States, works on Buddhism in its various forms arise to meet the perceived need. Sometimes new works will arise from new academic concerns. Of course, some scholarship is not impacted by political factors and continues along in its own quiet manner.

Textbooks on World Religions

Fisher, Mary Pat, and Robert Luyster. *Living Religions*. New York: Prentice Hall Press, 1990. ISBN 0-13-538604-7.
  This is the most recent text on world religions recommended here. Other texts, such as Noss and Noss's *A History of the World's Religions*,

are revisions with new material, but are not new throughout. The focus in *Living Religions* is on how religions provide meaning that transforms men and women. Each chapter provides historical detail about the founder or the early development of the religious tradition, discusses spiritual disciplines and contemporary rituals and practices, and offers a section that features an interview with a devout member of the faith.

Living Religions begins with a criticism of earlier scholarship that focused upon classical texts and detached erudition. The authors caution the reader that, despite its great learning, Western scholarship did not often have a sympathetic understanding of the religions it studied, and did not treat them with the necessary respect. Despite some oversimplification and notable exceptions, such as H. Gibb in his treatment of Islam or A. Basham's exploration of Hinduism, there is much truth to this criticism, in that most European scholars were Christians or secularists who did not see the faiths they studied as sources of inspiration for themselves. Likewise, the tone of much scholarship reflects the influence of the Enlightenment and its general distrust of the supernatural and the mystical phenomena that are essential ingredients in most religions.

However, one must balance this criticism by acknowledging the debt owed these same scholars for demystifying and demythologizing elements of these traditions, and for revealing such errors as inaccurate dating of scripture, excessive claims concerning miracles and powers, mythical elaboration of the lives of saints and founders, general confusion of myth with fact, and a prescientific understanding of the historical evolution of religious traditions.

Chapter 1 gives a sympathetic summary of the human need for religion and discusses mystical encounters with the sacred. It also treats the theme of women in religion, the differences between fundamental and liberal interpretations of faith, and the destructive side of organized religion. Chapter 2 gives a lively look at contemporary primal (preliterate) traditions. Chapters 3–12 look at the usual inventory of world religions, while chapter 13 deals with new religious movements, including millenarian movements, nature spirituality, Baha'i, the occult, metaphysical study, and interfaith dialogue.

Refreshingly current, this spirited work will promote vigorous discussion. A glossary of terms is included, and bibliographies of resources that incorporate customary scholarship are provided with each chapter, adding to customary scholarship a large number of works that testify to the living experience found within the different religions.

Hutchison, John A. *Paths of Faith*. 4th ed. New York: McGraw-Hill, 1991. ISBN 0-07-031543-4.

First published in 1969 and now in its fourth edition, *Paths of Faith* is a lucid introduction to the religions of the world appropriate for a college-level audience. The book can be supplemented with selections from primary sources (such as scriptures or theologies) of the religion under study.

Hutchison's method is existential—he sees the religions of the world answering basic universal questions such as: Who am I? Where am I going? Does life have a meaning? Why do the wicked prosper? and Is death the end? Human beings are understood to be naturally religious in the sense that they require an answer to these questions, or their lives become meaningless.

The author organizes religions into three categories: cosmic traditions, or polytheism; acosmic traditions, or transcendent monism; and historical religion, or theism. Chapter 1 provides a general introduction on how to be a student of religion and distinguishes between the disciplines of philosophy, theology, and religious studies. Chapter 2 offers a brief look at Native American and African preliterate traditions and ancient Mesopotamian, Egyptian, and Greek religions. Chapters 3–16 discuss each of the major religions (based on number of adherents or historical importance) in comprehensible prose, emphasizing doctrine as the basis for understanding each tradition's response to the fundamental questions of ultimate meaning. Significant holidays and rituals are discussed alongside the historical development of ideas.

In Chapter 17, *Paths of Faith* departs from the usual pattern of texts on world religion and considers the evolution of modern religious criticism, from the Renaissance to the twentieth century. Chapter 18 offers a prospectus on the future of religion. The new edition has a thoroughly updated bibliography, an excellent glossary of terms, and a reworked "issues and questions" section at the end of each chapter suitable for use in group discussion. This work has done well in both church schools and secular institutions and has been consistently praised for its objectivity and style.

Nielsen, Niels C., Jr., et al. *Religions of the World.* 2d ed. New York: St. Martin's Press, 1988. ISBN 0-312-00308-0.

Religions of the World presents world religions in their social, cultural, and geographic context. Now in its second edition, *Religions of the World* reflects recent scholarship in its presentation, and balances the customary emphasis on doctrine with substantial material on myth, ritual, and folk traditions. On the whole, this work is superior in its concern for relevant historical and political detail. Its format includes boxed features that contain descriptions of special rites and ceremonies. It offers an abundance of illustrations displaying art (black-and-white pictures), photographs, maps, and timelines, all of which add to the usefulness of the text. However, because this book was coauthored, the style is not consistent. Some essays are stronger than others, though all are competent and informative.

The introduction offers an excellent discussion of the problem of defining religion; gives an overview of theories about the origin of religion; and distinguishes between theological, philosophical, psychological, sociological, and anthropological interpretations in a serviceable manner. An updated bibliography with some annotation is provided at the back of the book.

Part 1 covers such religions of antiquity as Egyptian, Mesopotamian, Greek, Roman, Persian (Zoroastrian), Celtic, Germanic, and Scandinavian. Its discussion of preliterate traditions is richer than discussions found in most introductory texts, and includes illustrations from Africa, Brazil, and Melanesia. Part 2 covers the history of Hinduism, from the Indus Valley civilization to contemporary religious leaders; the treatment of the caste system is quite good. Part 3 covers the development of Buddhism, while part 4 treats the religions of China and Japan, including Sikhism and Jainism (within the subcontinent). Part 5 discusses the evolution of the Jewish tradition to the present. Part 6 handles the history of Christianity, including the secular philosophies and intellectual revolutions that were born in the European-Christian arena. Part 7 covers the evolution of Islam, including a brief discussion of Black Muslims in the United States and Muslim militant revivalism throughout the world. This is an important contribution for those seeking a deeper cultural look into world religions.

Noss, John B., and David S. Noss. *A History of the World's Religions.* 9th ed. New York: Macmillan, 1993. ISBN 0-02-388471-1.

Now in its ninth edition, this magisterial work, first published in 1949, has been thoroughly upgraded to incorporate new developments in the field of comparative religion. The new edition uses inclusive language, has a revised bibliography, has a glossary of terms at the end of each chapter, and includes throughout the text material on female deities and the role of women in religion. For its quantity and precision of information, this text is perhaps the most impressive of all introductions that have been widely used in American colleges. It remains a model of objectivity, but is less existential than Hutchison's approach and less personal in conveying what a religion means to believers than Huston Smith's *The Religions of Man.*

Chapter 1 offers helpful categories with which to understand preliterate traditions, while chapter 2 discusses bygone religious cultures that have left their mark on the West, including Mesopotamian, Greek, Roman, Celtic, and Teutonic. Chapters 3–18 tell the story of the larger traditions of South Asia, East Asia, and the Middle East (including Judaism and Christianity). As a reference work, or as a text, this is an invaluable source of information.

Smith, Huston. *The World's Religions.* Rev. ed. New York: HarperCollins, 1991. ISBN 0-06-250799-0; 0-06-250811-3pa.

This is the single best book for those who wonder why an intelligent human being belongs to a religion other than one's own, and how that religious basis influences his or her worldview. Originally published in 1958, this text has been revised and includes new bibliographies and updated gender language. Wilfred Cantwell Smith, one of the senior statespersons of world religions, indicated that this work was the first adequate textbook ever written on world religions because of its ability to present the world as believers of different religions see it. The religions treated include Hinduism, Buddhism, Confucianism, Taoism,

Islam, Judaism, and Christianity. Fewer traditions are dealt with than in other texts, but those that are discussed are treated in an extraordinarily insightful manner. Smith's writing style has nothing of a textbook feel; it is graceful, literary, and clear. This is a book for those who desire eloquent presentation, insight, and enjoyment. Recommended for high school to college readers.

Methodological Approaches to the Study of World Religion

The importance of methodology has been discussed in the introductory essay.

Textbooks on Methodology

De Vries, Jan. *Perspectives in the History of Religions*. Berkeley, CA: University of California Press, 1977. ISBN 0-06-080972-8.

Broader than most surveys, this is both a history and an evaluation of the methods used to study religion. Part 1 includes an overview of approaches from classical antiquity, the Christian apologists, the Middle Ages, the Renaissance, and the eighteenth century. Part 2 treats the contributions of the nineteenth-century Romanticists, while part 3 deals with the notable theories of the later nineteenth and twentieth centuries. Part 4 treats special problems in the study of magic, sacrifice, and myth. The epilogue reflects on the past and considers the future of the history of religions as a discipline. This college-level text should be required reading for understanding the advances and blind alleys in the academic comprehension of religion.

Eliade, Mircea. *The Sacred and the Profane: The Nature of Religion*. Magnolia, MA: Peter Smith, 1983. ISBN 0-8446-6080-9.

The effect of this seminal work on the field of religious study cannot be overstated. Eliade is one of the giants in comparative religion in the twentieth century and has been the primary force in the University of Chicago's approach to the study of religion. *The Sacred and the Profane* explores the significance of religious myth, symbolism, and ritual to life and culture. Its method is a form of structuralism. Eliade finds that certain symbolic motifs reoccur in religious life across the globe. This fact leads him to postulate categories that can be universally applied to religious life. These include the notion of the sacred versus the profane (the ordinary), sacred space, sacred times, the sacredness of nature, and the loss of the sense of the holy in contemporary thinking. His work has interesting parallels with the writings of Carl Jung, and offers fruitful ways of understanding "primitive" (preliterate) cultures; earlier mythic ways of perceiving the world; art, including modern art; and dreams and contemporary visions. This text is highly recommended for the college-level reader.

James, William. *The Varieties of Religious Experience*. New York: Random House, 1990. (Vintage-Library of America Series). ISBN 0-679-72491-5.

This is *the* classic work on the psychology of religion. Although this book is dated (originally published in 1902), it would be negligent not to bring the most influential of all texts in this field to the reader's attention. Its author is known not only as the father of the scientific study of religious experience, but is considered by many to be America's greatest philosopher. James set a standard of literary presentation in the social sciences that has never been equaled. His examples of religious experience are still fresh and dynamic; his vocabulary, such as the "sin sick soul" and the "healthy minded," is the source of many stock phrases in the field. Naturally, the years have created a large gap in information and new developments, yet one can still find vivid accounts of the conversion process that make later descriptions seem crude. James's discussion of religious pathology seems perennially relevant.

This is a work for the industrious; it is long and philosophically sophisticated, but will still stimulate the mind as almost no other work can. For those who desire a more contemporary resource to supplement James's, Wayne E. Oates's *The Psychology of Religion*, unfortunately now out of print, should be consulted, as should David Wulff's recent *Psychology of Religion: Classic and Contemporary Views*.

Lessa, William A., and Evon Z. Vogt, eds. *Reader in Comparative Religion: An Anthropological Approach*. 4th ed. New York: Harper-Collins, 1979. ISBN 0-06-043991-2.

This is an expert compendium of articles dealing with almost all aspects of religious life and encompassing and illustrating the full range of methods used. As the most distinguished collection of articles on preliterate traditions available, it features articles by respected representatives of contemporary and classical approaches. For college-level readers. See page 25 for a fuller analysis of this title.

O'Dea, Thomas F. *The Sociology of Religion*. 2d ed. New York: Prentice Hall Press, 1983. ISBN 0-13-821066-7; 0-13-821058-6pa.

Those who want a text of brief statement and clear presentation, with an appreciation of religion's function in shaping cultural behavior, will welcome O'Dea's presentation. Because of the amount of material covered in a short space, the style is a bit condensed, but it moves rapidly to the point.

Chapters include: 1) "The Functionalist Approach," which presents topics such as functional theory, the function of religion and magic, and religion and social causation; 2) "The Religious Experience," which deals with the sacred, the extraordinary, the phenomenon of charisma, ultimacy, meaning and relationship, and the problem of projection; 3) "The Institutionalization of Religion," which deals with cult, rationalization of belief patterns, and religious organizations; 4) "Religion and Society," which treats religion and social stratification, contemporary conversion, conversion and cultural prestige, and the church and the world; 5) "Religion and Conflict," which addresses the secularization of culture and dilemmas in the institutionalization of religion; and 6) "Ambiguity and Dilemma," which deals with religion and magic, religion as a central element in culture, and religion and society.

Almost every topic is handled in a way that shows familiarity not only with sociological but with significant theological writings. This work is ideal for those with backgrounds in religious studies or theology. Milton Yinger's *Scientific Study of Religion* (now out of print) is a useful supplement to this text.

Otto, Rudolf. *The Idea of the Holy*. 2d ed. New York: Oxford University Press, 1950. ISBN 0-19-500210-5.

First published in German in 1917 and in English in 1923, this classic has greatly influenced thinking about the nature of religious experience. Written at a time when naturalistic philosophy dominated Continental research, Otto demonstrated that religion in its purest form is neither ethics nor doctrine but something unique, an encounter with what he called the numinous—the sacred power or the holy. The study of religion thus has a unique object, and the different religions may be defined by the manner in which they encounter the holy.

Otto discusses how the holy is neither rational nor irrational, but superrational, and argues that human beings have a unique religious faculty that allows them to experience the holy. Several chapters analyze the components of the numinous: the numinous in art, in the Old and New Testaments, in Luther, in "primitive" traditions, in Buddhism and the Bhagavad Gita, and as a category of experience built into the human psyche. This is an advanced work, but one that remains timely in its response to reductionistic theories of the religious life. College level.

Smart, Ninian. *Worldviews: Crosscultural Explorations of Human Beliefs*. New York: Scribner's, 1983.

Smart divides the global religious map into worldviews and argues that a religion is a worldview, as are ideologies such as communism. Portions of a religion, such as belief systems and rituals, are expressions of the worldview and have an intimate relation with each other because each part expresses in some way the underlying vision of reality. Each religion expresses itself in at least six dimensions: in religious experience, in myth, in doctrine that reflects on myth, in ethics, in ritual, and in social expression. To understand different worldviews, the student of world religion should be a participant-observer, one who enters into the faith (worldview) of another to imaginatively reconstruct it as a way of seeing the world. Only then will one be able to understand why others find excellence in a path of faith other than one's own.

In the last chapter, Smart discusses the increasing global interpenetration of the world faiths. This is a stimulating book, clear and precise, and it presents ideas that have had significant academic influence. Smart puts into simple language many of the ideas expressed in his *The Phenomenon of Religion*, an earlier work (now out of print) on methodology that masterfully shows the logical relationship of all scholastic approaches to the study of religion. For the student interested in Smart's worldview analysis, this earlier work should be consulted as a reference for further research. College level.

Smith, Wilfred Cantwell. *The Meaning and End of Religion*. Minneapolis, MN: Augsburg Fortress, 1991. ISBN 0-8006-2475-0.

This modern classic revolutionized thinking about how to speak about and how to study religions. Smith criticizes the use of the word *religion*, finding it means different things to different people and is too vague. Though most scholars have been reluctant to give up the word, they have long listened to Smith's analysis. Religion can mean: 1) a religion, such as Christianity or Hinduism, that one belongs to and that has a history; 2) piety, as in the colloquial phrase, "Have you got religion?" 3) the ideal religion of a theologian who speaks of what his religion should mean—that is "true" Christianity or "true Hinduism," as opposed to the actual historical religion with its many denominations, aberrations, and conflicting doctrines; and 4) all of the above together.

Smith asks us to reject the idea that religion has an unchanging essence. The question, "What is Christianity?" does not allow for a simple answer. Christianity has been many things and continues to evolve, like a human being, with the passage of time. Though there are enduring themes such as the centrality of Christ, exactly how this centrality is understood and how it relates to other parts of the religion—to polity, forms of spirituality, relationships to the state, notions of priesthood, leadership, and so on—varies from age to age. Intellectual precision therefore requires the asking of more specific questions, such as: What did Christianity mean to the first Christians? What did it mean to Lutherans in the sixteenth century? What does it mean to Lutherans in the United States today? What does it mean to women in contemporary Denmark? In this way, the student is not lost in an abstracted understanding of the faith.

Smith wishes to replace the concept of religion with two categories, "faith" and "cumulative tradition." Faith refers to the vital experiential side of religion. Cumulative tradition refers to the observable aspects of a tradition, such as organization, customs, laws, rituals, and so on. Smith is a personalist and, more than any scholar in the twentieth century, he has corrected the objectivist concern with facts by insisting that one cannot begin to understand the faith of another until one sees the world through the eyes of the other. College level.

Streng, Frederick. *Understanding Religious Life*.

See annotation on page 8 for an analysis of Streng's experiential method.

Women and Religion

The 1970s and 1980s were times of creativity and self-definition for feminist scholarship, and the role of women in religious life began to be a concern in the church and temple due to growing political organization on the part of feminist intellectuals. There was also a sense that the time had come for women to take their place in the religious institution, that women's liberation was providential and necessary.

Out of this ferment came not only increasing ordination of women and an increasing number of women with doctorates in religious studies, but a systematic exploration of the role of women in both primal traditions and world religions. Scholarly concern focused on the unwritten and uncelebrated contributions of women, and on the way religion defined and circumscribed female possibilities in religious and secular culture (including the problem of oppression in patriarchal societies, that is, in all known large and powerful civilizations). For this reason, feminist research sometimes focused on preliterate societies that were smaller, less hierarchical, and less militant in orientation than the larger, patriarchal religions. In such societies, the role of woman as maker and life-bearer was held in high esteem and was reflected in positive female myths and rituals. Male anthropologists had long overlooked the significance of these rituals; even though information had been gathered, it was overshadowed by concern with male myths and rites that often included the official myths of the tribe, of which men were customarily the custodians.

Feminist scholarship was often polemical, and articles regarding other times and their traditions therefore reflected the struggle of sexual politics in contemporary society. But a maturity soon became apparent which demonstrated that a significant number of women scholars had mastered the sensitivity and objectivity that the phenomenological (descriptive) method of study demanded, even while maintaining a critique of male-based power structures.

Rita Gross, one of the editors of *Unspoken Worlds: Women's Religious Lives in Non-Western Cultures* and the contributor of an important essay in Arvind Sharma's *Women in World Religions*, challenges religious studies to move beyond an androcentric approach that one often finds in official religious scriptures and move into the actual society to discover what "women actually do, think, or feel."

Gone are the more radical voices of feminist criticism that were so incensed by the muffled voice of women in the world religions that they found religion a mere ideology for male dominance, renounced all known religions in favor of new female-created ones, or remained within a tradition but thought of it in terms of subjugation.

There is, of course, truth in stereotypes of female oppression, whether in the Hindu *sati*, Muslim *purdah*, Christian witchcraft trials, or Chinese footbinding, and focusing on the extreme may be useful in identifying important themes but does not actually tell us the actual situation of the majority of women in most world religions during the extent of its history. Feminist scholarship has become methodologically complex and now recognizes the degrees of freedom and opportunities for self-development that have been available to women in either the heart or the periphery of a tradition.

The importance of writing about a two-sexed view of humanity cannot be overestimated. Its effect on scholarship is as important intellectually as it is morally. Unhappily, much of the contributions of women to religious life have been irrevocably lost, and attempts to rediscover the unwritten history of women in ancient myth or in comparisons with contemporary primal societies may never fully succeed. Attempts to uncover this buried history proceed to this day, but at this point it is impossible to know how effective such an excavation will be. At present, female scholars have made a significant improvement not only in redressing an imbalance in scholarship, but also by writing lively essays that present the living quality of women's religious life throughout the world.

Textbooks on Women and Religion

Carmody, Denise L. *Women and World Religions.* 2d ed. New York: Prentice Hall Press, 1989. ISBN 0-13-962424-4.

This concise and useful text is an excellent supplement to an introductory course in world religions. Carmody acquaints the reader with basic themes from the religions of the world and discusses how these have been used to abet or frustrate women's self-fulfillment. She also skillfully shows how equalitarian religious ideals are distorted in the development of patriarchal religion. Unlike more radical authors, Carmody has considerable appreciation for the spiritual and intellectual achievements of traditional religion. She combines this with an accurate portrait of women's actual life in the religions of the world, as opposed to their theoretical existence in the minds of traditional male theologians.

Carmody's work is always up-to-date and includes material that is on the cutting edge of scholarship. Like many feminist writers, she does not withhold normative statements, but this does not detract from the accuracy of her work. Instead, a prophetic critique of the treatment of women infuses her discussion of the major religious traditions in an equitable manner. Given her theological and biblical training, Carmody's work in world religions speaks very well to church audiences. Highly recommended as a strong and balanced presentation of sensitive material. College level.

Falk, Nancy A., and Rita M. Gross, eds. *Unspoken Worlds: Women's Religious Lives in Non-Western Cultures.* Belmont, CA: Wadsworth, 1989. (McGill Studies in the History of Religions). ISBN 0-534-09852-5.

This is a text that Mircea Eliade, the dean of twentieth-century religious studies at the University of Chicago, called "useful, necessary, and important for the history of religions and the history of culture."

It is a brilliant collection of stimulating articles, arranged topically. Section 1, "Encounter: Two Extraordinary Women," includes interviews with women of spiritual authority. One of these women, Julia, is a diviner in East Africa; the other, Mother Guru Jnanananda, is a saint and expert on the meaning of liberation in the Hindu Advaita Vedanta tradition. Section 2, "Women Explode: Ritualized Rebellion for Women," includes articles on possession and sickness, and shows how each of these conditions is a socially accepted way of manifesting the despair of female oppression.

Section 3, "In the Wings: Rituals for Wives and Mothers," contains material on the rituals of significant times in the lives of women. This section incorporates material on Hindu childbirth rituals; Hindu household rites; the *habisha* rituals, which are a variety of Hindu rituals for middle-aged women performed during a stage in the life cycle that involves making vows to gain something in this world and in the next; death rituals for black Carib women in the coastal villages of Central America; and an article titled "The Controversial Vows of Urban Muslim Women in Iran." Section 4, "Up Against the Wall: Women in Male Dominated Systems," contains material on Islam and tribal women in Iran, the role of prophetesses in the new religions of Japan, the treatment of the Empress Wu by Chinese historians, and the reasons for the disappearance of nunneries from ancient Indian Buddhism.

To offer positive positions on male/female relationships in the religious world, section 5, "Success Stories: Women and Men in Balance or Equality," shows examples of traditions where religious life has reached a respectful harmony between male and female contributions to religious life. Included are articles on the accomplished women in Tantric Buddhism of medieval India and Tibet, and on women of spiritual prestige among Native American Iroquois. Section 6, "Womb Envy: Male Domination and Woman's Power," sets out to demonstrate male respect and awe before female sacral power in the realm of fertility, and shows how this reverence balances male domination in other areas; this section uses Australian aboriginal culture as its focus. The areas covered are wide ranging; many articles are fresh and suggest new work to be done. The material takes the reader to several cultural worlds and through many expressions of female spirituality. This work is a cosmopolitan example of the new scholarship. College level.

King, Ursula, ed. *Women in the World's Religions, Past and Present.* New York: Paragon House, 1987. (God, The Contemporary Discussion Series). ISBN 0-913757-32-2; 0-913757-33-0pa.

This work grew out of a call for papers on or about women in the religions, from an historical, contemporary, or comparative point of view. Therefore, the methods used in these articles are mixed with historical and descriptive works blended with normative positions. The response by able theologians and historians was generous and became the core of this collection. Most articles concern the Christian faith, but other pieces deal with the topics of women in African traditional religions, women in Buddhism, women in the Hare Krishna movement, evangelical feminism, and Unification theology and women. These are welcome additions to the growing body of scholarship on women and religion, especially the material on evangelicalism and new religious movements.

Some of the questions addressed are: What do theology and spiritual writings teach concerning women? How do religious traditions use female symbolism? To what degree do women participate in the rituals and decision-making bodies of their tradition? and Why is female religious experience rarely reflected in official theology, but more substantially found in mystical and spiritual writings?

Three overarching categories organize the division of this book: 1) historical and systematic perspectives; 2) contemporary perspectives; and 3) feminist reflections. The last category addresses topics such as: goddesses, witches, androgeny, and beyond; sex, dependency, and religion from a Buddhist perspective; and women and philosophies of interconnectedness. The significance of feminist conceptuality to the transformation of contemporary religious consciousness is also addressed. Much of this text makes fascinating reading, and for the reader who desires a collection on women and religion that combines factual presentations on past and contemporary religious life with new directions in theology, this is an excellent resource. College level.

Sharma, Arvind, ed. *Women in World Religions.* Albany, NY: State University of New York Press. 1987. ISBN 0-88706-374-8; 0-88706-375-6pa.

This book features a collection of articles that deal with the role and treatment of women in world religions and in one preliterate tradition—aboriginal Australia. Objective and sensitive to the difficulty of discussing the role of women in religion in so short a format, this work is evidence of the maturing of scholarship in this area. Each author is a specialist in her field. The material covered is similar to that found in Carmody's *Women and World Religions,* but the selections are larger and have considerably more information. Carmody contributes an article on Jewish attitudes toward women.

The methods used are phenomenological and historical, and each author avoids stereotypical presentations of male/female relationships. An interesting article by Jane I. Smith on Islam explodes formulaic thinking about women and Islam and invites the reader to consider a new woman who is both Muslim and concerned with women's rights. One of the leading theologians of the Christian tradition, Rosemary Ruether, offers an article on the role of women in Christianity. College level.

Primal Traditions

Although primal or preliterate traditions are largely the domain of anthropology, findings in that field become material for reflection in comparative religion and theology. The word *primitive* is no longer used because of its connotations of inferiority. Primal traditions were once thought of as religions of the past whose preliterate status left them ill prepared for survival in the modern age. A steady erosion of traditions in the missionary camps of Islam and Christianity has long been observed. But as the modern world becomes more sensitive to the rights of minorities, and as dominant cultures accept the philosophy of pluralism, smaller tribal cultures in some areas are entering a period of creative adaptation.

We have already seen how feminist thought has found a greater respect for social and religious equality in some preliterate traditions. Other researchers have been impressed with the complexity and sophistication of primal symbol systems, of primal spirituality, of the sensitivity of these traditions to the religious value of the earth, of the wisdom reflected in rites of passage, and of the achievement of harmonious interpersonal relationships.

Many nineteenth- and early-twentieth-century classics on primal religions sought out the earliest manifestations of religion, and their findings exist as permanent contributions to the discipline of the history of religions. Introductions to world religions, depending on their length, usually contain a small section on preliterate traditions. The traditions usually referred to are Native American and African, indicating that the author is American. The present reviewer has followed this pattern with the following offerings.

Textbooks on Primal Traditions

Gill, Sam D. *Beyond the primitive: The Religions of Nonliterate Peoples.* New York: Prentice Hall Press, 1982. (The Prentice-Hall Series in World Religions). ISBN 0-13-076034-X.

This work is a sensitive study of primal traditions; it is ideal for discussion groups, given its brevity and clarity. As the title indicates, Gill finds fault with what most persons mean by the word *primitive*; in chapter 1 he provides an excellent discussion of why he chose the term *nonliterate* instead. Chapter 2 shows how primal cultures experience space and time differently than literate cultures. Chapter 3 discusses the importance and power of art to express primal beliefs. Chapter 4 speaks of the legacy of early hunting societies and the effect of the invention of agriculture. Chapter 5 deals with the importance of story-telling and myth for oral traditions. Chapter 6 analyzes the function of ritual in rites of passage and annual rites, with interesting material on the roles of shamans and clowns.

The role of the traditions in the present is emphasized in chapter 7, which discusses the problem of confronting and affirming modernity, and the variety of responses that have occurred, such as the ghost dance movement of the Great Plains Indians. Chapter 8 contains concluding remarks and expresses hope that the variety, complexity, and abiding dignity of the traditions have been perceived by the reader. For the advanced high school or college reader taking his or her first look at the nature of nonliterate traditions, Gill's *Beyond the Primitive* is an excellent starting place.

————. *Native American Religions: An Introduction*. Belmont, CA: Wadsworth, 1982. (The Religious Life of Man Series). ISBN 0-534-00973-5.

Gill exhibits the same sympathy in this work that he does in his introduction to nonliterate traditions. American Indians are not strangers to the author, and so he writes for at least three audiences: Native Americans, non-Native Americans, and non-Americans (especially Europeans). His intention is to present a humane and academic understanding of these traditions by giving the reader an appreciation for the diversity and complexity of Native American traditions.

Chapter 1 begins with creation myths among representative tribes such as the Zuni, Seneca, and Navajo, with a discussion of the trickster figure and the cosmic significance of Indian art. Chapter 2 treats the oral nature of the tradition in poetry and performance. Chapter 3 deals with religious paintings, masks, clowns, and other symbols. Chapter 4 is an exploration of the Native American life cycle, from birth to puberty to death, using the metaphor of the journey. Chapter 5 discusses bear, corn, winter, and other themes that are central to many tribal ceremonies. Chapter 6 considers the problems of modernization and the changes that have occurred among the Rio Grande Pueblos, the Yaqui, and the Plains Tribes since the coming of Europeans and Christianity. As part of his concluding remarks in chapter 7, Gill offers a summary of his intention in writing each chapter and gives a helpful bibliography for further research.

The clear presentation of *Native American Religions* makes it an excellent place for the high-school reader to begin. Though the material is presented in a straightforward, nontechnical manner, it shows a sophisticated comprehension of the subject.

King, Noel Q. *African Cosmos: An Introduction to Religion in Africa*. Belmont, CA: Wadsworth, 1986. (The Religious Life of Man Series). ISBN 0-534-05334-3.

As Western scholarship has recently come to know, African religion is rich in ethics, myth, and spirituality. Many of its ideas prepare the reader for a fuller understanding of the worldview contained in the Hebrew scriptures. The author presents several major religious systems common to equatorial Africa, those religions he has personally studied with African intellectuals who are familiar with both their own traditions and Western ways of thought and scholarship. The traditions treated include: the Yoruba of Nigeria; the Akan of Ghana; the religious world of Bantu-speaking peoples, including the religion of the Ganda and the Swahili; and the religions of the "Luo" river-lake peoples, including the Dinka, the Nuer, and the Acholi.

The central concern of African traditions are described as "woman and man, their fullness of being and power, their health in the widest sense." Around this center, the author analyzes themes that continually circulate in African values: doctrines about God; the greater and lesser spirits; the ancestors; the nature of being human; the "faceless powers" (sorcery, magic, fetishes, blessings and curses); and means of fellowship with the spirit world (prayer, divination, rituals, sacrifice, and mysticism). This is the focus found in the first five chapters. Chapter 5 is especially interesting in its treatment of spirit possession by gods and deceased humans, and of the nature of African "witchcraft."

A new approach informs chapter 6, "Enter Jesus and Muhammad," which tells the story of the Islamization and Christianization of much of Africa. It analyzes the Africanity that both traditions manifest under the impress of traditional culture (note that the author has also written a separate work, *Christian and Muslim in Africa*). Chapter 7 deals with post-colonial Africa and how the central motifs of African religion continue to survive in both traditional religion and in African Christianity and Islam.

This is an important work for the churches, with an extensive bibliography and recommendations for exploring African art, music, and dance. Helpful material on slides, video, and museums is also offered at the end of the text. A must for those interested in African traditions, this text is appropriate for both high school and college readers.

Lessa, William A., and Evon Z. Vogt, eds. *Reader in Comparative Religion: An Anthropological Approach*. 4th ed. New York: Harper-Collins, 1979. ISBN 0-06-043991-2.

This is the standard work for those seeking a thorough introduction to the various aspects of primal religion. The reader is offered a collection of essays rather than a single narrative; however, each section opens with brief explanatory introductions that organizes the work topically. Articles are a blend of classical (nineteenth-century, early-twentieth-century) and contemporary scholarship. The contributors represent many of the most significant scholars in the field, past and present. Because each of its four editions alters the selections somewhat, the individual looking for a particular article must on occasion refer to an earlier edition. This is necessary to keep abreast with developments, but can be frustrating in that first-rate material must inevitably be edited or replaced.

Reader in Comparative Religion is a large volume, with more than 400 pages of double-columned print. Contents include articles on: 1) the origin and development of religion; 2) the function of religion in human society; 3) the interpretation of symbolism; 4) the analysis of myth; 5) the symbolic analysis of ritual; 6) the purposes of shamanism; 7) interpretations of magic, witchcraft, and divination; 8) the meaning of ghosts and ancestor worship; and 9) dynamics in religion, such as nativistic revivals and millenarianism. Although the work is too large to be used as a reader for church groups, individual articles can be discussed. This collection will demonstrate the intellectual range and depth of the discipline to a person unfamiliar with the study of primal religions. College level.

Sullivan, Laurence E., ed. *Native American Religions: North America*. New York: Macmillan, 1989. (Religion, History, and Culture: Selections from The Encyclopedia of Religion). ISBN 0-02-897402-6.

This is a reference work with selections on history, culture, and religion taken from the monumental *Encyclopedia of Religion*. In part 1, information on different ritual practices, beliefs, and customs is provided for tribes and regions of the country. Part 2 discusses mythic themes, tricksters, drama, iconography, music, sun dance, ghost dance, potlatch, and modern religious movements. For the person who needs to find facts on single tribes or regions, this work is required reading. However, given its encyclopedic style, it is not recommended for straightforward reading, even though each of the topics treated in part 2 makes for excellent reading by itself. The bibliographies on specific tribes are significant contributions for one hoping to research a geographic area or pursue an interest in a specific tribe's religion. The same thoroughness is found in the bibliographies of part 2. Essential for scholarship, this book is also appropriate for high school and college readers.

Underhill, Ruth M. *Red Man's Religion: Beliefs and Practices of the Indians North of Mexico*. Chicago: University of Chicago Press, 1965. ISBN 0-226-84167-7.

Although published in 1965, many scholars consider *Red Man's Religion* to be the first adequate text treating Native American religion. Written in nontechnical language, the text is intended for "those making their first acquaintance with the First Americans." Nonetheless, there are suggestions in this volume that experts have found useful. Twenty-three chapters form the external organization of this work. Most of them deal with various rituals, from hunting and gathering to war, planting, and the sun dance.

Chapter 1 discusses the Indian perception of the supernatural, as does chapter 3, which deals with the impersonal concept of sacred power among different tribes. Chapter 2 handles the problem of Indian origins and geographic dispersion. Chapter 4 discusses creation and world origin beliefs. Chapter 5 discusses the spirit world. Chapter 6 has important information on woman power. Chapter 7 contains material on attitudes toward the dead. Chapter 9 deals with religious specialists such as medicine man, shaman, and priest. Chapter 10, "The Vision," contains material on the vision quest.

Remaining true to the significance of ritual for American Indians, chapters 11–22 focus on rituals of great importance. Chapter 23 discusses the modern religious movements that emerged as a response to European dominance, such as Christianity, the ghost dance millenarian movement, movements of coexistence, and the peyote cult. Informative, sympathetic, and easy to access, this work is an enjoyable entrance into Native American religion.

Hinduism

Hinduism was the focus of much textual research during the nineteenth century, when grammars of Sanskrit aided scholars in their successful efforts to reconstruct the Indo-European tree of languages. Turn-of-the-century missionary Vivekananda brought to America and

Europe an interest in this tradition, although the Bhagavad Gita had already made an impression on writers like Emerson and Whitman. Popular Hindu notions were spread through the Theosophical Movement, continuing the West's fascination with India. The 1960s found a Hindu revival in the United States, Great Britain, and, to a lesser degree, the Continent as part of the counterculture. Besides producing popular works of sketchy (and sometimes dubious) content, this period also produced pieces of excellent quality. The following books are a sample of the fairly large number of works available. Less technical pieces have been emphasized, as readings with a large volume of Sanskrit terms can dispirit the reader.

Textbooks on Hinduism

Embree, Ainslee T., and Stephen Hay, eds. *Sources of Indian Tradition*. 2d ed. New York: Columbia University Press, 1989. 2 vols. ISBN 0-231-06650-3 (vol. 1); 0-231-06651-1pa. (vol. 1); 0-231-06414-4 (vol. 2); 0-231-06415-2pa. (vol. 2).

This work contains selections from Hindu writings of all periods, including early Buddhist, Jain, and Sikh writings. For the reader who wishes to study primary scriptural and philosophical sources, this is the finest collection available.

Kinsley, David R. *Hinduism: A Cultural Perspective*. 2d ed. Englewood Cliffs, NJ: Prentice-Hall, 1993. (Prentice-Hall Series in World Religions). ISBN 0-13-395732-2.

This book is part of the Prentice-Hall Series in World Religions, which presents a religious worldview in many cultural facets so that the reader will see the unity of vision that informs art, politics, belief, ritual, and other aspects of the tradition. The method is a synthetic one that "encourage[s] an understanding of the worldview, lifestyle, and deep dynamics of religious cultures in practice as they affect real people."

The introduction (chapter 1) takes the reader to Benares to see Hindu culture operating in the lives of ordinary people. Chapter 2 gives an historical outline of five periods in the development of Hinduism, offers some historical scenes from the great epics, and introduces two saints from the past. Chapter 3 deals with dissent in the tradition. Chapter 4 gives illustrations of art as revelation. Chapter 5 discusses central Hindu beliefs and presents Shankara and Gandhi as representative thinkers. Chapter 6 addresses the topic of worship and gives examples, including a discussion of goddess worship. Chapter 7 explains the social structure of the caste system and the stages of life, and explores the nature of pollution and purity for different castes. Chapter 8 reviews some of the great gods and offers a synopsis of the Hindu vision.

This work, clear and replete with living, modern examples, takes the reader to modern India to observe Hindu life in action. It is an excellent introduction and a corrective to earlier works that emphasized belief systems or philosophy to the exclusion of the total religious culture. Kinsley's work is ideal as an introductory text for the advanced high school level and beyond.

Koller, John M. *The Indian Way.* New York: Macmillan, 1982. ISBN 0-02-365800-2.

This work is an idealistic presentation of the Indic path from a philosophical and spiritual perspective. Koller, more than other writers, is able to help the reader discover the various answers that India's saints and sages have given to the question, "Who am I?" The answer is almost always, "I am Divine," even though the precise meaning of divinity differs, and the best ways to attain it are disputed. Koller guides us through the usual introductory material: Indic and Vedic beginnings, caste and individual norms, the Upanishads and liberation, and so on. Also appealing are his treatments of the ideals and distinctions between the different paths to liberation in chapters that discuss the Jaina vision, the way of the Buddha, Yoga, the Bhagavad Gita, devotional Hinduism, and systematic philosophy. Koller also includes an important discussion of Islam in India and the faith of the Sikhs. *The Indian Way* is rounded off with the reformation of modern Hindu spirituality in the nineteenth and twentieth centuries (Koller calls it a renaissance), and offers prospects for the future.

This is philosophy at its most approachable and is highly recommended for the beginner. Works like Kinsley's *Hinduism: A Cultural Perspective* or A. L. Basham's *The Wonder That Was India* (out of print, but still a significant reference work) might be read in conjunction with this text to give students a larger cultural foundation. At times, Koller confuses the ideal of religion with its less-than-perfect manifestation in society, but this is the sign of one who is in love with the ideal, one who is an able guide to show us religion at its best. For those hoping to continue their exploration of the intricacies of India's philosophies, Koller's suggestions for further reading are valuable. College level.

Prabhavananda, Swami, and Christopher Isherwood, trans. *The Song of God: Bhagavad Gita.* New York: NAL/Dutton, 1954. ISBN 0-451-62757-1.

Called the "Bible of India," the Bhagavad Gita is the foremost work for spiritual formation in Hinduism. It has inspired many in Western traditions, maintains a perennial freshness, and elicits numerous translations. The translation one chooses is largely a matter of aesthetics, but this translation is valuable because it is a collaboration between a literary person and a Hindu scholar. If looking for a superior work of scholarship from a Western critical perspective, Frank Edgerton's translation contains penetrating essays that form an invaluable commentary, but Edgerton's literary effort is inferior.

Prabhavananda and Isherwood's easy style make the Gita a delight to read, though their interpretation of the Advaita Vedantic (a school of Hindu philosophy) is questionable. Originally part of the massive epic the *Mahabharata*, the Gita is an insertion by an unknown sage who summarizes the paths of Hinduism in a discussion between

Krishna and the great warrior Arjuna on the plain of Kurukshetra before a tragic battle of mythic proportion.

Radhakrishnan, Sarvepalli. *The Hindu View of Life*. Cambridge, MA: Unwin Hyman, 1988. ISBN 0-04-294115-6.

In this short work, the basic themes of Hinduism are presented by a grand master of scholarship. Having taught at Oxford for years, Radhakrishnan was unique in his ability to compare Eastern and Western philosophical traditions. He is to be credited more than any person in the twentieth century for bringing a logical and systematic treatment of Indic philosophy to the West. The methodology found in *The Hindu View of Life* is philosophical and idealistic. It gives both the ideas that inspire Indian religion and the ideals that underly its complex social structure.

Chapter 1 contains a succinct and penetrating presentation of Hindu religious experience. Chapter 2 deals with the Hindu solution to the problem of religious disagreement and conflict. Chapters 3 and 4 discuss the nature of the Hindu *dharma*.

The concept of *dharma* includes morality, etiquette, and the proper ways of behaving, given one's place in life, age, sex, caste, occupation, and level of spiritual development.

Radhakrishan writes in clear language; he has the wisdom of a pastor in presenting his message for different audiences, and his familiarity with Western spirituality makes his comparisons to Hinduism precise and informative. Highly recommended for the advanced high school level and up, this text is for those who wish to quickly penetrate the heart of a tradition.

Zaehner, Robert C. *Hinduism*. New York: Oxford University Press, 1962. ISBN 0-19-888012-X.

This work provides a masterful entrance into the historical reconstruction of classical Hinduism by one of the twentieth-century's greatest comparative religionists. Zaehner uses Hindu scripture to reveal India's developing understanding of God (personal and impersonal), *dharma* (duty and cosmic law), *moksha* (spiritual liberation), *bhakti* (devotional love of God), and the continuity of Hindu ethics through 2,500 years. Gandhi is shown to be an embodiment of classical Hindu ethics, and the reader is given one of the finest presentations of quality critical scholarship blended with philosophical appreciation. This is a work for those who have some familiarity with Hindu tradition. College level.

Jainism

The Jain tradition, founded by Nattaputta Vardhamāna Mahāvīra (540-463 B.C.E.), is a vital community of India (though small—less than 4 million) known for charity and education, and having a distinct vision of reality that makes it interesting both to members of Western religions and to the 80 percent of the Hindu population who are theists. Jainism rejected the Hindu scriptures and their concepts of God for its own understanding of the ultimate state of consciousness (*moksha*). In Jain cosmology, the gods themselves are bound by the wheel of karma and thus cannot guide humankind to the other shore of freedom. The gods are not as significant in Jainism as are great individuals such as Mahāvīra, who is known as a fordfinder, one who finds and crosses over the river of time into the eternity of one's higher self.

In Jain teaching, salvation is secured only through rigorous effort, and Mahāvīra himself practiced an almost unimaginable asceticism. The tradition is famous for these practices, especially in the monastic part of the community, and has affirmed the practice of voluntary starvation for those who are spiritually prepared to leave the world of karma. Laypersons are expected to meditate and deprive themselves in lesser ways, and support the community of monks. One of the most famous of the Jain virtues is *ahimsa*, or harmlessness, a theme made popular in the West by Gandhi, who derived it from his early exposure to Jains.

Today, many Jains are educated professionals and businesspersons who play down the more extreme elements of the tradition, but who cultivate *ahimsa*, practice charity to animals and people, and are committed to vegetarianism.

Textbooks on Jainism

Jaini, Padmanabh S. *The Jaina Path of Purification.* Berkeley: University of California Press, 1979. ISBN 0-520-03459-7.

Acknowledged as one of the finest works in the field, Jaini balances mature scholarship with a sympathetic grasp of the goals of Jainism. Much Jain scholarship draws on a very technical philosophical and scriptural vocabulary that makes readability in English cumbersome. Jaini couches his in-depth scholarship in a fluent and easy style, making this work an excellent text. Nine chapters include material on Mahavira and the foundations of the movement; the first disciples and the Jaina scriptures; the nature of reality; the mechanism of bondage; the first awakening; the path of the layman; rituals and ceremonies; the mendicant path; and Jaina society through the ages. Included is an impressive bibliography, a list of translations, and a list of modern works.

If the reader has time for only one work on Jainism, this is the one. College level.

Roy, Ashim Kumar. *A History of the Jainas.* Columbia, MO: South Asia Books, 1984. ISBN 0-8364-1136-6.

Clear and concise, this brief introduction covers some of the same material developed by Jaini on Mahāvīra and the development of the movement, but also includes other important issues, especially the legendary history of fordfinders (liberated teachers) prior to Mahāvīra, the problem of schisms and separate scriptures, and a clear discussion of the differences that divide the Digambaras from the Shvetambaras. The appendices provide useful information on the different canonical scriptures, the mythical and historical list of fordfinders, and the lists of pontiffs of the different sects. This is a college-level work, given its many scriptural and historical references. It does not read as evenly as Jaini's *The Jaina Path of Purification*, but contains information of the utmost importance for a rounded reading of Jainism.

Sikhism

The Sikh tradition is unique in the history of religion—it is the only syncretistic religion to survive a span of many centuries. Its success can, in large part, be traced to the spiritual genius of its founder, Guru Nanak, one of the greatest religious personalities on record. Nanak's dates (1469–1539 C.E.) place him in India (near modern day Lahore) at a time when Muslim *sufis* (devotional mystics) and Hindu *bhaktis* (devotional mystics) sang songs of praise in the same villages to the Personal Lord of the Universe. Often, the followers of these saints worshipped at the same shrines and sang in the same processions.

Somewhat earlier than Nanak, the saintly poet Kabir (1440–1518 C.E.), though born a Muslim, had described himself as "a child of Rama and Allah" and sought reconciliation between Hindu and Muslim. Nanak was able to formalize this reconciliation into a theology that drew on ideas from both Muslim and Hindu sources. Seeing that different names of God, like Allah or Shiva, divided people, Nanak called his God "True Name," thus bypassing centuries of conditioned response. His ministry began with a prophetic call that reminds one of the call of the Hebrew prophets or of Muhammad. In his preaching, Nanak combined notions of the world as *maya* (illusion) with the belief of the world as God's creation, and he combined the image of God as Lord with more impersonal names for ultimate reality. He accepted revelation from a personal God, yet preached reincarnation.

After the death of Nanak, a line of nine gurus provided the organizational stability and spiritual leadership the fledgling community required. By the time of the sixth guru, Har Govind, this pacifist group was transformed into a theocratic fighting force, prepared to defend their way of life against Muslim persecution. With the assassination of the last guru, Gobind Singh, the focus of authority was placed in sacred scripture, the Adi Granth, a collection of the writings and poems of Nanak, the gurus, and other mystics, including Kabir.

Textbooks on Sikhism

Cole, William Owen, and Piara Singh Sambhi. *The Sikhs: Their Religious Beliefs and Practices*. New York: Routledge, Chapman and Hall, 1989. (Library of Religious Beliefs and Practices). ISBN 0-415-04028-0.

This work is a superior and readable introduction to the Sikh tradition. Chapters deals with: 1) the religious background of Guru Nanak; 2) the place of the ten gurus in the Sikh religion; 3) the Sikh scriptures; 4) the Gurdwara and Sikh worship; 5) Sikh religious thought; 6) daily life, ceremonies, and festivals; 7) ethics; 8) the attitude of Sikhism toward other religions; and 9) Sikhism from 1708 to 1976 (including material on Sikhs in Canada and the United States). The appendices provide population statistics, the structure of the Adi Granth, and most importantly, a copy of the *Rehat Maryada*, or guide to the Sikh way of life, which is a statement of faith, ethics, and practice approved in 1945. Included are a glossary of terms, an annotated bibliography together with additional bibliography, plus (rare for a work of this quality) important materials for audiovisual aids to the study of Sikhism. College level.

McLeod, W. H. *The Sikhs: History, Religion and Society*. New York: Columbia University Press, 1989. ISBN 0-231-06814-X.

This work is a mature accomplishment by a seasoned scholar of the Sikh tradition. Each chapter exhibits considerable reflection on problems that arise in adequately interpreting Sikhism, and is appropriate for a college-level readership. Chapters include: 1) "The Sikhs"; 2) "The Origins of the Sikh Tradition"; 3) "Sikh Doctrine"; 4) "Who Is a Sikh?"; 5) "The Literature of the Sikhs"; and 6) "Sikhs in the Modern World." McLeod presents an excellent glossary of terms and a selected bibliography.

Buddhism

Buddhism is increasingly becoming an American religion, especially on the West coast where there is a large Asian-American population. In its devotional forms, Buddhism has had some success as a missionary religion, and has exercised considerable influence among intellectuals as a philosophy with an impersonalist concept of ultimate reality (*dharma*), and a mystical technique to attain it in Zen. Within the last twenty-five years, the West's one-sided preoccupation with the Zen tradition of Buddhism is being corrected by interest in the Theravada tradition (Southern Buddhism); the Vairocana tradition (Tibetan Buddhism as practiced by the Dalai Lama); and the Amida tradition, a Buddhism of salvation by grace, in both its Japanese and Chinese (Omito) forms.

Modern scholarship continues to explore the vast area of Buddhist history, and able scholars from Sri Lanka, Japan, the United States, and Europe lead the field. Japan, having mastered the techniques of modern research from Germany in the nineteenth and early twentieth centuries, is an important contributor to the growing global sophistication about the history and varieties of Buddhism. In relation to Christian churches, Christian/Buddhist dialogue is proceeding in a serious manner, and Buddhist concepts are beginning to appear in the writings of Christian theologians, such as John Cobb's *Beyond Dialogue: Toward a Mutual Transformation of Christianity and Buddhism*.

Textbooks on Buddhism

Beyer, Stephan. *The Buddhist Experience: Sources and Interpretations.*
Belmont, CA: Wadsworth, 1974. (The Religious Life of Man Series).
ISBN 0-8221-0127-0.
This work brings together a collection of Buddhist tales, scripture,
and philosophy organized around the categories of virtue, meditation,
and wisdom. A helpful sampling to complement Robinson and
Johnson's *The Buddhist Religion.*

Fields, Rick. *How the Swans Came to the Lake: A Narrative History of
Buddhism in America.* Boston: Shambala, 1992. ISBN 0-87773-
631-6.
Fields tells the story of Buddhism in America in eminently readable prose. He tells about the migrations of ethnic forms of Buddhism,
and also about the development of an American Buddhism. This is an
important work for distinguishing between the various strands of
Buddhism that now flourish in North America, and for showing the
various ways in which Buddhism found new life on foreign shores. High
school level and beyond.

Hopkins, Jeffrey, and Anne C. Klein. *The Tantric Distinction: An
Introduction to Tibetan Buddhism.* Boston: Wisdom, 1984. ISBN
0-86171-023-1.
Perhaps no other form of Buddhism has seemed as mysterious to
the West than the Tantric form. Since the exile of the Dalai Lama from
Tibet, and the relocation of large numbers of Tibetans to the West, the
problem of misinformation has been corrected. Jeffrey Hopkins, the
scholar and personal interpreter for the Dalai Lama, and Anne Klein
have written a readable and understandable introduction that makes
this tradition real and capable of being appreciated by a nonscholarly
audience. Advanced high school level and up.

Kalupahana, David. *A History of Buddhist Philosophy: Continuities
and Discontinuities.* Honolulu: University of Hawaii Press, 1992.
ISBN 0-8248-1384-7; 0-8248-1402-9pa.
Buddhism can be misrepresented in two major ways, either as a
philosophy detached from experience or as an experience detached from
philosophy. The influence of Zen in America has often had the effect of
so emphasizing the immediate experiential dimension of Buddhist
contemplation that the powerful philosophical tradition that supports
Buddhism has not been given proper voice. Kalupahana's *A History of
Buddhist Philosophy* corrects this imbalance and allows the breadth of
the philosophical history of Buddhist thought to influence the reader.
His presentation uses both Western and Buddhist categories of
thought, enabling a person with some background in Western philosophy
to easily appropriate the themes of Buddhism. Because this is a philosophical work, it is college level.

Kapleau, Philip. *The Three Pillars of Zen: Teaching, Practice and Enlightenment*. New York: Doubleday, 1980. ISBN 0-385-14786-4.

The late D. T. Suzuki introduced Westerners to Zen a generation ago (1940s to 1960s). His writings are standards in the field, and the beginner with some philosophical background is still advised to seek out his *An Introduction to Zen Buddhism*, or the collection of essays edited by William Barrett, *Zen Buddhism: Selected Writings of D. T. Suzuki*. Still, a generation of American students has been educated without much background in philosophy. Philip Kapleau's *The Three Pillars of Zen* nicely avoids this problem, and in doing so makes Zen come alive for the reader. His compilation, translations, introductions, and notes make this tradition accessible and an enjoyable discovery for the reader. The book is dedicated to his teachers, as is proper, for Kapleau is a *roshi* (a recognized Zen teacher who has personally realized the truth of Zen), and *roshis* receive their title by undergoing a strenuous apprenticeship to other *roshis*.

Part 1 provides the introductory lectures of Kapleau's master, Yasutani-Roshi, on Zen training. It also provides Yasutani-Roshi's commentary on the *koan*, the paradox used to train Buddhist monks; Mu, a traditional nondiscursive syllable whose utterance signifies the awakening of the Bodhi-mind or mind of illumination; private interviews with ten Westerners; and the sermon of One-mind by fourteenth-century Zen master Bassui, with Bassui's letters to his disciples, including laypersons. Both the private interviews and the letters reveal the personal side of Zen that has been lacking in prior treatments. This is ground-breaking material that takes the reader into the spiritual core of a tradition that has been difficult to document.

Part 2 provides eight contemporary enlightenment experiences by Japanese and Westerners, plus the moving letters of a saintly twenty-five-year-old woman to her master, Harada-Roshi, as she is dying, including his eloquent comments.

In part 3, one finds the famous "Ten Oxherding Pictures" with commentary, material on Dogen's "Being-Time," *zazen* (meditation) postures, and notes on Zen vocabulary and Buddhist doctrine. The material varies in difficulty; letters and interviews can be approached at the high school level, whereas the commentaries on doctrine are more appropriate for college level. If a person has time to read only one book on Zen, this is it.

La Fleur, William R. *Buddhism: A Cultural Perspective*. New York: Prentice Hall Press, 1988. (Prentice-Hall Series in World Religions). ISBN 0-13-084724-0.

The Prentice-Hall Series in World Religions aims to present the worldview of religious cultures by showing how its disparate parts express the underlying total vision of reality. Part 1 offers a concise history of Buddhism, up to the founding of its major forms. It also discusses "difficult places along the middle path"; that is, material on religious dissent, the role of women, the friction with Confucianism in China, and a section on Buddhist poetry. The section on poetry gives the reader an insight into the series, which does not pretend to offer customary introductory material, but proceeds by giving "cameo" portraits into personalities, movements, and historical moments that reveal the spirit of the religions as "they affect real people." Part 2 discusses classical and modern Buddhist philosophy; the Buddha as a model and the way rituals reflect this; the *sangha,* or Buddhist community; and Buddhism's response to modernity.

This is a lively work that successfully demonstrates the spirit of a religion in its choices of people, problems, and movements, including the choice of self-immolation made by monks during the Vietnam War and its religious meaning. Recommended for high school level and beyond.

Robinson, Richard H., and Willard L. Johnson. *The Buddhist Religion: A Historical Introduction.* 3d ed. Belmont, CA: Wadsworth, 1982. (The Religious Life of Man Series). ISBN 0-534-01027-X.

This book is considered by most experts in the field to be the best introduction to Buddhist faith, designed to be used with Steven V. Beyer's supplementary reader *The Buddhist Experience: Sources and Interpretations.* However, Robinson's work certainly stands on its own. Part 1 is an insightful presentation of the first centuries of the Buddhist pilgrimage which discusses the antecedents of Buddhism; Gautama's (the historical Buddha) enlightenment and his teachings; the development of Indian Buddhism; the rise of the Mahayana tradition; the Mahayana soteriology (concept of salvation); the rise of Tantric Buddhism; and the fall of Buddhism in India. The in-depth understanding and sympathetic treatment of material on doctrine and salvation in Mahayana is unusual in an introductory text. Part 2 addresses the spread of Buddhism and its developments in Southeast Asia, East Asia, the Tibetan cultural region, and the West, and offers a synoptic commentary on the past, present, and future of Buddhism. Designed for the college reader.

Chinese Religion

China began its religious journey with elements of manaism (reverence for and use of sacred power) and animism (spirits ensouling the forces of nature). By the sixth to fifth centuries B.C.E., it had been transformed into a philosophical culture, with the names of Confucius (Master Kung) and Lao Tzu becoming legendary. Confucianism continued the moral ordering of society begun by Confucius, whose concern was to rebuild the humanity of a civilization lost in centuries of feudal warfare. To this end, he advocated a return to the noble pattern of the ancients; the cultivation of the liberal arts, including poetry, music, and history; and moral work on the self. Confucius organized a school, praised the subtle work of ritual, insisted that people think of the duties of their station in life, and composed sayings for moral edification. In all this, he insisted that he was not an innovator but one called to return society to the Tao, the way things are (the Chinese version of natural law), if the human enterprise was to succeed.

Lao Tzu (also named "old boy," if historical) is an older contemporary of Confucius, who also saw the good life that awaited the individual in a return to the Tao. But whereas the Tao of Confucius requires moral control, social responsibility, and the maintenance of ritual, Lao Tzu's program calls for a withdrawal from moral control to discover the spontaneous goodness of human nature. Ritual was rejected as artificial and contrary to nature, and urban life was seen as too citified and lacking in the simple virtue of the rural town. The guiding concept was a return to nature in order to find the Tao, whereas for Confucius the Tao was present in complex and sophisticated society as well as in the countryside.

These two philosophies have often been thought of as complementary sides of the Tao. The usual synthesis between them, as well as with Buddhism, which had begun to influence thought by the second century C.E., is expressed in the adage "In social life a Confucianist, in retirement a Taoist, and in death a Buddhist." Buddhism brought a joyful vision of life after death into the Chinese theater, and an intense spirituality that aimed higher than either Confucianism, which is a wisdom of this world, or Taoism, which in its early form did not enjoy the supernatural vistas of Buddhism.

Western scholars have long debated whether Confucianism or Taoism should be counted as religions or philosophies. They are, in fact, both; and in their later organized forms they contain rituals, morality, myths, beliefs, and all the other ingredients of religion. Confucius believed in life after death, a morality inscribed in the heart of man by Heaven (his term for the Divine), and a sense of being called to a sacred mission. The *Tao Te Ching*, a work ascribed to Lao Tzu or his school, posits an invisible spiritual power that is the fountain of being and the source of the nature of things; salvation consists in conformity to this mysterious reality.

Textbooks on Chinese Religion

Chan, Wing-tsit, trans. and comp. *A Source Book in Chinese Philosophy*. Princeton, NJ: Princeton University Press, 1963. ISBN 0-691-01964-9.

This compendium contains a large selection of documents with short and useful introductions by the acknowledged interpreter of Chinese philosophy to the West. This is an important work that, if used in conjunction with Overmeyer's sociological approach or Thompson's cultural emphasis, will provide a broad and balanced view of Chinese religion.

de Bary, William T., et al. *Sources of Chinese Tradition*. New York: Columbia University Press, 1960. 2 vol. ISBN 0-231-08602-4pa. (vol. 1); 0-231-08603-2pa. (vol. 2).

These volumes give the reader access to classical writings in religion (Buddhism), philosophy, art, and economics. Also included are selections on Chinese history written by Chinese historians, including Chinese reactions to the West, modernist movements, and Chinese communism. Much of this material is hard to find elsewhere (e.g., sections from schools of Chinese Buddhism). The original sources provide quick insight into the spirit of earlier ages, with helpful brief introductions. This collection also serves as a useful background work to Japanese culture. As with the Wing-tsit Chan's *A Source Book in Chinese Philosophy* (Chan is also a major contributor to this collection), de Bary's selection can be used to supplement any introductory text to Chinese religion.

Fingarette, Herbert. *Confucius—The Secular As Sacred*. New York: HarperCollins, 1972. ISBN 0-06-131882-2.

The *Analects* of Confucius do not normally make exciting reading for most Westerners, who find in them a combination of biblical proverbs and the common sense epigrams of Ben Franklin. Fingarette does what no other scholar has; he makes Confucius exciting for the Western nonscholar, by revealing the depth in his thought. Confucius is portrayed as a social and religious reformer with insights still useful to modern people. Highly convincing; for high school level and up.

Overmeyer, Daniel L. *Folk Buddhist Religion: Dissenting Sects in Late Traditional China*. Cambridge, MA: Harvard University Press, 1989. (Harvard East Asian Series, no. 83). ISBN 0-317-55369-0.

Many contemporary scholars have expressed the need for understanding and appreciating the "little traditions," those movements that were separate from the dominant religions of the majority or the powerful. Some were prohibited; others were ignored. China often proscribed traditions that were at variance with established Confucianism and, at times, even attacked Buddhism as being anti-Chinese. Overmeyer gives a constructive analysis of a variety of proscribed folk Buddhist movements, or "secret societies," and the populist or peasant values they represented.

Thompson, Laurence G. *Chinese Religion: An Introduction*. 4th ed. Belmont, CA: Wadsworth, 1984. (The Religious Life of Man Series). ISBN 0-534-09270-5.

This is a cultural introduction to Chinese religion and although it treats the three different movements—Confucianism, Taoism, and Buddhism—it focuses upon the way these elements have influenced on Chinese culture: the family, the community, the state, intellectuals, and festivals. An important ending chapter on religion under communism rounds off the work. Thompson offers an excellent analysis of the historical development of religious themes within the orbit of Chinese culture, an important corrective to earlier works that overemphasized philosophy and doctrine. Thompson provides an extensive bibliography for this work, and also has edited and contributed to a helpful supplementary reader, *The Chinese Way in Religion*. Both works are appropriate for college level.

————. *The Chinese Way in Religion*. Belmont, CA: Wadsworth, 1973. (The Religious Life of Man Series). ISBN 0-8221-0109-2.

This work is an important collection of primary sources and secondary articles in the areas of: 1) ancient Chinese traditions, 2) Taoism, 3) Buddhism in China, 4) religion and the state, 5) family religion, 6) popular religion, and 7) religion under communism. Designed to complement Thompson's *Chinese Religion: An Introduction*. College level.

Waley, Arthur. *The Analects of Confucius*. New York: Random House, 1989. ISBN 0-679-72296-3.

This is a standard translation of the *Analects* by one of the major figures in the field. For high school level and beyond.

————. *Three Ways of Thought in Ancient China*. Stanford, CA: Doubleday, 1939. ISBN 0-8047-1169-0.

This work, by one of the most outstanding scholars of Chinese culture in the twentieth century, presents a classic statement on the ways Confucianism, Taoism, and Buddhism—at first contradicted, but later fused with one another. This is a clear introduction to the themes that have supplied the foundation for 2,000 years and more of Chinese thought. College level.

————. *The Way & Its Power: A Study of the Tao Te Ching & Its Place in Chinese Thought*. New York: Grove/Weidenfeld, 1988. ISBN 0-8021-5085-3.

The author offers a clear, easy to read, mystical rendering of the *Tao Te Ching*, with commentary and historical analysis of its influence. College-level commentary.

Welch, Holmes. *Taoism: The Parting of the Way*. Boston: Beacon Press, 1966. ISBN 0-8070-5973-0.

The classic statement of Taoism by Lao Tzu, the *Tao Te Ching*, is notoriously difficult to translate. Its poetic structure allows for different translations, depending on whether one evaluates the work as a piece of philosophy or as a work of mysticism. Welch mentions the mystical interpretation by Waley, but prefers a philosophical reading. Welch adds important material on the development of popular magical Taoism. This important scholarly work, appropriate for college level, gives the reader insight into many aspects of Taoism.

Wright, Arthur F. *Buddhism in Chinese History*. Stanford, CA: Stanford University Press, 1959. ISBN 0-8047-0546-1; 0-8047-0548-8pa.

This is a short work that tells of the introduction, the appropriation, and the development of Buddhism in China. It is crucial for understanding the unique flavor and doctrines of Far Eastern Buddhism, from its earlier Indic and Southeast Asian forms. The author shows the initial resistance to Buddhism and its final synthesis with indigenous Chinese philosophy and worldview. This text is a sound and well-written account for high school level and beyond.

Japanese Religion

The study of Japanese religion is fascinating because of its combination of elements: Shintoism, Buddhism, Confucianism, folk religion, new religions, and Taoism. Japan has entered the twentieth century with a scientific worldview that essentially destroyed a literalistic interpretation of Shinto scripture for intellectuals, causing a massive failure of traditional faith. Buddhism, however, has seen a significant revival and maintains its vitality. Shintoism itself, the only indigenous Japanese religion, has shown itself adaptable in its demythologized form as a religion of natural beauty, ceremonial elegance, and the expression of the unique Japanese character.

Zen and Shin Buddhism have been discussed in the section on Buddhism. Nevertheless, an understanding of many elements in Japanese culture requires an exploration of how Zen has influenced the tea ceremony, floral arrangement, the aesthetic sense in general, and even the martial arts. For this background, one should turn to D. T. Suzuki's *Zen and Japanese Culture.*

If an earlier generation of scholarship displayed more concern for Zen and Shintoism (in large part because of its fusion with Japanese nationalism in World War II), contemporary scholarship has been more interested in Japanese folk traditions and festivals, and recently with the place of women in Japanese religious life. For information on the latter, see the section on women and religion. The following books offer the reader important insight into Japanese religious existence.

Textbooks on Japanese Religion

Blacker, Carmen. *The Catalpa Bow: A Study of Shamanistic Practices in Japan.* 2d ed. Cambridge, MA: Unwin Hyman, 1986. ISBN 0-04-398008-2.

Belief in the supernatural and the spirit world has always been a part of popular Japanese religion, and this work is the first comprehensive study of shamanistic practices that analyzes traditional shamanism found in both classical literature and contemporary practice. College level.

de Bary, William T., et al., ed. *Sources of Japanese Tradition.* New York: Columbia University Press, 1958. 2 vols. ISBN 0-231-02254-9 (set); 0-231-08604-0pa. (vol. 1); 0-231-08605-9pa. (vol. 2).

William de Bary has put together an indispensable collection of historically significant documents from religion, philosophy, and literature, with short and lucid introductions. This is an ideal supplementary reader for any introduction to Japanese religion. It will give the reader access to primary material and a "feel" for the original. College level.

Earhart, H. Byron. *Japanese Religion: Unity and Diversity*. 3d. ed.
   Belmont, CA: Wadsworth, 1982. (The Religious Life of Man Series).
   ISBN 0-534-01028-8.
   The development of all the traditions of Japan (including Christianity) are discussed and united by showing the persistence of unifying
themes in Japanese culture. Divided into seventeen sections, this
sophisticated overview is highly recommended for its brief, perceptive
discussion of both old and new traditions, and for its excellent material
on religion in postwar Japan and religious life in contemporary Japan. If
the reader has special interests in a particular religion or theme,
Earhart's elaborate annotated bibliography and references to research
materials are essential for further research. College level.

———. *Religion in the Japanese Experience: Sources and Interpretations*. Belmont, CA: Wadsworth, 1974. ISBN 0-8221-0104-1.
   Designed to be read in conjunction with the author's *Japanese
Religion*, this compilation of essays and original materials offers information on art, family, nation, new religions, festivals, Shintoism,
Buddhism, Confucianism, Taoism, Christianity, and modernity. Although
either of Earhart's volumes can be read without the other, the combination leads to a rich understanding of the spirit of Japan.

Ellwood, Robert S., and Richard Pilgrim. *Japanese Religion: A Cultural
   Perspective*. New York: Prentice Hall Press, 1985. (Prentice-Hall
   Series in World Religions). ISBN 0-13-509282-5.
   This short, enjoyable work, designed to cover areas of culture often
overlooked in treatments that emphasize history and beliefs, gives
brief snapshots of important people, movements, and rituals that
capture the "soul" of Japan. After a brief overview of religious history,
the authors demonstrate the importance of art; discuss counterculture
movements, such as Nichiren Buddhism and Tenrikyo; provide illustrations of model religious rituals; discuss patterns of religious community; and analyze both change and continuity in Japanese life.
Though less thorough than Kitagawa's history or Earhardt's presentation, this text faithfully shares the flavor of the tradition with the
reader who has limited time. High school level and up.

Hori, Ichiro, Joseph M. Kitigawa, and Alan L. Miller, eds. *Folk Religion
   in Japan: Continuity and Change*. Chicago: University of Chicago
   Press, 1983. (Midway Reprint Series). ISBN 0-226-35335-4.
   This collection of essays has had a significant influence on scholarship through its analysis of the complex fabric of folk religion and its
demonstration of the importance of folk religion to understanding
Japanese culture. This contribution discusses the local quality of a
religion and shows how it is often as important in forming religious
lives as the larger traditions, if not more so. College level.

Kitagawa, Joseph M. *On Understanding Japanese Religion*. Princeton, NJ: Princeton University Press, 1987. ISBN 0-691-07313-9; 0-691-10229-5pa.

America's leading historian of Japanese religion and a member of the respected Chicago School of Religious Studies, Kitagawa guides the reader through the development of Japanese religion in its multifaceted variety. This work includes material on Shintoism and the new religions, and is to be consulted for its objectivity and clarity. College level.

Suzuki, D. T. *Zen and Japanese Culture*. Princeton, NJ: Princeton University Press, 1959. ISBN 0-691-01770-0.

This work is a brilliant presentation of the influence that Zen, though it has only a small following, has had on Japanese attitudes toward life as expressed in the tea ceremony, in flower arrangement, in the understanding of aesthetic space, and in the mental discipline of the martial arts. College level.

Zoroastrianism

Today, Zoroastrianism is a small religion with membership of only approximately 100,000 people. It was originally located in what is now Iran, but in the seventh century its adherents fled Muslim persecution to the Bombay area of India, where they are known as Parsis (from Pars, the Iranian province from which the word *Persia* is also derived). A remnant known by the pejorative name Gabars (infidels) remain in Iran, but call themselves Boh-dinan (followers of the good law).

Many scholars believe that the impact of this tradition on Judaism and Christianity was enormous, coloring the demonology, angelology, and eschatology (images of life after death and the end of the world) of post-Exilic Judaism and thus early Christianity. Images from various apocalypses such as the Book of Revelation seem to be of Zoroastrian ancestry.

Once thought to espouse a complete dualism of good and evil, with two gods sharing in the creation of the world, this tradition has been shown by the research of Robert Zaehner to be monotheistic in the original teachings of Zoroaster (628–551 B.C.E.). Even in Zoroastrianism's later, dualist form, the good god Ahura Mazda overcomes the evil Angra Mainyu at the end of time.

Zoroastrianism is an ethical religion that shares with Judaism, Christianity, and Islam a prophetic sense of warfare against evil. As a community, Zoroastrians are known for both their charity and their commitment to education; they remain a creative minority of India with a distinct identity.

Textbooks on Zoroastrianism

Boyce, Mary. *Zoroastrians: Their Beliefs and Practices*. New York: Routledge Kegan Paul, 1986. (Library of Religious Beliefs and Practices). ISBN 0-7102-0156-7.

The author gives a detailed historical account of the development of Zoroastrianism, including material on the pre-Zoroastrian polytheism against which Zoroaster preached and fought. With an excellent current bibliography, this text is for advanced high school level and beyond.

Hinnells, John R. *Zoroastrianism and the Parsis*. New York: State Mutual Book & Periodical Service, 1985. ISBN 0-7062-3973-3.

This is a readable and direct presentation of Zoroastrian beliefs, practices, and history with useful illustrations. For high school level and up.

Pavry, Jal D. *Zoroastrian Doctrines of a Future Life from Death to the Individual Judgment*. 2d ed. New York: A M S Press, 1965. ISBN 0-404-50481-7.

This work contains a fascinating analysis of Zoroastrian eschatology, which had considerable influence on Jewish, Christian, and Muslim beliefs about the end of time, the nature of judgment at death, and the nature of judgment in general.

Zaehner, Robert C. *The Teachings of the Magi: A Compendium of Zoroastrian Beliefs*. New York: Oxford University Press, 1976. ISBN 0-19-519857-3.

The Magi in the title refers to priests who taught Zoroastrianism in its dualistic post-Zoroaster form. Zaehner has argued that Zoroaster was originally a monotheist, but that later speculation on the power of evil turned his religion into a dualism with deities of good and evil of almost equivalent power. In this work, Zaehner analyzes Zoroastrianism as it was understood for 1,500 years in its teachings on God, the Devil, the origins of the universe, the reasons for imperfection, the nature of the human condition, the purpose of religion, and the ethical teachings that support the purpose of religion. Having presented these, Zaehner considers Zoroastrian sacraments, sacrifice, the fate of the soul at death, and the end of the world. A brilliant scholar, Zaehner does more than tell the story of this religion; he reveals its foundational philosophy and shows the consistency of its vision. College level.

Judaism

Christians have often been under the mistaken impression that they understand Judaism because Christianity can be seen as either a Jewish reform movement or a Jewish heresy. Therefore, in traditional seminary education, Judaism has usually been studied as a portion of Christian tradition, or as backdrop for New Testament analysis. As a result, knowledge of the Jewish tradition from the second century on has been incomplete, except in specialized scholarly works. The importance of Judaism's impact on Christianity and Islam is well known, however, and like other minority religious cultures such as Zoroastrianism or Sikhism, the Jewish tradition continues to exist as a creative minority making contributions beyond its numbers.

Textbooks on Judaism

Anderson, Bernard. *Understanding the Old Testament.* 4th ed. New York: Prentice Hall Press, 1986. ISBN 0-13-935925-7.
    This readable survey covers the period from the Exodus to the beginning of the first century. In presenting the material, Anderson avoids the twin perils of literalism, which reads the Hebrew scriptures as straight history rather than theology, and Continental skepticism, which overrates the literary and theological dimension of the scriptures by failing to give archaeological evidence its place, thus underrating the value of historical material in the scriptures. Anderson's format weaves together literary, historical, theological, and archaeological research. Each chapter draws upon readings from the Hebrew scriptures and follows the unfolding of the biblical story. This is a standard history that is useful for advanced high school level and beyond.

Bright, John. *A History of Israel.* 3d ed. Louisville, KY: Westminster/John Knox, 1981. ISBN 0-664-21381-2.
    This history draws strongly on archaeology and literature to reconstruct the world of Israel's origins and follow its development to the end of the Old Testament period. The clear style of this work disguises the fact that the author draws on a full range of critical scholarship. This is a standard work used in many introductory college courses.

Heschel, Abraham Joshua. *God in Search of Man: A Philosophy of Judaism.* New York: Farrar, Straus & Giroux, 1976. ISBN 0-374-51331-7.
    If the student has time for only one work on the spiritual and foundational teachings of Judaism, this work will do. Used for over thirty years by instructors of theology and world religions, it maintains a freshness and provides direct insight into the heart of the Jewish intellectual understanding of the Divine. High school level and above.

———. *The Prophets.* New York: HarperCollins, 1971. 2 vols. ISBN 0-06-131421-8pa. (vol. 1); 0-06-131557-5pa. (vol. 2).
    This is a brilliant and readable introduction to the prophets, with a discussion of the contribution of each. Also included is an analysis of the unique philosophy that underlies the prophetic corpus, including the meaning of the wrath of God; the prophetic pathos; the nature of prophecy and ecstasy; the problem of prophecy and psychosis; and the

role of prophets, priests, and kings. Highly recommended for its scholarly and sympathetic insight into the prophetic worldview. College level.

Küng, Hans. *Judaism: Between Yesterday and Tomorrow*. New York: Crossroad, 1992. ISBN 0-8245-1181-6.

This is an unusual work in that it combines history, theology, and ethics. Hans Küng is among the most important religious thinkers in the twentieth century. In this work, he divides the history of the Jewish faith into the past that is still present, the challenges of the present, and the possibilities for the future.

Part 1 is a theological reflection on Jewish history that contains an excellent summary (167 pages) of the history of the Jewish faith. Part 2 summarizes the challenges of the present: the Holocaust, the dispute between Christians and Jews, and the problems of Jewish identity today. Part 3 speaks of new possibilities for peace between Muslims and Jews in the Middle East based on what Küng calls a "real-utopian vision" of peace. His hope is based on three postulates: 1) No world survival without a world ethic; 2) No world peace without religious peace; 3) No religious peace without religious dialogue. This work, like others by Küng, is an encyclopedia of learning, and can be read both in separate sections and in chapters of particular interest. The writing style is clear and the language is nontechnical, but the author's breadth of learning may presuppose some college background from the reader. For those concerned with the Jewish future, this is an important work.

Sachar, Howard. *The Course of Modern Jewish History*. New York: Random House, 1990. ISBN 0-679-72746-9.

Sachar has written an objective and interesting study that is a standard for this time period of radical Jewish transformation. Readable and comprehensive. College level.

——. *A History of Israel from the Rise of Zionism to Our Time*. New York: Alfred A. Knopf, 1979. ISBN 0-394-73679-6.

Israel is once again at the center of the world stage. Sachar's work is considered by many to be the best study of the state of Israel. The author reveals the complexity of Zionism and traces the vicissitudes in the creation of the state of Israel and its continuing problems into the 1970s. This is important foundational reading for a controversial topic. College level.

——. *A History of the Jews in America*. New York: Random House, 1993. ISBN 0-679-74530-0.

A commanding presentation of the Jewish experience in America, from colonial days to the present. Twenty-five chapters unify this monumental work. Some representative chapter titles include: "The Germanization of American Jewry," "The Americanization of German Jewry," "Survival in the Immigrant City," "The Zionization of American Jewry," "The Triumph of Democratic Pluralism," and "Defining a

Relationship with the Jewish State." Beautifully written, this large work should intimidate no one, as each of its chapters can be read as small works that are clear and precise within themselves. A wonderful resource for high school level and beyond.

Trepp, Leo. *Judaism: Development and Life.* 3d ed. Belmont, CA: Wadsworth, 1982. ISBN 0-534-00999-9.

This work is well written, sensitive, and a model of clarity for introductory texts. Dr. Trepp has given both Jews and non-Jews a concise look into Jewish history and contemporary life. Written from a conservative-traditional perspective that regards all Jewish denominations as legitimate religious expressions, this work is intended for the general reader with no background. In addition to traditional introductory material, Trepp offers informative chapters on Judaism and America, the Holocaust, and restored Christian-Jewish dialogue. This work includes an excellent bibliography and can be used for study at the advanced high school level.

Islam

Recent historical events have proven the importance of a new understanding of Islam as it moves toward post-colonial self-definition. Older studies of this faith tended to be objective but expressed little feeling or sensitivity to the Islamic worldview.

For several centuries, Islam was the only religion to threaten the borders of Christendom. The West responded in the nineteenth century by colonializing all Muslim nations to varying degrees. This history of rivalry and misunderstanding between the two faiths can be clarified, and hopefully overcome, with the aid of comparative religion. More recent treatments show that Western scholars can study Islam from within, in its institutions of higher learning under Muslim scholars, and with an appreciation for its vision of the divine will. However, tension exists between Western scholarship and many Muslim traditionalists who do not accept the findings of Western scholarship on *hadith* (sayings of the Prophet) or on historical influences upon the Prophet.

Textbooks on Islam

Arberry, Arthur J. *The Koran Interpreted.* New York: Macmillan, 1955. 2 vols. ISBN 0-02-083260-5pa. (set).

Most Western scholars find Arberry's translation the most poetically rewarding translation of the Qur'an (Koran) in the English tongue. Muslims have always claimed that the peculiar beauty of the Qur'an could not be captured in translation. Those who know the spirit of the Arab language agree. However, this inability to communicate its beauty has led to the Qur'an falling on unsympathetic ears in the West. Arberry has come the closest to correcting this aesthetic problem.

Cragg, Kenneth, and Marston Speight. *Islam from Within: Anthology of a Religion*. Belmont, CA: Wadsworth, 1980. (The Religious Life of Man Series). ISBN 0-87872-212-2.

This is an anthology that will supplement any of the major introductions to Islam with primary source material. It is filled with material from Muslim writers on the Qur'an, on scriptural interpretation, on the nature of worship, on religious law, on theology, on religious art, on saints and mystics, and on contemporary issues. Many of the selections are not easy to find in other works. This collection makes the riches and diversity of Islamic thought available to the Western reader. College level.

Denny, Frederick Mathewson. *An Introduction to Islam*. New York: Macmillan, 1985. ISBN 0-02-328520-6.

This introduction to Islam, by a scholar who has spent much time at Muslim centers of higher learning, is the most useful now available. Denny's work is not only objective, but it helps the reader understand the Muslim worldview. Denny covers the history of Islam, the Prophet's life, and Muslim doctrine and law, and offers a large section on Sufism. Particularly interesting are chapter 14, on the Islamic life cycle and the family, including discussions of divorce, marriage, inheritance, death rituals, and mourning; and chapter 15, on the ideals and realities of Islamic community life, including material on the mosque, marketplace, re-creation, official Islam versus popular Islam, saint veneration, and Shi'ite rituals. Islam is approached as a total culture, not merely a religion in the narrower sense. The final chapter points to reform movements in the past and present that have reshaped, or are reshaping Islam today. This college-level text has an excellent bibliography and glossary of terms.

Esposito, John L., ed. *Voices of Resurgent Islam*. New York: Oxford University Press, 1983. ISBN 0-19-503339-6; 0-19-503340-Xpa.

Prior to 1940, the majority of Islamic lands had been colonized to some degree by the West. Islam today is in the process of creating a post-colonial identity. This process sometimes takes a violent form, while, at other times, it finds peaceful expression. In both instances, the problem of self-identity comes from conflict with intellectual or material forces derived from the West, such as democracy, free market capitalism, socialism, individualism, human rights, women's rights, scientific worldview, cultural imperialism, and technological development.

Esposito has selected sixteen essays by Western and Muslim scholars that explain the dynamics of a resurgent post-colonial Islam. Included are Khomeini's Islam, Qaddafi's Islam, the search for Arab identity, democracy and the Islamic state, Islam and Zionism, and American perceptions of Islam. For someone who wishes to broaden their intellectual horizons beyond the clichés of popular magazines and news reports and look into the ideologies and purposes of another civilization, this is an important work. It demonstrates how Islam is inextricably political and religious at the same time. A significant study for those in government, Near Eastern history, political science, and international relations. College level.

Esposito, John L., and John J. Donohue, eds. *Islam in Transition*. New York: Oxford University Press, 1982. ISBN 0-19-503022-2; 0-19-503023-0pa.

This selection of essays represents the range of debate over modernist issues that one finds in contemporary Islam. Part 1 includes material on Islam and patriotism, nationalism, and social change. Part 2 continues the discussion of nationalism, adding responses to socialism and the secular state. Part 3 analyzes the modernization of Islamic law, the changing status of women and the family, and the nature of Islamic economics. Part 4 discusses the reemergence of Islam and its significance for legal and political life in Egypt, Pakistan, and Iran. For those who hope to understand the variety of Muslim perspectives and how they differ from (or are similar to) Western viewpoints, *Islam in Transition* offers a quick entrance. College level.

Gibb, H. A. R. *Mohammedanism: An Historical Survey*. 2d ed. London, New York: Oxford University Press, 1953. ISBN 0-19-500245-8.

This now classic introduction to Islam is short and precise. No other work has caught the essentials of Islam in so objective and critical a manner. In a presentation on the development of Islam, Gibb covers the topics of the early expansion of Islam, Muhammad, the Qur'an, doctrine and ritual, *hadith, shariah*, orthodoxy, Sufism, and Islam in the modern world. He reveals the basics of the faith with impressive depth. Highly recommended for the person who is in need of a short but reliable work. For its essential grasp of Islam and Islam's problems in adapting to the modern world, this work has not been surpassed. College level.

Hodgson, Marshall G. S. *The Venture of Islam: Conscience and History in a World Civilization*. Chicago: University of Chicago Press, 1974. 3 vols. ISBN 0-226-34678-1 (vol. 1); 0-226-34680-3 (vol. 2); 0-226-34681-1 (vol. 3); 0-226-34683-8, P716pa. (vol. 1); 0-226-34684-6, P717pa. (vol. 2); 0-226-34685-4, P718pa. (vol. 3).

This work is well known for its magisterial presentation of the course of Islamic history, covering the entire range of civilizations that Islam has molded. Hodgson considers Islam from religious, economic, and sociological perspectives. Volume one treats the rise of Islam to the dissipation of the Baghdad caliphate; volume two discusses medieval Islam up to 1503; volume three takes the reader through the Ottoman Empire and colonialism to the modern period. At present, this work is the most ambitious history of Islam available by a single hand. This is a college-level text and not an easy read, due to its wealth of erudition, but if reading for information on a particular movement, cultural area, or time period, *The Venture of Islam* is invaluable.

Martin, Richard C. *Islam: A Cultural Perspective*. New York: Prentice
    Hall Press, 1982. (Prentice-Hall Cultural Perspective Series).
    ISBN 0-13-506345-0.

The Prentice-Hall Cultural Perspective Series aims to present
each religion as a living culture and so treats material often overlooked
by other introductory texts. Its historical presentation of the tradition
is brief, but it compensates by offering examples from ritual, art, and
representative thinkers that reveal the tone and spirit of the tradition.
Especially interesting are chapters on Islamic art, forms of worship,
the interplay of religion and society, and the tension between the
traditional and the modern. Vivid in examples and style, *Islam: A
Cultural Perspective* is a state-of-the-art presentation of newer trends
in the field of comparative religion. High school level and beyond.

Robinson, Neal. *Christ in Islam and Christianity*. Albany: State Univer-
    sity of New York Press, 1991. ISBN 0-7914-0558-3; 0-7914-0559-1pa.

The theological status of Jesus of Nazareth is crucial for understanding the distinctions between Christianity and Islam, because
both faiths recognize Jesus as the Messiah. However, the term *messiah*
has radically disparate meaning for the two traditions. Robinson has
clarified these distinctions by offering chapters on "Jesus in the
Qur'an," "Muhammad and the Christians," "Muhammad and Jesus,"
"Jesus' Return in the Qur'an," "The Representation of Jesus in Sufi
Commentary," and other material that compares traditional Muslim
and Christian apologetics and polemics about the nature of the Messiah.
An important work for those who wish to understand how the interpretation of the person of Jesus both unites and divides the earth's two
most populous religious traditions. Advanced high school to college
level.

Schimmel, Annemarie. *Mystical Dimensions of Islam*. Chapel Hill:
    University of North Carolina Press, 1974. ISBN 0-8078-1271-4.

The Sufis of Islam have inspired religious persons of several faiths
for centuries. Their mystical writings and practices have revealed
profound spiritual resources within the Islamic peoples. Sufic religious
poetry is among the most elegant on earth in both the Arabic and
Persian tongues. Annemarie Schimmel has written the most thorough
analysis of this tradition available in English, from both an historical
and a doctrinal perspective. *Mystical Dimensions of Islam* displays
enormous erudition coupled with sympathy and comprehension. This
work is a must for those with a serious interest in the mystical
dimension of life. College level.

Smith, Jane I. *The Islamic Understanding of Death and Resurrection*.
    Albany: State University of New York Press, 1981. ISBN 0-87395-
    506-4; 0-87395-507-2pa.

The Qur'an, despite its proclamation of resurrection, makes little
if any reference to the intermediate state between death and resurrection at the end of the world. From the third century on, traditionalists

have enormously amplified eschatological material and formed an Islamic vision of life after death. Smith and Haddad discuss the development of these views and show how they have been altered in recent times. They also make an excellent case for demonstrating how patriarchal notions of an afterlife reveal an abusive understanding of women. Chapters contrast the classical understanding of the state between death and resurrection (the *barzakh*) with modern concepts, and the classical notions of eschaton (the end), judgment, and final dispensation with those held by Muslims today. Although a work of thorough scholarship, *The Islamic Understanding of Death and Resurrection* reads well. An important contribution to the study of eschatology. College level.

Watt, W. Montgomery. *Muhammad: Prophet and Statesman*. New York: Oxford University Press, 1974. ISBN 0-19-881078-4.
Watt's biography of the Prophet of Islam emphasizes Muhammad's creative response to the political and social forces around him without minimizing the significance of his religious vision. This is a work that critically reconstructs events; it will satisfy both the rigorous historian and the person of reasoned piety. One does not find herein the Muhammad of legend, but instead an extraordinary religious and cultural leader. Recommended for advanced high school and college levels.

Christianity

Although Christianity is well known in its popular contemporary forms, few members of the faith are aware of the complex development of church history behind its dominant American forms, Orthodox forms, or the ancient forms found in the Middle East, such as the Jacobite or Coptic churches.

The discipline of church history made an early contribution to the study of world religions in its analysis of the different forms of Christianity. Both Protestant and Catholic apologists claim the support of Christian tradition. Centuries of dispute persuaded church historians to stop viewing the past through denominational blinders and step into the clearer light of objectivity. The points made on both sides of the debate were often one-sided; over the generations, this was corrected. In this manner, a professional concern for rigorous scholarship in church history was developed that later overflowed into the discipline of comparative religion.

Textbooks on Christianity

Ahlstrom, Sydney. *A Religious History of the American People*. New Haven, CT: Yale University Press, 1972. ISBN 0-300-01762-6.
Comprehensive and readable, this is a monumental effort that surpasses previous introductions. Although a serious work of considerable length, this text can be used without prior knowledge in the field

for information on the development of specific movements and churches in America. College level, though portions are accessible for high school research.

————, ed. *Theology in America: The Major Protestant Voices from Puritanism to Neo-Orthodoxy.* New York: Macmillan, 1967. ISBN 0-672-60118-4.
This able work reveals the uniqueness of American religious thought. Although most American denominations have European origins, American thinkers have given theology a unique coloring that reflects the religious concerns and experience of living in the New World. Ahlstrom offers selections that introduce the thoughts of the theological shapers of the American religious mind. Included are Thomas Hooker, Jonathan Edwards, Charles Hodge, Ralph Waldo Emerson, Horace Bushnell, William James, Walter Rauschenbusch, H. Richard Niebuhr, and others. This is a well-written work with an important selection of texts for the study of vital issues in American religious history. College level.

Atiya, Aziz S. *History of Eastern Christianity.* Millwood, NY: Kraus Reprint & Periodicals, 1980. ISBN 0-527-03703-6.
The majority of Christians in the West are unaware that seven million native Christians live in Egypt, or that 45 percent of Lebanon is Christian, nor are they aware of the distinct teachings or history of these ancient forms of Eastern Christianity. Even the numerically large Greek and Russian Orthodox churches receive little press in North American Christian writing. Atiya's work corrects this lacuna in the scholarship about the Christian tradition. He discusses the development of the Orthodox churches and their smaller relatives, the Monophysite churches (including the Coptic, Jacobite, and Armenian) and the Nestorian Church. College level.

Carmody, John, and Denise Carmody. *Roman Catholicism.* New York: Macmillan, 1989. ISBN 0-02-319390-5.
Roman Catholicism, once accused of being pre-modern and medieval in outlook, is now, in its post–Vatican II period, more progressive in social outlook and theology than many of its accusers. The rapid change in Catholic tradition calls for a book that explains current Catholic positions. The Carmodys have met this need and have written a book in four parts that cover: 1) Catholic history up to the present (a brief but effective exposition in 100 pages); 2) the Catholic worldview of creation, incarnation, redemption, and eschatology; 3) Catholic ritual and ethics; and 4) contemporary trends dealing with peace and social justice, the role of women in the church, internationalism, and issues of tension between conservative and liberal Catholics. In a clear and sophisticated presentation of material often shrouded in technical theology, the Carmodys offer the reader a large overview of the Catholic position, without neglecting minority and dissenting voices. For the average reader (advanced high school), this may be the best introduction

to Catholicism now available, and is certain to become a standard work in introductory college courses.

Dillenberger, John, and Claude Welch. *Protestant Christianity: Interpreted Through Its Development.* 2d ed. New York: Macmillan, 1988. ISBN 0-02-329601-1.

The authors cover Protestantism from the late medieval period to the twentieth century's ecumenical movement and have provided a must-read for those interested in understanding the development of the many strands of Protestantism. Subjects include Luther and Calvin, the Anabaptist tradition, Puritanism and the Quakers, Pietism, the Great Awakening and John Wesley, the American Church Tradition, the formation of Liberal Theology, the Social Gospel, twentieth-century developments in Protestant thought, and the ecumenical movement. The last chapter answers the important question, "What is Protestantism?" by analyzing the elements of the Protestant perspective that are found in most of its manifestations. College level.

Gonzalez, Justo L. *A History of Christian Thought.* rev. ed. Nashville, TN: Abingdon, 1988. 3 vols. ISBN 0-687-17185-7(set); 0-687-17182-2 (vol. 1); 0-687-17183-0 (vol. 2); 0-687-17184-9 (vol. 3).

This comprehensive history of Christian theology was written for those without formal training in theology. Because Christianity is called an "orthodox" faith (one that places considerable importance on correct formulations of faith) by historians of world religions, it is fitting to make the history of doctrinal thought available, and explain the importance of changing doctrine in the march of the centuries. Gonzalez has achieved this in three volumes, organized accordingly: 1) from the beginnings to the Council of Chalcedon; 2) from St. Augustine to the eve of the Reformation; and 3) from the Protestant Reformation to the twentieth century. This is challenging material, but it is suitable for one who has done some work in theology or world religions. A good mix of Protestant, Catholic, and Eastern Orthodox developments, this is an accessible college-level text, and could be read at an advanced high school level.

Hick, John, and Brian Hebblethwaite, eds. *Christianity and Other Religions: Selected Readings.* Minneapolis, MN: Wm. Collins, 1981. ISBN 0-8006-1444-5.

The study of world religions and the advent of dialogue between different faiths has led to continuous discussion concerning the status of Christianity's relation to other religions, and has raised the issue of exclusivism versus universalism once again for churches. Hick and Hebblethwaite have gathered together the voices of several theologians on this disputed issue, and allow the reader to find his or her own position by reflecting with major thinkers on the problem. College level.

Kimball, Charles. *Striving Together: A Way Forward in Christian-Muslim Relations*. Maryknoll, NY: Orbis Books, 1991. ISBN 0-88344-691-X.

Both Christianity and Islam have striven, often against each other, to spread their understanding of the will of God to the rest of the world. Kimball asks if there is a way to strive together, to work with one another to overcome centuries of mutual misperception. He begins his work with a discussion of the obstacles and opportunities that await Christian-Muslim relations, then provides background to Christian readers on the nature of Islam and an historical summary of Christian views on Islam and Muslim views on Christians. He discusses the important problem of exclusivism and ends by calling for a theology of pluralism. The last chapter outlines practical ways to further Christian-Muslim relations. This work is useful for its brevity, clarity, and hopefulness about the future of interreligious cooperation. Advanced high school level.

Lossky, Vladimir. *The Mystical Theology of the Eastern Church*. Crestwood, NY: Saint Vladimir's Seminary Press, 1976. ISBN 0-913836-31-1.

While the Protestant tradition sought the Kingdom of God, the Eastern Church sought the Vision of God. Drawing on Pauline mysticism, both the Greek and Russian expression of Orthodoxy developed the meaning of St. Paul's concept of "Christ in us" in their meditations and life. Lossky describes the theology that expresses this centuries-old approach to Christian spirituality and biblical interpretation. College level.

MacHaffie, Barbara J. *Her Story: Women in Christian Tradition*. Minneapolis, MN: Augsburg Fortress, 1986. ISBN 0-8006-1893-9.

The enormous contribution of women to Christianity has been overlooked by historians focusing on the public arena, where power and official leadership have been largely a male possession. MacHaffie shows women of spirit who have preserved, aided, challenged, and brought dignity to the church despite the hindrances of patriarchal bias. This is a significant supplement and correction to one-sided histories. College level.

Pelikan, Jaroslav. *Jesus Through the Centuries: His Place in the History of Culture*. New Haven, CT: Yale University Press, 1985. ISBN 0-300-03496-2.

To speak of Jesus is to speak of a person who actually lived in the first century, but who has been interpreted and viewed through the lens of each succeeding century. The good shepherd of the time of the catacombs, the Pantocrator of late-Greek theology, or the Jesus of St. Thomas Aquinas or Martin Luther reflect a Jesus refracted through the needs and the categories of a particular age. Pelikan shows the many faces of Jesus through the ages in an historical tour of the Christian tradition. His analysis is both analytical and appreciative. College level.

Tyson, Joseph B. *The New Testament and Early Christianity*. New York: Macmillan, 1984. ISBN 0-02-421890-1.

This work is an objective survey of the early church (beginning to 185 C.E.) in light of its Jewish and Hellenistic context. Part 1 discusses the problems of weighing historical evidence in scripture and other sources for this period. Part 2 analyzes the Roman and Jewish ambience of the early church. Part 3 discusses the value of the Gospels for historical research and the special problems that this poses for an historian. Part 4 discusses early Jewish Christianity as evidenced in the Acts of the Apostles, and discusses the unique characteristics of Pauline Christianity. The last section, part 5, addresses the nature of Christianity from 70 C.E. through 185 C.E., with developments in late-Pauline, late-Jewish, Johannine, Gnostic, and Marcionite expressions. The Christian response to Roman persecution and the character of early Catholic Christianity are also discussed. Tyson raises the kinds of questions that anyone interested in the beginning phase of Christianity or in the problems that surround its study should address. College level.

Walker, Williston, Richard A. Norris, David W. Lotz, and Robert T. Handy. *A History of the Christian Church*. 4th ed. New York: Macmillan, 1985. ISBN 0-02-423870-8.
To one with a seminary background, Walker is no stranger. His successful *History of the Christian Church*, first copyrighted in 1918 and revised and expanded into its fourth edition in 1985, has been the standard one-volume introduction to church history for generations. Readable, though crammed with information, Walker provides a quick, sophisticated look at the movements in Western Christianity, with some coverage of Eastern traditions. The bibliography has been revised and is one of the best guides for further research on a figure, movement, or period. College level.

Ware, Timothy. *The Orthodox Church*. New York: Viking Penguin, 1963. ISBN 0-14-020592-6.
This is an insightful introduction to the history, doctrine, rites, and mystical teachings of the Orthodox Church. Ware's knowledge of the tradition is sympathetic and informed, and this work comes recommended by scholars of the Orthodox traditions. College level.

Conclusion

The increase in awareness about comparative religion, and the increase in direct contact between members of different faiths, will pressure older theologies that were formulated within a narrower cultural ambience and a smaller range of acquaintances, to adapt and reflect these new awarenesses. Classical Christian theology in the Roman Empire gathered insights from Greek and Roman philosophers. This process is beginning again with a peaceable empire the size of humankind. The future will be different than the past, but its shape is unknown, for the mix of ingredients is novel. Comparative religion will continue to explore the nature of religion in its full, global variety. For those who study theology in this new cosmopolitan spirit, the discipline of comparative religion will be essential in its role as translator between traditions. In time, whatever is found to be true in one tradition will probably be incorporated in some manner into the theological thinking of other traditions. Pluralistic tendencies will no doubt continue, and the contributions of women will receive the understanding they merit. The primal traditions will also be explored and appreciated for their contributions to the total religious experience of humankind.

References

Each of the introductory texts in world religions have generous and updated bibliographies for the major world religions, and most have some information on smaller traditions. For more specific works on special areas of research, the student should consult introductory texts to the different world religions. For research on the components of religion, such as ritual, myth, belief, art, ethics, and so on, one should consult the bibliographies of the introductions to religious studies as well as works on methodology. Several works mentioned in the above essay are also useful reference works but are either out of print or supplemental to works reviewed within the essay.

Textbooks

Basham, A. L. *The Wonder That Was India: A Survey of the Indian Sub-Continent Before the Coming of the Muslims*. New York: Grove Press, 1959.
This is the most complete survey of Indian culture available, with sections on philosophy, religion, daily life, dynasties, art, and other subjects.

Cobb, John B., Jr. *Beyond Dialogue: Toward a Mutual Transformation of Christianity and Buddhism*. Philadelphia: Fortress Press, 1982.
A contemporary theologian discusses the West's attempt to understand Buddhism over the past 100 years and suggests that it is time to appropriate concepts from Buddhism into Christianity. For those interested in the contemporary interaction of world religions, this is a state-of-the-art work dealing with the results of dialogue.

King, Noel. *Christian and Muslim in Africa*. New York: Harper & Row, 1971.
The author describes Christianity and Islam in Africa both as shapers of religious thought and as being molded by prior African worldviews.

Oates, Wayne. *The Psychology of Religion*. Waco, TX: Word Books, 1973.
This general introduction deals with developments in the study of religion that postdate the writing of William James, including

developments in psychoanalysis, psychedelics, the phenomenon of glossolalia, dream research, and more.

Smart, Ninian. *The Phenomenon of Religion.* New York: Herder and Herder, 1973.
Professor Smart demonstrates how the many methodologies used to study religion interface with one another.

Suzuki, D. T. *An Introduction to Zen Buddhism.* New York: Grove Press, 1964.
Suzuki's work has long been acknowledged as a brilliant philosophical introduction to Zen.

————. *Zen Buddhism: Selected Writings of D. T. Suzuki.* William Barrett, ed. New York: Doubleday, 1956.
This is a representative collection from the corpus of Suzuki's many writings on Zen.

Yinger, J. Milton. *The Scientific Study of Religion.* New York: Macmillan, 1970.
Dr. Yinger has given the reader the most thorough available presentation of how sociologists study religion.

Encyclopedias

Encyclopedias are important reference tools. Some of the more significant ones follow.

The Encyclopaedia of Islam. 6 vols. H. A. R. Gibb et al., eds. Leiden, Holland: E. J. Brill, 1960- .
Because this work is still in progress, the student may need to consult the earlier work that it is designed to replace. The earlier work is currently in print under the name *E. J. Brill's First Encyclopaedia of Islam*, H. A. R. Gibb et al., eds. (Leiden, Holland: E. J. Brill, 1987). However, for access to the purely religious aspects of Islam, *Shorter Encyclopaedia of Islam*, H. A. R. Gibbs and J. H. Kramers, eds. (Leiden, Holland: E. J. Brill, 1974) is easier to use and contains all articles found in the earlier encyclopedia and its supplement that relate to religion and law.

The Encyclopedia of Religion. Mircea Eliade, ed. New York: Collier/ Macmillan, 1987.
This is the most recent and complete work for reference in world religions, with 2,750 signed articles by 1,400 international scholars.

The Encyclopedia of the Jewish Religion. R. J. Zwi Werblowsky and Geoffrey Wigoder, eds. New York: Holt, Rinehart & Winston, 1966.
This is a standard and thorough compilation of articles.

New Catholic Encyclopedia. Rev. William J. McDonald, ed. New York: McGraw-Hill, 1981.

Regarding the Catholic faith, this is the most important modern reference.

The New Encyclopaedia Britannica. 15th ed. Philip Goetz, ed. Chicago, London: Encyclopaedia Britannica, 1990.

For articles on each of the world religions, and on aspects of religious traditions such as symbol, ritual, myth, and so on, this edition is highly recommended.

Media

Media has become an important complement to teaching world religions. Unfortunately, most introductory texts do not include this information. Cole and Sambhi have an excellent selection on audiovisual guides for the study of Sikhism in *The Sikhs: Their Religious Beliefs and Practices.* Noel King's *African Cosmos* gives an unusually rich and varied selection of audiovisual aids following a bibliography entitled "Art, Music, the Dance, and Discography, Slide Libraries, and Museum Crawling." Roger Schmidt, in *Exploring Religion*, provides a significant media guide that treats several religions, including the conceptual and social dimensions of religion. Some recommendations follow:

Media Resources

The Christians (McGraw-Hill Films). A set of thirteen films that survey the history of Christianity. Produced by the BBC, each film is 39 minutes long.

Heritage: Civilization and the Jews (WNET-TV). A set of nine films on Jewish history with Abba Eban as host. Each film is 50 minutes in length.

The Long Search (Time-Life Multi-Media). Thirteen films introduce the major living religious traditions. This set has long been popular in introductory college courses. Produced by the BBC, each film is 50 minutes long.

Religions of South Asia (Dr. David Knipe, University of Wisconsin). Fifteen videocassettes explore the religions of India, Tibet, and Pakistan.

Religious America (Yale University Media Design Studio). Thirteen films produced by the BBC on contemporary religion in the United States. Each is approximately 30 minutes long.

2

Trends in
Contemporary
Jewish Literature

Peter J. Haas

Introduction

Judaism is a fully developed and highly diverse contemporary religious culture that has undergone, and continues to undergo, great change from generation to generation. This is a fundamental point that must always be kept in mind when trying to understand the issues behind modern Jewish literature. All too often, non-Jews, and Christians in particular, tend to assume that modern Jewish religion and culture are little more than a modified version of Old Testament religion or of the Pharisaic religion presented by the New Testament. Nothing could be further from the truth. A true understanding of the issues and struggles in contemporary Judaism is possible only if the religious and cultural heritage of modern Jews is seen in its own terms. For that reason, anyone interested in learning more about contemporary Judaism must have some acquaintance with the experiences of Jews and Judaism over the last 2,000 years. With this in mind, the first section of this chapter recommends books that can help provide the basic background necessary for placing contemporary Judaism in context.

I have divided the remainder of this chapter into thematic divisions that reflect the more or less natural categories of the literature. I start off with the Holocaust because it has deeply influenced every aspect of Jewish life and thought for the last fifty years. None of the issues of contemporary Judaism can be understood separate from the experience of being the targeted victims of the most powerful civilization in twentieth-century Europe. What so profoundly affects Jewish thought today is not only the loss of nearly one-third of the world's Jews, leaving virtually no Jewish family untouched, but also the sense of betrayal in light of Christian silence and sometime acquiescence. An overwhelming preoccupation with survival, and a strong commitment to self-reliance leading to, among other things, a revival of traditional Jewish piety and spirituality, are all reactions to the horrors of the Holocaust. I therefore discuss this material first.

I follow my discussion of the Holocaust with literature on the State of Israel, because the rebirth of the State of Israel is linked in many minds, Jewish and Christian, with the Holocaust. This is in part correct, because the State was declared in the aftermath of the Holocaust, because many of the survivors of the Holocaust found refuge there after the war, and because the Holocaust has become an integral part of Israeli political thought and rhetoric. However, it should be kept in mind that the Zionist movement predates the Holocaust by nearly a century, and its efforts to establish a new Jewish life in the Land of Israel were well underway by the 1940s. So despite its later association with the Holocaust, the Zionist movement that led to the creation of the State of Israel has its own roots and history in the pre-Holocaust world. It was based on the deep conviction that in the face of both rising secularism and rising ethnic nationalism in Europe, Judaism could not survive unless it had its own homeland. It was the profound conviction of Zionism, repeated over and over again in Jewish circles, that Jewish life in the Diaspora (Jewish communities outside Israel) could not be expected to survive.

This claim on the part of Zionists in the late nineteenth century and throughout the twentieth century was received with mixed emotions by Jews who chose not to migrate to Palestine but to live in the Diaspora, especially American Jews. To be sure, Jews in America were sympathetic to the Zionist cause. After all, the Jews who came to North America in the nineteenth and twentieth centuries were themselves either refugees from European oppression and anti-Semitism, or the descendants of such refugees. There was thus a good deal of resonance in the American Jewish community for the Zionist claim that European Jewry was facing a crisis in the modern world, and that establishing a Jewish homeland had to be a priority of all Jews. Despite this emotional commitment, however, North American Jews, by and large, rejected the Zionist program in deed. There was a strong sense among American Jews that things were different here, that in the land of opportunity and religious freedom, Jews could survive and prosper as Jews. Thus, while American Jews have been deeply committed to the survival and welfare of the State of Israel, few have felt the need to move there themselves. This dissociation has caused an ongoing debate between Israelis and American Jews about the legitimacy of an ongoing Diaspora community in the face of a revitalized Jewish State.

While American Jews are vocal in their claims about the vitality and future security of Jewish life in the United States, demographic data have been suggesting that matters are much less certain. As American Jews move further away from their European roots with each generation, there is an increasing rate of secularization, assimilation, and intermarriage. There is an ever-growing body of literature examining the sociology of American Judaism and analyzing what the demographic trends mean. I survey some of this literature in the next section.

The rising rate of assimilation and intermarriage in the United States has had an unforeseen result. While it is often the case that partners in an intermarriage remain unaffiliated, or that each remains loyal to his or her prior religious upbringings, the sheer rate of intermarriage has resulted in a significant number of non-Jewish spouses becoming active in Jewish religious and communal affairs. In many, although not in all, of these cases, the non-Jewish spouse formally converts to Judaism. These "Jews by Choice" have become a significant element in the makeup of the Jewish community, and their increasing presence has raised questions about whether or not the Jewish community ought to engage more actively in systematic outreach programs, about the role of conversion in the community, and about how to make these new converts feel more welcome. Because most such conversions are done in the United States under Reform auspices, and because these are consequently not recognized by Orthodox rabbis (nor by the State of Israel), the issue of "Jews by Choice" has been the subject of sometimes acrimonious debate, not only among Jewish denominations in America, but between American Jews and Israelis.

Partly because of this influx of people of non-Jewish background into the community, partly as a reaction to the increased secularization of American life, and partly because of the increased mobility and rootlessness of Americans, there has been a growing interest among many Jews in the long tradition of Jewish spirituality. Beginning in the late 1960s, there has been a steady interest in how to create a rich and spiritually meaningful Jewish life for oneself outside the bounds of traditional Orthodoxy, and even outside the bounds of formal religious organizations altogether. Many books examine the role traditional *halachah* (Jewish law) can play in nurturing one's religious life from this perspective, while others address questions about the meaning of human life, suffering, and death. All draw on traditional Judaic resources and so represent a renaissance of Jewish religious life in the midst of an increasingly secular society.

I close this essay with a section on women in Judaism. As Jewish women have moved into the work force, and especially into the professions, they have demanded greater participation in the spiritual life of Judaism. This has taken several forms: the ordination of women into the rabbinate (by the Reform and Reconstructions branches, and recently by the Conservative movement); leadership positions in secular Jewish organizations; and the recovery of specifically female spirituality. Because so much of Jewish life is governed by *halachah* that have been devised by males, there are also now attempts to rewrite *halachah* from the female perspective. I touch on these themes in the closing section of this essay.

Introductions to Judaism

It is important that anyone approaching Judaism for the first time have some basic grasp of the vocabulary and structure of Judaic life and culture. Nearly all of the books surveyed in this chapter are written by Jewish writers addressing Jewish issues for a Jewish audience. By their very nature, they make certain basic assumptions concerning their readers' knowledge about Judaism that are foreign to Christians and others coming from non-Judaic backgrounds. For this reason it is important to have some orientation in contemporary Judaism. There are several brief introductions to Judaism that could serve this purpose. One old standby is Milton Steinberg's *Basic Judaism* (1947). Although dated, it is still a standard introduction. Somewhat more detailed, but still relatively short, is Roy Rosenberg's *The Concise Guide to Judaism* (1990). For those with questions about why certain Jewish customs are as they are, there is Alfred Kolatch's *The Jewish Book of Why* (1981), which lists questions often asked by Jews (and non-Jews) about particular practices or customs and offers short explanations. For those looking for a more in-depth orientation to Judaism, including Jewish history, a solid standby is Leo Trepp's *Judaism: Development and Life* (1982). This was written as a college textbook and so covers history as well as rituals and life-cycle events. A more detailed handling of many topics, in more of an encyclopedic rather than narrative form, is Joseph Telushkin's *Jewish Literacy: The Most Important Things to Know About the Jewish Religion, Its People and Its History* (1991). Any of these resources will give the reader a minimally adequate orientation to the history and culture of Judaism.

There are also some excellent video introductions. For a brief introduction to some aspects of contemporary Judaism, there is *Judaism: The Chosen People*, part of the Long Search series done for British television, narrated by Ronald Eyre. For those who are interested in more in-depth reading, there are a number of different resources. A well-written, illustrated coffee-table history of Jews and Judaism is Chaim Potok's *Wanderings* (1978). With its detailed discussions and many illustrations, this book provides a sense of the unique and often isolated, but also immensely rich, development of Jewish religious and cultural life. An even more powerful introduction to the flow of Jewish civilization, albeit with a not-always-subtle Zionist prejudice, is the PBS videotape series Heritage: Civilization and the Jews narrated by Abba Eban. There is also a companion coffee-table book to this series of the same name (1984).

Several rather hefty textbooks are available on Judaism. One, *An Introduction to Judaism: A Textbook and Reader* by Jacob Neusner (1991) is meant for college courses in Judaism. It is well written, and its narrative is often built around selections from traditional text. For those willing to work through it, this text will provide a modern academic reading of the development of Jewish civilization by one of the most prolific writers on Judaism today. A more traditional handling of Jewish history, but also somewhat drier, is Robert Seltzer's *Jewish People, Jewish Thought: The Jewish Experience in History* (1980). This is a comprehensive review of Jewish history and is best suited for those who already have some acquaintance with the subject. Somewhat less technical and more readable, but still comprehensive, is Paul Johnson's *A History of the Jews* (1987). Finally, I can mention *Judaism: A People and Its History* (1989) edited by Robert Seltzer. This is a collection of articles on various aspects of Judaism and Jewish culture written originally for the *Encyclopedia of Religion* (1987), edited by Mircea Eliade. Because each chapter was written originally as a self-standing article, the collection as a whole does not read smoothly, and there is also a certain unevenness in coverage and on the perspective brought to the material by each individual author. This would serve best as a reference for those interested in a detailed discussion of specific aspects of Judaica.

Holocaust

It is a matter of fact that the mass extermination of Jews in Europe fifty years ago has deeply affected every development within contemporary Judaism. The basic outlines of the Holocaust can be quickly sketched. Adolf Hitler and the National Socialist party came to power in Germany in 1933 in the midst of severe economic, social, and political crises. Drawing on centuries of Christian anti-Semitism, Hitler identified Jews as the source of all problems, not only in Germany but in the world, and felt it was his duty to once and for all rid the world of what he saw as the root of all evil. Hitler's notion of Aryan superiority led to the institutionalization of race warfare as the ideological basis for all German policy, domestic and foreign. From 1933 on, the full power of the German state was directed at isolating Germany's racial enemies. By 1935, Jews had been deprived of all legal rights in Germany: they lost citizenship, were fired from all government posts, were forbidden to practice most professions, and were systematically uprooted and moved to newly constructed "ghettos." In November 1938, the "Kristallnacht" riots destroyed every Jewish institution, synagogue, and business that was still operating in Germany. By the beginning of World War II in 1939, the once-prosperous Jewish community in Germany had been reduced to one-third of its former size (mostly through emigration) and to utter poverty. Those Jews who remained were virtual prisoners of the state.

As Nazi Germany expanded, first into Austria and then into Czechoslovakia, the Jews of those countries were immediately subjected to the same process that had destroyed German Jewry. Within months, the Jewish communities of these countries were stripped of all rights, lost their businesses and homes, and were being arrested and sent to ghettoes or labor camps. The invasion of Poland brought the massive Jewish community of that country under Nazi control. These Jews suffered under a double disability; they were both Jews and Poles. During the first few months of German occupation, German troops, and especially the S.S., the Nazi party's racial shock troops, engaged in a massive campaign of terror and killing, designed to destroy both Polish and Jewish cultures. Hundreds of thousands of people were summarily shot or sent into overcrowded ghettoes where they were left to die of disease and starvation.

The invasion of Poland provoked France and Britain to declare war on Germany, beginning World War II. The outbreak of war sealed the fate of Europe's Jews. Those countries that had offered refuge for Jews fleeing the Nazis—Holland, Belgium, France, and later the Balkans—all fell under Nazi control and, with them, the remaining Jews of Europe. These people were also rounded up and sent to concentration centers, often with the cooperation of local authorities.

Unable, and unwilling, to deal with the millions of Jews they had thus rendered impoverished and homeless, the Nazis developed new schemes for reducing their numbers. When Hitler invaded Russia in 1941, for example, mobile killing units (Einsatzgruppen) entered villages and shot anyone identified as a Jew. When this proved too slow and cumbersome, fixed-site killing centers were established, at first using diesel engine exhausts to kill truckloads of victims at a time. Out of these experiments grew the gas chambers at Treblinka, Lublin, Sobibor, and finally, Auschwitz. At these places the able-bodied were separated from their families and sent to labor camps; the others—the old, the infirm, children—were immediately gassed. As Jews were shipped to these killing centers from around Europe, the communities they left behind were systematically ransacked. Synagogues, ritual objects, prayer books, and manuscripts were all destroyed so that nothing of Jewish life and culture would remain. In all, some 5.5 to 6 million Jews were killed during the Nazi occupation, along with an equal number of other people the Nazis considered undesirable—gypsies, homosexuals, political prisoners, and so forth. In addition, the cultural legacy of nearly 2,000 years of Jewish life in Europe was destroyed.

The impact of the Holocaust on Jewry is hard to overstate. The great centers of Jewish thought and learning, those of Germany, Hungary, and Poland, were utterly destroyed. The centers of Jewish life shifted either to America or to the nascent, and as yet underdeveloped, community in Palestine. Zionists, who had been arguing that Western culture was bankrupt and that Jewish life in the West was at peril, were vindicated, while those who had argued for accommodation with Western culture and religion were busy burying their dead and trying to reconstruct what was left of their lives. Jewish thinkers and communal leaders who thought that Judaism and Christianity could work together to help bring about a better world were shocked and betrayed by the sustained silence of virtually all Christian religious institutions in the West throughout the long period of Nazi occupation. And Jewish theologians wondered about the silence of G-d.

There are a number of books available on the Holocaust, its pre-Hitlerite roots, and its aftermath. For a relatively brief overview, a classic, if somewhat dated, account is Lucy Dawidowicz's *The War Against the Jews 1933–1945* (1986). Another good, fairly straight historical review is Yehuda Bauer's *A History of the Holocaust* (1982). Both of these are relatively short histories written for a popular readership. There are a number of more massive histories for those interested in a more detailed treatment of the Holocaust in all of its complexity. Two general histories stand out: Nora Levin's *The Holocaust: The Destruction of European Jewry, 1933–1945* (1968), and Martin Gilbert's *The Holocaust: A History of the Jews of Europe During the Second World War* (1986). There is also a detailed three-volume description of the organization of the Nazi war against the Jews in Raul Hilberg's *The Destruction of the European Jews*, 3rd ed. (1985).

As courses in the Holocaust have become more common on college campuses, college-level textbooks have become available. Two that deserve particular mention are Richard L. Rubenstein and John Roth's *Approaches to Auschwitz: The Holocaust and Its Legacy* (1987), which takes an historical approach to the subject, and Peter J. Haas's *Morality After Auschwitz: The Radical Challenge of the Nazi Ethic* (1988), which takes a more philosophical approach. In addition to these, two new books offer different kinds of approaches to understanding the Holocaust. One of these, Michael Berenbaum's *The World Must Know: The History of the Holocaust as Told in the U.S. Holocaust Memorial Museum* (1993) is based on the exhibit in the new Holocaust Memorial Museum in Washington, D.C. The second, a useful guide for teachers and others, is Abraham Edelheit's *History of the Holocaust: A Handbook and Dictionary* (1993).

The importance of the Holocaust to this essay, of course, is not in the historical facts themselves, but the meaning they have been given in modern Jewish thought. As mentioned above, the Holocaust brought into question almost all of pre-Holocaust modern Jewish thought. One major concern is the question of how modern Jews should relate to the G-d who remained silent at Auschwitz. Two radically different approaches have emerged. One, set forth powerfully in Richard Rubenstein's classic *After Auschwitz* (1966), argues that the G-d of classic theology is dead. Rubenstein's argument is that the notion of an all-powerful deity who will intervene to save people has been shown to be false and that, as a consequence, Jews (and others) must outgrow their childlike dependence on G-d and take responsibility for their own lives and community. Diametrically opposed to that viewpoint is that of Eliezer Berkovits in works such as *Faith After the Holocaust* (1973) and *With God in Hell* (1979). In both of these works, Berkovits, an Orthodox rabbi, draws on medieval Jewish theological speculation to account for the apparent absence of G-d during the Holocaust. In brief, his claim is that G-d does at times withdraw the divine self from involvement in human affairs in order to provide room for human moral freedom and responsibility. The Holocaust represents one of those periods of divine eclipse. Yet, G-d's covenant with the People of Israel remains in effect. That this is so even after the Holocaust, Berkovits argues, is demonstrated by the ultimate survival of the Jews and the emergence of a reborn state of Israel.

Probably the most popular Jewish writer dealing with the Holocaust is Eliezer Wiesel, himself a survivor of Auschwitz and a recent winner of the Nobel Peace Prize. He is probably best known for the short autobiographical account of his experiences in *Night* (1960). After publishing *Night*, Wiesel began to explore possible human responses to the horrors of the Holocaust through his writing. His next book, *Dawn* (1970), explored the possibility of revenge; then *The Accident* (1970) considered suicide; the subject of madness was taken up in *The Town Beyond the Wall* (1970); and finally, Wiesel addressed memory in *Beggar in Jerusalem* (1970). Wiesel has written many more books, all suffused with the sadness of the Holocaust. For those interested in following this remarkable writer in more detail, a good overview of his thought and message is Robert McAfee Brown's study *Elie Wiesel: Messenger to All Humanity* (1983).

Formal theological speculation has been only one arena for the expression of Jewish reaction to the Holocaust. There also have been some attempts to place the Holocaust in some larger philosophical framework. The foremost Jewish writer in this regard has been Emil Fackenheim. Building on the Hegelian dialectic, Fackenheim, in *God's Presence in History* (1970) and *The Jewish Return into History* (1978), argues that the Holocaust represents the logical culmination of secular thought and demonstrates the need for a new and higher synthesis. He sees this synthesis residing in what he sees as a new command from G-d: to fight for communal survival. There have been other Jewish philosophical reactions to the Holocaust. For those interested in a brief but solid overview of Jewish theological reactions to the Holocaust, including Rubenstein, Fackenheim, Berkovits, and Wiesel, I suggest Dan Cohn-Sherbok's *Holocaust Theology* (1990). A somewhat academic and detailed, but valuable, analysis of the impact of the Holocaust on modern Jewish thought can also be found in Steven Katz's *Post-Holocaust Dialogues: Critical Studies in Modern Jewish Thought* (1983). A broader attempt to describe the overall effect of modern Western culture and history, including the Holocaust, on contemporary Jewish thought is Jacob Neusner's *Death and Rebirth of Judaism: The Impact of Christianity, Secularism and the Holocaust on Jewish Faith* (1987).

Jewish-Christian Dialogues

A number of books attempted to assess the impact of the Holocaust on the way post-Holocaust Jews have related to the outside world. Obviously, one of the areas of most interest has been Jewish relations with Christianity. There have been a number of Christian theologians who have looked closely at Christian theological implication in the Holocaust, and who have tried to rethink the Christian theological heritage, especially as it relates to Judaism, in light of the Holocaust. This has led to serious theological dialogue between Christians and Jews for the first time. An early appraisal of this dialogue is Abraham J. Peck's short book, *Jews and Christians After the Holocaust* (1982). This collection of essays is somewhat superficial but gives a good sense of the areas and themes of Jewish-Christian dialogue. These have included in particular a recognition that Christian supercessionism and triumphalism—that is, the idea that Christianity somehow completes, supercedes, or triumphs over Judaism—not only played a significant role in establishing a theological rationale for the Holocaust, but may have prevented Christians from entering into a true dialogue with Judaism. Several contemporary Christian thinkers have tried to reformulate Christian thought to eliminate this supercessionism. One of these earliest writers is Roy Eckardt, who wrote his landmark book, *Long Night's Journey into Day: Life and Faith After the Holocaust,* (1982) with his wife Alice L. Eckardt. Christian supercessionism is rooted in the New Testament. Norman Beck, in *Mature Christianity: The Recognition and Repudiation of the Anti-Jewish Polemic of the New Testament* (1985), takes a programmatic look at these texts with the aim of laying a new foundation for Christian approaches to Judaism. Building on this, a monumental effort to achieve a systematic rethinking of the Jewish people in a more traditional Christian theological scheme is Paul Van Buren's multivolume work *A Theology of the Jewish Christian Reality* (1980). Of particular relevance in this regard is volume 3, *A Christian Theology of the People Israel* (1983). Many of the themes of this new literature are analyzed in Geoffrey Wigoder's *Jewish-Christian Relations Since the Second World War* (1988). And a recent discussion in which a rabbi and a Christian thinker describe how each religion thinks of the other is Randall Falk and Walter Harrelson's *Jews & Christians: A Troubled Family* (1990).

The dialogue has probably moved further with the Roman Catholic Church than with any other Christian body. One example of this new approach is Franz Josef van Beeck's *Loving the Torah More than God? Towards a Catholic Appreciation of Judaism* (1989). To catch up on what has been happening in the Catholic-Jewish dialogue, see John Oesterreicher's *The New Encounter: Between Christian and Jews* (1986), or more recently, Leon Klenicki and Eugene Fisher's *In Our Time: The Flowering of Jewish-Catholic Dialogue* (1990).

Israel

With the destruction of the European centers of Judaism, two new centers of Jewish life have emerged to fill the void, one in North America and the other in Palestine (Israel), each with a different history and based on different ideologies. As a result, a tension between these two communities has emerged in contemporary Jewish life that has yet to be resolved. This tension has brought into question all aspects of Jewish life: whether being Jewish is primarily a religious identity (America) or primarily a national identity (Israel); whether authentic Jewish culture is essentially pluralistic (America, where there are several "denominations": Orthodox, Conservative, Reform, Reconstructions, and Hasidic, and secular Jewish institutions such as community centers) or essentially monolithic (Israel, where "authentic" Jewish life is defined by the Orthodox rabbinate); whether anyone raised as a Jew and identifying as a Jew is Jewish (America, with its growing population of Jews by Choice), or only those fitting Talmudic criteria (Israel); whether true Judaism can be lived in a Diaspora, that is, an exilic condition (America) or only in the Holy Land (Israel); whether authentic Jewish prayer and scholarship can be performed in any language (America, where English predominates) or only in Hebrew (Israel). Because there are often several possible positions on either side and because the debate takes place as much within America and Israel as between them, the ongoing discussions have been complex and at times emotional. In addition, the argumentation often turns around fine points of interpretation concerning

Jewish history or Jewish law (*halachah*). As a result, this aspect of Jewish life is extremely difficult to convey to outsiders. There are very few books or surveys on the subject because these debates are still raging within the Jewish community. In what follows, then, I will try to point the reader to some general resources.

As a minimum beginning, it is necessary to understand the basic differences in the history and ideology between the Israeli and the American Jewish communities. There are several books that outline the history of the Zionist movement and the growth of the State of Israel. A good general overview from pre-state settlements through the 1948 war and beyond is Abba Eban's *My Country: The Story of Modern Israel* (1972). A lengthy, but very readable, retelling of the history of Zionism and the founding of the State of Israel is Conor Cruise O'Brian's *The Siege: The Saga of Israel and Zionism* (1986). As an Irish diplomat, O'Brian was particularly impressed by the ability of the Israelis to revive an ancient culture and language and successfully create a state. There are two good scholarly accounts; one is by British historian Martin Gilbert, *Exile and Return: The Struggle for a Jewish Homeland* (1978). The other is Howard Morley Sachar's two-volume *A History of Israel*. For those interested in a Christian perspective, there is James Rudin's *Israel for Christians: Understanding Modern Israel* (1983). A somewhat dated but still useful all-around reference is *The Encyclopedia of Zionism and Israel* (1971), edited by Raphael Patai.

The history of the State of Israel really begins over a century and a half ago with the birth of the modern Zionist movement in Europe. To be sure, there has been a significant population of Jews in the Holy Land since at least the Middle Ages, but these were almost exclusively pious mystics who hoped to spend their last days in the holy cities of Jerusalem, Tiberias, Safed, or Hebron. As nationalistic and ethnic tensions increased in central and eastern Europe in the middle of the last century, however, a new breed of Jewish settlers emerged. Many Jewish thinkers, primarily radical Jewish students, became convinced that Jewish life in Europe, and especially in Czarist Russia, had no future. For these radicals, the only solution was for Jews to establish a modern, secular, ethnic homeland of their own. By the 1870s, these students had taken the step of organizing a colonization society, called *Hibbat Zion*, to establish and support autonomous Jewish farming villages in what was then the Turkish province of Syria (now modern Israel). Not surprisingly, these young, urban Russian idealists were unable to succeed as farmers in the harsh climate and difficult conditions of Turkish Palestine. By 1890, nearly all of their settlements had failed, and the immigrants were able to survive only through philanthropic projects funded by wealthy Jews in the United States and Europe. Despite their failure as farmers, however, these early pioneers did succeed in establishing the core of a revitalized modern Jewish society in Palestine.

In addition, their actions sparked a philosophical debate about the nature and character of the new homeland. A number of theories emerged that shaped the course of future events. These diverse philosophical and political theories, lumped together as "Zionism," have been the subject of several studies. One of the standard references is Arthur Hertzberg's *The Zionist Idea* (1972). Hertzberg provides excerpts from the speeches and writings of major Zionist thinkers from the mid-nineteenth century on, with appropriate introductions. Together, these selections illustrate the range of Zionist thought from the religious Zionism of Orthodox rabbis to the Communist Zionism of the 1920s to the political theorists of the new state: Weizmann, Jabotinsky, and Ben Gurion. A historical overview of this debate is provided by Walter Laqueur in *A History of Zionism* (1972).

Meanwhile, a mass exodus of Jews from Czarist Russia was underway in the wake of the repressive May Laws imposed by the government in 1881. Nearly 3 million Russian Jews, along with Jews from Poland and Rumania, fled their homelands between 1880 and World War I. Aware of the fate of the Jews who had tried to make a living in Palestine, the vast majority of these immigrants traveled West, some settling in Europe but most, some 90 percent, choosing to emigrate to America. The Jews who chose to go to America rather than follow the Zionist idealists to the Holy Land, nonetheless felt a duty to help those of their brethren who did choose to rebuild the Jewish homeland. The burgeoning American Jewish community thus became a major source of support for the early Zionist settlement activity, a relationship that still exists today.

The Zionist movement underwent a crucial change in the 1890s. Just as the older Zionist settlement societies were becoming overwhelmed by failure, a visionary arose who not only saw the need for an international systematical effort to organize a return to Zion, but had the charisma to actually put his vision into institutional form. This visionary, Theodore Herzl, is regarded as the true founder of modern Zionism. He organized a World Zionist Congress in 1896 and, over the next few years, put together an executive agency and a fund-raising apparatus. Although he himself was eventually ousted by the World Zionist Congress (for, among other things, agreeing with the British to establish the Jewish homeland in Uganda), his catalytic efforts had dramatic results. The World Zionist Organization proceeded to purchase land, drain swamps, train farmers, organize settlements (the first successful kibbutz was established in 1909), and begin the creation of a modern social infrastructure. By World War I, some 200,000 Jewish farmers and workers had been successfully settled, the kibbutz movement was showing remarkable success, new towns and cities (such as Tel Aviv) were beginning to appear, and the rudiments of a self-sustaining, largely socialist economy were in place.

By the end of World War I, when Great Britain inherited the region from the now-defunct Turkish empire, the Jewish community was organized and able to work with the British to begin the process of creating a modern state. An excellent scholarly treatment of this early period of settlement and the evolution of Zionist thought and organization can be found in David Vital's three-volume work on the development of Zionism: *The Origins of Zionism* (1975). It covers the Hibbat Zion period; *Zionism: the Formative Years* (1982) covers Herzl's impact in the early twentieth century; and *Zionism: The Crucial Phase* (1987) carries the story up to the Balfour Declaration in 1917.

The growth of the modern Jewish settlement in Palestine coincided with the birth of Arab nationalism. In the wake of World War I and the collapse of the Ottoman Turkish empire, the entire region fell under the control of Great Britain. The modern Middle East, with all its tensions and conflicts, is the creation of subsequent European, especially British, policy. From the point of view of the Jewish settlement (*yishuv*), emigration out of Europe continued slowly throughout the 1920s and more quickly in the 1930s, bringing for the first time middle-class Jewish settlers from Western Europe, who brought with them ideas of democracy and a devotion to capitalism. As a result, the social, political, and economic development of the Jewish settlement increased, becoming more diversified and complex. Yet the political situation deteriorated rapidly, fueled by the continued expansion of the Jewish community and the rise of Arab nationalism in the 1920s. The result was ever-increasing tensions, conflicts, and violence. The political background of this seemingly endless conflict is masterfully described in David Fromkin's *A Peace to End All Peace* (1989). Fromkin shows that British policies in the early 1920s, when the present national boundaries in the Middle East were drawn up, were based on British misunderstandings of the Middle East and so set the stage for continued turmoil and unrest. While bad for the Arab world, the increasing anarchy of the Middle East fostered internal cohesion within the beleaguered Jewish community and the eventual creation of Jewish self-defense forces.

By the 1930s, social violence between Jewish and Arab communities reached a state of virtual civil war, including strikes and full-scale rioting. In an attempt to keep the situation under control, and mindful of their many ties to other Arab governments, the British government took a decidedly pro-Arab position. Jewish immigration was severely restricted. As a result, throughout World War II, when there was virtually no asylum offered anywhere for Jews hoping to flee the Nazis, the British maintained a strict embargo of all Jews trying to enter Palestine, often interning refugees in detention camps in Cyprus or Africa. Yehuda Bauer has chronicled much of this in *Flight and Rescue: Brichah* (1970). British immigration policy convinced the Jewish settlers that they would have to throw out the British and establish an independent country. At the conclusion of the war, then, both Arab nationalists and Jewish settlers turned against the British. Soon, the British government lost all control of the region and, in 1947, agreed to withdraw from Palestine, dividing the land between a Jewish homeland and an Arab homeland. After a fierce war in 1947–48, a cease-fire was declared and the land held by the Jewish defense forces was declared to be the State of Israel.

The 1947–48 War of Israeli Independence and the subsequent transition to statehood were trying times for the Jewish settlers. The nature of the war is portrayed in moving terms in Larry Collins and Dominique Lapierre's *O Jerusalem!*, an account of the battle for Jerusalem. The problems of establishing statehood are covered in a collection of scholarly articles on various topics edited by Laurence J. Silberstein, *New Perspectives on Israeli History: The Early Years of the State* (1991). A classic study of the character of the pioneering generation that brought Israel into being and their children who were born in their own homeland is Amos Elon's *The Israelis: Founders and Sons* (1971). A more recent scholarly treatment of this transition is Tom Segev's *The First Israelis* (1986). One of the key politicians in the struggle for statehood was Chaim Weizmann. Weizmann was instrumental in getting the British government to issue the Balfour Declaration in 1917, and he continued to lead the political struggle for independence, culminating in his service as the first president of the state. His story is told by Norman Rose in *Chaim Weizmann: A Biography* (1986).

In its early years, the new state was near collapse. The economy was in shambles, with severe rationing in effect, and the military situation—the armies of Syria, Jordan (the Arab League), Iraq, and Egypt were regrouping—appeared hopeless. On top of this, the settlers felt it was their responsibility to offer a home not only to refugees from Europe, but also to the nearly 1.5 million Jews expelled by Arab countries. Most arrived with no money, no education, and no skills. This placed a tremendous burden on the social and educational resources of the fledgling State. Only gradually, and with generous help from the American Jewish community, were these difficulties overcome. Gradually, the new immigrants were educated, jobs were created, and the economy improved, largely through government-sponsored industrial programs. By the Six-Day War in 1967, Israel was able to field a modern, Westernized, well-equipped army. The decisive Israeli victory that resulted had a profound effect on both Israeli and American Jews.

Reaction to the Six-Day War demonstrates two themes in particular. On the one hand, both the Israeli and the American Jewish communities derived tremendous pride from the accomplishments of the Jewish state. In only twenty years, the Jews of Israel had taken in hundreds of thousands of refugees and built a modern Western democratic state. On the other hand, there was the passivity of the Western world in the face of what had at first looked like the imminent destruction of Israel. As Arab rhetoric grew more strident and bellicose in the months leading up to the war, and as Arab armies, led by Egypt, began to mobilize, the Western democracies held back support from Israel. This increased a sense in both the Israeli and American Jewish communities that Jews could not depend on others for survival, but had to develop their own power. Jews realized the vulnerability of the State of Israel and felt a new commitment to unity and political activism to ensure Jewish survival and a renewed interest in the Holocaust.

By the late 1980s, this new closeness was beginning to unravel. There are a number of reasons for this. One, the passing of the generation of Holocaust survivors and the coming to the fore of a new generation in both Israel and America who do not share the memory of European roots. Second, the defeat of the Labor government in Israel in 1977, and the ascendancy of the Likud block, which represented a kind of strident Israeli nationalism that was foreign to most American Jews. Third, the growing power of the Orthodox rabbinate under successive

Likud governments. This rabbinate pursued a policy of systematically delegitimating liberal Judaism, Reform and Conservative, which represent the bulk of American Jews. Finally, the increasing success of the Israeli economy made Israel less dependent on American Jewish support and so less willing to consult with, or work in accord with, American Jewish leaders. For all these reasons, among others, the relation between Israel and the American Jewish community is particularly complex.

There are few books that deal with how contemporary American and Israeli Jews relate to each other. From the Zionist perspective, there is Hillel Halkin's *Letters to an American Jewish Friend: A Zionist's Polemic* (1977). The point of the book is that, with the creation of the State of Israel, the future of authentic Jewish life is now in the Middle East, not in America, and that American Jews who wish to preserve their Judaism must move to Israel. Obviously, American Jews have, by and large, rejected this argument, although there are a few books that explicitly expound the American perspective. The American Jewish community's image of itself and its more positive view of its own destiny is usually covered along the way in books dedicated to American Jewish history as a whole. I discuss these books in the next section. One attempt to place American Jewish relations with Israel within the larger American context is Edward B. Glick's *The Triangular Connection: America, Israel, and American Jews* (1982).

There have also been some attempts to understand how the historical emergence of Israel worked to shape the American Jewish agenda, including *Vision Confronts Reality: Historical Perspectives on the Contemporary Jewish Agenda* (1989) edited by Ruth Kozodoy, David Sidorsky, and Kalman Sultanik. There is only one important American Jewish thinker who has tried to place the American Jewish perception of Israel into a larger frame of American Jewish religiosity in general. This is Jacob Neusner in *The Jewish War Against the Jews: Reflection on Golah, Shoah and Torah* (1984). In this title, *golah* is the Israeli word for "exile" (Diaspora) and *shoah* is the Israeli word for the Holocaust. A more general discussion of the nature and character of Jewish life as it is developing outside Israel is Howard Morley Sachar's *Diaspora: An Inquiry into the Contemporary Jewish World* (1985).

The Palestinian-Israeli conflict has been a major topic of concern to Judaism. The development of the conflict from the 1920s on is the subject of Ian J. Bickerton and Carla L. Klausner's *A Concise History of the Arab-Israeli Conflict* (1991). For a more impressionistic account of what the conflict has meant to Israelis and Arabs, particularly in Lebanon, see Thomas Friedman's *From Beirut to Jerusalem* (1989). A reading of this conflict from a decidedly liberal Jewish perspective is Marc Ellis's *Beyond Innocence and Redemption: Confronting the Holocaust and Israeli Power: Creating a Moral Future for the Jewish People* (1990). Citing the Holocaust as an example, Ellis argues that power can degenerate into corruption—therefore, American Jewish pride in the military power of Israel is misplaced pride.

American Judaism

Jews in America have enjoyed a degree of acceptance that is quite possibly the greatest since the pre-Christian Parthian empire of Babylonia. As a result, Jews as individuals have, by and large, thrived in America, achieving notable social, educational, and economic success. Along with this success, Jews have founded a range of Jewish educational, artistic, political, social, religious, and cultural institutions. Yet at the same time, American Jews have become more and more assimilated into American life and culture. This has set up an unusual paradox. While Jewish institutions, associations, religious organizations, and journals are thriving, the Judaic content of these is steadily declining. This has led to increasing concern about the future of Judaism in America and heated communal discussions on how to ensure the survival of Judaism among Jews. Jews in America are caught in a squeeze: They do not want to jeopardize their social position and yet want to maintain a distinct Judaic identity. In many ways, the American Jewish community today seems to be growing toward both extremes: increased assimilation, with its attendant "dropping out" of organized Jewish life by some; and a revival of Orthodoxy, or at least traditional Jewish lifestyle and spirituality, among others.

The tensions inherent in American Jewish life can be understood in part on the basis of the history of the community. There are several good and brief introductory histories on Jews in America. Nathan Glazer's *American Judaism*, 2d ed. (1972) is a standard short history that will give the reader a basic overview of the history of the American Jewish community. Also helpful is Joseph Blau's *Judaism in America: From Curiosity to Third Faith* (1976). A more popular written history of Jewish life in North America is Max Dimont's *The Jews in America: The Roots, History and Destiny of American Jews* (1978). Two rather substantial histories of the Jewish experience in America have just been written. A rather comprehensive history in one volume is Howard Morley Sachar's *A History of the Jews in America* (1992). The most comprehensive treatment can be found in The Jewish People in America, a five-volume series published by Johns Hopkins Press (1992).

A completely overlooked aspect of Jewish life in America is the role of Jews in the Westward expansion. Irving Howe and Kenneth Libo present a collection of photographs and personal accounts of Jewish pioneers in *We Lived There, Too: In Their Own Words and Pictures— Pioneer Jews and the Westward Movement of America, 1630–1930* (1984). For an overall view of the demographics and organizations of North American Jewry, consult *The American Jewish Yearbook*, published annually by the Jewish Publication Society.

Jews arrived in North America in the early days of colonization, often fleeing the Inquisition. There are reports of a small Jewish community (about twenty people) in New Amsterdam as early as the 1620s. Yet Jewish emigration to the New World was only a trickle throughout the seventeenth and eighteenth centuries. Most of those who came were descended from Spanish Jews and were highly assimilated into Western culture. Except for the occasional synagogue, there was virtually no organized Jewish life in America until well into the nineteenth century.

One element that changed this was a steady stream of Jewish immigrants from Germany beginning around 1830. Although the flow was relatively small, it was steady, increasing the American Jewish population to between 200 and 250 thousand people over the next fifty years. Most of these German Jewish immigrants were not strictly orthodox. They tended to work as peddlers or small shopkeepers in the little towns of the Southeast and Midwest. A few prospered, laying the groundwork for the great Jewish department stores of the late nineteenth century, but only gradually did enough Jews assemble in any particular area for a proper burial society to be organized. Synagogues and other Jewish organizations (such as B'nai B'rith) slowly followed. Only after the Civil War, and largely as a response to that war, did local Jewish organizations begin to band together into something akin to "national" organizations. Yet even so, the small, isolated Jewish communities were hard to organize: the first rabbinic seminary in the United States did not graduate its first class until 1878. A wonderful account of the great New York German Jewish families who made their name in banking and finance is Stephen Birmingham's *Our Crowd* (1967).

By far, the most significant factor in the creation of the contemporary Jewish community in America was the immigration of masses of East European Jews (mostly Russian, but with significant complements from Rumania and Poland) beginning in 1881. These Jews came from heavily Jewish villages and regions in East Europe, and were only lightly, if at all, assimilated into Western culture. In contrast to the earlier German Jewish immigrants, these spoke Yiddish, ate only Kosher food, were required to be within walking distance of Orthodox synagogues, and kept Jewish religious law meticulously. Between 1880 and 1920, 2.5 million East European Jews arrived in North America, swamping the established and highly Americanized German Jewish community already there. The East European Jews felt little in common with German Jews who, from the East European Orthodox perspective, were practically indistinguishable from Gentiles. East European Jews and their children lived in Jewish neighborhoods (creating such famous ghettos as New York's Lower East Side), patronized kosher butchers and delicatessens, and created their own network of synagogues (Conservative and Orthodox, as opposed to German Reform), communal institutions, political organizations, and the like. Although the immigrants or their children tended over time to give up their strictly Orthodox lifestyle (only about one in ten American Jews today is Orthodox), they nonetheless clung to Jewish cultural and ethnic identity. Many of their organizations thus became dedicated to secular Jewish culture. It is this group that has given the American Jewish community the particular ethnic and organizational character it has today. Irving Howe and Kenneth Libo compiled a collection of pictures and documentary excerpts illustrating the lives of these immigrants in East Europe in *World of Our Fathers* (1976). A companion volume by the same editors, *How We Lived: A Documentary History of Immigrant Jews in America, 1880–1930*

(1979), deals with the immigration of East European Jews and the new life they created in America, making extensive use of original documents and photographs. An account of the rise of some of these immigrants is *The Rest of Us: The Rise of America's East European Jews* (1984), Stephen Birmingham's companion to his study of German Jewish families.

Tensions between German and Russian Jews persisted through the 1940s. A number of factors have led to the decline of this dichotomy and the creation of an American Judaism, including the increased Americanization of the descendants of the East European immigrants; increased intermarriage between Jews from German and Russian heritages; the Holocaust; and concern for the survival and welfare of Israel, especially after the tense period leading up to the Six-Day War in 1967. The last twenty years have seen, on the one hand, an explosion in special-interest Jewish organizational activity (*The American Jewish Yearbook* lists over 300 national Jewish organizations, from B'nai B'rith to the Yiddish Scientific Research Organization), and attempts to achieve some national organizational cohesion on the other. At the same time, there is increasing concern with the secularization of Jewish life (Jews without Judaism) and attempts to reintroduce Jewish religion and spirituality in such bastions of Jewish secular culture as Jewish community centers.

Several studies try to understand and present to the reader an understanding of the forces that have shaped and continue to shape the particular experience of Jews in the United States. A basic academic, but quite readable, history of the major Jewish denominations and how they took shape in North America is Marc Lee Raphael's *Profiles in American Judaism: The Reform, Conservative, Orthodox, and Reconstructionist Traditions in Historical Perspective* (1989). One segment of American Judaism that is often ignored in these studies, because it seems to defy being American, is that of Hasidic Jews. The Hasidic community in New York is the subject of a descriptive ethnography by Solomon Poll, *The Hasidic Community of Williamsburg* (1973).

Jacob Neusner has put together a two-volume collection of essays exploring various aspects of American Jewish life, *Understanding American Judaism: Toward the Description of a Modern Religion* (1975). He has also published a college textbook that covers much of the same ground, *American Judaism: Adventure in Modernity* (1978). Other studies focus on the nature of contemporary American Jewish life in general. One excellent scholarly approach, written by an American sociologist now living in Israel, is Charles Liebman's *The Ambivalent American Jew: Politics, Religion and Family in American Jewish Life* (1976). More impressionistic and upbeat is Charles Silberman's *A Certain People: American Jews and Their Lives Today* (1984). Silberman's thesis is that, not only have Jews achieved remarkable material success, but they have done so without abandoning their Judaism, and in fact have become acceptable as Jews in all aspects of American life. Yet many Jewish intellectuals and thinkers worry about the future viability of American Jewish life. A well-written discussion of the character of the American Judaism that is now taking shape is Stuart E. Rosenberg's *The New Jewish Identity in America* (1985). The concerns and hopes of a prominent contemporary Jewish communal leader and writer who worries about the religious and spiritual content of American Jewish lives in the midst of material success are expressed in Leonard Fein's *Where Are We? The Inner Life of American Jews* (1988).

Jews by Choice

One of the consequences of Jewish assimilation into American life is an increasing rate of intermarriage between Jews and non-Jews. A recent study has concluded that, in more than 50 percent of marriages involving a Jewish person, the spouse is non-Jewish. Exactly what this means for the future character of Jewish life in America has become a highly emotional and hotly debated topic. One immediate result has been that, in a significant number of cases, the non-Jewish partner has converted to Judaism (become a "Jew by Choice") and has taken on the responsibility of raising a Jewish family. Though conversions to Judaism have always taken place, the sheer number of Jews by Choice today has raised a number of unprecedented issues: whether or not active outreach programs should be instituted to encourage the non-Jewish partner to convert to Judaism; what can be done to better integrate Jews by Choice into the community; and finally, what role non-converted spouses should have, if any, in Jewish religious and communal life. These questions get to the very heart of what it means to be a Jew and so have raised fundamental issues of definition not only within the American Jewish community, but between the North American Jewish community and Israel.

Although suppressed over the last two millennia, proselytization has been a part of Judaism since the beginning. Abraham, of course, converted to Judaism, and Ruth, the great-grandmother of King David, stands as a model of the ideal convert when she swore to Naomi, "your G-d is my G-d and your people my people." Throughout the Biblical period, diverse groups of people were conquered by the Biblical Israelites and converted to Judaism. Even after Judea lost its independence under the Romans, Jewish proselytization continued. There are estimates that, at the time of the birth of Christianity, some 10 percent of the population of the Roman empire were Judaizers (often called "God-fearers"). Exactly what this meant is unclear, but all evidence points to widespread proselytization by Jews into late antiquity. This activity stopped only when Christianity became the state religion of Rome and reduced Judaism to a persecuted religion. By the Middle Ages, conversion to Judaism was at times considered to be a capital offense. Gradually this restriction became a virtue. Rabbinic tradition stressed the importance of Jewish distinctiveness and regarded conversion to be appropriate only for those few Gentiles chosen by G-d. Prospective converts were put off and warned of the difficulties of becoming part of the covenant community. Only the most persistent and dedicated were allowed to actually undergo conversion. Upon conversion, of course, the proselyte was considered fully Jewish in every way.

Rabbinic literature thus regards conversion as a rare event that is to be taken with only the utmost care and dedication. Whatever the real rate of conversion since Roman times, the attitude has been that Jews formed a tightly endogenous group in which there was very little foreign blood. It was precisely on this basis that, in the nineteenth century, the Zionist movement could claim that Jews comprised a nation, not a religion. It was also, of course, the basis for the Nazi's racial classification of the Jews.

Although the issue is far from settled, it seems that, in fact, conversions to Judaism never entirely ceased. The fact that North African Jews look North African, that German Jews look German, and that Polish Jews look Polish, is strong evidence of this. Arthur Koestler published a study entitled *The Thirteenth Tribe: The Khazar Empire and Its Heritage* (1976), in which he claimed that most East European Jews were not derived from Semitic stock at all, but from a Turkic tribe, the Khazars, converted in the eleventh century. Although his hypothesis has been rejected by nearly all historians and demographers, it illustrated nonetheless how open the question of the "racial purity" of Jews really is.

The question of conversion and the Jewish attitude toward it has been reopened in this generation because of the prevalence of interdating and intermarriage in America. In many such cases, the Jewish partner remains dedicated to Judaism. Because the Jewish upbringing of the children depends heavily on Judaic practice in the home, would it not make sense to be open to the non-Jewish spouse converting? Given the high rate of divorce in American families and the large number of children being brought up under no particular religious faith, would it not make sense to try to create in a family a commitment to religion and religious values? Increasingly, Jewish religious and communal leaders have been discussing the possibility more openly and receptively. The Reform movement in Judaism has begun a modest program of outreach to give guidance to rabbis facing intermarried couples who express an interest in maintaining a Jewish home. There are strong countervailing forces: 2,000 years of tradition and a bedrock aversion to applying any pressure, psychological or otherwise, to prospective converts. Everyone seems to agree that a conversion, to be valid, must grow out of true conviction and years of study and reflection.

Although only a small proportion of non-Jewish spouses undergo formal conversion to Judaism, the sheer number of such cases means that people converted to Judaism are no longer an oddity. However, the psychological and social implications of these conversions is still not fully understood. From the point of view of the new converts, the transition can be especially trying. They must leave behind childhood memories and, at times, family connections to enter a complex social and religious culture with associations and attitudes that are second-nature to born Jews but are entirely new to them. They lack the childhood holiday memories and familial associations that so often make the Jewish community work. Jews by Choice often complain that it takes them years to stop feeling like strangers in the Jewish community. Several books have appeared in which Jews by Choice articulate their personal struggles. One of the earliest of this genre is Devorah

Wigoder's *Hope Is My House* (1966). A more recent, excellent discussion is that of Lydia Kukoff in *Choosing Judaism* (1981). Kukoff, herself a Jew by Choice, once headed the outreach program for the Reform synagogue movement. She thus brings a good deal of personal experience to her writing. A moving story is that of Paul Cowan and Rachel Cowan. Paul was an alienated Jew who, through his intermarriage, rediscovered his Jewish heritage. His own renewal eventually led to the conversion of his wife to Judaism. Their story is told in *Mixed Blessings: Marriage Between Jews and Christians* (1987). A lyrical account of the route to becoming a Jew by Choice, this time by an African-American writer, is Julius Lester's *Love Song: Becoming a Jew* (1988).

Many Jews by Choice discover that the decision to convert is only the first stage of a long process. After conversion, there is an ongoing struggle to fit in and learn the intricacies of Jewish religious and communal life. Part of the difficulty is that Jews by Choice often feel that they are not fully accepted by born Jews. A good practical discussion of these issues, addressed to the Jew by Choice, is Lena Romanoff's *Your People, My People: Finding Acceptance and Fulfillment as a Jew by Choice* (1990). Because most Jews by Choice convert in the Reform movement, most of the books dealing with this phenomenon come from this perspective. One book that addresses conversion from a more traditional perspective is Maurice Lamm's *Becoming a Jew* (1991).

Of course, not all spouses of an intermarriage convert to Judaism. But even so, many Jewish partners continue to be active in Jewish religious and communal life. This often leads to difficulties, conflicts, and misunderstandings later on, especially if there are children involved. A number of books attempt to deal with the practical problems posed by inter-religious marriages. Egon Mayer, a respected sociologist, has written a sociological study of Jewish-Christian intermarriage entitled *Love and Tradition: Marriage Between Jews and Christians* (1985). One of the earliest books aimed at the actual people involved, written by a renowned Jewish scholar of the Jewish origins of Early Christianity, is Samuel Sandmel's *When a Jew and Christian Marry* (1977). Two good books addressing the practical problems of mixed-marriage families in the 1990s are Susan Weideman Schneider's *Intermarriage: The Challenge of Living with Differences Between Christians and Jews* (1989) and Steven Carr Reuben's *But How Will You Raise the Children? From First Date to First Grandchild—A Practical Guide to Coping with the Emotional, Psychological and Personal Issues of Interfaith Marriages* (1987).

Spirituality

Although this section is titled "Spirituality," the reader must be aware at the outset that this topic is directed much more toward practice and less toward theology than most Christians might expect. Because of its own particular style, Christianity often tends to want to reduce religion to matters of theology, doctrine, or creed. That is, from a Christian perspective, the most important question concerning one's religion is, "What do you believe?" This is not the case for Judaism. Jewish religiosity has from Biblical times been focused more on practice than on theology. This is not to say that there is no theology within Judaism or that Jews do not care about philosophical questions. There is an immense body of literature on both counts. It is fair to say, however, that for most Jews, the important issue in defining their Judaism is what they do, how they regard the *halachah* (Jewish religious practice, norms, or laws). Thus, Jews are often perplexed by Christian interest in what Jews think about God, Messiah, salvation, life after death, and the like, because these are not terribly important questions to Jews. Jews are much more concerned with how one responds to the Sabbath, whether or not one remains Kosher, what one does during the Jewish holidays, how one deals with one's neighbor, and the like. For this reason, the books mentioned below deal primarily with issues of how one should respond in day-to-day life to the will of God, rather than with philosophical or theological issues.

A very general treatment of what it means to be Jewish, and the kinds of personal issues that this raises, is James Kugel's *On Being a Jew* (1990). A similar, very accessible guide is David C. Gross's *How to Be a Jew* (1989). Along these same lines is Leo Trepp's *The Complete Book of Jewish Observance* (1980). Finally, I can mention two reissues of books by Hayim HaLevy Donin, *To Be a Jew: A Guide to Jewish Observance in Contemporary Life* (1972, 1991) and *To Pray as a Jew: A Guide to the Prayerbook and the Synagogue Service* (1980, 1991).

In terms of the specific issues that are part of contemporary Jewish religious dialogue, a rather massive collection of important writings on a variety of divisive topics within the Jewish community is William Berkowitz's *Dialogues in Judaism: Jewish Dilemmas Defined, Debated and Explored* (1991). A briefer overview of some of these issues is Israel Shenker's *Coat of Many Colors: Pages from Jewish Life* (1985). For those interested in the development of rabbinic Judaism, there is Jacob Neusner's anthology, *Understanding Rabbinic Judaism: From Talmudic to Modern Times* (1974).

One route into contemporary Jewish religion and spirituality is to look at the different forms or denominations of Judaism that have emerged in North America. In general, there are five. Those Jews who have retained the traditional pattern of worship and lifestyle most fully make up Orthodoxy, about 10 percent of all North American Jews. Orthodox Jews regard traditional *halachah* to be revelatory and unchanging. At the other end of spectrum is Reform Judaism, which claims that Jews are a part of the society in which they are found and are different only in the religion of their homes. For Reform Jews, *halachah* is an expression of inner religiosity and thus can and must change according to the culture in which Jews live. Reform Jews tend to be the most politically liberal and culturally assimilated. They comprise some 40 percent of affiliated Jews. A slightly smaller denomination is Conservative Judaism, which agrees with Reform that Jewish law can change over time, but also holds that the bulk of Jewish tradition remains binding. Conservative Jews tend, as a group, to be more traditional in worship and practice than Reform Jews, but more assimilated and liberal than Orthodox Jews. A fourth denomination appeared in America in the 1930s under the impact of the writings of Mordecai Kaplan. This movement, called Reconstructionism, is close to Conservative Judaism in overall attitude (Mordecai Kaplan was a Conservative rabbi) but places more emphasis on Jewish culture. True Conservative Judaism places greater emphasis on Jewish religion. Finally, I should mention Hasidism, an outgrowth of East European mystical pietism of the eighteenth century. Most Hasidic communities in North America were established in the aftermath of the Holocaust in the late 1940s and early 1950s. These groups are most reminiscent of Amish communities in that they continue to wear traditional black raiment, often live in isolated communities, and shun much of modern culture. There are several sects active in the United States, each regarding its spiritual leader (the rebbe) as divinely appointed and inspired. The largest and most prominent on the American scene today, largely due to its proselytizing activity among other Jews, is the Lubavitch, or Habad, sect.

For general background to the Jewish denominations in North America, I have already mentioned Marc Lee Raphael's historical survey, *Profiles in American Judaism* (1989). A more popular and impressionistic approach can be found in Gilbert S. Rosenthal's *Four Paths to One God: Today's Jew and His Religion* (1973). There are several studies that deal with the various denominations. For liberal, or Reform Judaism, there is Daniel Syme's *Why I Am a Reform Jew* (1989) and the work of the major Reform Jewish thinker Eugene Borowitz, *Liberal Judaism* (1984). The meaning of being a Conservative Jew is described beautifully in Herman Wouk's *This Is My God: The Jewish Way of Life* (1970). Because traditional practice is important for Conservative Jews, a good resource for the nature of the ideal life for Conservative Jews is Isaac Klein's *A Guide to Jewish Religious Practice* (1979). A good overall review of the development of this brand of Judaism is Herbert Rosenblum's *Conservative Judaism: A Contemporary History* (1983). The Reconstructionist movement, although relatively new, has also been the subject of recent studies, often centered on the thought of its founder, Mordecai Kaplan. See, for example, Emanuel Goldsmith et al., *The American Judaism of Mordecai M. Kaplan* (1990). For information on Orthodoxy, there are a number of books discussing Jewish lifestyle. One standard is Hayim HaLevy Donin's *To Be a Jew* (1972, 1991), and *To Pray As a Jew* (1980, 1991). Less technical is Alfred Kolatch's *The Jewish Home Advisor* (1981). A scholarly but quite engaging description of Orthodox Jewish life, especially the ritual of Talmud study, is William Helmreich's *The World of the Yeshiva: An Intimate Portrait of Orthodox Jewry* (1982).

Several notable studies on Hasidism have appeared in recent years. A brief but valuable overview is Milton Aron's *Ideas and Ideals of the Hasidim* (1969). For those interested in the historical development of the movement, there is Harry M. Rabinowitz's *Hasidism: The Movement and Its Masters* (1988). An interesting look at the nature of the relationship between the individual Hasid (follower) and the rebbe (sect leader) is in Zalman Meshullam Schechter-Shalomi's *Spiritual*

Intimacy: A Study of Counseling in Hasidism (1991). Hasidism has also been at the center of a revival of Jewish meditation. One contemporary guide to this revival is Aryeh Kaplan's *Jewish Meditation: A Practical Guide* (1985). An excellent source for traditional Jewish spirituality is the two-volume set *Jewish Spirituality*, edited by Arthur Green for the series World Spirituality: An Encyclopedic History of the Religious Quest . Volume 1 is subtitled *From the Bible to the Middle Ages* (1987), and Volume 2 is subtitled *From the Sixteenth-Century Revival to the Present* (1987).

One phenomenon that has deeply affected the Jewish community in North America and in Israel is the revival of Orthodoxy and fundamentalism in the younger generation, which had at one point seemed alienated from religion. Such a person is often referred to as a *baal teshuvah*, that is, one who has returned in repentance. The nature of that revival is the subject of M. Herbert Danziger's *Returning to Tradition: The Contemporary Revival of Orthodox Judaism* (1987). The impact this conversion to Orthodoxy can have on a family is beautifully told in Agi L. Bauer's *"Black" Becomes a Rainbow: The Mother of a Baal Teshuvah Tells Her Story* (1991). This revival has also had major influence in Israel, especially among heretofore completely secularized Israelis. Several excellent studies have appeared. A more impressionistic account of the *baal teshuvah* movement is found in Janet Aviad's *Return to Judaism: Religious Revival in Israel* (1983). A scholarly examination of the effect of such conversion on Israeli society is Charles Liebman and Eliezer Don-Yehiya's *Religion and Politics in Israel* (1984). Although new converts to Orthodoxy tend to be socially and politically conservative, there are Orthodox voices in Israel looking for accommodation between different streams of Judaism and secular Israeli society. One of the major voices in moderate Israeli Orthodoxy is David Hartman; see his *Conflicting Visions: Spiritual Possibilities of Modern Israel* (1990).

Although most guides to Jewish life and spirituality focus on the practical, as noted at the beginning of this section, there is a theological and philosophical tradition as well. A general review of classical Jewish thought is provided in the collection of writings and essays edited by Jacob Neusner, *Understanding Jewish Theology: Classical Issues and Modern Perspectives* (1973). For those interested in the twentieth-century Jewish thought of people such as Martin Buber and A. J. Heschel (among others), there is Eliezer Berkovits's *Major Themes in Modern Philosophies of Judaism* (1974) and, more recently, Norbert Samuelson's *An Introduction to Modern Jewish Philosophy* (1989).

Women in Judaism

Until recently, almost all studies of Jews and Judaism have assumed that the story of Judaism is told through its men. This view has begun to change, and new studies are emerging on the role of women. In fact, while men dominated (and still dominate to a large extent) the religious life of Judaism, women have always dominated (and still do to a large extent) the domestic life of Judaism. Given the importance of the home in Jewish religious practice, the influence of women has been considerable. The current literature on women in Judaism can thus be divided into two subcategories: the recovery of the role of women in classical Jewish society, and the emerging call by Jewish women for greater presence in the religious life of the Jewish community. I shall look at each of these in turn.

Much of modern feminist thought in Judaism has been aimed at recovering the role women traditionally have played in Jewish culture. Two good orientations to this field are Judith Reesa Baskin's *Jewish Women in Historical Perspective* (1991) and, from a theologian's perspective, Eliezer Berkovits's *Jewish Women in Time and Torah* (1990). An early look at the role of women in American Jewish life is Charlotte Baum's *The Jewish Woman in America* (1976). A more recent study looking at the issue is Sylvia Fishman's *A Breath of Life: Feminism in the American Jewish Community* (1993). For an overall sourcebook for the study of the history of Jewish women in America, there is Jacob R. Marcus's *The American Jewish Woman, 1654–1980* (1981). A more recent attempt to understand, in particular, the effect of the East European immigration on Jewish women is Sidney Stahl Weinberg's *The World of Our Mothers: Lives of Jewish Immigrant Women* (1988), which is a general historical treatment. For a personal discussion of what it is like to be a Jewish woman in America, there is Letty Cottin Pogrebin's *Deborah, Golda, and Me: Being Female and Jewish in America* (1991). The choices facing Jewish women in America are the subject of Susan Weideman Schneider's *Jewish and Female: Choices and Changes in Our Lives Today* (1984).

Beyond the recovery of women's role in Jewish culture, there are attempts to rethink Jewish theology and practice to make them more responsive to the needs of Jewish women. The most prominent Jewish feminist theologian is Judith Plaskow. Her discussion of the possibility of a Jewish feminist theology can be found in her *Standing Again at Sinai: Judaism from a Feminist Perspective* (1990). But traditional Judaism has had its effect on Jewish women as well. One book that addresses the role traditional Judaism can play in fulfilling the lives of modern American Jewish women is Blu Greenberg's *On Women and Judaism: A View from Tradition* (1981). A study of what attracts some modern Jewish women to traditional Judaism is Debra Renee Kaufman's *Rachel's Daughters: Newly Orthodox Jewish Women* (1991). Along these lines, a wonderful description of the encounter between a modern assimilated Jewish woman and the deep religiosity she finds in the New York Hasidic community is Lis Harris's moving personal account in *Holy Days: The World of a Hasidic Family* (1985).

One problem faced by traditional Jewish women is that the synagogue is almost exclusively male-oriented. The recovery of a feminist spirituality is the aim of Tamar Frankiel in *The Voice of Sarah: Feminine Spirituality and Traditional Judaism* (1990). An historical look at Jewish women's spirituality is Ellen Umansky and Dianne Ashton's *Four Centuries of Jewish Women's Spirituality* (1992).

In an attempt to recover their spirituality, many women have organized their own prayer groups. One analysis of the *halachic* (traditional Jewish legal) basis for this movement is Avraham Weiss's *Women at Prayer: A Halachic Analysis of Women's Prayer Groups* (1989). There has also been interest in the possibility of ordaining women as rabbis. While this has now become commonplace in the Reform and Reconstructionist movements, it has been a matter of some debate and contention in the Conservative movement. The Conservative movement's consideration of the issue has been published as *The Ordination of Women As Rabbis: Studies and Responsa* (1988), edited by Simon Greenberg.

Those wishing to do further reading on this issue should consult *The Jewish Women's Study Guide* (1987), compiled by Sue Levi Elwell. A more scholarly resource is Inger Marie Ruud's *Women and Judaism: A Select Annotated Bibliography* (1988).

References

The American Jewish Yearbook. Philadelphia: Jewish Publication Society.

Aron, Milton. *Ideas and Ideals of the Hasidim*. New York: Citadel, 1969.

Aviad, Janet. *Return to Judaism: Religious Revival in Israel*. Chicago: University of Chicago Press, 1983.

Baskin, Judith Reesa. *Jewish Women in Historical Perspective*. Detroit: Wayne State University Press, 1991.

Bauer, Agi L. *"Black" Becomes a Rainbow: The Mother of a Baal Teshuvah Tells Her Story*. New York: Feldheim, 1991.

Bauer, Yehuda. *Flight and Rescue: Brichah*. New York: Random House, 1970.

———. *A History of the Holocaust*. New York: Franklin Watts, 1982.

Baum, Charlotte. *The Jewish Woman in America*. New York: Dial, 1976.

Beck, Norman. *Mature Christianity: The Recognition and Repudiation of the Anti-Jewish Polemic of the New Testament*. Cranbury, NJ: Susquehanna University Press, 1985.

Berenbaum, Michael. *The World Must Know: The History of the Holocaust As Told in the U.S. Holocaust Memorial Museum*. Boston: Little, Brown, 1993.

Berkovits, Eliezer. *Faith After the Holocaust*. New York: KTAV, 1973.

———. *Jewish Women in Time and Torah*. Hoboken, NJ: KTAV, 1990.

——. *Major Themes in Modern Philosophies of Judaism*. New York: KTAV, 1974.

——. *With God in Hell*. New York: Sanhedrin, 1979.

Berkowitz, William, ed. *Dialogues in Judaism: Jewish Dilemmas Defined, Debated and Explored*. Englewood Cliffs, NJ: Jason Aronson, 1991.

Bickerton, Ian J., and Carla L. Klausner. *A Concise History of the Arab-Israeli Conflict*. Englewood Cliffs, NJ: Prentice-Hall, 1991.

Birmingham, Stephen. *Our Crowd*. New York: Dell, 1967.

——. *The Rest of Us: The Rise of America's East European Jews*. Boston: Little, Brown, 1984.

Blau, Joseph. *Judaism in America: From Curiosity to Third Faith*. Chicago: University of Chicago Press, 1976.

Borowitz, Eugene. *Liberal Judaism*. New York: UAHC, 1984.

Brown, Robert McAfee. *Elie Wiesel: Messenger to All Humanity*. Notre Dame, IN: Notre Dame University Press, 1983.

Cohn-Sherbok, Dan. *Holocaust Theology*. San Francisco: Harper & Row, 1990.

Collins, Larry, and Dominique Lapierre. *O Jerusalem!* New York: Simon & Schuster, 1972.

Cowan, Paul, and Rachel Cowan. *Mixed Blessings: Marriage Between Jews and Christians*. New York: Doubleday, 1987.

Danziger, M. Herbert. *Returning to Tradition: The Contemporary Revival of Orthodox Judaism*. New Haven, CT: Yale University Press, 1987.

Dawidowicz, Lucy. *The War Against the Jews, 1933–1945*. New York: Bantam Books, 1979; New York: Seth Press, 1986.

Dimont, Max. *The Jews in America: The Roots, History and Destiny of American Jews*. New York: Simon & Schuster, 1978.

Donin, Hayim HaLevy. *To Be a Jew: A Guide to Jewish Observance in Contemporary Life*. New York: Basic, 1972; repr. 1991.

——. *To Pray As a Jew: A Guide to the Prayerbook and the Synagogue Service*. New York: Basic, 1980; repr. 1991.

Eban, Abba. *My Country: The Story of Modern Israel*. New York: Random House, 1972.

Eckardt, Roy, and Alice L. Eckardt. *Long Night's Journey into Day: Life and Faith After the Holocaust*. Detroit: Wayne State University Press, 1982.

Edelheit, Abraham. *History of the Holocaust: A Handbook and Dictionary*. Boulder, CO: Westview Press, 1993.

Eliade, Mircea, ed. *Encyclopedia of Religion*. New York: Macmillan, 1986.

Ellis, Marc. *Beyond Innocence and Redemption: Confronting the Holocaust and Israeli Power: Creating a Moral Future for the Jewish People*. San Francisco: Harper & Row, 1990.

Elon, Amos. *The Israelis: Founders and Sons*. New York: Holt, Rinehart & Winston, 1971.

Elwell, Sue Levi. *The Jewish Women's Study Guide*. Lanham, MD: University Presses of America; Fresh Meadows, NY: Biblio Press, 1987.

Fackenheim, Emil. *God's Presence in History*. New York: New York University Press, 1970.

——. *The Jewish Return into History*. New York: Schocken Books, 1978.

Falk, Randall, and Walter Harrelson. *Jews & Christians: A Troubled Family*. Nashville, TN: Abingdon Press, 1990.

Fein, Leonard. *Where Are We? The Inner Life of American Jews*. New York: Harper & Row, 1988.

Fishman, Sylvia. *A Breath of Life: Feminism in the American Jewish Community*. New York: Free Press, 1993.

Frankiel, Tamar. *The Voice of Sarah: Feminine Spirituality and Traditional Judaism*. San Francisco: HarperCollins, 1990.

Friedman, Thomas. *From Beirut to Jerusalem*. New York: Farrar, Straus & Giroux, 1989.

Fromkin, David. *A Peace to End All Peace*. New York: Henry Holt, 1989.

Gilbert, Martin. *Exile and Return: The Struggle for a Jewish Homeland*. Philadelphia: J. B. Lippincott, 1978.

——. *The Holocaust: A History of the Jews of Europe During the Second World War*. New York: Holt, Rinehart & Winston, 1986.

Glazer, Nathan. *American Judaism*, 2d ed. Chicago: University of Chicago Press, 1972.

Glick, Edward B. *The Triangular Connection: America, Israel, and American Jews*. Boston: Allen & Unwin, 1982.

Goldsmith, Emanuel, et al., eds. *The American Judaism of Mordecai M. Kaplan.* New York: New York University Press, 1990.

Green, Arthur, ed. *Jewish Spirituality: From the Bible to the Middle Ages,* vol. 1. World Spirituality: An Encyclopedic History of the Religious Quest series. New York: Crossroad, 1987.

———. *Jewish Spirituality: From the Sixteenth-Century Revival to the Present,* vol. 2. World Spirituality: An Encyclopedic History of the Religious Quest series. New York: Crossroad, 1987.

Greenberg, Blu. *On Women and Judaism: A View from Tradition.* Philadelphia: Jewish Publication Society, 1981.

Greenberg, Simon, ed. *The Ordination of Women As Rabbis: Studies and Responsa.* New York: Jewish Theological Seminary of America, 1988.

Gross, David C. *How to Be a Jew.* New York: Hippocrene, 1989.

Haas, Peter J. *Morality After Auschwitz: The Radical Challenge of the Nazi Ethic.* Philadelphia: Fortress Press, 1988.

Halkin, Hillel. *Letters to an American Jewish Friend: A Zionist's Polemic.* Philadelphia: Jewish Publication Society, 1977.

Harris, Lis. *Holy Days: The World of a Hasidic Family.* New York: Collier, 1985.

Hartman, David. *Conflicting Visions: Spiritual Possibilities of Modern Israel.* New York: Schocken Books, 1990.

Helmreich, William. *The World of the Yeshiva: An Intimate Portrait of Orthodox Jewry.* New York: Free Press, 1982.

Heritage: Civilization and the Jews. New York: Summit, 1984.

Heritage: Civilization and the Jews series. PBS video series.

Hertzberg, Arthur. *The Zionist Idea.* New York: Antheneum, 1972.

Hilberg, Raul. *The Destruction of the European Jews,* 3d ed. New York: Holmes & Meier, 1985.

Howe, Irving, and Kenneth Libo. *How We Lived: A Documentary History of Immigrant Jews in America, 1880–1930.* New York: NAL, 1979.

———. *We Lived There, Too: In Their Own Words and Pictures—Pioneer Jews and the Westward Movement of America, 1630–1930.* New York: St. Martin's Press/Marek, 1984.

———. *World of Our Fathers.* New York: Harcourt Brace Jovanovich, 1976.

The Jewish People in America series. 5 vols. Baltimore, MD: Johns Hopkins University Press, 1992.

Johnson, Paul. *A History of the Jews*. New York: Harper & Row, 1987.

Judaism: The Chosen People. The Long Search video series. 50 min.

Kaplan, Aryeh. *Jewish Meditation: A Practical Guide*. New York: Schocken Books, 1985.

Katz, Steven. *Post-Holocaust Dialogues: Critical Studies in Modern Jewish Thought*. New York: New York University Press, 1983.

Kaufman, Debra Renee. *Rachel's Daughters: Newly Orthodox Jewish Women*. New Brunswick, NJ: Rutgers University Press, 1991.

Klein, Isaac. *A Guide to Jewish Religious Practice*. New York: KTAV, 1979.

Klenicki, Leon, and Eugene Fisher, eds. *In Our Time: The Flowering of Jewish-Catholic Dialogue*. New York: Paulist Press, 1990.

Koestler, Arthur. *The Thirteenth Tribe: The Khazar Empire and Its Heritage*. New York: Random House, 1976.

Kolatch, Alfred. *The Jewish Book of Why*. Middle Village, NY: Jonathan David, 1981.

———. *The Jewish Home Advisor*. Middle Village, NY: Jonathan David, 1981.

Kozodoy, Ruth, David Sidorsky, and Kalman Sultanik, eds. *Vision Confronts Reality: Historical Perspectives on the Contemporary Jewish Agenda*. New York: Herzl Press; Rutherford, NJ: Fairleigh Dickinson University Press, 1989.

Kugel, James. *On Being a Jew*. San Francisco: Harper, 1990.

Kukoff, Lydia. *Choosing Judaism*. New York: UAHC, 1981.

Lamm, Maurice. *Becoming a Jew*. Middle Village, NY: Jonathan David, 1991.

Laqueur, Walter. *A History of Zionism*. New York: Holt, Rinehart & Winston, 1972.

Lester, Julius. *Love Song: Becoming a Jew*. New York: Henry Holt, 1988.

Levin, Nora. *The Holocaust: The Destruction of European Jewry, 1933–1945*. New York: Thomas Y. Crowell, 1968.

Liebman, Charles. *The Ambivalent American Jew: Politics, Religion and Family in American Jewish Life*. Philadelphia: Jewish Publication Society, 1976.

Liebman, Charles, and Eliezer Don-Yehiya. *Religion and Politics in Israel*. Bloomington: Indiana University Press, 1984.

Marcus, Jacob R., ed. *The American Jewish Woman, 1654–1980*. New York: KTAV; Cincinnati, OH: American Jewish Archives, 1981.

Mayer, Egon. *Love and Tradition: Marriage Between Jews and Christians*. New York: Plenum Press, 1985.

Neusner, Jacob. *American Judaism: Adventure in Modernity*. New York: KTAV, 1978.

———. *Death and Rebirth of Judaism: The Impact of Christianity, Secularism and the Holocaust on Jewish Faith*. New York: Basic, 1987.

———. *An Introduction to Judaism: A Textbook and Reader*. Louisville, KY: Westminster/John Knox, 1991.

———. *The Jewish War Against the Jews: Reflection on Golah, Shoah and Torah*. New York: KTAV, 1984.

———. *Understanding American Judaism: Toward the Description of a Modern Religion*. New York: KTAV, 1975.

———. *Understanding Jewish Theology: Classical Issues and Modern Perspectives*. New York: KTAV, 1973.

———. *Understanding Rabbinic Judaism: From Talmudic to Modern Times*. New York: KTAV, 1974.

O'Brian, Conor Cruise. *The Siege: The Saga of Israel and Zionism*. New York: Simon & Schuster, 1986.

Oesterreicher, John. *The New Encounter: Between Christian and Jew*. New York: Philosophical Library, 1986.

Patai, Raphael, ed. *The Encyclopedia of Zionism and Israel*. New York: McGraw-Hill, 1971.

Peck, Abraham J. *Jews and Christians After the Holocaust*. Philadelphia: Fortress Press, 1982.

Plaskow, Judith. *Standing Again at Sinai: Judaism from a Feminist Perspective*. New York: Harper & Row, 1990.

Pogrebin, Letty Cottin. *Deborah, Golda, and Me: Being Female and Jewish in America*. New York: Crown, 1991.

Poll, Solomon. *The Hasidic Community of Williamsburg*. New York: Schocken Books, 1973.

Potok, Chaim. *Wanderings*. New York: Alfred A. Knopf, 1978.

Rabinowitz, Harry M. *Hasidism: The Movement and Its Masters*. Northvale, NJ: Jason Aronson, 1988.

Raphael, Marc Lee. *Profiles in American Judaism: The Reform, Conservative, Orthodox, and Reconstructionist Traditions in Historical Perspective*. San Francisco: Harper & Row, 1989.

Reuben, Steven Carr. *But How Will You Raise the Children? From First Date to First Grandchild—A Practical Guide to Coping with the Emotional, Psychological and Personal Issues of Interfaith Marriages*. New York: Pocket Books, 1987.

Romanoff, Lena. *Your People, My People: Finding Acceptance and Fulfillment As a Jew by Choice*. Philadelphia: Jewish Publication Society, 1990.

Rose, Norman. *Chaim Weizmann: A Biography*. New York: Viking, 1986.

Rosenberg, Roy. *The Concise Guide to Judaism*. New York: NAL, 1990.

Rosenberg, Stuart E. *The New Jewish Identity in America*. New York: Hippocrene, 1985.

Rosenblum, Herbert. *Conservative Judaism: A Contemporary History*. New York: United Synagogues of America, 1983.

Rosenthal, Gilbert S. *Four Paths to One God: Today's Jew and His Religion*. New York: Bloch, 1973.

Rubenstein, Richard. *After Auschwitz*. Indianapolis, IN: Bobbs-Merrill, 1966.

Rubenstein, Richard L., and John Roth. *Approaches to Auschwitz: The Holocaust and Its Legacy*. Atlanta: John Knox, 1987.

Rudin, James. *Israel for Christians: Understanding Modern Israel*. Philadelphia: Fortress Press, 1983.

Ruud, Inger Marie. *Women and Judaism: A Select Annotated Bibliography*. Garland Reference Library of Social Science series. New York: Garland, 1988.

Sachar, Howard Morley. *Diaspora: An Inquiry into the Contemporary Jewish World*. New York: Harper & Row, 1985.

———. *A History of Israel: From the Rise of Zionism to Our Time*. New York: Alfred A. Knopf, 1991.

——. *A History of the Jews in America*. New York: Alfred A. Knopf, 1992.

Samuelson, Norbert. *An Introduction to Modern Jewish Philosophy*. New York: State University of New York Press, 1989.

Sandmel, Samuel. *When a Jew and Christian Marry*. Philadelphia: Fortress Press, 1977.

Schechter-Shalomi, Zalman Meshullam. *Spiritual Intimacy: A Study of Counseling in Hasidism*. Northvale, NJ: Jason Aronson, 1991.

Schneider, Susan Weideman. *Intermarriage: The Challenge of Living with Differences Between Christians and Jews*. New York: Free Press, 1989.

——. *Jewish and Female: Choices and Changes in Our Lives Today*. New York: Summit, 1984.

Segev, Tom. *The First Israelis*. New York: Free Press; London: Collier Macmillan, 1986.

Seltzer, Robert. *Jewish People, Jewish Thought: The Jewish Experience in History*. New York: Macmillan, 1980.

——. *Judaism: A People and Its History*. New York: Macmillan, 1989.

Shenker, Israel. *Coat of Many Colors: Pages from Jewish Life*. Garden City, NY: Doubleday, 1985.

Silberman, Charles. *A Certain People: American Jews and Their Lives Today*. New York: Simon & Schuster, 1984.

Silberstein, Laurence J. *New Perspectives on Israeli History: The Early Years of the State*. New York: New York University Press, 1991.

Steinberg, Milton. *Basic Judaism*. New York: Harcourt Brace and World, 1947.

Syme, Daniel. *Why I Am a Reform Jew*. New York: Donald Fine, 1989.

Telushkin, Joseph. *Jewish Literacy: The Most Important Things to Know About the Jewish Religion, Its People and Its History*. New York: William Morrow, 1991.

Trepp, Leo. *The Complete Book of Jewish Observance*. New York: Behrman House, 1980.

——. *Judaism: Development and Life*, 3d ed. Belmont, CA: Wadsworth, 1982.

Umansky, Ellen, and Dianne Ashton, eds. *Four Centuries of Jewish Women's Spirituality*. Boston: Beacon, 1992.

van Beeck, Franz Josef. *Loving the Torah More Than God? Towards a Catholic Appreciation of Judaism.* Chicago: Loyola University Press, 1989.

Van Buren, Paul. *A Christian Theology of the People Israel,* vol. 3 of *A Theology of the Jewish Christian Reality.* New York: Seabury, 1983.

———. *A Theology of the Jewish Christian Reality.* New York: Seabury, 1980.

Vital, David. *The Origins of Zionism.* Oxford, England: Clarendon, 1975.

———. *Zionism: The Crucial Phase.* Oxford, England: Clarendon; New York: Oxford University Press, 1987.

———. *Zionism: The Formative Years.* Oxford, England: Clarendon; New York: Oxford University Press, 1982.

Weinberg, Sidney Stahl. *The World of Our Mothers: Lives of Jewish Immigrant Women.* Chapel Hill: University of North Carolina Press, 1988.

Weiss, Avraham. *Women at Prayer: A Halachic Analysis of Women's Prayer Groups.* Hoboken, NJ: KTAV, 1989.

Wiesel, Eliezer. *The Accident.* New York: Avon Books, 1970.

———. *Beggar in Jerusalem.* New York: Avon Books, 1971.

———. *Dawn.* New York: Avon Books, 1970.

———. *Night.* New York: Avon Books, 1969.

———. *The Town Beyond the Wall.* New York: Avon Books, 1969.

Wigoder, Devorah. *Hope Is My House.* Englewood Cliffs, NJ: Prentice-Hall, 1966.

Wigoder, Geoffrey. *Jewish-Christian Relations Since the Second World War.* Manchester, England: Manchester University Press, 1988.

Wouk, Herman. *This Is My God: The Jewish Way of Life.* New York: Pocket Books, 1970.

3
Contemporary Catholic Spirituality for "Everyperson"

Fr. Michael Tracey

Introduction

The Second Vatican Council (1962–65) has become a milestone in the recent history of Catholicism. The implications of the Council are still being realized in the Catholic Church's understanding of itself and its mission today. But to understand these implications, it is necessary to understand the Catholic spirituality that motivated Vatican II. Undeniably, Catholic spirituality is shaped by Catholic identity, and Catholic identity is rooted in a historical journey of 2,000 years. This journey has been directed by a keen sense of scripture and tradition. It is also necessary to understand the Catholic sensibility, the Catholic religious "style," before we can fully appreciate Catholic spirituality. In their book, *How to Save the Catholic Church* (1985), Fr. Andrew Greeley and Mary Greeley Durkin suggest:

> The Catholic religious experience is sacramental: it encounters God in the events, objects, and persons of every day. The Catholic imagination is analogical: it pictures God as being similar to these events, objects, and persons. The Catholic religious story is cosmic: it believes in happy ends in which grace routs both evil and injustice. The Catholic religious community is organic: it is based on a dense network of local relationships that constitute the matrix of everyday life.

According to John Carmody and Denise Carmody, in their book *Christian Uniqueness & Catholic Spirituality* (1990):

> The great trigger to spiritual searching, historically, has been dissatisfaction and suffering. Tasting ashes or wormwood, people have resolved to find genuine nourishment for their souls. Encountering evil or harsh fate, people have left their old sense of reality behind and set out to find something deeper, something so profound that it might make death and injustice penultimate. To be human was to be realistic about one's world. To be wise was to know, in ways that pacified one's soul and made one a guide and comfort to others, what was possible in both human affairs and intercourse with more than human powers. (P. 12)

An evening meal is the product of many hours of work. The gourmet blends many ingredients together to produce the final product. The recipient's taste buds are stimulated as mind, body, and spirit are nourished in a way that a TV dinner cannot match. In the same way, present Catholic lay spirituality is the product of a gourmet, the Holy Spirit, who blends together satisfying nourishment to feed the hungers, passions, and tastes of the receptive diners. Here we list the ingredients, the themes, trends, milestones, and essential works, of the recipe for contemporary Catholic spirituality for "everyperson."

The first major development in Catholic spirituality is the development of lay spirituality. When Donna Hanson, a lay Catholic, addressed Pope John Paul II in San Francisco on September 18, 1987, she told him, "The lay members of our church are now among the best educated and the most highly trained in the world. Yet we hunger for spiritual education and formation. We long for structures in which to truly share responsibility." Lay spirituality is one of the main areas undergoing change in today's Roman Catholic Church. Laypeople desire direct experiential knowledge of God, not only knowledge about God. Catholics have passed from an era of information to an era of infusion. There is a reemphasizing of philosophical-theological approach to spirituality, and this quest is reflected in a return to the classics—the works of St. John of the Cross and St. Teresa of Avila, for example.

In the past, lay spirituality was a lesser version of priestly spirituality, which in turn was a version of monastic spirituality. Today, a unique lay spirituality is developing in its own right. We in America have moved beyond being an immigrant Catholic Church to being the American Catholic Church. This new individuality and identity will reflect how we develop and embrace our own spirituality.

Historically, the concept of an inward journey has been flavored by various movements in the Catholic Church, particularly Cursillo (a weekend lay retreat movement), Marriage Encounter (a weekend experience to deepen communications in marriage), and the Charismatic movements (a movement that opens up a variety of prayer forms to the lay person) as well as Eastern spirituality. Yet there is something disturbing about these movements in that they are basically inward-looking organizations. From the 1930s and the time of the Second Vatican Council, the American Catholic Church was characterized by special-focus, action-oriented movements, designed to influence and help the outside world. These movements included Catholic Interracial Council, Catholic Organization for International Peace, Catholic Worker Movement, and Young Christians Students Movements. But all of these groups have disappeared. The problems that inspired these movements are being addressed through other bodies, such as the National Conference of Catholic Bishops, and in particular through diocesan agencies. Why has the focus changed? Is it a reflection on our sense of powerlessness over society, our lack of faith in our power to shape society? Is it part of the individualization of American society so thoroughly discussed by Robert Bellah et al. in their book *Habits of the Heart* (1987)?

The second development in the Catholic Church is the emergence of small Christian communities that possess transforming power over society. Basically a Latin American phenomenon (Comunidads de Base), these communities are formed in the context of liberation theology, which tries to change oppressive structures and society. Similarly, the RENEW movement, founded in Newark, New Jersey, in 1978 by Fr. Thomas Kleissler, is based on a concept of small-group spirituality strongly influenced by the Latin American movement, which empowers people to act upon the challenges presented by the Gospel. The RENEW experience has had a powerful and transforming effect on its participants both locally and internationally. Small groups continue to meet, to hear, and respond to the Lord's call. The concept of small Christian communities will continue to have far-reaching implications for our spirituality.

The third development has been in the area of Scripture studies. Many movements and educational opportunities have opened up the riches of the Scriptures to the ordinary person, providing more opportunities for individuals to share, discuss, and pray the Scriptures.

The fourth development has been in the area of prayer. In the past, clerical spirituality (and, prior to that, monastic spirituality) did not fit into the vocation of the layperson in the world. Today, a lay spirituality is developing in its own right. Its prayer form is for the marketplace, not the rectory or monastery. The multiplicity of books on this topic attests to the depth of the spiritual hunger. The popularity of the Enneagram, retreats, and the participation in workshops on prayer, spiritual direction, and other such topics further support this development.

A fifth development in the Catholic Church is the integration of the behavioral sciences (such as psychology) with Catholicism. These sciences have provided us with a more in-depth understanding of the human person and his or her growth process. Rather than working in opposition to each science, as in the past, Catholicism now recognizes that science can complement spirituality.

A sixth development is that of social consciousness, which is an extension of the development of lay spirituality. More and more Catholics are involved in promoting social change through, for example, St.

Vincent de Paul charities, food banks, political activism, social justice, and ecology. Yet many Catholics are still uncomfortable with the social gospel. The greatest challenge here is to engender a sense of belonging and being responsible for a larger reality.

A seventh development in the Catholic Church is in the area of marriage and family life. Present estimates are that one-third of children in the United States will have divorced parents by their eighteenth birthday. The diminution of Catholic schools and the increase of inter-religious marriages (where one partner is not Catholic) have contributed to this trend. Religious socialization in such an inter-religious marriage is very different than in a marriage between two Catholics. The changing role of women in the church and the quality of the relationship between men and women in the church is critical.

An eighth development in today's Catholicism is the slow transition from a spirituality based on a fall/redemption motif to one based on a creation-centered motif. The former is based on the sin of humanity needing redemption, while the latter is based on the idea of blessing or creation. The former emphasizes humanity's fallenness, the latter humanity's place in a divine order. The former position's greatest proponent was St. Augustine, the latter's major proponent was Meister Eckhart. This transition from a fall/redemption motif to a creation-centered motif is just beginning to have far-reaching consequences in the continuing development of lay spiritualities.

Finally, probably one of the most significant contributions to the ongoing development of a lay spirituality in today's Catholic Church is the tremendous increase of ministries. This explosion of ministries, coming from the decline of vocations to the priesthood and religious life, has increased interest in spirituality. This development's main pillar is a new sense of vocation among Catholics. Catholics are becoming more aware of their call to ministry as part of their baptismal commitment. Many Catholics consider spirituality a high priority because they are living a personal, intentional faith life that they want to develop.

The hunger for spiritual formation and education is shared, not by troublemakers and reformers, but by committed people, sharing a need, seeking a voice, and asking for direction, nourishment, and participation.

Themes, Trends, and Milestones

In the introduction, I have briefly defined the Catholic sensibility and how that sensibility gives rise to a particular flavor of spirituality. I have also indicated some of the trends that have shaped and continue to shape the contours of Catholic spirituality for everyperson. I will now try to delineate particular forms of lay spirituality: Lay spirituality in general, psychology and spirituality, the tension between contemplation and action, feminine spirituality, masculine spirituality, liberation spirituality, journey spirituality, story spirituality, creation-centered spirituality, and small-group spirituality.

Lay Spirituality in General

Lay spirituality cannot be understood without understanding the history of the church that created it. This background will help identify the factors that support or hinder lay spirituality. The early church was a very uncomplicated network of people spreading the Good News. All the baptized were called to holiness and, hence, to spirituality. Yet three things hindered this call to holiness. The first hindrance to growth were heresies such as Gnosticism (in 140 A.D.), Montanism (in 150 A.D.), and Manichaenism (in 275 A.D.). One of the adverse effects of these heresies was dualism, which minimized matter and stressed spirit. Second, the development of monasticism perpetuated a "flight from the world" mentality that encouraged those called to holiness to withdraw from common life and concerns—an emphasis that separated ordinary people from the spirituality of the church. Third, institutionalization of the church made a sharp distinction between the leaders and the followers. The leaders became elitists, while the role of the baptized was diminished. Monastic spirituality became the model for all spirituality. As previously indicated, priests became mini-monks, and laypeople who exercised their spirituality became mini-priests. The influence of monasticism continued until the 1600s.

The decline of monastic influence was replaced by schools of spirituality, such as the Benedictine, Franciscan, Dominican, and Augustinian. Mystics like John of the Cross (1542–1591) and Teresa of Avila (1515–1582) provided a better balance between prayer and action while developing a spirituality accessible to all. St. Francis de Sales (1567–1622), who wrote the classic *Introduction to the Devout Life* (1609), reflects on this trend in his introduction:

> Nearly everyone who has written about the spiritual life has had in mind those who live apart from the world, or at least the devotion they advocate would lead to such retirement. My intention is to write for those who have to live in the world and who, according to this state, to all outward appearances have to live an ordinary life. (P. 18)

Twentieth-century spirituality developed from biblical, liturgical reform. There emerged Catholic biblical scholars who began to make the scriptures understandable to the ordinary Catholic. In Europe, prior to the Second Vatican Council, pioneers were already laying the groundwork for the liturgical reform that would result from the Council. Outstanding laypersons such as Jacques Maritain, Dorothy Day, Jean Vanier, Frank Sheed, Frank Duff, and Friedrick von Hugel brought the fledging lay spirituality to the workplace. The Second Vatican Council drew from the emerging trends in spirituality, and once again recognized and emphasized the call to holiness of all the baptized, because of their baptism.

Since Vatican II, lay spirituality has undergone many changes. A systematic, formal, individual type of spirituality has been replaced by a more vital, less systematic, and less formal spirituality, oriented more toward personal responsibility. Parish-based spirituality, guided by the local pastor, has been replaced by a global vision based less on method and more on personal meaning. A spirituality based on personal devotions has been replaced by a spirituality that is Christocentric, ecclesial, liturgical, both individual and communal, contemplative, and ministerial. According to Leonard Doohan, in his book *The Lay-Centered Church* (1984), there are four major trends in spirituality today: ecclesial, incarnational, service, and liberational. We will explore each in some detail.

Ecclesial Thrust

The ecclesial thrust emphasizes a sense of church, community awareness, and prayer in the life of the people who are the church. The way we view church colors is the way we see our own spiritual development. In the past, the hierarchical model of church was emphasized. The hierarchical model perpetuated an us/them mentality. This model provided a sense of security, reinforced a sense of solidarity, and supported continuity between past and present. Its liabilities included scant evidence in Scripture for this type of model. It stifled creativity, led to elitism among the hierarchy, and left no room for diversity or dialogue with other religions.

Other models of church have been developed by theologians such as Avery Dulles in his *Models of Church* (1974). These models include church as sacrament, herald, and servant. Dulles's latest model is one of a community of disciples. He suggests that, because of such factors as the genuine eagerness for prayer, the quest for the transcendent, the attraction of the person of Jesus, the evolution of lay movements, the decline in religious vocations, the upsurge in interest in various ministries, ignorance and misunderstanding of church dogmas, and, finally, the decline of the Catholic schools system, we must rethink our understanding of church. He suggests that the community of disciples model is best suited to meet the needs of today's Catholic.

In *A Church to Believe In* (1984), Dulles explains:

> The disciple is by definition one who has not yet arrived, a learner trying to comprehend strange words and unravel puzzling experiences. To be a disciple is to be under authority and correction. It is to be still on the way to full conversion and blessedness of life. . . . The concept of discipleship makes it clear that each member of the church is under personal obligation to appropriate the Spirit of Jesus. Church membership, so conceived, is neither a passive acceptance of a list of doctrines, nor abject submission to a set of precepts, but rather the adventure of following Jesus in new and ever changing situations. (P. 10)

The discipleship model of church has brought about among the laity a growing awareness of what it means to be church. Various movements emphasizing conversion and renewal have overflowed into a more global awareness of a sense of brotherhood and sisterhood, and a sense of responsibility for our world.

Incarnational Thrust

In past decades, the church defined itself in opposition to the world. It saw the world as evil and corrupt. The church challenged people to focus on God and not be trapped by the world. Nowadays, we have shifted from an either/or mentality to a both/and approach. Rather than seeing the world as evil, the church now sees the world as being redeemable. This approach affirms the goodness of creation as stressed in the creation story in Genesis. According to Doohan in *The Lay-Centered Church* (1984), "Incarnational spirituality is a spirituality of influential presence. It implies a positive appreciation of the world and a self-insertion into the world to sanctify and redeem it" (p. 7). The writings of Teilhard de Chardin and Matthew Fox have discussed this new incarnational thrust. We will discuss the contribution of Matthew Fox to creation-centered spirituality later. Briefly stated, creation-centered spirituality places all living organisms within the economy of redemption and the matrix of creation.

Service Thrust

Lay spirituality has become more service-oriented because of differing ecclesiologies and new understandings of ministry. Under the umbrella of evangelization, the service thrust to spirituality deals with personal lifestyles and commitment to public presence and office. Many laypersons have committed themselves to protecting and developing human rights, the right-to-life movement, peacemaking, and have become volunteers for service overseas and in poorer regions at home. This service thrust creates its own tensions, particularly the tension between contemplation and action. We will deal more fully with that tension later.

Liberational Thrust

As a people, we have become more aware of social, structural, and cosmic sin. Our interconnectedness leads to a greater awareness that spirituality is not individualistic but must be authenticated by a commitment to social justice. The liberational thrust of Catholicism contains three key trends. The first is the healing, on an individual, personal level, of such addictions as compulsiveness, competitiveness and possessiveness. This healing is also communal. The second component is often called "contestation," which is a personal or organized struggle against the injustices of society. A final component of the liberational thrust is the adoption and development of new attitudes of creativity, imagination, and hope. This attitude leads to more creative ways of looking at world problems, offering solutions and alternatives. We will discuss the liberational form of spirituality in more detail later.

Resources on Catholic Lay Spirituality

Bacik, James J. *The Glorious Mystery: Finding God in Ordinary Experience.* Cincinnati, OH: St. Anthony Messenger Press, 1984. ISBN 0-86716-072-1.

James Bacik, professor of theology at Fordham University, has written this book for individuals engaged in "the quest for meaning in the midst of absurdity, for commitment in the face of multiple options, for a deeper life amidst the temptation to superficiality" (p. 6). Blending speculation and practicality, he offers excellent advice and theological insight on such a search for meaning.

Broccolo, Gerald T. *Vital Spiritualities.* Notre Dame, IN: Ave Maria Press, 1989. ISBN 087793-417-7.

This popular, readable book suggests that there are many ways of being spiritual. The author defines spirituality as "a way of coping with life, of viewing and experiencing life." He believes that the way we view God, world, others, and self shapes our spirituality. He contrasts the ideal with the real, where we can find holiness in the midst of everyday struggles. He calls on the church to recognize a "plurality of spiritualities" as he tries to bring the reader to identify the holy in their life.

Carmody, John Tully, and Denise Ladner Carmody. *Christian Uniqueness & Catholic Spirituality.* Mahwah, NJ: Paulist Press, 1990. ISBN 0-8091-3197-8.

In their preface, this husband and wife team writes:

> [We] take neither "orthodox" nor "traditional" restrictively or oppressively. We are not concerned to sniff out doctrinal deviance or meet a litmus test devised in Rome. But we are concerned to reflect about the Jesus who has been the treasure of traditional Christian faith, because so much of the best prayer and service to the poor has centered on him. (P. 3)

The book is expansive in that it discusses ways in which holiness is manifested in Hinduism, Buddhism, and other comparative religions. The authors present a more balanced view of the uniqueness of Christ, from Scriptural and historical points of view. Because of this more balanced view of Christ's uniqueness, the reader is given an accurate taste of Catholic spirituality in the context of male/female spirituality, social justice, and creation-centered spirituality. Though at times tedious, this book provides clarification and a fresh approach to our relationship to Christ and spirituality.

Doohan, Leonard. *The Lay-Centered Church: Theology & Spirituality*. Minneapolis, MN: Winston Press, 1984. ISBN 0-86683-808-2.

Leonard Doohan is a professor of theology at Gonzaga University, Spokane, Washington. Gonzaga University has one of the largest centers of spirituality in the United States and Canada. Doohan considers four aspects of the place of the laity in the church today. First, he reviews the writings on the laity since Vatican Council II, in particular the writings of Rahner, Congar, and Schillebeeckx. Doohan shows that all Catholics share in a common priesthood, and suggests that laypersons do not simply *belong* to the church, nor do they *have a role* in the church, because they *are* the church through their baptism. Second, he deals with the developments and changes in attitudes in church structures since Vatican II. He identifies the church's strengths and weaknesses in understanding the laity. He also develops three major areas of concern: ecclesial responsibility, spiritual life and growth, and mission and ministry. Third, Doohan discusses the church as family, challenging the laity to acknowledge and appreciate their everyday experiences, knowledge, and skills. Finally, Doohan reviews developments in spirituality, identifying some of the trends we have already spoken of earlier in this essay. *The Lay-Centered Church* is an excellent synthesis of current theologies on the life and role of the laity in the church. It provides the reader with a definite perspective on trends, milestones, and attitudes of a rapidly developing, lay-centered church.

Finley, Mitch. *Catholic Spiritual Classics*. Kansas City, MO: Sheed & Ward, 1989. ISBN 1-55612-058-3.

Reading the spiritual classics, such as those by John of the Cross and Theresa of Avila, can be a tedious task for the newcomer. This short book gives a concise but brief introduction to such western spiritual classics. Rather than laboriously review all the details of these works, Finley gleans from them key ideas, garnished with fresh insights and little-known pieces of information. Consequently, this book would be excellent for someone who may be curious about the great spiritual classics but has been overwhelmed by their complexity. It provides a bait to invite the reader deeper into the lives and thoughts of these spiritual mystics and writers.

Fox, Matthew. *On Becoming a Musical Mystical Bear: Spirituality American Style*. Mahwah, NJ: Paulist Press, 1976. ISBN 0-8091-1913-7.

Matthew Fox is a Dominican priest who has written extensively on creation-centered spirituality. His aim in *On Becoming a Musical Mystical Bear* is:

> To present the groundwork for a spirituality that is non-repressive and non-ideological. One that frees instead of coerces, and that does so by rejecting ideological or uncritically accepted (usually piously approved) terminology. (P. xi)

Though written in 1976, this book touches a responsive chord in people's lives. Many readers will find themselves nodding in approval and saying, "That's me!" because Fox speaks to what Catholics feel deep down in their hearts. Fox states that every cultural crisis produces corresponding spiritual crises. These crises have challenged us to learn to "unpray" before we can truly pray. Unpraying is the realization that true prayer is not saying prayers, not withdrawal from or acquiescence to a culture, not asking God to change things, not talking to God, and not an exceptional experience. Instead, life is mystery, and prayer is a psychological and socially radical response to life. This book will give the reader a fresh start to becoming a Musical Mystical Bear—American style, to taking his or her rightful place within God's creation.

Green, Thomas H. *Opening to God*. Notre Dame, IN: Ave Maria Press, 1976. ISBN 087793-136-4.

Thomas Green, a Jesuit priest, spent many years ministering in the Philippines. This is his first book in a series of books on various aspects of the spiritual life, and it has become a classic. It is much more than a "how-to" handbook on prayer. It combines the fundamentals of the Christian tradition with the insights of today. The book is a blend of a rich tradition, spontaneity, and today's practical experience. It is the building block upon which all his other books stand.

Kempis, Thomas À. *The Imitation of Christ*. Translated by William C. Creasy. Notre Dame, IN: Ave Maria Press, 1990. ISBN 087793-411-8.

Creasy offers a modern translation of this classic written by Thomas À. Kempis, who died in 1471. The book offers profound insights into a person's relationship with God. It has appeared in hundreds of editions and guided millions on their journey toward God. This is timeless and classic companion for anyone who is seriously interested in their own spiritual journey.

Rolheiser, Ronald. *Spirituality for a Restless Culture*. Mystic, CT: Twenty-Third, 1991. ISBN 0-89622-469-4.

Rolheiser is vice-dean of theology at Newman Theological College, Edmonton, Canada. He suggests that we are a restless society filled with fear and guilt. We fear losing life, heath, job, loved ones, security, respect, and youthfulness. We are guilt-ridden because of things we have done or not done. The book is a series of reflections that shed light on such restlessness, longing, fears, and guilt. Chapters include reflections on passion, love, sex, virginity, daily prayer, social justice, and the need for community. In the preface, the author states the purpose of the book:

> [It] is for those who struggle to make this life, such as it is, enough. It is for those who ache to be outside themselves, with the headaches and heartaches behind them. It is dedicated to those who struggle with restlessness, guilt, and obsessions, who struggle to taste their own coffee and who struggle to feel the consolation of God.

Warnke, James W. *Becoming an Everyday Mystic*. St. Meinrad, IN: Abbey Press, 1990. ISBN 0-87029-230-7.

This simple, popular book deals with discovering God in the "extraordinary ordinary." It explains, in nontechnical language, mysticism, and opens up the wisdom of such spiritual giants as St. Thérèse of Lisieux, Thomas Merton, Dorothy Day, and Catherine DeHueck Doherty to the ordinary person. The book makes the reader more aware of the presence of God in their everyday routine and decision making. Woven throughout the book is the thread of love that is an invitation-response challenge expected of everyone.

Audio Resources on Catholic Lay Spirituality

Muto, Susan A. *Formative Spirituality for Laity*. Notre Dame, IN: Ave Maria Press. audiocassette. 56 min.

Susan Muto is well-known for her treatment of lay spirituality. Her cassette offers some practical suggestions on how our everyday lives suggest avenues, often unnoticed, for in-depth spiritual formation. Based on the fact that we are all part of God's work of art, we are called to become a new creation and to find deeper meaning in our lives.

Nouwen, Henri J. M. *The Lonely Search for God*. Notre Dame, IN: Ave Maria Press, 1978. 2 audiocassettes. 2 hrs. 30 min.

In this cassette series, Nouwen leads the listener through a process in his or her search for God. The process means converting from hostility to hospitality, from illusion to prayer, and from loneliness to solitude. Nouwen shows that this conversion process is accomplished alone, but through a genuine, caring, open Christian community.

Psychology and Spirituality

In the past, psychology and religion have had an unhealthy distaste for each other. For too long, the two disciplines have been compartmentalized and competitive. The new sciences, behavioral sciences, took care of the natural; the church took care of the supernatural. The behavioral sciences took care of human needs, while the church took care of divine (spiritual) needs.

The dichotomy between the body and the spirit, the natural and the supernatural, is being bridged gradually. Science and religion are beginning to come together to complement rather than antagonize each other. The split between science and religion was a split in human experience. Today, most Catholics agree that the foundation for both the behavioral sciences and religion is human experience. C. S. Lewis suggested that "to discover God is not to discover an idea but to discover oneself."

In our century, psychologists such as Sigmund Freud, Carl Jung, Victor Frankl, William James, Abraham Maslow, and others have helped us to better understand the human experience. Based on that understanding of the human experience, the church is better able to help us understand the religious experience of the human person.

In *Sensing Your Hidden Presence* (1987), Ignacio Larranaga writes:

> Technology and all the human sciences will be able to resolve the majority of human needs, but they will never be able to give a proper answer to the fundamental question regarding the meaning of life. When we are confronted by our own mystery, when we experience the strangeness of "being there," being in the world as consciousness, then the central question will be raised, challenging our path: Who am I? Where do I come from? Is there a future for me, and what is it? In other words, What is the ultimate meaning of my existence? These questions obligate us to make a great leap into the Absolute. (P. 33)

Perhaps the greatest contribution to the developmental approach to human growth was made by Eric Erickson, Carl Jung, Gordon Allport, Gail Sheehy, Daniel Levinston, and James Whitehead and Evelyn Whitehead. Erickson helped us understand the eight stages of human growth, while Jung made us more aware of the *anima* and the *animus*, and especially the "shadow" that is part of the inner struggle for maturity. Allport showed us personality as a dynamic complexity of traits in the process of becoming, while Sheehy, Levinston, and the Whiteheads reflected on the patterns in human growth. By understanding the contributions of these psychologists, we can come to a more complete understanding of our own spiritual journey and developmental stages.

Today, much psychology has value to the study of spirituality. Personality inventories can give initial clues as to where one might look for that central learning that shapes one's spirituality. Psychology can also give information about where and how spiritual development may be blocked. We also have available, from both Western and Eastern religious traditions, scores of techniques to help with prayer, meditation, body-awareness, imaging, journal-keeping, and other contemporary issues.

Because spirituality involves the whole person, it can be related to every area of human behavior. Interest in the relationship between psychology and spirituality has increased enormously in the last decade. Both psychology and spirituality have built-in dangers when they relate to each other. Spirituality can be naïve and destructive when it flies in the face of healthy psychology. At the same time, spirituality loses its significance when it capitulates completely to psychology. A delicate balance is needed.

Through its study of human growth, psychology has provided us with insights on how we move from one stage of development to another. The central challenge is how we understand and manage change. Change threatens past accomplishments and disrupts stability. It often feels like loss, failure, or (for the Christian) sin. In their book

Christian Life Patterns (1982), Evelyn Whitehead and James Whitehead suggest that the "ultimate criterion of religious maturity is neither good intentions nor a well-rounded personality. It is instead, the ability to be loving and generative, and to discover within the unexpected turns and crosses of adult life a meaning that is, at bottom, a gift" (p. xxv).

Resources on Psychology and Spirituality

Grant, W. Harold, Magdala Thompson, and Thomas E. Clark. *From Image to Likeness: A Jungian Path in the Gospel Journey.* Mahwah, NJ: Paulist Press, 1983. ISBN 0-8093-2552-8.

For the past decade, these three authors have conducted retreat workshops based on the Gospel as illuminated through Jungian personality types. They have employed the Myers-Briggs Type Indicator (MBTI) to help individuals identify their personality type and corresponding spiritual path. The Myers-Briggs Type Indicator is the creation of Isabel Myers and her mother, Katheryn Briggs. Using Carl Jung's psychological types, Myers and Briggs devised this indicator as a tool for identifying sixteen different personality patterns. There are four dimensions on the scale: introvert or extrovert, intuitive or sensate, thinking or feeling, and judging or perceiving.

The book develops four basic models: the journey from image to likeness; the four Jungian functions; a developmental typology that predicates four stages of growth toward wholeness; and, finally, the triad of solitude, friendship, and society as it expresses the human reality that must be developed as part of the journey from image to likeness.

The basic premise of the book is that we are made in God's image. This premise is a call to holiness, wholeness, perfection, fullness, and glory. This call to holiness begins with an attitude of attentiveness. This attentiveness is brought about through simplicity of heart and an openness to sensing that "is the function by which we meet or encounter both God and every creature in their self-presentation to us." By paying attention to our encounters, we journey to the truth that makes us free, endowing us with a joyful heart, because we cannot imagine the fullness of God's love for us, nor can we imagine our final incorporation into God.

The appendix, which provides a summary of the correlation of the sixteen types and brief descriptions of each type in each of the four periods of development, provides an excellent opportunity to refresh our understanding of Jungian personality types.

Groeschel, Benedict J. *Spiritual Passages: The Psychology of Spiritual Development.* New York: Crossroad, 1984. ISBN 0-8245-0628-6.

Benedict Groeschel, O.F.M., is director of the Office for Spiritual Development of the Archdiocese of New York and teaches pastoral psychology at Fordham University and Iona College. He is well known for his retreat work and television shows. His book attempts to "relate some of the sounder insights of contemporary psychology to the classic outline of the spiritual journey contained in the immense and fascinating literature of spirituality." Groeschel merges tested psychological insights and Christian spiritual tradition. This is not a bedtime book; rather, it is to be read slowly (with frequent underlining) and digested in small quantities.

Spiritual Passages is divided into two parts: "The Psychology of Spirituality" and "A Psychological Understanding of the Three Ways." The former deals with human development and spirituality, the latter with the three stages of the spiritual life: Purgation, Illuminative, and Unititive. The book integrates academic and meditative approaches to spirituality. This book is written not for the bookshelf but for the heart. Gilbert K. Chesterton indicated that our relationship with God is the only subject important enough to argue about. *Spiritual Passages* will give the reader more food for argument.

Larranaga, Ignacio. *Sensing Your Hidden Presence: Toward Intimacy with God.* New York: Image Books, 1987. ISBN 0-385-24021-X.

Originally published in Spanish in 1979, this book has become a classic for anyone seriously interested in their spiritual journey. Our image of God can be thwarted by our fears, cultures, interests, weakness, limitations, and ignorance. Larranaga offers "a means for those who want to initiate, or to recover, their relationship with God, and for those others who wish to advance further into the unfathomable mystery of the living God."

The book amplifies prayer from Scriptural, psychological, and experiential points of view. A generous array of recognizable signposts, insights, meditations, and personal experiences are strewn throughout the book so that the reader can integrate them into his or her own spiritual journey. Practical exercises on silence, adoration, contemplation, meditation, consolation, desolation, and illumination wait to satisfy the hungry heart.

Michael, Chester P., and Marie C. Norrisey. *Prayer and Temperament: Different Prayer Forms for Different Personality Types.* Charlottesville, VA: The Open Door, 1984. ISBN 0-940136-01-5.

Are you wondering what is the most appropriate prayer form for you? This book may give you the answer. Using the Myers-Briggs Type Indicator, the authors show that there is a close connection between personality types and prayer and spirituality. The book is the result of a study conducted by the authors with more than 400 participants from the United States, Canada, and Australia.

The organization of the book is straightforward and easy to follow. First, it gives an overview of the history and development of the theory of personality followed by a brief description of how temperament has affected the development of prayer and spirituality. Second, individual chapters delineate the five types of personal prayer found in Christian tradition: Benedictine, Augustinian, Franciscan, Thomistic, and Ignatian. Third, the role of the shadow in prayer is explored. Finally, the authors discuss how the theory of temperament relates to public prayer. The authors provide some excellent prayer suggestions for the different forms of prayer and a summary appendix describing the different types. This book is an excellent tool to help the person who is frustrated with prayer but wonders why. Yet the authors caution that the relationship of temperament and prayer needs to be taken with certain reservations. The conclusions drawn are never to be taken absolutely. The authors caution the reader not to become "stifled with just one type of prayer. Enjoy the riches of all the different kinds of prayer, by, at least occasionally, making an effort to practice those forms of prayer which require extra psychic energy and effort on your part. Your pains will be handsomely rewarded" (p. 121).

Welch, John. *Spiritual Pilgrims: Carl Jung & Teresa of Avila*. Mahwah, NJ: Paulist Press, 1982. ISBN 0-8091-2454-8.

If you wonder what the psychology of Jung and the spirituality of Teresa of Avila have in common, this book will surprise you. You will be even more surprised at the way Jung's types complement Teresa's mystical experience, documented in her book *The Interior Castle*.

Welch, a Catholic priest and faculty member at Washington Theological Union, begins the first chapter of this book with this interesting statement:

> We can grow in awareness of the images which deeply affect us in our lives. They can be discovered, listened to, and incorporated into our ongoing story. In our dreams, in our loves, on our journeys, we are being addressed by images. They are inviting us to enter more deeply into our lives, to allow our stories to unfold. (P. 7)

The images used by Teresa in *The Interior Castle* include: castle, water, journey, serpent, devil, butterfly, marriage, and Christ. Welch takes all these images and shows how they can be interpreted by Jungian psychology. For Teresa, these images are vehicles for entering more deeply into her own experiences. Jung's theory is that such images are expressions of the collective depths of the psyche we share with one another.

The journey within is very difficult and is at times disconcerting. Yet this book provides a road map that will guide our journey from darkness to light, death to birth, trauma to healing, hurt to healing, and despair to hope.

Whitehead, Evelyn Eaton, and James D. Whitehead. *Christian Life Patterns*. New York: Image Books, 1982. ISBN 0-385-15131-4.

This husband-and-wife theologian team has written several books, including *The Emerging Laity* and *Seasons of Strength*. *Christian Life Patterns* is an in-depth sketch of the dynamics of maturing to adulthood, from psychological, theological, and spiritual viewpoints. Theology, psychology, and human experience are combined to guide the reader to a more mature adult faith. This combination is a healthy dose of God's abiding presence and grace in the individual's life. The reader should find an unhurried atmosphere and quiet environment where he or she can soak up the book's contents. An addendum to the book provides various exercises and thought-provoking activities to help the reader better integrate the book into his or her own faith journey. The book challenges the reader to rethink concepts such as change, crisis, conversion, growth, sexuality, intimacy, maturity, and generativity. It is proof that a marriage of spiritual, theological, and psychological concepts not only works but stimulates growth.

Audio Resources on Psychology and Spirituality

Groeschel, Benedict. *Principles of Spiritual Development*. Notre Dame, IN: Ave Maria Press. 2 audiocassettes. 2 hrs., 29 min.

The author of *Spiritual Passages* (1984), mentioned above, uses a blend of humor and seriousness to explore some basic truths: Original Sin, repentance, the Cross, and others. He uses the stages of human development to delineate the call of the Gospel to conversion.

Sweeney, Richard J. *Spirituality and the Seasons of Adulthood*. Cincinnati, OH: St. Anthony Messenger Press. 4 audiocassettes.

Sweeney is a Catholic priest, a doctor in spiritual theology, and is a licensed counselor. He identifies the spiritual issues and challenges a person is likely to encounter at various phases of the adult life cycle. These challenges are discussed within the context of spiritual growth.

Themes include: "Introduction to Spirituality and the Seasons of Life," "Spiritual Tasks of Early Adulthood," "Spiritual Tasks of the Mid Years," and "Spiritual Tasks of the Late Years."

———. *Understanding Your Dreams*. Cincinnati, OH: St. Anthony Messenger Press. 2 audiocassettes. ISBN A0250.

This series of audiocassettes, which draws on the works of Jung, Freud, contemporary psychology, and classical spiritual writers, relates the world of dreams to the ongoing task of personal and spiritual development. The tapes answer the most basic questions about dreams. Themes include: "The Role of Dreams," "Five Steps Toward Understanding," "Frequent Images and Motifs," and "Ways to Verify Understanding."

———. *You and Your Shadow*. Cincinnati, OH: St. Anthony Messenger Press. 2 audiocassettes with guide. ISBN A5450.

These audiocassettes explore Jung's "shadow" and help us to understand how it colors our relationships and emotions. They offer practical ways to discover and embrace the shadow and to harness its energy for spiritual and personal growth.

Contemplation and Action

Perhaps we should begin by defining the terms *contemplation* and *action*. Thomas Merton, the world's best-known Trappist monk, struggled with the issue of contemplation and action in his own life. In his book *New Seeds of Contemplation* (1961), he attempts to define contemplation:

Contemplation is always beyond our own knowledge, beyond our own light, beyond explanations, beyond discourse, beyond dialogue, beyond our own self. To enter into the realm of contemplation one must in a certain sense die: but this death is in fact the entrance into a higher life. It is a death for the sake of life, which leaves behind all that we can know or treasure as life, as thought, as experience, as joy, as being. . . . Contemplation is also the response to a call: a call from Him who has no voice, and yet Who speaks in everything that is, and Who most of all, speaks in the depths of our own being: for we ourselves are words of His. (P. 2)

Action has two components: *awareness*, which is openness to what is true and real in the human and the divine, and *freedom*, which is the responsive dimension, the ability to say "yes" freely to God.

There has always been a tension between contemplation and action. This tension can have two dangerous results. *Quietism,* which is retreat into long periods of prayer instead of action, or *activism,* which is to plunge into action with no time or energy for prayer. Merton warns us about the dangers of activism:

There is a pervasive form of contemporary violence. The rush and presence of modern life are a form of its innate violence. To allow oneself to be carried away by a multitude of conflicting concerns, to surrender to many projects, to want to help everyone in everything is to succumb to violence. The frenzy of the activist destroys his own inner capacity for peace. It destroys the fruitfulness of his own work because it kills the root of inner wisdom which makes work fruitful. (P. 66)

The real challenge is creating a balance between contemplation and action in the life of the adult Christian. But how can we go from a position of either contemplation or action to one that balances both? Robert Kinast suggests a possible bridge between contemplation and action. He calls it a "spirituality of engagement" and writes that this kind of spirituality is a spirituality "in which life experiences are the source or starting point for the encounter with God. The engagement in real-life situations leads the minister to reflection on the experience, which in turn leads to an identification with God's action in Scripture and to prayer and sharing with others."

Ministry, or action, is not delivering services but empowering people. It is mainly about relationships, and is enhanced by the contemplative awareness that seeks and discovers God in each person. This discovery allows one to treat the other person with compassion. Spiritual writer Henri Nouwen, in his book *The Way of the Heart* (1981), describes this compassion as the

fruit of solitude and the basis of all ministry. The purification and transformation that takes place in solitude manifest themselves in compassion. It is in solitude that we realize that nothing human is alien to us. In solitude our heart of stone can be turned into a heart of flesh; a closed heart into a heart that can open itself to all suffering people in a gesture of solitude. (Pp. 33–34)

Resources on Contemplation and Action

Doohan, Leonard. *Leisure: A Spiritual Need*. Notre Dame, IN: Ave Maria Press, 1991. ISBN 0-87793-433-9.

The leisure industry in the United States generates $300 billion annually, yet it often leaves us empty and unfulfilled. Leonard Doohan, Professor of Religious Studies at Gonzaga University, Spokane, Washington, approaches leisure from a spiritual rather than commercial point of view. Leisure is a topic that is often discussed but seldom realized without a certain guilt. The book, while accepting that many of us feel an obligation to work to improve our quality of life, suggests that we need to complement that search with a healthy attitude about the necessity of leisure. The book discusses the need for leisure, its nature, how leisure is part of spiritual development and prayer, and the helps and hindrances to a leisurely approach to prayer. This book is a must for anyone who is interested in "wasting time" constructively. A suggested caveat: read it at a leisurely pace.

Green, Thomas H. *Weeds Among the Wheat Discernment: Where Prayer & Action Meet*. Notre Dame, IN: Ave Maria Press, 1984. ISBN 0-87793-318-9.

Green's books, beginning with *Opening to God* (1976) and ending with his latest, *Drinking from a Dry Well* (1991), lead the reader from learning to pray to the more advanced issues of learning how to deal with discernment and desolation. This book is not for the novice because it is laden with content and thought processes that will undoubtedly baffle the beginner. The purpose of the book is to translate the basic meaning and principles on the art of discernment. Discernment is an art that is learned by doing. The book has three parts: discernment from a biblical perspective; discernment from the perspective of John of the Cross and Teresa of Avila; and, finally, a chapter on "weeds," based on Jesus's parable of the weeds (Matt. 13:24–30). Though the book may be most beneficial to those engaged in spiritual direction, it does offer some pertinent insights to the ordinary person who is willing to truly discern its message.

Kelsey, Morton T. *Discernment: A Study in Ecstasy & Evil*. Mahwah, NJ: Paulist Press, 1978. ISBN 0-8091-2129-8.

Kelsey, an Episcopal priest and theologian, answers the basic question, "How can I discern the touch of God upon my life?" This book guides the reader through the process of discernment. The author approaches discernment from a Scriptural point of view as well as the "slaying in the spirit" mentality. He also looks at discernment critically from language, myth, and psychological "evil" points of view. In conclusion, he applies his finding to discernment in counseling. This books become a valuable tool, not only for understanding discernment but for helping the professional and nonprofessional lead people from evil to ecstasy.

————. *The Other Side of Silence*. Mahwah, NJ: Paulist Press, 1976. ISBN 0-8091-1956-0.

Kelsey is an Episcopal priest and theologian who teaches at Notre Dame University. His main thesis is that we live in an age when many people are setting themselves up as self-styled gurus in the art of meditation; many others have turned to Eastern disciplines, to Zen, to Yoga, to transcendental meditation, and to New Age spirituality. Many of these people fail to realize the depth and wealth of methods and experiences available within Christianity. In his introduction, Kelsey writes:

> Jesus offered a way for common people to encounter and experience God. His way is not just for intellectuals or the full-time professionals or the particularly adept. It is for everyone, particularly people like the publican who do not think they have a chance and those whom life has beaten down. Simple people and beginners can have a genuine encounter with God. It is a matter of learning to respond to the presence and love of God which He already offers us. It is very much like Dante's conception of heaven, in which each person has a particular place, while everyone who enters at all also has some basic experience of the whole of the heavenly spheres. (P. 1)

Kelsey provides one simple way in which encounter with God is possible: meditation. This approach has been tested in classrooms at Notre Dame and in many conferences around the world. In the book, you not only learn about meditation, you engage in it. The author leads you through creating the basic climate for meditation, preparing you for the inward journey, and discerning the images of meditation. This book is both a classic and practical road map of the journey into meditation and silence.

Merton, Thomas. *New Seeds of Contemplation*. New York: New Directions Books, 1961. ISBN 0-8112-0099-X.

Thomas Merton, the internationally-known activist and contemplative monk, personifies the inner tension between contemplation and action. His best selling autobiography, *The Seven Story Mountain* (1970), traces the restlessness of his early life. This restlessness was a lifelong gift and challenge. Merton was a mixture of action and contemplation, of piety and secularity, of protest and sympathy. He was filled with contradictions: the impulse toward both anarchy and discipline; the desire to escape affection and the desperate need for it; he was a bystander and a participant; he was skeptical and full of faith; and he desired both solitude and fame.

Perhaps we get a glimpse of this contradictory man in his book *No Man Is an Island* (1955), where he writes that "we do not live more fully merely by doing more, seeing more, tasting more, and experiencing more. . . . Some of us need to discover that we will not begin to live more fully until we have the courage to do and see and taste and experience much less." (P. 191)

Like most of Merton's books, *New Seeds of Contemplation* probes the inner depths of the spirit, showing how every moment of our life is pregnant with hope and possibilities. The chapters are short, but each is packed with insight that belongs not in the head but in the heart. A sampling of this insight includes: "We do not detach ourselves from things in order to attach ourselves to God, but rather we become detached from ourselves in order to see and use all things." Another insight suggests, "The contemplative is not isolated in himself, but liberated from his external and egotistic self by humility and purity of heart—therefore there is no longer any serious obstacle to simple and humble love of other men."

Audio Resources on Contemplation and Action

Rohr, Richard. *Letting Go: A Spirituality of Subtraction*. Cincinnati, OH: St. Anthony Messenger Press. 8 audiocassettes. 60 min. each. ISBN A4200.

Richard Rohr, founder of the Center for Action and Contemplation in Albuquerque, New Mexico, is a Franciscan priest, popular speaker, and retreat master. Rohr believes that, in our culture, "the good life" means getting *more*. This series of audiocassettes challenge the listener to "subtract"—to let go of what hinders us. Themes include: "Making Room for Freedom: Liberating the Affluent," "At Home in the Wrong House: Living with God and Mammon," "Yes to God: Travelling Through Self to Acceptance," "Silence and Willing Service: Delving into Mystery," "What Is the Good Life? Breaking Out of the Consumer Trap," "Beyond Our Cultural Biases: Siding with the Cosmic Christ," "Leaving Security Behind: Finding a New Center," and "Surrendering: Giving Everything We Are." This series is a daring call to surrender materialism and be free.

Feminine Spirituality

Diana Hayes, a theologian at Georgetown University, spoke at a symposium entitled "The Wisdom of Women," sponsored by the U.S. Catholic Bishops Committee on Women in Society and the church. She stated:

> We are very good at waiting. As women we have waited for centuries for our husbands, our fathers, our sons, our brothers, for all of the men in our lives to listen to the message we bring, a message of love and peace, of justice and true equality, of the shared humanity of all God's creations, of hope in a truly shared life in church and society. This is the message

we, as women, have been the unheard and ignored bearers of from time immemorial. In all truth we have been waiting, with Mary Magdalene, since Christ's death and resurrection for our words of wisdom to not only be heard but to be believed. . . . The wisdom of women must be a multicolored, multihued tapestry which startles those who behold it into a new consciousness, a new understanding of what it truly means to be one in Christ Jesus. (*Catholic News Service*, December 20, 1990, p. 449)

I do not wish to debate the issues of the feminist movement or to give a thumbnail sketch of feminine theology. Chapter 5 deals with Feminism and Theology. Rather, I presume that the reader is aware of some of the writings and discussion on women in society and theology. I propose to outline some resources that will better enable women to reflect their unique wisdom in prayer and spirituality.

In the past, Catholic spirituality was one of repression and righteousness. Our religion has developed the Father God concept, not a Mother God concept. The patriarchal image of God presented in the creation story has permitted a cataract to grow, thus clouding our vision and perception. We inherited the world legitimatized by Genesis. Through the clouded lens, we have believed that *man* rules over and names creation, while *woman* is the bearer of children as well as the instrument through which sin and death came into the world.

Today, we are aware of our rootedness in past myths and how they formed our approach to spirituality; and how we break through to new approaches and insights. Obviously, a new spirituality is called for—a feminine spirituality. And women are helping bring about many changes in the Catholic Church's approach to spirituality. What are ingredients of this change? First of all, ours must be a spirituality of *passion*. This means a change from a spirituality based on power, control, and dominance to one based on sexuality, affectivity, intensity, creativity, and a passion for life. For this spirituality of passion to become rooted, it needs *imagination*. We have lost our capacity to wonder. We need to approach the same old problems, not with the same old solutions, but with a new resilience and intensity that is both creative and imaginative. It reminds one of the old Jewish proverb, "Faced with two alternatives, always choose the third."

The final ingredient of this emerging feminine spirituality is *solidarity*. In a society premised on a male "divide and conquer" mentality, it is imperative that what is learned and experienced through struggles, obstacles, trials, and errors become the redeeming feature of a more balanced feminine spirituality.

Resources on Feminine Spirituality

Chittister, Joan. *WomenStrength: Modern Church, Modern Women*. Kansas City, MO: Sheed & Ward, 1990. ISBN 1-55612-373-6.

Joan Chittister, executive director of A.I.M. (the Alliance for International Monasticism), is a widely published author and lecturer. In this book, she includes sixteen essays on women, women's role in the church, social ministry, justice and peace, spirituality, and activism. The book is filled with insights on women as icon, rebel, and saint, and includes reflections on Moses' mother and Pharaoh's daughter. It also includes a challenging letter to the American bishops about wrestling with the possibility of nuclear war and also some insights on peacemaking. The book concludes with essays on the spirituality of St. Benedict and the future of Benedictine women. The book is a fresh collection of the thoughts, aspirations, and challenges of women today, seen through their strengths and contributions.

Conn, Joann Wolski, ed. *Women's Spirituality*. Mahwah, NJ: Paulist Press, 1987. ISBN 08091-2752-0.
This book provides women with some of the many resources they need to develop a new and refreshing feminine spirituality. The book blends insights from feminine psychology and classical spirituality. It shows how the marriage of the two disciplines can lead the searcher to greater maturity in her faith journey.

Harris, Maria. *Women and Teaching*. Mahwah, NJ: Paulist Press, 1988. ISBN 08091-2991-4.
This book deals with the spirituality of pedagogy, focusing on teaching as a form of spirituality. Five different themes resonate throughout the lives of the women who are featured: silence, remembering, ritual mourning, artistry, and birthing. For the reader who is interested in the women of western classics, they are available from Paulist Press. The Classics of Western Spirituality series provides an in-depth view of Western mysticism. Each book deals with a particular classic spiritual writer, including Catherine of Genoa, Catherine of Siena, Julian of Norwich, Teresa of Avila, and many more. They would be a welcome addition to the reader committed to spirituality.

Leckey, Dolores. *Women and Creativity*. Mahwah, NJ: Paulist Press, 1991. (Madeleva Lecture Series on Spirituality). ISBN 08091-3259-1.
Leckey is executive director of the Office of the Laity of the National Conference of Catholic Bishops. This short book (64 pages) is part of the Madeleva Lecture Series on Spirituality. Leckey's key question is: How do women channel their creativity? According to Leckey, they do so in a structured community, such as convent, workplace, or home; through a common cause, such as the women's movement; and especially through solitude and quiet study. Leckey singles out the places that female spirituality has flourished: The church, in spite of its male leadership; the religious community; and the home. Her message is succinct, engaging, and entertaining as well as challenging to the reader who is called upon to raise his or her own consciousness.

Audio Resources on Feminine Spirituality

Dorgan, Margaret. *Guidance in Prayer from Three Women Mystics.*
    Kansas City, MO: Credence Cassettes. 7 audiocassettes. 7 hrs.
    ISBN AA1173.
    Margaret Dorgan, a Carmelite nun, opens up the lives of three
female mystics: Julian of Norwich, Teresa of Avila, and Thérèsa of
Lisieux. In response to growing interest in feminism and the fascination with mysticism, Dorgan applies the lives, thought patterns, and
prayer styles of these three mystics to the listener's life. What results
is a richer spirituality and a greater appreciation for the feminine
religious experience.

Froehle, Virginia Ann. *In Her Presence.* Cincinnati, OH: St. Anthony
    Messenger Press. 2 audiocassettes with guidesheet. ISBN A4400.
    Froehle presents a series of ten guided, imagery-based medita-
tions on feminine images of God drawn from Scripture and tradition.
These guided-imagery experiences help us to understand and respect
both the masculine and feminine within ourselves and society. These
audiocassettes are most suited for groups but can be used for private
meditation and prayer.

Miles, Midge. *Stories in Our Souls.* Kansas City, MO: Credence Cassettes.
    6 audiocassettes. 5 hrs. ISBN AA1765.
    The author leads the listener through dramatic stories of women
in the Gospels that reflect the universal experience of women. Side
two of each audiocassette provides reflections for individual listeners
to help integrate the richness of the feminine religious experience into
their own lives.

Ruether Radford, Rosemary, et al. *WomenSharing.* Cincinnati, OH: St.
    Anthony Messenger Press. 2 audiocassettes. ISBN A5400.
    Nine of the most influential women in the church—Rosemary
Radford Ruether, Theresa Kane, Dianne Neu, Jeanette Rodriguez,
Mary Luke Tobin, Renny Golden, Terry Hamilton, Silvia Cancio, and
Frances Wood—discuss God, Jesus, self, prayer, and service.
    The authors talk about their personal journeys to God and with
God. Their testimonials are stimulating, challenging, articulate, and
often moving.

Masculine Spirituality

In the past, spirituality in the Catholic Church has been male-oriented.
The vast majority of writing on spirituality was from men, mostly men
who lived solitary lives in monasteries. Yet, one has to wonder if such
spirituality was, in fact, truly a masculine spirituality. Rather, it was
written from a male point of view, but with the expectation that it be
applied to both male and female.

The development of a feminine spirituality has challenged the church to rethink its male spirituality as well. Very little has been written about male spirituality, mainly because of the male stereotypes prevalent in our society. Men are not expected to be overly religious or spiritual, unless they are full-time professionals in the church. They are expected to be tough, cynical, and emotionless. If men showed an interest in spirituality, they commensurately showed a sign of weakness, of dependence. To develop a male spirituality, we must first recognize that men have an innate need for God. Admitting and expressing this need may be more difficult, though. Additionally, any male spirituality must take into account the whole person and must be integrated into every aspect of a man's life. Because of the lingering fear of stereotyping, men and women are reluctant to specify particular qualities or characteristics that are feminine or masculine. Both have fears, and yet both wish to be comfortable with their own developing identities.

Some women resent the gender barriers they encounter in business as they advance into leadership positions. Many men resent the fact that there is nothing clear about sexual behavior today. Consequently, many men decide not to become caught up in the emotional fodder by deciding not to become involved emotionally.

Resources on Masculine Spirituality

Carmody, John. *Toward a Male Spirituality*. Mystic, CT: Twenty-Third, 1990. ISBN 0-89622-410-4.

Carmody, a senior research fellow at the University of Tulsa, Oklahoma, is the author of several books on spirituality. The book is both a confession and guide. It is a confession of the author's own struggles and hopes for a male spirituality. It is also a guide in that it highlights some ways to serve a new and more realistic male spirituality. In his introduction, Carmody sets the tone by stating:

> I think men and women have differences, but that these differences should weigh less than what they hold in common. I think that each of us goes to God as a unique individual, shaped by genes, sex, family upbringing, social conditioning, education, and the gifts of the Holy Spirit who is not a generic Paraclete, but a Comforter treating us as distinctive individuals—she could no more abandon us than her nursing children. (P. 4)

Carmody takes some very basic Christian concepts and finds in them the potential for a more authentic male spirituality. His basic starting point is love: love of God, love of self, love of neighbor. In the final part of the book, he deals with some recent trends in spiritualities for men: moving into mystery, spirituality and holism, sexuality and spirituality, and personality types.

He concludes his books most poignantly, writing:

> Christian spirituality, for men or women, is never about
> worthiness. Always it is about grace. What God has done in
> creation, salvation, and divinization is always undeserved.
> At times the proper attitude is thanksgiving and wonder that
> God could be so good. Compared to the goodness of God, the
> follies, even the evils, of human beings are at best secondary.
> (P. 112)

Pable, Martin W. *A Man and His God*. Notre Dame, IN: Ave Maria
    Press, 1988. ISBN 0-87793-380-4.

Pable argues that there is a real spiritual hunger among men. They
are interested in reading about spiritual growth. Unfortunately, most
of what is written does not speak to their concerns. In this small book
(144 pages), Pable connects the Gospel with issues that confront men
today: the search for meaning, fulfillment, friendship, marriage, work,
and the drive for success. At the same time, Pable suggests ways men
can live harmonious lives.

Audio Resources on Masculine Spirituality

Rohr, Richard. *The Father and I Are One*. Kansas City, MO: Credence
    Cassettes. 4 audiocassettes. 3 hrs. 44 mins. ISBN AA2307.

Rohr, the director of the Center for Action and Contemplation in
Albuquerque, New Mexico, is a very popular speaker, workshop leader,
and spiritual director. His series of audiocassettes deal with the healing
of sexuality, the illness of which often stunts one's spiritual growth. He
discusses some of the cultural and individual problems Americans face in
trying to attain sexual maturity. He shows the listener how these problems are actually spiritual problems. We must heal them if we are to
continue our spiritual journey. Though the talks deal predominantly with
men, certain parts of the material speak to both men and women. Women
can begin to understand some of the stereotypes men labor under, and
discover some ways to help men get beyond such stereotypes.

Titles in the series include: *Human Sexuality*, *The Wild Man*, *The
Ego*, and *A Fatherless World*.

———. *A Man's Approach to God*. Cincinnati, OH: St. Anthony Messenger
    Press. 4 audiocassettes with guide. 90 min. each. ISBN A2800.

These tapes were recorded at a retreat given by the author to a
group of men trying to discover their own unique spirituality. Themes
include: "The Hero's Journey," "Creators of Life," "The Boy and the Old
Man," and "The GrandFather."

At the end of each talk, there is an opportunity to reflect on some
thought-provoking questions. A program guide is included. This is a
series of tapes that will not gather dust on your shelf, but will be shared
and listened to many times.

———. The Spirit in a Man series. Kansas City, MO: Credence Cassettes. 4 audiocassettes. 4 hrs. ISBN AA2182.

This series of four cassettes is primarily addressed to a male audience and addresses our entire male-oriented culture. He shows how destructive this culture is both to men and women. He critiques the current system and then outlines how the spirit calls us to move beyond it to discover an authentic maleness that is demanded and supported by the Gospels.

Liberation Spirituality

In 1971, Fr. Gustavo Gutierrez, a Peruvian psychologist, theologian, and author, wrote the highly influential A *Theology of Liberation.* While some critics said the work was imbued with Marxist concepts, others hailed its message of hope, clothed in a new idiom. Originally developed in Latin America in the 1960s, liberation theology is a controversial religious thought that has gained widespread acceptance, especially in Latin America. To many, it is the duty of Christians to support the rights of the poor and oppressed. But among its extremist proponents, liberation theology has been used as an apologia for revolutionary upheaval in the Third World that strives to link the imperatives of Christian charity with the dictates of Marxist class struggle.

What distinguishes liberation theology from the mainstream of church thinking is its strong emphasis on social change. Two new voices in particular, who now are household names, surfaced with the new movement, Leonardo Boff from Brazil and Jon Sobrino from El Salvador. In general, however, the official church, particularly the Vatican, has looked upon their work with censure.

From the viewpoint of Liberation Theology, Christians are called upon to build the Kingdom. This involves participating in the struggles for the liberation of those oppressed by others. We are called by the Spirit of Truth that will set us free (John 16:13), leading us to complete freedom. This spirituality brings us into solidarity with all people, committing ourselves to liberation so that the Lord may lead us in His own unique way to salvation.

A spirituality of liberation must be centered on conversion to the neighbor, the oppressed person, the exploited social class. To be converted is to commit oneself to the process liberating the oppressed, through analysis of the situation and action to be taken to remedy that situation. This conversion is a lifetime process; otherwise, what is gained can easily be lost. Because conversion is both a call and a practical involvement in an unjust situation, conversion involves a change in social and political structures. Without a change in these structures, there is no authentic conversion.

Another aspect of liberation spirituality is a sense of gratitude, the realization that everything is a gift from God. Because all is gift, we cannot adopt a passive attitude, but must actively work for the beneficial use of all God-given talents. When we encounter obstacles that hinder the full use of gifts, it is easy to become discouraged, so an attitude of prayer is imperative.

Finally, being challenged to conversion because of the gratuitous nature of God, we must be persons of joy, of hope. This allows us to encounter others more intimately despite obstacles. Liberation spirituality is a call to live the Magnificat (Luke 1:47–49), which assures us that the powerful will be dethroned and the lowly exalted, where the rich are sent away empty and the needy are filled.

Resources on Liberation Spirituality

Paulsell, William O. *Tough Minds, Tender Hearts*. Mahwah, NJ: Paulist Press, 1990. ISBN 0-8091-3148-6.

Paulsell takes six modern prophets of social justice (Martin Luther King Jr., Simone Weil, Dag Hammarskjold, Dorothy Day, Dietrich Bonfoeffer, and Dom Helder Camera) and portrays their deep spirituality and social activism. In each portrait, Paulsell shows how these modern prophets used the Gospel "call to freedom" as an instrument to bring about social change.

Tastard, Terry. *The Spark in the Soul*. Mahwah, NJ: Paulist Press. ISBN 0-8091-3154-4.

Most of the material written about liberation theology to date has had very little to say about liberation spirituality itself. Tastard allows the reader to discover a fresh approach to this kind of spirituality. He takes four dynamic figures: St. Francis of Assisi, Evelyn Underhill, Meister Eckhard, and Thomas Merton, and shows how, from their vantage point, spiritual liberation can take place through a mix of love of God and commitment to social change.

Audio Resources on Liberation Spirituality

Sobrino, Jon. *What I Learned in El Salvador They Didn't Teach Me in St. Louis*. Kansas City, MO: Credence Cassettes. audiocassette. 50 min. ISBN AA2295.

Jon Sobrino is an internationally known liberation theologian from El Salvador. This talk was given at the Pax Christi Conference in 1989. This is a very personal account of his journey into liberation theology and its implications in sharing the Gospel with the poor in the Third World.

Journey Spirituality

During the past decade, there has been a tremendous increase in the number of "nothing books" published. These books are filled with blank pages so the writer can commit to paper his or her inmost thoughts and ideas in a personal journal. In a sense, these books are sophisticated diaries. Most writers use them to plot their days. Over a period of time, they reflect the many ways a person grows and changes.

Journal-keeping is a popular and insightful pastime. Pope John XXIII, who convened the Second Vatican Council, kept a journal, which was published after his death. It gives us a rare glimpse into the man whose actions revolutionized the Catholic Church.

Numerous workshops on journaling have provided participants with some guidance on how to approach journal-keeping. Journal-keeping is a unique form of prayer, because it allows the writer to communicate the personal thoughts that become prayers. Committing one's thoughts to paper allows a more transparent view of life's journey.

Journal-keeping is also an opportunity in prayer to heal the broken places in our lives. It allows us to understand the hurt, and draw renewed strength from the healing power of expressing those hurts.

One of the most famous journal-writers was Anne Frank, the Jewish girl whose diary recounts her family's experience hiding from the Nazis during the Second World War. She found journal-keeping emotionally balancing, courageously affirming, and spiritually enriching. She wrote, "I can shake off everything if I write; my sorrows disappear, my courage is reborn."

Resources on Journey Spirituality

Hutchinson, Gloria. *Christ Encounters*. Notre Dame, IN: Ave Maria Press, 1988. ISBN 0-87793-378-2.

The concept of a thirty-day retreat has been very popular among many Catholics, but participation in such an experience is impossible for the average person. In this book, Hutchinson brings the thirty-day retreat into the home, where the ordinary person can find the time and opportunity to commune with Jesus in his or her own familiar surroundings.

This retreat journal allows the participant to respond daily to encounters with the Lord. Hutchinson suggests thirty minutes each day as the ideal commitment. The format of the book is very simple: Each day is clearly mapped out. A Scripture theme is suggested daily, some reflections on the Scripture passage are given, and space is provided for the participant to consider and act upon what he or she has prayed about. For those who do not have the time or resources to participate in a thirty-day retreat, this book is an ideal substitute that allows the participant to journey deeper into the heart of Christ.

Hutson, Joan. *My Heart's Journal*. Notre Dame, IN: Ave Maria Press, 1991. ISBN 0-87793-449-5.

Jesus had a special place in his heart for the child. He also challenged us to discover the child within by allowing ourselves to experience the wonder and trust of a child. This delightful spiral-bound book will help the reader accomplish the task.

This book brings out the child in us. Its pages provide words of comfort for the lonely, peace for the restless, and gentle reproach and forgiveness for the angry. Whatever your mood or disposition, you will find this book enriching. It also provides spaces for you to record your child heart. The book is a wonderful gift to self or others.

Koontz, Christian. *Evoked by the Scriptures*. Kansas City, MO: Sheed & Ward, 1989. ISBN LL1320.

————. *The Living Journal*. Kansas City, MO: Sheed & Ward, 1990. ISBN LL1370.

Both books address journal-keeping, but they differ in their approach. *Evoked by the Scriptures* deals with keeping a Scriptural journal. It helps the participant journey through anger, violence, addictions, dependencies, ignorance, and illusions toward greater inner freedom and spiritual maturity. It is a how-to book that draws strength from the Scriptures for the journey. It connects Scripture and life in a very practical way.

The Living Journal is a tool that encourages readers to explore their inner life, helping them encounter and explore Ultimate Mystery. It provides techniques for gathering the facts and occurrences of each day, and helps readers not only pay attention to those events but integrate them in a more profound way into their consciousness.

Link, Mark. The Challenge Program series. Allen, TX: Tabor, 1988. ISBN 0-89505-654-2.

The Challenge Program series is made up of three books: *Challenge, Decision*, and *Journey*. Together they form an integral thirty-eight week meditation program based on St. Ignatius Loyola's *Spiritual Exercises* (1548). The first book, *Challenge*, treats the first "week" of the exercises. The second book, *Decision*, treats the second "week," and the third book, *Journey*, treats the third and fourth "weeks" of the exercises.

Link, a teacher and prolific writer, leads the participant through the exercises with clarity, vision, and purpose. In the introduction, he sets the tone by answering some basic questions and approaches. He addresses where, when, and how you should use the exercises in meditation, and he discusses the three P's: preparation, presence, and prayer.

O'Shea, Donagh. *Take Nothing for the Journey*. Mystic, CT: Twenty-Third, 1990. ISBN 0-89622-444-9.

This book evolved from O'Shea's three-month journey through Ireland, during which he lived in a tent. Along the way, the author discovered many prayer-filled experiences, which he committed to paper. These themes revolve around two basic realities: time and place. The book, though simple, is profound in that these basic realities can produce much food for thought and personal reflection.

Progoff, Ira. *At a Journal Workshop*. New York: Dialogue House Library, 1975. ISBN 0-87941-006-X.

The "intensive journal" process was created by Ira Progoff in 1966. Since then, through books and workshops, its reputation has spread worldwide. The primary reason for its success is that journal-keeping is an effective way for all persons, regardless of age, social, and educational background, to begin their journey and draw everything into focus. It is especially valuable for persons going through transition times and times of uncertainty.

The book deals with such areas as beginning the process of intensive journaling; the dynamics of journal feedback; privacy; imagery; daily logs; check-lists; time components; life-history; and a series of chapters on encountering others, works, body, dreams, society, and self.

The book is designed to provide techniques through which the participants can discover within themselves resources for coping, and spiritual maturity they might not have known they possessed. The book is not an answer, but a tool, a process that enriches the journey to an awareness and perception not previously known.

Story Spirituality

Buried inside the rubble of societal conditioning in every adult, there is the "child." The world of a child is the world of wonder, newness, anticipation—a world filled with stories with happy-ever-after endings. We have discovered that the "once upon a time" story is timeless. Story is our attempt to resonate and represent our experience of life, love, and relationships. Through a retelling of the Christian story, we are able to encounter ourselves in our own story. Our story is our identity; it marks the stepping stones of our path through life.

The rediscovery of story can be attributed to many factors. First, there has been a trend to go back to the ultimate source—God in Jesus. Jesus didn't preach theological doctrines, dogmas, positions, or treatises. Instead, he told stories. They didn't need clarification, because their message was obvious to the audience of the time. Second, the growing awareness of the influences of the left and right sides of the brain, and the reemphasis on the creative right brain has helped to bring story back into focus. Left-brain people are more logically oriented, they tend to clarify, define, and bring closure to things. Right-brain people are more imaginative and creative, the prophets, poets, and pastors who never lost the capacity to wonder, enjoy, be amazed, and take delight in the mystery that surrounds them. Third, some social commentators suggest that we have rediscovered story as a reaction to television, which is devoid of personal contact. Fourth, because we live in a computer age, where things are processed at lightning speed, and we are inundated with facts, figures, trends, we are forced to always react to outside factors. The story—our own story—gives us more control and allows us to renew our interest in traditional values.

Our story is very much intertwined with God's. God's story shapes us to the extent that we accept it, allow it, and listen to it with our hearts. Unless we hear God's story, we can't be formed, transformed, created, and recreated.

Stories will always be popular because they contain the stuff of human existence. They heighten our curiosity and demand repetition. They are bridges that connect people of all cultures, age groups, and ethnic backgrounds into a common universal human family. Stories help us to remember, to reflect on the power of the word. They are both the basis of hope and the power of escape from the boredom of life.

Resources on Story Spirituality

Bausch, William J. *Storytelling: Imagination and Faith*. Mystic, CT: Twenty-Third, 1984. ISBN 0-89622-199-7.
This valuable introduction to storytelling by a pastor in Colts Neck, New Jersey will fire your imagination. These stories will charm and challenge. Be sure to indulge as proscribed: in small doses, and keep a highlighter close at hand. The book is for the child in you that anticipated Santa at Christmas. A brief preview of what this bag holds is the story of the little boy who ran into the house announcing that his pet turtle had rolled over and died. He was inconsolable. His mother called her husband; when he came home, he gathered up the tearful boy in his arms as he sat in front of the dead turtle and told him that maybe they could have a funeral for the dead turtle. Yes, and not only that, but they would bury him in a little tin candy box. By this time, the boy had stopped crying and was listening intently. "Then," chimed the mother, "we can have a party afterwards. Wouldn't that be nice?" By this time, the boy was smiling. Encouraged, the father went on: "Yes, and we'll have balloons and some of your friends over, and everything." The boy was grinning from ear to ear. But then, to the surprise of all, the turtle rolled back on its legs and began slowly moving away. The boy looked startled and then exclaimed, "Oh, daddy, let's kill it." (Pp. 43–4)
This above story reflects escapism. At times, escapism allows us to flee from the loneliness we often experience, even though we are surrounded by loved ones who always have, to some degree, a love-hate relationship with us. Escapism is a good thing at times. It takes it away from our immediacy and gives us a chance to regroup, reform, and reenter life.
The author not only tells you about stories, he puts you at the center of them. The book is about stories, while at the same time being a story itself. Subjects covered include the characteristics of story; its paradoxes; Scripture as story; Jesus and story; theology and story; spirituality and story; and, most of all, *your* story.

De Mello, Anthony. *The Song of the Bird*. New York: Image Books, 1984. ISBN 0-385-19615-6.
Fr. Anthony De Mello was a Jesuit priest who spent his life ministering in his native India. An insightful and prolific writer of stories and thoughts that fire up the imagination, his books have become best-sellers in Catholic circles.
The Song of the Bird is a collection of 124 stories about various aspects of life, including freedom, peace, love, joy, and hope, from a variety of traditions, both ancient and modern. Each teaches an eternal truth. A story is a delightful way to begin each day. They are sure to share the complexion of each day and, eventually, your life.

Other De Mello books include *One Minute Wisdom* (1986), *Well-springs, Taking Flight* (1988) and *The Heart of the Enlightened* (1991), all of which are available from Image Books.

Donze, Mary Teresa. *Touching a Child's Heart*. Notre Dame, IN: Ave Maria Press, 1988. ISBN 0-87793-290-5.
   The author draws on her thirty-five years as a teacher, using her expertise, enthusiasm, and experience to challenge parents and teachers to use storytelling to teach children about God. This short book (88 pages) is full of hints, suggestions, techniques, and sample stories. It will allow parents and teachers to not only call forth the child's sense of wonder but also their own.

Fahy, Mary. *The Tree That Survived the Winter*. Mahwah, NJ: Paulist Press, 1989. ISBN 0-8091-0432-6.
   This beautifully illustrated and sensitively written book is for adults who have experienced a winter in their lives. It is a story of courage and healing, compassion and growth, affirmation, and the indomitability of the human spirit. Most of all, it is a story of hope that reminds the reader that no matter how devastating the winter experience, there is survival, healing, and hope.

Paulus, Trina. *Hope for the Flowers*. Mahwah, NJ: Paulist Press. ISBN 0-8091-1754-1.
   A classic, this book has touched the lives of thousands of people. Beautifully illustrated, it explodes with hope for everyone. It is "a tale—partly about life, partly about revolution, and lots about hope." You will read the book in a few minutes, but you will live its hopeful message for a lifetime. *Hope for the Flowers* is a parable, open-ended and full of surprises from cover to cover. It finds a home with a child as well as an adult. It is so great that you don't have to talk about it. It is a must gift for yourself and for the special people in your life.

Shea, John. *Stories of God: An Unauthorized Biography*. Chicago, IL: Thomas More Press, 1978. ISBN 0-88347-085-3.
   Theologian John Shea was one of the first to develop the concept of story within the overall context of theology. He begins his preface by stating:

> If God made man because he loves stories, creation is a success. For humankind is addicted to stories. No matter what our mood, in reverie or expectation, panic or peace, we can be found stringing together incidents, and unfolding episodes. We turn our pain into narrative so we can bear it; we turn our ecstasy into narrative so we can prolong it. We tell our stories to live. (P. 7)

The Christian strategy has always been to gather folks, break the bread, and tell the stories. Shea begins by helping us understand ourselves as storytellers. Then he reflects on how Christian symbols are woven into stories of God: Symbols of rescue and covenant, judgment and apocalypse, resurrection and parousia, hope and justice. As a theologian, Shea carefully picks his way through what is best in Catholicism and Protestantism to retell the Christian story in a new light. The result is a remarkable synthesis of theology and spirituality.

Creation-Centered Spirituality

The Catholic Church has recently experienced a shift in orientation from a fall-redemption theology to a creation-centered theology. This change continues to have a dramatic influence on how the church views itself and its role in the world. Creation-centered theology speaks volumes to social justice, liberation theology, the feminist movement, and ecological awareness. Because of this shift in emphasis, hope replaces despair and creativity replaces cynicism.

Fall-redemption and creation-centered spiritualities are studies in contrast. Fall-redemption is patriarchal; creation-centered is feminist. Fall-redemption theology advocates control of body and discipline of passions, while creation-centered theology advocates birthing, ecstasy, *eros*, and the celebration of passion. Fall-redemption theology stresses God as Father; creation-centered theology stresses God as Mother. Fall-redemption spirituality sees death as a consequence of sin, while creation-centered spirituality sees it as a natural event. Fall-redemption theology emphasizes original sin, but creation-centered theology emphasizes original blessing. Fall-redemption spirituality traces its origin back to St. Augustine (354–430 A.D.), while creation-centered spirituality traces itself back to the ninth century B.C., to the Yahwish or J source in the first book of the Bible. There are other notable differences, too numerous to mention here. Probably the best known proponent of creation-centered spirituality today is the Dominican priest and theologian Matthew Fox, whose works we refer to more in-depth in the following resources.

Resources on Creation-Centered Spirituality

de Waal, Esther. *Every Earthly Blessing: Rediscovering the Celtic Tradition. Celebrating a Spirituality of Creation*. Ann Arbor, MI: Servant, 1991. ISBN 0-89283-762-4.

Esther de Waal, who taught history at Cambridge and Nottingham Universities in England and studied Celtic spirituality, wrote this book as part of her own search for identity. Of Scottish extraction herself, she studied Celtic spirituality as part of her search. Her book is a succession of themes: monks and hermits, pilgrims and exiles, universe, creation, sin and sorrow, salvation, the Cross, and a world made whole.

She suggests that, if we neglect our heritage, we neglect our soul. In the past, the Catholic Church has often imposed Romanism in place of a local culture, rather than affirming and enhancing the belief systems already inherent in the culture. Celtic spirituality is creation spirituality at its best. In it, we are co-creators with God.

The author reflects this spirituality when she says that

> life was lived at two levels—the practical tasks of daily life are done for their own sake carefully and competently, but simultaneously they become signs of God's all-encompassing love. A thing is done well not only for itself but because of the part that it plays in God's world. . . . The Celtic way of seeing the world is infused with the sense of the all-pervading presence of God. This is God's world, a world to be claimed, affirmed, and honored. (P. 7)

Personally, I found the book enriching because, as I am of Celtic background, it helped me understand and appreciate my own spirituality and its roots. It will do the same for others with Celtic roots.

Donders, Joseph G., and Elizabeth Byrne. *Original Joy*. Mystic, CT: Twenty-Third, 1988. ISBN 0-89622-388-4.

Original Joy is creation spirituality at its best, freeing the playful within us. The book extols life in its primal innocence and beliefs, and encourages the reader to explore the simple, perhaps long-abandoned ideals within us. The authors show how our educational system often fosters a hostile, if not destructive, worldview. They suggest how we can redirect that negativism so we can once again rediscover the child within. The playful message is reinforced throughout the book by insightful quotes from some of the great thinkers of our time.

Fox, Matthew. *Original Blessings*. Santa Fe, NM: Bear, 1983. ISBN 0-939680-07-6.

Fox's book is a primer in creation spirituality. He suggests that we need a new, creation-centered paradigm. His reasons include: the ecological and unemployment crises, scientific awakening, global ecumenism, justice and liberation movements, hope versus pessimism, religious transformation, rediscovery of the right-brain approach, the fact that the creation-centered approach was the original approach, and a sense of community.

For anyone interested in an extensive and exciting way of looking at their faith journey, this book is required reading. The book is long and difficult reading, but that should not deter the reader from exploring a new vision and direction in spirituality. It presents four paths and twenty-six themes that help the reader discover a very old and creative form of spirituality. The book is a kind of dialogue between two forms of spirituality: One that has a short history, yet is deeply entrenched in the minds of people; the other, a newly discovered but very ancient form of spirituality. *Original Blessings* is less a book and more a program; it is theory fed by practice and practice fed by theory. What is most assuring is that many people have been living creation-centered spirituality without knowing the concepts. Now they have the primer.

————, ed. *Western Spirituality: Historical Roots, Ecumenical Routes.* Santa Fe, NM: Bear, 1981. ISBN 0939680-017.

The best known proponent of creation-centered spirituality gathered seventeen influential scholars to discuss various aspects of creation-centered theology. They discuss it from a biblical perspective as well as from the perspectives of the early , Celtic spirituality, politics, Native American spirituality, yoga, and mysticism.

Fox, in the introduction, reflects on the authors' experiences and backgrounds. He says of them that

> all have been tempered by racial, economic, sexual, and political injustices. They are critical and qualified thinkers who are young at heart, though they vary in age and familiarity to the reading public. Their spiritual visions are people-oriented, politically conscious, and earthy. Each and every one is living an alternative lifestyle and has resisted hiding behind pillars of security whether they derive from the comfort of piety or the comfortable benefits that only academia can bestow. (P. 18)

Small-Group Spirituality

In the past two decades, small-group movements have played a central role in the development of the Catholic . Through the Charismatic Movement, thousands of people have been able to hear the promptings of the Holy Spirit and lead a more enriching prayer life. Through Marriage Encounter, many couples have had their marriages renewed and have been given a process through which to deepen their communications. Through Cursillo, many adults have been able to deepen their faith commitment, and through the RENEW process, thousands around the world have discovered the depth and beauty and applications of the Scriptures as they gather in small groups to share their faith.

The above-mentioned movements have touched a responsive chord in the lives of many Catholics. They have discovered fulfillment and opportunity to develop toward a more mature faith and prayer life.

Why are small groups so appealing? People join small faith-sharing groups because they have a desire to grow. Life is a process of growth, but often we become stagnant and need a breath of fresh air, new ideas, new challenges that will help us on the journey.

People join a small faith-sharing group because they wish to be part of a community, to experience life together, to share, to pray, to support each other, to challenge and be challenged, and to find the support and strength to reach out in service to others.

To be successful, small faith-sharing groups need five elements. The first of these is prayer, which is the lifeline of any support group. Prayer keeps the group focused, provides strength to its members, clarifies its purpose, and directs its energy. People have a desire to pray and need to be exposed to various forms of prayer and opportunities to pray.

The second element is sharing. Sharing life and faith in a small-group setting provides an opportunity to develop relationships that are rooted in Christ. These relationships provide an alternative to the individualism of society. In small faith-sharing groups, there is a great opportunity to share more deeply one's faith journey, one's faith, and one's actions. Sharing enables the building of self and other in faith, support, and relationship.

The third ingredient is that of mutual support. To live the message of our faith, we need the support of others. Unfortunately, many forces in society erode such support. Consumerism and alienation threaten to divide us; mutual support strengthens in fellowship, friendship, charity, and service for one another. Mutual support is the answer to the alienation that so many experience.

The fourth ingredient is learning—learning more about God's revelation in one's life, the world, the Scriptures, and the church is vital to spiritual growth.

Finally, there is the service dimension. A small group can become smug and closed, unless it is involved in outreach. The Gospel message is a challenge, not just to talk about, but to act upon. The challenge is to reach out in service through charity and justice to others.

Resources on Small-Group Spirituality

Baranowski, Arthur. *Called to Be Church Program*. Cincinnati, OH: St. Anthony Messenger Press, 1988. ISBN B5980.

This is a unique, tested program on how to restructure Catholic parishes into smaller communities. There are various parts to the program, including *Creating Small Faith Communities*, a plan for restructuring and renewing Catholic life; *Pastoring the "Pastors,"* a step-by-step training manual for leaders of the basic Christian communities; and *Praying Alone and Together,* an eleven-week prayer module for small groups. All the above are available separately. And there is also a video, *Creating Small Faith Communities*, that introduces the concept.

The "Called to Be Church" process allows people to have a greater sense of belonging and caring within their parish structure, and provides the opportunity for them to support one another in their faith development.

The series is basically for parish leadership but can be read by individuals who want to discover the potential for parishes. The *Praying Alone and Together* module would be an ideal prayer resource for individuals or groups intent on developing their prayer life.

Kleissler, Thomas A. *Small Christian Communities*. Mahwah, NJ: Paulist Press, 1992. ISBN 0-8091-3217-6.

The creator of the RENEW process and his team explain their hopeful vision for the future of small groups. This book presents practical and concrete approaches that will lead to small communities becoming a lasting and vibrant asset to parishes in years to come. An auxiliary book, *Resources for Small Christian Communities: A Vision of Hope*, provides specific sessions and processes for pastoral leaders and small-group leaders.

Tracey, Michael. *Pater Noster.*

———. *A Change of Pace*

———. *Don't Miss Your Calling*

———. *God, Are You Listening?*

———. *Happy Are. . .*

———. *Journeys*

———. *There Is a Time*

———. *You Better Believe It!*

All of the above titles are available upon request from the author.

Fr. Michael Tracey served as Director of the RENEW program for the Diocese of Biloxi, Mississippi, 1986–1989. He has developed several small-group, faith-sharing programs for groups interested in coming together to reflect, pray upon, and act upon certain Scriptural themes. *Pater Noster* is a six-week faith-sharing program that allows groups to appreciate more deeply the Lord's Prayer. *Journeys* offers a group the opportunity to mirror their own spiritual journey in the light of the Emmaus story (Luke 24:13–35). *A Change of Pace* is another six-week program, based on the Lenten themes of fasting, deserting, transforming, liberating, nurturing, and rising. *Don't Miss Your Calling* treats a Christian vocation in the context of Jeremiah's vocation (Jer. 1:4–10). *God, Are You Listening?* is also a six-week program on prayer from an unusual perspective. *Happy Are. . .*, an eight-week program, allows a group to explore the eight Beatitudes (Matt. 5:3–10). *There Is a Time*, an eight-week program, reflects on Ecclesiastes 3:1–8. *You Better Believe It!* is a six-week program on faith as a process. These programs have been used successfully in various parishes and dioceses throughout the United States and Canada. Their format is simple, making it easy for the leader to guide the participants through the process.

Westley, Dick. *Redemption Intimacy.* Mystic, CT: Twenty-Third, 1980. ISBN 0-89622-123-7.

Westley, professor of philosophy at Loyola University, Chicago, provides a new perspective for the journey to adult faith. His book challenges the reader to journey beyond religion, to faith and into a personal relationship with God who raises up and heals all of humanity.

The appendix of the book is a treasure of principles for base communities, practical suggestions for dialogue and faith-sharing groups, the aims and goals of such groups, and suggested formats and themes that small groups can use in integrating the contents of the book into the rest of their spiritual journey.

Conclusion

Someone once defined Americans as "people who are born in the country, where they work with great energy so they can live in the city, where they work with greater energy so that someday they can live in the country again." This definition tells us a great deal about who we are, what we do, and why we do it. It is a poignant comment on the culture that largely forms our spirituality. Culture and spirituality are not separate entities but parts of the same fabric. The function of spirituality is not to protect us from our culture but to enable us to leaven it, stretch it, bless it, and break it open to the present designs of God.

We have made quantum leaps in space and in science. Science has changed many aspects of life, death, sex, birth, and war. We have made ourselves militarily powerful but personally broken. Feminism has challenged our stereotypes, the supremacy of men, our myths, and our dreams, and presented us with the possibility of discovering a new identity.

Individualism has permeated every aspect and institution of our society. Yet we are social beings, and we experience a tension between individualism and community. We are fractured, not only because of our individualism, but also because we have lost the power to link the personal with the public dimension of life. We have forgotten how to make private spirituality the stuff of public policy in a world that is dangerously private and individualistic.

Because of this dichotomy, many commentators call for a "spirituality of engagement" or a "spirituality of contemplative co-creation." The challenge is to connect the private with the public, the individual with the communal, and the contemplative with the action. It is much easier to state the question than to attempt the answer. Perhaps we have to digest the question before we can find the answer.

To discover the answer, we must discover the roots of our journey and take from them what supports us on our individual journeys. From St. Anthony of the Desert, the first Christian monk, we learn the need for discipline. From St. Patrick, we learn the importance of listening to our dreams. From St. Teresa, we learn about the interior rooms of our souls. And from Thomas Merton and Dorothy Day, we learn that prayer and social justice are two sides of the same coin.

Catholic spirituality has always had a tension between prayer and action. This is a healthy tension, providing checks and balances to keep the sojourner on journey. That tension serves as a prism through which Christian spirituality is a distinct inner-to-outer movement. It is a movement from solitary interiority to societal action in the service of others.

All are called to holiness. That call is expressed differently, depending on a person's life situation. It is an openness to the sacred in the human heart and this openness demands a discerning spirit. In this essay, I have briefly addressed the multifaceted dimensions of lay spirituality. I have stated some of the contributing factors that become the road maps toward a more authentic, integrated, and wholesome spirituality. These contributing factors are not isolated trends or incidents. Rather, they are expressions of the presence of the Holy Spirit at work. Their diversity reflects their unity of purpose, the universal call to holiness.

Lay spirituality, whether it be from a psychological or theological, a male or female, a contemplative or active point of view, whether it be liberation, journey, story, or creation-centered spirituality, and whether it be experienced individually or in a group setting, is a lived experience.

The Sufis say that there are two ways to study honey. One way is to do it intellectually, by examining all its properties. The other way is to simply taste it. Both are important, but no amount of study will enable us to know the sweetness of honey without tasting it. And no amount of intellectualizing will enable us to know God apart from being open to know and serve Him in others.

Contemporary Catholic spirituality for "everyperson" is a multifaceted, never-ending process of letting go of old ideas and old ways of seeing things that may stand as obstacles to a more intimate experience of God. No matter what our present stage of the journey, no matter how satisfied we may feel about our journey's images, direction, and content, God is always beyond them and God beckons us to continue the journey.

An old Hassidic story reflects the nature of our ever-developing spiritual path. A pious Jew approached a noted rabbi for some advice on the spiritual journey.

> "Teach me," he implored the rabbi, "the way to God."
> "There is no one way to God," replied the learned rabbi. "Each person has a way to God that is best for him or her. You must find out what that way is for you and then commit yourself to it with all your love, strength, and will."

References

Bellah, Robert, et al. *Habits of the Heart*. New York: Harper, 1987.

Carmody, John Tully, and Denise Ladner Carmody. *Christian Uniqueness & Catholic Spirituality*. Mahwah, NJ: Paulist Press, 1990.

de Sales, Francis. *Introduction to the Devout Life*. Translated by Michael Day. 1609. Reprint, New York: Dutton, 1961.

Doohan, Leonard. *The Lay-Centered : Theology & Spirituality*. Minneapolis, MN: Winston Press, 1984.

Dulles, Avery. *A Church to Believe In: Discipleship & the Dynamics of Freedom*. Mahwah, NJ: Paulist Press, 1984.

———. *Models of the Church*. Garden City, NJ: Doubleday, 1974.

Fox, Matthew. *On Becoming a Musical Mystical Bear: Spirituality American Style*. Mahwah, NJ: Paulist Press, 1976.

Greeley, Andrew, and Mary Greeley Durkin. *How to Save the Catholic*. San Francisco: Viking Penguin: Harper & Row, 1985.

Green, Thomas H. *Opening to God*. Notre Dame, IN: Ave Maria Press, 1976.

Hayes, Diane. "Origins." *Catholic News Service* 20, no. 28 (December 20, 1990): 449.

Larranaga, Ignacio. *Sensing Your Hidden Presence: Toward Intimacy with God*. New York: Image Books, 1987.

McBrien, Richard. *Catholicism*. Minneapolis, MN: Winston Press, 1981.

Merton, Thomas. *The Seven Story Mountain*. Garden City, NJ: Doubleday, 1970.

Nouwen, Henri. *The Way of the Heart*. New York: Seabury Press, 1981.

Whitehead, Evelyn Eaton, and James D. Whitehead. *Christian Life Patterns*. New York: Image Books, 1982.

Further Reading

Berry, Thomas. *The Dream of the Earth*. San Francisco: Sierra Club Books, 1988.

Brennan, Patrick. *The Evangelizing Parish*. Allen, TX: Tabor, 1987.

Freeman, Laurence. *Light Within: The Inner Path of Meditation*. New York: Crossroads, 1987.

Greeley, Andrew. *The Catholic Myth*. New York: Charles Scribner's Sons, 1990.

Gustin, Marilyn. *You Can Know God: Christian Spirituality for Daily Living*. Liguori, MO: Liguori, 1993.

Hassel, David. *Radical Prayer*. Mahwah, NJ: Paulist Press, 1983.

Kennedy, Eugene. *Tomorrow's Catholics—Yesterday's Church*: New York: Harper & Row, 1988.

Merton, Thomas. *Contemplative Prayer*. Garden City, NJ: Doubleday, 1971.

Moore, Thomas. *Care of the Soul: A Guide for Cultivating Depth and Sacredness in Everyday Life*. New York: HarperCollins, 1992.

Navone, John. *Tellers of the Word*. New York: Jesuit Educational Center, 1981.

Nouwen, Henri. *Reaching Out*. New Jersey: Doubleday, 1975.

Pollard, Miriam. *The Laughter of God: At Ease with Prayer*. Wilmington, DE: Michael Glazier, 1986.

Rahner, Karl. *Encounter with Silence*. Mahwah, NJ: Paulist Press, 1972.

Rohr, Richard, and Andreas Ebert. *Discovering the Enneagram*. New York: Crossroads, 1991.

Savary, Louis M., and Patricia H. Berne. *Kything: The Art of Spiritual Presence*. Mahwah, NJ: Paulist Press, 1988.

Shea, John. *An Experience Named Spirit*. Chicago: Thomas More, 1980.

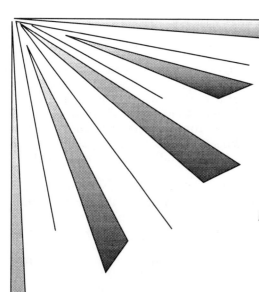

4

The Religion of Islam

A.K.M. Aminul Islam and Gordon Welty

Introduction

Of all the manifestations of man's intellectual and sociocultural life, none is so elusive of definition as religion. Yet none is more important. There are many different religions in this world. Of these, about a dozen may be considered as major, or world, religions. Amongst the world religions, Islam is the youngest, but also one of the largest, with about three-quarters of a billion devotees (Muslims). Most Muslims live in the Middle East, Africa, and Asia, but some do live in Europe, the Americas, and even in Australia and New Zealand. The wide variety of Muslims worldwide, together with a dynamic and colorful founder and a rapid period of expansion, make Islam one of the most interesting as well as important of all world religions. Unfortunately, Islam's reception in the West has been tinged with fear and misunderstanding. For example, the continuing crises in the Middle East seem to be reflected in American popular opinion as a series of latter-day Crusades. The fear Americans hold towards Islam and the resulting deaths in the Middle East are, in part, due to a misunderstanding of Islam. A better understanding of Islam might help remedy this fear and ease relations.

Unfortunately for Western study of Islam, the vast portion of the literature on the Islamic religion is written by Muslims in non-Western languages—Arabic, Persian, Urdu, and so on. Very little of this literature is ever translated into any Western language, let alone into English. Therefore, most material on Islam is forever inaccessible to English-speaking readers.

Therefore, the following bibliographic essay on contemporary literature on Islam foregrounds Muslim authors in English, where possible, and highlights throughout that literature which is sensitive to the Muslim perspective. It reviews all aspects of Islam, from the time of the Prophet to the present, insofar as these aspects are addressed in English-language books that have been published during the past two decades or so. Such publications should be readily accessible to English-speaking readers.

There are a number of reference works that provide a detailed introduction to the Muslim countries of the Middle East, North Africa, South Asia, and Indonesia today. Two that are to be recommended in particular are the *Asia Yearbook*, an annual published in Hong Kong by the Far Eastern Economic Review, and *The Middle East and North Africa*, also an annual published in London by Europa Publications. From the Atlas mountains of the Maghreb (the West), the civilization of Islam can be traced across the southern half of the Mediterranean. Its influence runs down both sides of the Red Sea and throughout the Arabian Peninsula. It sweeps across the Arabian Sea and the Bay of Bengal to the islands of Indonesia. In the north, Islam follows the ancient caravan routes across the Central Asian steppes until it reaches almost to the Great Wall of China. For a further presentation of the geography of the Islamic world, yesterday and today, the reader can consult William Brice's *An Historic Atlas of Islam* (1981).

Yet, Islam did not achieve any political or territorial unity, despite the fact that its followers were certainly identifiable by a set of finite attributes. These attributes—the language of the Qur'an, directional place of worship, distinctive mannerisms, and prescribed food habits—provided Muslims with a cohesiveness, a clear-cut, articulate, and self-confident identity, but that cultural unity did not translate to political unity or power.

The religion of Islam is based on strict monotheism, subordination to one and only one God (Allah), the sole and sovereign ruler of the universe. Islam rejects any concept of a plurality of the godhead, be it a duality, such as the Manichaean doctrine of Ormazd (Light, Good) and Ahriman (Matter, Evil); a Trinity, such as the Christian notion of God the Father, God the Son, and God the Holy Spirit; or a polytheism such as that of the Hindu religion. The adherents of Islam are known as Muslims, meaning "Submitters to the Will of Allah." In some literature, the adherents of Islam have also been referred to as "Muhammadans." This reflects a Western prejudice that assumes every world religion involves the worship of its founder, just as Christianity involves the worship of Jesus of Nazareth, Son of God. The title Muhammadans is a misnomer, because the adherents of Islam do not worship the man, Muhammad the Prophet, but are the Submitters to the Will of Allah, the One and Only.

Muslims all over the world believe that, although Allah has made himself known through a series of prophets through ages, his last and fullest revelation was to and through the Prophet Muhammad in the seventh century A.D. Muhammad the Prophet taught Muslims that they have only one life to live, and their conduct in life will determine how they will fare through their eternal existence.

The Life of the Prophet

Sigmund Freud, in his *Moses and Monotheism* (1939), observed that many of the founders of religions spent at least a portion of their formative years in homes without a father figure. This was the case in the lives of Moses, Confucius, Menicius, and others. Muhammad was not an exception. In A.D. 570, when Muhammad was born into the Hashemite clan of the Quraishi tribe, who controlled the Ka'aba in Mecca, his father, Abdullah, was already dead; his mother, Amina, died when Muhammad was only six years old. Muhammad was raised and reared by his uncle, Abu Talib, the leader of the Quraish tribe.

When Muhammad was twenty-five, Gabriel, an archangel of Allah, came to him and conveyed God's command to him: "Proclaim! in the name Of thy Lord and Cherisher" (96:1–15).[1] Muhammad did not have any formal education and was illiterate. The adherents of Islam make much of that fact, and of the miracle of the revelation of the Qur'an that came to Muhammad through the angel Gabriel. Muhammad conveyed to his listeners what Gabriel revealed to him. These revelations eventually were written down to become the scripture of Islam, the Qur'an. This text was canonized a few years after the death of the Prophet, and Muslims stress that this process was completed before the possibility of substantial human error creeping into the text. Thus, as a result of these revelations, adherents find the presence of Allah in the Holy Writ.

Through these revelations, Muhammad was to preach that he was the last of a series of prophets that had included, among others, Abraham, Moses, and Jesus of Nazareth. For the Muslim account of Jesus of Nazareth in particular, see Edward Geoffrey Parrinder's *Jesus in the Qur'an* (1965), or see the Sufi account in Javad Nurbakhsh's *Jesus in the Eyes of the Sufis* (1983). Thus, at the very inception of Islam it was clear that Islam did not deny the validity of other religions, but rather proclaimed that what others began, Islam brought to completion. Muhammad also did not claim divinity; he was like any other man, and he died like any other man.

Muhammad the Prophet converted his wife, Khadijah, the first Muslim ever. He then proceeded to preach his religion in Mecca, converting the idolaters in the face of tremendous opposition. His subsequent converts included Ali ibn Abu Talib, his first cousin; Zayed ibn Thabit, a former slave whom Muhammad adopted as his son and who became the Prophet's secretary; and Abu Bakr, a friend of Muhammad. Initially, Abu Talib, Muhammad's uncle and Ali's father, gave the Prophet all the protection he needed from the hostile rich merchants and powerful clan leaders of Mecca. But later, the opposition to Muhammad crystallized, and he had to advise some of his followers to leave Mecca and take refuge in the Christian Kingdom of Abyssinia (what is now Ethiopia). After the death of Abu Talib in 619, opposition to

Muhammad became even greater and, by 622, he himself had to take refuge in Yathrib, later named Medina, a city about 250 miles north of Mecca. The life of the Prophet during the Meccan period has been presented in *Muhammad at Mecca* (1953), a widely recognized study by W. Montgomery Watt. The journey from Mecca to Medina is known as *Hijrah* (the Migration). Muslims begin their calendars with the date of that journey, whereupon the subsequent years are listed as A.H. (Anno Hegirae). A thorough discussion of the calendars can be found in *Muslim and Christian Calendars* (Freeman-Grenville and Greville 1977).

Following Muhammad's arrival at Medina, conflicts continued to brew between his group and the people of Mecca. One such encounter was the Battle of Badr in March, A.D. 623, where seventy Meccans were killed and the Muslims took many prisoners and booty. At the same time, Muslims came into conflict with the Jewish population of Medina. The Jews, who refused to accept Muhammad as the Prophet of God, frequently supported the Meccans against the Muslims. Reluctantly, Muhammad had to expel the Jews from Medina. The final break between the Muslim and Jewish community in Medina came when a Jewish matron, Zaynab, invited Muhammad and his followers to dinner and fed them poisoned lamb. Tradition has it that Muhammad ate only a little of the meat, but he suffered for the rest of his life, and never fully recovered from the effects of the poison. The complex relationship between the early Muslims and the Jews has been treated by Arent J. Wensinck in *Muhammad and the Jews of Medina* (1975).

Ten years after the Muslim migration to Medina, Muhammad returned to Mecca as a conqueror, where he destroyed all the idols of Ka'aba and invited Meccans to embrace Islam, which they almost all did. After that, Islam grew stronger and stronger. All this period, from the Hijrah up to the death of the Prophet, has been treated in the complementary volume to *Muhammad at Mecca*, *Muhammad at Medina*, by W. Montgomery Watt (1956).

A noteworthy biography of the Prophet, based on the earliest Arabic sources, is Martin Lings's *Muhammad* (1983). Finally, two Egyptian authors have written well-known biographies of the Prophet, now available in English—Tawfik al-Hakim's *Muhammad* (1985) and Muhammad H. Heykal's *The Life of Muhammad* (1976).

The Five Pillars of Islam

Diversity in Islamic practices by Muslims in different distant parts of the world may puzzle a casual observer, but the core beliefs and practices that bind Muslims into a solid bond are not hard to decipher. Five essential and obligatory practices spell out the way of life of all Muslims. These Five Pillars of Islam make one a Muslim, regardless of ethnic background or linguistic affiliation.

I. *Shahadah*

The First Pillar of Islam is the *Shahadah* (Creed of Islam), the profession of faith. The creed of Islam leads a Muslim in the straight path, which he declares explicitly, but in a very brief and simple fashion that "there is no God but The God (Allah) and Muhammad is His Messenger (the Prophet)." The Holy Qur'an begins with:

> In the name of Allah, Most Gracious, Most Merciful
> Praise be to Allah,
> The Cherisher and Sustainer of the Worlds . . . .
> Show us the straight path
> The way of those on whom
> Thou hast bestowed Thy Grace. (1:1, 6–7)

This proclamation, which Muslims call *Kalimah*, is the first and foremost prerequisite for becoming a Muslim. Kalimah affirms Islam's uncompromising attitude of monotheistic faith, that there is no god but Allah (God), and this faith brings a sense of oneness, belongingness—or *Tawhid* (Unity)—to the believers.

Additionally, the *Kalimah* declares the affirmation of the Prophet as the Messenger of God (*Rasul-i Allah*); the authenticity and the validity of his teachings, as the last in a series of prophets. This also implies that, although Muhammad was the final prophet, superseding all others such as Abraham, Moses, Ishmael, Idris (Enoch), and Isa (Jesus), and although he delivered the final message of Allah, his predecessors are also to be greatly honored. Two studies of the *Shahadah* and its context are Michael Cook's *Early Muslim Dogma: A Source-Critical Study* (1981) and Arent J. Wensinck's *The Muslim Creed* (1965). For insight into the Shi'ite understanding of this Pillar, see *Jihad and Shahadat* (1986), by Mahmud Taleqani et al.

II. *Salat*

The Second Pillar of Islam is *Salat* (Prayer), which helps a Muslim keep things in proper perspective, as the Qur'an asks a Muslim to "be constant." *Salat* reminds the Muslim to express gratitude toward Allah five times a day, as the *Muazzin* calls for prayer:

> Allah is great! Allah is great!
> There is no God but Allah,
> And Muhammad is his Prophet!
> Come to prayer, come to success
> Nothing deserves to be worshipped except Allah.
> [At dawn, the Muslim adds: Prayer is better than sleep.]

Of the Five Pillars of Islam, it is this second one, the *Salat*, that the Qur'an most emphatically and frequently directs Muslims to observe.

Prayer, according to Islamic teachings, is the remembrance of Allah and expression of gratitude, and without this sense of gratitude, everything else becomes meaningless. In this sense, and only in this sense, following the four other Pillars of Islam becomes secondary to a Muslim.

Five times a day—as he wakes up in the morning, at mid-day, in the afternoon, as the sun sets, and again before going to bed—a Muslim is expected to say his prayer with complete devotion, subordinating himself to Allah, as he must have faith that there is no higher activity than prayer, there is no greater protection against evil and the forces of evil than prayer.

The five daily liturgical prayers of the Muslims are preceded by ritual purification called *Ozu*. Facing Mecca, every Muslim is expected to perform this prayer through prostrations and recitations from the Holy Qur'an. For a Muslim, there is no way to avoid these obligatory prayers. In addition, there is a *Jumma* prayer, to be performed on Friday noon at a congregation. Islam also requires Muslims to pray on all other occasions of life, such as birth, marriage, death, initiations, and so on. For more information on Muslim prayer, see Constance Padwick's *Muslim Devotions: A Study of Prayer Manuals* (1961).

III. *Sawm*

The Third Pillar of Islam is *Sawm* (Fasting), fasting during the sacred month of *Ramadan*, the month in which it is said that the Qur'an was revealed to the Prophet. Muslim fasting during this month is very different from the short-term fasting of the Jew's Day of Atonement, or the Catholic avoidance of meat during Lent. *Sawm* is undoubtedly the most stringent fast of all, one that surpasses the fasting practiced by any other religion of the world.

Muslims during this month not only abstain from food and drink from dawn to sunset, they also refrain from any kind of sexual activity, either explicit or implicit. Because Muslims follow a lunar month, Ramadan comes at different times of the year; in tropical areas of the world, particularly in the summer, the fast is a very arduous and tedious experience.

This third principle of Islam reminds Muslims that they (as humans) are in fact helpless creatures in need of the perpetual and sustaining nourishment of God. Fasting for a month also gives Muslims the experience of hunger, inspiring them to be compassionate towards the deprived. Only the sick, men in action (war), pregnant women, and people traveling are exempted from fasting. All of this has been discussed in *Fasting* by Muhammad I. el-Geyoushi (n.d.) and *Fasting* by el-Bahay el-Kholi (1967).

IV. *Zakat* and *Sadakat*

The Fourth Pillar of Islam is *Zakat* and *Sadakat* (Charity). A Muslim is expected to sacrifice two percent of his total assets (not income) every year for the welfare of the needy. This amount, *Zakat*, may also be spent to support schools, hospitals, mosques, or any other institution that serves the entire community. This Fourth Pillar of charity acknowledges the reality of the distinction between 'haves' and 'have-nots', and lays down a religious responsibility on the well-to-do followers of Islam to support their less fortunate religious brethren.

A Muslim, though obligated by religious injunction, is free to choose not to pay, though very few do, as they read in the Qur'an:

> Establish regular Prayer
> And give regular Charity;
> And obey the Messenger,
> That ye may receive mercy. (24:56)

and

> Those who give in Charity, men and women,
> and loan to Allah a Beautiful Loan,
> It shall be increased manifold,
> and they shall have a liberal reward. (57:18)

Muslims have faith that their generosity will bring Allah's generosity to them in return. This fourth principle of Islam is similar to the biblical tithe, encouraging the individual to donate a fixed portion of savings for good causes, such as the freeing of slaves and relief of the poor. For more information on *Zakat*, refer to *Social Justice in Islam*, by Mahmud Ahmad (1982), and Farishta Zayas's *The Law and Philosophy of Zakat* (1960). Charity above and beyond this amount is *Sadaqat*. A good source for information on *Sadaqat* is Ghulam Sarwar's *Islam: Beliefs and Teachings* (1982).

V. *Hajj*

The Fifth Pillar of Islam is *Hajj* (Pilgrimage), considered the culminating experience of a Muslim's life. All Muslims are expected to perform pilgrimage to Mecca once in their lifetimes, if they can afford it. One can get a sense of the Pilgrimage in the late nineteenth century in *A Shi'ite Pilgrimage to Mecca, 1885–1886*, by a Persian notable, M. Mohammad H. Farahani (1990).

Pilgrimage takes place during *Dhu'l Hijja*, the twelfth month on the Muslim calendar. Every year, depending on the political and economic conditions of the world, anywhere from 2 to 2- million Muslims arrive in Mecca.

This annual congregation began 1,400 years ago, long before any comparable universal congregation of any other religion or creed. It is a unique congress at which not only the leaders of the nations meet, but also the people themselves congregate and come to know and rely on one another. The basic impression given by the Pilgrimage is one of the globalness of belief in Allah. Muslims pay homage to this universality of Islam by gathering in Mecca. It is at Pilgrimage that Muslims from all over the world, of every race and color, come to know the power of unified belief. It is here they realize the potential of their spiritual might. For more information on the Fifth Pillar of Islam, refer to Ali Shariati's *Hajj* (1977).

Universality of Islamic Religion

One of the fundamental differences between the Islamic doctrine and other religious practices is that no one, such as a priest, is needed to act as an intermediary between Allah and a Muslim, and neither are traditional and elaborate rituals such as the Hindus, Buddhists, Jains, and others practice. However, *Ulama*, scholars of Islamic scriptures, and *Maulvi*, religious teachers, are respected because they answer theological and legal questions.

In villages of Indonesia, India, Pakistan, and Bangladesh, the religious functionary is the *Mullah*, a lesser teacher, or the *Imam*, leader of congregational prayer. An Imam is similar in function to a priest in the Christian religion; he is one who manages the mosque, delivers Friday sermons, leads the congregation in prayers, officiates at Ramzan (Ramadan) and other special days, and tenders ethical advice. He operates the mosque school and teaches Arabic, so people can read the Qur'an, and interprets Muslim law. He or his wife may also teach Arabic to the girls. The Imam also serves the family, for instance, by validating a marriage by asking the groom's guardian three times if he accepts the bride, or by reciting the Qur'an near the deceased at a funeral.

Islamic Sects

Until the death of Muhammad the Prophet, the sense of a single community for all Muslims was undisturbed; they were all bound by a common faith and idealism, though rather pragmatic in nature. The Prophet's teachings and his galvanizing and dynamic presence unified all Muslims into a consolidated single community (the *Ummah*). However, within a few years of the Prophet's death, the community began to lose its bond, and gradually, profound differences emerged. As is usually the case, the first crack in the bond showed up shortly after the death of the Prophet, during the reign of Uthman, the third *caliph* (successor or deputy of the Prophet) of Islam, one who was accused of misrule and nepotism.

Uthman was assassinated as he sat reading the Qur'an, whereupon Muhammad's son-in-law and cousin, Ali, was named as the Fourth Caliph. Those who were instrumental in Ali's attaining the caliphate later became rebellious. They are known as *Kharijites*, from the Arabic word *khuruj*, meaning "dissent" or "rebellion." This Kharijism left a permanent mark on latter-day Islam, although the movement itself was rather short-lived. For further discussion of sects in Islam, see Fuad Khuri's *Imams and Emirs* (1970).

After the Kharijite movement, a more powerful sect based on rational theology emerged in the Muslim world. Popularly known as *Mutazilites*, this movement preceded the four permanent schools of jurisprudence in Sunni Islam. During the eighth and ninth centuries, Greek philosophical and scientific works were being translated into Arabic. At the same time, Muslims entered into controversies with theological dualists (e.g., the Gnostics or the Manichaeans). Mutazilites believed that divine predestination of human acts was incompatible with God's justice and with human responsibility. They emphasized the role of reason. But, in the early ninth century, the Mutazilite rationalists began to persecute their opponents. During the tenth century, the reaction against the Mutazilites culminated in the formulation and subsequent general acceptance of a set of theological propositions that became *Sunni*, or "Orthodox" Muslim theology. This theological development was initiated by Ali al-Ash'ari (A.D. 873–935), an early Muslim theologian whose contribution has been discussed by Richard Joseph McCarthy in *The Theology of al-Ash'ari* (1953).

Sunni Islam

Early schisms in Islam, like those associated with the Kharijites and Mutazilites, raised a number of issues that formed the foundation on which the Sunni (Orthodox) position has been laid. The Arabic term *sunnah* means "well-marked path," or the path or way of the majority. The meaning implies that the righteous way is the way of the majority (conventional), and not the ones indicated in the periphery by sectarians. This was reconfirmation of the Qur'anic doctrine that emphasized the uniqueness of the Muslim community from other sectarian and communal groups. The infallibility of the Scripture was reestablished, and at the same time, schismatics were condemned and dissident groups were labeled heretical. Yet, the Sunni's catholicity of outlook did not ignore the Prophet's saying: "differences of opinion among my community are a blessing."

The Sunnis constitute approximately 85 percent of all the Muslims in the world. These orthodox Muslims try to follow the path of Islam as it was established and directed by the Prophet, as it was encoded in the *Shari'ah* (the Islamic Law). The Shari'ah is based upon the statements of the Holy Qur'an. Difficulties arise in the sense that what was apparently the righteous way to live in the Arabian desert during the seventh and eighth centuries might not appear to be the best way in the tropical rain forests in later days. The Shari'ah is amplified by the *Hadith*, the sayings and activities of the Prophet and his *Ashab* (companions), which augment the statements of the Qur'an. Thus, it became important for Sunni Muslims to collect *Hadith* that had not been recorded in the Qur'an. *Mujtahids* (learned Muslims) had to interpret those acts and sayings to use as guides for problems not anticipated in the holy book. For the literature on Sunni Hadith, see especially

Munawar Ahmad Anees's *Guide to the Sira and Hadith Literature in Western Languages* (1986) and Muhammad Mustafa Azami's *Studies in Hadith Methodology and Literature* (1977). For three well-known collections of Hadith, see the *Salih Muslim*, by M. Muslim ibn al-Hajjaj (1971–75), the *Salih Bukhari* in M. Muhammad Ali's *A Manual of Hadith* (1951), and *Gardens of the Righteous*, by Iman Nawawei (1975). A Sufi account of the Hadith is provided by Javad Nurbakhsh in volume 2 of *Traditions of the Prophet: Ahadith* (1984). For further discussion of Hadith, see Gautier H. A. Juynboll's *Muslim Tradition* (1983) and Arent J. Wensinck's *Handbook of Early Muhammadan Tradition* (1971).

A third element in the development of Shari'ah is *Ijma* (consensus), which amounts to the shared understandings of the primary and secondary sources—the Qur'an and the Hadith, respectively—held by the *ulama* (the Sunni religious authorities). Finally, a fourth basis of the Shari'ah is *Qiyas* (analogy), where an understanding based on Qur'an and Hadith is extended to a new situation, insofar as the new case has the same cause as the original cause.

In the Holy Qur'an, for instance, it states:

> As to the thief,
> Male or female,
> Cut off his or her hands:
> A punishment by way
> Of example, from Allah,
> For their crime:
> And Allah is Exalted in Power,
> Full of Wisdom. (5:38)

It is widely recognized today that such punishments are not deemed appropriate outside the establishment of a truly Islamic state with its comprehensive provisions for social security. Similarly, it is not appropriate to institute Islamic prescriptions (e.g., punishments) in the absence of the others, merely to legitimate what remains fundamentally an un-Islamic regime. As a result, in many Muslim countries, flogging has replaced the chopping off of the arms of thieves. This solution was a new understanding of the traditional practices. These interpretations of Qur'anic laws came to be known as *Fatwas* (literally "advice"). Use of human reason for interpreting the Qur'anic law resulted in the growth of a number of schools of thought, at least one of which every Sunni Muslim must choose to follow.

There are actually four different schools of interpretation of the Shari'ah, concentrating in roughly four different geographical regions of the world. Hanbalites, the smallest, the followers of Ahmad ibn-Hanbal (d. A.D. 855) are found today mostly in Saudi Arabia, and are considered the most conservative. The Shafiites are the followers of Muhammad ibn Idris Al-Shafii (767–820), and are scattered throughout Africa and Asia, particularly in Egypt, Syria, India, and Indonesia (see al-Shafii's *Islamic Jurisprudence* [1961]). The Malikites, the followers of Abu Abdullah Malik ibn-Anas (716–795), are the second largest school and are found only in northern and western Africa, and also in upper regions of Egypt. The largest group is known as Hanifites, followers of Abu-Hanifah (700–767), and are found in western Asia, India, Pakistan, Bangladesh, and also in lower Egypt. Sometimes, a fifth school, known as the Zahiris, is mentioned in this context. These followers of Dawud ibn-Khalaf (d. 855) believed in a completely literal interpretation of the Qur'an and Hadiths. This school has died out. The schools of Sunni jurisprudence are discussed further in Joseph Schacht's *Introduction to Islamic Law* (1964).

Sufism

The Holy Qur'an states:

Allah is the First
And the Last,
The Evident (*Zahir*)
And the Hidden (*Batin*). (57:3)

Many have understood this *ayat* (verse) to suggest that the formalism of Shari'ah (the Islamic Law) must be complemented by an inward aspect. This amounts to a call for mysticism.

Islam, according to the teachings of the Prophet Muhammad, opposes any kind or form of esoterism or monasticism, yet, paradoxically, these aspects entered Islam through the agency of one of Muhammad's favorites, Ali, the Fourth Caliph of Islam, and through his family, especially Ja'far al-Sadiq (A.D. 699–765), the Sixth Imam of Shi'a Islam. Thus the rigor of Shari'ah (the Islamic Law) came to be supplemented by the inner feeling. The word *sufi* and the practice of Sufism in Islam actually emerged in the eighth century, associated with the name of Hasan al-Basri (642–728). Another early figure, the pious woman Rabiah al-Adawiyyah (713–801), is discussed by Margaret Smith in *Rabia the Mystic and Her Fellow Saints in Islam* (1984). For further biographical details on Sufi masters, see Farid al-Din Attar's *Muslim Saints and Mystics* (1966); there is a discussion of a number of prominent Sufi women in Javad Nurbakhsh's *Sufi Women* (1983).

The word *sufi* originates from the Arabic *suf*, which means "wool." The mystic wearing woolen garments or woolen headgear was called *Sufi*. These people possess esoteric or special knowledge of the deity, hence they are also known as "Gnostics" or "Theosophists." In a sense, mysticism is the genus, and Sufism is one of the species of this genus. These mystics experience an inner feeling of oneness with Allah. The outward differences that they manifest can perhaps be traced to the social and natural environment wherein the mysticism originates.

In Egypt, Turkey, Persia (Iran), and in the subcontinent of India (India, Pakistan, Bangladesh), esoteric Muslims who value the inner doctrine that goes beyond the external forms (represented by the straightforward meaning of the Qur'anic words) are customarily known as *Fakirs* or *Darvishes*. The Arabic Fakir and the Persian Darvish are the equivalent of the Sanskrit word *sadhu*; all of these mean "beggar"—although not all beggars are Fakirs, Darvishes, or Sadhus by any stretch of the imagination. Rather, the latter have abandoned any earthly possessions and have dedicated their lives to the effort to achieve "union with the Beloved," who is Allah (see Nurbakhsh's *Spiritual Poverty in Sufism* [1984]).

The doctrine of Sufism has two distinct principles or traditions, *Ahad* (the Unity) and *Tariqat* (the Path). The followers of Ahad reject any kind of pantheism, insisting on the supremacy of the One and Only God (Allah). Tariqat doctrine is more liberal in the sense that its followers believe that "the ways unto Allah are as the numbers of souls of men." The followers of Tariqat, who predominate in the villages of Pakistan and Bangladesh, hold that there is a direct relationship between the crises of life and a world of supernatural beings and unseen forces, and that systematic ritual can link men and supernatural beings in order to modify or, if necessary, control events causing uncertainty, pain, or fear.

Islamic Sufism is suffused with symbolism, as Dr. Javad Nurbakhsh has documented in his multivolume work, *Sufi Symbolism* (1984–1990). In the writings of the Persian poets Shams al-Din Hafez, Jalal al-Din Rumi, and Nizami Ganjavi, among others, Allah has been symbolically portrayed as Eternal Beauty, just as in the Vaishnava literature of Hinduism (these are the worshippers of Krishna, a reincarnated form of Vishnu, the Protector). This symbolism was the primary reason Sufi Islam was readily accepted by the Hindus of Eastern India. Therefore, Islam came to Eastern India (Bengal) not through the might of the Muslim sword, but through Sufi Darvishes, who resembled Hindu Sadhus in their many practices and lifestyle.

Thus, this branch of "localized Sufism" in the subcontinent of India became indistinguishable from localized Hindu mystics known as *Sadhus*. In its form and features, this Sufism is similar to Indian mysticism, Vaishnavism, or even the cult of Krishna. There is extensive literature available in English on Sufism: For further reading, see R. S. Bhatnagar's *Dimensions of Classical Sufi Thought* (1984); Henry Corbin's *The Men of Light in Iranian Sufism* (1978); Seyyed Husayn Nasr's *Sufi Essays* (1973), and *Sadr al-Din Shirazi [Mulla Sadr] and His Transcendental Theosophy* (1978); Javad Nurbakhsh's *Murad wa Murad: Master and Disciple in Sufism* (1977), *Masters of the Path* (1980), and *Sufism*, volumes 1–5 (1981–1991); Fazlur Rahman's *The Philosophy of Mulla Sadra* (1975); and Annemarie Schimmel's *Islam in the Indian Subcontinent* (1980).

The Rashidun Caliphs

When Muhammad died in A.D. 632, the Muslim community (Ummah) was led by four caliphs in turn: Abu Bakr (632–634), Umar (634–644), Uthman (644–656), and finally Ali ibn Abu Talib (656–661). There were a number of questions regarding succession, some of which had emerged as early as 632. Nonetheless, the leadership provided by these four caliphs is universally recognized by Muslims, hence these four are referred to as *Rashid* (i.e., "Upright" or "Rightly Guided") caliphs. During this period, Islam consolidated itself in Arabia, then expanded throughout much of Persia in the east and across the fertile crescent through Egypt in the West. During the Battle of Agrabah in Yamamah (633), against the forces of the false prophet Musaylimah, a large number of the Ansar (companions of the Prophet) were killed. These Muslims had heard and memorized the recitations of the Prophet, and the seriousness of this loss was quickly recognized by Umar, who suggested that Caliph Abu Bakr have the Qur'an canonized, so that no first-hand knowledge of the Prophet would be lost. The definitive text of the Qur'an was actually established during the caliphates of Umar and Uthman, by a committee headed by Zayed ibn Thabit, who had been the Prophet's secretary.

The Muslim world, the *Dar al-Islam* (the Abode of Peace) continued to encroach upon the *Dar al-Harb* (the Abode of Conflict). The capital of the Muslim world remained in Medina until Ali moved it to Kufah in 657. When Ali, cousin and son-in-law of the Prophet, was assassinated in Kufah in 661 by a Kharijite named Ibn Muljam, the leadership of the Muslim community was taken over by members of the Umayyad clan, relatives of Uthman, the Third Caliph. The Umayyads retained the leadership of the Ummah until 750.

The remarkable expansion of Islam into Persian and Byzantine territory after the death of the Prophet is treated in *The Early Islamic Conquests*, by Fred M. Donner (1981). For an account of the life of Ali, who also is known as the First Imam of Shi'a Islam, see Syed Husain M. Jafri's *Origins and Early Development of Shi'a Islam* (1979); Ali's writings and sermons are available in Ali ibn Abu Talib's *Nahjul Balagha* (1967).

The Umayyad Caliphs

When the Umayyad clan assumed the leadership of the Ummah in A.D. 661, the capital was shifted from Kufah to Damascus. The first Umayyad caliph was also one of the greatest of this lineage, Mu'awiyah. When Mu'awiyah died in 680, he was followed by several short-lived and largely ineffectual caliphs. During this period, a series of succession struggles between the Umayyads and the *Alids*, the descendants of the slain Ali, ensued. Ali's second son, grandson of the Prophet, Husayn, opposed Mu'awiyah's successor and son, Yazid. Husayn and most of his family were killed by Yazid's forces under the command of one Shamir ibn Dhu'l Jawshan at Karbala in 680. The only son of Husayn to survive the massacre—because he was too ill to fight—was Ali al-Zaki, known as the Fourth Imam of Shi'a Islam. These deaths at Karbala were to become centrally symbolic to the subsequent development of Shi'ite Islam, amounting to the Passion (*Taziyah*) of Islam.

Another great Umayyad caliph was Abdelmalik, who reigned from 685 to 705. During his reign, the Muslims built the magnificent "Dome of the Rock" in Jerusalem, which remains even today the finest example of Umayyad architecture, almost perfect in its proportions and balance. The expansion of Islam continued across North Africa, finally reaching Morocco by 708. Muslim forces, under the leadership of first Tarif and then Tarik, crossed over to Spain in 710, and all of Spain was captured by 713. During the same period, Muslim forces entered the Indus Valley and occupied Multan—situated in the present-day Punjab province in Pakistan—by 714.

A final great Umayyad caliph was the pious and good Umar II, sometimes referred to as the Fifth Rashid caliph, who sought to renew Islam and rejuvenate the Muslim world. He initiated the iconoclasm policy so influential in the Byzantine world. Umar's reign, however, lasted only from 717–720, when he died suddenly at age thirty-nine.

After Umar, the Umayyads experienced a period of decline. Charles Martel defeated the Muslims at the Battle of Tours in 732, representing the turning point of Umayyad fortunes in Western Europe. Finally, as though to underscore the reality of the period of decline, there were four caliphs in the year 744 alone! Walid II was caliph as 744 began. He was a dissolute ruler who happened to be a good poet. He was assassinated as he sat reading the Qur'an. The assassination of Caliph Uthman had exacerbated the question of succession in 656; that of Walid ibn Yazid likewise exacerbated the question in April 744. When the charismatic leader Abu Muslim Marwazi began the great revolt of the Abbasids in June 747, the Umayyads suffered defeat after defeat, until their last caliph, Marwan II, was killed in 750 after fleeing to Egypt. This ended the period of the Umayyad caliphs, except for the good fortune of Rahman, who escaped to Cordova, Spain, where, in 756, he began another Umayyad dynasty that continued to rule there until 1031.

There are a number of good books on the Umayyad period, including *The First Dynasty of Islam*, by Gerald R. Hawting (1986), and *Islamic History, A.D. 600–750, A New Interpretation*, by Muhammad A. Shaban (1971). For Islamic Spain (711–1492 A.D.), see the introduction to *Muslim Spain*, by Anwar G. Chejne (1974) and Thomas F. Glick's *Islamic and Christian Spain in the Early Middle Ages* (1978).

The Abbasid Caliphs

Having eliminated the Umayyads, the Abbasid clan established one of its own, Abu-al-Abbas, as caliph. The capital of the Muslim world was returned to Kufa during his reign. When he died of smallpox in A.D. 754, he was succeeded by his brother, Abu Jafer, who lived until 775. Abu Jafer, who took the royal name Caliph Mansur ("the winner"), founded a new capital city, Baghdad, in 762. This was to be the cultural center of the Muslim world for several centuries.

Mansur's grandson, Harun, became caliph in 786. Having taken the royal name Caliph Rashid ("The Upright," not to be confused with the earlier Rashidun caliphs), he ruled until 809. This period is widely considered to be the Golden Age of the Abbasid caliphs. Rashid began the policy of bringing large numbers of Muslim Turks from Central Asia into the government and army in Baghdad. During this era, the Muslim world began to experience pressures because of the enormous distances from the East (Afghanistan) to the West (Morocco). In the most distant regions, Alids established *Shi'ite* regimes, that is to say *Shi'a* (Partisans) *of Ali*, in opposition to the established caliphate. The Idrisid dynasty was established around 788 in what is today Morocco, and the Aghlabid dynasty was established in what is now Algeria around 800, effectively separating themselves from the central government in Baghdad. At this time, though, this separation reflected more of a political opposition than a well-defined theological stance. Several Abbasid caliphs during this period arranged dynastic marriages between their daughters and the leading Alids.

Baghdad continued to flourish during the entirety of this period. When Rashid's son Ma'mun ("The Trusted One") became caliph in 819, his "School of Translation" sought to encompass within the World of Islam all the cultural products of every civilization. The great Muslim scientist, al-Farghani, for example, estimated the circumference of the globe within one or two percent of its true value. During Ma'mun's reign, the Mutazilite rationalism flourished as well. Ma'mun died in 833, having appointed his brother Ishak his successor. Several presentations on the early Abbasid dynasty are Hugh Kennedy's *The Early Abbasid Caliphate* (1981), Jacob Lassner's *The Shaping of Abbasid Rule* (1980), and Muhammad A. Shaban's *Islamic History, A.D. 750–1055, A New Interpretation* (1976).

Ishak ruled from 833 to 842 under the name Caliph Mu'tasim ("Refuge in God"). Despairing of modifying the continuing orthodoxy in Baghdad, this Mutazilite constructed a new capital in Samarra, sixty miles up the Tigris River, where it would remain for more than half a century.

The Caliph Mu'tawakkil restored Islamic orthodoxy by 850. But by then the Abbasid world had begun a long period of decline, until a Buyid dynasty of Shi'ite orientation occupied Baghdad in 945 and rendered the caliph a figurehead. A few decades later, the Fatimid dynasty, Isma'ili Shi'ites, claimed direct descent from Fatima, daughter of the Prophet, wife of Ali ibn Abu Talib, mother of Hassan and Husayn. These Isma'ilis took control of Egypt and founded Cairo in 969, and then al-Azhar Madrasa (University) in 973 as a center of Isma'ili Shi'ite theology. Al-Azhar was to become, and still is today, the oldest continuously functioning university in the world (see Janet Cairo Abu-Lughod's *1001 Years of the City Victorious* [1971]; also A. Chris Eccel's *Egypt, Islam and Social Change* [1984]). In this weakened condition, the Muslim world began to receive setbacks from Europe: the Christian Reconquista of Spain began in 1000, and the Wars of the Cross, the Crusades, were initiated in 1095. A standard work on the Crusades is Stephen Runciman's *A History of the Crusades* (1987). For the view of the Crusades from the Arab standpoint, see Francesco Gabrieli's *Arab Historians of the Crusades* (1978), and Amin Maalouf's *The Crusades*

Through Arab Eyes (1985). Finally, an assessment of the cross-cultural impact of the Crusades is provided by W. Montgomery Watt's *The Influence of Islam on Medieval Europe* (1972).

The Fatimids in Cairo were replaced by a Sunni dynasty, the Ayyubids, in 1171. The most famous of this lineage was Salah al-Din (Saladin), who began the drive to rid Palestine of Crusaders. Saladin's forces drove the Crusaders from Jerusalem in 1187, from Antioch two years later, and he signed a peace treaty with Richard Coeur de Lion in 1191. For further reading on this illustrious Muslim leader, see Malcolm Cameron Lyons and D. E. P. Jackson's *Saladin: Politics of Holy War* (1982).

The weakened Muslim world was to suffer even greater setbacks, however. In 1219, the Mongols, under the leadership of Genghis Khan, entered Muslim Central Asia and began a period of unparalleled destruction. By 1258, Baghdad itself was totally devastated by Genghis's grandson, Hulagu Khan. Meanwhile, in 1250, the Ayyubids were replaced in Cairo by the Mamluks under Aybak. The Mamluks met the Mongols at Ayn Jalut (the Spring of Goliath) in Palestine in September 1260, where the Muslims finally stalled the predations of the Mongol hordes. For further studies of the Mongols, see David Ayalon's *Studies on the Mamluks of Egypt* (1977), *The Mamluk Military Society* (1979), and *Outsiders in the Lands of Islam* (1988); David Morgan's *The Mongols* (1987); and John Joseph Saunders's *History of the Mongol Conquests* (1971).

The displacement of the center of the Muslim world from Baghdad provided an opening for three great Muslim dynasties to flourish during the sixteenth and seventeenth centuries—the Ottoman dynasty, the Mughal dynasty in India, and the Safavid dynasty in Persia (Iran). The first, the Ottoman, provided the basis on which the caliphate would continue even into the twentieth century. The second, the Mughal, generated an intriguing interrelationship between Islam and another world religion, Hinduism. The third, the Safavid, provided the basis upon which Shi'a Islam would become fully institutionalized in Iran. We will consider each of these in turn.

Ottoman Caliphs

Turkish Muslim tribes began migrating out of Central Asia during the tenth century. By 1300, a Turkish leader, Osman (Turkic for Uthman, the third caliph), established a dynastic state in the northwest corner of Anatolia. The capital was first established at Bursa, in Asia Minor. After these Turks captured Gallipoli and further territory on the European side of the Dardanelles, their capital was shifted to Edirne (Adrianople). At this point, Constantinople, capital of the Byzantine Empire, was completely surrounded by the new Muslim state. This rapidly developing state was called "Ottoman" by the West, which had difficulty transliterating "Osman." The head of state—each and every one a patrilineal descendant from Osman—was called sultan ("the powerful"), a title that the fourth Ottoman, Bayezid, received from the Abbasid caliph who resided in Cairo.

This was to become one of the longest lasting and most important dynasties in history, stretching from 1300 until 1922. In May 1453, Ottoman troops under Sultan Mehmed II captured Constantinople, putting an end to the Byzantine Empire at last. This great city was renamed Istanbul ("the city") and became the Ottoman capital. Mehmed's grandson, Selim, defeated the Mamluks of Egypt in 1517 and incorporated their territories into the Ottoman Empire. Selim also acquired the title of caliph from the last (nominal) Abbasid in Cairo, Muhammad Abu Jafer, whose royal name was Mu'tawakkil III. The union of the secular power of the sultan with the religious stature of the caliph made Istanbul truly the "world city" of the sixteenth and seventeenth centuries. Minorities of the Religions of the Book were protected in Millets (religious communities) wherein their own law prevailed.

Selim's son was the greatest of the Ottoman lineage, Suleyman (i.e., Solomon). Under his leadership, Ottoman forces captured Budapest in 1525 and threatened all of Europe. Ottoman troops reached the gates of Vienna in 1529 (and again in 1683). Indeed, the Ottoman expansion was a profound stimulus to the Lutheran Reformation in Germany. For further reading on the greatest of all Ottomans, see Antony Bridge's *Suleiman the Magnificent* (1983), and Harold Lamb's *Suleiman* (1951). Upon Suleyman's death in 1566, the Ottoman sultans (caliphs) showed a marked decline in ability, although the Empire and the caliphate retained a significant role in both European politics and the Muslim world until after World War I. The Ottoman Empire has been discussed in Rifa'at Ali Abou-el-Haj's *Foundation of the Modern State: The Ottoman Empire* (1991), Robert Dankoff's *The Intimate Life of an Ottoman Statesman* (1991), Halil Inalcik's *The Ottoman Empire* (1978), Resat Kasaba's *The Ottoman Empire and the World Economy: The 19th Century* (1988), Mehmet Fand Köprülü's *Origins of the Ottoman Empire* (1992), and in Sanford Shaw and Ezel K. Shaw's *History of the Ottoman Empire and Modern Turkey* (1976–77).

The Mughals of India

Islam came to India, the ancient homeland of Hinduism, in the eighth century A.D. In 711, the same time that Muslim troops under Tarik crossed from North Africa to Spain, a young Muslim named Muhammad bin Qasim entered the Indus Valley (what is now Pakistan) as a conqueror. Since then, Islam has penetrated all parts of the subcontinent. Although Arab traders began to convert the Indians as early as the seventh century, the actual flood of conversion occurred in the eleventh century, when the Central Asian Muslims—Turks, Afghans, Persians, and Mongols—came into India in successive waves beginning around 1000.

The initial invaders were fierce, as the Muslims sought to pillage, collect booty, and slay the infidels to earn the title *Ghazi* (Warrior for the Faith). However, the soldiers of Islam soon realized that the local inhabitants of the subcontinent, the Hindus, were totally unable to protect themselves against the forces of Islam. The Muslim penetration of India accelerated from the eleventh century onwards, coming in huge waves at intervals. First came the Turks, next the Afghans, followed by the Persians, and finally the Mongols, known in India as the *Mughals*.

In the eleventh and twelfth centuries, India failed to absorb the Muslim invasions as it had in more ancient times. Thereupon, the Muslims began to carve out sultanates (principalities) for themselves in India, known as the Delhi Sultanates (until 1526). The Turk and Afghan Muslim sultans (who had come before), though fierce, could not fully consolidate their kingdoms.

The Mughals were a particular class of Mongols who claimed a distinct ethnicity that was actually the result of free intermarriage between themselves and Turks, Persians, and other Muslims of western Asia. The first Mughal to consolidate his rule in India was Babur, the architect of a glorious empire based in Delhi after 1526. In his *Memoirs*, he expressed a deep contempt for the Indians (Hindus), saying they were a people of "few charms," lacking "genius and capacity"; lacking manners, good horses, and good grapes; and lacking good bread, hot baths, and colleges. In short, the Muslim attitude toward the Hindus was disdain, an attitude not conducive to acculturation.

It was not until Babur's grandson, Akbar (1556–1605), came to power that the Mughal Empire became more magnanimous. Emperor Akbar realized that he would not be accepted by the subject populace unless he abandoned the aggression of his predecessors for a path of conciliation. His mother tongue was still Turkic, the language of his ancestor Timur, who had been nurtured on the banks of the Oxus, but Akbar's state language was Persian, laced with Arabic freely drawn from the holy Qur'an. Although Akbar was not attracted to Qur'anic dogmatism, still his thought was directly Islamic.

Akbar's doctrine, *Din-i Ilahi* (the Divine Faith), sought to bring understanding between Islam and the existing religions of India. This doctrine, while it antagonized the Muslim orthodoxy, in fact later suggested that there might be a systematic way to guide infidels toward the path of Islam at a comfortable pace. It represented a distinctive form of Islamic culture and institutions. Many Bengali and Urdu writers, and even some Hindi writers, accused Akbar of deviating drastically from the way of Islam, especially when he exempted the Hindus from paying *jizya* (the head tax levied on non-Muslims in Islamic countries).

Subsequently, this tax was reimposed on non-Muslims by Akbar's great-grandson, Aurangzib, who came to the throne in 1658. Aurangzib was a stern Muslim who felt that any of his subjects following another religion should be given two choices: converting to Islam or death. This led to widespread tax resistance and Hindu revivalism. The Mughal Empire went into a period of decline following his death in 1707, leading to a devastating series of foreign interventions. Nader Shah, the ruler of Persia, sacked Delhi in 1739. The British defeated the

Bengalis at Plassey in 1757. Warren Hastings began to consolidate British authority in India fifteen years later, leading to the colonial rule that would last until after World War II.

The heritage of this colonial period was continuing tension between the Hindu and the Muslim religious communities. Yet the fact remains that Hindus and Muslims have been living in the subcontinent since the seventh century, when the Muslims were the intruders and the Hindus were the indigenes. Until the middle of the eighteenth century, Hindus were under Muslim rule; during this long period, acculturation was an ongoing process that changed both Hindu and Muslim life. The process of conversion and mixed marriage continues to this day, and these as well as immigration from other Muslim countries are responsible for the huge number of Muslims presently in the subcontinent. For further reading on Muslim India, see Aziz Ahmad's *An Intellectual History of Islam in India* (1969), K. N. Chowdhury's *Asia Before Europe: Economy and Civilization of the Indian Ocean from the Rise of Islam to 1750* (1990), S. Mohammed Ikram's *Muslim Civilization in India* (1964), Aminul K. M. Islam's *Victorious Victims* (1978), M. Mujeeb's *The Indian Muslims* (1967), and Annemarie Schimmel's *Islam in the Indian Subcontinent* (1980).

The Safavids of Iran

The third great Muslim dynasty of the sixteenth and seventeenth centuries was that of the Safavids in Iran. This dynasty was descended from a Sufi master, Ishaq Safi al-Din (d. 1334), who lived in Azerbaijan—the dynasty was named *Safavid* after "Safi." Safi al-Din's descendant, Ismail ibn Haydar, was raised in a Shi'ite community near the Caspian Sea. His family called themselves *Alid*—descendants of Ali ibn Abu Talib—and Ismail himself was initially characterized as the reincarnation of the Hidden Imam, *al-Mahdi* (see Ghulam Sarwar's *History of Shad Ismail Safawi* [1939]).

While still very young, Ismail took advantage of the political disorganization in Persia following the Mongol conquests, and by 1501 had unified the territory. He proclaimed Shi'a Islam as the state religion. This Safavid and Shi'ite expansionism threatened the eastern domains of the Ottoman sultans, including Bayezid II and Selim I. Finally, Selim attacked Ismail Shah at Chaldiran near the Safavid capital of Tabriz in 1514; the Ottomans prevailed and occupied Tabriz. Defeat constituted a major setback to Ismail's pretensions to divinity. For more information on Ismail and the Safavids, see Roger M. Savory's *Iran Under the Safavids* (1980).

Theological retrenchment followed. Ismail Shah began to bring Shi'ite theologians to Iran; one of the first of these was Shaykh Muhaqqiq al-Karaki, who proselytized actively for Shi'a Islam—and against the Sunnis—throughout Iran. Ismail's successors to the Safavid throne—especially Tahmasp Shah (1524–1576), Abbas I Shah (1588–1629), and Abbas II Shah (1642–1666)—supported further Shi'ite theological development. When Abbas I moved the capital city to Isfahan in

1597, another great Shi'ite theologian, Shaykh Baha'i, helped develop the city plan. The efforts of Mulla Shushtari, who promoted the education of Shi'a religious students in the *Madrasas* there, also helped Isfahan become a religious center. The School of Isfahan was founded by Mir Damad, and reached its peak in the person of Mulla Sadra (compare to Seyyed Hossein Nasr's *Sadr al-Din Shirazi [Mulla Sadr] and His Transcendental Theosophy* [1978]). By 1624, the struggles between Safavids and Ottomans turned in favor of the Shi'ites; Baghdad and Iraq were captured by the forces of Abbas I.

After the death of Abbas I, Safavid fortunes declined. The Ottomans recaptured Baghdad in 1638, and Sultan Murad IV and Safi Shah signed the Treaty of Zuhab the next year, which established a general peace and recognized Ottoman authority over the Shatt al-Arab waterway that divided them. It is worth mentioning that the British established an imperial outpost the same year in Basra; these two issues—authority over the waterway and Western intervention in southern Iraq—eventually led to the Iran-Iraq War, and "Operation Desert Storm" of our own days. When the great-grandson of Abbas I came to the throne as Abbas II Shah in 1642, the decline was temporarily halted, but it resumed with his death in 1666. Within Iran, the weak successors of Abbas II were no match for one of the greatest of the Shi'ite Ulama, Shaykh Majlisi. This theologian sought to suppress not only Sufi mysticism in Shi'a Islam, but also Sunni Islam throughout all of Safavid territory. This triggered a revolt within the Safavid domains by (Sunni) Afghanis, who would finally capture Isfahan in 1722, ending the Safavid dynasty (see Laurence Lockhart's *Fall of the Safavi Dynasty* [1958]).

By the time he died at the close of the seventeenth century, Majlisi had set the Shi'a firmly on the course of formalism and external forms, denying the significance of an inner doctrine. He set the Shi'a just as firmly to restricting itself to Iranians and to the intolerance of Sunnis. This development could function as an element of what today's social scientists would call "nation-building"; it also ultimately contributed to the downfall of the Safavid regime. Finally, Majlisi had firmly established the independence of the ulama against the Iranian throne, and this tension would ultimately culminate in the Iranian Revolution in our own times.

When the Safavid dynasty fell, a brilliant military leader named Nader Khan emerged to save Iran from its powerful neighbors. He proclaimed himself Nader Shah in 1736 and sought to reestablish Sunni Islam throughout Iran, in place of the Shi'ite Islam of the discredited Safavids. But Shi'a Islam was too firmly established to be quickly uprooted, and Nader Shah was assassinated in 1747 before his plans could come to fruition. See Laurence Lockhart's biography, *Nader Shah* (1938), for more information.

Imami Shi'ite Islam

The form of Shi'a Islam with the most adherents in the Middle East is known as "Twelver," or *Imami* Shi'ite Islam; it recognizes twelve Imams, or spiritual leaders of the Umma, after the Prophet. There are four interrelated features of Imami Shi'ite Islam that differentiate it from Sunni Islam, with which it shares many basic features. These are the doctrine of the *Imamate*, the doctrine of the *Hidden Imam*, the doctrine of *Ijtihad* (Interpretation), and finally, the doctrine of *Taqlid* (Imitation). We will discuss each of these in turn. For more information on Imami Shi'ite Islam, see Moojan Momen's *Introduction to Shi'i Islam* (1985).

The Imamate

While the Sunni believe the leadership of the Umma rests with any Muslim who is deputized to lead, called the caliph, the Shi'a believe that valid leadership of the Umma rests only with the *Ahl al-Bayt* (the People of the Prophet's House), that is to say, with Ali and Fatima and their progeny. These will be the spiritual leaders of the Ummah, and are known as Imams. The Imams have included: first, Ali; second, Hasan; third, Husayn; fourth, Ali al-Zaki; fifth, Muhammad al-Baqir; sixth, Ja'far al-Sadiq; seventh, Musa al-Kazim; eighth, Ali al-Rida; ninth, Muhammad al-Taqi; tenth, Ali al-Hadi; eleventh, Hasan al-Askari; and twelfth, Muhammad al-Madhi (b. A.D. 869).

The Imam is inspired by divine illumination both to guide humanity and to provide proof of Allah to humanity. It should be noted that any temporal leader (be that a king, an emperor, a caliph, or whatever) who differs from the perfect leadership provided by the Imam must be spurious. This point is crucial for understanding the tension that lately characterized the relationship between the Shi'ite ulama and the Iranian monarchy, tension leading to overthrow of the Pahlavi dynasty in 1979.

The Hidden Imam

Because of the inherent tension between the Imamate and the caliphate (first the Umayyads and then the early Abbasids), many Imams met violent ends. The tenth and eleventh Imams were imprisoned by the caliphs in Samarra as Islamic orthodoxy was being restored. They communicated with their followers through intermediaries. When Hasan al-Askari died in 874 A.D., his son Muhammad was a child; he made his one and only public appearance at his father's funeral. Thereafter, the twelfth Imam, Muhammad al-Malidi, went into *ghaybah* (occultation, i.e., concealment), and also communicated to his followers through intermediaries, called the *bab* ("gate"), including Uthman al-Amri, who had been an intermediary for Imam Hasan. This period is known as the Lesser Occultation. In 941, this period of *ghaybah* passed over to a new period, the Greater Occultation, when the Imam still lived but no longer communicated through a *bab*. The

Shi'a movement maintains that the period of Greater Occultation miraculously continues to the present time. Shi'a doctrine holds that this Hidden Imam will reappear as the *madhi* (the messiah) to lead the forces of Good against the forces of Evil just before the Final Judgement.

Ijtihad

With the passage of time, the absence of leadership implied by the Greater Occultation became increasingly problematic to the Shi'a followers. Then the Shi'a ulama began to assume more and more of the functions of leadership of the Umma. When the Safavids came to power in the sixteenth century, Muhaqqiq al-Karaki argued successfully that the Shi'a ulama were the *Na'ib* (representatives) of the Hidden Imam, thereby assuming an intermediary role similar to that of the long-absented *bab*. As such, the ulama came to be recognized as capable of *ijtihad* (interpretation), whereby contemporaneous problems of the Umma were creatively addressed in light of Islamic Law and the Tradition of the Prophet and the Imams by the ulama. Those mullahs (religiously learned ones) whose interpretations are sought and respected are known as *mujtahid*. By the end of the eighteenth century, Shaykh Bihbahani had established the primacy of *ijtihad* in the development of the Shi'ite law. This secured the position of the ulama against the Qajar dynasty, which had restored the monarchy in nineteenth-century Iran. For further readings on the Shi'a law, see Hassein Modarresi Tabatabai's *An Introduction to Shi'i Law: A Bibliographic Study* (1984).

Taqlid

The vast majority of Shi'ites, who are not mujtahid, cannot themselves exercise *ijtihad*, because they would end in error. Hence they must engage in *taqlid* (emulation), following the model established by one of their contemporary mujtahid. This dialectic of creativity and emulation creates the potential for a tremendous popular mobilization throughout the Shi'ite Umma. If the leading mujtahids, who in recent years have come to be called *ayatollah* ("the sign of Allah"), are accommodating to the political regime, it will be greatly strengthened. If the ayatollahs are opposed to the regime, the masses may turn against it, and it may collapse. This has been discussed with respect to the Iranian Revolution of 1979 in *The Turban for the Crown* by Said Amir Arjomand (1988).

Two Islamic Heresies

Before turning to the topic of Islam in the modern era, it will perhaps be worthwhile to mention two heresies of Islam that have recently presented themselves—the Ahmadiyya Movement, which originated in what is today Pakistan, and the Baha'i Movement, which originated in Iran.

The *Shari'ah* holds that there are two ways a Muslim can renounce the faith: *ridda*, converting from Islam to another religion, and *irtidad*, falling from Islam into unbelief. Two religious movements that began within Islam are now considered heresies by virtually all Muslims, interlacing both the element of unbelief, by questioning the finality of Muhammad's prophecy, and the element of conversion to another religion. We will briefly discuss both of these heresies, and indicate some literature for further study.

The Ahmadiyya Movement

Orthodox Muslims regard the Ahmadiyya Movement (Qadianism) as a dangerous heresy that has, in the name of Islam, done more to undermine its foundations than have any individual apostates or dissenters. Following Pakistan's decision in the 1970s to declare its adherents a non-Muslim group, most Muslim countries no longer recognize the right of Qadianis to describe themselves as Muslims. They are forbidden to enter the holy city of Mecca for the annual *hajj*. Few Muslims knowingly intermarry with them, and in Pakistan—where the heresy originated—Ahmadis are apt to be viewed with great suspicion.

The movement was launched by Mirza Ghulam Ahmad in 1889 in the town of Qadian, in the Punjab, when that was still part of India. Ahmad (1835–1908) claimed that he was the recipient of divine revelation in the manner of the Prophet Muhammad, and that he had been sent into the world in the power and spirit of Jesus Christ. His revelations were later compiled into an addendum to the Qur'an, which are discussed in *The Essence of Islam*, by Ghulam Ahmad (1979).

Ghulam Ahmad of course insisted on calling himself a Muslim; his followers do so to this day. But in claiming to be a prophet himself, Ahmad repudiated what is considered one of the fundamental principles of Islam, namely, that Muhammad was the last of the divinely inspired prophets, and that the Qur'an was the last of the Divine Books. The doctrine of *risalat* (the prophetic mission), founded on the belief that Muhammad was the last of the prophets, is as basic to Islam as is *tawhid* (faith in the unity of *Allah*). To reject either doctrine is to strike at the heart of Islam. While there are those who would not interfere with Ahmadism as a separate cult, it is its claim to be Islamic that is challenged and has frequently led to violence. In the 1950s, soon after the establishment of Pakistan as a new state, anti-Ahmadiyya riots caused so many casualties that martial law had to be imposed in Punjab.

The Ahmadiyya conception of prophecy turns on the subtle interpretation of a verse in the Qur'an. The sect maintains that the verse leaves room for the appearance of prophets after Muhammad, a view that no orthodox Muslim will accept. Ahmadis say that the channel of communication between Allah and humanity is always open for the transmission of new messages. Ghulam Ahmad's mastery of Arabic, the language in which he wrote his revelations, lent him the appearance of legitimacy in the eyes of his followers, but orthodox Muslims counter this by pointing out that such use of Arabic itself is a rebuttal of Ahmad's pretensions. There has been no prophet who has used any language but his own to communicate his message.

The Ahmadiyyas are divided into two basic factions: those who accord to Ghulam Ahmad the full status of *nabi* (prophet), and those who believe he was only a *mujaddid* (a reformer). Neither position is countenanced by the mainstream of Islamic thought.

Not only did Ghulam Ahmad claim to have received revelations from Allah, but he also advanced a new account of the fate of Jesus of Nazareth. He taught that Jesus did not die on the cross, but was taken down unconscious and, when revived, continued secretly to see his disciples for the next forty days. When Jesus' wounds were fully healed, he left Palestine to preach among the lost tribes of Israel, and eventually arrived in Kashmir.

Jesus, the Ahmadiyyas further believe, lived to a venerable age, passing away when he was 120 years old. His tomb is also said to have been located. Mirza Ghulam Ahmad believed himself to be not only a prophet, but also Jesus reincarnate. No orthodox Muslim, let alone Christian, accepts this account. Even those who anticipate the reappearance of Jesus as Messiah do not think that the Ahmadiyyan account has any historical basis.

When Ghulam Ahmad died in 1908, a disciple was elected his *khalifa* (deputy) in the same way as Abu Bakr succeeded the Prophet as his khalifa. When the Khalifa died in 1941, the Ahmadiyyas split into two groups: one elected a khalifa based in Lahore, Mirza Bashiruddin Mahmud Ahmad (1889-1965), while the other group installed a son of the first khalifa in the office at Qadian. The current headquarters of the Ahmadiyya Movement is in Rabwa, Pakistan. For more information on this movement, see *Invitation to Ahmadiyyat*, by Bashiruddin M. Ahmad (1980).

Doctrinally, the Ahmadiyyas purport to accept all the principal Islamic beliefs, and purport to accept the Qur'an. Their liturgy, form of prayer, and other practices are identical with those followed by the Muslim community. They subscribe to the importance of congregational prayer and hold service on Fridays, again like the Muslims. Their mosques, as they call them, have the same architectural features as mosques proper, characterized by minarets and domes. They insist on fasting as an obligatory duty, and also believe in the *hajj*, even though Saudi Arabia doesn't permit them to enter during the pilgrimage time. But their affirmations of faith—called *kalimas*—are worded differently, and Ghulam Ahmad is invariably invoked as intercessor in their prayers.

In recent times there has been a tendency to present Mirza Ghulam Ahmad as only a reformer, not the promised Messiah, whom many Muslims eagerly await. To this end, innumerable miracles have been attributed to Ahmad, but the claim that Ghulam Ahmad was a prophet is not stressed, if it is mentioned at all; rather, his services in the advancement of Islam are highlighted. Care is taken to say that his revelations were due to *ilham* (saintly inspiration) rather than *wahi* (prophetic inspiration). But the retreat from wahi to ilham is interpreted by orthodox Muslims as a ploy to lull the suspicions of the Muslim community and to deceive the unwary, for no saint in Islam ever claimed the status that Ghulam Ahmad claimed.

It is impossible to say with any certainty how large the Ahmadiyya community is, because in many non-Muslim countries (and also, interestingly enough, in Bangladesh) they identify themselves as Muslims. Ahmadiyya missionaries in Africa are known to have achieved considerable success, with perhaps as many as half a million converts in East Africa. For further reading, see the sociological studies of Yohanan Friedmann, *Prophecy Continuous* (1989), and that of Antonio R. Gualtieri, *Conscience and Coercion* (1989).

The Baha'i Movement

Baha'ism, a cult born in the nineteenth century, shows some similarities to the Ahmadiyya Movement in that it owes its origin to a new conception of prophetic inspiration. It rejects the belief that Muhammad was the last of the inspired prophets, maintaining instead that the door of communication between Allah and humanity will always be open, with successive prophets receiving direct revelations from Allah. Like the Ahmadiyya Movement, it began as a reform tendency within Islam—Shi'a Islam, in this case—when its founder, Mirza Ali Muhammad (1819–1850), a native of Shiraz in Iran, claimed to be the long-awaited Imam who was to pave the way for the advent of One greater than himself. At this point it could be understood as one of the more extreme positions of Shi'ism, stressing the tension between mosque and Qajar court.

During this period of great social and economic stress in Iran, Ali Muhammad assumed the name Bab ud-Din (Gate of the Faith) and was initially hailed as a religious leader. The response to his preaching soon led him to announce drastic changes in Islam itself, to abrogate Islamic laws, and finally to replace the Qur'an with a new holy book, the *Bayan* (the Explanation). The Qur'an, he announced, was no longer suited to the needs of the age (see his writings in Ali Muhammad Shirazi's *Selections from the Writings of the Bab* [1976]). This heretical position, as well as uprisings by his followers, produced an immediate response: The Bab was denounced as an apostate and eventually shot in the public square of Tabriz on July 9, 1850. After Babis made several attempts on the life of Shah Nasir al-Din, eighteen chosen disciples that the Bab had sent to preach his message and to proclaim the advent of the One whom Allah shall Manifest were also executed. For further reading on this subject, see *The Bab: The Herald of the Day of Days*, by Hasan Muraggar Balyuzi (1973).

The next chapter in the history of the cult is marked by a struggle over succession to the Bab, a struggle which was resolved by the appearance, in 1863, of the One whose advent was predicted by the Bab. Husayn Ali Nuri (1817–1892), one of the disciples of the Bab who had been exiled to Baghdad, came forward to claim that he was the Imam who had been expected by his master. He styled himself *Baha'Allah*

(Glory of God), and from that point onwards, Babism came to be known as Baha'ism. As has frequently been the case in messianic religious movements that experience defeat or setbacks (for example, the Anabaptists), revolutionary fervor came to be replaced by doctrines of political acquiescence, if not doctrines calling for no political involvement at all. For further reading, see *Baha'u'llah: The King of Glory*, by Hasan Muraggar Balyuzi (1980).

Baha'Allah seems to have been an extremely energetic man, and is reputed to be the author of several hundred books. The three basic ones written in Baghdad are *Hidden Words*, *Seven Valleys*, and *Kitab i-Iqan* (*The Book of Certitude*). These constitute the Baha'i Movement's scripture, and the rest are commentaries on Baha'Allah's teachings. See *Gleanings from the Writings of Baha'u'llah* (1983) for the writings of Baha'Allah. The entire Baha'i canon consists of the writings of the Bab, those of Baha'Allah, and those of his eldest son, Abdul Baha. The latter was named Abbas (1844–1921) and succeeded Baha'Allah in 1892, taking the name Abdul Baha (servant of Baha). The Baha'i Movement finally relocated its headquarters to Haifa, at that time an Ottoman city, where it remains today.

During World War I, Abdul Baha worked for the Allies from within Ottoman territory, and was rewarded with knighthood in 1920 (see his *Some Answered Questions* [1981]). The last testament of Sir Abdul Baha was *The Divine Plan,* which was an exposition on his father's teachings (see Hasan Muraggar Balyuzi's *Abdul-Baha* [1971]). Shoghi Effendi, Baha'Allah's grandson, succeeded Abdul Baha in 1921. After he died in 1957, the leadership of the Baha'i Movement was finally settled into a council in 1963.

Baha'i teaching stresses internationalism. The movement looks forward to the establishment of a single world order based on Baha'i principles, which will come about through the work of the Chosen One. One of the interesting goals of the Baha'i Movement is the development of an international language as a means of global understanding, so it supports the dissemination of Esperanto, an artificial international language. Baha'is believe in the Unity of God, accept all prophets, and maintain that all religions teach the same truth and that their differences are superficial. The Baha'i Movement condemns all superstition, advocates equal rights for men and women, and insists its teachings are compatible with science. Baha'i teaching rejects polygamy, discourages divorce, and bans asceticism and religious mendicancy. Baha'is do not have a hereditary priesthood, and even dispense with religious ritual altogether.

Baha'is characterize their movement as "an independent worldwide religion" with several million members, and its role in the United Nations lobbying efforts provides it with a further measure of influence. Because of the persecutions Baha'i have suffered in Iran, relations between Baha'ism and Islam have always been strained. Like the Ahmadiyya Movement, the Baha'i Movement is not permitted to proselytize in Muslim countries—again with the exception of Bangladesh and India. In India, the Baha'i Movement is thriving; the Baha'i temple in New Delhi has been called the Taj Mahal of the twentieth century.

Baha'i has had more success in the United States than elsewhere; there is a Baha'i temple on Lake Michigan near Chicago. One of the reasons Baha'ism is tolerated, and even encouraged, in the West is its injunction against political rebellion and its call to its followers to obey the government under which they find themselves, a doctrine calculated to serve the interests of any government in power.

The Baha'i Movement does not pose as great a threat to Islam as the Ahmadiyya Movement, as it does not proselytize as aggressively as Qadianism, but it is not discounted either, because it is viewed as tending to erode the foundations of Muslim faith. While the Ahmadiyya Movement persists in claiming that it is still orthodox Islam, the Baha'is no longer consider it necessary to preserve any link with Islam, and usually represent themselves as devotees of a completely separate religion. For further reading on the Bahai Movement, see *Studies in Babi and Baha'i History*, by Moojan Momen (1982), and Peter Smith's *The Babi and Baha'i Religions* (1987).

The Great Game

By the end of the eighteenth century, the three great Muslim dynasties—the Ottoman, the Mughal, and the Safavid—had entered periods of decline, and in the case of Iran, the Safavid dynasty had ended completely. At this critical point, a major shift took place in the balance of forces among the European Great Powers that was to have enormous impact on Dar al-Islam.

The fall of Montcalm at Quebec in 1759, and the defeat of Lally at Pondicherry in January 1791, ended any grandiose French colonial aspirations in North America or in the Indian subcontinent. This was affirmed in the Treaty of Paris in 1763. These colonial adventures, the expenses they incurred, and the defeats they occasioned also contributed to the fiscal crisis and loss of confidence in France which would result in the end of the Bourbon monarchy itself.

Ironically, the establishment of English hegemony in North America and in India had an unexpected effect, and assured the end of the first British Empire based in the original thirteen colonies, and the redirection of British, as well as French colonialism, toward the Orient. Within two decades of the Treaty of Paris, which relieved the English colonies of threats from France, the colonial oligarchs of the thirteen colonies raised a war of independence that ended with Cornwallis's surrender at Yorktown. Thus the first British Empire gave way almost immediately to the second British Empire. This empire had already been firmly anticipated during Robert Clive's and Warren Hastings's several governorships in Bengal, and was formalized by the younger William Pitt in his 1784 India Act. This fixed not only the eastern end of the English trade-route to the Orient, but the shape of the British Empire itself. The issue of the control of the middle of the British Empire—*ou les extremes se touchent*—thus came to be raised to the level of worldwide significance that the Middle East retains today, long surviving even the empire itself. The struggle among the Great Powers of Europe for hegemony in the Middle East was known as the "Great Game" (see Edward Ingram's *The Beginning of the Great Game in Asia* [1979], and *Commitment to Empire* [1981]). This Great Game led to the European assault on the Islamic world, complete with colonialism and oppression—long before the significance of petroleum reserves in the Middle East was recognized.

The end of the first British Empire unleashed forces of messianic republicanism in Europe, forces that had been stifled in oligarchic North America. In August 1704, the British secured Gibraltar, which at the time served only the trading interests of the Levant Company in the eastern Mediterranean. The French Revolution of 1789 transformed all this.

Republicanism threatened the British Empire throughout. Napoleon Bonaparte's Egyptian expedition in 1798 was incorrectly but widely taken by the English to be a thrust at India. Interestingly enough, Napoleon proposed a canal at Suez in his invasion plans. At the end of the first stage of the Great Game, the second British Empire was secured against the French threat, as its great enemy was exiled on St. Helena, a station in the middle of the trade route to India. The British sought to prevent any further threats to the Empire through Egypt by invading it in 1807, but were defeated and driven out by Ottoman forces under the command of Muhammad Ali, who went on to become the great modernizer of Egypt. By 1830, in part as an effort to stifle republicanism by distracting and draining off its surplus population, France began to colonize Algeria. The Great Powers were to follow the lead of France in colonial ventures into the Middle East.

A second stage in the Great Game involved British moves to counter what was perceived as a Russian thrust at India, or at the least toward a "warm water port." This led to British intervention in Iranian and Ottoman affairs—including the Anglo-Iranian Treaty of 1809—culminating in the Crimean War of 1854. By the middle of the nineteenth century, the British Empire and Russia had divided Iran into spheres of influence. Tsarist Russia had captured and annexed all Iranian territory east of the Caspian Sea (what is today known as Muslim Central Asia) and all Ottoman territory north of the Danube (what is today known as Romania and the Ukraine).

The Suez Canal was completed in 1869 at the height of the Second Empire of Louis Bonaparte, nephew of Napoleon I. With Gibraltar, Malta, and the Aden Protectorate, Britain controlled the major sea approaches to the Canal. Yet the fear of new French expansionism made the British uneasy; Sedan and the sack of Paris after the Commune of 1871 relieved these fears. As a third stage in the Great Game, Prime Minister Benjamin Disraeli's government purchased the Egyptian shares of the Suez Canal in 1875. This is the same Disraeli who, in his hackneyed 1847 novel *Tancred*, recognized that only the middle of the Second British Empire was fixed and that the end-points were indifferent. In the novel, Disraeli's character proposed that Queen Victoria shift the capital from London to Delhi! The British finally invaded and occupied Egypt in September 1886, to remain until the 1950s.

The fourth stage in the Great Game involved British opposition to Imperial Germany's plans to build the Berlin-to-Baghdad railway, with Basra as its southernmost station. By 1899, Britain established a protectorate over the Ottoman territory of Kuwait, effectively cutting Basra off from the sea. This elevated the al-Sabah dynasty there to a prominence it has held to the present time.

Within a decade, oil would be discovered in nearby Khorramshahr, Iran, and the significance of the Great Game would pale in the face of Great Power rivalry for this resource. The British fleet began to be converted from coal to oil by 1911, and the British Admiralty became a controlling partner in the Anglo-Persian Oil Company in 1914. As significant as the thrusts and repartees of the Grand Game, the struggle over petroleum was even more rewarding for the imperialist victors, and it is estimated that Great Britain didn't pay anything for the Iranian oil extracted between 1914 and 1951.

The Muslim Response

The Muslim response to the European assault on Dar al-Islam, as well as to centuries of deprivation, took a number of forms. During the nineteenth century, these were largely limited to reformism, such as that of Muhammad Ali in Egypt (see Aden Rivlin's *The Agricultural Policy of Muhammad Ali in Egypt* [1961]; Afaf Lutfi Marsot's *Egypt in the Reign of Muhammad Ali* [1984]), and the Tanzimat era in the Ottoman Empire (see Roderic H. Davison's *Reform in the Ottoman Empire* [1963]; Carter V. Findley's *Bureaucratic Reform in the Ottoman Empire* [1980]). Of course, there were also outbreaks of fundamentalist revolt as well, such as that of the Mahdi Movement in Sudan (compare to Peter Holt's *The Mahdist State in the Sudan* [1970]).

In the twentieth century, as the depth and the intention of the Great Power assault on Islam became more evident, Muslims responded with an even wider range of alternatives. These later responses can be explicated by considering two dimensions—on the one hand, the relevance of Islamic identity; on the other hand, the relation of Islam to the West.

At one extreme is the secularism of Kamal Ataturk's republican transformation of Turkey. When the Allies defeated the Ottomans at the end of World War I, they sent troops into Anatolia. The nationalist forces of Ataturk beat back this invasion, ended the Ottoman sultanate (in 1922) and caliphate (in 1924), and proclaimed a secular Turkish republic. The secularization campaign that Ataturk initiated effected a sharp distinction between religion and state, wherein Islam was treated as a matter of personal faith rather than the institutional and cultural core of social order. For more information on the Turkish republic, see *Turkey in Crisis*, by Berch Berberoglu (1982), *State and Class in Turkey*, by Caglar Keyder (1987), and *Islam and Political Development in Turkey*, by Binnaz Toprak (1981). This campaign, undertaken as a matter of survival of the Turkish people, modernized Islam in order to enhance relations with the West; in the eyes of some, this jettisoned crucial features of Islamic identity. A rather weak echo of this campaign is found in the modernization policies of Reza Shah Pahlavi in Iran, described in Shahrough Akhavi's *Religion and Politics in Contemporary Iran* (1980).

At the other extreme is the pan-Islamic position of the Iranian Revolution of 1979 among Shi'ites, or that of the Egyptian *Ikhwan al-Muslimun* (Muslim Brotherhood) among the Sunnis. These movements strive for the cultural, political, and economic unification of all Muslims, for the reestablishment of Islam in erstwhile Muslim territories such as Spain, and ultimately, for the expansion of Islam around the globe. As Sayyid Qutb, the famous Egyptian advocate of the Muslim Brotherhood, has put it in his *Milestones* (1964), the Muslim's obligation is to revive Islam through holy *jihad* (struggle for Allah), and to establish *al-Hakimiyyah* (the lordship of Allah on earth). In the face of this lordship, any object of veneration (flag, country, ideology, etc.) is heretical and must be opposed absolutely. Such movements just as clearly reject the West as Ataturk's republicanism sought to emulate it. This thought culminated in the October 1981 assassination of Anwar Sadat by the so-called "Jihad" Movement. For further reading, see *The Neglected Duty*, by Johannes Jansen (1986), and *The 'Jihad': An 'Islamic Alternative' in Egypt*, by Nemat Guenena (1986).

Most Muslims take positions that do not lie at either of these extremes—on the one hand, Islamic identity is increasingly espoused; on the other hand, the West is not yet fully rejected. Now, the search for Islamic identity no longer seems to require the institution of the caliphate. This, combined with the deepening ambivalence toward the West and its secular campaigns, suggests that the institutionalization of this Islamic identity is yet to be fully developed. That institutionalization, when it is finally realized, will probably be something quite new and different. It will probably be some institutional form that the West will find unfamiliar.

It has been especially troubling to a great many Muslims that the third most sacred site of Islam, the Dome of the Rock in Jerusalem, should come under the control of non-Muslims, and that religious access to this site has been denied to the hundreds of millions of Muslims in the world. This, combined with concern about the oppression of Palestinians, and the further extension of colonialism in the form of Zionism, have led to conflict between a number of Muslim states and Israel during the last half of the twentieth century. This conflict has served to provide a concrete reference point for the grievances of Muslims against the West. The West is viewed as espousing sectarianism as a fundamental political credo, and yet it actively—hence hypocritically—supports the establishment of a particular religion in the Middle East—namely that of the Israelis. The Muslim recognition of this hypocrisy has done much to undermine the legitimacy of secular experiments such as that of Ataturk.

More recently, of course, the West has been viewed as pursuing its own very limited interests, at the expense of the Muslim world. The West—particularly the United States and Great Britain—have been perceived as unleashing tremendous military force on behalf of the Kuwaitis in their dispute with Iraq, while conveniently overlooking the much older claim of the Palestinians in their dispute with Israel (see some of the discussions in Gordon Welty's *Linkages to the Middle East* [1991]). Large numbers of Muslims have become convinced that the West has no sense of justice—only of its own national, material interests.

Most recently, the West has exacerbated this with its ill-advised intervention in Somalia, where the pretense of Western humanitarianism rapidly gave way to the reality of gun-boat (or gun-ship) diplomacy. Many Muslims wonder why the West has not sought to act as decisively on behalf of Muslim refugees and dissidents in Bosnia, in the former Yugoslavia. Large numbers of Muslims are becoming convinced that the West not only lacks a sense of justice—it doesn't even have a sense of benevolence.

Overall, if one were to hazard a judgment about the future of Islam, one would expect that this dynamic world religion will continue to grow and thrive—it is presently the fastest growing religion in the United States. And, perhaps unfortunately, one is led to expect that conflict will continue to grow between the Muslim world and the West.

Notes

1. All Quranic references are to Abdullah Yusuf Ali, *The Holy Qur'an* (Brentwood, MD: Amana, 1989).

References

Abou-el-Haj, Rifa'at Ali. *Foundation of the Modern State: The Ottoman Empire*. Albany, NY: SUNY Press, 1991.

Abu-Lughod, Janet Cairo. *1001 Years of the City Victorious*. Princeton, NJ: Princeton University Press, 1971.

Ahmad, Aziz. *An Intellectual History of Islam in India*. Edinburgh, Scotland: Edinburgh University Press, 1969.

Ahmad, Bashiruddin M. *Invitation to Ahmadiyyat*. Boston: Routledge Kegan Paul, 1980.

Ahmad, Ghulam. *The Essence of Islam*. London: London Mosque, 1979.

Ahmad, Mahmud. *Social Justice in Islam*. New Delhi: Adam, 1982.

Akhavi, Shahrough. *Religion and Politics in Contemporary Iran*. Albany, NY: SUNY Press, 1980.

al-Hakim, Tawfik. *Muhammad*. Cairo: Al-Adab Press, 1985. 309p.

al-Shafii, Muhammad ibn Idris. *Islamic Jurisprudence: Shafii's Risala*. Baltimore: Johns Hopkins University Press, 1961.

Ali ibn Abu Talib. *Nahjul Balagha*. Poona, India: Fine Arts Printing Press, 1967.

Ali, Abdullah Yusuf. *The Holy Qur'an*. Brentwood, MD: Amana, 1989.

Ali, M. Muhammad. *A Manual of Hadith [Salih Bukhari]*. Lahore, Pakistan: Ahmadiyya Anjuman Ishaat-Islam, 1951.

Anees, Munawar Ahmad. *Guide to the Sira and Hadith Literature in Western Languages*. New York: Mansell, 1986.

Arjomand, Said Amir. *The Shadow of God and the Hidden Imam*. Chicago: University of Chicago Press, 1984.

————. *The Turban for the Crown*. New York: Oxford University Press, 1988.

Attar, Farid al-Din. *Muslim Saints and Mystics*. Chicago: University of Chicago Press, 1966.

Ayalon, David. *The Mamluk Military Society*. London: Variorum Reprints, 1979.

————. *Outsiders in the Lands of Islam*. London: Variorum Reprints, 1988.

————. *Studies on the Mamluks of Egypt*. London: Variorum Reprints, 1977.

Azami, Muhammad Mustafa. *Studies in Hadith Methodology and Literature*. Indianapolis, IN: Islamic Teaching Center, 1977.

Baha'Allah. *Gleanings from the Writings of Baha'u'llah*. Wilmette, IL: Baha'i Publications Trust, 1983.

Baha, Abdul. *Some Answered Questions*. Wilmette, IL: Baha'i Publications Committee, 1981.

Balyuzi, Hasan Muraggar. *Abdu'l-Baha*. Oxford, England: George Ronald, 1971.

————. *The Bab: The Herald of the Day of Days*. London: George Ronald, 1973.

————. *Baha'u'llah: The King of Glory*. London: George Ronald, 1980.

Berberoglu, Berch. *Turkey in Crisis.* London: Zed Press, 1982.

Bhatnagar, R. S. *Dimensions of Classical Sufi Thought.* Delhi, India: Motilal Banarsidas, 1984.

Brice, William C. *An Historic Atlas of Islam.* Leiden: E. J. Brill, 1981.

Bridge, Antony. *Suleiman the Magnificent.* New York: Franklin Watts, 1983.

Chejne, Anwar G. *Muslim Spain.* Minneapolis, MN: University of Minnesota Press, 1974.

Chowdhury, K. N. *Asia Before Europe: Economy and Civilization of the Indian Ocean from the Rise of Islam to 1750.* Cambridge, England: Cambridge University Press, 1990.

Cook, Michael. *Early Muslim Dogma: A Source-Critical Study.* New York: Cambridge University Press, 1981.

Corbin, Henry. *The Men of Light in Iranian Sufism.* Boulder, CO: Shambala, 1978.

Dankoff, Robert, trans. *The Intimate Life of an Ottoman Statesman.* Albany, NY: SUNY Press, 1991.

Davison, Roderic H. *Reform in the Ottoman Empire, 1856–1876.* Princeton: Princeton University Press, 1963.

Donner, Fred M. *The Early Islamic Conquests.* Princeton, NJ: Princeton University Press, 1981.

Eccel, A. Chris. *Egypt, Islam and Social Change: Al-Azhar in Conflict and Accommodation.* Berlin: Klaus Schwarz, 1984.

el-Geyoushi, Muhammad I. *Fasting.* Cairo: Wahba Book Shop, n.d.

el-Kholi, el-Bahay. *Fasting.* Cairo: Supreme Council for Islamic Affairs, 1967.

Farahani, M. Mohammad H. *A Shi'ite Pilgrimage to Mecca, 1885–1886.* Austin, TX: University of Austin Press, 1990.

Findley, Carter V. *Bureaucratic Reform in the Ottoman Empire.* Princeton, NJ: Princeton University Press, 1980.

Freeman-Grenville, Stewart Parker Greville. *Muslim and Christian Calendars.* Totowa, NJ: Rowman and Littlefield, 1977.

Freud, Sigmund. *Moses and Monotheism*. London: Hogarth Press, 1939.

Friedmann, Yohanan. *Prophecy Continuous*. Berkeley: University of California Press, 1989.

Gabrieli, Francesco. *Arab Historians of the Crusades*. Berkeley: University of California Press, 1978.

Glick, Thomas F. *Islamic and Christian Spain in the Early Middle Ages*. Princeton, NJ: Princeton University Press, 1978.

Gualtieri, Antonio R. *Conscience and Coercion*. Montreal: Guernica, 1989.

Guenena, Nemat. *The 'Jihad': An 'Islamic Alternative' in Egypt*. Cairo: American University in Cairo Press, 1986.

Hawting, Gerald R. *The First Dynasty of Islam*. Carbondale, IL: SIU Press, 1986.

Heykal, Muhammad H. *The Life of Muhammad*. Indianapolis, IN: American Trust, 1976.

Holt, Peter. *The Mahdist State in the Sudan*. Oxford, England: Clarendon Press, 1970.

Ikram, S. Mohammed. *Muslim Civilization in India*. New York: Columbia University Press, 1964.

Inalcik, Halil. *The Ottoman Empire*. London: Variorum Reprints, 1978.

Ingram, Edward. *The Beginning of the Great Game in Asia, 1828–1834*. Oxford, England: Oxford University Press, 1979.

———. *Commitment to Empire*. Oxford, England: Oxford University Press, 1981.

Islam, Aminul K. M. *Victorious Victims*. Boston: G. K. Hall, 1978.

Jafri, Syed Husain M. *Origins and Early Development of Shi'a Islam*. London: Longman, 1979.

Jansen, Johannes. *The Neglected Duty*. New York: Macmillan, 1986.

Juynboll, Gautier H. A. *Muslim Tradition*. New York: Cambridge University Press, 1983.

Kasaba, Resat. *The Ottoman Empire and the World Economy: The 19th Century*. Albany, NY: SUNY Press, 1988.

Kennedy, Hugh. *The Early Abbasid Caliphate*. Totowa, NJ: Barnes & Noble, 1981.

Keyder, Caglar. *State and Class in Turkey*. New York: Verso, 1987.

Khuri, Fuad. *Imams and Emirs*. London: Saqi, 1970.

Köprülü, Mehmet Fuad. *Origins of the Ottoman Empire*. Albany, NY: SUNY Press, 1992.

Lamb, Harold. *Suleiman*. Garden City, NY: Doubleday, 1951.

Lassner, Jacob. *The Shaping of Abbasid Rule*. Princeton, NY: Princeton University Press, 1980.

Lings, Martin. *Muhammad*. New York: Inner Traditions International, 1983.

Lockhart, Laurence. *Fall of the Safavi Dynasty*. Cambridge, England: Cambridge University Press, 1958.

———. *Nader Shah*. London: Luzac, 1938.

Lyons, Malcolm Cameron, and D. E. P. Jackson. *Saladin: Politics of Holy War*. Cambridge, MA: Cambridge University Press, 1982.

Maalouf, Amin. *The Crusades Through Arab Eyes*. New York: Schocken Books, 1985.

Marsot, Afaf Lutfi. *Egypt in the Reign of Muhammad Ali*. Cambridge, England: Cambridge University Press, 1984.

McCarthy, Richard Joseph. *The Theology of al-Ash'ari*. Beirut: Imprimat Catholique, 1953.

Momen, Moojan. *Introduction to Shi'i Islam*. New Haven: Yale University Press, 1985.

———. *Studies in Babi and Baha'i History*. Los Angeles, CA: Kalimat Press, 1982.

Morgan, David. *The Mongols*. Oxford, England: Basil Blackwell, 1987.

Mujeeb, M. *The Indian Muslims*. Montreal: McGill University Press, 1967.

Muslim ibn al-Hajjaj, M. *Salih Muslim*. 4 vols. Lahore, India: Sh. Muhammad Ashraf. 1971–75.

Nasr, Seyyed Hossein. *Sadr al-Din Shirazi [Mulla Sadr] and His Transcendental Theosophy*. Tehran: Imperial Iranian Academy of Philosophy, 1978.

———. *Sufi Essays*. Albany, NY: SUNY Press, 1973.

Nawawei, Iman. *Gardens of the Righteous*. London: Curzon Press, 1975.

Nurbakhsh, Javad. *Jesus in the Eyes of the Sufis*. London: Khaniqahi-Nimatullahi, 1983.

———. *Masters of the Path*. New York: Khanigahi-Nimatullahi, 1980.

———. *Murad wa Murad: Master and Disciple in Sufism*. Tehran: Khanigahi Nimatullahi, 1977.

———. *Spiritual Poverty in Sufism [Faqr va Faqir]*. New York: Khaniqahi-Nimatullahi, 1984.

———. *Sufi Symbolism*. 4 vols. New York: Khaniqahi-Nimatullahi, 1984–1990.

———. *Sufi Women*. New York: Khaniqahi-Nimatullahi, 1983.

———. *Sufism: Fear and Hope*. Vol. 2. New York: Khaniqahi-Nimatullahi, 1982.

———. *Sufism: Meaning, Knowledge, and Unity*. Vol. 1. New York: Khaniqahi-Nimatullahi, 1981.

———. *Sufism: Submission, Contentment*. Vol. 3. London: Khaniqahi-Nimatullahi, 1985.

———. *Sufism*. Vol. 4. London: Khaniqahi-Nimatullahi, 1988.

———. *Sufism*. Vol. 5. London: Khaniqahi-Nimatullahi, 1991.

———. *Traditions of the Prophet: Ahadith*. Vol. 1. New York: Khaniqahi-Nimatullahi, 1981.

———. *Traditions of the Prophet: Ahadith*. Vol. 2. New York: Khaniqahi-Nimatullahi, 1984.

Padwick, Constance. *Muslim Devotions: A Study of Prayer Manuals.* London: SPCK, 1961.

Parrinder, Edward Geoffrey. *Jesus in the Qur'an.* London: Faber and Faber, 1965.

Perry, John R. *Karim Khan Zand.* Chicago: University of Chicago Press, 1979.

Qutb, Sayyid. *Milestones.* Cedar Rapids, IA: Unity, 1964.

Rahman, Fazlur. *The Philosophy of Mulla Sadra.* Albany, NY: SUNY Press, 1975.

Rivlin, Helen. *The Agricultural Policy of Muhammad Ali in Egypt.* Cambridge, MA: Harvard University Press, 1961.

Runciman, Stephen. *A History of the Crusades.* 3 vols. Cambridge, England: Cambridge University Press, 1987.

Sarwar, Ghulam. *History of Shah Ismail Safawi.* New York: AMS Press, 1939.

———. *Islam: Beliefs and Teachings.* London: Muslim Educational Trust, 1982.

Saunders, John Joseph. *History of the Mongol Conquests.* London: RKP, 1971.

Savory, Roger M. *Iran Under the Safavids.* Cambridge, England: Cambridge University Press, 1980.

Schacht, Joseph. *Introduction to Islamic Law.* Oxford, England: Clarendon Press, 1964.

Schimmel, Annemarie. *Islam in the Indian Subcontinent.* Leiden, Netherlands: E. J. Brill, 1980.

———. *Mystical Dimensions of Islam.* Chapel Hill: University of North Carolina Press, 1975.

Shaban, Muhammad A. *Islamic History, A.D. 600–750, A New Interpretation.* Cambridge, England: Cambridge University Press, 1971.

———. *Islamic History, A.D. 750–1055, A New Interpretation.* Cambridge, England: Cambridge University Press, 1976.

Shariati, Ali. *Hajj.* Bedford, OH: Free Islamic Literatures, 1977.

Shaw, Sanford, and Ezel K. Shaw. *History of the Ottoman Empire and Modern Turkey*. Cambridge, England: Cambridge University Press, 1976–77.

Shirazi, Ali Muhammad (the Bab). *Selections from the Writings of the Bab*. Haifa, Israel: Baha'i World Center, 1976.

Smith, Margaret. *Rabia the Mystic and Her Fellow Saints in Islam*. New York: Cambridge University Press, 1984.

Smith, Peter. *The Babi and Baha'i Religions*. Cambridge, England: Cambridge University Press, 1987.

Tabatabai, Hossein Modarresi. *An Introduction to Shi'i Law: A Bibliographic Study*. London: Ithaca Press, 1984.

Tabatabai, Muhammad Husayn. *Shi'ite Islam*. Albany, NY: SUNY Press, 1975.

Taleqani, Mahmud, et al. *Jihad and Shahadat*. Houston, TX: IRIS, 1986.

Toprak, Binnaz. *Islam and Political Development in Turkey*. Leiden, Netherlands: E. J. Brill, 1981.

Watt, W. Montgomery. *The Influence of Islam on Medieval Europe*. Edinburgh, Scotland: Edinburgh University Press, 1972.

——. *Muhammad at Mecca*. Oxford, England: Clarendon Press, 1953.

——. *Muhammad at Medina*. Oxford, England: Clarendon Press, 1956.

Welty, Gordon, ed. *Linkages in the Middle East: Opportunities for Justice and Peace*. Dayton, OH: University of Dayton Review, 1991.

Wensinck, Arent J. *Handbook of Early Muhammadan Tradition*. Leiden, Netherlands: E. J. Brill, 1971.

——. *Muhammad and the Jews of Medina*. Freiburg/Breisgau, Germany: K. Schwarz, 1975.

——. *The Muslim Creed*. New York: Barnes & Noble, 1965.

Zayas, Farishta. *The Law and Philosophy of Zakat*. Damascus, Syria: al-Jadidah Printing Press, 1960.

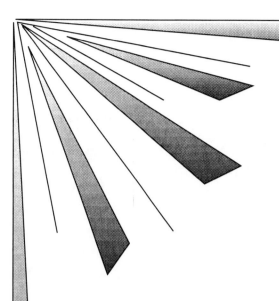

Part 2

The Literature of Liberation

5
Feminist Liberation Theology

Rev. Shelley Davis Finson

Introduction

What is feminist liberation theology? Simply put, theology is language about God, our faith experience documented. Feminist liberation theology is about the faith experience of women. The goal of feminist liberation theology is a "liberative praxis"—action informed by reflection. It addresses the need for radical transformation of the church as well as the social/economic/political structures that oppress women and other marginalized persons. The systems that deprive women of full status within the church also deprive women of God-given dignity.

Humans are constantly searching for ways to share our experience of that which many call God, but which others name the Spirit, Goddess, Sustainer, the Divine, Energy, Comforter, Creator, the Other, Rush of Wind, Friend, Provider, and other names. Language—verbal, written, bodily, or pictorial—is our means for such communication. Feminist liberation theology is about women doing theology based on their unique experience as women. It is a revolutionary activity because, as Rosemary Radford Ruether states in *Sexism and God-Talk Towards a Feminist Theology* (1983), it explodes the long held assumption that classical theology, including its codified traditions, is based on universal experience (p. 16).

170

Why Is Feminist Theology Important?

In the foreword of *A Different Heaven and Earth* (1974), Sheila Collins reflects on the experience of researching the book and her conversations with other women. As a result of those conversations she wrote the following about theology:

> Theology must come out of experience. Form cannot be separated from content. Theologizing can be done by anyone, with or without theological degrees; if women were ever to get into the pulpits in any number, the Book would no longer be kept from the people; the mysteries would be brought down from the cross and the pulpit for all to examine. (P. 10)

Feminist liberation theology is important because it is about change, and most importantly, it is about women's lives. It has grown out of the conviction of women that there is an urgent need to transform patriarchy, which is the interstructuring of sexism, racism, class-exploitation, and colonialism in women's lives.

In the last twenty years, there has been a rapid increase in the publication of feminist liberation theology. By and large, these works have come from white, North American women. Gradually, however, there has developed a steadily increasing stream of work from women of different races and from different parts of the world.

Feminist liberation theology begins in those places where women are suspicious that what they are being taught as universal truth is in fact something created out of male experience. But can we speak meaningfully about female experience as something fundamentally different from male experience? This was the central question for Valerie Saiving in her groundbreaking essay, "The Human Situation" (1979). She examined the distinctions between the experience of men and the experience of women as they occur in any human society, and she recognized that women's way of being in the world is radically different from men's. Saiving's examination of the theological categories of sin and redemption revealed that these are indeed experienced differently by women and by men. Women's sin lies, not in being proud, but rather in their self-effacing, submissive, or subservient behavior. Redemption for women lies, not in relying on their relationship to males, but in their ability to stand-up for themselves and to honor themselves as full persons, second to none.

Saiving's work stands as a milestone marking the beginning of the current wave of feminist liberation theology. As we will see in the "Women and History" section of this essay, women have always contributed to the life and work of the church. Although few records of their written theological contribution exist, we know, for instance, that Paula, with Jerome, established a monastery that she led until her death in A.D. 404. Saint Lioba, an Anglo-Saxon nun in the eighth century, was both a scholar and an abbess. (See Rosemary Radford Ruether and Eleanor McLaughlin's *Women of Spirit* [1979].)

Since 1960, feminist theologians have been challenging the core symbolism of Western religion and theology. Like other liberation theologies, feminist liberation theology strives to hold theology accountable to the modern world—the struggle of women for dignity and power. It began with the realization that the Christian tradition does not support the liberation of women. The exclusive language of the faith, the barriers to woman's full participation in the Christian hierarchy, and misogynist interpretations of Scripture exemplify the discrimination inherent in the Christian tradition.

Ultimately, feminist liberation theology is about liberation for all humankind. In the foreword of Letty Russell's early contribution to feminist liberation theology, *Human Liberation in a Feminist Perspective—A Theology* (1974), the writer said that like other liberation theologies, feminist theology will make white male theologians insecure because "feminist theology requests and urges men to give up their male chauvinistic pride so that they may be set free to become fully human" (p. 11).

The task of feminist liberation theology is to reconstruct theology, so that it truly reflects the life experience of all humankind. Therefore, it acknowledges and challenges the principalities and powers that exist in our relations between women and men, white people and people of color, young and old, heterosexual and homosexual, privileged and poor.

A variety of perspectives can be found on any one subject within feminist theological literature. Anne E. Carr, in "Is a Christian Feminist Theology Possible?" (1982), explains how this variation within feminist religious scholarship reflects the variety of perceptions of the depth and pervasiveness of sexism within Christianity. Writers included in this chapter bring their own worldview, religious experience, and institutional affiliation, which influence their perspective, to their arguments. Elizabeth Schüssler Fiorenza, in "Changing the Paradigms" (1990), has pointed out that the recent infusion of theology from Third World women has meant that Euro-American feminist theologians have been alerted to the necessity of addressing the "invisibility of doubly oppressed women."

Feminist liberation theology is still in its infancy, yet over the last two decades there has been a burst of energy and scores of voices taking up the debate.

Structure of the Chapter

The goal of this chapter is to provide a general overview of the literature available in the area of feminist liberation theology, including books, articles, theses, a few study guides, and music resources. Many of the books are collaborative efforts and reflect an ecumenical or interdenominational perspective. The chapter also provides an historical perspective on the development of the literature over the period of 1970 to 1994, and demonstrates the themes that have emerged during that time. Much has happened during that period, and the field of feminist liberation theology is rapidly deepening and widening. For example, the University of Toronto Press published an extensive resource of over 3,000 items—Shelley Davis Finson's *Women and Religion: A Bibliographic Guide to Christian Feminist Theology* (1991).

Although divided into sections, most of the articles and books cited in this bibliographic review could be listed under a single general heading, feminist liberation theology, revealing that much of the subject matter is interconnected. For example, issues related to the ordination of women could also be included in the section "Ministry of Women," or items on reflections on spirituality could be listed in the "Theology" section. The inter-disciplinary nature of feminist liberation theology makes absolute categorization difficult. Also, since the late 1960s, there has been a range of issues identified within the lives of some Christian women related to the institutional church—these include pastoral and ministerial concerns, language and doctrinal aspects of theology, biblical interpretation, and worship experience (liturgy).

This chapter is, therefore, organized to facilitate easy identification of topic areas with the appropriate resources cited. In a few instances, for reasons already indicated, some of the resources are cited in more than one section.

References

Carr, Anne E. "Is a Christian Feminist Theology Possible?" *Theological Studies* 43, no. 2 (June 1982): 279–97.

Collins, Sheila D. A. *Different Heaven and Earth*. Valley Forge, PA: Judson, 1974.

Finson, Shelley Davis. *Women and Religion: A Biographic Guide to Christian Feminist Liberation Theology*. Toronto: University of Toronto, 1991.

Fiorenza, Elisabeth Schüssler. "Changing the Paradigms." *Christian Century* (September 5–12, 1990): 797–800.

Ruether, Rosemary Radford. *Sexism and God-Talk Towards a Feminist Theology*. Boston: Beacon, 1983.

Ruether, Rosemary Radford, and Eleanor McLaughlin, eds. *Women of Spirit: Female Leadership in the Jewish and Christian Traditions*. New York: Simon & Schuster, 1979.

Russell, Letty M. *Human Liberation in a Feminist Perspective—A Theology*. Philadelphia: Westminster, 1974.

Saiving, Valerie. "The Human Situation: A Feminine View." In *Womanspirit Rising: A Feminist Reading in Religion*," edited by Carol P. Christ and Judith Plaskow. San Francisco: Harper & Row, 1979.

Sexism in the Church

The challenge to patriarchal Christian religion and practice has come from the Christian feminist movement within the church itself. Besides reflecting on the interpretation of Scripture and the meaning for women of the stories within Scripture, this movement, in the early period of the 1970s and 1980s, stirred several women to write about their experience of the church. The experience of sexism pervades all denominations.

Sara Bently Doely edited *Women's Liberation and the Church* (1970), a volume of essays that represented a pioneering effort to portray the new demand by women for meaningful participation in the life of the church. The contributors addressed topics including "Women's Liberation and the Church," "A Christian Perspective on Feminism," and "Education for Liberation: Women in the Seminary and Women in Ministry." Four years later, Alice Hageman edited a collection of papers called *Sexist Religion and Women in the Church: No More Silence* (1974). This collection of papers came out of a Women's Caucus of Harvard Divinity School's symposium designed to break the silence of women's voices in theological education, bringing together speakers such as Beverly Wildung Harrison, Letty Russell, Nelle Morton, Mary Daly, Gail Shulman, and Theresa Hoover.

Throughout the 1970s and 1980s, many have been committed to improving the position of Christian women in their respective churches. Much of their work has been inspired by the struggles of the contemporary women's movement. Several titles from this period express the growing concern: Arlene Swidler's *Woman in a Man's Church: From Role to Person* (1972); Nancy Van Vureen's *The Subversion of Women As Practiced by Churches, Witch-Hunters, and Other Sexists* (1973); Mary Durkin's *The Suburban Woman: Her Changing Role in the Church* (1975); Clare Fischer, Betsy Brennema, and Anne Bennet's *Women in a Strange Land* (1975); Bernard Braxton's *Sex and Religion in Oppression: Sexual and Religious Exploitation of Women, Anti-Abortion, Anti-Lesbianism and Wife-Beating* (1978); Jill Briscoe's *Prime Rib and Apple* (1978); Mary Papa's *Christian Feminism: Completing the Subtotal Woman* (1981). A highly commendable book that brings together much of the analysis that has taken place about sexism in the church is a volume by Bärbel von Wartenberg-Potter, *We Will Not Hang Our Harps on the Willows: Engagement and Spirituality* (1987). It is particularly useful because it recognizes the interconnections of all structures of oppression, including race, class, and gender.

Yet another book of note is by Margaret Wold, *The Shalom Woman* (1974). Wold was an enthusiastic participant at the Consultation of the World Council of Churches (1975) held in West Berlin in 1974. Many women who were disturbed by their growing awareness of the sexist nature of the church gained confirmation of their suspicions from this event. Margaret Wold took this opportunity to reach out to women functioning in traditional roles. She viewed herself as a reconciling voice within the growing women's movement in church. The story of her personal journey into wholeness and into a feminist spirituality spoke of a promise of newness for the Body of Christ.

In 1976, Elizabeth Verdesi published her thesis about the role of the women's organizations in the United Presbyterian Church, provocatively titled *In, But Still Out: Women in the Church*. This was the first of a number of testimonies concerning women's experience in specific denominations. Sonja Johnson received some publicity in the early 1980s after she published a frank account of her experience as a woman within the Mormon Church, *From Housewife to Heretic* (1981). Joan Ohanneson, in *Woman* (1980), and Sheelagh Conway, in *A Woman and Catholicism* (1987), wrote about their experiences in the Roman Catholic Church.

In the early 1980s, several reports were issued from denominational national church offices attempting to address women's issues in the church. These included *Daughters and Sons* (1981) and *The Changing Roles of Women and Men* (1984), by the United Church of Canada, and *Partners in the Mystery of Redemption*, by the National Conference of Catholic Bishops (1988).

The World Council of Churches, building on their report *Sexism in the 1970s* (1975), published several other documents focusing on the community of women and men in the church (1978; 1983). The Subunit on Women and Church and Society of the World Council also produced a report, "Orthodox Women: Their Role and Participation in the Orthodox Church, Report on the Consultation of Orthodox Women, 11–17 September 1976, Agapia, Romania" (New York: World Council of Churches, 1979).

The full impact of feminism on the church has become visible in journals during the 1980s and 1990s. A brief overview of article titles provides a sense of the concerns: "Feminism in Different Voices" by Marcia Bunge (1988); "Christianity and Feminism" by William Hasker (1988); "The Web of Relationship: Feminists and Christians" by Diane Yeager (1988); "The Feminist Movement in and on the Edge of the Churches in the Netherlands" by Lieve Troch (1989); "Christian Feminism" by Coleen Samuel (1989); "Catholic Feminism: Its Impact on United States Catholic Women" by Rosemary Rader (1989); "A Brief History of Christian Feminism" by Janette Hassey (1989); "Differing Theories, Same Old Praxis: Some Feminist Thoughts on Right Wing Religion" by Denise Ackerman and Mary Armour (1989); and "Christian Feminists in the Soviet Union" by Mary Ann De Trana (1990). Besides providing a history of feminism in the church, these articles also speak to the tension that many women experience, tension between their faith and their recognition of the power of feminism as a movement for social change.

Women have not simply critiqued the church and religion, they have also been developing resources that point to signs of hope. In *A Map of the New Country* (1983), Sara Maitland, an English Anglo-Catholic, looked at the efforts of Christian feminists over the previous fifteen years and suggested that, because of their insights, women were in "a unique position to prophesy to their respective churches." Mary Jo Weaver, a Roman Catholic in the United States, offered a new perspective in *New Catholic Women: A Contemporary Challenge to Traditional Religious Authority* (1985). Joan Chittister, also a strong Roman Catholic voice in the United States, has written two visionary books, *Winds of Change: Women Challenge the Church* (1986), and *WomanStrength: Modern Church, Modern Woman* (1990). Two authors have presented new understandings of the impact of a feminist perspective on women and the church in the 1990s—Marie-Eloise Rosenblatt in *Where Can We Find Her?* (1991), and Letty M. Russell in *Church in the Round* (1993).

Several publications that demonstrate the new developments in feminist liberation theology recognize interconnections of all structures of oppression, including race, class, and gender. Dorthee Sölle, a leading activist for justice and peace in Germany, has written the inspiring text *The Strength of the Weak: Towards a Christian Feminist Identity* (1984), which tackles the question of what it means for Christian women to claim the label "feminist." She begins:

> Meaning and credibility have become scarce. The demand exceeds the supply. We all talk not only about an economic and technological crisis but also about an ideological crisis, a lack of meaning in our private lives, a lack of credibility in public life. (P. 11)

In her last chapter, "Who Am I?," Sölle offers texts and meditations on the question of identify and calls us to examine our own lives and ask ourselves how we live them:

> How can I live so that it is really I who live my life? How can I keep my life from being dictated and lived for me by compulsions and routine? How can I become one with myself? Who am I? (P. 166)

In her more recent book, *The Window of Vulnerability: A Political Spirituality* (1990), Sölle turns to how the women's movement has drawn "the connections between male dominance and war, between maleness and self-identification with the warrior, between lust and violence." Sölle asserts there is a connection between how we live our lives and our spirituality.

Two Catholic scholars address the current situation in the Roman Church. Mary Ellen Sheehan's work, "Institutional Relationships" (1989), provides a feminist analysis of the church's authority and the role of women as reflected in recent statements by bishops in the church. Sandra Schneiders, in "Strangers, Rivals, or Partners?" (1986), clarifies the language and concerns of feminist spirituality, and describes the tension that exists because of the treatment of women by the church. She reminds us that patching is not enough; old practices must be replaced.

A welcome development in the 1990s is the publication of books that bring together writings of women across faiths. Paula Cooey,

William Eakin, and Gay McDaniel's *After Patriarchy: Feminist Transformations of the World Religions* (1991) includes writings by Muslim, Buddhist, and Jewish women. Maura O'Neill's *Women Speaking, Women Listening: Women in Interreligious Dialogue* (1990) is a collection of readings on sexism and various aspects of religion. The articles in *Women, Religion and Sexuality* (1991), commissioned by the World Council of Churches, are studies of the teachings of major religious and faith traditions and their impact on women.

Any liberation movement provokes reaction, and there are always concerns about extremism and even anarchy. Shirley Rogers Radl (1983), a long-time activist in the population control movement, raised some disturbing questions about the Religious New Right in the United States. She probes into the war raging against freedom of women to control their bodies and to redefine the family. Most striking of all is her analysis of the connection between fanatical religious groups and the business interests that support them. Elaine Storkey, in *What's Right with Feminism* (1985), interprets the polarization within the church:

> Right-wing attitudes within the church (although not seen as right-wing by their adherents but as politically neutral!) continue their challenge and attack of contemporary feminism in a strident, often aggressive manner. Probably, among the Evangelical and reformed Christians in the United States and Britain, this would even remain the pervasive attitude. The majority of Christians would react with irritation to the very notion of woman's oppression. Most would not be able to image how feminists can even posit this suggestion. The whole idea is ludicrous. What are those women on about? (Pp. 113–14)

In 1987, Betty Steele, a Canadian, wrote *The Feminist Take Over: Patriarchy to Matriarchy in Two Decades.* In it she surveys what she describes as the "take-over" of feminism. Perhaps the most scathing treatment of feminist liberation theology to date comes from Donna Steichen in *Ungodly Rage* (1991). The cover of her book describes how she exposes the hidden face of Catholic feminism, "revealing its theoretical and psychological roots in loss of faith." She asserts that most Catholic nuns, who have control of lay education, now practice another religion—witchcraft and Goddess religion. The rise of this neo-sexism coincides with recent attacks from Canadians on women faculty who teach in the area of feminist liberation theology.

There is every indication that this vigorous debate will not be resolved in the near future. Throughout this essay, the resources listed will assist the reader in identifying and considering their own faith in relationship to the numerous theological issues that have been raised by the current trends in feminist liberation theology. All the works mentioned here are evidence of the vision that women have for a church and a religion without sexism.

References on Sexism and the Church

Ackerman, Denise, and Mary Armour. "Differing Theories, Same Old Praxis: Some Feminist Thoughts on Right Wing Religion." *Journal of Theology for Southern Africa*, no. 69 (December 1989): 53–59.

Braxton, Bernard. *Sex and Religion in Oppression: Sexual and Religious Exploitation of Women, Anti-Abortion, Anti-Lesbianism and Wife-Beating*. Washington, DC: Verta, 1978.

Brisco, Jill. *Prime Rib and Apple*. Grand Rapids, MI: Zondervan, 1978.

Bunge, Marcia. "Feminism in Different Voices: Resources for the Church." *Word and World: Theology for Christian Mission* 8 (Fall 1988): 321–26.

Chittister, Joan D. *Winds of Change: Women Challenge the Church*. Kansas City, MO: Sheed & Ward, 1986.

———. *WomanStrength: Modern Church, Modern Woman*. Kansas City, MO: Sheed & Ward, 1990.

Conway, Sheelagh. *A Woman and Catholicism*. Toronto: Paperjacks, 1987.

Cooey, M. Paula, William R. Eakin, and Gay B. McDaniel, eds. *After Patriarchy: Feminist Transformations of the World Religions*. Maryknoll, NY: Orbis Books, 1991.

———. *Women Speaking, Women Listening: Women in Interreligious Dialogue*. Maryknoll, NY: Orbis Books, 1990.

De Trana, Mary Ann. "Christian Feminists in the Soviet Union." *St. Vladimir's Theological Quarterly* 34, no. 1 (1990): 88–93.

Doely, Sarah Bentley, ed. *Women's Liberation and the Church: The New Demand for Freedom in the Life of the Christian Church*. New York: Association, 1970.

Durkin, Mary G. *The Suburban Woman: Her Changing Role in the Church*. New York: Seabury Press, 1975.

Fischer, Clare Benedicks, Betsy Brenneman, and Anne McGrew Bennet, eds. *Women in a Strange Land: Search for a New Image*. Philadelphia: Fortress Press, 1975.

Hageman, Alice L., comp. and ed. *Sexist Religion and Women in the Church: No More Silence*. New York: Association, 1974.

Hasker, William, ed. "Christianity and Feminism." *Christian Scholar's Review* 17, no. 3 (1988): 231–323.

Hassey, Janette. "A Brief History of Christian Feminism." *Transformation: An International Dialogue on Evangelical Social Ethics* 6, no. 2 (1989): 1–5.

Johnson, Sonia. *From Housewife to Heretic*. New York: Doubleday, 1981.

Maitland, Sara. *A Map of the New Country: Women and Christianity*. London: Routledge Kegan Paul, 1983.

National Conference of Catholic Bishops. "Partners in the Mystery of Redemption: A Pastoral Response to Women's Concerns for Church and Society, First Draft. March 23, 1988." Washington, DC: United States Catholic Concerns, 1988.

Ohanneson, Joan. *Woman: Survivor in the Church*. Minneapolis, MN: Winston, 1980.

O'Neill, Maura. *Women Speaking, Women Listening: Women in Interreligious Dialogue*. Maryknoll, NY: Orbis Books, 1990.

Papa, Mary Bader. *Christian Feminism: Completing the Subtotal Woman*. Chicago: Fides/Claretian, 1981.

Rader, Rosemary. "Catholic Feminism: Its Impact on United States Catholic Women." In *American Catholic Women: A Historical Exploration*, edited by Karen Kennelly. New York: Macmillan, 1989.

Radl, Shirley Rogers. *The Invisible Woman: Target of the New Religious Right*. New York: Delta, 1983.

Rosenblatt, Marie-Eloise, ed. *Where Can We Find Her? Searching for Woman's Identity in the New Church*. New York: Paulist Press, 1991.

Russell, Letty M. *Church in the Round: A Feminist Interpretation of the Church*. Louisville, KY: Westminster/John Knox, 1993.

Samuel, Coleen. "Christian Feminism." *Transformation: And International Dialogue on Evangelical Social Ethics* 6, no. 2 (1989): 1–31.

Schneiders, Sandra. "Strangers, Rivals, or Partners?" *Horizons: Journal of the College Theology Society* 13 (Fall 1986): 253–74.

Sheehan, Mary Ellen. "Institutional Relationships: Religious Life in the Ur Church." *The Way Supplement* 65 (Summer 1989): 18–89.

Sölle, Dorothee. *The Strength of the Weak: Toward a Christian Feminist Identity*. Translated by Robert Kimber and Rita Kimber. Philadelphia: Westminster, 1984.

———. *The Window of Vulnerability: A Political Spirituality*. Minneapolis, MN: Augsburg Fortress, 1990.

Steele, Betty. *The Feminist Take Over: Patriarchy to Matriarchy in Two Decades*. Richmond Hill, Ontario: Irwin, 1987.

Steichen, Donna. *Ungodly Rage: The Hidden Face of Catholic Feminism*. San Francisco: Ignatius, 1991.

Storkey, Elaine. *What's Right with Feminism*. Grand Rapids, MI: William B. Eerdmans, 1986.

Swidler, Arlene. *Woman in a Man's Church: From Role to Person*. New York: Paulist Press, 1972.

Troch, Lieve. "The Feminist Movement in and on the Edge of the Churches in the Netherlands: From Consciousness-Raising to Woman-Church." *Journal of Feminist Studies in Religion* 5 (Fall 1989): 113–28.

United Church of Canada. Interdivisional Task Force on Changing Roles of Women and Men in Church and Society. "Daughters and Sons of God." Toronto: United Church of Canada, 1981.

————. Division of Mission in Canada. "The Changing Roles of Women and Men: A Report of the Task Force on the Changing Roles of Women and Men in Church and Society." Toronto: Division of Mission in Canada, United Church of Canada, 1984.

Van Vureen, Nancy. *The Subversion of Women as Practiced by Churches, Witch-Hunters, and Other Sexists*. Philadelphia: Westminster, 1973.

Verdesi, Elizabeth Howell. *In, But Still Out: Women in the Church*. Philadelphia: Westminster, 1976.

Von Wartenberg-Potter, Bärbel. *We Will Not Hang Our Harps on the Willows: Engagement and Spirituality*. (The Risk Book Series.) Geneva: World Council of Churches, 1987.

Weaver, Mary Jo. *New Catholic Women: A Contemporary Challenge to Traditional Religious Authority*. San Francisco: Harper & Row, 1985.

Wold, Margaret. *The Shalom Woman*. Minneapolis, MN: Augsburg Fortress, 1974.

World Council of Churches Conference (Sheffield, Yorkshire, 1981). "The Community of Women and Men in the Church." Edited by Constance F. Parvey. Geneva: World Council of Churches, 1981 (Sheffield, Yorkshire); Philadelphia: Fortress Press, 1983.

————. "The Community of Women and Men in the Church: A Study Program." New York: Friendship, 1978.

———. "Sexism in the 1970s: Discrimination Against Women: A Report of a World Council of Churches Consultation, West Berlin, 1974." Geneva: World Council of Churches, 1975.

World Council of Churches. "Orthodox Women: Their Role and Participation in the Orthodox Church, Report on the Consultation of Orthodox Women, 11–17 September 1976, Agapia, Romania." New York: World Council of Churches, 1979.

———. *Women, Religion, and Sexuality: Studies on the Impact of Religious Teachings on Women.* Philadelphia: Trinity Press International, 1991.

Yeager, Diane. "The Web of Relationship: Feminists and Christians." *Soundings: An Interdisciplinary Journal* 71 (Winter 1988): 485–513.

Zikmund, Barbara Brown. "Women and the Church." In *Altered Landscapes: Christianity in America, 1935–1985*, edited by David Lotz. Grand Rapids, MI: William B. Eerdmans, 1989.

Theology

Early Beginnings

The initial theme of feminist liberation theology was the challenge to sexism in the traditional theology of mainline Christianity. A candid critique came from Mary Daly in her searing message about the church and patriarchal religion, *The Church and the Second Sex* (1968). In her next work, *Beyond God the Father: Towards a Philosophy of Woman's Liberation* (1973), she portrays feminists' experience in this patriarchal world. Her phrase, "if God is male, then male is God," became a touchstone for those who were already harboring suspicions about language for God.

In 1974, Rosemary Radford Ruether edited a collection of essays called *Religion and Sexism: Images of Women in the Jewish and Christian Traditions.* This was the first textbook in feminist liberation theology to bring together material that was entirely new, addressing a wide range of topics. The description on the cover describes the work of the volume as an

> attempt to fill a growing need for a more exact idea of the role of religion, especially in the Judeo-Christian tradition, in shaping the traditional cultural images that have degraded and suppressed women.

This book sets out many of the issues that were to be developed in the ensuing years.

Feminist Hermeneutical Methods or Theories of Interpretation of the Bible

Letty M. Russell introduced her book *The Liberating Word: A Guide to Nonsexist Interpretation of the Bible* (1976) with this statement about hearing the Word of God:

> The universal message of God's love for all humankind will continue to be heard through the power of the Holy Spirit, but the fashion in which it is heard depends on our willingness to speak and act the Word in ways concretely addressed to the struggles and longings of women and men today. Today, that speaking and acting no longer ignores the existence of women as part of the people of God. (Pp. 14–15)

Such early literature introduced the significance of the reader, past and present, to the interpretation of Scripture. What did the author intend the readers of that day to hear? Whom were they addressing, and what was happening at the time of the writing? Exegesis, the attempt to understand the material in the context of the original readers, is followed by hermeneutics, the attempt to discern the message for today. Many questions are raised here. What brings us to read Scripture in the first place? Who are we? Are we female or male? Rich or poor? Free or captive? Just as the social status, gender, religious beliefs, and current events surrounding the writers and readers of the past influenced their interpretations of the Scriptures, so these same factors govern what will be heard by us today. For instance, the words of Scripture addressed to those in the early church who were persecuted for their faith will have poignant meaning for the people of Korea, imprisoned for their witness today. The battered woman will hear St. Paul's injunctions with respect to relationships between women and men with a different ear than the woman who lives in safety.

The beginnings of the process of liberating Scripture from past assumptions and readings can be found in writings of the 1970s. Phyllis Tribble plays an important role in this period because of her discerning presentation of feminist issues in her ground-breaking articles: "Depatriarchalizing in Biblical Interpretation" (1973), "The Bible and Women's Liberation" (1974), and "Women in the Old Testament" (1976). In 1978, Tribble wrote her major study, *God and the Rhetoric of Sexuality*. In this work, she focuses on the familiar stories of Creation and of Ruth, examining the text's own concern for language and for speech. She describes her work this way: "Using feminist hermeneutics I have tried to recover old treasures and discover new ones in the household of faith" (p. xvi). The female imagery that she finds provides insights hitherto unknown.

Elisabeth Schüssler Fiorenza was another early contributor to the effort of developing a feminist critical hermeneutical method. Her first articles, including "Women in the New Testament" (1976) and "Women in the Pre-Pauline and Pauline Churches" (1978), foreshadowed what was later to be published in her two compelling books: *In Memory of Her: A Feminist Reconstruction of Christian Origins* (1983), and *Bread Not Stone: The Challenge of Feminist Biblical Interpretation* (1984). No one spells out the task of feminist critiquing, exploring, challenging, and visioning better than Elizabeth Schüssler Fiorenza. In her newest publication, *But She Said* (1992), she offers strategies for feminist biblical interpretation as she explores the story of women like Miriam, Mary of Magdala, Prisca, and Sophia.

It was during the 1980s that several others joined the work of developing different methods for a feminist interpretation of the Bible. They asked whether or not the Bible is revelatory for women, and if so, what approaches to interpretation of the text provide a message of liberation rather than subjugation to women. The range of articles listed in the references provide a sense of the methodological issues being addressed at this time: Katherine Sakenfeld's "Old Testament Perspective" (1982); Cheryl J. Exum's "The Mothers of Israel" (1986); Paula Milne's "Eve and Adam; Is a Feminist Reading Possible?" (1988); Carolyn Osiek's "The Feminist and the Bible" (1989); Sandra M. Schneiders's "Feminist Ideology Criticism and Biblical Hermeneutics" (1989); and Elaine Wainwright's "In Search of the Lost Coin" (1989).

For those readers who are interested in exploring in greater depth issues connected to the Bible and authority, and a developing feminist hermeneutic, there are several other books listed in the references: Mary Ann Tolbert's *The Bible and Feminist Hermeneutics* (1983); Adela Yarbo Collins's *Feminist Perspectives on Biblical Scholarship* (1985); Alver Michelsen's *Women, Authority and the Bible* (1986); Elisabeth Moltmann-Wendel's *A Land Flowing with Milk and Honey* (1986) and *Humanity in God* (1983); Alice L. Laffey's *An Introduction to the Old Testament* (1988); Anne E. Carr's *Transforming Grace* (1988); Ann Loades's *Feminist Theology* (1990); and Teresa Elwes's *Women's Voices* (1992).

Language About God

Resources regarding inclusive language and liturgy can be found in the "Language and Liturgy" section of this chapter. This section looks at the way we have named God.

Because language must be authentic to human experience, how we describe our experience of God is a central issue for feminist theologians. It was not until the 1980s that several articles were published dealing with how we image God, what metaphor we use for God, and what our tradition has said by how we address God. (See Kari Borrensen's "God's Image, Man's Image?" [1983]; Elizabeth Johnson's "The Incomprehensibility of God and the Image of God, Male and Female" [1984]; James Edwards's "Does God Really Want to Be Called Father?" [1986]; and Sally Cunneen's "Mother Church, Mother World, Mother God" [1987].)

Numerous exceptional books were published that explored and developed radically new ways of naming God. These include: Sallie McFague's *Metaphorical Theology: Models of God in Religious Language*

(1982); Isabel Heyward's *The Redemption of God: A Theology of Mutual Relation* (1982); Marianne Micks's *Our Search for Identity: Humanity in the Image of God* (1982); Alen Lewis's *The Motherhood of God* (1984); Elisabeth Moltmann-Wendel's *Humanity in God* (1983); and Elizabeth Johnson's *She Who Is: The Mystery of God in Feminist Discourse* (1993).

In the 1980s, scholars began to apply the new hermeneutical methods (ways of interpreting) to specific themes or women in Scripture. In a particularly powerful yet disturbing book, *Texts of Terror: Feminist Readings of Biblical Narratives* (1984), Phyllis Tribble combines the discipline of literary criticism with the hermeneutics of feminism to focus on four variations on the theme of terror in the Bible. She examines the abuse and rejection of Hagar in Genesis, the rape of Tamar in 2 Samuel, and the extravagant violence against the unnamed women and the inhuman sacrifice of the daughter of Jephthah, both in Judges.

Letty Russell, in *Household of Freedom: Authority in Feminist Theology* (1987), uses a feminist hermeneutic as a tool for scriptural analysis to study issues of authority, which she calls "legitimate power in the context of Christianity."

A more recent contribution to the discourse on a feminist hermeneutic comes from a Canadian scholar, Pamela Dickey Young, who assesses the work of theologians such as Fiorenza, Russell, and Ruether in her book *Feminist Theology/Christian Theology In Search of Method* (1990). She offers her own criteria concerning the place of Christian tradition, biblical authority, and women's experience as source and norm of theology.

A few of the many non-English publications on feminist liberation theology have been translated into English, including one by German feminist scholar Luise Schottroff. Using a social-historical method, she has written a stimulating set of essays titled *Let the Oppressed Go Free* (1991), addressing perspective on the New Testament.

Perhaps the most valuable contribution to the 1990s is *The Women's Bible Commentary*, which seeks out all the women found in Scripture. This is a collection of writing that takes seriously how biblical texts portray the experiences and lives of women in Jewish and Christian communities. The authors not only expose the androcentric bias of the original writer, but they also present how women's perspective influences the interpretation of biblical text.

Voices of Women from Asia, Africa, and Other Third World Countries

In the introduction to a book with the compelling title *Let the Weak Be Strong: A Woman's Struggle for Justice*, by Cho Wha Soon (1988), Letty Russell wrote, "The only way to have my perspective opened to new horizons is to open myself to the suffering and pain of my sisters in the Third World" (p. 2). Gradually, the voices of feminist theologians from countries other than North America are being heard on this continent through their books and articles. Marianne Katoppo's *Compassionate and Free* (1979) was one of the first such voices to be heard in America. In the opening pages, Marianne Katoppo asks the question, "Why is it so difficult to concede that Asian women may have their own insights to contribute to the richness of Asian theology?" (p. 7). She follows with this challenging poem:

> I am—You are
> I am free—You are free
> But—where I am, what I am, You cannot be
> Where you are, what you are, I cannot be
> Am I encroaching on your freedom?
> Are you intruding on mine?
> Have I the right to be what I am?
> Can we be fully human: You and I,
> each in our own way?

Throughout the book, Katoppo draws on the Bible and the contemporary reality of life for women in Asia to develop Asian women's theology.

In 1986, the World Council of Churches published two valuable books. The first, *New Eyes for Reading*, edited by John Pobee and Bärbel von Wartenberg-Potter (1986), gathers together biblical and theological reflections by women from Africa, Asia, and Latin America. The second is a startling account of women's struggle for justice in Namibia, Caroline Allison's *It's Like Holding the Key to Your Own Jail* (1986). In the chapter "The Work of the Churches," Allison speaks of the role of the church in a country that is embroiled in a revolution:

> Over ninety percent of the Namibia population are church-going Christians. Because of their unwavering support for the national liberation struggle and their commitment to true independence, the black church of Namibia, organized under the umbrella of the CCN, have suffered violent abuse at the hands of the military. (P. 42)

Another major contribution toward the development of global feminist liberation theology was the book edited jointly by Letty Russell, Kwok Pui-lan, Ada María Isasi-Díaz, and Katie Geneva Cannon (1988). This personal history and perspective of African, Asian, Anglo-American, and Latin American women is titled *Inheriting Our Mothers' Gardens: Feminist Theology in Third World Perspective* (1988). Each story is an account of how women recognize the gifts and the shortcomings of their inheritance from their mothers.

Yet another outstanding collection of original essays from Third World Protestant and Catholic women is *With Passion and Compassion: Third World Women Doing Theology*, by Virginia Fabella and Mercy Amba Oduyoye (1989), which covers a range of topics, including new insights into the Bible, Christology, and spirituality.

A significant challenge to traditional theology and the churches emerged from an Asian woman, Chung Hyun Kyung, a professor of systematic theology at Ewha Women's University, Seoul, Korea, who takes the everyday, concrete life experience as source for building religious meaning in *Struggle to Be the Sun Again* (1990). Susan Brooks Thistlethwaite and Mary Potter Engel have co-edited a textbook called *Lift Every Voice: Constructing Christian Theologies from the Underside* (1990). This is clearly a breakthrough, because it not only brings together voices—black, Hispanic, feminist, Latin American, and others from around the world—but it also makes available, in one volume, the insights and perspectives of many oppressed peoples undertaking the serious task of developing theologies of liberation. It is powerful text because it re-envisions Christian theology from the perspective of oppressed people.

Womanist Voices

A new development in feminist liberation theology in the late 1980s was the challenge to white feminist perspective by womanist scholars. *Womanist* is a term used by Alice Walker in *Making Face, Making Soul* (1990, 370), referring to a woman-of-color feminist. As Judith Plaskow and Carol Christ point out in the introduction of their book *Weaving the Visions: New Patterns in Feminist Spirituality* (1989), "women's experience" had too often meant "white, middle-class women's experience," in just the way that "human" too often means "men."

Two womanist scholars, Katie Cannon and Delores Williams, began to introduce womanists' concerns. "The Emergence of Black Feminist Consciousness," by Cannon, was included in the *Feminist Interpretation of the Bible*, edited by Letty Russell (1985), and Delores Williams's "Womanist Theology: Black Women's Voices" was included in *Christianity and Crisis* (1987). In 1989, both scholars contributed essays to the recent book *Weaving the Visions New Patterns in Feminist Spirituality*, edited by Plaskow and Christ (1989), which combines the diverse and complex experience of women and spirituality.

In 1989, Jacquelyn Grant published her thesis, "White Women's Christ and Black Women's Jesus," in which she sets out the limitations of feminist liberation theology this way:

> Feminist theologians are white in terms of their race and in terms of the *nature of the sources* they use for the development of their theological perspectives. Although there are sharp differences among feminist theologians . . . they are *all* the *same* race and the influence of their race has led them to similar sources for the definition of their perspective on the faith. Of course, chief among the sources is women's experience. . . . White women's experience and black women's experience are not the same. (P. 193)

In 1993, Delores Williams published *Sisters in the Wilderness: The Challenge of Womanist God-Talk*, in which she describes the slavery experience of black women whose lives, like Hagar's, are focused on survival, not liberation.

In 1988, Renita J. Weems published *Just a Sister Away—A Womanist Vision of Women's Relationships in the Bible*. We have become accustomed to stories about the relationships between Naomi and Ruth, or Elizabeth and "the Blessed Virgin" Mary. Stories about Lot's wife and her daughters, or Jephthah's daughter and the "mourning woman" are less familiar. What is new is the way Weems interprets the relationships between the women. She uses the best of feminist biblical criticism and the best of African-American oral tradition to reclaim and reconstruct the stories. Questions for discussion at the end of each chapter are another valuable feature of this book.

The end of the 1980s saw the beginning of the critique of white Christian feminists' racism emerging in the literature. In *Sex, Race and God*, Susan Thistlethwaite (1989), influenced by Audre Lord's work, set about to answer these questions:

> What happens to white feminism if we begin to give up *all* the master's tools and not just some? What happens when the differences between black women and white women become the starting point for white feminist theology? (P. 2)

Thistlethwaite places before us superb insights as one woman reckons with her own whiteness.

Christology—The Meaning of Jesus

The meaning of Jesus is yet another crucial topic explored by feminist liberation theologians. Rosemary Radford Ruether dealt with this theme as early as the 1970s, when she published "The Messianic Code" in *Commonweal, A Review of Public Affairs, Religion, Literature, and the Arts* (1970). Later she wrote an occasional paper for the United Methodist Church titled *Christology and Feminism: Can a Male Savior Help Women?* (1976), and she published a series of lectures under the title *To Change the World, Christology and Cultural Criticism* (1981). In her book, *Sexism and God-Talk: Towards A Feminist Theology* (1983), she has a major section dealing with the question "Can a male Saviour save women?" Ruether traces the evolution of the understanding of the Messiah. She looks at the ancient near-Eastern roots, the Hebraic prophetic thought, and Jesus' own interpretation of the tradition of a coming Reign of God. She reminds us:

> The transformation of Christian reflection on Jesus into orthodox Christology takes place over the five centuries during which the Christian church itself is transformed from a marginal sect within the messianic renewal movement of

first-century Judaism into the new imperial religion of a Christian Roman Empire. (P. 123)

Ruether does not cast Jesus aside; on the contrary, she affirms the person of Jesus of Nazareth as a positive model of redemptive humanity. Nonetheless, she raises serious questions that make reading her work disturbing and rewarding.

Rosemary Radford Ruether plainly has made an enormous contribution to the field of feminist liberation theology. In 1988, Mary Hembrow Snyder published her useful thesis *The Christology of Rosemary Radford Ruether: A Critical Introduction* (1988). While this volume traces the Christology of Ruether, it also introduces the reader to the implications of her theology for ecumenism, spirituality, salvation, theological method, and the church's self-understanding.

In 1994, Ellen K. Wondra published her thesis, *Humanity Has Been a Holy Thing*. This book brings together the contemporary discussion on feminist methodology, and poses criteria for an adequate feminist Christology.

In most recent times, the Christological debate has included imaging the crucified woman. Just such an image resides on the grounds of Emmanuel Theological College, Toronto. This powerful and distressing sculpture has caused enormous controversy; its story is told by Doris Dyke in *Crucified Woman* (1991).

Books are being written now with the purpose of transmitting this new scholarship to children. Lois Wilson, the first woman Moderator of the United Church of Canada, has provided two such resources. The first, *Miriam, Mary and Me: Women in the Bible, Stories Retold for Children and Adults* (1991), draws on Wilson's global experience to open up the world to children. The second, *Telling Her Story: Theology out of Women's Struggles* (1992), is a small companion book that serves as a tool for teachers, parents, and all who need to tell stories to those who come after us.

Several other authors have also been raising questions and challenges about the Christian interpretation of Jesus the Christ, and they have come to other conclusions. See for instance: Marjorie Suchocki's *God, Christ, Church* (1982); Patricia Wilson-Kastner's *Faith, Feminism and the Christ* (1983); Sharon Ringe's *Jesus, Liberation, and the Biblical Jubilee Images for Ethics and Christology* (1985); Rita Brock's *Journeys by Heart* (1988); Isabel Heyward's *Speaking of Christ* (1989); and Mary Grey's *Feminism, Redemption and the Christian Tradition* (1990).

Feminist Ethics

In 1985, a one-volume collection containing many of the works written by Beverly Wildung Harrison during the 1970s and 1980s was published. The cover of *Making the Connections: Essays in Feminist Social Ethics* (1985) makes a very clear statement about why feminist liberation theologians want to formulate new ethical theory.

During the past thirty years, ethical theory has become increasingly abstract and removed from everyday life. This is certainly so in Anglo-American ethics, where analytic preoccupations with the logic of ethical language have reinforced earlier abstractionism. (Jacket Cover)

Beverly Wildung Harrison develops a feminist ethic that addresses the everyday life of women and men. Such issues as "The Effect of Industrialization on the Role of Women in Society," "Sexuality and Social Policy," "Theology and Morality of Procreative Choice," and "Misogyny and Homophobia" are discussed in this superb collection of essays.

Prior to Harrison's publication, the literature in this area was largely confined to articles. Early discourse explored the nature or method of actually doing ethics with a feminist liberation vision— Eleanor Haney's "What Is Feminist Ethics?" (1980); Carol Robb's "A Framework for Feminist Ethics" (1981); and Mary Elizabeth Hunt's "Transforming Moral Theology" (1986). Margaret Farley set out some of the issues for theological schools when she began her article "Feminist Ethics in the Christian Ethics Curriculum" (1984) by stating:

The incorporation of feminist issues and feminist methods and sources into a Christian ethics curriculum is at once a simple and complex enterprise. It is simple because a feminist approach to ethics can be made explicit at almost every juncture in the curriculum. It is complex because feminist ethics is, like most other general approaches to ethics, pluralistic. (P. 361)

By the late 1980s, there was a whole range of articles written on all kinds of ethical issues, such as work (Katie Cannon's "Emergence of Black Feminist Consciousness" [1985]); sexual ethics, marriage, and divorce (Lis Cahill's "Sexual Ethics, Marriage and Divorce" [1986]); abortion (Mary Kenny's "Abortion" [1986]); reproductive choice (Virginia Mollenkott's "Reproductive Choice" [1988]); clergy and sexual abuse in counseling (Mary Pellauer's "Sex, Power, and the Family of God" [1987]); and sex and power (Carole Pateman's "Sex and Power" [1990]). Feminists were making a major contribution to the study of ethics. In 1986, Elizabeth Bettenhausen addressed the Annual of the Society of Christian Ethics with her outstanding paper, "The Concept of Justice and a Feminist Lutheran Social Ethic."

Karen Lebacqz's *Professional Ethics: Power and Paradox* (1985) is an extraordinary contribution to the dialogue about how power functions within relationships between professionals and those who seek support or counsel. She exposes the significance of the existence of issues such as confidentiality and privilege and provides helpful insights that can provide guidelines to a professional relationship.

A pioneering reader in feminist ethics, designed for undergraduate courses as well as seminary or graduate-level courses, was published in 1985. *Women's Consciousness, Women's Conscience* by Barbara Adolsen, Christine Gudorf, and Mary Pellauer contains contributions from black, Hispanic, and Jewish women, as well as studies by radical and mainstream Christians, Jews, and post-Christians. One of the intriguing papers is that of Starhawk, a well-known scholar of the Goddess Religion. Her paper, entitled "Ethics and Justice in Goddess Religion" (1985), explores and clarifies "the ethics and morality inherent in a worldview centered on immanent divinity found within nature, human beings, and the world" (p. 193). She suggests that, regardless of whether or not a religion of the Great Goddess existed in prehistoric times, there is one today. Whether or not women actually ruled in matriarchies cannot be proven, but they are taking power today. Whether or not witchcraft, as practiced today, has its roots in the Stone Age, is not the issue; what is important is that the branches of the religion of the Great Goddess reach into the future.

Another useful teaching resource is *Embodied Love Sensuality and Relationship As Feminist Values*, by Paula Cooey, Sharon Farmer, and Mary Ellen Ross (1987), a collection of writings that focuses on the infinite number of ways in which "the embodiment and the material realm impoverishes, for both men and women, our ethical values, our ability to relate, and our ability to communicate" (p. 2). In the introduction, Sharon Farmer states:

> The assumption that women are more embodied, more tied to our bodies, than are men, begins with the fact that we are physically different from men: that we menstruate, lactate, and bear children. These physical differences have served as primary reasons, in the Jewish and Christian traditions, for women's exclusion from the priesthood and from ritual functions. (Pp. 1–2)

This book is another example of a collaborative work by a whole generation of new thinkers with diverse backgrounds and unique contributions.

Isabel Carter Heyward, one of the first women priests in the Episcopal Church, U.S.A., and professor of Theology at Episcopal Divinity School, has written numerous compelling books. Outstanding among them are two concerning ethics: *Our Passion for Justice: Images of Power, Sexuality, and Liberation* (1984), which is a collection of her essays, sermons, lectures, and liturgical poetry spanning a six-year period, and *Touching Our Strength: The Erotic As Power and the Love of God* (1989). The latter work, as the author states,

> is not about either sex or God as these terms have denoted particular traditional points of reference: to male and female reproductive/pleasure organs and their manipulation, or to an anthropomorphic deity to whom we ascribe absolute power. It is about sex and God as we are able to re-image both as empowering sparks of ourselves in relation. (P. 3)

Sharon D. Welch has drawn from African-American women's litera-ture for her insightful work *A Feminist Ethic of Risk* (1990). Focusing on the everyday life and the wider society, Welch examines what it means to work for social transformation in the face of seemingly insurmountable suffering and evil, and our own sense of despair over defeats. This book provides hope as it develops a clear analysis and offers new paths for the white middle-class to stand in solidarity with others.

A new contribution to the theological ethics comes with the publi-cation of Marilyn Legge's thesis *The Grace of Difference: A Canadian Feminist Theological Ethic* (1992). This is a study of immense impor-tance, as it explores questions of economic justice in the day-to-day realities of Canadian women. Three Canadian novels, *In Search of April Raintree*, *The Diviners*, and *Obasan* serve as the voice of women's experience as they explore women's experience for its theological and ethnic dimensions.

Other items in the references that address the field of feminist ethics include Katie Cannon's "Resources for a Constructive Ethic in the Life and Work of Zora Neale Hurston" (1985); Beverly Harrison's *Our Right to Choose* (1985); Susan Parsons's "The Intersection of Feminism and Theological Ethics" (1988); Ether Bruland's "Evangelical and Feminist Ethics" (1989); and Lois Daly's *Feminist Theological Ethics* (1994).

Theological Education

"Is Theological Education Good for Any Woman's Health?" is the title of a pointed article in *Newsletter of the Center for Women and Religion,* co-authored by Beverly Wildung Harrison with Robert Martin (1978). The article looks at the issue of women and theological educa-tion. During the past twenty years, there has been a radical increase in the number of women entering theological school. On many cam-puses, women make up at least 50 percent of the student body, and in some instances, as much as 80 percent. With this influx of women, theological education has been tested, critiqued, and challenged in its treatment of women and women's issues.

Women's experience in theological schools has sometimes been the catalyst for feminist consciousness. In some instances, women do not feel welcome in seminaries. There is often an absence of women authors in curricula, or a dearth of women professors. The language of community worship is often non-inclusive, and women are invisible in readings (see Pamela Milne's "Women and Words" [1989]). There may be an underlying assumption that, although women are involved in theologi-cal studies, they will probably not make professional use of this knowl-edge, and as a consequence, they can have difficulty finding employment once they graduate.

As more women entered the theological education system, they began to write about the experience of going back to school (see Marna McKenzie's "Going Back to Seminary" [1972] and Margaret Maxey's

"To Catholic Women Contemplating Theological Education" [1972]); life as a lesbian student (see Anne Gilson's "Therefore Choose Life" [1985]); the experience of being a women in field education (see Arabella Meadow-Rogers's "Women in Field Education" [1975]); and of being supervised by male clergy (see Marilyn Mayse and Paula Teague's "Women Supervised by Men" [1987]).

Several doctoral theses and articles written on the experience of women in theological education are listed in the references: Carol Bohn's "Women in Theological Education" (1981); Maryanne Confoy's "Women and Theological Education" (1983); Christa Klein's "Women's Concerns in Theological Education" (1985); Mary Boys's "Women As Leaven" (1986); and Shelley Finson's "On the Other Side of Silence" (1986).

In the 1980s, two volumes were published that specifically addressed issues raised by the presence of women in theological education. The first, the Cornwall Collective's *Your Daughters Shall Prophesy: Feminist Alternatives in Theological Education* (1980), begins with this statement:

> From storefront churches to the Vatican, feminists are chal-
> lenging the institutions of patriarchal religion. We recognize
> that the church has played (and plays) an enormous role in the
> creation and maintenance of a sexist society—not only in the
> obvious sexism of worship and of Sunday school, but in the
> structures and process of theological education. (P. 1)

Chapters in this volume include "Constituency: What We Learn Is Shaped by Those with Whom We Learn"; "Racism and the Responsibility of White Women in Theological Education"; "Marginality, Alternative Structures, and Leadership Styles"; and "Power and Institutional Change." Besides discussing women's experience of theological education, the Collective has included some feminist alternative models of doing theological education. Three of these are the Seminary Quarter at Grailville, Ohio; Black Women in Ministry Boston Theological Institute, and the Center for Women and Religion of the Graduate Theological Union, California. These models have motivated some theological schools to reexamine their model of theological education.

The second volume to address issues of women's theological education is *God's Fierce Whimsy: Christian Feminism and Theological Education* by the Mudflower Collective (1985). This was a research project of seven women—black, Hispanic, and white Christians—all of whom were involved in theological education as educators and learners. This is a disturbing and remarkably inspiring book, as women of such diversity show what theological education can be and, from a feminist point of view, must be if Christians are truly interested in human well-being and in knowing how to serve the common good.

References on Theology

Adolsen, Barbara Hilkert, Christine E. Gudorf, and Mary D. Pellauer. eds. *Women's Consciousness, Women's Conscience: A Reading in Feminist Ethics*. Minneapolis, MN: Seabury Books, 1985.

Allison, Caroline. *It's Like Holding the Key to Your Own Jail: Women in Namibia*. Geneva: World Council of Churches, 1986.

Bennet, Anne McGrew. *From Woman-Pain to Woman-Vision: Writing in Feminist Theology*. Edited by Mary E. Hunt. Minneapolis, MN: Augsburg Fortress, 1989.

Bettenhausen, Elizabeth. "The Concept of Justice and a Feminist Lutheran Social Ethic." In *Annual of the Society of Christian Ethics*. Dallas, TX: Society of Christian Ethics, 1986- .

Birnbaum, Lucia Chiavola. *Black Madonnas: Feminism, Religion, and Politics in Italy*. Boston: Northeastern University, 1993.

Bohn, Carol R. "Women in Theological Education: Realities and Implication." Ed.D. diss., Boston University School of Education, 1981.

Borrensen, Kari Elisabeth. "God's Image, Man's Image? Female Metaphors Describing God in the Christian Tradition." *Temenos: Studies in Comparative Religion Presented by Scholars in Denmark, Finland, Norway and Sweden* 19 (1983): 17–32.

Boys, Mary C. "Women As Leaven: Theological Education in the United States and Canada." In *Christianity Among World Religions (Concilium 183)*, edited by Hans Küng and Jürgen Moltmann. Edinburgh, Scotland: T. & T. Clark, 1986.

Brock, Rita Nakashima. *Journeys by Heart: A Christology of Erotic Power*. New York: Crossroad, 1988.

Bruland, Ether Byle. "Evangelical and Feminist Ethics: Complex Solidarities." *Journal of Religious Ethics* 17 (Fall 1989): 139–60.

Cahill, Lis Sowle. "Sexual Ethics, Marriage and Divorce." *Theological Studies* 47, no. 1 (March 1986): 102–17.

Cannon, Katie Geneva. "Emergence of Black Feminist Consciousness." In *Feminist Interpretation of the Bible*, edited by Letty M. Russell. Philadelphia: Westminster, 1985.

———. "Moral Wisdom in the Black Women's Literary Tradition." In *Weaving the Visions: New Patterns in Feminist Spirituality*, edited by Judith Plaskow and Carol Christ. New York: Harper & Row, 1989.

————. "Resources for a Constructive Ethic in the Life and Work of Zora Neale Hurston." *Journal of Feminist Studies in Religion* 1, no. 1 (Spring 1985): 37–51.

Carr, Anne E. *Transforming Grace: Christian Tradition and Women's Experience.* San Francisco: Harper & Row, 1988.

Carr, Anne, and Elisabeth Schüssler Fiorenza, eds. *Motherhood: Experience, Institution, Theology.* (Concilium, Religion in the Eighties 206). Edinburgh, Scotland: T. & T. Clark, 1989.

Chinnici, Rosemary. *Can Women Re-Image the Church?* New York: Paulist Press, 1992.

Collins, Adela Yarbo, ed. *Feminist Perspectives on Biblical Scholarship.* Atlanta, GA: Scholars, 1985.

Confoy, Maryanne. "Women and Theological Education." *Lutheran Theological Journal* 17 (August 1983): 14–18.

Cooey, Paula M., Sharon A. Farmer, and Mary Ellen Ross. *Embodied Love: Sensuality and Relationship as Feminist Values.* New York: Harper & Row, 1987.

Cornwall Collective. *Your Daughters Shall Prophesy: Feminist Alternatives in Theological Education.* New York: Pilgrim, 1980.

Culleton, Beatrice. *In Search of April Raintree.* Winnipeg: Pemmican, 1983.

Cunneen, Sally. "Mother Church, Mother World, Mother God." *Cross Currents: A Quarterly Review to Explore the Implications of Our Times* 37, nos. 2–3 (Summer–Fall 1987): 129–39.

Daly, Lois K., ed. *Feminist Theological Ethics: A Reader.* Louisville, KY: Westminster/John Knox, 1994.

Daly, Mary. *Beyond God the Father: Toward a Philosophy of Women's Liberation.* Boston: Beacon, 1973.

————. *The Church and the Second Sex.* New York: Harper & Row, 1968.

Douglass, Jane Dempsey. *Women, Freedom and Calvin.* Philadelphia: Westminster, 1985.

Drorah, Setal E. "Feminist Insights and the Question of Method." In *Feminist Perspectives on Biblical Scholarship,* edited by Adela Yarbo Collins. Atlanta, GA: Scholar, 1985.

Dumais, Monique. *Diversité des Utilsations Féministes du Concept Experiences des Femmes en Sciences Religieuses.* No. 32. Ottawa: I.C.R.E.F/C.R.I.A.W., 1993.

Dyke, Doris J. *Crucifies Woman*. Toronto: United Church, 1991.

Edwards, James R. "Does God Really Want to Be Called Father?" *Christianity Today* 30, no. 3, (February 21, 1986): 27–30.

Elwes, Teresa, ed. *Women's Voices: Essays in Contemporary Feminist Theology*. London: Marshall Pickering, 1992.

Exum, Cheryl J. "The Mothers of Israel: The Patriarchal Narratives from a Feminist Perspective." *Bible Review* 11, no. 1 (Spring 1986): 60–67.

Fabella, Virginia, and Mercy Amba Oduyoye, eds. *With Passion and Compassion: Third World Women Doing Theology*. New York: Orbis Books, 1989.

Farley, Margaret Ann. "Feminist Ethics in the Christian Ethics Curriculum." *Horizons: The Journal of the College Theology Society* 11 (Fall 1984): 361–72.

Finson, Shelley Davis. "On the Other Side of Silence: Patriarchy, Consciousness and Spirituality—Some Women's Experience of Theological Education." D.Min. diss., Boston University School of Theology, 1986.

Fiorenza, Elisabeth Schüssler. *Bread Not Stone: The Challenge of Feminist Biblical Interpretation*. Boston: Beacon, 1984.

———. *But She Said: Feminist Practitioners of Biblical Interpretation*. Boston: Beacon, 1992.

———. *Discipleship of Equals: A Critical Feminist Ekklesia-logy of Liberation*. New York: Crossroads, 1993.

———. *In Memory of Her: A Feminist Reconstruction of Christian Origins*. New York: Crossroad, 1983.

———. "The Will to Choose or to Reject: Continuing Our Critical Work." In *Feminist Interpretation of the Bible*, edited by Letty M. Russell. Philadelphia: Westminster, 1985.

———. "Women in the New Testament." *New Catholic World* 219 (November–December 1976): 256–60.

———. "Women in the Pre-Pauline and Pauline Churches." *Union Seminary Quarterly Review* 33, no. 3 (Spring 1978): 153–66.

Froehle, Virginia Ann. *In Her Presence: Prayer Experiences Exploring Feminine Images of God*. Cincinnati, OH: St. Anthony Messenger, 1987.

Grey, Mary C. *Feminism, Redemption and the Christian Tradition.* Mystic, CT: Twenty-Third, 1990.

Gilson, Anne. "Therefore Choose Life [Lesbian Seminarian Personal Statement]." *Witness* 68, no. 9 (September 1985): 22.

Grant, Jacquelyn. "White Women's Christ and Black Women's Jesus: Feminist Christology and Womanist Response." (American Academy of Religion Series, no. 64). Edited by Susan Thistlethwaite. Atlanta, GA: Scholars Press, 1989.

Hampson, Margaret Daphne. *Theology & Feminism.* Oxford, England: Blackwell, 1990.

Haney, Eleanor Humes. "What Is Feminist Ethics?" *Journal of Religious Ethics* 8, no. 1 (Spring 1980): 115–24.

Harrison, Beverly Wildung. *Our Right to Choose: Toward a New Ethic of Abortion.* Boston: Beacon, 1985.

———. *Making the Connections: Essays in Feminist Social Ethics.* Edited by Carol Robb. Boston: Beacon, 1985.

Harrison, Beverly Wildung, and Robert Martin Jr. "Is Theological Education Good for Any Woman's Health?" *Center for Women and Religion Newsletter* 4 (Winter 1978): 6–10.

Heine, Susanne. *Matriarchs, Goddesses, and Images of God: A Critique of Feminist Theology.* Translated by John Bowden. Minneapolis, MN: Augsburg Fortress, 1989.

Heyward, Isabel Carter. *Our Passion for Justice: Images of Power, Sexuality, and Liberation.* New York: Pilgrim, 1984.

———. *The Redemption of God: A Theology of Mutual Relation.* Lanham, MD: University Press of America, 1982.

———. *Speaking of Christ: A Lesbian Feminist Voice.* Edited by Ellen C. Davis. New York: Pilgrim, 1989.

———. *Touching Our Strength: The Erotic As Power and the Love of God.* San Francisco: Harper & Row, 1989.

Hunt, Mary Elizabeth. "Transforming Moral Theology—A Feminist Ethical Challenge." In *Christianity Among World Religions (Concilium 183)*, edited by Hans Küng and Jürgen Moltmann. Edinburgh, Scotland: T. & T. Clark, 1986.

Johnson, Elizabeth A. "The Incomprehensibility of God and the Image of God, Male and Female." *Theological Studies* 45, no. 3 (September 1984): 441–65.

———. *She Who Is: The Mystery of God in Feminist Discourse*. New York: Crossroad, 1993.

Katoppo, Marianne. *Compassionate and Free: An Asian Woman's Theology*. New York: Maryknoll, 1979.

Kenny, Mary. "Abortion: What the Female Philosophers Say." *Grail: An Ecumenical Journal* 2, no. 1 (March 1986): 23–42.

King, Ursula. *Feminist Theology from the Third World: A Reader*. Maryknoll, NY: Orbis Books, 1994.

Klein, Christa Ressmeyer. "Women's Concerns in Theological Education." *Dialog: A Journal of Theology* 24, no. 1 (Winter 1985): 25–31.

Koqawa, Joy. *Obasan*. Toronto: Lester & Orpen Dennys, 1981.

Kyung, Chung Hyun. *Struggle to Be the Sun Again: Introducing Asian Women's Theology*. New York: Orbis Books, 1990.

LaCugna, Catherine Mowry. *Feminist Theology: The Essentials of Theology in Feminist Perspective*. San Francisco: Harper & Row, 1993.

Laffey, Alice L. *An Introduction to the Old Testament: A Feminist Perspective*. Philadelphia: Fortress Press, 1988.

Lawrence, Margaret. *The Diviners*. Toronto: McClelland and Stewart, 1974.

Lebacqz, Karen. *Professional Ethics: Power and Paradox*. Nashville, TN: Abingdon, 1985.

Legge, Marilyn J. *The Grace of Difference: A Canadian Feminist Theology Ethic*. (American Academy of Religion series, no. 80). Edited by Susan Thistlethwaite. Atlanta, GA: Scholars, 1992.

Lewis, Alen E., ed. *The Motherhood of God*. Edinburgh, Scotland: St. Andrew's, 1984.

Loades, Ann, ed. *Feminist Theology: A Reader*. London: SPCK, 1990.

Long, Grace D. *Passion and Reason: Womenviews of Christian Life*. Louisville, KY: Westminster/John Knox, 1993.

Maxey, Margaret N. "To Catholic Women Contemplating Theological Education: Quo Vadis?" *Theological Education* 8, no. 4 (Summer 1972): 260–68.

Mayse, Marilyn, and Paula Jeanne Teague. "Women Supervised by Men." *Journal of Supervision and Training in Ministry* 9 (1987): 35–41.

McFague, Sallie. *Metaphorical Theology: Models of God in Religious Language*. Philadelphia: Fortress Press, 1982.

McKenzie, Marna. "Going Back to Seminary: An Old Wife's Tale." *Theological Education* 8, no. 4 (Summer 1972): 257–59.

Meadow-Rogers, Arabella. "Women in Field Education: Some New Answers to Old Questions." *Theological Education* 11, no. 2 (Summer 1975): 301–7.

Mickelsen, Alver, ed. *Women, Authority, and the Bible*. Downers Grove, IL: InterVarsity, 1986.

Micks, Marianne H. *Our Search for Identity: Humanity in the Image of God*. Philadelphia: Fortress Press, 1982.

Milne, Paula. "Eve and Adam: Is a Feminist Reading Possible?" *Bible Review* 4, no. 3 (June 1988): 12–22.

———. "Women and Words: The Use of Non-Sexist, Inclusive Language in the Academy." *Studies in Religion / Sciences Religiuses* 18, no. 1 (1989): 25–35.

Mollenkott, Virginia Ramey. "Reproductive Choice: Basic to Justice for Women." *Christian Scholar's Review* 17, no. 3 (1988): 286–93.

Moltmann-Wendel, Elisabeth. *A Land Flowing with Milk and Honey: Perspectives on Feminist Theology*. New York: Crossroad, 1986.

Moltmann-Wendel, Elisabeth, and Jürgen Moltmann. *God—His and Hers*. New York: Crossroad, 1991.

———. *Humanity in God*. New York: Pilgrim, 1983.

Mud Flower Collective. *The God's Fierce Whimsy: Christian Feminism and Theological Education*. New York: Pilgrim, 1985.

Newsom, Carol A., and Sharon H. Ringe, eds. *The Women's Bible Commentary*. Louisville, KY: Westminster/John Knox, 1992.

Oddie, William. *What Will to God? Feminism and the Reconstruction of Christian Belief*. London: SPCK, 1984.

Oduyoye, Amba, and Musimbi R. A. Kanyoro, eds. *The Will to Arise: Women, Tradition and the Church of Africa*. New York: Orbis, 1992.

Osiek, Carolyn. "The Feminist and the Bible: Hermeneutical Alternatives." *Religion and Intellectual Life* 6 (Spring–Summer 1989): 96–109.

Parsons, Susan F. "The Intersection of Feminism and Theological Ethics: A Philosophical Approach." *Modern Theology: A Quarterly*

Journal of Systematic and Philosophical Theology 4, no. 3 (April 1988): 251–66.

Pateman, Carole. "Sex and Power." *Ethics: An International Journal of Social, Political and Legal Philosophy* 100 (January 1990): 398–407.

Pellauer, Mary D. "Sex, Power, and the Family of God: Clergy and Sexual Abuse in Counselling." *Christianity and Crisis: A Christian Journal of Opinion* 47, no. 2 (February 16, 1987): 47–50.

Plaskow, Judith, and Carol Christ, eds. *Weaving the Visions: New Patterns in Feminist Spirituality*. San Francisco: Harper & Row, 1989.

Pobee, John S., and Bärbel von Wartenberg-Potter, eds. *New Eyes for Reading Biblical and Theological Reflections by Women from the Third World*. Geneva: World Council of Churches, 1986.

Ringe, Sharon H. *Jesus, Liberation, and the Biblical Jubilee Images for Ethics and Christology*. Philadelphia: Fortress Press, 1985.

Robb, Carol S. "A Framework for Feminist Ethics." *Journal of Religious Ethics* 8, no. 1 (Spring 1981): 48–68.

Rosenblatt, Marie-Eloise, ed. *Where Can We Find Her? Searching for Woman's Identity in the New Church*. New York: Paulist Press, 1991.

Ruether, Rosemary Radford. *To Change the World: Christology and Cultural Criticism*. London: SCM, 1981.

———. "Christology and Feminism: Can a Male Savior Help Women?" United Methodist Board of Higher Education and Ministry, Occasional Paper 1. Nashville, TN: United Methodist Center, 1976.

———. "The Messianic Code." *Commonweal* 91 (January 16, 1970): 423–25.

———, ed. *Religion and Sexism Images of Women in the Jewish and Christian Traditions*. New York: Simon & Schuster, 1974.

———. *Sexism and God-Talk: Toward a Feminist Theology*. Boston: Beacon, 1983.

Ruether, Rosemary Radford, and Eleanor McLaughlin, eds. *Women of Spirit Female Leadership in Jewish and Christian Traditions*. New York: Simon & Schuster, 1979.

Russell, Letty. *Church in the Round: Feminist Interpretation of the Church*. Louisville, KY: Westminster/John Knox, 1993.

————, ed. *Feminist Interpretation of the Bible*. Philadelphia: Westminster, 1985.

————. *Household of Freedom: Authority in Feminist Theology*. Philadelphia: Westminster, 1987.

————. *The Liberating Word: A Guide to Nonsexist Interpretation of the Bible*. Philadelphia: Westminster, 1976.

Russell, Letty, Kwok Pui-lan, Ada María Isasi-Díaz, and Katie Geneva Cannon, eds. *Inheriting Our Mothers' Gardens: Feminist Theology in Third World Perspective*. Louisville, KY: Westminster, 1988.

Sakenfeld, Katherine. "Old Testament Perspective: Methodological Issues." *Journal for the Study of the Old Testament* 22 (February 1982): 68–71.

Schneiders, Sandra M. "Feminist Ideology Criticism and Biblical Hermeneutics." *Biblical Theology Bulletin* 19 (January 1989): 3–10.

Schottroff, Luise. *Let the Oppressed God Free: Feminist Perspectives on the New Testament*. Translated by Annemair S. Kidder. Louisville, KY: Westminster/John Knox, 1993.

Snyder, Mary Hembrow. *The Christology of Rosemary Radford Ruether: A Critical Introduction*. Mystic, CT: Twenty-Third, 1988.

Soon, Cho Wha. *Let the Weak Be Strong: A Woman's Struggle for Justice*. Bloomington, IN: Meyer Stone, 1988.

Starhawk. "Ethics and Justice in Goddess Religion." In *Women's Consciousness, Women's Conscience: A Reader in Feminist Ethics*, edited by Barbara Adolsen, Christine Gudorf, and Mary Pellauer. Minneapolis, MN: Seabury Books, 1985.

Stevens, Maryanne, ed. *Reconstructing the Christ Symbol: Essays in Feminist Christology*. New York: Paulist Press, 1993.

Suchocki, Marjorie. *God, Christ, Church: A Practical Guide to Process Theology*. New York: Crossroad, 1982.

————. "The Unmale God: Reconsidering the Trinity." *Quarterly Review: A Scholarly Journal for Reflection on Ministry* 3, no. 1 (Spring 1983): 33–49.

Tamaz, Elsa, ed. *Through Her Eyes: Women's Theology from Latin America*. Maryknoll, NY: Orbis, 1989.

Thistlethwaite, Susan Brooks. *Sex, Race and God: Christian Feminism in Black and White*. New York: Crossroad, 1989.

Thistlethwaite, Susan Brooks, and Mary Potter Engel, eds. *Lift Every Voice: Constructing Christian Theologies from the Underside*. San Francisco: Harper & Row, 1990.

Tolbert, Mary Ann, ed. *The Bible and Feminist Hermeneutics*. Chico, CA: Scholars, 1983.

Tribble, Phyllis. "The Bible and Women's Liberation." *Theology Digest* 2, no. 1 (Spring 1974): 32–37.

——. "Depatriarchalizing in Biblical Interpretation." *Journal of American Academy of Religion* 41, no. 1 (March 1973): 30–48.

——. *God and the Rhetoric of Sexuality*. Philadelphia: Fortress Press, 1978.

——. *Texts of Terror: Literary-Feminist Readings of Biblical Narratives*. Overtures to Biblical Theology series, no. 13. Philadelphia: Fortress Press, 1984.

——. "Women in the Old Testament." In *Interpreter's Dictionary of the Bible, Supplementary Volume*. Nashville, TN: Abingdon, 1976.

Van Wijk-Bos, Johanna W. H. *Reformed and Feminist: A Challenge to the Church*. Louisville, KY: Westminster/John Knox, 1991.

Von Wartenberg-Potter, Bärbel. *We Will Not Hang Our Harps on the Willows: Engagement and Spirituality*. Geneva: World Council of Churches, 1987.

Wainwright, Elaine. "In Search of the Lost Coin: Towards a Feminist Biblical Hermeneutic." *Pacifica: Australian Theological Studies* 2 (June 1989): 135–50.

Walker, Alice. *Making Face, Making Soul: Haciendo Caras Creative and Critical Perspectives by Women of Color*. Edited by Gloria Anzaldua. San Francisco: Aunt Lute Foundation Books, 1990.

Weems, Renita J. *Just a Sister Away: A Womanist Vision of Women's Relationships in the Bible*. San Diego, CA: Lura Meida, 1988.

Welch, Sharon D. *A Feminist Ethic of Risk*. Minneapolis, MN: Augsburg Fortress, 1990.

Williams, Delores S. *Sister in the Wilderness: The Challenge of Womanist God-Talk*. Maryknoll, NY: Orbis Books, 1993.

——. "Womanist Theology." In *Weaving the Visions: New Patterns in Feminist Spirituality*, edited by Judith Plaskow and Carol Christ. New York: Harper & Row, 1989.

——. "Womanist Theology: Black Women's Voices." *Christianity and Crisis: A Christian Journal of Opinion* 47, no. 3 (March 2, 1987): 66–70.

Wilson, Miliam Lois. *Miriam, Mary and Me: Women in the Bible, Stories Retold for Children and Adults.* Winnipeg, Manitoba: Hignell, 1991.

——. *Telling Her Story: Theology out of Women's Struggles.* The McGeachy Papers, vol. 4. Toronto: United Church, 1992.

Wilson-Kastner, Patricia. *Faith, Feminism and the Christ.* Philadelphia: Fortress, 1983.

Wondra, Ellen K. *Humanity Has Been a Holy Thing: Towards a Contemporary Feminist Christology.* Lanham, MD: University Press of America, 1994.

Young, Pamela Dickey. *Feminist Theology / Christian Theology in Search of Method.* Minneapolis, MN: Fortress, 1990.

Biblical Themes and
Feminist Liberation Theology

In the 1970s, many feminist voices questioned whether Scripture any longer held authority for women. They asked: "Is the Bible hopelessly sexist? How can so many stories of abuse of women be 'good news' for women?"

Long before 1970, however, in the late nineteenth century, a feisty woman with roots in the old-school Presbyterian Church, Elizabeth Cady Stanton, wrote the following in *The Women's Bible* (1898):

> I have long heard so many conflicting opinions about the Bible—some saying it taught woman's emancipation and some her subjection . . . the thought came to me that it would be well to collect every biblical reference to women in one small compact volume, and see on which side the balance of influence really was. (Pp. 389–90)

Cady Stanton organized a committee of thirty women scholars "for a thorough revision of the Old and New Testament, and to ascertain what the status of woman really was under the Jewish and Christian religion" (p. 390). The women who formed the "revising committee" were from the United States and England, and had competency in Latin, Greek, and Hebrew. Their task was to illustrate how the Bible was used as a means of justifying women's subordination to men through divine sanction. Their motivation grew out of their own struggle for women's suffrage, and the recognition that their cause was being hindered by the claims of clergy who justified their resistance to women's rights by quoting the Bible. In 1898, the committee published *The Woman's Bible,* and it was republished in 1974. In the introduction, Cady Stanton wrote, "The canon law, the Scriptures, the creeds and codes and church discipline of the leading religions bear the impress of fallible man" (p. 13).

The foresight of these women continues today as women within the Christian tradition respond to the influence of the movement for Christian feminism.

In the 1970s, several very readable publications addressed the question of how to study, teach, and interpret the Bible from the standpoint of women. Two books from the evangelical biblical viewpoint are Letha Scanzoni and Nancy Hardesty's *All We're Meant to Be: Biblical Feminism for Today* (1974), and Virginia Ramey Mollenkott's *Women, Men and the Bible* (1977). *All We're Meant to Be*, written for church study groups and women's groups, raises critical questions about the interpretation of contentious biblical passages related to Christian anthropology. What does it mean to be created female and male? What does it mean to be created in the likeness of God? How are men and women to relate to each other? *Women, Men and the Bible*, also directed at the local congregation, includes two tapes and a study guide. This very clear book addresses such themes as, "Is God masculine?"; freedom from stereotypes; interpreting the Bible; and doctrines and human equality.

Later, several volumes explored the lives of women in the Bible, and the relationship of women to Jesus. Writers such as Alicia Craig Faxon in *Women and Jesus* (1973), Rachel Conrad Wahlberg in *Jesus According to a Woman* (1975), and *Jesus and the Freed Women* (1978), and Leonard Swidler in *Biblical Affirmation of Woman* (1979) interpreted the stories from the point of view of the women in the stories, and from the point of view of women as readers. All of these books bring a new perspective to the importance of women's contributions to the nascent Christian community.

For many, a relationship to Mary, the Mother of Jesus, has been pivotal to their faith, and yet this relationship is less than simple. Throughout the two decades of feminist revisioning, many have reflected on this association. In 1977, Rosemary Radford Ruether wrote *Mary, the Feminine Face of the Church.* In the same year, Andrew Greeley, a Roman Catholic priest, theologian, and sociologist, published *The Mary Myth: On the Femininity of God* (1977). The theme of associating Mary with the feminine dimension of the church, or as the face of God, was repeated ten years later by Leonardo Boff in the *Maternal Face of God: The Feminine and Its Religious Expressions* (1987).

A collaborative statement by Protestant and Roman Catholic scholars was issued in a book edited by Raymond Brown, *Mary in the New Testament* (1978), acclaimed as a significant ecumenical achievement in American biblical scholarship. The complexity of the figure of Mary for the church is also explored in several articles. Marina Warner in *Alone of Her Sex* (1976) discusses Mary as part myth and cult, and Mary Malone in *Who Is My Mother?* (1984) describes her as Mother. Elizabeth Johnson develops the theme in "Mary and the Female Face of God" (1989) as she describes her as Mother.

Recent publications develop the liberation theme. They seek ways of understanding Mary that free her from patriarchal trappings and align her with the community of the poor and oppressed. The task of attempting to understand the role of Mary for Christian faith continues to challenge scholars and devotees. (See Frances Jegen's *Mary According to Women* [1985]; Ivone Gerbara and Maria Bingenemar's *Mary, Mother of God, Mother of the Poor* [1989]; and Leland White's "Mary— Woman in the Mediterranean" [1990].)

The 1970s closed with a fascinating book by Elaine Pagels, *The Gnostic Gospels* (1979). She ended the book with this statement:

> It is the winners who write history—their way. No wonder, then, that the view point of the successful majority has dominated all traditional accounts of the origin of Christianity. (P. 142)

Pagels demonstrates the possibility that Christianity might have developed in very different directions if the winners had not written history. She offers new insights, disturbing to some and exciting to others, to the meaning of Jesus and the origins of Christianity.

In the 1980s, several volumes focused on specific women and their role in the New Testament—Elizabeth Tetlow's *Women and Ministry in the New Testaments* (1980); Hanice Nunnally-Cox's *Foremothers* (1981); Nancy Hardesty's *Great Women of Faith* (1982); Ann Johnson's *Miryam of Nazareth* (1984), and *Miryam of Judah* (1987); Dianne Bergant's "Biblical Update" (1986); Margaret Wold's *Women of Faith and Spirit* (1987); and Carol Meyers's *Discovering Eve* (1988). An imaginative approach is brought to the study of the Bible by Colleen Ivey Hartsoe in her book *Dear Daughter—Letters from Eve and Other Women in the Bible* (1987). She images what the women in Scripture might have written to the women in the pew today. This small volume also provides questions to assist the reader in going deeper into the text. Yet another kind of approach to Scripture is in *The Women of Genesis: From Sarah to Potiphar's Wife*, by Sharon Jeansonne (1990). This brings contemporary biblical scholarship to the study of Scripture and, through close attention to literary features of the texts, reveals God's involvement in history and portrays human failure, freedom, and strength. With the growing movement of women in the churches, and the struggle to deal with the sexism of the writers and interpreters of Scripture, denominational church offices began to develop task forces and assign staff to develop ways of responding. The National Council of the Churches of Christ Task Force on Sexism in the Bible commissioned Letty Russell to produce a resource for the "Bible-reading and Bible-studying community." This small selection of accessible essays, *The Liberating Word: A Guide to Nonsexist Interpretation of the Bible* (1976), focused on biblical authority and interpretation, interpreting patriarchal traditions, images of women, changing language, and the church.

After this early flowering, the agenda of the literature clearly shifted from the focus on woman to texts dealing with the method of biblical interpretation. This ongoing interrogation of the biblical text has led to further exposure of the many dimensions of misogyny in Scripture and its use in the church. Mary Hayter, a deaconess of the Church of England, made a major contribution to the issue of women and Scripture when she wrote *The New Eve in Christ: The Use and Abuse of the Bible in the Debate About Women in the Church* (1987). Conscious of the way leadership in her own denomination has used Scripture to block women's full participation in the life and work of the church, Hayter inquires into such issues as the "Sexuality of God and the Nature of Priesthood" and "Woman's Status and Function in Ministry." Several of the texts used in the controversial ordination debate are attributed to the Apostle Paul. In particular, there are the texts that refer to "headship," as in 1 Corinthians 11: 2–16. This is regularly interpreted to illustrate that women are subordinate to men, and that men have been given prerogative to exercise authority over women. Hayter reexamines these passages and the assumptions on which that understanding has been based, and she offers alternative interpretations. She points out that the root meaning of "headship" is "source"; it does not have the idea of descending hierarchy but rather refers to origin (p. 120). Further discussion of biblical interpretation may be found in the "Theology" section of this essay.

In the 1990s we see feminist scholarship building on the past studies of the Bible and the work of depatriachalizing Scripture, and turning to focus on specific women or books in the Bible. *The Women in Genesis*, by Sharon Jeansonne (1990) looks at women like Sarah, Rebekah, and Dinah. Ita Sheres rewords the exploits of Dinah in *Dinah's Rebellion: A Biblical Parable for Our Time* (1990). Katheryn Pfisterer Darr provides a critical, rabbinical, and feminist perspective of the stories of Ruth, Esther, and Hagar in *Far More Precious Than Jewels* (1991). Savinah Teubal has written a fascinating piece of detective work on the Hebrew texts in *The Lost Tradition of the Matriarchs* (1990).

All of these volumes illustrate how the faith and lives of biblical women can be an encouragement to women today.

References on the Bible

Bellie, Alice Ogden. *Helpmates, Harlots, and Heroes: Women Stories in the Hebrew Bible.* Louisville, KY: Westminster/John Knox, 1994.

Bergant, Dianne, ed. "Biblical Update: Esther and Judith." *Bible Today: A Periodical Promoting Popular Appreciation of the Word of God* 24, no. 1 (1986): 6–23.

Boff, Leonardo. *The Maternal Face of God: The Feminine and Its Religious Expressions.* San Francisco: Harper & Row, 1987.

Brown, Cheryl Anne. *No Longer to Be Silent: First Century Jewish Portraits of Biblical Women*. Louisville, KY: Westminster/John Knox, 1992.

Brown, Raymond E., ed. *Mary in the New Testament: A Collaborative Assessment by Protestant and Roman Catholic Scholars*. Philadelphia: Fortress Press, 1978.

Darr, Katheryn Pfisterer. *Far More Precious Than Jewels*. Louisville, KY: Westminster/John Knox, 1991.

Exum, Cheryl J. *Fragmented Women: Feminist (Sub)versions of Biblical Narratives*. Valley Forge, PA: Trinity, 1993.

Faxon, Alicia Craig. *Women and Jesus*. Philadelphia: United Church, 1973.

Gerbara, Ivone, and Maria Clara Luchetti Bingenemar. *Mary Mother of God, Mother of the Poor*. New York: Orbis Books, 1989.

Greeley, Andrew M. *The Mary Myth: On the Femininity of God*. New York: Seabury Press, 1977.

Hardesty, Nancy. *Great Women of Faith*. Nashville, TN: Abingdon, 1982.

Hartsoe, Colleen Ivey. *Dear Daughters—Letters from Eve and Other Women in the Bible*. Wilton, CT: Morehouse-Barlow, 1987.

Hayter, Mary. *The New Eve in Christ: The Use and Abuse of the Bible in the Debate About Women in the Church*. Grand Rapids, MI: William B. Eerdmans, 1987.

Jeansonne, Sharon Pace. *The Women of Genesis: From Sarah to Potiphar's Wife*. Minneapolis, MN: Fortress, 1990.

Jegen, Frances Carol, ed. *Mary According to Women*. Kansas, MO: Leaven, 1985.

Johnson, Ann. *Miryam of Judah: Witness in Truth and Tradition*. Notre Dame: Ave Maria, 1987.

———. *Miryam of Nazareth: Woman of Strength and Wisdom*. Notre Dame: Ave Maria, 1984.

Johnson, Elizabeth A. "Mary and the Female Face of God." *Theological Studies* 50 (Summer 1989): 500–526.

Korsak, Mary Phil. *At the Start . . . Genesis Made New*. Louvain, Belgium: European, 1992.

Malone, Mary T. *Who Is My Mother? Rediscovering the Mother of Jesus*. Dubuque, IA: W. C. Brown, 1984.

Meyers, Carol. *Discovering Eve*. Oxford: Oxford University Press, 1988.

Mollenkott, Virginia Ramey. *Women, Men, and the Bible*. Nashville, TN: Abingdon, 1977.

Nunnally-Cox, Hanice. *Foremothers: Women of the Bible*. New York: Seabury Press, 1981.

Pagels, Elaine. *The Gnostic Gospels*. New York: Random House, 1979.

Ruether, Rosemary Radford. *Mary, the Feminine Face of the Church*. Philadelphia: Westminster, 1975.

Russell, Letty M., ed. *The Liberating Word: A Guide to Nonsexist Interpretation of the Bible*. Philadelphia: Westminster, 1976.

Scanzoni, Letha, and Nancy Hardesty. *All We're Meant to Be: Biblical Feminism for Today*. Rev. ed. Nashville, TN: Abingdon, 1974.

Sheres, Ita. *Dinah's Rebellion: A Biblical Parable for Our Time*. New York: Crossroad, 1990.

Stanton, Elizabeth Cady. *Eighty Years and More*. (Reprinted from the T. Fisher Unwin Edition of 1898.) New York: Schocken Books, 1971.

———. *The Women's Bible*. New York: European, 1898.

Swidler, Leonard J. *Biblical Affirmation of Woman*. Philadelphia: Westminster, 1979.

Tetlow, Elizabeth M. *Women and Ministry in the New Testament*. New York: Paulist Press, 1980.

Teubal, Sarina J. *Hagar the Egyptian: The Last Tradition of the Matriarchs*. San Francisco: Harper & Row, 1990.

Wahlberg, Rachel Conrad. *Jesus According to a Woman*. New York: Paulist Press, 1975.

———. *Jesus and the Freed Women*. New York: Paulist Press, 1978.

Wainwright, Elaine Mary. *Toward a Critical Reading of the Gospel of Matthew*. Berlin: De Bruyter, 1991.

Warner, Marina. *Alone of Her Sex: The Myth and Cult of the Virgin Mary*. New York: Alfred A. Knopf, 1976.

White, Leland, ed. "Mary—Woman in the Mediterranean." *Biblical Theology Bulletin* 21 (Summer 1990): 46–94.

Wold, Margaret. *Women of Faith and Spirit: Profiles of Fifteen Biblical Witnesses*. Minneapolis, MN: Fortress, 1987.

Language and Liturgy

This section of the review of feminist liberation theology literature will include resources that address questions such as: Why is inclusive language necessary? What is inclusive language? and What are the implications for how we name God, how we name the Trinity, and how we read Scripture? Brian Wren's poem "The Main Question," in *What Language Shall I Borrow? God-Talk in Worship: A Male Response to Feminist Theology* (1989, 2) asks the question this way:

> Then how
> can we name and praise God
> in ways less idolatrous,
> more freeing,
> and more true
> to the Triune God
> and the direction of love
> in the Anointed One, Jesus?

As early as 1974, Letty Russell in *Human Liberation from a Feminist Perspective*, reminded us that language reflects the experience of our lives and the patterns of our social behavior. Later, Sallie McFague in *Metaphorical Theology* (1982) said that language is not something superficial, but is the human world, for what is not named is not thought. The following quotation from *Weaving the Visions*, by Judith Plaskow and Carol Christ (1989), sets out one of the fundamental contentions underpinning the inclusive language discussion by feminist liberation theologians:

> A growing number of people feel they have been denied full humanity by a pattern of exclusion of English usage. Consider, for example, the traditional English use of the word "man." A man is a male human being, as opposed to a female human being. But in common usage, "man" has also meant "human being," as opposed to "animal." No word that refers to a female person identifies her with humanity. (P. 163)

When religious language is male-centered, a great many women have difficulty seeing their own woman-centered spiritual experience as authentic, and as a consequence, that experience is truncated. For a more detailed reflection on the consequences of non-inclusivity and spirituality, refer to the section "Women's Spirituality" in this chapter.

The 1970s and 1980s Discussion of Feminism and Language

The inclusive language debate has been a lively and often acrimonious one in most churches. Early discussion was largely on the negative effects on women's experience in worship and Bible study. An overview of the titles from some of the articles give the flavor of the discussions: "Ye That Are Men Now Serve Him . . ." or "Did We Really Sing That in Chapel This Morning?," by Joan Forsberg (1976); "The Image of God in Man: Is Woman Included?," by Maryann Horowitz (1979); "Scripture Readings: God-Language and Non-Sexist Translation," by Madeleine Boucher (1984); and "Naming God in Public Prayer," by Mary Collins (1985). In 1975, Walter Burkhardt edited *Women: New Dimensions*, which includes an essay that sets out the early language debate.

Congregations have split over the issue of inclusive language. Pastors have been asked to resign, and people have left the church because they cannot, with integrity, remain. In "Inclusive Language Re-examined," Joseph Beaver (1988), another linguistic scholar, speaks for some when he says, "inclusive language, while well-intentioned, has turned out, and will turn out for most people to be a fad . . . what we 'mean' when we relate to each other is what is truly important" (p. 303).

Many denominational offices responded to the tension by producing useful study kits and guidelines designed to assist people in working on the issue of inclusive language within the parish or congregation. Such material would be readily available through those offices. Another institutional response was the provision of alternative liturgical material such as "The Supplemental Liturgical Text Prayer Book Studies 30," and the "Commentary on the Prayer Book Studies 30," written by the Standing Liturgical Commission of the Episcopal Church (1989). For more resources refer to "Feminist Liturgies" in the section following.

The Late 1980s Through the Present

From the late 1980s through the present, there has been a spate of articles all calling for the re-examination of the possibilities and problems of inclusive language. As the inquiry proceeds, it is becoming abundantly clear that there are a multitude of theological issues involved. Geoffrey Wainwright, Pheme Perkins, and David Bossman make this same point in "An Inclusive Language Lectionary" (1984). The programmatic name of God as "Father" and "Mother" makes for difficulty and confusion with regard to the traditional, Christological significant veneration of Mary as "Theotokos," the "God-bearer," "the Mother of God" (p. 29).

How we address God is not simply an issue of personal preference, but rather, is rooted in our understanding of the beginnings of Christianity. Feminist liberation theologians are asking: Who decided on the language we have used in the past, and who ought to decide today? What was happening when the church opted to use the form "Father, Son, and Holy Spirit"? What happens if we use the inclusive form of "Creator, Redeemer, and Sustainer"? Who has the right to tamper with tradition?

Sallie McFague, in *Models of God: Theology for an Ecological, Nuclear Age* (1987), offers a metaphorical understanding of our language about God: "The essence of metaphorical theology, however, is precisely the refusal to identify human constructions with divine reality" (p. 22).

God is not a Father, but rather, God is like a Father. God is not a Mother, but God can be like a Mother.

In the 1980s, several books were published that incorporate a chapter addressing the subject of inclusive language: Rosemary Ruether's *Woman-Church* (1985); Judith Weidman's *Christian Feminism Visions of a New Humanity* (1984); Marie Bingemer's "The Trinity from the Perspective of Woman" (1988); and Barbara Darling-Smith's "A Feminist Christological Exploration" (1988). Besides these, the references contain several journal articles, each of which would provide useful grist for the mill of the inclusive language debate: Steven Mills's "New Names for God" (1985); Roland Frye's "Language for God and Feminist Language" (1989); Gordon Dalbery's "A Problem of Inclusive Language" (1988); Alan Jones's "Men, Women and Sex" (1988); Megan Walker's "The Challenge of Feminism to the Christian Concept of God" (1989); Robert Lerner and Stanley Rothman's "Newspeak, Feminist Style" (1990); Bonnie Thurston's "Language, Gender and Prayer" (1992); and Charles Cosgrove's "The First Attempt to Use Gender Inclusive Language in English Bible Translation" (1993). In addition, there are a growing number of volumes dealing specifically with topics emerging out of the inclusive language debate. These include *God As Father?*, by Johannes-Batist Metz and Edward Schillebeeckx (1981); *Our Search for Identity: Humanity in the Image of God*, by Marianne Micks (1982); *The Father-hood of God in an Age of Emancipation*, by Willem Adolt Visser't Hooft (1982); *What Will Happen to God? Feminism and the Reconstruction of Christian Belief*, by William Oddie (1984); *The Divine Mother: A Trini-tarian Theology of the Holy Spirit*, by Donald Gelpi (1984); *Is God the Only Reliable Father?*, by Diane Tennis (1985); and *God Beyond Gender: Feminist Christian God Language*, by Gail Ramshaw (1995).

Changing the Scripture has been difficult for many. This is most clearly seen in the response to The Inclusive Language Lectionary Committee's *The Inclusive Language Lectionary* (1983), which provides weekly lectionary Bible readings in inclusive language. Ronald Allen (1988) expresses both appreciation and caution about the changes to the *Lectionary* readings:

> Inclusive language translation . . . helps recover those aspects of the sacred writings that contribute to a vision of justice seen in the gospel. . . . Not every effort to use inclusive language when translating the Bible is theologically sound or scripturally appropriate. (P. 15)

Other responses to *The Inclusive Language Lectionary* can be found in the references: Leslie Keylock's "God Our Father and Mother" (1983); Ben Patterson's "The God of NCC Lectionary Is Not the God of the Bible" (1984); Burton Throckmorton's "Why the Inclusive Language Lections?" (1984); Janice Shepherd's "Language, Sex and Lectionary" (1984); Robert Jenson's "The Inclusive Lectionary" (1984); Patrick Miller's "The Inclusive Language Lectionary" (1984); Mark Olson's "Comparing Two Inclusive Language Lectionaries" (1984); Ann

Johnson's *Miryam of Nazareth* (1984); Beclee Wilson and Edwina Hunter's "Celebration of the Inclusive Language Lectionary" (1984); Virginia Mollenkott's "A Unity That Affirms Diversity" (1986); Janet Schaffran and Pat Kozak's *More Than Words* (1986); Marie Uhr's "The Portrayal of Women in the Lectionary" (1988); Calvin Mercer's "Contemporary Language and the New Translation of the Bible" (1990); Gail Ramshaw's "An Inclusive Language Lectionary" (1984); Barbara Field's "Positioning Women As Subordinate" (1991); Jean Campbell's "Lectionary Omissions" (1993); Sharon Hels's "The Revised Common Lectionary" (1993); and Carol Schlueter's "The Gender Balance of Texts from the Gospels" (1993).

As *The Inclusive Language Lectionary,* and others like it, become more widely used, there will undoubtedly be more discussion about the change to inclusive language. Other Bible-related resources include a new translation of The Psalms in Gary Chamberlain's *The Psalms* (1984), and Johanna Bos's *Ruth, Esther, Jonah* (1986), which provides preaching notes.

Feminist Liturgies

An incredible number of resources—books, tapes, music, revised hymns, and liturgies—have come out of the struggles to find a way to transform liturgy, so that both women and men can experience the message as inclusive.

The early publications were welcomed by those who were searching for alternatives. Important works include *Sistercelebrations: Nine Worship Experiences* (1974), edited by Arlene Swidler, and *Women and Worship: A Guide to Non-Sexist Hymn, Prayers, and Liturgies* (1974), edited by Sharon and Thomas Neufer-Emswiler. Both of these publications have services that can be adapted to a variety of situations. The Ecumenical Women's Center published *Because We Are One People* (1975), a book of traditional hymns rewritten in inclusive language that was quickly followed by *Sing a Womansong* (1975), a collection of fifty original songs. The rewriting of hymns is a useful and effective method for struggling with inclusive language. Grace Moore wrote a series of short reflections called *The Advent of Women* (1975), and Janice Grana collected some marvelous women's poetry in *Images: Women in Transition* (1976). One poem that stands out is "Minnie Remembers," in which an aging woman remembers her life as a youngster and as a young married woman with children of her own.

Linda Clark, Marian Ronan, and Eleanor Walker published a very usable book called *Image-Breaking, Image-Building: A Handbook for Creative Worship with Women of Christian Tradition* (1981). One of the chapters deals with raising the issue of inclusive language in the congregation. In 1983, the United Church of Canada published a volume called *Women, Work and Worship*, by Shirley Davy (1983), which contains reflections on women's work and worship in the church, past and present; it's a moving history and a valuable resource for today. In *No Longer Strangers*, by Iben Gjerding and Katherine Kinnamon

(1983), four Christian organizations based in Geneva, Switzerland brought together resources for women and worship written by women in different parts of the world. Another joint venture was a booklet of resources, *Celebrating Women*, by Janet Morley and Hannah Ward (1986), published by the Women in Theology and the Movement for the Ordination of Women, a group based in England. A collection of liturgies from two Roman Catholic women, Schaffran and Kozak, *More Than Words* (1986) also provides an excellent list of examples of God images and a discussion on God-language.

One of the most prolific contributors of resources for worship is Ruth Duck. Along with others, she has provided words and music for liturgies to celebrate all occasions, including: *Bread for the Journey* (1981); *Everflowing Streams*, with coauthor Mike Bausch (1981); and *Touch Holiness*, with coauthor Marene Tirabassi (1990). One of several resources developed by Women's Alliance for Theology is called *Women Church Celebrations: Feminist Liturgies for the Lenten Season*, by Diann Neu (1985). Rosemary Radford Ruether, in *Woman-Church Theology and Practice* (1985), has gathered together several liturgies— "Ritual of Divorce," "Coming of Age Ritual," "Coming-Out Rite for a Lesbian," and "Covenant Celebration." Miriam Therese Winter, a Medical Mission Sister, was inspired by women's struggles throughout the world to write *Woman Prayer, Woman Song* (1987), a book of rituals. Of particular poignancy is the "Mass for the Missing," a ritual for political dissenters kidnapped by the state. She has recently produced another fine book, *WomanWord: A Feminist Lectionary and Psalter* (1990), which is based on women of the New Testament. An exciting resource brought together by the World Council of Churches is *Churches in Solidarity with Women* (1988), a selection of prayers, poems, songs, and stories written by women from around the world. This is one of several resources created to celebrate the beginning of the Ecumenical Decade of the Churches in Solidarity with Women.

In 1993, two exciting books were published. The first, *Women at Worship*, edited by Marjorie Procter-Smith and Janet Walton (1993), a collection of essays, is comprised of original ceremonies, liturgies, and rites from a wide variety of tradition. The second, *To Make and Make Again Feminist*, by Charlotte Caron (1993), a theologian in Western Canada, is described on the book cover as weaving together a rich tapestry of feminism and religious ritual, social justice, and spirituality, integrating them with a vision and practice of feminist ritual theology.

The Christian feminist movement in the church has often inspired and been inspired by music. In the 1970s, Carol Etzler began the decade with two fine records for women in the church, *Sometimes I Wish* and *Woman River*. Since the 1970s, Carolyn McDade has produced cassettes and songbooks about women's struggle towards liberation. Some of her work, produced in the 1980s, includes *This Tough Spun Web*; *Rain Upon Dry Land*; *The Best of Struggles*; and *We Come with Our Voices: Sister Carry On*. Her newest collection of songs, on tape with sheet music, has just been released under the title *Songs for Congregational Singing* (1991). Recently, a young Canadian woman,

Linnea Good, together with Patti Powell, has produced cassettes and books of songs that speak to women in the church—*A Word to Begin With* (1989). These three women, Etzler, McDade, and Good, continue to inspire us to celebrate and remain in the struggle as they travel through the United States and Canada leading workshops and offering their vision of the church and the world. There is an abundance of material available, some of which is available in church book rooms, much of which can be found in women's bookstores.

References on Language and Liturgy

Allen, Ronald. "Inclusive Language: Possibilities and Problems." *Christian Ministry* 19:15 (July-Aug. 1988): 18-19.

Beaver, Joseph. "Inclusive Language Re-examined." *Dialog: A Journal of Theology* 27 (Fall 1988): 301–3.

Bingemer, Marie Clara. "The Trinity from the Perspective of Woman." In *Faith Born in the Struggle for Life: A Rereading of Protestant Faith in Latin America Today*, edited by D. Kirkpatrick. Grand Rapids, MI: William B. Eerdmans, 1988.

Bos, Johanna W. H. *Ruth, Esther, Jonah.* (Knox Preaching Guides.) Atlanta, GA: John Knox, 1986.

Boucher, Madeleine. "Scriptural Readings: God-Language and Non-Sexist Translation." In *Language and the Church: Articles and Designs for Workshops*, edited by A. Withers. New York: Nation Council of Churches of Christ in U.S.A., 1984.

Burkhardt, Walter, ed. *Women: New Dimensions.* New York: Paulist Press, 1975.

Campbell, Jean. "Lectionary Omissions [Biblical Women and Feminine Imagery]." *Witness* 76 (May 1993): 22.

Caron, Charlotte. *To Make and Make Again Feminist: Ritual Theology.* New York: Crossroad, 1993.

Chamberlain, Gary. *The Psalms: The New Translation for Prayer and Worship.* Nashville, TN: Upper Room, 1984.

Church of England Liturgical Commission. *Making Women Visible: The Use of Inclusive Language with the A.S.B.* Report by the Liturgical Commission of the General Synod of the Church of England. London: Church House, 1989.

Clark, Linda, Marian Ronan, and Eleanor Walker. *Image-Breaking, Image-Building: A Handbook for Creative Worship with Women of Christian Tradition.* New York: Pilgrim, 1981.

Collins, Mary. "Naming God in Public Prayer." *Worship* 59, no. 4 (July 1985): 291–304.

Cosgrove, Charles H. "The First Attempt to Use Gender Inclusive Language in English Bible Translation." *Journal of Ecumenical Studies* 30 (Spring 1993): 263–68.

Dalbery, Gordon. "A Problem of Inclusive Language." *Witness* 71 (July–August 1988): 20–21.

Darling-Smith, Barbara. "A Feminist Christological Exploration." In *One Faith, Many Cultures: Inculturation, Indigeneration, and Contextualization,* edited by Ruy O. Costa. Maryknoll, NY: Orbis Books, 1988.

Darr, Katheryn Pfisterer. *Far More Precious Than Jewels: Perspective on Biblical Women.* Louisville, KY: Westminster/John Knox, 1991.

Davy, Shirley. *Women Work and Worship in the United Church of Canada.* Toronto: Division of Mission in Canada, United Church of Canada, 1983.

Duck, Ruth C., ed. *Bread for the Journey: Resources for Worship.* New York: Pilgrim, 1981.

Duck, Ruth C., and Marene C. Tirabassi, eds. *Touch Holiness: Resources for Worship.* New York: Pilgrim, 1990.

Duck, Ruth C., and Mike G. Bausch, eds. *Everflowing Streams.* New York: Pilgrim, 1981.

Ecumenical Women's Center. *Because We Are One People.* Chicago: Ecumenical Women's Center, 1975.

———. *Sing a Womansong.* Chicago: Ecumenical Women's Center, 1975.

Engelsman, Joan Chamberlain. *The Feminine Dimension of the Divine.* Philadelphia: Westminster, 1979.

Etzler, Carole. *Sometimes I Wish.* R.R. #1, Box 1420, Vergennes, VT 05491.

———. *Women River.* R.R. #1, Box 1420, Vergennes, VT 05491.

Field, Barbara L. "Positioning Women as Subordinate: The Semiosis of the Weekly Lectionary in the Anglican Church." *St. Mark Review* 144 (Summer 1991): 16–21.

Forsberg, Joan Bate. " 'Ye That Are Men Now Serve Him . . .' or 'Did We Really Sing That in Chapel This Morning?' " *Reflection: Journal of Opinion at Yale Divinity School* 74, no. 1 (1976): 3–4.

Frye, Roland. "Language for God and Feminist Language: A Literary and Rhetorical Analysis." *Interpretation: A Journal of Bible and Theology* 43 (January 1989): 45–57.

Gelpi, Donald. *The Divine Mother: A Trinitarian Theology of the Holy Spirit*. Lanham, MD: University of America, 1984.

Gjerding, Iben, and Katherine Kinnamon. *No Longer Strangers: A Resource for Women and Worship*. Geneva: World Council of Churches, 1983.

Good, Linnea, with Patti Powell. *A Word to Begin With*. Cassette and book. Self-published, 1989. Available from 258 Church St., Fredericton NB E3B 4E4, Canada.

Grana, Janice. *Images: Women in Transition*. Nashville, TN: Upper Room, 1976.

Hammerton-Kelley, Robert. *God the Father: Theology and Patriarchy in the Teaching of Jesus*. Philadelphia: Fortress Press, 1979.

Hardesty, Nancy. *Inclusive Language in the Church*. Atlanta, GA: John Knox, 1987.

Hels, Sharon J. "The Revised Common Lectionary." *Quarterly Review: A Scholarly Journal for Reflection on Ministry* 13 (Summer 1993): 37–70.

Horowitz, Maryann Cline. "The Image of God in Man: Is Woman Included?" *The Harvard Theological Review* 72 (July–October 1979): 175–206.

Inclusive Language Lectionary Committee. Appointed by the Division of Education and Ministry, National Churches of Christ in the U.S.A. *Inclusive Language Lectionary: Readings for Year A.B.C.* Atlanta, GA: John Knox, 1983–1987.

Jenson, Robert W. "The Inclusive Lectionary." *Dialog: A Journal of Theology* 23 no. 1 (Winter 1984): 4–6.

Johnson, Ann. *Miryam of Nazareth: Woman of Strength and Wisdom*. Notre Dame, IN: Ave Maria, 1984.

Jones, Alan W. "Men, Women and Sex: Make Way for the Image of God!" *Worship* 62, no. 1 (January 1988): 25–44.

Keene, Jane A. *A Winter's Song: A Liturgy for Women Seeking Healing from Sexual Abuse in Childhood*. New York: Pilgrim, 1991.

Keylock, Leslie R. "God Our Father and Mother: A Bisexual Nightmare from the National Council of Churches." *Christianity Today* 27, no. 17 (November 11, 1983): 23–24.

Lebans, Gertrude. *Out of the Fire: Worship and Theology of Liberation.* Dundas, Ontario: Artemis Enterprises, 1992.

Lerner, Robert, and Stanley Rothman. "Newspeak, Feminist Style." *Commentary* 89 (April 1990): 54–56.

Lutheran Church of America. *Guidelines for Inclusive Language,* n.d. Available from L.C.A. Office for Communication, 231 Madison Ave., New York, NY 10016.

McDade, Carolyn. *This Tough Spun Web*; *Rain Upon Dry Land*; *The Best of Struggles*; *We Come with Our Voices: Sister Carry On*; and *Songs for Congregational Singing.* Cassettes and books. Available from c/o 19 Brown Street, Wareham, MA 02571.

McFague, Sallie. *Metaphorical Theology: Models of God in Religious Language.* Philadelphia: Fortress Press, 1982.

——. *Models of God: Theology for an Ecological, Nuclear Age.* Philadelphia: Fortress Press, 1987.

Mercer, Calvin R. "Contemporary Language and the New Translation of the Bible." *Religious & Public Education* 17 (Winter 1990): 89–98.

Metz, Johannes-Batist, and Edward Schillebeeckx, ed. *God As Father?* (Concilium 143). Edinburgh, Scotland: T. & T. Clark, 1981.

Micks, Marianne H. *Our Search for Identity: Humanity in the Image of God.* Philadelphia: Fortress Press, 1982.

Miller, Patrick D. "The Inclusive Language Lectionary." *Theology Today* 41 (Fall 1984): 26–33.

Mills, Steven. "New Names for God." *PMC: The Practice of Ministry in Canada* 2, no. 3 (Autumn 1985): 10–11.

Mollenkott, Virginia R. "A Unity That Affirms Diversity: An Inclusive Language Lectionary." *Ecumenical Trends* 15, no. 11 (January 1986): 9–10.

Moore, Grace. *The Advent of Women: Twenty-Five Meditations.* Valley Forge, PA: Judson, 1975.

Morley, Janet, and Hannah Ward. *Celebrating Women.* Wilton, CT: Morehouse-Barlow, 1986.

Neu, Diann. *Women and the Gospel Traditions: Feminist Celebrations.* Silver Spring, MD: Waterworks, 1991.

――――. *Women Church Celebrations: Feminist Liturgies for the Lenten Season*. Washington, D.C.: Women's Alliance for Theology, Ethics and Ritual, 1985.

Neufer-Emswiler, Sharon, and Thomas Neufer-Emswiler. *Women and Worship: A Guide to Non-Sexist Hymns, Prayers, and Liturgies*. New York: Harper & Row, 1974.

Oddie, William. *What Will Happen to God? Feminism and the Reconstruction of Christian Belief*. London: SPCK, 1984.

Olson, Mark. "Comparing Two Inclusive Language Lectionaries." *Other Side* 20, no. 150 (March 1984): 34.

Patterson, Ben. "The God of NCC Lectionary Is Not the God of the Bible." *Christianity Today* 28, no. 2 (February 3, 1984): 12–13.

Plaskow, Judith, and Carol Christ. *Weaving the Visions: New Patterns in Feminist Spirituality*. San Francisco: Harper & Row, 1989.

Procter-Smith, Marjorie, and Janet R. Walton, eds. *Women at Worship: Interpretations of North American Diversity*. Louisville, KY: Westminster/John Knox, 1993.

Ramshaw, Gail. "The First Testament in Christian Lectionaries." *Worship* 64 (November 1990): 494–510.

――――. *God Beyond Gender: Feminist Christian God Language*. Minneapolis, MN: Fortress, 1995.

――――. "An Inclusive Language Lectionary." *Worship* 58, no. 1 (January 1984): 29–37.

Ruether, Rosemary Radford. *Woman-Church: Theology and Practice of Feminist Liturgical Communities*. New York: Harper & Row, 1985.

Russell, Letty M. *Human Liberation from a Feminist Perspective: Theology*. Philadelphia: Westminster, 1974.

Schaffran, Janet, and Pat Kozak. *More Than Words: Prayers and Ritual for Inclusive Communities*. Cleveland, OH: Offset Printing, 1986.

Schlueter, Carol J. "The Gender Balance of Texts from the Gospels: The Revised Common Lectionary and the Lutheran Book of Worship." *Currents in Theology & Mission* 20 (June 1993): 177–86.

Shepherd, Janice M. "Language, Sex and Lectionary [reply to B. Throckmorton]." *Christian Century* 101, no. 28 (September 26, 1984): 875–76.

Standing Liturgical Commission. *Commentary on Prayer Book Studies 30*. New York: Church Hymnal, 1989.

————. *Supplemental Liturgical Texts: Prayer Book Studies 30*. New York: Church Hymnal, 1989.

Swidler, Arlene, ed. *Sistercelebrations: Nine Worship Experiences*. Philadelphia: Fortress Press, 1974.

Tennis, Diane. *Is God the Only Reliable Father?* Philadelphia: Westminster, 1985.

Throckmorton, Burton H. "Why the Inclusive Language Lections?" *Christian Century* 101, no. 24 (August 1–8, 1984): 742–44.

Thurston, Bonnie Bowman. "Language, Gender and Prayer: The Importance of Naming God." *Lexington Theological Quarterly* 27 (January 1992): 3–9.

Uhr, Marie Louis. "The Portrayal of Women in the Lectionary." *Saint Mark's Review* 135 (Spring 1988): 22–25.

United Church of Canada. Interdivisional Task Force on Changing Roles of Women and Men in Church and Society. *Daughters and Sons of God*. Toronto: General Council Office of United Church of Canada, 1981.

United Methodist Publishing House. *Guidelines for Eliminating Racism, Ageism, Handicappism and Sexism, prepared by the General Council in Ministries*. Nashville, TN: United Methodist Publishing House, 1984.

Visser't Hooft, Willem Adolt. *The Fatherhood of God in an Age of Emancipation*. Geneva: World Council of Churches, 1982.

Wainwright, Geoffrey, Pheme Perkins, and David M. Bossman. "An Inclusive Language Lectionary: Three Views." *Biblical Theology Bulletin: A Journal of Bible and Theology* 14, no. 1 (January 1984): 28–35.

Walker, Megan. "The Challenge of Feminism to the Christian Concept of God." *Journal of Theology for Southern Africa* 66 (March 1989): 4–20.

Weidman, Judith W., ed. *Christian Feminism Visions of a New Humanity*. San Francisco: Harper & Row, 1984.

Wilson, Beclee Newcomer, and Edwina Hunter. "Celebration of the Inclusive Language Lectionary [sermon]." *Journal of Women and Religion* 3, no. 21 (Summer 1984): 5–11.

Winter Miriam Therese. *Woman Prayer, Woman Song: Resources for Ritual*. Oak Park, IL: Meyer Stone, 1987.

———. *WomanWord: A Feminist Lectionary and Psalter*. New York: Crossroad, 1990.

Wren, Brian. *What Language Shall I Borrow? God-Talk in Worship: A Male Response to Feminist Theology*. New York: Crossroad, 1989.

World Council of Churches. Ecumenical Decade 1989–1998. *Churches in Solidarity with Women (Prayers and Poems, Songs and Stories)*. Geneva: World Council of Churches, 1988.

Women's Spirituality

This review of the literature related to spirituality will cover a cross-section of writings both historical and recent. This section will also weave together the writing of women belonging to the Christian and Jewish faiths, as well as women who are a part of neither tradition. To make a distinction between these authors would be to set up a false dichotomy because many of the women are influenced by one another's work. It is not my intention to deny the differences that exist between them; in this review I have chosen to recognize their similarities, namely, their intent to clarify patriarchy, feminist consciousness, and spirituality.

Women's Movement

The influence of the secular women's movement is evident in the increase of literature in books, newspapers, and journals. Judy Davis and Juanita Weaver explain, in their chapter in *The Politics of Women's Spirituality* (1982), that the division between cultural feminism and political feminism results from patriarchal thinking that sets out false dualisms:

> The so-called division between cultural feminism and political feminism is a debilitating result of our oppression. It comes from the patriarchal view that the spiritual and the institution operate in separate realms. (P. 372)

Today, women are defining new spheres of knowledge and experience about spirituality and are also reclaiming stories of women in the past. They are forging a new understanding of what it means to integrate the body and mind; material and spiritual; subjective and objective; faith and reason; and self and other.

Feminist Spirituality

What is spirituality, and what does it mean for feminist women? Some writers speak about "feminine spirituality": Rosemary Haughton in *Feminine Spirituality* (1976); Susan Muto in "Foundations of Feminine

Spirituality" (1980); and Theodore Letis in "Feminine Spirituality" (1982–83). Other writers use the language of "feminist spirituality": Patricia Schechter in "Feminist Spirituality and Radical Political Commitment" (1981); Anne Carr in "On Feminist Spirituality" (1982); Christin Weber in *Womanchrist* (1987); Joan Chichester in "A Full Picture of God" (1987); and Judith Plaskow and Carol Christ in *Weaving the Visions* (1989). This difference generally reflects whether or not the writer consciously integrates a feminist analysis in her description of women's experience (see Shelley Finson's "Feminist Spirituality Within the Framework of Feminist Consciousness" [1987]). A feminist understanding would make no separation between the person, political, and spiritual.

Two volumes stand out from the 1970s: *Becoming Woman: The Quest for Wholeness in the Female Experience* (1977), by Penelope Washbourne and *Kiss Sleeping Beauty Good-Bye* (1979), by Madonna Kolbenschlag. The first recognizes that women's experience of "becoming" is both a personal and a political process. The author points out that the crisis periods in a woman's life, menstruation, marriage, menopause, and others, can be moments that are deeply spiritual (p. 4). The second work describes women's spirituality in society as having been used to

> provide the moral and spiritual uplift in the masculine world . . . woman's mythical moral and spiritual influence amounts to little more than the effect a band of cheerleaders might have on the execution of a football game. Cheerleaders do not affect strategy. (P. 181)

Kolbenschlag continues by pointing out that women tend to use religion for therapeutic reasons—a religious experience for a woman is "like applying a poultice to herself" (p. 148).

Eleanor Haney covered many complex themes, including spirituality and sexuality, and ecology and economic justice, in her *Vision and Struggle: Meditations on Feminist Spirituality and Politics* (1989).

Diane Mariechild is the author of a fascinating book called *MotherWit* (1981), in which she says that the spiritual is a dimension of self that we come in touch with through dreams, myths, intuition, hunches, feelings, and visions. Elizabeth Dodson Gray edited *Sacred Dimensions of Women's Experience* (1988), and here again, connections are made between women's lives and their spirituality.

Other works included in the bibliography that discuss feminist spirituality are: *Feminist Spirituality and the Feminine Divine*, by Anne Carson (1986); *Sophia: The Future of Feminist Spirituality*, by Susan Cady et al. (1986); *A Discipleship of Equals: Towards a Christian Feminist Spirituality*, by Francis Eigo (1988); *Spirituality and Personal Maternity*, by Joann Conn (1988); *Reclaiming the Connection: A Contemporary Spirituality*, by Kathleen Fischer (1990); *The Voice of Sarah: Feminine Spirituality and Traditional Judaism*, by Tamar Frankiel (1990); and *Defecting in Place: Women Claiming Responsibility for*

Their Own Spiritual Lives, by Miriam Winter, Adair Lummis, and Allison Stokes (1994).

In Search of the Goddess and Reclaiming Wicca

Much of the feminist critique of religion is focused on the language used to describe God. For a discussion of this, see "Language and Liturgy" in this essay. This evaluation of language is rooted in the belief that a female deity or divine principle is necessary if women's experience is to be included in a religious worldview. Sara Maitland, an English Christian laywoman, makes the connection between feminine language and spirituality in her early book *A Map of a New Country: Women and Christianity* (1983):

> Reclaiming the feminine in worship helps me to reclaim myself as a person created uniquely in the image of God, female. Now I know with my whole being that I am connected to God . . . and that the realization of this connection is the reason for which I was born. (P. 132)

It is not surprising, therefore, that the religion of the Great Goddess is undergoing rebirth. The Goddess is *not* a female version of the patriarchal god. There are many Goddesses. Carol Christ (1979), describes the meaning of the Goddess symbol as a divine female, who symbolizes the life, death, and rebirth energy in culture and nature in personal and communal life. As a symbol, the Goddess legitimates the affirmation and beauty of female power.

Literature on the Goddess is considerable. A few of the works from the 1970s include: Charlene Spretnak's *Lost Goddesses of Early Greece: A Collection of Pre-Hellenic Myths* (1978); Marija Gimbutas's *The Goddess and Gods of Old Europe, 6500–3500 B.C.: Legends and Cult Images* (1982); and Carol Christ's *Laughter of Aphrodite: On a Journey to the Goddess* (1987).

The Politics of Women's Spirituality, by Charlene Spretnak (1982) has a marvelous variety of views on spirituality. It brings together women who themselves have produced some valuable books in the area of spirituality.

Two interesting publications written for women studies courses, but quite accessible, came out in the 1990s: *Whence the Goddesses: A Source Book,* by Mirian Dexter (1990) and *The Reflowering of the Goddess,* by Gloria Orenstein (1990). Dexter examines "the accrual of characteristics, powers, and functions among goddesses throughout ancient Europe and other areas" (p. ix). Orenstein makes striking links between art, literature, history, and spirituality.

Witchcraft is also gaining favor as an expression of women's spirituality. The term *wicca* is the ancient form of the word "witchcraft." Naomi Goldenberg, in "Feminist Witchcraft" (1982), describes the wicca religion as the "first modern theistic Religion to conceive of its deity mainly as an internal set of images and attitudes" (p. 213). Most followers accept the notion of the Great Goddess, who appears in the three forms of the maiden, the mother, and the crone. Two early publications that are still favorites of many are *Witches, Midwives and Nurses: A History of Women Healers* (1973), by Barbara Ehrenreich and Deidre English, and *Dreaming the Dark* (1982), by Starhawk. Also, there are two popular magazines that cover many aspects of women's spirituality: *Chrysalis: A Magazine of Women's Culture* and *Woman-Spirit Magazine*. These can be located at women's bookstores and are often available in the reading room of libraries.

Christian Women As Models for Spirituality

Rosemary Radford Ruether and Eleanor McLaughlin, in *Women of Spirit* (1979), both strongly insisted that women from the distant past can speak to today's women seeking models for their spirituality. They say, "The spirituality of the women who are called holy . . . was a source of wholeness, meaning, power and authority . . . power out of holiness" (p. 23). Women did find "their place" within patriarchal religion; the Christian tradition, under certain conditions and at certain times, has been supportive of women. For example, the Middle Ages (1050–1400) was a time when many women found meaningful spiritual experiences in the ascetic or cloistered life. In an earlier article, "Christ My Mother" (1975), Eleanor McLaughlin made the connections between the spirituality of medieval women and their use of feminine imagery for Jesus. Ellen Macek wrote "The Emergence of a Feminine Spirituality in the Book of Martyrs" (1988), and Mary Giles edited *The Feminist Mystic* (1982); both works provide marvelous insights to women of the past. Fiona Bowie has edited *Beguine Spirituality* (1990), a wonderful volume of writings of three Beguine women, Mechthild of Magdeburg, Beatrice of Nazareth, and Hadewijch of Brabant. These thirteenth-century writings are clearly a model for contemporary feminists' efforts today. Women are also searching into the lives of women in the more recent periods of history. Phyllis Mack, in "Gender and Spirituality in Early Quakers" (1989), examined the experiences of early Quaker women, and discussed the links between gender and spirituality. Amanda Porterfield and Barbara Welter, in *Feminine Spirituality in America* (1980), turned to American women in history for signs of feminine spirituality.

Spirituality Today

The function of Christian spirituality has often been to paint women as passive or recipient. Consequently, throughout the feminist liberation literature there is much critique of the damage done to women by this Christian tradition. Joann Wolski Conn, in "Women's Spirituality" (1980), focused on the central issue for women who try to relate to the Christian tradition:

At the heart of the problem of women's spirituality is a subtle but divisive twist of the patristic theme: "The glory of God is humanity fully alive." Women in the Christian tradition have unfortunately been led to believe that God is glorified by their humanity only partially alive, because they have been restricted to roles that limit their capacities for self-direction and restrict their ability to experience self-esteem. (P. 293)

The two roles, being sex object and living for another, simply submerge the identity of women in the identities, needs, and interests of others.

Some of the writers in the 1980s and 1990s have developed a specific interest in relationship to spirituality. For instance, in the early 1980s there was a gathering of Jewish and Christian feminist theologians, and the outcome of that event is a fine collection of essays, *Women's Spirit Bonding*, by Janet Kalven and Mary Buckley (1984). Women are showing an interest in women's spiritual journey. Nell Morton wrote the inspiring book *The Journey Is Home* (1986), which includes part of her own journey as well as a series of papers far ahead of their time. Two other writers with similar interest highlight women's changes: Theresa King O'Brien, in *The Spiral Faith* (1988), brought together a series of essays and interviews on women's spirituality, and JoAnne Cooney Cripe, in "Integrative Relationality" (1989), looked at themes of transition in women's faith development. Kathlene Fischer shows how a feminist perspective transforms both the context of spiritual direction in *Women at the Well: Feminist Perspectives on Spiritual Direction* (1988). Marjorie Hewitt Suchocki and Dorothee Sölle both have featured an earth-based spirituality in "Earthsong, Godsong" (1989) and *The Window of Vulnerability* (1990), respectively. Naomi Southard discusses spiritual resources for Asian-American women in "Recovering and Rediscovered Images" (1989).

The very fact that it has had to find expression in a patriarchal society has truncated the spirituality of women. Yet, throughout history, there is evidence that women have claimed their own expressions of the spiritual dimensions of their lives, though often at great cost. The creative potential of women is found in the unfolding discovery of spirituality for women in our time. Refer to both the "Women and History" and "Ministry of Women" sections of this essay for a wide range of works that are clear expressions of women's creative witness to their faithfulness.

References on Women's Spirituality

Bowie, Fiona, ed. *Beguine Spirituality: Mystical Writings of Mechthild of Magdeburg, Beatrice of Nazareth, and Hadewijch of Brabant.* New York: Crossroad, 1990.

Cady, Susan, Marian Ronan, and Hal Taussig. *Sophia: The Future of Feminist Spirituality.* San Francisco: Harper & Row, 1986.

Carr, Anne E. "On Feminist Spirituality." *Horizons: The Journal of the College Theology Society* 9, no. 1 (Spring 1982): 96–103.

Carson, Anne. *Feminist Spirituality and the Feminine Divine: An Annotated Bibliography*. Trumansburg, NY: Crossing, 1986.

Chichester, Joan. "A Full Picture of God: A Look at Feminist Spirituality." *Sojourner* 16 (July 1987): 34–37.

Christ, Carol P. *Laughter of Aphrodite: On a Journey to the Goddess*. San Francisco: Harper & Row, 1987.

Christ, Carol P., and Judith Plaskow, eds. *Womenspirit Rising: A Feminist Reader in Religion*. San Francisco: Harper & Row, 1979.

Chrysalis: A Magazine of Women's Culture. Los Angeles, CA: Winter Soltice, 1978. Quarterly.

Conn, Joann Wolski. *Spirituality and Personal Maturity*. New York: Paulist Press, 1989.

———. "Women's Spirituality: Restrictions and Reconstruction." *Cross Currents* 30 (Fall 1980): 293–307.

Cripe, Jo Anne Cooney. "Integrative Relationality: Themes of Transition in Women's Faith Development." *Journal of Women and Religion* 8 (Winter 1989): 4–20.

Davis, Judy, and Juanita Weaver. "Dimensions of Spirituality." In *The Politics of Women's Spirituality*, edited by Charlene Spretnak. New York: Anchor, 1982.

Dexter, Mirian Robbins. *Whence the Goddesses: A Source Book*. New York: Pergamon, 1990.

Downing, Christine. *The Goddess: Mythological Representations of the Feminine*. New York: Crossroad, 1984.

Ehrenreich, Barbara, and Deidre English. *Witches, Midwives and Nurses: A History of Women Healers*. Old Westburg, NY: Feminist, 1973.

Eigo, Francis A., ed. *A Discipleship of Equals: Towards a Christian Feminist Spirituality*. Villanova, PA: Villanova University Press, 1988.

Finson, Shelley Davis. "Feminist Spirituality within the Framework of Feminist Consciousness." *Studies in Religion / Sciences Religieuses: A Canadian Journal* 16, no. 1 (1987): 65–77.

Fischer, Kathleen. *Reclaiming the Connections: A Contemporary Spirituality*. Kansas City, MO: Sheed & Ward, 1990.

———. *Women at the Well: Feminist Perspectives on Spiritual Direction*. New York: Paulist Press, 1988.

Frankiel, Tamar. *The Voice of Sarah: Feminine Spirituality and Traditional Judaism*. San Francisco: Harper & Row, 1990.

Giles, Mary E., ed. *The Feminist Mystic, and Other Essays on Women and Spirituality*. New York: Crossroad, 1982.

Gimbutas, Marija. *The Gods and Goddesses of Old Europe, 7000–3500 B.C.: Legends and Cult Images*. Los Angeles: University of California Press, 1982.

Goldenberg, Naomi. "Feminist Witchcraft: Controlling Our Own Inner Space." In *The Politics of Women's Spirituality*, edited by Charlene Spretnak. New York: Anchor, 1982.

Gray, Elizabeth Dodson, ed. *Sacred Dimensions of Women's Experience*. Wellesley, MA: Roundtable, 1988.

Haney, Eleanor H. *Vision and Struggle: Meditations on Feminist Spirituality and Politics*. Portland, ME: Astarte Shell, 1989.

Haughton, Rosemary. *Feminine Spirituality: Reflection on the Mysteries of the Rosary*. New York: Paulist Press, 1976.

Kalven, Janet, and Mary Buckley. *Women's Spirit Bonding*. New York: Pilgrim, 1984.

King, Ursula. *Women and Spirituality: Voice of Protest and Promise*. New York: New Amsterdam, 1989.

Kolbenschlag, Madonna. *Kiss Sleeping Beauty Good-Bye*. New York: Doubleday, 1979.

Letis, Theodore P. "Feminine Spirituality: Eve Shakes an Angry Fist at Yahweh, But He Triumphs Through the Son." *Journal of Christian Reconstruction* 9, nos. 1 and 2 (1982–83): 182–200.

Macek, Ellen. "The Emergence of a Feminine Spirituality in the Book of Martyrs." *Sixteenth Century Journal* 19, no. 1 (1988): 66–80.

Mack, Phyllis. "Gender and Spirituality in Early Quakerism, 1650–1665." In *Witnesses for Change: Quaker Women Over Three Centuries*, edited by Elizabeth Brown and Susan Mosher Stuard. New Brunswick, NJ: Rutgers University, 1989.

Maitland, Sara. *A Map of the New Country: Women and Christianity*. London: Routledge Kegan Paul, 1983.

Mariechild, Diane. *MotherWit: A Feminist Guide to Psychic Development*. Freedom, CA: Crossing, 1981.

McLaughlin, Eleanor. "Christ My Mother: Feminine Naming and Metaphor in Medieval Spirituality." *Nashotah Review* 15 (1975): 228–48.

Mollenkott, Virginia R. *Sensuous Spirituality: Out From Fundamentalism*. New York: Crossroad, 1992.

Monaghan, Patricia. *The Book of Goddesses and Heroines*. New York: E. P. Dutton, 1981.

Morton, Nell. *The Journey Is Home*. Boston: Beacon, 1986.

Muto, Susan Annette. "Foundations of Feminine Spirituality." *Witness* 67, no. 2 (February 1980): 5–9.

O'Brien, Theresa King, ed. *The Spiral Faith: Essays and Interviews on Women's Spirituality*. St. Paul, MN: YES, 1988.

Orenstein, Gloria Feman. *The Reflowering of the Goddess*. New York: Pergamon, 1990.

Plaskow, Judith, and Carol Christ, eds. *Weaving the Visions: New Patterns in Feminist Spirituality*. San Francisco: Harper & Row, 1989.

Porterfield, Amanda, and Barbara Welter. *Feminine Spirituality in America: From Sarah Edwards to Martha Graham*. Philadelphia: Temple University, 1980.

Ruether, Rosemary Radford, and Eleanor McLaughlin, eds. *Women of Spirit: Female Leadership in the Jewish and Christian Tradition*. New York: Simon & Schuster, 1979.

Schechter, Patricia. "Feminist Spirituality and Radical Political Commitment." *Journal of Women and Religion* 1, no. 1 (Spring 1981): 51–60.

Sölle, Dorothee. *The Window of Vulnerability: A Political Spirituality*. Minneapolis, MN: Augsburg Fortress, 1990.

Southard, Naomi P. F. "Recovering and Rediscovered Images: Spiritual Resources for Asian-American Women." *Asian Journal of Theology* 3 (October 1989): 624–38.

Spretnak, Charlene. *The Lost Goddesses of Early Greece: A Collection of Pre-Hellenic Myths*. Boston: Beacon, 1978.

———, ed. *The Politics of Women's Spirituality: Essays of the Rise of Spiritual Power with the Feminist Movement*. New York: Anchor, 1982.

Starhawk. *Dreaming the Dark: Magic, Sex and Politics*. Boston: Beacon, 1982.

——. *The Spiral Dance: A Rebirth of the Ancient Religion of the Great Goddess.* San Francisco: Harper & Row, 1979.

Suchocki, Marjorie Hewitt. "Earthsong, Godsong: Women's Spirituality." *Theology Today* 45 (January 1989): 392–402.

Umansky, Ellen, and Dianna Ashton, eds. *Four Generations of Jewish Women's Spirituality: A Source Book.* Boston: Beacon, 1992.

Washbourn, Penelope. *Becoming Woman: The Quest for Wholeness in Female Experience.* New York: Harper & Row, 1977.

Weaver, Mary Jo. "Springs of Water in a Dry Hand: A Process Model of Feminist Spirituality." In *A Discipleship of Equals*, edited by F. Eigo. Villanova, PA: Villanova University Press, 1988.

Weber, Christin Lore. *Womanchrist: A New Vision of Feminist Spirituality.* San Francisco: Harper & Row, 1987.

Winter, Miriam Terese, Adair Lummis, and Allison Stokes. *Women Claiming Responsibility for Their Own Spiritual Lives.* New York: Crossroad, 1994.

Women and History

There is a flourishing interest in women and religious history, as witnessed by the ever-increasing number of theses, articles, and books being written on the subject. What gets recorded in the histories, who is included, and how history is written, all are central concerns of feminist liberation theology.

Women's invisibility in traditional history means that writers today are challenged to write women back into history. The topics generally divide into two areas: the general history of women in the church, and specific women who stand out in the life of the church.

General History of the Women in the Church

Georgia Elma Harkness opened up the 1970s with her *Women in Church and Society* (1971), an historical and theological inquiry. This was followed by two very readable publications. The first was by Elise Boulding, *The Underside of History* (1976), which introduced the idea of women's history as the "underside of history." The second is Rosemary Radford Ruether and Eleanor McLaughlin's collection of essays, *Women of Spirit: Female Leadership in the Jewish and Christian Traditions* (1979). From 1981 to 1986, Rosemary Radford Ruether and Rosemary Skinner Kellar edited three volumes of *Women and Religion in America*. These works are all fascinating reading for history buffs!

Some of the book titles from the 1970s and 1980s give a sense of the focus for writers of women's history: *Not in God's Image: Women in History from the Greeks to the Victorians*, by Julia O'Faolain and Lauro Martines (1973); *Our Struggle to Serve: The Stories of Fifteen Evangelical Women*, edited by Virginia Hearn (1979); *Women, Church and State*, by Matilda Gage (1980); *Women in the Middle Ages: The Lives of Real Women in a Vibrant Age of Transition*, by Frances Gies and Joseph Gies (1980); *Her Story: Women in Christian Tradition*, by Barbara MacHaffie (1986); *Religion in the Lives of English Women, 1760–1930*, edited by Gail Malmgreen (1986); *Holy Feast and Holy Fast: The Religious Significance of Food to Medieval Women*, by Caroline Bynum (1987); and *Passionate Women: Two Medieval Mystics*, by Elizabeth Dreyer (1989).

In 1991, Clarissa Atkinson provided a wonderful study of motherhood as she looked at styles of child-rearing and family life in the Middle Ages in *The Oldest Vocation*.

An overview of articles written during the 1980s suggests a few themes that were of interest for historians. The ascetic woman is a fairly common theme: "The Conversion of Women to Ascetic Forms of Christianity," by Ross Kraemer (1980); "Ascetic Renunciation and Feminine Advancement: A Paradox of Late Ancient Christianity," by Elizabeth Clarke (1981); and "Women and Asceticism in the 4th Century: A Question of Interpretation," by Jean Simpson (1988) are examples. Women's involvement in mission is a second focal point for writers; works include: "Zealous Evangelists: The Woman's Auxiliary to the Board of Mission," by Mary Donovan (1982) and "Sisters All: Feminism and the American Women's Missionary Movement," by Shirley Garrett (1982). The history of women's organizations is a third focus; titles include: "Women in Groups," by Anne Boylan (1984); "Sisterhoods of Service and Reform: Organized Methodist Women in the Late 19th Century—An Essay on the State of Research," by Carolyn Gifford (1985); "The Leadership of Nuns in Immigrant Catholicism," by Mary Ewans (1988); and "Colorizing Church History: A History That Ignores Women and Ministry," by Ruth Tucker (1992).

The history of women's religious communities has proven to be an intriguing topic for many thesis writers. These include the evolution of religious communities in Canada from 1639–1973, by Joan Marguerite (1974); the role of women in monastic life in early medieval England and Ireland, by Carmine Bell (1975), and the part women took in the development of the monastic ideals of the Gilbertine Order in 1131, by Ellen Barrett (1986). In 1978, Margaret Williams wrote *Society of the Sacred Heart–History 1800–1975*, which traces the development of that society. The lives of the founders of religious orders have also provided intriguing thesis topics. Two such works include the story of Mary Josephine Rogers (a Maryknoll Sister), by Mary Kennedy (1980), and the influence of St. Elizabeth Seton (the founder of the Sisters of Charity), by Rose Marie Padovano (1984).

How history has been written is also of concern to feminist liberation theology. Elizabeth Schüssler Fiorenza wrote a chapter that focused on the method of writing about women in early church history in *Critical History and Biblical Faith: New Testament Perspective* (1979). Mary Sudman Donovan discussed a more inclusive historiography in her work about women and mission, "Women and Mission" (1984). In 1989, Halver Moxnes edited a special issue of *Studia Theologica: Scandinavian Journal of Theology* that included a chapter titled "Feminist Reconstruction of Early Christian History."

In the 1980s, the history of women in denominations became a subject of interest to scholars in the field of women's history. For instance, Donald Gorrell (1980) discussed a woman's rightful place in United Methodist history. Lois Boyd and Douglas Brackenridge (1983) followed with a study of two centuries of women's struggle for status in the Presbyterian Church. Nadine Frantz and Lauree Hersch Meyer (1985) celebrated the contributions of Brethren women. Mary Donovan (1986) traced the different ministries of women in the Episcopal Church from 1850 to 1920. Margaret Bacon (1986) studied the mothers of feminism in the Quaker tradition. Marjorie Procter-Smith (1985) studied women in the Shaker community, Maureen Beecher (1987) explored the sisterhood of women in Mormon history and culture, and Linda Huebert Hecht (1992) investigated the significance of Anabaptist women and religious change.

In the 1990s, historians show an interest in women as part of historical movements. These include Betty Deberg's (1990) study of gender as a factor in the first wave of American fundamentalism; Porterfield's (1992) study of female piety and the rise of religious humanism, revivalism, and feminism in the age of Finney; and Carol Deven's (1992) study of women's involvement in the Christian Missionary Movement from 1630 to 1900.

Specific Women in History

Women's history in the church goes back to its very beginning. Many historians who have studied church history have overlooked or ignored the contributions of women like Mary Magdalene, Dorcas, and Phoebe—women who accompanied Jesus in his ministry, or who were there as the nascent Christian community began to develop, often in *their* homes. In 1984, Mary Hammack published a much needed dictionary of many outstanding women who played decisive roles in the development of Christianity.

Recovery of that history is still a major task confronting researchers and writers. Patricia Wilson-Kastner and colleagues produced a fascinating book, *A Lost Tradition* (1981), which sets out the lives of women writers of the early church. During the 1980s, there were several publications written on early Christian martyrs, such as *Melanie*, by Elizabeth Clarke (1985), and *Perpetua*, by Rebecca Lyman (1989), and on many of the mystics, such as *Catherine of Siena*, by Suzanne Noffke (1980); *Margery Kempe*, by Clarissa Atkinson (1983);

Hildegard of Bingen, by Matthew Fox (1985); *Simone Weil*, by Laurie Brands (1983); and the unique character *Joan of Arc*, by Anne Barstow (1986) and by Nadia Margolis (1990). They provide fascinating reading for those interested in biographies.

A recent publication that engages the reader is titled *Prayer with Julian of Norwich*, by Gloria Durka (1989), which provides a window into the spirituality of a unique woman. A comment from the cover reads that this is "a quiet argument for women's rights."

Women's more recent history is particularly important to preserve. For instance, there was Ida Miller's (1978) work about the life of Frances Elizabeth Willard, who was dedicated to the Women's Temperance Movement; Margaret Littlehales's (1982) work about the vision of Mary Ward, who opened up frontiers in urban social work; and Robert Coles's (1987) work about the faith of Dorothy Day, a vibrant Roman Catholic social activist. All these stories are available to inspire women of today.

Books published in the 1990s include a wonderful contribution to our understanding of our foremothers, by tracing the religious social thought of three great ladies, Elizabeth Cady Stanton, Susan B. Anthony, and Anna Howard Shaw in Mary Pellauer's book *Toward a Tradition of Feminist Theology* (1991).

There is a growing body of feminist historical literature that reconstructs the events of history in such a way that it calls into question the very foundations of our belief. Three of these works include *The Lady Was a Bishop*, by Joan Morris (1973), *When God Was a Woman*, by Merlin Stone (1976), and *The Chalice and the Blade*, by Riane Eisler (1987). Each of these books leaves us with important questions: Were there women bishops? Was God once known as Mother? Are the very roots of Christianity patriarchal, and thus pivotal in the destruction that pervades our world? A feminist re-envisioning of history may find the answers to these questions.

References to Women and History

Atkinson, Clarissa. *Mystic and Pilgrim: The Book and the World of Margery Kempe*. Ithaca, NY: Cornell University Press, 1983.

——. *The Oldest Vocation: Christian Motherhood in the Middle Ages*. Ithaca, NY: Cornell University Press, 1991.

Bacon, Margaret Hope. *Mothers of Feminism: The Story of Quaker Women in America*. New York: Harper & Row, 1986.

Barrett, Ellen Marie. "From the Zeal of Seven Women: The Evolution and Monastic Ideals of the Gilbertine Order, 1131." Ph.D. diss., New York University, 1986.

Barstow, Anne Llewellyn. *Joan of Arc: Heretic, Mystic, Shaman*. (Studies in Women and Religion, 17). Lewiston, NY: Edwin Mellen Press, 1986.

Beecher, Maureen Ursenbach, and Lavina Fielding Anderson. *Sisters in Spirit: Mormon Women in Historical and Cultural Perspective.* Urbana: University of Illinois Press, 1987.

Bell, Carmine Jane. "The Role of Monastic Women in the Life and Letters of Early Medieval England and Ireland." Ph.D. diss., University of Virginia, 1975.

Boulding, Elise. *The Underside of History: A View of Women Through Time.* Boulder, CO: Westview, 1976.

Boyd, Lois A., and Douglas R. Brackenridge. *Presbyterian Women in America: Two Centuries of a Quest for Status.* (Presbyterian Historical Society Contributions to the Study of Religion, 9). Westport, CT: Greenwood, 1983.

Boylan, Anne M. "Women in Groups: Analysis of Women's Benevolent Organizations in New York and Boston, 1797–1840." *Journal of American History* 71, no. 3 (December 1984): 497–523.

Brands, Laurie Elizabeth. "The Spiritual Journey of Simone Weil and the Vision That Emerged from It." Ph.D. diss., University of Notre Dame, 1983.

Bynum, Caroline Walker. *Holy Feast and Holy Fast: The Religious Significance of Food to Medieval Women.* Berkeley: University of California Press, 1987.

Clarke, Elizabeth A. "Ascetic Renunciation and Feminine Advancement: A Paradox of Late Ancient Christianity." *Anglican Theological Review* 63, no. 3 (July 1981): 240–57.

———. *The Life of Melanie the Younger: Introduction, Translation and Commentary.* (Studies of Women and Religion, 14). Lewistown, NY: Edwin Mellen Press, 1985.

Coles, Robert. *Dorothy Day: A Radical Devotion.* Reading, MA: Addison-Wesley, 1987.

Deberg, Betty. *Ungodly Women and the First Wave of American Fundamentalism.* Minneapolis, MN: Fortress, 1990.

Deven, Carol. *Separate Confrontation: American Indian Women and the Christian Mission, 1630–1900.* Berkeley: University of California Press, 1992.

Donovan, Mary Sudman. *A Different Call: Women's Ministries in the Episcopal Church, 1850–1920.* Wilton, CT: Morehouse-Barlow, 1986.

————. "Women and Mission: Toward a More Inclusive Historiography." *Historical Magazine of the Protestant Episcopal Church* 53 (December 1984): 297–305.

————. "Zealous Evangelists: The Woman's Auxiliary to the Board of Mission." *Historical Magazine of the Protestant Episcopal Church* 51 (December 1982): 371–83.

Dreyer, Elizabeth. *Passionate Women: Two Medieval Mystics.* New York: Paulist Press, 1989.

Durka, Gloria. *Praying with Julian of Norwich.* Winona, MN: Saint Mary's, 1989.

Eisler, Riane. *The Chalice and the Blade.* San Francisco: Harper & Row, 1987.

Ewans, Mary. "The Leadership of Nuns in Immigrant Catholicism." In *The American Catholic Religious Life: Selected Historical Essays,* edited by Joseph Michael White. New York: Garland, 1988.

Fiorenza, Elizabeth Schüssler. "The Study of Women in Early Christianity: Some Methodological Consideration." In *Critical History and Biblical Faith: New Testament Perspective,* edited by T. Ryan. Villanova, PA: College Theological Society, 1979.

Fox, Matthew. *Illuminations of Hildegard of Bingen.* Santa Fe, NM: Bear; Mahwah, NJ: Paulist Press, 1985.

Franz, Nadine, and Lauree Hersch Meyer, eds. "Women Contribution to the Church." Special Issue of *Brethren Life and Thought: A Quarterly Journal Published in the Interests of the Church of the Brethren* 30 (Winter 1985): 4–63.

Gage, Matilda Joselyn. *Woman, Church and State.* Watertown, MA: Persephone, 1980.

Garrett, Shirley S. "Sisters All: Feminism and the American Women's Missionary Movement." In *Missionary Ideologies in the Imperialist Era: 1800–1920,* edited by Torben Christiansen and William R. Hutchinson. Aboulevarden, Denmark: Aros, 1982.

Gies, Frances, and Joseph Gies. *Women in the Middle Ages: The Lives of Real Women in a Vibrant Age of Transition.* Toronto: Fitzhenry and Whiteside, 1980.

Gifford, Carolyn De Sevarte. "Sisterhoods of Service and Reform: Organized Methodist Women in the Late 19th Century—An Essay on the State of Research." *Methodist History* 24 (October 1985): 15–30.

Gorrell, Donald K., ed. *'Women's Rightful Place': Women in United Methodist History*. Dayton, OH: United Theological Seminary, 1980.

Hammack, Mary L. *A Dictionary of Women in Church History*. Chicago: Moody, 1984.

Harkness, Georgia Elma. *Women in Church and Society: A Historical Theological Inquiry*. Nashville, TN: Abingdon, 1971.

Hearn, Virginia, ed. *Our Struggle to Serve: The Stories of Fifteen Evangelical Women*. Waco, TX: Word Books, 1979.

Hecht, Linda Huebert. "Women and Religious Change: The Significance of Anabaptist Women." *Studies in Religion / Sciences Religieuses* 21 (November 1992): 57–66.

Kennedy, Mary Therese. "A Study of the Charism Operative in Mary Josephine Rogers (1882–1955), Founder of the Maryknoll Sisters." Ph.D. diss., Saint Louis University, 1980.

Kraemer, Ross S. "The Conversion of Women to Ascetic Forms of Christianity," *Signs: Journal of Women in Culture and Society* 6, no. 2 (Winter 1980): 289–307.

Littlehales, Margaret. *Mary Ward: A Woman of All Seasons*. London: Clarke, 1982.

Lyman, Rebecca. "Perpetua: A Christian Quest for Self." *Journal of Women and Religion* 8 (Winter 1989): 26–33.

MacHaffie, Barbara J. *Her Story: Women in Christian Tradition*. Philadelphia: Fortress Press, 1986.

Malmgreen, Gail, ed. *Religion in the Lives of English Women, 1760–1930*. London: Croom Helm, 1986.

Margolis, Nadia. *Joan of Arc in History, Literature & Film: A Selected Annotated Bibliography*. New York: Garland, 1990.

Marguerite, Jean. "Évolution des Communautés Religieuses de Femmes au Canada, 1639–1973." Ph.D. diss., University of Ottawa, 1974.

Miller, Ida Tetrault. "Frances Elizabeth Willard: Religious Leader and Social Reformer." Ph.D. diss., Boston University Graduate School, 1978.

Morris, Joan. *The Lady Was a Bishop: The Hidden History of Women with Clerical Ordination and the Jurisdiction of Bishops*. New York: Macmillan, 1973.

Moxnes, Halvor, ed. "Feminist Reconstruction of Early Christian History." *Studia Theologica: Scandinavian Journal of Theology* 43, no. 1 (Special Issue, 1989): 1–163.

Noffke, Suzanne, ed. *Catherine of Siena: The Dialogue.* (Classics of Western Spirituality). Mahwah, NJ: Paulist Press, 1980.

O'Faolain, Julia, and Lauro Martines. *Not in God's Image: Women in History, from the Greeks to the Victorians.* New York: Harper & Row, 1973.

Padovano, Rose Marie Bernadette. "The Influence of Elizabeth Seton Reflected in Dimensions of Her Charism and Educational Ministry: A Renewal Program." D.Min. diss., Drew University, 1984.

Pagels, Elaine. *The Gnostic Gospels.* New York: Vintage Books, 1981.

Pellauer, Mary D. *Toward a Tradition of Feminist Theology: The Religious Social Thought of Elizabeth Cady Stanton, Susan B. Anthony, and Anna Howard Shaw.* Brooklyn, NY: Carlson, 1991.

Porterfield, Amanda. *Female Piety in Puritan New England.* New York: Oxford University Press, 1992.

Procter-Smith, Marjorie. *Women in Shaker Community and Worship: A Feminist Analysis of the Uses of Religious Symbolism.* (Studies in Women and Religion, 16). Lewiston, NY: Edwin Mellen Press, 1985.

Ruether, Rosemary Radford, and Eleanor McLaughlin, eds. *Women of Spirit: Female Leadership in the Jewish and Christian Traditions.* New York: Simon & Schuster, 1979.

Ruether, Rosemary Radford, and Rosemary Skinner Keller, eds. *Women and Religion in America.* 3 vols. San Francisco: Harper & Row, 1981–1986.

Simpson, Jean. "Women and Asceticism in the 4th Century: A Question of Interpretation." *The Journal of Religious History* 15 (June 1988): 38–60.

Stone, Merlin. *When God Was a Woman.* New York: Dial, 1976.

Tucker, Ruth. "Colorizing Church History: A History That Ignores Women and Ministry." *Christianity Today* 36 (July 20, 1992): 20–23.

Williams, Margaret. *The Society of the Sacred Heart—History 1800–1975.* London: Darton, Longman and Todd, 1978.

Wilson-Kastner, Patricia, J. Ronald Kastner, Ann Millin, Rosemary Rader, and Jeremiah Reddy. *A Lost Tradition: Women Writers of the Early Church.* Washington, DC: University of America Press, 1981.

Ministry of Women

Most of the books published in the general area of women's ministry did not appear until the 1980s and early 1990s, corresponding with the influx of women into full-time, paid, accountable ministry.

Ministry is the response to God's call. In the biblical and historical sections of this chapter there are many accounts of the faithful ministry of women in the church and society. Many historians have turned to the Christian Bible to explore the biblical foundations of women's ministry: Elizabeth Tetlow (1980); Elizabeth Clarke (1983); Barbara MacHaffie (1986); Ruth Tucker and Walter Liefeld (1987); and Joann Conn (1987).

Still other historians celebrate women's ministry as they reflect on the contributions they have made to the church. Two titles that illustrate this celebration are *American Protestant Women in World Mission: History of the First Feminist Movement in North America*, by R. Pierce Beaver (1980), and *No Time for Silence: Evangelical Women in Public Ministry Around the Turn of the Century*, by Janette Hassey (1986).

But what is the impact of feminist consciousness on women's understanding and experience of ministry? Letty Russell discusses this in her two ground-breaking books, *The Future of Partnership* (1979) and *Growth in Partnership* (1981), which reflect on "partnership" in ministry. She explains her understanding of partnership in her introduction of *Growth in Partnership*:

> Partnership may be described as a new focus of relationship in which there is continuing commitment and common struggle in interaction with a wider community contact. Partnership is always growing and dying, for it is human interrelationship that is never static. (P. 18)

Additional resources that examine the working relationship between the sexes include a book by Fran Ferder and John Heagle, *Partnership: Women and Men in Ministry* (1989), and two articles: "Partners in Ministry," by Stephanie Frey and Laurence Wholrabe (1988); and "Men and Women Ministering Together," by Kenneth Himes (1990).

Denominational publications seem to address the nature of this debate most often. For example, *Review and Expositor: A Baptist Theological Journal* included an article "Women in Ministry: The Distaff of the Church," by Sara Anders (1983), and *Dialogue: Journal of Mormon Thought* included two notables articles, one titled "Ministering Angels: Single Women in Mormon Society," by Lavina Anderson (1983), and the more recent, "Mormon Women and the Right to Wage Work," by Vella Evans (1990). *The Expository Times* has a reflection on "Female Ministry in the Salvation Army," by Douglas Clarke (1984), and *The Unitarian Universalist Christian* discusses the "Women in Ministry Program of the National Council of Churches of Christ," by D. Arakawa (1986). A survey article reflecting on "The Ministry of Women:

Past, Present, and Future," by Phyllis Anderson (1985) can be found in the *Lutheran Theological Seminary Bulletin*. A reflection on "Women in the Catholic Church of Canada," by Elizabeth Lacelle (1985) can be found in the *Ecumenist: A Journal Promoting Christian Unity*, and the *Brethren Life and Thought* has an article titled "Women as Missionaries," by Mary Eikenberry (1985).

Lynn Rhodes published her valuable thesis as *Co-creating: A Feminist Vision of Ministry* (1987). In it, she interviews several women clergy who identify themselves as feminists. They tell her how they handle issues of authority, how they understand mission, salvation, and their own vocation. Rhodes speaks about women struggling with a tradition that has often been used against women's freedoms and equality. She reminds us that, because women have stories of their own, faith experiences, and ways of talking about God entering into their lives, they are also authors of tradition. This small paperback is essential reading for any woman thinking about ministry. It discusses the profound questions that face all women in ministry, particularly those who have developed feminist consciousness.

The following is a summary of some of the titles from articles and booklets that illustrate the range of issues that women encounter in ministry: "Celibacy in the Men's Church," by Nadine Foley (1980); "Summary of the Discussion: Women and Power in the Church," by Anne Carr (1982); "Black Women and the Church," by Jacquelyn Grant (1982); "Call Me by My Name," by Mary Gibson et al. (1983); "Women in Ministry in the Small Congregation," by Lynne Josselyn (1983); "Women in Authority: Operating out of a Different Perspective," by Jean Armstrong (1984); "Women in Ministry Research Report," by Janet Silman (1984), a report on sexual harassment of women in ministry; "Psychological Androgyny and Self-Esteem in Clergywomen," by Katherine Flagg (1984); *Women, Decision Making and the Future*, by Barbara Clowse (1985); *Women in Parish Ministry: Stress and Support*, by Marian Coger (1985); "Deacons [lesbian] Suspended" [unsigned] (1986); "Clergywomen and Senior Pastorates," by Carole Carlson (1988); "Ministry from a Single Perspective: Assets and Liabilities," by Carolyn Crawford (1988); "On Power and Gender," by Daphne Hampson (1988); "Keeping Our Balance: Work, Family and Self," edited by Sharon Baker-Johnson (1988); "Power Struggles, Equality Quests, and Women in 'Ecclesia'," by Carole Rayburn (1989); "Women in Ministry: Estrangement from Ourselves," by Susan Dunfee (1989); and "Women in Ministry," by Ellen Leonard (1990).

As issues of women in the church have been addressed by women, they have encouraged their denominations to respond by way of changing structures, building networks, and providing resources. We still are in the early days of realizing the impact that the increased number of women entering full-time ministry will have, both for ministry and for the larger church.

The diversity of women's roles and the spiritual power that women demonstrated in Jesus' time and in the church that they have served have often been forgotten. This is seen nowhere more clearly than in the history of deaconesses. Diaconal ministry in many denominations has been the one area where women have long been established. Three wonderful histories of the lives of deaconesses are included in this section because they reveal the myriad of places where deaconesses have served the church. Janet Grierson published a short history of Anglican deaconesses, *The Deaconess* (1981), in which she not only traces the development of the Order in the Church of England, but sets this against the ministry of women in early centuries of the church. Nancy Hardy recorded in her work, *Called to Serve—A Story of Diaconal Ministry in the United Church* (1985), the struggles of deaconesses in her denomination to find recognition for their contribution. And Aimé Georges Martimort, in *Deaconesses* (1986), has provided a detailed history of deaconesses, from the early church on. Each of these histories attests to the fact that these women had to continuously struggle to have their ministry recognized, and to claim just treatment by the church that they so lovingly served.

Also included in the bibliography are several articles that trace the roots and significance of Diaconal ministry, such as Sister Philsy's "Diakonia of Women in the New Testament" (1983).

It is to be hoped that one outcome of the Ecumenical Decade of the Churches in Solidarity with Women will be that all women's ministries, lay or ordered, paid or voluntary, will indeed be recognized as the work of the Holy Spirit.

References on the Ministry of Women

Anders, Sara F. "Women in Ministry: The Distaff of the Church." *Review and Expositor: A Baptist Theological Journal* 80 (Summer 1983): 427–36.

Anderson, Grace M. *A Study of Women in Ministry*. Burlington, Canada: Trinity, 1990.

Anderson, Lavina Fielding. "Ministering Angels: Single Women in Mormon Society." *Dialogue: Journal of Mormon Thought* 16, no. 3 (Autumn 1983): 59–72.

Anderson, Phyllis Brosch. "The Ministry of Women: Past, Present, and Future." *Lutheran Theological Seminary Bulletin* 65, no. 4 (Fall 1985): 35–44.

Arakawa, D. "Women in Ministry Program of the National Council of Churches of Christ." *Unitarian Universalist Christians* 41, no. 1 (Spring 1986): 20–21.

Armstrong, Jean. "Women in Authority: Operating Out of a Different Perspective." *PMC: The Practice of Ministry in Canada* 1, no. 3 (September 1984): 20–21.

Baker-Johnson, Sharon, ed. "Keeping Our Balance: Work, Family and Self." *Daughters of Sarah* 14, no. 2 (March–April 1988): 3–27.

Beaver, R. Pierce, ed. *American Protestant Women in World Mission: History of the First Feminist Movement in North America*. Rev. ed. Grand Rapids, MI: William B. Eerdmans, 1980.

Carlson, Carole. "Clergywomen and Senior Pastorates." *Christian Century* 105, no. 1 (January 6–13, 1988): 15–17.

Caron, Charlotte. "The Significance of Women in Ministry." *Touchstone: Heritage and Theology in a New Age* 4, no. 1 (Spring–Summer 1986): 59–75.

Carr, Anne E. "Summary of the Discussion: Women and Power in the Church." *Proceedings of the Catholic Theological Society of America* 37 (1982): 128–29.

Chilcost, Paul Wesley. *John Wesley and the Women Preachers of Early Methodism*. Methuen, NJ: Scarecrow, 1991.

Clarke, Douglas. "Female Ministry in the Salvation Army." *Expository Times* 95 (May 1984): 232–35.

Clarke, Elizabeth A. *Ascetic Piety and Women's Faith: Essays of Late Ancient Christianity*. (Studies in Women and Religion, 20). Lewiston, NY: Edwin Mellen Press, 1986.

———. *Women in the Early Church*. Wilmington, DE: Michael Glazer, 1983.

Clowse, Barbara Barksdale. *Women, Decision-Making and the Future*. Atlanta, GA: John Knox, 1985.

Coger, Marian. *Women in Parish Ministry: Stress and Support*. New York: Alban Institute, 1985.

Conn, Joann Wolski. "A Discipleship of Equals: Past, Present & Future." *Horizons* 14 (Fall 1987): 232–61.

Crawford, Carolyn A. "Ministry from a Single Perspective: Assets and Liabilities." *Journal of Pastoral Care* 42, no. 2 (Summer 1988): 117–23.

"Deacons Suspended" [self-acknowledged Lesbians, Anglican Church of Canada]. *Christian Century* 103, no. 11 (April 2, 1986): 322.

Dunfee, Susan Nelson. "Women in Ministry: Estrangement from Ourselves." *Quarterly Review: A Scholarly Journal for Reflection on Ministry* 9 (Summer 1989): 52–74.

Eikenberry, Mary. "Women as Missionaries." *Brethren Life and Thought* 30 (Winter 1985): 90–94.

Evans, Vella Neil. "Mormon Women and the Right to Wage Work." *Dialogue: A Journal of Mormon Thought* 23, no. 4 (Winter 1990): 45–63.

Felder, Cain J. "The Bible, Black Women and Ministry." *Journal of Interdenominational Theological Center* 12 (Fall 1984–Fall 1985): 9–21.

Ferder, Fran, and John Heagle. *Partnership: Women and Men in Ministry*. Notre Dame: Ave Maria, 1989.

Flagg, Katherine. "Psychological Androgyny and Self-Esteem in Clergy-women." *Journal of Psychology and Theology* 12, no. 3 (Fall 1984): 222–29.

Foley, Nadine. "Celibacy in the Men's Church." In *Women in a Men's Church (Concilium 134)*, edited by Virgil Elizondo and Norbert Greinacher. Edinburgh, Scotland: T. & T. Clark, 1980.

Frey, Stephanie, and Lawrence R. Wohlrabe. "Partners in Ministry: Men and Women." *Word and World: Theology for Christian Ministry* 8, no. 4 (Fall 1988): 366–73.

Gibson, Mary Irwin, Shirley Herman, Maureen Kabwe, Faye Mount, and Allison Stewart Patterson. "Call Me by My Name" [issues involved in being a woman in ministry]. *Arc* 10, no. 2 (Spring 1983): 24–41.

Grant, Jacquelyn. "Black Women and the Church." In *All the Women Are White, All the Blacks Are Men, But Some of Us Are Brave*, edited by Gloria T. Hull, Patricia Bell Scott, and Barbara Scott. Old Westbury, NY: Feminist, 1982.

Grierson, Janet. *The Deaconess*. London: CIO, 1981.

Hampson, Daphne. "On Power and Gender." *Modern Theology: A Quarterly Journal of Systematic and Philosophical Theology* 4, no. 3 (April 1988): 234–50.

Hardy, Nancy. *Called to Serve—A Story of Diaconal Ministry in the United Church of Canada*. Toronto: Division of Ministry, Personnel, and Education, United Church of Canada, 1985.

Hassey, Janette. *No Time for Silence: Evangelical Women in Public Ministry Around the Turn of the Century*. Grand Rapids, MI: Zondervan, 1986.

Himes, Kenneth. "Men and Women Ministering Together: A Report from Participant Observers." *New Theology Review* 3 (August 1990): 63–70.

Ide, Arthur Frederick. *Women As Priest, Bishop and Laity in the Early Catholic Church to 440 A.D.* Mesquite, TX: Ide House, 1984.

Josselyn, Lynne. "Women in Ministry in the Small Congregation." In *New Possibilities for Small Churches*, edited by Douglas Alan Walrath. New York: Pilgrim, 1983.

Lacelle, Elizabeth J. "Women in the Catholic Church of Canada." *Ecumenist: A Journal Promoting Christian Unity* 23, no. 4 (May– June 1985): 49–54.

Leonard, Ellen. "Women in Ministry." *Grail* 6 (July 1990): 344–53.

MacHaffie, Barbara J. *Her Story: Women in Christian Tradition.* Philadelphia: Westminster, 1986.

Marimort, Aime Georges. *Deaconesses: An Historical Study,* translated by K. D. Whitehead. San Francisco: Ignatius, 1986.

Muir, Elizabeth Gillian. *Petticoats in the Pulpit: The Story of Early Nineteenth-Century Methodist Women Preachers in Upper Canada.* Toronto: United Church, 1991.

Philsy, Sister. "Diakonia of Women in the New Testament." *Indian Journal of Theology* 32 (January–June 1983): 110–18.

Rayburn, Carole A. "Power Struggles, Equality Quests, and Women in 'Ecclesia.'" *The Journal of Pastoral Counseling* 24, no. 2 (1989): 145–50.

Rhodes, Lynn Nell. *Co-creating: A Feminist Vision of Ministry.* Philadelphia: Westminster, 1987.

Russell, Letty M. *The Future of Partnership.* Philadelphia: Westminster, 1979.

———. *Growth in Partnership.* Philadelphia: Westminster, 1981.

Silman, Janet. *Women in Ministry Research Report.* Toronto: Division of Ministry, Personnel, and Education, United Church of Canada, 1984.

Tetlow, Elizabeth M. *Women in Ministry in the New Testament.* New York: Paulist Press, 1980.

Tucker, Ruth A., and Walter Liefeld. *Daughters of the Church: A History of Women in Ministry from New Testament Times to the Present*. Grand Rapids, MI: Zondervan, 1987.

The Ordination Debate

The ordination debate within the churches elicited an extraordinary number of articles and books during the 1970s and 1980s. In 1976, Marianne Micks and Charles Price edited a volume of essays titled *Towards a New Theology of Ordination*, but unquestionably the debate goes back much further. The church's disapproving stance on the ordination of women was challenged by many voices when Antoinette Brown Blackwell (1825–1921) in the United States and Lydia Gruchy in Canada (1894–1992) prepared themselves for ordination and were refused. Both women were eventually ordained: Antoinette Brown Blackwell was ordained into the Congregational Church in 1852; later she became a Unitarian minister. Lydia Gruchy was ordained into the newly formed United Church of Canada in 1936. Other resources on the ordination of women include: Nellie McClung's *In Times Like Those* (1915); Elsie Culver's *Women in the World of Religion* (1967); E. T. James's *Notable American Women* (1971); Sidney Ahlstrom's *A Religious History of the American People* (1972); and David Jones's "The Ordination of Women in the Christian Church" (1989).

Male Support of Ordination of Women

As with the issue of God-language, many of those discussing the ordination of women are male voices. One early champion of the cause was the Lutheran scholar Krister Stendahl, who wrote *The Bible and the Role of Women* (1966). His work in hermeneutics, the Bible, and the role of women laid the groundwork for ensuing discussions. Others such as Eric Lionel Mascall (1972), Caroll Stuhlmueller (1978), and Paul Jewett (1980) have continued the debate.

Women's Voices

Women's voices often speak from their own desire to be ordained. Emily C. Hewitt (1973) and Isabel Carter Heyward (1976) were two women who would later be among the eleven women "irregularly ordained" in the Episcopalian Church on July 29, 1974. Their ordinations were recognized in 1976, and today there are approximately 1,500 Episcopal women priests. The Anglican Church of Canada began ordaining women to the priesthood in 1977; the Anglican community in Australia ordained their first woman priest in 1992.

At an historic event in 1976, Roman Catholic women gathered in Detroit to declare their "call" to full participation in their denomination. Two thousand people came together to hear Sister Nadine Foley proclaim that the question of women's ordination is not just a woman's issue, but a fundamental issue in the life of the church. Anne Marie Gardiner (1976) edited the proceedings of that conference.

Two books reflect on the struggle of women to claim full participation in the life of the Anglican Church of England. In *Sharing a Vision* (1978), Phoebe Willetts reflects on her struggle to claim full participation, suggesting that her relationship to the church is like an apartheid based on sex not color. In *Pilgrimage to Priesthood* (1983), Elizabeth Canham discusses her desire for recognition as a priest. She was finally ordained as an Episcopal priest in the United States of America.

Church Officials Speak

Naturally, official bodies of the church are also part of this debate. The Vatican (Catholic Church) produced the *Declaration on the Question of the Admission of Women to the Ministerial Priesthood* (1976), which reiterated the Catholic Church's policy against ordaining women priests. One of the central arguments against women being priests is that the priest is to be an image of Christ (male), and a woman obviously could not represent such an image. Leonard Swidler and Arlene Swidler swiftly edited a response in *Women Priests: A Catholic Commentary on the Vatican Declaration* (1977). This comprehensive collection of writings by leading Roman Catholic scholars responds to this issue with such essays as "Ordination and the Ministry Willed by Jesus," and "The Apostleship of Women in Early Christianity."

The Church of England (1973, 1987, 1988) published several reports on the ordination question.

Dialogue with Catholic and Orthodox Churches

The ordination of women is also problematic for dialogue with the Orthodox communions. An early reflection on women's ordinations and orthodox views was provided by Constantine Tsirpanlis (1984). Movement by the church toward endorsing the ordination of women has occasioned dialogue between the Metropolitan (1989) and the Archbishops (1989).

The roots of the argument against the ordination of women are set out in the Ecumenical Patriarchate's (1989) summary of ecclesiastical positions: Jesus did not select women as Apostles; Theotokos (the mother of God) did not exercise the function of sacramental priesthood; the Apostolic Tradition did not ordain women; Pauline teachings do not support the ordination of women; women cannot provide the image of the maleness of Christ.

Alyson Peberdy, in her book *Women Priests?* (1988), reminds us of the issue of women's ordination in the context of Anglican-Roman Catholic dialogue. These concerns are also discussed in *One in Christ: A*

Catholic Ecumenical Review, by Robert Runcie (1989), a former Archbishop of Canterbury.

The debate regarding the ordination of women as rabbis has produced at least one volume edited by Simon Greenberg (1988). This includes studies and responses from a variety of Conservative Jewish scholars.

World Council Support

An ecumenical perspective on the ordination of women began as early as 1970 with a conference in Switzerland. Almost ten years later, Constance Parvey published the Faith and Order paper, "Ordination of Women in Ecumenical Perspective: Workbook for the Church's Future" (1980).

More recent ecumenical reflections can be found in "Introducing the Ecumenical Decade for Churches in Solidarity with Women," by Emilio Castro (1988), and "Unity and Renewal in Feminist Perspective," by Letty Russell (1988), in *Mid-Stream: An Ecumenical Journal*.

The Experience of Ordained Women

Women who have been ordained are beginning to reflect on their experience in books such as *Womanpriest: A Personal Odyssey*, by Alla Bozarth-Campbell (1978), and *Call Accepted: Reflections on Woman's Ordination in the Free Churches*, by Rosemary Wakelin (1988). Other reflections in journal articles describe the ramifications for women who have chosen to function in ministry in a patriarchal system; authors include: Suzanne Hiatt (1979), Rosemary Ruether (1980), Sally Eaton (1982), Mary Simpson (1985), Meg Wheatley-Pesci (1985), Carol Mork (1987), Roberta Morris (1987), and Pamela Darling (1988).

The first national examination of the attitudes toward ordained women in most mainline denominations in the United States was published in 1983 by Jackson Carroll, Barbara Hargrove, and Adair Lummis. This groundbreaking study includes research with the American Baptist Church in the United States, the American Lutheran Church, the Anglican Christian Church (Disciples of Christ), the Lutheran Church in America, the Church of Christ, the United Methodist Church, and the United Presbyterian Church. Questions that they raised in the study include: What kinds of careers are women able to carve out in the church? How are ordained women accepted? What institutional obstacles remain? The authors recognize that, in the final analysis, what counts is the ministry and mission of the churches these women serve. Yet they recognize that, until the blocks are removed from women and other marginalized groups, the fullness of this ministry and mission cannot be realized.

Two further studies include a progress report of ordained women in the Presbyterian Church, United States, by Patricia McClung (1984), and an analysis by the Lutheran Church of ordained women in the life of their denomination by Frances Maher (1975). The United

Church of Canada has ordained women for more than fifty years, and a reflection on this experience was written by Deborah Marshall (1986) at the time of that anniversary. Edward Lehman (1987) made a study of women clergy in England, and Mary Donovan (1988) surveyed the experience of women priests in the Episcopal Church.

Recent works include Gail Gabbert's (1990) research of the experiences of sixty-nine women in ministry in ten denominations. Her work focuses on employment and other ordination issues. *God Calls, Man Chooses: A Study of Women in Ministry*, by Grace Anderson (1990) is a study that focuses on the experience of women in four mainline Canadian churches. Two current publications continue the study of issues surrounding women's ordination: *Women's Ordination* (1991) and *The Churches Speak on Women's Ordination* (1991), both edited by J. A. Melton and Gary Ward. The first brings together the current official statements from religious bodies and ecumenical organizations. The second discusses the politics and feminist praxis associated with the priesthood.

The Debate Continues

The recent election of the first woman bishop in the Episcopal Church in the United States made news both in and out of the church. Pamela Darling (1989) voices the concern of many when she writes:

> For both traditionalists and the "feminist cabal" they fear, Barbara Harris' ordination to the episcopate symbolizes the beginning of a new order for church and society. If the process of change is to continue, if she is not to be tokenized by a self-protecting structure of power and privilege, we must find ways to win the hearts of those who fear change, to call to conversion those whose privilege binds them to the dysfunction and evils of the old order, and speak plainly the eternal Word of God's saving love. (P. 11)

There are several recent articles and books about this historic occasion in the references; authors include: Peter Steinfels (1988), May Malanie (1989), Myrtle Langley (1989), Jennifer Chapman (1989), and Jacqueline Field-Bibb (1991).

In the 1990s, we have seen two other women made bishops, one in Australia and the other in Canada.

Not every woman has a call to ordained ministry. In fact, today, many would say that lay ministry is far more appropriate. But there are those who know the call to ordained ministry and so the ordination debate will continue until all women have the choice of whether or not to be ordained.

References on the Ordination Debate

Ahlstrom, Sidney E. *A Religious History of the American People*. New Haven: Yale University Press, 1972.

Anderson, Grace M. *God Calls, Man Chooses: A Study of Women in Ministry*. Burlington, Canada: Trinity, 1990.

Bozarth-Campbell, Alla. *Womanpriest: A Personal Odyssey*. New York: Paulist Press, 1978.

Canham, Elizabeth. *Pilgrimage to Priesthood*. London: SPCK, 1983.

Carroll, Jackson W., Barbara Hargrove, and Adair T. Lummis. *Women of the Cloth: A New Opportunity for the Churches*. San Francisco: Harper & Row, 1983.

Castro, Emilio, ed. "Introducing the Ecumenical Decade for Churches in Solidarity with Women." *The Ecumenical Review* 40 (January 1988): 104–10.

Catholic Church. Congregation pro Doctrina Fidei. *Declaration on the Question of the Admission of Women to the Ministerial Priesthood*. Vatican City: Catholic Church, 1976.

Chapman, Jennifer. *The Last Bastion: Women Priests, the Case for Against*. London: Methuen, 1989.

Chapman, Mark. "The Ordination of Women Evangelical and Catholic." *Dialog: A Journal of Theology* 28 (Spring 1989): 133–36.

Church of England. Advisory Council of the Church's Ministry. *The Ordination of Women to the Priesthood*. London: Church Information Office, 1973.

———. General Synod House of Bishops. *The Ordination of Women to the Priesthood: First Report by the House of Bishops*. London: Church of England General Synod, 1987.

———. *The Ordination of Women to the Priesthood: Second Report by the House of Bishops*. London: General Synod of the Church of England, June, 1988.

Culver, Elsie Thomas. *Women in the World of Religion*. Garden City, NY: Doubleday, 1967.

Darling, Pamela. "Episcopal Visitors: Symbols of Institutional Sexism." *Witness* 71, no. 9 (September 1988): 8–10.

———. "Patriarchy Strikes Back." *Witness* 73 (April 1989): 9–11.

Donovan, Mary S. *Women Priests in the Episcopal Church: The Experience of the First Decade*. Cincinnati, OH: Forward Movement, 1988.

Eaton, Sally. "Womanpriest: Coming into Full Power." *Journal of Women and Religion* 2, no. 1 (Spring 1982): 15–20.

Ecumenical Patriarchate. "Conclusion of the Inter-Orthodox Consultation on Women and the Question of Ordination." *Ecumenical Trend* 18 (March 1989): 36–42.

Edwards, Denis. "The Ordination of Women and Anglican-Roman Catholic Dialogue." *Pacifica: Australia Theological Studies* 1 (June 1988): 125–40.

Field, Barbara. "Betty Is a Prime Number: Matching Metaphors of Priesthood and Womanhood." *Pacifica: Australia Theological Studies* 3 (June 1990): 172–86.

Field-Bibb, Jacqueline. *Women Toward Priesthood: Ministerial Politics & Feminists Praxis*. Cambridge, England: Cambridge University Press, 1991.

Fitzgerald, Kyriaki. "Inter-Orthodox Theological Consultation on Women in the Church." *Ecumenical Trends* 18 (March 1989): 33–36.

Gabbert, Gail. "Women in Ministry: Employment and Ordination Issues." D.Min. diss. Chicago: Lutheran School of Theology, 1990.

Gardiner, Anne Marie, ed. *Women and Catholic Priesthood: An Expanded Vision. Proceedings of the Detroit Ordination Conference*. New York: Paulist Press, 1976.

Greenberg, Simon, ed. *The Ordination of Women as Rabbis: Studies and Responses*. New York: The Jewish Theological Seminary of America, 1988.

Hewett, Emily C. *Women Priests: Yes or No?* New York: Seabury, 1973.

Heyward, Isabel Carter. *A Priest Forever*. New York: Seabury, 1976.

Hiatt, Suzanne. "More Women Priests, Bishops Still Angry." *Witness* 62, no. 7 (July 1979): 4–6.

James, E. T., ed. *Notable American Women, 1605–1950*. Vol. 2. Cambridge, MA: Belknap of Harvard University, 1971.

Jewett, Paul. *The Ordination of Women: An Essay on the Office of Christian Ministry*. Grand Rapids, MI: William B. Eerdmans, 1980.

Jones, David A. "The Ordination of Women in the Christian Church: An Examination of the Debate, 1880–1893." *Encounter* 50 (Summer 1989): 199–217.

Langley, Myrtle. "One Baptism, One Ministry: The Ordination of Women in Unity in Christ." *Transformation: An International Dialogue on Evangelical Social Ethic* 6, no. 2 (1989): 27–31.

Lehman, Edward C. *Women Clergy in England: Sexism, Modern Consciousness, and Church in Viability*. (Studies in Religion and Society, 16). Lewiston, NY: Edwin Mellen Press, 1987.

Maher, Frances, ed. "The Ordination of Women in Lutheran Churches: Analysis of an LWF Survey." *LWF Documentation*, no. 18 (March 1984): 1–36.

Malanie, May A. "The Ordination of Women: The Churches' Responses to Baptism, Eucharist, and Ministry." *Journal of Ecumenical Studies* 26 (Spring 1989): 251–69.

Marshall, Deborah. "Ministry of Women" [50th anniversary of ordination of women]. *Exchange: For Leaders of Adults* 10, no. 3 (Spring 1986): 31–33.

Mascell, Eric Lionel. *Women Priests?* London: Church Literature, 1972.

McClung, Nellie. *In Times Like These*. Toronto: McLeod and Allen, 1915.

McClung, Patricia Austin. "Twenty Years of the Ordination of Women: A Progress Report." *Presbyterian Church U.S. Seminary Bulletin* 99 (May 1984): 15–21.

Melton, J. A., and Gary I. Ward, eds. *The Churches Speak on Women's Ordination*. Detroit: Gale Research, 1991.

———. *Women's Ordination: Official Statements from Religious Bodies and Ecumenical Organizations*. Detroit: Gale Research, 1991.

Micks, Marianne H., and Charles P. Price, eds. *Towards a New Theology of Ordination: Essays on the Ordination of Women*. Somerville, MA: Greeno, Hadden, 1976.

Mork, Carol J. "Women's Ordination and the Leadership of the Church." *Word and World: Theology for Christian Ministry* 7, no. 4 (Fall 1987): 374–79.

Morris, Roberta. "Canadian Women 'Re-vision' Priesthood." *Catholic New Times* 11, no. 12 (June 14, 1987): 1, 14.

Parvey, Constance F., ed. "Ordination of Women in Ecumenical Perspective: Workbook for the Church's Future." (Faith and Order Paper, 105). Geneva: World Council of Churches, 1980.

Patterson, Torquie. "The Ordination of Women: A Contribution to the Debate with the CPSA." *Journal of Theology for South Africa* 66 (March 1989): 21–33.

Peberdy, Alyson, ed., *Women Priests?* (Women and Religion series). Basingstoke, England: Marshall Pickering, 1988.

Ruether, Rosemary Radford. "Why Males Fear Women Priests: Historical Analysis." *Witness* 63 (July 1980): 19–21.

Runcie, Archbishop Robert, and Pope John Paul II. "The Ordination of Women: Letter Between Canterbury and Rome." *One in Christ: A Catholic Ecumenical Review* 25, no. 1 (1989): 91–94.

Russell, Letty M. "Unity and Renewal in Feminist Perspective." *Mid-Stream: An Ecumenical Journal* 27 (January 1988): 55–56.

Schaefer, Mary. "Forum: Ordination Women." *Worship* 63 (September 1989): 467–71.

Simpson, Mary Michael. "She Is the Vicar, I Am the Canon." *Sisters Today* 56, no. 5 (January 1985): 17–36.

Steinfels, Peter. "Advocate of Equality: Barbara Harris." *New York Times* 137 (September 26, 1988): 8.

Stendahl, Krister. *The Bible and the Role of Women: A Case in Hermeneutics*. Philadelphia: Fortress Press, 1966.

Stuhlmueller, Caroll, ed. *Women and the Priesthood: Future Directions*. Collegeville, MN: Liturgical, 1978.

Swidler, Leonard, and Arlene Swidler, eds. *Women Priests, a Catholic Commentary on the Vatican Declaration*. New York: Paulist Press, 1977.

Thumra, Jonathan. "Biblical Base of Women Ministry in the Context of Traditional and Cultural Heritage." In *Church, Ministry and Mission: Essays in Honor of the Reverend K. Incotemjen Aier, General Secretary of the Baptist Churches in North East India,* edited by Renthy Keitzer. Guwahati, Assam: Council of Baptist Churches in North East India, 1988.

Tsirpanlis, Constantine N. "An Orthodox View on Women's Ordination." *Orthodox Thought and Life* 1, no. 2 (1984): 16–18.

Wakelin, Rosemary. *Call Accepted: Reflections on Woman's Ordination in the Free Churches.* London: Movement for the Ordination of Women, 1988.

Watson, John. "A Coptic Orthodox Message to Lambeth: An Ecumenical Note." *Coptic Church Review: A Quarterly of Contemporary Patristic Studies* 10 (Summer 1989): 50–52.

Wheatley-Pesci, Meg. "An Expanded Definition of Priesthood: Some Present and Future Consequences." *Dialogue: A Journal of Mormon Thought* 18, no. 3 (Fall 1985): 33–42.

Willetts, Phoebe. *Sharing a Vision.* Cambridge, England: James Clarke, 1978.

Ziziolas, Metropolitan John. "Address to the 1988 Lambeth Conference." *Sourosk: A Journal of Orthodox Life and Thought* 35 (February 1989): 29–35.

Women and Preaching

There have been many women preachers throughout history, though they are perhaps not well known. Among them are Ann Marbury Hutchinson (1591-1643), a religious activist and popular speaker who was persecuted for her beliefs, documented by Selena William (1981); Lucretia Mott (1793-1880), a remarkable Quaker minister and leader in the American anti-slavery movement, documented by Lucretia Mott (1989); and Rebecca Jackson (1795-1871), a powerful, black, visionary Shaker preacher, documented by Rebecca Jackson (1981). Paul Chilcote (1991) has recently written a book about the history of Methodist women preachers and their relationship with John Wesley. In *Petticoats in the Pulpit* (1991), Elizabeth Muir tells fascinating stories about women preachers in Canada, and why women like Elizabeth Dart Eynon (1792-1857), Mary Ann Lyle (1797-1862), and Jane Woodill Wilson (1824-1893), once strong voices from pulpits in Canada, were virtually silenced.

Since the late 1970s and into the 1990s, there have been several interesting collections of women's sermons published. Church Employed Women of the National Council of Churches provided *Women in the Pulpit* (1978); in the same year, Helen Gray Crotwell edited *Women and the Word—Sermons.* A group of Protestant, Catholic, and Jewish women brought together a wonderful collection of sermons by women, *Spinning a Sacred Yarn: Women Speak from the Pulpit* (1982). Ella Pearson Mitchell edited the collection *Those Preachin' Women: Sermons by Black Women Preachers* (1985). From her introduction we can catch a sense of the conviction with which this woman speaks about preaching: "The hour is come. As a daughter of God I feel the weight of the mantle, and so I must proclaim the message as best I can" (p. 11).

It was in the 1980s that articles or chapters about women preachers began to appear. Jualynne Dodson's chapter, "Nineteenth Century A.M.E. Preaching Women" (1981), is included in a book by Thomas Keller. In it, Dodson discussed women's involvement on the cutting edge of church policy. A question that emerged during this period was, "How does having a woman preacher influence preaching?" This question has been explored by Marjorie Procter-Smith (1987), who makes the following claim:

> Brought vividly into the pulpit, the solidarity with all the women in the world can help the church not only to confront and transcend its own complicity in the oppression of women, but also to identify with all those who suffer and struggle against oppression. (P. 8)

Other journal writings dealing with the discussion of women as preacher have been included in the references; authors include: Maxine Walaskay (1982), Barbara Zikmund (1984), Cheryl Sanders (1986), Patricia Yeaman (1987), Edwina Hunter (1987), and Nancy Sehested (1988).

Feminist scholars in the area of homiletics (preaching) are posing questions and exploring issues of method, content, context, and hermeneutics. Three valuable textbooks are recent additions in this vein to the literature concerning women and preaching. *The Power to Speak* (1989), by Rebecca Chopp, opens up the important discussion of feminism, language, and God in the context of preaching. Christine Smith explores several strands of feminist thought and insight as she develops "weaving" as the metaphor for preaching. In her most recent book, *Preaching As Weeping, Confession, and Resistance: Radical Responses to Radical Evil* (1992), Smith reflects on her Third-World experience and focuses on preaching, on what she describes as the "larger social context." Topics she tackles include handicappism, ageism, heterosexism, and white racism. The closing lines from her first book, *Weaving the Sermon: Preaching in a Feminist Perspective* (1989), capture the vision of the potential in women's preaching:

> As women preachers in the Christian church weave together expanded understandings of what it means to be human, the critique and vision of feminism, and the good news of faith, it is my hope that communities might feel compelled to change as they are invited to new life. (P. 150)

The 1990s began with a collection of sermons edited by David Albert Farmer and Edwina Hunter titled *And Blessed Is She* (1990), as well as Annie Lally Milhaven's *Sermons Seldom Heard* (1991). In 1992, Carol Norén's book *The Women in the Pulpit* became available. This unique examination of women as preachers asks some of the same questions raised by earlier writers: How does a woman experience the call to preach? Who are her role models? How does she exercise authority?

What does she disclose of herself when she preaches? Norén's insights are based on careful research from interviews with women preachers of various denominations. Although the books are engaging, they still leave us with questions that can only be answered as the increasing number of women entering our pulpits find their way. For example, "Is there something different about women's preaching?" The opportunity to hear a woman preach is still quite rare, so that, for many, this question remains unanswered. What seems to be shared by those of us who have heard women preach is that it can be both an astonishing and an awesome experience. We do know that many women preachers, rather than working alone, come together in small clusters with laypeople or with their female colleagues to collaborate on preparing sermons.

References for Women and Preaching

Chilcote, Paul Wesley. *John Wesley & the Women Preachers of Early Methodism*. Scarecrow Press, 1991.

Chopp, Rebecca. *The Power to Speak: Feminism, Language, God*. New York: Crossroad, 1989.

Church Employed Women. *Women in the Pulpit*. New York: Church Employed Women, 1978.

Crotwell, Helen Gray, ed. *Women and the Word—Sermons*. Philadelphia: Fortress Press, 1978.

Dodson, Jualynne. "Nineteenth Century A.M.E. Preaching Women: Cutting Edge of Women's Inclusion in Church Policy." In *Women in New World: Historical Perspective on the Wesleyan Tradition*, vol. 1, edited by Hilah F. Thomas and Rosemary Skinner Keller. Nashville, TN: Abingdon, 1981.

Farmer, David Albert, and Edwina Hunter, eds. *And Blessed Is She: Sermons by Women*. San Francisco, CA: Harper & Row, 1990.

Hunter, Edwina. "Weaving Life's Experiences into Women's Preaching." *Christian Ministry* 18, no. 5 (September–October 1987): 14–17.

Jackson, Rebecca. *Gifts of Power: The Writings of Rebecca Jackson, Black Visionary, Shaker Eldress*. With an introduction by Jean McMahon Humez. Amherst: University of Massachusetts Press, 1981.

Milhaven, Annie Lally, ed. *Sermons Seldom Heard: Women Proclaim Their Lives*. New York: Crossroad/Continuum, 1991.

Mitchell, Ella Pearson, ed. *Those Preachin' Women: Sermons by Black Women Preachers*. Valley Forge, PA: Judson, 1985.

Mott, Lucretia. *Lucretia Mott: Her Complete Speeches and Sermons.* (Studies in Women and Religion, 4). Edited by Dana Green. Lewiston, NY: Edwin Mellen Press, 1980.

Muir, Elizabeth Gillian. *Petticoats in the Pulpit: The Story of Early Nineteenth-Century Methodist Women Preachers in Upper Canada.* Toronto: United Church, 1991.

Norén, Carol M. *The Women in the Pulpit.* Nashville, TN: Abingdon, 1992.

Procter-Smith, Marjorie. "Why Women Should Preach." *Homiletic: A Review of Publications in Religious Communication* 12 (1987): 5–8.

Sanders, Cheryl J. "The Woman as Preacher." *Journal of Religious Thought* 43, no. 1 (Spring–Summer 1986): 6–23.

Sehested, Nancy Hastings. "By What Authority Do I Preach?" [extemporaneous speech before the Shelby County Baptist Association, October 19, 1987]. *Sojourners* 17, no. 2 (February 1988): 24.

Smith, Christine M. *Preaching As Weeping, Confession, and Resistance: Radical Responses to Radical Evil.* Louisville, KY: Westminster/John Knox, 1992.

———. *Weaving the Sermon: Preaching in a Feminist Perspective.* Louisville, KY: Westminster/John Knox, 1989.

Spinning a Sacred Yarn: Women Speak from the Pulpit. New York: Pilgrim, 1982.

Walaskay, Maxine. "Gender and Preaching." *Christian Ministry* 13, no. 1 (January 1982): 8–11.

William, Selena. *Divine Rebel: The Life of Anne Marbury Hutchinson.* New York: Holt, Rinehart & Winston, 1981.

Yeaman, Patricia A. "Prophetic Voices: Differences Between Men and Women." *Review of Religious Research* 28, no. 4 (June 1987): 367–76.

Zikmund, Barbara Brown. "Women As Preachers: Adding New Dimensions to Worship." *Journal of Women and Religion* 3, no. 2 (Summer 1984): 12–16.

Pastoral Care of Women and by Women

Three significant characteristics stand out when one does an overview of the resources for feminist theology in the area of pastoral care of women and by women. The first is that the literature base is very small; second, the themes of sexual violence and abuse and women and poverty stand out; and third, these themes are quite new to pastoral theology.

Sexual Violence and Abuse

Marie Fortune (1983) opens her book *Sexual Violence, the Unmentionable Sin* with a quote from clergymen whom she interviewed: "But no one ever comes to me with this problem" (p. xi). Women pastors, however, are more frequently approached with situations of sexual violence and abuse. A small, but useful book, *Keeping the Faith* (1987) includes answers to questions that abused women are likely to raise about the passages of Scripture that have been used to keep women in a place of submission. Marie Marshall Fortune, well known for her writing workshops for ministers on violence and sexual abuse, has also provided several valuable readings and resources (1983, 1987, 1989). In 1991, the Center for the Prevention of Sexual & Domestic Violence prepared the video recording "Not in My Church," which can be borrowed for educational workshops with congregations.

Pastoral ministry by women, and for women, like the history of women in the church, seems to be a favorite area for thesis research. Several theses that address the issues of sexual violence and abuse began appearing in the 1980s. These include "Wife Abuse and Christian Faith," by James Alsdurf (1985); "Coping Successes and Failures in Incested Daughters," by Neil Carter (1986); "A Feminist Christian Approach to the Sexual Abuse of Children by Family Members," by Virginia Doherty (1984); and "A Therapeutic Approach to Adult Victims of Sex Abuse," by Virginia Maitland (1988).

There are several books that examine church and theology in relationship to violence and sexual abuse. One recent valuable contribution to the feminist critique of theology and abuse is the controversial book *Christianity, Patriarchy, and Abuse* (1989), edited by Joanne Brown and Carole Bohn. The essay topics include: "And a Little Child Will Lead Us: Christology and Child Abuse"; "The Transformation of Suffering: A Biblical and Theological Perspective"; and "Theological Pornography: From Corporate to Communal Ethics." Elizabeth Bettenhausen wrote in the foreword that several of these essays describe how Christian theology "has long imposed upon women a norm of imitative self-sacrifice based on the crucifixion of Jesus of Nazareth. Powerlessness is equated with faithfulness" (p. xii). Clearly, the task facing feminist theologians is whether or not suffering can be given meaning without sanctioning it. What about the violent death of Jesus of Nazareth? How can abuse survivors come to a ritual that offers symbolism of sacrifice and death?

Pastoral Care: Violence and Sexual Abuse

In the 1980s, several books appeared that were specifically focused on issues of pastoral care, violence, and abuse. Carol Bingham (1986) and Rita-Lou Clarke (1986) both discuss the role of clergy with battered women. A handbook for clergy and religious professional, *Sexual Assault and Abuse* (1987), by Mary Pellauer, Barbara Chester and Jane Boyagian, also deals with the issue. *Abuse and Religion: When Praying Isn't Enough*, by Anne Hoirton and Judith Williamson (1988) deals with the question of prayer, and *Pastoral Care for Survivors of Family Abuse*, by James Leehan (1989) speaks to the families of the abused. Marshall Scott discusses resources for victims of incest and parental abuse in the *Journal of Pastoral Care* (1988).

Obviously, the concern about abuse in the church itself, and especially abuse by male clergy, has to be addressed. Maria Fortune has recently published *Is Nothing Sacred?* (1989), which deals with this issue. Two articles from the late 1980s that also look at clergy abuse are "Blaming Women for the Sexually Abusive Male Pastor" (1988), by Ann-Janine Morey, and "Power and Abuse: Working Toward Healthier Relationships in the Church" (1989), by Bert Katscheke-Jennings. Karen Lebacqz (1985, 1991), professor of ethics, has published two insightful books about ethics for those working in congregational ministry.

Most mainline institutional churches have now developed policies and procedures to deal with the very disturbing fact that some of those in positions of responsibility in the church are abusing its members. The fact that two fundamentalist Christian organizations have provided their members with books on such abuse is encouraging, because research seems to indicate that many survivors of abuse were raised in homes with traditional values and roles for men and women (see James Alsdurf and Phyllis Alsdurf's *Battered into Submission* [1989]; Cathy Sutton and Howard Green's *A Christian Response to Domestic Violence* [1985]).

Joy Bussert (1986) wrote a book for the Lutheran Church in America, and it provides extremely pertinent material for congregations. The book itself deals with the theology of suffering and the ethic of empowerment. The several appendices include: a) "Letter from a Battered Wife"; b) "A Batterer's Perspective"; c) "Study Questions"; d) "Action Checklist"; e) "Sample Workshop"; f) "Sample Litany"; and g) "Selected Resources and Directories."

The Anglican Church of Canada (Task Force of the Women's Unit) provides the book *Violence Against Women: Abuse in Society and Church, and Proposals for Change* (1987). The Women's Inter-Church Council, a Canadian National ecumenical women's organization, has put together a comprehensive packet of materials, *Hands to End Violence* (1989). Both are designed for use by local congregations and also include teaching material for professors of theological education.

Concilium, edited by Elisabeth Schüssler Fiorenza and Mary Shawn Copeland (1994), dedicated an entire volume to violence against women. It includes articles such as "Violence and Justice"; "African-American Women in Three Contexts of Domestic Violence"; and "Ecclesiastical Violence: Witness and History."

Women and Poverty

Another new major area of concern for pastoral theology and care is women and poverty. The literature available is still primarily in the form of articles. Throughout many countries, including Canada and the United States, women have been using the Ecumenical Decade of the

Churches in Solidarity with Women (1989-1998) as an opportunity to struggle with issues of affluence and poverty. The Presbyterian Women U.S.A. held a conference to discuss the issue, resulting in the work "Women and Economic Justice," by Mildred Brown and Sydney Brown (1986). *Sojourners* published two articles on women and poverty in their March 1986 issue. In one of these, Joyce Hollyday views the poverty of women from a biblical perspective; in the other, Vicki Kemper raises the concern that poor women are getting poorer. Likewise, Barbara Ehrenreich (1986) examines causes of women's poverty, and Constance Parvey (1987) raises the issue of homeless women. Pamela Couture (1991) published an outstanding book titled *Women's Poverty, Family Policy & Practical Theology*. She points to the connection of American family policy and its contribution to the growth of women's poverty. Given the economic disadvantages of women throughout the world, it is likely that the poverty of women will need to be a topic that stays at the forefront for those who are doing pastoral care.

Gender and Pastoral Care

What specifically do women bring to pastoral ministry? The discussion of this issue began in the 1980s with an article by Edward Morgan, "Implications of the Masculine and the Feminine in Pastoral Ministry" (1980). Two women developed their theses with the focus of women's specific contribution to pastoral care in mind: "Women's Experiences: Implications for Theology and Pastoral Care," by Theresa McConnell (1981) and "In Their Own Words: Women Defining Ministry Toward a Feminist Theology of Pastoral Care," by Laurie Holmen (1985). Mary Seidal wrote a thesis titled "The Melody of Life: A Theological Interpretation on Women's Experience Integrated with Pastoral Ministry" (1990). These writings would suggest that women are consciously working at answering the question of the uniqueness of women's experience in the context of pastoral ministry.

Much of the other written material at this stage is in article form. Ruth Armstrong (1982, 1985) wrote two pieces related to women's experience of pastoral work, and Katherine Flagg (1984) discusses clergywomen's self-esteem. The significance of gender in pastoral care is an area where women's experience has yet to be fully explored. Christine Downing (1989) captured something of the urgency to get on with the research in this area when she titled her recent article "Gender Anxiety."

Maxine Glaz and Jeanne Stevenson Moessner have brought out an incisive collection of essays in *Women in Travail and Transition: A New Pastoral Care* (1991). In this work, the writers argued for greater awareness of women's experience to provide better pastoral care. The introduction sets out the purpose of the book as addressing

> basic questions intrinsic to the psychology of women . . . [as giving] a hearing to women experiencing particular crises,

> including women who are suffering battering or sexual
> abuse, struggling with divorce or the loss of a partner . . .
> [and] posits a new model of ministry that better expresses
> women's growing self-understanding both as ministers and
> as persons who cry—silently or aloud—for ministry. (P. 6)

Pastors will know from their pastoral experience, if not from their own lives, that women's self-esteem is often low. Carroll Saussy has recently published in the Women's Studies series, *God Images and Self-Esteem: Empowering Women in Patriarchal Society* (1991). One of the suspicions that motivated Saussy's research of several groups of women and men was that "what some people call 'faith in God' or 'faith in Jesus Christ' might be an escape from faith itself" (p. 13). This will be an important resource for every pastor, seminary student and teacher, and woman who is striving to develop self-esteem in a world that is frequently hostile.

Consequences of Feminist Consciousness

Both the *Journal of Supervision* and the *Journal of Pastoral Counseling* have articles that discuss the consequences of feminist consciousness, by Julia Jewett and Emily Haight (1983) and Eileen Gavin (1982), respectively. The development of feminist consciousness has given rise to the very interesting discussion about the relevance or validity of traditional psychological theories and practices related to women. For instance, are the works of Freud and Jung helpful to a feminist study of the religion? Naomi Goldenberg's 1982 book *The End of God* saw a significant contribution made by Freud and Jung. However, Alison Stokes's *Ministry After Freud* (1982), and the articles by Judith Van Herik (1982) and Roselyn Ann Karaban (1987), each raise serious questions when they apply feminist critical analysis to classical psychoanalysis in general. This inquiry is obviously not yet resolved!

Other Emerging Themes in Pastoral Care

Journal articles in the field of pastoral care of women and by women reveal several themes, not only from a feminist perspective, but also in new areas of concern for pastoral theology. Themes and their authors include: gender roles, by S. Scott Bartchy (1984); female chaplain's contributions to breast cancer management, by Jann Clanton (1984); depression, by Linda Bailey (1984); miscarriage, by Swanee Hunt (1984); anger, by Naomi Goldenberg (1986); and anorexia, by Gail Corrington (1986); suicide among gay men and lesbian women, by Judith Saunders and S. M. Valente (1987); faith development and women, by Lavinia Bryne (1988); and the impact of AIDS on women and persons of color, by Annette Johnson (1989). A more substantial literature base in terms of books related to these issues from a feminist theological perspective is yet to be published.

References for Pastoral Care of Women and by Women

Alsdurf, James. "Wife Abuse and Christian Faith: An Assessment of the Church's Response." Ph.D. diss., Fuller Theological Seminary School of Psychology, 1985.

Alsdurf, James, and Phyllis Alsdurf. *Battered into Submission: The Tragedy of Wife Abuse in the Christian Home.* Downers Grove, IL: InterVarsity, 1989.

Angelica, Jade Christine. *A Moral Emergency: Breaking the Cycle of Child Sexual Abuse.* Kansas City, MO: Sheed & Ward, 1993.

Armstrong, Ruth M. "Women As Pastoral Counselors." *Pastoral Psychology* 31, no. 2 (Winter 1982): 129–34.

———. "Women Pastors and the Idealization of Suffering." *Pastoral Psychology* 34, no. 2 (Winter 1985): 77–81.

Bailey, Linda. "Today's Women and Depression." *Journal of Religion and Health* 22, no. 1 (Spring 1984): 30–38.

Bartchy, S. Scott. "Jesus, Power and Gender Roles." *TSF Bulletin* 7, no. 3 (January–February 1984): 2–4.

Berry, Jason. *Lead Us Not into Temptation: Catholic Priests and the Sexual Abuse of Children.* New York: Doubleday, 1992.

Bingham, Carol F., ed. *Doorway to Response: The Role of Clergy in Ministry with Battered Women.* Springfield, IL: Interfaith Committee Against Domestic Violence, 1986.

Brewer, Connie, ed. *Escaping the Shadows, Seeking the Light: Christians in Recovery from Childhood Sexual Abuse.* San Francisco: Harper & Row, 1991.

Brown, Joanne, and Carol Bohn, eds. *Christianity, Patriarchy, and Abuse: A Feminist Critique.* New York: Pilgrim, 1989.

Brown, Mildred McKee, and Sydney T. Brown, eds. "Presbyterian Women Address the Feminization of Poverty" [Selected proceedings from the Conference of Women and Economic Justice, Washington, DC, October 4–6, 1984]. *Church and Society* 76, no. 3 (January–February 1986): 3–54.

Bryne, Lavinia. "Faith Development and Women." *Month: Review of Christian Thought and World Affairs* 21, no. 6 (June 1988): 746–48.

Bussert, Joy. *Battered Women: From a Theology of Suffering to an Ethic of Empowerment.* New York: Lutheran Church in America, 1986.

Carter, Neil Charles. "Coping Successes and Failures in Incested Daughters: Emotional Burdens, Background Factors and Religious Resources." Ph.D. diss., Boston University, 1986.

Center for the Prevention of Sexual & Domestic Violence. "Not in My Church." Videorecording, written and directed by Maria Gargiulo. Seattle, WA: Michi Pictures, 1991.

Clanton, Jann Aldredge. "The Female Chaplain's Contributions to Breast Cancer Management." *Journal of Pastoral Care* 38, no. 3 (September 1984): 195–99.

Clarke, Rita-Lou. *Pastoral Care of Battered Women*. Philadelphia: Westminster, 1986.

Corrington, Gail. "Anorexia, Asceticism and Autonomy: Self-Control As Liberation and Transcendence." *Journal of Feminist Studies in Religion* 2, no. 2 (Fall 1986): 51–62.

Couture, Pamela. *Women's Poverty, Family Policy & Practical Theology*. Pennsylvania: Abingdon, 1992.

Doherty, Virginia. "A Feminist Christian Approach to the Sexual Abuse of Children by Family Members." D.Min. diss., Boston University School of Theology, 1984.

Downing, Christine. "Gender Anxiety." *Journal of Pastoral Care* 43 (Summer 1989): 152–61.

Ehrenreich, Barbara. "The Root Causes of Women's Poverty and What We Can Do." *Church and Society* 76, no. 3 (January–February 1986): 19–28.

Feldmeth, Joanne Rose, and Midge Wallace Finley. *We Weep for Ourselves and Our Children: A Christian Guide for Survivors of Child Sexual Abuse*. San Francisco: Harper & Row, 1990.

Fiorenza, Elisabeth Schüssler, and Mary Shawn Copeland. *Violence Against Women (Concilium)*. Maryknoll: Obis, 1994.

Flagg, Katherine. "Psychological Androgyny and Self-Esteem in Clergywomen." *Journal of Psychology and Theology* 12, no. 3 (Fall 1984): 222–29.

Fortune, Marie Marshall. *Is Nothing Sacred? When Sex Invades the Pastoral Relationship*. New York: Harper & Row, 1989.

———. *Keeping the Faith: Question and Answers for the Abused Woman*. New York: Harper & Row, 1987.

———. *Sexual Violence, the Unmentionable Sin: An Ethical and Pastoral Perspective*. New York: Pilgrim, 1983.

Gavin, Eileen. "Stress and Conflict of Catholic Women in Relation to Feminism." *Journal of Pastoral Counseling* 17, no. 1 (Spring–Summer 1982): 9–13.

Glaz, Maxine, and Jeanne Stevenson Moessner, eds. *Women in Travail and Transition: A New Pastoral Care.* Minneapolis, MN: Augsburg Fortress, 1991.

Goldenberg, Naomi R. "Anger in the Body: Feminism, Religion and Jungian Psychoanalytic Theory." *Journal of Feminist Studies in Religion* 2, no. 2 (Fall 1986): 39–50.

———. *The End of God: Important Directions for a Feminist Critique of Religion in the Works of Sigmund Freud and Carl Jung.* Ottawa: University of Ottawa Press, 1982.

Halsey, Peggy. *Abuse in the Family: Breaking the Church's Silence.* New York: United Methodist Church Office of Women in Crisis, 1984.

Heggan, Carolyn Halderread. *Sexual Abuse in Christian Homes and Churches.* Scottsdale, PA: Herald, 1993.

Heitritter, Lynn, and Jeanette Vought. *Helping Victims of Sexual Abuse: A Sensitive Biblical Guide for Counselors, Victims, and Families.* Minneapolis, MN: Bethany House.

Hoirton, Anne L., and Judith A. Williamson, eds. *Abuse and Religion: When Praying Isn't Enough.* Lexington, MA: Lexington Books, 1988.

Hollyday, Joyce. "You Shall Not Afflict: A Biblical Perspective on Women and Poverty." *Sojourners* 15, no. 3 (March 1986): 26–29.

Holmen, Laurie Proctor. "In Their Own Words: Women Defining Ministry Toward a Feminist Theology of Pastoral Care." D.Min. diss., School of Theology at Claremont, 1985.

Hunt, Swanee. "Pastoral Care and Miscarriage: A Ministry Long Neglected." *Pastoral Psychology* 32 (Summer 1984): 265–78.

Jewett, Julia, and Emily Haight. "The Emergence of Feminine Consciousness in Supervision" [clinical pastoral education]. *Journal of Supervision and Training in Ministry* 6 (1983): 164–74.

Johnson, Annette. "The Impact of AIDS on Women and Persons of Color: Ethical and Theological Problems." In *AIDS Issues: Confronting the Challenge of Ethical and Religious Problems,* edited by D. Hallman. New York: Pilgrim, 1989.

Karaban, Roslyn Ann. "Jung's Concept of the Anima/Animus: Enlightening or Frightening?" *Bangalore Theological Forum* 19 (October–December 1987): 291–300.

Katscheke-Jennings, Bert. "Power and Abuse: Working Toward Healthier Relationships in the Church." *American Baptist Quarterly* 8 (December 1989): 268–75.

Kemper, Vicki. "Poor and Getting Poorer: Women Struggle for Survival." *Sojourners* 15, no. 3 (March 1986): 62–71.

Lebacqz, Karen. *Professional Ethics: Power & Paradox*. Nashville, TN: Abingdon, 1985.

Lebacqz, Karen, and Ronald G. Barton. *Sex in the Parish*. Louisville, KY: Westminster/John Knox, 1991.

Leehan, James. *Pastoral Care for Survivors of Family Abuse*. Louisville, KY: Westminster/John Knox, 1989.

Maitland, Virginia. "A Therapeutic Approach to Adult Victims of Sexual Abuse." D.Min. diss., Andover Newton Theological School, 1988.

McConnell, M. Theresa. "Women's Experiences: Implications for Theology and Pastoral Care." D.Min. diss., Lutheran Northwestern Theological Seminary, 1981.

Morey, Ann-Janine. "Blaming Women for the Sexually Abusive Male Pastor." *Christian Century* 105, no. 28 (October 5, 1988): 866–69.

Morgan, Edward. "Implications of the Masculine and the Feminine in Pastoral Ministry." *Journal of Pastoral Care* 34, no. 4 (December 1980): 268–77.

Parvey, Constance E. "Homeless Women: Priorities." *Christianity and Crisis: A Christian Journal of Opinion* 47, no. 4 (March 6, 1987): 94–96.

Pellauer, Mary D., Barbara Chester, and Jane Boyagian. *Sexual Assault and Abuse: A Handbook for Clergy and Religious Professionals*. San Francisco: Harper & Row, 1987.

Saunders, Judith M., and S. M. Valente. "Suicide Risk Among Gay Men and Lesbians: A Review." *Death Studies* 11, no. 1 (1987): 1–24.

Saussy, Carroll. *God Images and Self-Esteem: Empowering Women in a Patriarchal Society*. Louisville, KY: Westminster/John Knox, 1991.

Scott, Marshall S. "Honor Thy Father and Mother: Scriptural Resources for Victims of Incest and Parental Abuse." *Journal of Pastoral Care* 42 (Summer 1988): 139–48.

Seidal, Mary. "The Melody of Life: A Theological Interpretation on Women's Experience with Pastoral Ministry." D.Min. diss., Consortium of Theological Schools, 1990.

Stokes, Alison. *Ministry After Freud*. New York: Pilgrim, 1982.

Sutton, Cathy A., and Howard Green. *A Christian Response to Domestic Violence: A Reconciliation Model for Social Workers*. St. David, PA: North American Association of Christians in Social Work, 1985.

Task Force of the Women's Unit of the Anglican Church of Canada. *Violence Against Women: Abuse in Society and Church, and Proposals for Change*. Toronto: Anglican Book Centre, 1987.

Van Herik, Judith. "The Feminist Critique of Classical Psychoanalysis." In *The Challenge of Psychology to Faith (Concilium 156)*, edited by Steven Kepnas and David Tracey. Edinburgh, Scotland: T. & T. Clark, 1982.

Women's Inter-Church Council. *Hands to End Violence*. Toronto: Women's Inter-Church Council, 1989.

Conclusion

The past twenty years have seen extraordinary changes in women's consciousness. What women thought were personal situations of misfortune or distress are now recognized as pervasive and systematic forms of structural oppression of sexism, racism, and class exploitation. Without this feminist consciousness, we simply replicate what patriarchy has taught us, and our spirituality will remain distorted. Unquestionably, the significance of the flood of writings in feminist liberation theology is witness to the fact that many of the vices that the church denounces reside too comfortably within itself. Feminist liberation theology provides alternatives to traditional ways of thinking about our experience of God, ourselves, and each other. Writers not only search out new frontiers, but they rejoice and celebrate the strength and wisdom of women in the past. Feminist theologians lift up the liberating strands that can be found even in patriarchal tradition, serving to remind us of the power of the liberating Spirit. These writings represent voices that are calling their sisters and brothers to join in the quest for a new vision and praxis that will create a just world order.

Libraries today show such listings as Feminist Liberation Theology, Sexism in Language, Femininity of God, and Goddesses. Many theological schools support a Women's Caucus, and some even have ongoing committees to undergird the feminist commitment on campus. Theological faculties in schools in several countries including Canada, England, Germany, Korea, South Africa, and the United States have women scholars who identify themselves as feminists and who teach courses in feminist liberation theology. In Boston, the Episcopal Divinity School now offers a Doctor of Ministry degree in feminist liberation theology, and the Women's Theological Center provides a one-year course of study toward a Master of Divinity. The Women and Religion Center in

Berkeley, California has long provided courses and opportunities for reflection in the area of feminist theological studies.

The leadership in the Christian Feminist Movement includes both laywomen and clergywomen and those men committed to standing with their sisters against sexism. At the local church level, a quiet revolution is taking place. Regular conferences and workshops provide women with an opportunity to talk with other women. The boundaries are breaking down as women of different ages, classes, and races are coming together to pursue their faith with renewed vigor. An exciting new development is the dialogue between women who identify themselves as feminists, talking with their sisters across faith lines and with those who are Goddess worshippers or members of Wicca.

The structural changes within the church are slow in coming. Indeed, many women have given up the hope that the church will ever respond to them and their spiritual and material needs. The resources in this chapter represent the work of those who have not given up and who are committed to calling the church to faithfulness and accountability.

I am grateful to Alice Harrison, Gwyn Griffith, Vicki Hall, Joyce Meadows, and Barbara Rumscheidt for their feedback and help during the process of producing this essay.

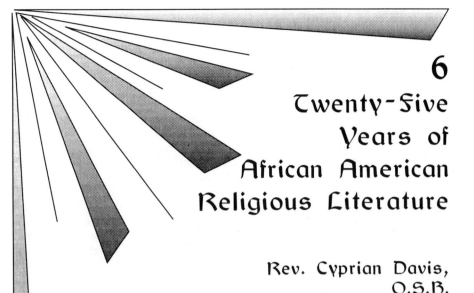

6
Twenty-Five
Years of
African American
Religious Literature

Rev. Cyprian Davis,
O.S.B.

Introduction

The publication of the three-volume encyclopedia *The American Religious Experience: Studies of Traditions and Movements* (1988), edited by Charles Lippy and Peter Williams, provides a broad survey of the phenomenon of religion among black Americans. The first volume, which is made up of "The African Heritage in Caribbean and North American Religions," by Leonard Barret, and "Black Christianity in North America," by Albert Raboteau, brings an historical overview of religious movements among African descendants in the West Indies and Mexico, as well as the continental United States. In the second volume, "Black Militant and Separatist Movements," by Lawrence Mamiya and C. Eric Lincoln treats black religious traditions outside of the Protestant and Catholic churches; and "Black Religious Thought," by James Cone treats the beginnings and evolution of black theology. The scope and focus of these articles provide the major divisions for an article on African-American religious literature, namely history, theology and religious thought, and religious movements outside the main Christian traditions.

History of African American Religious Tradition

The seminal work for black religious history in the United States is Albert Raboteau's *Slave Religion*, published in 1978. Covering the entire period between Africa and emancipation, Raboteau discusses the institutions, the practice, the beliefs, and the worship of a people shackled in the body, but free in heart and mind. Milton Sernett covers the same period from a different vantage point, that of Protestant evangelicalism, in *Black Religion and American Evangelicalism: White Protestants, Plantation Missions, and the Flowering of Negro Christianity, 1787–1865* (1975). In the same historical perspective, David Wills and Richard Newman have edited a series of articles on the missionary activity of African Americans in the first three-quarters of the nineteenth century in a book titled *Black Apostles at Home and Abroad: Afro-Americans and the Christian Mission from the Revolution to Reconstruction* (1982). Walter Williams breaks new ground in *Black Americans and the Evangelization of Africa: 1877–1900* (1982), a study of black American missionaries in the nineteenth century who left the United States for Africa, bringing with them the culture of American Protestantism and the sympathy of their shared racial heritage. Williams concludes that African-American missionary work promulgated an interest in Africa that resulted in the growth of a Pan-African sentiment.

Afro-American Religious History: A Documentary Witness, edited by Milton C. Sernett (1985), a selection of primary source texts arranged in chronological order, gives a solid historical foundation to the study of black religion from Africa to the Black Power Movement. C. Eric Lincoln has compiled another collection of contemporary texts centering on black religion, *The Black Experience in Religion: A Book of Readings* (1974). Lincoln wrote a commentary piece, "The Black Church Since Frazier," in the reissue of E. Franklin Frazier's famous analysis, *The Negro Church in America* (1974). In Lincoln's opinion, the church that Frazier described had its roots in the slavery of the rural South, but it had become middle class and assimilationist in the urban North. This church no longer exists. In its place has come a church reborn in the Civil Rights Movement and the emergence of Black Power. C. Eric Lincoln continues his dialogue on black religion and the Black Church, describing it as "a unique cultural precipitate, born of the peculiar American interpretation of the faith and the black American response" in a collection of his lectures, *Race, Religion, and the Continuing American Dilemma* (1984). Most recently, C. Eric Lincoln and Lawrence Mamiya published a monumental analysis of the Black Church and black religion in the United States, *The Black Church in the African American Experience* (1990). Lincoln and Mamiya conduct an historical and sociological analysis of various Protestant churches that are black in constitution or in extensive membership. While they examine the roots and contemporary situation of the Black Church and explore social institutions and black religious thought, they scarcely mention black Roman Catholics.

In the past two decades, several works have been published that reveal the radical and militant roots of the Black Church prior to the Civil War. David Swift, in *Black Prophets of Justice: Activist Clergy Before the Civil War* (1989), studies the life and work of six black ministers, Presbyterian and Congregationalist, who fought against slavery from their pulpits. The best known of these six are Henry Highland Garnet, James Pennington, and Samual Cornish. In *Segregated Sabbaths: Richard Allen and the Emergence of Independent Black Churches. 1760–1840* (1973), Carol V. R. George assesses the life of Richard Allen, the founder of the African Methodist Episcopal Church, and one of the principal architects of what might be called the Black Church.

The publication of two major autobiographies shed valuable light on what the Black Church has become in the twentieth century. In 1987, *Born to Rebel: An Autobiography by Benjamin Mays*, the autobiography of a Baptist minister, president of Morehouse College in Atlanta, and mentor and inspiration of Martin Luther King Jr., was happily reissued by the University of Georgia Press. In 1979, another leading black clergyman, Howard Thurman (1899–1981) published his autobiography *With Head and Heart: The Autobiography of Howard Thurman* (1979). Thurman deserves to be celebrated as one of the top spiritual writers of this century. He has written more than twenty books that deal in one way or another with prayer, meditation, and the spiritual life. In his writings, Thurman shaped the contours of African-American spirituality. His autobiography recounts his life from Daytona, Florida, where he was born, until his retirement after a long career in education, ecumenism, preaching, and spiritual guidance.

Another valuable example of African-American religious biography can be found in the collection *Black Apostles: Afro-American Clergy Confront the Twentieth Century* (1978), edited by Randall Burkett and Richard Newman. Fifteen articles depict the lives and activities of black clergymen as diverse as Francis Grimké and Father Divine. In the same perspective, Randall Burkett also wrote *Black Redemption. Churchmen Speak for the Garvey Movement* (1978).

A different view of black religious experience is found in Gayraud Wilmore's *Black Religion and Black Radicalism: An Interpretation of the Religious History of Afro-American People* (1983). First published in 1973, Wilmore's book was thoroughly revised and printed as a second edition in 1983. He first surveys the religion of the slaves and its evolution into the mainline black churches of the beginning of this century, then traces the Black Church's rediscovery of its militant and survivalist roots in the Black Power Movement. Two years later, Wilmore edited with David Shannon a series of papers by black theologians dealing with the faith tradition of the Christian churches for the Faith and Order Commission of the World Council of Churches. This work, titled *Black Witness to the Apostolic Faith* (1985), nicely summarizes the usefulness of these volumes.

From the other side, Forrest Wood looks at how the Christian churches, both Protestant and Catholic, betrayed their basic beliefs in the face of slavery and racism. His book, *The Arrogance of Faith:*

Christianity and Race in America from the Colonial Era to the Twentieth Century (1990), surveys a wide variety of disciplines, including theology, anthropology, and geography, from Africa to North America, and a wide array of secondary sources to advance his thesis. Unfortunately, his hastily-drawn conclusions weaken at times the force of his arguments. In dealing with the Catholic Church's involvement in slavery and the papal decrees against the slave trade, Wood introduces much evidence, an abundance of which, at times, reveals a lack of historical precision. For example, Daniel O'Connell, a great Irish statesman and one of the best known Catholic laypersons of the nineteenth century, was viscerally opposed to slavery and did not hesitate to criticize Irish Americans for their pro-slavery stance. Wood, in *The Arrogance of Faith* (1990), disappointingly omits mention of the career of this astute Irish Catholic member of the British Parliament who became known as the "Great Liberator," and calls him an Irish American (p. 363). Wood, however, does correctly report the fact that the Jesuits in Maryland were slave owners, but without citing references of any kind, he singles out "Irish-born Michael H. Healy, president of Georgetown University and owner of a plantation in Georgia with sixteen hundred acres and seventeen slaves" (p. 356). Michael Morris Healy was an Irish-born planter who owned a plantation in the back country of Georgia. He had ten children by a slave woman. Three of those children, all slaves (technically), became priests, one even a bishop. One, Patrick Francis Healy, became a Jesuit and president of Georgetown University in 1874—and he was born a slave, not a slave owner.

The history of black Catholics has only just begun to be treated in articles and monographs. African-American participation in Roman Catholicism has been generally ignored by American church historians, Catholic as well as Protestant, and by the majority of African-American Protestant writers. Recent publications have revealed unmined treasure just below the surface. The question of slavery and the Catholic Church has been treated very briefly in a work that is more of an introduction than a definitive synthesis, *Slavery and the Catholic Church*, by John Maxwell (1975). Two important studies have concentrated on slave-holding by religious orders: " 'Splendid Poverty': Jesuit Slaveholding in Maryland, 1805–1838," by R. Emmett Curran in *Catholics in the Old South*, edited by R. M. Miller and J. L. Wakelyn (1983), and *Church and Slave in Perry County, Missouri. 1818–1865*, by Stafford Poole, C.M. and Douglas Slawson, C.M. (1986). Poole and Slawson give a detailed account of Vincentian slaveholding.

Currently, the only recent survey of the history of the black Catholic community in the United States is to be found in my own work, *The History of Black Catholics in the United States* (Davis 1990). The history of black priests in the United States has been recounted by Stephen Ochs in *Desegregating the Altar: The Josephites and the Struggle for Black Priests. 1871–1960* (1990). Ochs approaches the subject from the point of view of a religious community dedicated to the African-American apostolate and caught in the web of racism in American society. Ochs's work provides necessary background reading on this much neglected topic. Marilyn Nickels has studied one of the important lay movements among African-American Catholics and the unfortunate controversy between its prophetic leader, Thomas Wyatt Turner, and two Jesuit heroes of racial justice, John LaFarge and William Markoe, in *Black Catholic Protest and the Federated Colored Catholics, 1917–1933* (1988). The earlier activities of black Catholics, which resulted in the five black Catholic Congresses between 1889 and 1894, were documented for the first three congresses in 1889, 1890, and 1892 by Daniel Rudd, the editor of *The American Catholic Tribune* and the leader of this movement. The proceedings of these three congresses, *Three Catholic Afro-American Congresses*, first published in 1893, were reprinted by Arno Press in 1978. Finally, the late Albert Foley, S.J., who published the life of America's first black Catholic bishop, James Augustine Healy, in *Bishop Healy, Beloved Outcaste: The Story of a Great Man Whose Life Has Become a Living Legend* (1954), also wrote about the life of Bishop Healy's brother, Patrick, who became president of Georgetown University, in *Dream of an Outcaste: Patrick F. Healy, S.J.: The Story of the Slave-Born Georgian Who Became the Second Founder of America's Great Catholic University, Georgetown* (1989). Although it was known that Bishop Healy was black, the race of his brother, Patrick Healy, S.J., was not so widely known. It is ironic that an African-American presided over a great Catholic University (1874–1882) that did not admit black students until the middle of the twentieth century. Unfortunately, Foley's biographies of Bishop Healy and Patrick Healy, S.J. contain very little detailed documentation. Although it is very short, Dolores Labbe's study *Jim Crow Comes to Church: The Establishment of Segregated Catholic Parishes in South Louisiana* (1978), on racial segregation and parish churches in Louisiana should not be overlooked.

Sandra Smithson, a School Sister of St. Francis, has analyzed the situation of the African-American Catholic Community in *To Be the Bridge: A Commentary on Black / White Catholicism in America* (1984). Taking into consideration the historical failure of the American Church into evangelization of Blacks, she pointed out the possibilities for the Black Catholic community to become an instrument of healing and reconciliation in racial matters. This study was published almost a decade ago and its hopes have been only partially realized.

Theology and Religious Thought

The growing number of studies in black theology is one of the most significant developments in contemporary religious literature. Foremost among recent works is *Black Theology: A Critical Assessment and Annotated Bibliography*, compiled by James H. Evans Jr. (1987). Evans provides a thorough survey of books and articles on black theology and related issues under three headings: "Origin and Development of Black Theology"; "Liberation, Feminism, and Marxism"; and "Cultural and Global Discourse." Each area is preceded by a critical examination of the development of the discipline. Evans's entries are readable, succinct, and accurate.

Another major contribution to the field is the publication of a compilation of significant documents in *Black Theology: A Documentary History*. Edited by James Cone and Gayraud Wilmore (1993), this two-volume book covers foundation documents from the Civil Rights Movement and the Black Power struggle to the initial discourse of black theologians and the varied response to their writings, and concludes with the issues of women's role in theology, and Third-World theology. Wilmore and Cone supply a useful annotated bibliography.

Perhaps no one has helped to define and to promulgate the major issues of black theology as much as James Cone, who began this movement with the publication of *Black Theology and Black Power* (1969), *A Black Theology of Liberation* (1970), and *God of the Oppressed* (1975). In 1986, Cone published a second edition of *A Black Theology of Liberation*, an important work that provides a basic outline for a systematic approach to black theology. Earlier, Cone published a critical assessment of the black liberation theology movement and its connection to the Black Church in *For My People* (1984). In a closing chapter, Cone presents a vision of the future task for the black theologian in the Black Church. Cone's *Speaking the Truth: Ecumenism, Liberation, and Black Theology* (1986) is a collection of lectures, articles, and essays from 1975 to 1985, treating such issues as the nature of black theology and the history of the Black Church and the African-American community. In his *My Soul Looks Back* (1986), Cone looks at his own life and career, his intellectual and spiritual journey, and makes (as stated in the introduction) a "testimony" to the black church community.

James Deotis Roberts ranks with James Cone as a founder of the black theology movement. In a collection of essays brought together under the heading of *Black Theology Today* (1983), Roberts discusses method, contextualization, political and pastoral theology, and spirituality. In a work that is a more mature statement than *Black Theology Today*, Roberts continues his systematic treatment of black theology in terms of method, ecclesiology, ethics, and a theology of the Holy Spirit, in *Black Theology Today in Dialogue* (1987). In this work, Roberts establishes a vision and a framework for the future of black theology. Equally important is Major Jones's *The Color of God: The Concept of God in Afro-American Thought* (1987).

Three works approach black theology from a broader geographic perspective than just the Black Church in the United States. Theo Witvliet, a Dutch theologian, interpreted the African-American movement for Europeans in a work originally published in Dutch and translated into English in 1987 as *The Way of the Black Messiah*. Dwight Hopkins in *Black Theology, USA and South Africa. Politics, Culture, and Liberation* (1989), and Josiah Young in *Black and African Theologies. Siblings or Distant Cousins* (1986), both students of James Cone at Union Theological Seminary in New York, compared and contrasted black theology in the United States and black theology in South Africa.

Soul Theology: The Heart of American Black Culture (1986), by Henry Mitchell and Nicholas Cooper Lewter studies black theology not as liberation theology but as an embodiment of popular beliefs and practices. Using case studies, the authors seek to exemplify the basic religious themes of African-American religious life: God's providence, omnipotence, omniscience, and goodness; and humanity's destiny and equality. In his work *The Social Teaching of the Black Church* (1985), Peter J. Paris analyzes the social and ethical teachings of the Black Church, particularly the African Methodist Episcopal Church and the National Baptist Convention. For Paris, it is not the progressivism of liberation theology that characterizes the black religious experience, but the ambiguity, the strength, and the conservatism of black churches that helped define the religious consciousness of African-American Protestants. Earlier, Paris had studied the same issues as expressed by four black religious leaders, in his work *Black Leaders in Conflict: Martin Luther King, Jr., Malcolm X, Joseph H. Johnson, Adam Clayton Powell* (1978).

In *Black Socialist Preacher: The Teachings of Reverend George Washington Woodbey and His Disciple Reverend George W. Slater, Jr.* (1983) by Phil Foner, the biography of socialist preacher and activist George Washington Woodbey is an example of another type of black religious thought in a political context. In his lengthy introduction, Foner gives a useful biographical sketch of Woodbey's life, and in the rest of the book, collects the writings and speeches of one of America's first black socialist leaders. One of the newest black religious thinkers who is in the process of taking black theology into a dialogue with Marxist social philosophy is Cornel West. His book, *Prophesy Deliverance: An Afro-American Revolutionary Christianity* (1982), integrates Afro-American religious philosophy and its social and political implications from a Marxist perspective. More recently, West, now professor at Princeton University, has published *Prophetic Fragments* (1988) and *Race Matters* (1993).

Cain Hope Felder, a Scripture professor at the Howard University Divinity School, has also been responsible for a new and exciting contribution to scriptural study from a black perspective. This is important, because, for black theology to remain a viable discipline, it needs the contribution of Scripture scholarship. In *Troubling Biblical Waters: Race, Class, and Family* (1989), Felder looks at meaning, exegesis, and history in the biblical texts from the perspective of Africa and Africans, on the continent and abroad (i.e., United States, Europe, and other countries). In *Stony the Road We Trod* (1991), Felder has edited a collection of articles dealing with Scripture and the African worldview. The collection is the work of African-American biblical scholars who met regularly for a period of five years to discuss and collaborate in the field of biblical studies.

Black women are contributing important works to a growing collection of women's studies. Preferring the term *womanist* to differentiate the issues of women of color from those treated in feminist studies, black religious women introduce another aspect of black theology. The religious history of African women has been recounted in such works as William Andrews's *Sisters of the Spirit: Three Black Women's Autobiographies of the Nineteenth Century* (1986), and Harriet Jacobs's *Life of a Slave Girl, Written by Herself* (1987), the autobiographical story of a young slave girl who manages to escape the lecherous slave owner who keeps her as a concubine. The girl spends seven years hiding in a crawl space of her grandmother's house, until she finally makes her way North to New York. Jacobs first published the account of her life at the beginning of the Civil War. Like much writing by people subject to persecution, her religious experience is an essential part of her self-understanding.

Jacquelyn Grant contributes the first major study in womanist theology with her *White Women's Christ and Black Women's Jesus: Feminist Christology and Womanist Response* (1989). Grant's major premise is that the experience of white women is not the same as that of black women, that white women have had their part to play in the oppression of blacks, and that Jesus has a special significance in the womanist tradition. Grant believes that black women should seriously study the feminist analysis but not allow themselves to become part of the agenda of white women, who, she believes, are at times racist.

Finally, Gerald Davis analyzes one school of the black preaching tradition in a very well-written work, *I Got the Word in Me and I Can Sing It, You Know* (1985). In a similar vein, Jon Michael Spencer has shown the importance of black religious music as a source for black religious thought and liberation theology in *Protest and Praise: Sacred Music of Black Religion* (1990).

Spirituality in the African Tradition

Spirituality is the notion of how people respond to the action of the Holy Spirit: how they pray, how they practice virtue, how they discipline their appetites, and how they satisfy their thirst for God. Spirituality, as a word, is an abstraction; in reality, its expression is always in a cultural context. It is this cultural context that Robert E. Hood, an Episcopal priest and professor at New York's General Theological Seminary, writes in his recent work, *Must God Remain Greek? Afro Cultures and God-Talk* (1990). As Hood says, because "one may generalize and speak of Western culture and indeed mainstream Christian faith as descendants of Graeco-Roman thought, which . . . greatly shaped early and later Christian doctrines about God" (p. 6), we can speak of God as being Greek. Professor Hood points out the significance of this cultural bind for Africans and those of African descent in the Americas, for Native Americans, and for Asians. From the religious and spiritual points of view, they are rendered the "homeless, those whose cultures have not been shaped or greatly influenced by Graeco-Roman concepts and culture as found in European or Euro-American cultures and their attendant religion" (p. 2). Finally, he concludes that the Christian message in Africa, Latin America, the Caribbean, and the United States might enhance traditional Christian concepts.

Two articles in *The Study of Spirituality* (1986), edited by Cheslyn Jones, Geoffrey Wainwright, and Edward Yarnold, treat African and African-American spirituality, touching related issues brought out in Professor Hood's work. John S. Mbiti, in a chapter on African religions, takes his readers into the world of African prayer as expressed in the various traditional religions. "The spirituality which comes out of these prayers is an all-embracing spirituality; that is, the physical world is embraced in the . . . spiritual" (p. 514). James Cone, in the same study, treats African-American spirituality in the context of black worship. It is this worship, formed in the context of slavery, connected to its origins in Africa, and expressing longing and protest in the face of oppression and racism, that reveals the spirituality of black people.

Two other articles from a Roman Catholic perspective also delineate black spirituality. The Nigerian Dominican, Father Chris Nwaka Egbulem, describes African spirituality in *The New Dictionary of Catholic Spirituality* (1993). Father Egbulem gives seven characteristics of African spirituality: 1) God as active creator; 2) all reality is a whole, without dualism; 3) life as gift; 4) importance of community; 5) veneration of ancestors; 6) the strength of the spoken word; and 7) created nature and the human environment are sacred. In the same volume, Cyprian Davis treats African-American spirituality, spelling out four characteristics of African-American spirituality: it is contemplative, holistic, joyful, and communitarian.

The Legacy of Martin Luther King Jr.

Twenty-six years ago in 1968, the Reverend Martin Luther King Jr. was struck down in Memphis, Tennessee. The man who tore open the conscience of America and laid bare its soul left a spiritual legacy that was part dream, part hope, and part prophecy. It was also controversial. An increasing body of literature probes, analyzes, assures, critiques, and interprets King as prophet, religious leader, hero, martyr, and human being. Already the historiography is rich with numerous schools of interpretation. However, a thorough analysis of this literature demands a separate essay.

There are three major bibliographies of King literature. In 1977, William H. Fisher edited *Free At Last: A Bibliography of Martin Luther King, Jr.* Fisher's entries are divided into King's own writings, writings about King, writing about people and events surrounding King, and reviews of King's works. Eleven years later, Clayborne Carson wrote *A Guide to Research On Martin Luther King, Jr. and the Modern Black Freedom Struggle* (1989). A third bibliography, Steven F. Lawson's lengthy essay "Freedom Then, Freedom Now: The Historiography of the Civil Rights Movement," in *The American Historical Review*, demonstrates, among other things, a gradual shift in the critique of King's writings, especially regarding the authenticity of his sources. Carson writes:

> More recently, scholars have discovered that King liberally borrowed ideas for his sermons and writings from both black and white Protestant ministers, often without attribution, and that his published books were produced with the helping hands of ghostwriters. These findings do not diminish his contribution to the movement, but they do suggest that future researchers will have to look even more carefully to follow the myriad influences on King. (P. 461)

Lawson provides a much-needed service in one of the fastest growing areas of African-American history. Issues of originality and attribution of source material used by Dr. King were clouding Dr. King's contribution to African-American religious history and thought. Lawson's work helps to clarify Dr. King's unique role in recent history.

This unique role leads to the importance of the King biographies. Stephen Oates's *Let the Trumpets Sound: The Life of Martin Luther King, Jr.* (1982) remains the most complete account of the man and his mission. Oates's book does not completely replace the biography of King's earlier life, *King: A Critical Biography*, by David Lewis (1970), published shortly after the assassination, that depicts a King who had not yet become a legend. Although his review of King is insightful, Lewis was too close to his subject in time and in place for a solid historical assessment. David Garrow's recently published and controversial study *Bearing the Cross: Martin Luther King, Jr. and the Southern Christian Leadership Conference* (1986) assesses King's life in the context of the Southern Christian Leadership Conference, and frankly addresses King's limitations and mistakes. Garrow portrays the man, not the prophet; the pathfinder, not the hero.

The writings of Martin Luther King Jr. have been widely discussed in the last few years. In 1986, the study *A Testament of Hope: The Essential Martin Luther King, Jr.*, by James Melvin Washington was published. Two years later, a new edition of three meditations by King, *The Measure of a Man* (1988), summed up much of his spirituality.

Recently, David Garrow edited an eighteen-volume collection of documentation on King and his influence, *Martin Luther King, Jr. and the Civil Rights Movement* (1989). Even more recent studies place King within the intellectual climate of his time. They ask: "Who was King?" "What was the intellectual matrix of this man whose thoughts and ideals left a mark on the consciousness of America?" John Anbro, in *Martin Luther King, Jr.: The Making of a Mind* (1982), examines the thinkers and writers that influenced King's thinking. It is an intellectual biography of an influential preacher. James P. Hanigan did a similar study of the theological underpinnings of King's theories of nonviolence in *Martin Luther King, Jr. and the Foundation of Nonviolence* (1984).

The work *To See the Promised Land: The Faith Pilgrimage of Martin Luther King, Jr.* (1986), by Frederick Downing interprets King using the stages of development described by Erik Erikson and James W. Fowler. Some may see Downing's approach as more psychological than theological, especially in light of what he writes at the beginning of his study:

> Since Erikson and Fowler are two theorists who have given attention to the issues of faith and identity and have attempted to study what it means to be a religious person in a wholistic sense, it appears that the work of both theorists may be helpful in trying to clarify the nature and meaning of King's life. (Pp. 28–29)

Other writers, especially African Americans, insist that King cannot be understood or interpreted apart from his cultural and social roots. His roots are the Black Church, the African-American culture, and African-American society. King's cultural placement is one of the major premises of Lewis Baldwin's book *There Is a Balm in Gilead: The Cultural Roots of Martin Luther King, Jr.* (1991). Baldwin writes, "This book differs from previous scholarship on King in that it is the first extensive treatment of his roots in black folk culture, particularly that of the South" (p. 6). Baldwin and those who agree with him contend that King, "the black intellectual, maintained continuity with black mass culture in America" (p. 10). King's cultural roots were the South, his family, and the Black Church. Baldwin examines what he considers a fundamental theme in King's teaching: The Messianic role of the African-American people.

In the book *To Redeem the Soul of America: The Southern Christian Leadership Conference and Martin Luther King, Jr.* (1987), Adam Fairclough stresses the need to look at King's associates in order to interpret King. He writes:

> SCLC was not, as has frequently been asserted, a mere extension of [King's] personality. Neither in Montgomery at the time of the bus boycott, nor in subsequent years, did King build his own organizational base. SCLC was created *for* him but not *by* him. Moreover, the men (rarely women) who comprised SCLC were not ciphers or sycophants who paid blind obeisance to a charismatic leader . . . most of the people who worked with King were forceful individuals who did not hesitate to assert their own point of view. (P. 4)

Finally, attention is due to three works dealing with King and other thinkers and leaders. Walter E. Fluker's study *They Looked for a City: A Comparative Analysis of the Ideal of Community in the Thought of Howard Thurman and Martin Luther King, Jr.* (1984), contrasts the history and thought processes of these two African-American spiritual leaders. And James Cone in *Martin and Malcolm and America: A Dream or a Nightmare* (1991) puts together these two men who barely knew each other and generally disagreed with each other and yet affected each other and the course of American history.

Outside the Main Christian Traditions

Hans A. Baer writes about a little-known aspect of black religion in the United States in *The Black Spiritual Movement: A Religious Response to Racism* (1984). His subject is the Black Spiritual, or Spiritualist churches, which he characterizes as "thaumaturgical /manipulationist sects," adding that, "although Spiritual churches exhibit many of the features found in other black religious groups, their emphasis on the manipulation of one's present condition through magico-religious rituals and esoteric knowledge tends to differentiate them" (p. 9).

The best overview of nontraditional black religious churches is *Black Gods of the Metropolis* (1975), by Arthur Fauset. Although now dated, Fauset's book describes the religious organizations that grew up in northern cities as more and more Southern blacks moved northward and sought a religious home that was welcoming and supportive. That religious home included such charismatic leaders as Father Divine. In the past decade, three more complete studies of Father Divine have been written. Sara Harris's *Father Divine* (1971) is a revised edition of a book that originally appeared in the 1950s. As a journalist, Harris relied heavily on personal interviews with Divine himself, those associated with him, and those who had become disillusioned in his service. Her unflattering portrayal of Father Divine incurred his wrath—he cursed her work. Harris revised her work after Divine's death in 1965. Two later studies are more academic, and place Divine and his work in the context of the African-American struggle to adapt to a hostile society. Robert Weisbrot's *Father Divine and the Struggle for Racial Equality* (1983) is a look at the political and sociological factors in his religious work. Jill Watts, in *God, Harlem, U.S.A.: The Father Divine Story* (1992), examines the movement of Father Divine in a religious context, seeing him as the founder of a spiritual movement. Watts closes her study of Divine by examining the history of the movement after his death.

Islam has made an enormous advance in the African-American community in the last quarter century. Akbar Muhammad gives an overview of the various Islamic organizations in the United States in "Muslims in the United States. An Overview of Organizations, Doctrines, and Problems," in *The Islamic Impact* (1984), edited by Yvonne Yazbeck Haddad, Byron Haines, and Ellison Findly. Included in this overview is a brief history of the various African-American Islamic groups. The first writer to discuss the followers of Elijah Muhammad with objectivity and respect, and even to call them the "Black Muslims" was C. Eric Lincoln. His work *The Black Muslims in America* (1982) is still the best study on this particular movement. Shortly after the appearance of Lincoln's revised *The Black Muslims in America*, Clifton E. Marsh provided a new assessment of the black Muslim movement in *From Black Muslims to Muslims* (1984). Marsh recounts how the organization that Elijah Muhammad had headed became an orthodox Muslim community under his son Wallace Muhammad. The religious group is now known as the World Community of Al-Islam in the West. However, those members who rejected the evolution brought about by Wallace Muhammad followed the charismatic leadership of Louis Farrakhan. Farrakhan's organization became known as The Nation of Islam.

Conclusion

African-American religious literature has been abundant and diverse during the last quarter century. Unfortunately, there is not yet a complete bibliography for the period. Two bibliographies, however, will be useful in researching part of this period and the period preceding it. For the field of religious literature prior to 1975, see *The Howard*

University Bibliography of African and Afro-American Religious Studies (1977), compiled by Ethel Williams and Clifton Brown. For a resource covering the past twenty-five years, see Hans A. Baer's "Bibliography of Social Science Literature on Afro-American Religion in the United States," in *Review of Religious Research* (1988).

Finally, two publications give a broad overview of the African-American religious population. The first is a well-researched reference work edited by Wardell Payne, *Directory of African American Religious Bodies* (1991), and the other is the more narrowly focused *1984: Statistical Profile of Black Catholics* (1985).

The variety and the extent of religious literature concerning African Americans in the last quarter century provide ample evidence that the Black Church is still one of the most potent elements in the African-American community. Without some idea of this literature, the significance of the African-American community's contribution to contemporary American culture would remain underestimated and undervalued.

References

Anbro, John. *Martin Luther King, Jr.: The Making of a Mind.* Maryknoll, NY: Orbis Books, 1982.

Andrews, William. *Sisters of the Spirit: Three Black Women's Autobiographies of the Nineteenth Century.* Bloomington: Indiana University Press, 1986.

Baer, Hans A. "Bibliography of Social Science Literature on Afro-American Religion in the United States." *Review of Religious Research* 29 (1988): 413–30.

———. *The Black Spiritual Movement: A Religious Response to Racism.* Knoxville: University of Tennessee Press, 1984.

Baldwin, Lewis. *There Is a Balm in Gilead: The Cultural Roots of Martin Luther King, Jr.* Minneapolis, MN: Augsburg Fortress, 1991.

Burkett, Randall. *Black Redemption. Churchmen Speak for the Garvey Movement.* Philadelphia: Temple University Press, 1978.

Burkett, Randall, and Richard Newman, eds. *Black Apostles: Afro-American Clergy Confront the Twentieth Century.* Boston: G. K. Hall, 1978.

Carson, Clayborne. *A Guide to Research On Martin Luther King, Jr. and the Modern Black Freedom Struggle.* Stanford, CA: Stanford University Libraries, 1989.

Cone, James. *Black Theology and Black Power.* New York: Seabury, 1969.

——. *A Black Theology of Liberation*. New York: Seabury, 1970.

——. *A Black Theology of Liberation*. 2d ed. Maryknoll, NY: Orbis Books, 1986.

——. *For My People*. Maryknoll, NY: Orbis Books, 1984.

——. *God of the Oppressed*. New York: Seabury, 1975.

——. *Martin and Malcolm and America: A Dream or a Nightmare*. Maryknoll, NY: Orbis Books, 1991.

——. *My Soul Looks Back*. Maryknoll, NY: Orbis Books, 1986.

——. *Speaking the Truth: Ecumenism, Liberation, and Black Theology*. Grand Rapids, MI: William B. Eerdmans, 1986.

Cone, James, and Gayraud Wilmore, eds. *Black Theology: A Documentary History*. 2 vols. Vol. 1, 1966–1979. Vol. 2, 1980–1992. Maryknoll: Orbis Books, 1993. 2d ed. rev.

Curran, R. Emmett. " 'Splendid Poverty': Jesuit Slaveholding in Maryland, 1805–1838." In *Catholics in the Old South*, edited by R. M. Miller and J. L. Wakelyn. Macon, GA: Mercer University Press, 1983.

Davis, Cyprian. "African-American Spirituality." *The New Dictionary of Catholic Spirituality*. Collegeville, MN: Liturgical Press, 1993.

——. *The History of Black Catholics in the United States*. New York: Crossroad, 1990.

Davis, Gerald. *I Got the Word in Me and I Can Sing It, You Know*. Philadelphia: University of Pennsylvania Press, 1985.

Downing, Frederick. *To See the Promised Land: The Faith Pilgrimage of Martin Luther King, Jr.* Macon, GA: Mercer University Press, 1986.

Egbulem, Fr. Chris Nwaka. "African Spirituality." *The New Dictionary of Catholic Spirituality*. Collegeville, MN: Liturgical Press, 1993.

Evans, James H., Jr., comp. *Black Theology: A Critical Assessment and Annotated Bibliography*. New York: Greenwood Press, 1987.

Fairclough, Adam. *To Redeem the Soul of America: The Southern Christian Leadership Conference and Martin Luther King, Jr.* Athens, GA: University of Georgia Press, 1987.

Fauset, Arthur. *Black Gods of the Metropolis*. Philadelphia: University of Pennsylvania Press, 1975.

Felder, Cain Hope. *Troubling Biblical Waters: Race, Class, and Family*. Maryknoll, NY: Orbis Books, 1989.

————, ed. *Stony the Road We Trod*. Minneapolis, MN: Augsburg Fortress, 1991.

Fisher, William H., ed. *Free At Last: A Bibliography of Martin Luther King, Jr*. Metuchen, NJ: Scarecrow Press, 1977.

Fluker, Walter E. *They Looked for a City: A Comparative Analysis of the Ideal of Community in the Thought of Howard Thurman and Martin Luther King, Jr*. Lanham, MD: University Press of America, 1984.

Foley, Albert, S.J. *Bishop Healy, Beloved Outcaste: The Story of a Great Man Whose Life Has Become a Living Legend*. New York: Farrar, Strauss, 1954.

————. *Dream of an Outcaste: Patrick F. Healy, S.J.: The Story of the Slave-Born Georgian Who Became the Second Founder of America's Great Catholic University, Georgetown*. Tuscaloosa, AL: Portals Press, 1989.

Foner, Phil. *Black Socialist Preacher: The Teachings of Reverend George Washington Woodbey and His Disciple Reverend George W. Slater, Jr*. San Francisco: Synthesis, 1983.

Frazier, E. Franklin. *The Negro Church in America*. Rev. ed., with commentary by C. Eric Lincoln. New York: Schocken Books, 1974.

Garrow, David. *Bearing the Cross: Martin Luther King, Jr. and the Southern Christian Leadership Conference*. New York: Morrow, 1986.

George, Carol V. R. *Segregated Sabbaths: Richard Allen and the Emergence of Independent Black Churches. 1760–1840*. New York: Oxford University Press, 1973.

Grant, Jacqueline. *White Women's Christ and Black Women's Jesus: Feminist Christology and Womanist Response*. Atlanta, GA: Scholar's Press, 1989.

Haddad, Yvonne Yazbeck, Byron Haines, and Ellison Findly, eds. *The Islamic Impact*. Syracuse, NY: Syracuse University Press, 1984.

Hanigan, James P. *Martin Luther King, Jr. and the Foundation of Nonviolence*. Lanham, MD: University Press of America, 1984.

Harris, Sara. *Father Divine*. Rev. ed. New York: Collier Books, 1971.

Hood, Robert E. *Must God Remain Greek? Afro Cultures and God-Talk*. Minneapolis, MN: Augsburg Fortress, 1990.

Hopkins, Dwight. *Black Theology, USA and South Africa, Politics, Culture, and Liberation*. Maryknoll, NY: Orbis Books, 1989.

Jacobs, Harriet. *Life of a Slave Girl, Written by Herself.* Cambridge, MA: Harvard University Press, 1987.

Jones, Cheslyn. *The Study of Spirituality.* New York: Oxford University Press, 1986.

Jones, Major. *The Color of God: The Concept of God in Afro-American Thought.* Macon, GA: Mercer University Press, 1987.

Josephite Pastoral Center. *1984: Statistical Profile of Black Catholics.* Washington, DC: Josephite Pastoral Center, 1985.

King, Rev. Martin Luther, Jr. *The Measure of a Man.* Philadelphia: Fortress Press, 1988.

Labbé, Dolores. *Jim Crow Comes to Church: The Establishment of Segregated Catholic Parishes in South Louisiana.* New York: Arno Press, 1978.

Lawson, Steven F. "Freedom Then, Freedom Now: The Historiography of the Civil Rights Movement." *The American Historical Review* 96 (1991): 456–71.

Lewis, David. *King: A Critical Biography.* New York: Praeger, 1970.

Lincoln, C. Eric. "The Black Church Since Frazier." In *The Negro Church in America.* Edited by E. Franklin Frazier. New York: Schocken Books, 1974.

———, ed. *The Black Experience in Religion: A Book of Readings.* Garden City, NY: Anchor Press/Doubleday, 1974.

———. *The Black Muslims in America.* Rev. and reprinted. Westport, CT: Greenwood Press, 1982.

———. *Race, Religion, and the Continuing American Dilemma.* New York: Hill and Wang, 1984.

Lincoln, C. Eric, and Lawrence Mamiya. *The Black Church in the African American Experience.* Durham, NC: Duke University Press, 1990.

Lippy, Charles, and Peter Williams, eds. *The American Religious Experience: Studies of Traditions and Movements.* 3 vols. New York: Scribner's, 1988.

Marsh, Clifton E. *From Black Muslims to Muslims.* Metuchen, NJ: Scarecrow Press, 1984.

Maxwell, John. *Slavery and the Catholic Church.* Chichester, England: Barry Rose, 1975.

Mays, Benjamin. *Born to Rebel: An Autobiography of Benjamin Mays*. Athens, GA: University of Georgia Press, 1987.

Mbiti, John S. "African Religions." In *The Study of Spirituality*, edited by Cheslyn Jones. New York: Oxford University Press, 1986.

Mitchell, Henry, and Nicholas Cooper Lewter. *Soul Theology: The Heart of American Black Culture*. San Francisco: Harper & Row, 1986.

Muhammad, Akbar. "Muslims in the United States. An Overview of Organizations, Doctrines, and Problems." In *The Islamic Impact*, edited by Yvonne Yazbeck Haddad, Byron Haines, and Ellison Findly. Syracuse, NY: Syracuse University Press, 1984.

Nickels, Marilyn. *Black Catholic Protest and the Federated Colored Catholics, 1917–1933*. New York: Garland, 1988.

Oates, Stephen. *Let the Trumpets Sound: The Life of Martin Luther King, Jr.* New York: Harper & Row, 1982.

Ochs, Stephen. *Desegregating the Altar: The Josephites and the Struggle for Black Priests. 1871–1960*. Baton Rouge: Louisiana State University Press, 1990.

Paris, Peter J. *Black Leaders in Conflict: Martin Luther King, Jr., Malcolm X, Joseph H. Johnson, Adam Clayton Powell*. New York: Pilgrim Press, 1978.

———. *The Social Teaching of the Black Church*. Philadelphia: Fortress Press, 1985.

Payne, Wardell, ed. *Directory of African American Religious Bodies*. Washington, DC: Howard University Press, 1991.

Poole, Stafford, C. M., and Douglas Slawson, C. M. *Church and Slave in Perry County, Missouri. 1818–1865*. Lewiston, ME: Edwin Mellen Press, 1986.

Raboteau, Albert. *Slave Religion*. New York: Oxford, 1978.

Roberts, James Deotis. *Black Theology Today*. New York: Edwin Mellen Press, 1983.

———. *Black Theology Today in Dialogue*. Philadelphia: Westminster, 1987.

Rudd, Daniel, ed. *Three Catholic Afro-American Congresses*. Cincinnati, OH: American Catholic Tribune, 1893; New York: Arno Press, 1978.

Sernett, Milton C. *Black Religion and American Evangelicalism: White Protestants, Plantation Missions, and the Flowering of Negro Christianity, 1787–1865*. Metuchen, NJ: Scarecrow Press and American Theological Library Association, 1975.

————, ed. *Afro-American Religious History: A Documentary Witness*. Durham, NC: Duke University Press, 1985.

Shannon, David, and Gayraud Wilmore, eds. *Black Witness to the Apostolic Faith*. Grand Rapids, MI: W. B. Eerdmans, 1985.

Smithson, Sandra. *To Be the Bridge: A Commentary on Black / White Catholicism in America*. Nashville, TN: Winston Derek, 1984.

Spencer, Jon Michael. *Protest and Praise: Sacred Music of Black Religion*. Minneapolis, MN: Augsburg Fortress, 1990.

Swift, David. *Black Prophets of Justice: Activist Clergy Before the Civil War*. Baton Rouge: Louisiana State University Press, 1989.

Thurman, Howard. *With Head and Heart: The Autobiography of Howard Thurman*. New York: Harcourt Brace Jovanovich, 1979.

Washington, James Melvin. *A Testament of Hope: The Essential Martin Luther King, Jr.* San Francisco: Harper & Row, 1986.

Watts, Jill. *God, Harlem, U.S.A.: The Father Divine Story*. Berkeley: University of California Press, 1992.

Weisbrot, Robert. *Father Divine and the Struggle for Racial Equality*. Urbana: University of Illinois Press, 1983.

West, Cornel. *Prophesy Deliverance: An Afro-American Revolutionary Christianity*. Philadelphia: Westminster, 1982.

————. *Race Matters*. Boston: Beacon Press, 1993.

Williams, Ethel, and Clifton Brown, comps. *The Howard University Bibliography of African and Afro-American Religious Studies*. Wilmington, DE: Scholarly Resources, 1977.

Williams, Walter. *Black Americans and the Evangelization of Africa: 1877–1900*. Madison: University of Wisconsin Press, 1982.

Wills, David, and Richard Newman. *Black Apostles at Home and Abroad: Afro-Americans and the Christian Mission from the Revolution to Reconstruction*. Boston: G. K. Hall, 1982.

Wilmore, Gayraud. *Black Religion and Black Radicalism: An Interpretation of the Religious History of Afro-American People*. 2d ed. Maryknoll, NY: Orbis Books, 1983.

Wilmore, Gayraud, and David Shannon, eds. *Black Witnesses to Apostolic Faith*. Grand Rapids, MI: William B. Eerdmans, 1985.

Witvliet, Theo. *The Way of the Black Messiah*. London: SCM Press, 1987.

Wood, Forrest. *The Arrogance of Faith: Christianity and Race in America from the Colonial Era to the Twentieth Century*. New York: Alfred A. Knopf, 1990.

Young, Josiah. *Black and African Theologians. Siblings or Distant Cousins*. Maryknoll, NY: Orbis Books, 1986.

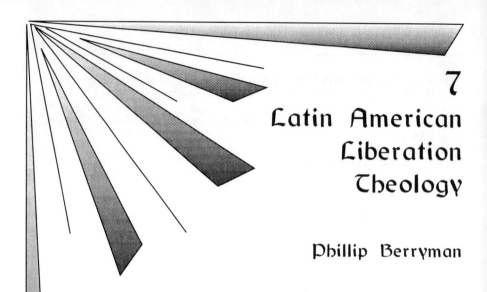

7
Latin American Liberation Theology

Phillip Berryman

Introduction

In the summer of 1988, Maryknoll, the missionary organization of the American Catholic Church, held a month-long seminar to honor the work of the Peruvian theologian Gustavo Gutierrez on the occasion of his sixtieth birthday, and thirtieth anniversary of his ordination as a priest. Theologians, Catholic and Protestant, male and female, and from several continents, presented dozens of papers. Saluting Gutierrez were several Catholic bishops from Brazil, China, and the United States, as well as Anglican Bishop Desmond Tutu of South Africa, and novelist and Holocaust survivor Elie Wiesel.

The seminar was not being held to honor Gutierrez alone, but celebrated Latin-American liberation theology as well, of which Gutierrez was one of the early formulators. At that meeting, a new edition of his own landmark work *A Theology of Liberation* (1988), first published in Spanish in 1971, was issued. Gutierrez himself would no doubt be the first to point out that Latin-American liberation theology is not primarily the work of individual theologians, but is rather the expression of an experience of Christian life among the poor, and of the church itself, as it seeks to approach and stand by the poor.

This theology did not arise in seminaries or university classrooms; it came about in the real world, often the Third World, and its unfolding has often been related to public events and struggles. In November 1989, members of El Salvador's armed forces gunned down six Jesuit priests, their housekeeper, and her daughter at the Central American University.

The most prominent of those killed, Ignacio Ellacuria, was a major figure in Latin-American liberation theology. He and his colleagues were murdered for his intellectual work, or more precisely, for the connections between his theology and his work as a priest.

That was not the only occasion when this kind of theology and the pastoral approach associated with it had a public impact in the 1980s. We need only recall the murder of Archbishop Romero of El Salvador in March 1980, and the rape and murder of four U.S. churchwomen in December of that year. Other events include Pope John Paul II's tour through Central America in 1983, and his confrontation with pro-revolutionary Christians in Nicaragua; the 1984–85 Vatican censures against Latin-American theologians (see Alfred Hennelly's *Liberation Theology* [1990]), especially the Brazilian Leonardo Boff; and the involvement of church figures in the peace processes in Central America. It is important to note, however, that liberation theology was not the only vital religious force in Latin America during these events. In terms of numbers, it was overshadowed by the remarkable growth of evangelical Protestantism.

A New Approach to Theology

Because the questions and context of Latin-American theology are rather different from those of North America, it is a good idea to consider the experience that has given rise to liberation theology. Until the 1960s, what theology there was in Latin America was largely that of Catholic seminaries, namely that of the Middle Ages and the Counter-Reformation. Although Latin-American concerns had little impact on Vatican Council II (1962–1965), the Council spurred Latin-American churchpeople to take a fresh look at their own continent and their own church.

As they did so, the reality of poverty became central to their reflections. They began to ask themselves questions: "What does the poverty of the vast majority of our people, in cities and the countryside, mean for the church and its mission?" "What is the Gospel message for these poor people?" "What new pastoral approaches should the church take to reach people—especially given the shortage of personnel (about 1 priest for every 10,000 Catholics, as opposed to the United States, where the ratio was about 1 per 1,000)?" In the late 1960s and early 1970s, many priests and sisters began to move to shantytowns and villages to live closer to the poor.

This self-questioning came at a time of crisis and questioning in Latin-American society when, as a whole, Latin-American social scientists were questioning the very paradigm of "development," which assumed that underdeveloped countries need only follow the path already laid out by developed countries. These new thinkers countered that such a path to development was impossible: The power wielded by industrialized countries kept Third-World countries in a subordinate role. What was needed by the Third World was, instead, liberation— breaking out from the existing structures, both international and national—so that countries and peoples could chart their own path toward a state of development that would enable all people to meet their basic human needs.

Thus, liberation theology arose at a crucial juncture, as church leaders unleashed a new critical spirit not only on issues within the church but on society at large. Many of these tendencies came to a head in the Catholic Church in Latin America at the meeting of bishops at Medellin, Colombia that was intended to provide guidelines on how the principles of Vatican II could be implemented in Latin America.

At Medellin, the bishops encouraged the formation of "Christian base communities," which were just beginning in a few places. These are small groups of people, generally in villages and poor neighborhoods, who, led by laypersons, meet to read and discuss the Scriptures, pray, and often to work together on community issues. Although they began as separate movements, liberation theology and the base-community approach to pastoral work soon came to influence each other.

Liberation theology is not so much a new theology—a new set of ideas about God, Christ, or even about how society should be changed— as it is a new approach to theology. Unlike their colleagues in Europe and North America, these Latin-American theologians do not teach in universities or divinity schools. They actually practice their theology with the poor, partly through their own pastoral work, and partly by conducting workshops for lay church leaders and other pastoral workers. Although the accent is strongly Roman Catholic, Protestants have played a significant role in liberation theology as well.

The first sketches of liberation theology appeared in the late 1960s and early 1970s, when it seemed possible that basic structural change in society might be a genuine possibility, at least in some countries such as Chile, where a socialist government was elected in 1970. In fact, however, the military overturned civilian governments and took over in country after country. In the mid-1970s, Brazil, Chile, Argentina, Uruguay, Paraguay, Bolivia, Peru, Ecuador, and most of Central America were under the control of unelected military governments. In a number of countries, with the media muzzled and political parties banned, corrupted, or rendered powerless, churchpeople and institutions played major roles in defending human rights.

By the end of the 1970s, these military dictatorships either began to loosen the reins or were forced out, and civilian government once more became the norm. Most, though, were saddled with enormous debts built up by the previous military regimes. To make matters worse, a recession in the industrialized countries lowered demand for Latin-American goods, and the continent as a whole suffered the worst depression since the 1930s.

With the Sandinista victory over the Somoza dictatorship, revolutionary change once more seemed possible in the tiny countries of Central America. However, the armies of Guatemala and El Salvador thwarted revolutionary movements by killing tens of thousands of their own citizens. United States' support for these governments and opposition to the Sandinistas—who, whatever their shortcomings, did not use mass murder as a routine political tool—frustrated efforts at revolution.

The fall of communism in Eastern Europe in 1989, and then in the Soviet Union in 1991, seemed to portend yet another major shift in the political climate of Central America. Latin-American governments were being told that capitalism and electoral democracy were the keys to progress, and under pressure from international financial institutions, were being forced to adopt austerity measures, cut back social spending, and privatize government assets. As governments sought to reshape their economies to take part in a proposed Western hemisphere free-trade zone, some were eager to portray liberation theology as the relic of a bygone era of romantic Marxist dreams.

When scrutinized more closely, however, such claims seemed premature to say the least. In the early 1990s, murder was still being used as a political tool in many parts of Latin America, even under formally democratic regimes. In Brazil, killers hired by large ranchers murdered hundreds of rural people. In Colombia, the army killed thousands of suspected leftists each year; and in Peru, civilians were being killed by both the army and the Shining Path guerrillas.

Most importantly, there was little prospect of dramatic improvement in the living conditions of the poor majority. Even if the liberalization of trade brought about economic growth, all indications were that little would trickle down to the poor. The poverty that had led to the first formulations of liberation theology was only more pressing twenty-five years later.

In short, since the inception of liberation theology, there have been notable shifts in the political background. Nevertheless, the plight of the poor, which was its starting point, has remained basically the same.

There have also been notable changes in the ecclesiastical background of Latin America. The first expressions of liberation theology prompted a backlash among the bishops, beginning around 1972. CELAM (the Latin American Bishops Conference) became a center of organized opposition to this new approach to theology. Therefore, when the bishops met at Puebla, Mexico in 1979, journalists were led to expect some kind of condemnation of liberation theology. However, the resulting documents (see John Eagleson and Philip Sharper's *Puebla and Beyond* [1979]) can be seen as something less than outright condemnation, and indeed, even a recognition of some of the themes liberation theologians have been arguing. At the time of Puebla, though, Pope John Paul II had been in office only a few months. Over the next decade, as part of a larger program of curbing what he and his advisors see as post-Vatican II excesses, he has acted against liberation theologians, most notably in the silencing of Leonardo Boff and the publication of Cardinal Ratzinger's 1984 document, which is a kind of summary of criticisms of liberation theology. Both of these actions are further discussed below.

This background in both Latin-American society and in the Latin-American Catholic Church should be kept in mind during the survey of the literature that follows. The procedure will be to discuss a number of works on the experience of Latin-American churches, the main themes of liberation theology as articulated by Gustavo Gutierrez, and then the work of major representative figures, followed by observations on overviews and critical works. I conclude with some observations on what I regard as the accomplishments and limitations of Latin-American liberation theology and its current challenges and prospects.

Experience of Churches and Christians

Because the experience of North American readers is generally far from that which gave rise to liberation theology, I have decided to include a number of works that, while directly theological, are helpful for understanding the context of this theology. A very good short overview of the Catholic Church in Latin America is *Crisis and Change: The Church in Latin America Today* (1985), by Edward Cleary. *Cry of the People: The Struggle for Human Rights in Latin America—The Catholic Church in Conflict with U.S. Policy,* by Penny Lernoux (1982) is a widely read account of the brutality of military regimes in a number of Latin-American countries, and of church involvement in the defense of human rights. A strength of the book is that Lernoux, who worked as a journalist in Latin America from the early 1960s until her death in 1989, devoting major attention to the church, draws material from all over the continent—Brazil, Chile, Central America—and tells stories in great detail, particularly of the martyrs. Almost a decade later, in *People of God: The Struggle for World Catholicism* (1989), she traced developments taking place in the Catholic Church under Pope John Paul II, including developments in the United States. She buttresses her case against present papal efforts to rein in experimentation and exploration, and reimpose narrow hierarchical control with numerous stories of real experiences. Her chapter on Nicaragua has greater balance than most writing during the period when she was writing. While sympathizing with the aims of the Sandinista revolution, she discerned that, to some extent, the pro- and anti-Sandinista partisans brought out the worst in each other.

Personal stories can offer important insight into the experience and vision underlying liberation theology. Much of the material during the last decade is from Central America. *Christians in the Nicaraguan Revolution* (1983), by Margaret Randall, and *Ministers of God, Ministers of the People* (1983), and *Revolutionaries for the Gospel* (1986), by Teofilo Cabestrero offer first-person testimony from Christians who participated in the overthrow of the Somoza dictatorship and in the efforts of the Sandinista government to make revolutionary changes. In *Don Lito of El Salvador* (1990), Maria Lopez Vigil presents the oral history of a peasant in El Salvador who is both a lay church leader and a militant organizer. *El Salvador: A Spring Whose Waters Never Run Dry* (1990), by Scott Wright et al. presents a collection of very short vignettes of the suffering of churchpeople in El Salvador. Renny Golden has gathered powerful stories of over a dozen Salvadoran women whose experience spans the 1980s in *The Hour of the Poor, The Hour of Women* (1990), a work that is especially important because, although women suffer most, and do most of the work in church organizations, men predominate in leadership positions.

Faith of a People (1986), by Pablo Galdamez is a short story of an urban parish in El Salvador, and *Death and Resurrection in Guatemala* (1986), by Fernando Bermudez gives a rural parish in Guatemala similar treatment. A more specific and more detailed account is Bernice Kita's *What Prize Awaits Us: Letters from Guatemala* (1988), a collection of letters by a Maryknoll sister in Guatemala from 1987 to early 1983. She and other sisters arrive at a peaceful Indian community, and begin to become familiar with them and to share their lives, while the violence of the Guatemalan army is overwhelming the country.

A number of Americans were themselves the victims of violence. In *Murdered in Central America* (1988), Donna Brett and Edward Brett offer well-researched accounts of eleven U.S. missionaries murdered in Central America. A well-known case is that of the three sisters and one laywoman who were raped and murdered by Salvadoran troops in December 1980; Ana Carrigan's *Salvador Witness* (1984) offers a full biography of one of the women, Jean Donovan.

A revealing personal account is *To Be a Revolutionary: An Autobiography* (1985), the memoir of Padre J. Carney, an American Jesuit who worked in rural Honduras for many years. Expelled from Honduras, he wrote this account of his slow radicalization as he saw people's efforts at development frustrated by the rich and powerful. In 1983, Carney reentered Honduras as chaplain to a group of guerrillas; they were soon detected by a Honduran army and its U.S. advisors. The official version was that when the guerrillas were surrounded, Fr. Carney and others died of starvation—but many suspect he was interrogated, tortured, and killed.

An important figure, not only in El Salvador but throughout Latin America, was Archbishop Oscar Romero of El Salvador, whose story many saw in the film *Romero* (with Raul Julia in the title role), which despite some liberties with specific details, presents clearly the basic dilemma of people of conscience in that country. James R. Brockman, S.J., sketches Romero's life in impressive detail in his *Romero: A Life* (1989). He also edited *The Violence of Love,* a collection of short passages of Romero's words that can be used for meditation (1988).

Several academic works provide information on the church in the larger region as well as in particular countries. Collections such as *Religion and Political Conflict in Latin America*, by Daniel Levine (1986), *The Progressive Church in Latin America*, by Scott Mainwaring and Alexander Wilde (1989), and *Church and Politics in Latin America*, by Dermot Keogh (1990) provide useful essays on individual countries as well as general trends. Mainwaring's *The Catholic Church and Power in Brazil, 1916–1985* (1986) studies institutional development of the church in Brazil, while Adriance's *Opting for the Poor* (1986) provides a shorter overview. While most writers emphasize church involvement on the side of social change, Emilio F. Mignone, in his *Witness to the Truth: The Complicity of Church and Dictatorship in Argentina* (1988), argues that, in his own Argentina, the Catholic hierarchy shamefully failed to confront the military in its "dirty war" of torture and the disappearance of thousands of Argentineans, including his own daughter.

Central America understandably has attracted a number of contributions. In *The Religious Roots of Rebellion: Christians in Central America Revolutions* (1984), Phillip Berryman surveys how Christians became involved in revolutionary movements, and attempts a sketch of liberation theology as exemplified in Central America. *The Catholic Church and Politics in Nicaragua and Costa Rica* (1989), by Philip J. Williams compares the Catholic Church in Costa Rica and Nicaragua. Dodson and O'Shaughnessy, in *Nicaragua's Other Revolution: Religious Faith and Political Struggle* (1990), argue that, contrary to the stereotypes, Sandinista Nicaragua should be seen as an experiment in a new kind of democracy, one that was having its impact on the churches. An advantage of Joseph Mulligan's *The Nicaragun Church and the Revolution* (1991) is that it covers events up to the period immediately after the Sandinista electoral defeat.

One tends to think of Latin America as Catholic; indeed, as recently as the 1960s, only 2 percent of the population was Protestant. However, evangelical Protestants, particularly pentecostals, are gaining converts very rapidly. Protestants are estimated to be more than 20 percent of the population in Guatemala and Chile, and 15 percent for the continent as a whole, including Brazil. Given low Catholic Mass attendance, there may be more Protestants than Catholics at church on Sunday morning in a number of countries. Anthropologist David Stoll, in *Is Latin America Turning Protestant?: The Politics of Evangelical Growth* (1990), and sociologist David Martin, in *Tongues of Fire: The Explosion of Protestantism in Latin America* (1990), analyze this phenomenon on the continent as a whole, invoking numerous local case studies. Martin argues that Protestantism will probably contribute to Latin-American development by encouraging habits of work, sobriety, and devotion to family, rather like early Methodism. Reading his work, however, one has the impression that most was done from a library, supplemented by some on-site interviewing. Stoll, who is an anthropologist, is closer to his subject, and is more interested in describing the phenomenon than in making grand projections. He believes that academics and the left, sympathizing with the political aims of liberation theology, have overlooked its rather limited success, and have been unwilling to confront the vitality of pentecostal religion. Nevertheless, rather than asserting that pentecostals are the winners, he believes that liberation theology and conservative Protestant religion are both legitimate parts of a movement of religious renewal, whose consequences are still unforeseeable.

An Initial Map

To present some characteristic themes and issues of liberation theology, I think it will be useful to pause over a single work, Gustavo Gutierrez's *A Theology of Liberation* (rev. ed. 1988). How the book came about is itself instructive. For years, during the 1950s and 1960s, Gutierrez had been a university chaplain and an informal advisor to many priests and sisters doing pastoral work. He had also met periodically with other theologians and with leaders of Catholic lay movements. In August 1968, Gutierrez gave a talk to a group of priests in the coastal fishing city of Chimbote. In that talk, he was reflecting as a theologian on the concerns he had been hearing and putting them into theological form. He suggested the need for a theology of human liberation. The ideas sketched at Chimbote soon grew into a more formal theological journal article, then into a presentation at an international symposium, and then into a book, published in Spanish in late 1971. Gutierrez's genius lay, I believe, in seizing the concerns of active Catholics—not necessarily a majority—and reflecting on them theologically.

The book opens with a consideration of what theology is all about. For instance, the theology of the early centuries of Christianity might be described as "wisdom," while the more systematic theology of scholasticism and modern times could be characterized as "rational knowledge." Gutierrez proposes that theology is taking on a new function, what he calls "critical reflection on praxis." He stresses that faith and commitment come first; theology only follows, and its mission is to aid faith and commitment. He does not claim that this new approach replaces the classic forms of theology, but simply that it is emerging as a legitimate way of carrying out the theological task.

Following this introductory chapter are several on the situation in Latin America and in the church (which to Gutierrez and other liberation theologians means the Catholic Church unless explicitly noted otherwise). Gutierrez first examines the notion of "development." Pointing to the work of Latin-American social scientists, he critiques the assumption that Latin-American countries need only follow in the steps of advanced countries. Latin Americans were realizing that underdevelopment was a structural relationship: Latin-American and other Third-World countries were part of an international division of labor, and hence in a situation of ongoing dependence. As long as such a relationship existed, catching up was impossible. The only way out for Third-World countries was to break free and chart their own economic and political course, in accordance with their own needs and requirements. At this time, many Latin Americans assumed that some kind of "revolution"—not necessarily violent—had to take place. Liberation was another term for this process, which people felt was already underway.

Gutierrez explicitly contrasts the word *development* to *liberation*, which he finds more dynamic and more biblical (not only in the event of Exodus, but in much of the dynamic of the Hebrew scriptures, and even more in the figure of Jesus). Early in his work, Gutierrez discusses the notion of liberation in terms of three levels: 1) the aspirations of the poor for better living conditions; 2) the human vocation to achieve freedom by building a more humane society; and finally, and most deeply, 3) the liberation wrought by Christ, freeing human beings from sin for communion with one another and with God. As articulated by Gutierrez, these are not "three parallel or chronologically successive processes," but rather "three levels of meaning of a single, complex process, which finds its deepest sense and its full realization in the saving work of Christ" (p. 25).

To restate the matter, Gutierrez and the other liberation theologians are convinced that a vast upheaval is underway in Latin America, that the people themselves are its major driving force, and that God is present in their suffering and struggle. They willingly accept the charge that this concept of liberation is "utopian"—that it is an ideal pulling humankind toward a future society more in accord with God's will.

Against this background, Gutierrez analyzes various kinds of pastoral approaches in the church. At the time of his initial writing, this was novel, as pastoral concerns normally had little impact on theology. An underlying issue of Gutierrez's work is the relationship between church and the larger society. Latin-American Catholicism was (and is) still emerging from "christendom," a model in which the boundaries of church and society were virtually the same. At Vatican II, the Catholic Church seemed to adopt a model in which the church acts within its own proper religious sphere, but Gutierrez and other liberation theologians were wary of fostering the view that there are, as it were, two histories, a worldly history and, alongside it, a salvation history. Opposed to this sort of dualism, theologians have insisted that there is only one world, one salvation, one history, in which God is at work. As recondite as it might seem, this difference in view has been a major concern among theologians.

Only after spending almost half of the book situating the issues (theology, development, situation of the church) does Gutierrez take up questions closer to the concerns of classical theology, such as creation, knowledge of God, Christ, the church, and the Sacraments. Here he shows himself quite conversant with the major currents of biblical research and theology. However, he largely ignores classical philosophical discussions of proofs for God or reflections on God's nature, and presents instead a Scriptural reflection that humankind itself is now God's temple, and that God is found in doing justice and serving one's neighbor (as in Matthew 25). In Latin America, the pastoral problem is not whether or not there is a God, as it often is in developed countries—few Latin Americans are atheists—but what kind of God is invoked.

One of Gutierrez's more original contributions is his discussion of poverty. The question is no doubt partly prompted by the fact that the wealth of a few and the poverty of many is often justified—implicitly and sometimes explicitly, and often by the privileged themselves—as the will of God (perhaps buttressed with the quote "Blessed are the poor in spirit"). Gutierrez develops a more complex notion of poverty: the Bible, he insists, views poverty as an evil and as generally the result of the oppression of some by others; however, it is just as clear that the Bible regards the poor and humble as more open to God; in a kind of synthesis of these seeming opposites, he proposes poverty as solidarity and protest, as exemplified in the Isaiah servant figure and even more in Jesus, who became poor so that we might become rich.

Gutierrez's book certainly does not cover all the major issues of liberation theology, and to some extent, it bears the marks of its era, not only in its bibliography but in its assumptions. Nevertheless, it remains quite valid as an overview of the major concerns of liberation theology, although some panoramic treatments are easier to read.

It is useful to reflect again on who Gutierrez's intended audience was—and who it was not. The primary intended audience was all those people who are on the frontlines of the church—priests, sisters, and some laypeople who devoted their lives to the church, and to working with and on behalf of the poor. Like liberation theology as a whole, this book is a defense of and rationale for a new kind of work in the church. A secondary but important audience are church authorities. Hence, a good deal of attention is paid to Vatican II and other official church documents (more than, say, would be typical of most Protestant theology). Yet another audience is perhaps theologians elsewhere, as is evidenced in Gutierrez's references to contemporary theologians, and some allusions to broader cultural and literary currents. Yet it is equally clear who is not Gutierrez's intended audience. Certainly, most of the Latin-American poor would have difficulty reading much of this work. Nor would it do much for an atheist or a Christian looking for an intellectual defense of Christian faith vis-à-vis secularism or atheism. By the same token, the typical, middle-class, North American churchgoer is by no means the intended audience. Those in the first world who approach this book or the others described here will have to make some effort to keep in mind the circumstances from which they arise and the audience for which they were intended.

Although this survey is largely focused on works in the 1980s, I will briefly note several other works dating from the first few years of liberation theology. Both Hugo Assmann's *Theology for a Nomad Church* (1976) and Ignacio Ellacuria's *The Mission of Christ and His Church* (1976) are similar to Gutierrez in that at the same time, and seemingly independent of his larger work, they elaborated similar maps of this new territory, although today all three works are largely of historical interest. Similarly, Enrique Dussel's *History and Theology of Liberation* (1976) and Juan Luis Segundo's *The Liberation of Theology* (1976) were certainly among the first to work in this new line. Rosino Gibellini's *Frontiers of Theology in Latin America* (1979) is still useful insofar as it gathers a number of essays from the first few years of the movement.

Jose Porfirio Miranda, a Mexican ex-Jesuit, is often linked to liberation theologians. In *Marx and the Bible* (1974), he used a great deal of erudition to argue the commonalities between the theories of Marx and Christianity—although he also unleashed his polemics against most embodiments of Marxism. Nevertheless, although some outsiders see Miranda as a liberation theologian, the theologians discussed here do not regard him as a colleague, perhaps because Miranda soon moved to an open expression of contempt for the institutional church, whereas the major liberation theologians have opted to work within it.

Leonardo Boff and Clodovis Boff

In 1985, the Vatican summoned a Brazilian Franciscan liberation theologian named Leonardo Boff to Rome to answer certain questions arising from his publications. In an unusual show of solidarity, two Brazilian cardinals accompanied Boff to Rome, showing their support of Boff's views, and that the Vatican's action was perceived as being aimed not only at an individual theologian, but at a good portion of the Brazilian clergy and episcopacy. At this same time, the Vatican issued a document fiercely critical of liberation theology (in Alfred Hennelly's *Liberation Theology* [1990], discussed below). Boff was silenced by the church; that is, he was ordered to stop publishing and teaching, and to step down from editing Brazil's main theological journal. Almost a year later that silence was lifted. The event drew the attention of the secular media to liberation theology.

That year of silence turned out to be only a hiatus in the activity of a very prolific writer—Boff is the author of approximately forty-five books written between 1971 and 1991, and coauthor of numerous others. What roused Vatican's ire was his book *Church: Charisma and Power: Liberation Theology and the Institutional Church* (1985), which raised serious questions about institutional Catholicism. Running through the book was the question of whether, in its institutional practice, the church exemplifies the ideals it professes in its proclamation, for example, with regard to human rights within the church. The Roman authorities cannot have been pleased when Boff quoted at great length the detailed comparison between the Vatican and the Kremlin, drawn by a Brazilian layman. Another work, *Ecclesiogenesis: The Base Communities Reinvent the Church* (1986), was focused first on considerations arising from the experience of base communities, but went on to raise explicitly the issue of women's ordination. To my knowledge, Boff is the only major male Latin-American theologian to deal with that issue at any length.

Boff also offered the first systematic Christology by a liberation theologian, *Jesus Christ Liberator; A Critical Christology for Our Time* (1978), although in many ways it still bears a strong European accent; that is, Boff's concern seems more to make Jesus credible to modern audiences than to draw out his social and political implications. That reticence, however, may reflect the fact that he was writing during the most repressive days of the military dictatorship in Brazil. A shorter work of Christology, *Passion of Christ, Passion of the World* (1987), centers on the meaning of Christ's death. Boff has also written the most systematic Latin-American study of the doctrine of grace, *Liberating Grace* (1979), which like his Christology, combines knowledge of the classical questions, an awareness of contemporary European theology, and an effort to relate this traditional theology to Latin America.

Boff is willing to venture into new terrain. Alone among Latin-American male theologians, he has explored the "feminine" side of God in the *Maternal Face of God: The Feminine and Its Religious Expressions* (1987), although one senses that he has not fully internalized the feminist critique of patriarchy. Those wishing to sample essays ranging over several areas of theology can consult shorter collections such as *When Theology Listens to the Poor* (1988). Although some of his works reflect considerable scholarship, Boff has also written devotional works, such as *The Lord's Prayer: The Prayer of Integral Liberation* (1983), his commentary on the Lord's Prayer.

Clodovis Boff, Leonardo's brother, has written the most thorough study of liberation theology's underlying method, *Theology and Praxis: Epistemological Foundations* (1987). Written in Europe as a dissertation, this work reflects the atmosphere of the mid-1970s with its frequent references to Monod, Ricoeur, Althusser, Bachelard, and other theologians, philosophers, and social thinkers. Upon returning to Brazil after his studies, Clodovis Boff seems to have made special efforts to ground his theology in pastoral experience. For several years, he spent one-half of each year teaching and the other half doing pastoral work in a remote corner of Brazil where rubber tappers worked (which region later gained worldwide attention due to the 1988 murder of Chico Mendes, the leader of the rubber tappers). Clodovis Boff's journal *Feet-on-the-Ground Theology: A Brazilian Journey* (1987) combines observation of life in the communities he visits, commentary on pastoral efforts, some poetic flights of fancy, occasional wry remarks, and pastoral musings. It is one of the best windows available into the mutual enrichment of pastoral work and theology.

Three books coauthored by the Boff brothers have the virtue of brevity: *Salvation and Liberation* (1984), essays on salvation and liberation, including a fictitious dialogue between a parish priest, a lay activist, and a theologian; *Liberation Theology: From Dialogue to Confrontation* (1986), a pair of essays on the liberation theology controversy as a result of the Vatican condemnation; and the short work *Introducing Liberation Theology* (1987).

Jon Sobrino and Ignacio Ellacuria

In the early morning of November 16, 1989, Salvadoran troops entered the UCA (Central American University), dragged six Jesuit priests out of their bed, and shot them, also murdering their cook and her daughter, who had taken refuge in their house, believing it was safer. Almost two years later, a Salvadoran jury found a colonel and a lieutenant guilty of the murder, but absolved the soldiers who had actually confessed to the killing, presumably because they acted under orders. This was the first instance in which a Salvadoran officer had been brought to justice for human rights violations, after a decade of war in which approximately 75,000 Salvadorans had lost their lives, the vast majority of whom were civilians killed by official forces or by death squads operating with impunity.

The leading figure among the murdered Jesuits was Ignacio Ellacuria, a philosopher and theologian and rector of the university. As noted above, one of his earlier works, *The Mission of Christ and His Church* (1976), can be regarded as one of the early systematic formulations of liberation theology. Hassett and Lacey's *Towards a Society That Serves Its People* (1991), a collection of the writings of three of those murdered, contains both theological and non-theological material by Ellacuria. For the details of the crime and some other selections, see *The Jesuit Assassinations* (1990), by El Rescate.

Had he not been giving a workshop in Bangkok, Jon Sobrino would undoubtedly have shared the fate of his colleagues. Like five of the murdered priests, he was also originally from Spain, but he had come to El Salvador in the 1960s. Within days of the murder, while still outside El Salvador, Sobrino wrote *Companions of Jesus: The Jesuit Martyrs of El Salvador* (1990), a highly personal theological reflection on the meaning of the life of his colleagues. While he devoted some pages to their personal qualities and on the political meaning of their deaths, he spoke of their vision of what a Christian university should do in a country like El Salvador, what kind of church they were striving for, and their theology. This work also has a number of essays by and about the murdered Jesuits.

Sobrino's *Christology at the Crossroads* (1978) is still the most systematic one-volume treatment by a Latin-American theologian, although like that of Boff noted above (1978), it still reflects his European theological training. Nevertheless, the accent is Latin American. For example, Sobrino sees Jesus' message, and the conflicts to which it gave rise, as integral to his Christology, and he presents the resurrection as God's vindication of Jesus' message over the powers of oppression. In a subsequent volume on Christology, *Jesus in Latin America* (1987), he responds to some questions raised about the first work, and reflects on Latin-American insight into Jesus.

Sobrino has also written frequently about the church, although *The True Church and the Poor* (1984) is more in the form of essays than a structured ecclesiology. This volume also contains an important essay on specific character of Latin-American theological method. Another collection, *Archbishop Romero: Memories and Reflections* (1990), gathers a number of essays and personal reflections on Archbishop Romero, with whom he had worked closely. As these titles indicate, Sobrino moves between spirituality and theology. Yet another spiritual work is a collection of essays, *Spirituality of Liberation: Toward Political Holiness* (1988). In the early 1980s, Sobrino and Juan Hernandez Pico reflected theologically on the phenomenon of church-to-church solidarity in *Theology of Christian Solidarity* (1985). All these writings are strongly biblical, and in them, one senses the presence of the suffering of the Salvadoran people.

Juan Luis Segundo

I admit to a special fondness for the work of the Uruguayan Jesuit, Juan Luis Segundo. In contrast to Gutierrez, Boff, Sobrino, and numerous others, who despite their variations in style, tend to overlap a good deal, Segundo has idiosyncratically pursued his own sets of questions. These are not simply his own ruminations, however, but the product of decades of dialogue with a group of laypeople in Montevideo. Perhaps because they are not themselves poor, but more or less middle-class and relatively well-educated, somewhat secularized interlocutors, Segundo's concerns have tended more toward the credibility of the church and its message than simply issues of solidarity with the poor. As early as 1962, Segundo noted in an article "The Future of Christianity in Latin America" that the theology he had learned did not prepare him to deal with the pastoral situation of Latin America, if the church is unable to evangelize the masses of people it baptizes (in Alfred Hennelly's *Liberation Theology* [1990]). The need for a pastoral approach to develop an adult faith is one of his constant themes, as can be seen in the work *The Hidden Motives of Pastoral Action: Latin American Reflections* (1978).

In an article reprinted in Hennelly (1990), Segundo makes the interesting observation that liberation theology has developed in two waves: the first in the 1960s, primarily in response to clergy and middle-class laypeople radicalized by their discovery of the poverty and injustice around them, and the second, characteristic of the 1970s, which reflected more direct contact with the poor, especially in base communities.

Segundo's major project for the 1980s is a series on Christology, *Jesus of Nazareth Yesterday and Today*, which in English, stretches out over five volumes. The hefty introductory volume, *Faith and Ideologies* (1984), however, does not even get to Christ, but is rather an extended discussion of foundational questions such as faith, knowledge, language, ideology, and particular ideologies. In this connection, he offers one of the most extensive head-on discussions of Marxism I recall seeing by a Latin-American theologian. Particularly incisive is his discussion of the effects of repressive government in Latin America. Rather than focus on the well-known barbarities of murder and torture, Segundo reflects on what happened to society, and especially to the middle classes, who supported an applauded military governments, at least for a time. He concludes that the "social ecology" destroyed by conflict has to be patiently rebuilt. To a degree, this may reflect the experience of Uruguay, where a once vibrant democracy had given way to a country with the highest per capita number of political prisoners in the world by the mid-1970s. I regard it as an example of Segundo's unwillingness to repeat clichés but to explore issues in his own way.

Segundo's concern in this series is not to engage in Christological debates, certainly not classical, and in a sense not even of those issues occupying theologians today. Rather, his central issue is "what contribution, if any, Jesus of Nazareth and the tradition stemming from him makes to the process of humanization." Each of the following volumes deals with Jesus from a particular angle: the synoptic Gospels (1985); St. Paul (1986); the spiritual exercises of Saint Ignatius Loyola (1987); and finally, from the standpoint of human evolution (1988). Although these works are demanding, they do not require the background of a professional theologian.

When the Vatican unleashed its 1984 attack on liberation theology, most theologians chose not to respond directly, asserting instead that what Cardinal Ratzinger was describing was a caricature of liberation theology, and even managing to say that the Vatican's action could serve to clarify matters. Such an approach was understandable, though perhaps a bit disingenuous. Segundo alone decided to respond directly to Ratzinger in the form of a short book, *Theology and the Church: A Response to Cardinal Ratzinger and a Warning to the Whole Church* (1985), even though he himself had not been publicly accused by the Vatican or the Uruguayan bishops. Besides responding to numerous individual points by Ratzinger, Segundo asserted that the structure of the cardinal's thought indicated that he had not really grasped the meaning of Vatican II. At one point, he goes so far as to say that if Ratzinger is right, he (Segundo) is wrong, and has been so for twenty-five years, as have been many bishops. With its rather relentless argumentation over church documents, this book may not strike a responsive chord in many readers, but it again attests to Segundo's independent spirit. Alfred T. Hennelly's *Theologies in Conflict: The Challenge of Juan Luis Segundo* (1979) is a good introduction to Segundo's earlier work.

The DEI School
(Hinkelammert, Assmann, Richard)

Forced to flee the brutal military crackdown after the September 1973 coup in Chile, the Brazilian Hugo Assmann and Franz Hinkelammert, a German economist who had been in Chile since the early 1960s, came together in San Jose, Costa Rica, to begin a small research and training institute. Since then, the DEI (Ecumenical Department of Investigation) has conducted intensive pastoral courses, organized occasional conferences, and published several dozen books. The DEI was joined by Pablo Richard, a Chilean, who became its director when Assmann returned to Brazil in the early 1980s.

Several characteristic themes have entered liberation theology largely through DEI's work. Hinkelammert, in *The Ideological Weapons of Death: A Theological Critique of Capitalism* (1986), a work originally published in 1977, seeks to get behind the appearances of social institutions to the underlying reality. For this purpose, he uses Marx's notions of fetishism to critique representative classical and modern economic and social thinkers and schools, such as Max Weber, Karl Popper, Milton Friedman, and representatives of Catholic social thought. Hinkelammert and others feel that, in unmasking the idolatry of modern social systems, they stand in continuity with the prophetic strain of the Bible concerned with the Molochs, who demand human sacrifice. In other words, modern social systems operate like gods, sacrificing the poor on the altars of their ideology, while proclaiming liberty. This line of thinking has been very influential among Latin-American theologians and pastoral workers, although many have not read Hinkelammert's dense prose. A series of papers presented by theologians, *The Idols of Death and the God of Life* (1983), was issued in a more biblically oriented presentation of the God of life in struggle with the idols of oppression.

Somewhat like Enrique Dussel, Richard, in his work *Death of Christendoms, Birth of the Church—Historical Analysis and Theological Interpretation of the Church in Latin America* (1987), presents a framework for understanding the past of the church in Latin America, to understand the present period and future possibilities. Though such a framework may be helpful, I suspect that historical research country by country will lead to a more complex formulation.

Scripture and Its Use

While most liberation theologians pay a great deal of attention to Scripture—and relatively little to, for example, the history of doctrine or speculative theology—J. Severino Croatto, an Argentinian, has reflected most specifically on how the read the Bible. In a work whose English title refers to the Exodus, but whose original title refers to hermeneutics, *Exodus* (1981), he ranges over aspects of Scripture often highlighted by liberation theologians (Exodus, creation, prophets, Christ, St. Paul), interested not simply in extracting their meaning but in illustrating how Scripture is to be understood today. A subsequent work, *Biblical Hermeneutics: Toward a Theory of Reading as the Production of Meaning* (1987), shows the influence of contemporary studies in semiotics.

Carlos Mesters, a Dutch priest, has worked for many years in Brazil, especially helping Christian communities with the Bible, even during the fierce repression of the early 1970s. He has written a number of simple but profound study guides for Bible groups. Although he is aware of contemporary scholarship, his need to explain things in terms understandable to semi-literate peasants has given him a very concrete style. His study *Defenseless Flower: A New Reading of the Bible* (1989) is a collection of several reflections on the use of the Bible. In Mesters, one feels closer to the pastoral grassroots than in many other writings of liberation theologians.

Gutierrez Again

It is perhaps somewhat surprising that Gustavo Gutierrez, who produced the most widely read early synthesis of liberation theology movement, has not produced an ambitious systematic theology. Although he could spend his whole time lecturing internationally by invitation, Gutierrez has continued to do parish work in a Lima *barrio*, perhaps precisely to avoid letting his theology get ahead of pastoral reality. His writings also give the impression of arising from particular circumstances rather than a long-range plan. His book *The Power of the Poor in History* is a collection of essays written in the 1970s, largely on the church, particularly in the period leading up to the Puebla meeting (1983). In a simply written volume, *We Drink From Our Own Wells:*

The Spiritual Journey of a People (1984), he explores the biblical basis of a newly emerging spirituality in Latin America. His commentary on the book of Job stays very close to the text, and is yet ultimately a question about the present of Latin America. It is not only Job's question ("If God is just, why am I suffering?"), but the question today: "How believe when the innocent suffer?" In a dialogue with European theologians and a reflection on theology and social sciences, he refines some points proposed in his earlier work (1990).

Two books about Gutierrez are especially helpful. Curt Cadorette, in *From the Heart of the People: The Theology of Gustavo Gutiérrez* (1988), sheds light primarily on the situation out of which Gutierrez's theology has emerged: his country Peru, the situation of the popular classes, and intellectual influences such as the novelist Jose Maria Arguedas and Jose Carlos Mariategui. With his usual graceful writing, Presbyterian theologian Robert McAfee Brown (1990) uses Gutierrez as a vehicle for dealing with not only Gutierrez's theology, but the import of liberation theology in general. He also presents a record of the Vatican's efforts to condemn Gutierrez and his response. The Orbis volume issuing from the celebration mentioned at the outset of this letter, *The Future of Liberation Theology*, by Marc Ellis and Otto Maduro (1989), also contains observations on Gutierrez.

Dialogue with Other Theologies

Parallel to the emergence of this Latin-American liberation theology, there also emerged black liberation theologies in the United States, the Caribbean, and in South Africa; feminist theology, first in the United States and Europe, and then elsewhere; and other Third-World theologies (including U.S. Latinos, and Native American religious movements). Most of these developments fall to other chapters in this book. Here I will note some examples of Latin-American participation in a wider theological dialogue.

In 1975, a conference on theology in the Americas held in Detroit brought together Latin-American, black, and feminist theologians in what was at first a surprisingly sharp clash: Latin-American theologians were accused of ignoring racism and sexism in their midst, while the Latin Americans thought black and feminist theologians failed to take seriously enough the class dimension of oppression (see Sergio Torres and John Eagleson's *Theology in the Americas* [1976]). Yet that and similar encounters led to the formation of EATWOT (Ecumenical Association of Third World Theologians) in 1976. In subsequent years, member theologians met on their own continents, and then in a series of meetings whose proceedings reflect a growing level of dialogue (see Sergio Torres and Eagleson's *The Challenge of Basic Christian Communities* [1981]; Virginia Fabella and Sergio Torres's *Irruption of the Third World* [1983] and *Doing Theology in a Divided World* [1985]; and K. C. Abraham's *Third World Theologies* [1990]). A women's group in EATWOT caucused at the 1986 meeting in Oaxtepec, Mexico and published its own set of papers, *With Passion and Compassion: Third*

World Women Doing Theology, by Virginia Fabella and Mercy Oduyoye (1988).

Mainstream theologians in Europe and North America have certainly been influenced by Latin-American and other liberation theologies. David Tracy observes, "It is now clear that the major breakthrough in Christian theology in the last decade [the 1970s] has been the explosive emergency of political and liberation theologies. . . . the theological landscape has been irretrievably changed." Tracy was writing the introduction to one volume in which U.S. theologians reflected on this impact, *The Challenge of Liberation Theology*, by Brian Mahan and L. Dale Richesin (1981). A decade later, when Thistlethwaite and Engel edited *Lift Every Voice: Constructing Christian Theologies from the Underside* (1990), a sampler of twenty essays in liberation theologies, their authors reflected a variety of struggles and experiences, from that of Native Americans, to a woman theologian from Hong Kong, to counselors of battered women; indeed, only one of the contributors was a Latin American.

Theology and Liberation Project

By 1980, although Latin-American liberation theology was a serious interlocutor with theology around the world, Latin-American Catholic seminaries continued to use European textbooks. Indeed, they had little choice; despite an outpouring of works, there was no single comprehensive and systematic presentation of theology from this new approach. A group of theologians brought together by the Chilean Sergio Torres proposed to remedy this lack.

At first, this group seems to have intended to produce a Latin-American counterpart to *Mysterium Salutis*, edited by Johannes Feiner and Magnus Löhrer (1970), three mammoth volumes put together by German-speaking theologians in the 1960s, widely used in seminaries. Reasoning, however, that Third-World seminarians and pastoral workers would find it difficult to pay for large, expensive volumes, they decided to produce a series of short paperbacks on specific topics. Taken altogether, these works would constitute a systematic library of the new theological approach.

As initially proposed, the project was impressive. The outline proceeded from more basic questions such as revelation and theological method; through classical questions such as God, Trinity, Christ, church, and Sacraments; and toward more specifically pastoral questions, such as work among indigenous peoples. Each of the several dozen Latin-American liberation theologians, mainly Catholic but some Protestant, working individually or in pairs or teams, accepted responsibility for certain individual topics. As originally conceived, the complete set of more than fifty volumes would be published in Spanish and Portuguese (as well as in translations) by the end of the 1980s. Because a large number of bishops publicly identified with the project, it was hoped that the series would be widely taught in seminaries and elsewhere.

This project has enabled the theologians to work collaboratively and to consult through periodic meetings. It must be confessed, however, that it has run into problems. The Vatican sought to halt the project, and while it was unsuccessful at stopping it completely, it was able to prevent bishops from being identified with it. Given the large number of titles, there is considerable overlap of material. It is also unrealistic to expect priests or sisters in pastoral work to buy and read so many books. Foreign publishers have found the market for translations disappointing. For the most part, the volumes do not represent fresh thinking, but are restatements of what has already been said.

Although only certain titles from this series are being selected for English translation, they should not be overlooked. Because this whole approach to theology is intended to serve the poor, one of the volumes of the series dealing with foundational issues, *The Bible, the Church, and the Poor*, by George Pixley and Clodovis Boff (1989), develops the many aspects of the topic from Scripture, the history of the church, and theological reflection. One of the most original contributions is that of Eduardo Hoonaert, a Belgian who has served in Brazil for many years. His *The Memory of the Christian People* (1988) approaches early Christianity, not as a scholar examining primary sources, but rather as one seeking what insight the pastoral experience of base communities may shed on the house churches of the early centuries, and, in turn, what that history may have to say to the church of the poor today.

Leonardo Boff's volume on the Trinity, *Trinity and Society* (1988), somewhat resembles his work on grace noted above (1979) insofar as it gives full weight to classical trinitarian doctrine and theology, while also drawing some of the consequences for Latin America. This is perhaps one of Boff's more important works, and is the first systematic study of the Trinity by a liberation theologian. Assigned the topic of God, the Chilean theologian Ronaldo Muñoz explores the traditional images of God in popular culture and religion, and how they are changing especially under the influence of urbanization. His modest observations in *The God of Christians* (1990) are thus grounded in his own dialogue with ordinary people in the shantytown in which he lives.

Pedro Trigo's volume *Creation and History* first questions traditional and contemporary approaches, noting that under the conditions of oppression and violence in Latin America, the starting point for a truly liberating theology cannot be a simple faith in the goodness of creation and in divine providence. This book has some of the most direct reflections on sin in the series. In dealing with what is often called theological anthropology, Jose Comblin, a Belgian who has worked in Brazil and Chile since 1958, offers a systematic reflection on the various dimensions of human life in *Retrieving the Human* (1990).

Although liberation theologians are insistent that Christian faith is a matter of practice rather than of mere belief, they have not produced many volumes of systematic ethical reflection. Moser and Leers's *Moral Theology* (1990) comes closest to the approach of theological ethics. The authors acknowledge the important advances made by the Catholic renewal, and then move on to the tendencies that require a specifically Latin-American approach. Enrique Dussel's approach to community ethics, *Ethics and Community* (1988), which is presented in a simple, almost catechetical manner, really amounts to a new set of analytical categories.

Many modern Catholic theologians tend to ignore the role of Mary, perhaps because of the excesses of what was once called "Mariology." Ivone Gebara and Maria Clara Binyemer approach the topic of Mary with respect and yet sophistication in *Mary, Mother of God, Mother of the Poor* (1989). They neither critique nor defend traditional doctrines, but rather explore their religious meaning. A later chapter in the book considers two of the major apparitions of Mary in Latin America: Guadalupe in Mexico and Aparecida in Brazil.

In its achievements and its shortcomings, this venture perhaps reveals much of the present status of Latin-American liberation theology and its future possibilities and challenges, to which we will return below.

Overviews

Curiously, although by the mid-1980s, dozens of volumes by and about liberation theologians had appeared, one would have been hard pressed to find a short readable overview of the phenomenon. That lack was remedied by several useful studies. In *Introducing Liberation Theology* (1987), a volume of less than 100 pages, Leonardo Boff and Clodovis Boff describe how liberation theology is carried out, its key themes, a brief history of the movement, and its extension beyond Latin America. Intended for non-theologians, and educated Brazilians who had heard about the movement through the media, their book is quite readable. One of the best contributions of this book is a discussion of the levels of theology, from grassroots poor people to pastoral workers to professional theologians. In another very short volume, *Liberation Theology: From Dialogue to Confrontation* (1986), reflecting the conflict with the Vatican (see below), the Boffs try to clarify basic issues of liberation theology. Roger Haight, in his *An Alternative Vision: An Interpretation of Liberation Theology* (1985), pays relatively little attention to the specifically Latin-American context and organizes his work along directly theological lines (e.g., faith, God, Christ, the Spirit, the church, the Sacraments, ministry, spirituality). *Liberation Theology: Essential Facts About the Revolutionary Movement in Latin America—and Beyond*, by Phillip Berryman (1987) seeks to deal with questions most asked by Americans. McGovern's *Liberation Theology and Its Critics: Toward an Assessment* (1989) may be the best single-volume treatment of the movement.

Several surveys by academics are useful. Approaching the subject from the standpoint of the sociology of knowledge, Christian Smith's *The Emergency of Liberation Theology: Radical Religion and Social Movement Theory* (1991) develops a history of how liberation theology was born and grew. In *Liberation Theology at the Crossroads: Democracy or Revolution?* (1990), Paul E. Sigmund organizes his overview around a thesis that there are, in effect, two strains in liberation theology, one of which uncritically accepts Marxist ideology, and another closer to the poor, especially in base communities. He believes this second tendency is prevailing, especially in its growing acceptance of democracy. Craig L. Nessan's *Orthopraxis or Heresy: The North American Theological Response to Latin American Liberation Theology* (1989) discusses the positions of approximately twenty-five North American theologians on liberation theology.

An extremely useful collection is Alfred T. Hennelly's *Liberation Theology: A Documentary History* (1990), which gathers about sixty articles and documents that trace the rise and development of liberation theology, especially relating to controversies within the Catholic Church. In addition, several collections may be mentioned. A good sampler of essays from the first decade of the movement is Gibellini's *Frontiers of Theology in Latin America* (1979). The 1988 celebration at Maryknoll described above resulted in *The Future of Liberation Theology: Essays in Honor of Gustavo Gutiérrez*, by Marc Ellis and Otto Maduro (1989), a publication of some fifty essays by theologians and others from around the world. Ellis and Maduro present fifteen of these essays in paperback form in *Expanding the View: Gustavo Gutiérrez and the Future of Liberation Theology* (1990).

The Critics

Liberation theology has had critics since the first writings appeared in the early 1970s. Indeed, a research center was set up in Bogotá, Columbia largely to counter its influence. Bishop (later Archbishop and Cardinal) Alfonso Lopez Trujillo used the apparatus of CELAM (Latin American Bishops Conference) to combat liberation theology, especially in preparation for the bishops' meeting at Puebla, Mexico in 1979. The election of Karol Wojtyla as John Paul II to the papacy, and the prominent involvement of Christians in the Sandinista movement and other revolutionary movements in Central America, gave added impetus to the arguments against liberation theology.

Indeed, the Vatican's 1984 "instruction" on liberation theology, authored by Cardinal Ratzinger, summarizes most of the objections against liberation theology (in Alfred Hennelly's *Liberation Theology* [1990], along with several related documents). Because this document is something of a compendium of arguments against liberation theology, I will describe its main outline. Widespread oppression is acknowledged as a fact, and the yearning for liberation and, indeed, liberation theology are acknowledged as legitimate. A major section summarizes liberation motifs from Scripture. After a great deal of praise for church workers among the poor, the document says that a particular kind of liberation theology "proposes a novel interpretation of both the content of faith and of Christian existence, which seriously departs from the faith of the church, and, in fact actually constitutes a practical negation" (p. 401). These theologies uncritically borrow from Marxism, which the document ridicules at some length, and propose a new interpretation of the faith "which is corrupting whatever was authentic in the general initial commitment on behalf of the poor" (p. 401).

Part of the document's arguing strategy is to push certain points to what seems to be their logical conclusion; for example, in the use of violence. The document purports to find numerous examples of this perverse new interpretation; for example, it is claimed that liberation theologians no longer believe in the real sacramental presence of Christ in the Eucharist, but see it simply as the celebration of the people's struggle.

Although the document itself does not mention particular theologians by name, Ratzinger elsewhere did in fact mention several. As already noted, Leonardo Boff was called to Rome and silenced for a year. Vatican efforts to get the Peruvian bishops to sanction Gutierrez were unsuccessful. Most Catholic liberation theologians tried to put the best face on the Vatican's actions, by saying that the whole process was part of a dialogue and would help theology itself deepen (but see Juan Luis Segundo's *The Historical Jesus of the Synoptics* [1985]). Boff's silence was lifted after about a year, and the Vatican issued a more positive statement on liberation themes in March 1986.

One consequence of the Vatican's actions was to turn the liberation theologians into celebrities, at least in Latin America, and bring their work to a wider audience. A negative effect, however, may have been the drain of their energy in defending their legitimacy vis-á-vis the Vatican, and that may have hindered them from devoting their best energy to reflection on changes going on in their own societies. The whole controversy is well-documented in Alfred Hennelly's *Liberation Theology* (1990). *Liberation Theology in Latin America* by Schall (1982) contains a long critical essay with many of the kinds of observations made by Ratzinger, as well as a collection of essays critical of liberation theology, including several by Pope John Paul II. A more mixed collection, including several fierce attacks on liberation theology's political assumptions, is *The Politics of Latin American Liberation Theology: The Challenge to U.S. Public Policy*, by Richard Rubenstein and John Roth (1988).

During the 1980s, Michael Novak of the American Enterprise Institute, tackled liberation theology with considerable zeal. Accepting the sincerity of the theologians and others doing pastoral work along liberation lines, Novak's *Liberation Theology and the Liberal Society* (1987) argues that true liberation will come not from the socialist society, which liberation theologians vainly imagine, but in learning from liberal (capitalist and democratic) societies. Contrary to the Latin Americans who believe (or assume) that the economies they experience in their countries are capitalist, Novak argues that Latin-American economies are statist or mercantilist. True capitalism has not even been tried. A 1985 debate, which Novak sponsored brought together U.S. academics from various disciplines and Latin Americans (see Novak's *Liberation Theology and the Liberal Society* [1987]). The presentations and debate focus largely on how to understand the reasons for Latin-American poverty. Significantly, those discussions make little reference to the writings of the theologians.

One would suspect that Latin-American evangelical Protestants would be fiercely opposed to liberation theologians. The most rapidly spreading Protestant churches—the Pentecostals—have little formal theology at all. Somewhat surprisingly, perhaps, is that non-pentecostal but conservative evangelicals tend to recognize some value in liberation theology and to take seriously their Biblical roots. In *Liberation Theology* (1985), Nuñez surveys the origin, method, and basic themes of liberation theology with fairness and respect. Similarly, Costas (1982), in reflecting on the meaning of the church's mission in *Christ Outside the Gate*, is by no means opposed to this kind of theology.

Prospects

Despite its title, *The Future of Liberation Theology: Essays in Honor of Gustavo Gutiérrez*, by Marc Ellis and Otto Maduro (1989), the volume gathering the papers of the 1988 meeting of Maryknoll, has little to say about "the future of liberation theology." The participants can hardly be faulted for not foreseeing the changes that would sweep Eastern Europe, the Soviet Union, and indeed the world within a year. Those events only confirmed the views of critics who believed that liberation theology was indeed in retreat.

Although the Latin-American theologians have produced no major post-1989 books thus far, they show few signs of undertaking major revisions of their work. Their immediate response has been to insist that their starting point has not been Marxism, but the plight of the poor. For the poor, there is no new "world order," and the basic problem of mass poverty remains as unresolved as ever, and perhaps even more retractable.

Nevertheless, I think the changing situation of the world and the churches raises some critical questions about the role of liberation theology. Before outlining some of these questions, however, I would like to summarize what liberation theology has meant for at least a significant sector of Christians in Latin America.

Liberation theology has provided a rationale for a whole generation of churchpeople who made a serious effort to share the lives of the poor. Methodologically, the effort to develop a uniquely Latin-American theology has "de-Europeanized" all theology, and made theologians realize that theology arises from a particular context. The centrality of the poor to Christianity has been emphasized. Reading the Scriptures from the experience of suffering and struggle has provided many fresh insights, for example, into the conflictive nature of Jesus' own life. Many themes from liberation theology have become part of the official discourse of the churches. Whatever the future brings, these Latin-American theologians have left their mark on their continent and on twentieth-century Christianity.

However, I believe that, despite their protestations of the validity of their basic stance for the poor, the events of 1989 through 1991, including those in Central America and especially the Sandinista electoral defeat in February 1990, call into question a fundamental conviction of liberation theologians, namely, that Latin America is on its way toward a qualitatively different kind of society. Indeed, chastened

by repressive military dictatorships, which in some countries eliminated a whole generation of youth leadership, the Latin-American left
of the 1980s accepted the existing democratic framework and largely
abandoned the dream of seizing political power and making revolutionary
changes. Although the shifting mood may have brought the left closer
to existing popular struggles for more immediate goals, it undeniably
indicated that revolutionary hopes were shrinking, if not evaporating.

To make the point sharper: when Gutierrez distinguished various
levels of liberation (improving material conditions of life, human beings
actively forging a new kind of society, communion with others and
ultimately with God), the assumption was that conditions called for a
radical reshaping of society and that present efforts were moving in
that direction. Today, however, is it still possible to believe that one's
own efforts are in any meaningful way contributing toward a new
model of society? What happens when there are no possible alternative
models on the horizon, when the whole world is increasingly one
market and offers no room for divergence—indeed when the fear is not
that of being in a subordinate role in the existing world order, but of
being left out of the emerging world order?

It is of course possible, even likely, that the end-of-communism
triumphalism of the early 1990s will look naïve within a few years.
Furthermore, a new generation of Latin-American activists and thinkers
may lead to fresh approaches to attacking poverty. The point here is
that to be faithful to its own methods, liberation theology cannot simply
repeat what has been said, but must make a renewed effort to understand the actual course of events, and their implications for the poor.

Although the writings of liberation theologians are replete with
references to its being based on "concrete reality," and though these
writings are aimed at people who are indeed working in *barrios* and
villages on a day-to-day basis, one does not find much of a sense of
Latin-American life in the writings. One could read many volumes, for
example, without finding evidence of one of the most important developments in recent decades, the rapid shift to urban life. In 1960, a
majority of Latin Americans were rural; today, two-thirds are urban
and the percentage is still rising. By the year 2000, four of the world's
ten largest cities (Mexico City, Sao Paulo, Rio de Janeiro, and Buenos
Aires) will be in Latin America, and 47 percent of Latin Americans will
live in cities of 500,000 or more. Liberation theologians, who claim to
be committed to being rooted in reality, might be expected to give more
evidence of serious reflection on this phenomenon. Similarly, one would
expect more attention to the mass urban culture, including movies,
soap operas, and soccer in a theology intended to be in dialogue with
the people.

A couple more examples may be in order. Although liberation
theologians make the obligatory nods toward the oppression of women,
I do not think they have been deeply affected by feminist thinking. They
oppose overt sexism, but show little awareness of deep-seated patriarchy
and its effects on women. A small but telling example is that, like other
Latin-American intellectuals, they continue to use the generic "man"
for human being. One finds little sense of the concrete lives of women

in their writings. For example, I have seen no observations on domestic violence. Additionally, one finds little sense of the theologians taking inspiration from what they observe in family life.

Another serious consideration, however, is the situation within the Roman Catholic Church. Although the Vatican's intervention in the mid-1980s probably changed few or no minds on the merits of its argument, Pope John Paul II and the conservative forces in the Vatican and the Latin-American hierarchy have continued to pursue their agenda, especially in the selection of bishops. Seminary education continues to be tightly controlled. Liberation theology continues to be very much a minority phenomenon within the church itself. It is my impression that the proportion of sisters and priests doing pastoral work along liberationist lines remains roughly the same as it was almost twenty years ago, that is, 10 percent or so. More tellingly, perhaps, it is questionable whether there is a younger generation of liberation theologians. Leonardo Boff, who is one of the youngest liberation theologians now publishing, is over fifty. An exception here are the women theologians, such as Elsa Tamez and Maria Clara Binyemer. In my own research in Central America, I found most pastoral workers along these lines to be of a similar age, and I find some circumstantial evidence for that elsewhere. If a new generation does not take up the movement, liberation theology and its associated pastoral work could end up as a movement characteristic of post-Vatican II years. It would certainly leave some permanent effects, but its own continuity is not assured.

More serious yet is a related fact that liberation theology and its kind of pastoral work has had only a modest impact on the lives of the very people they were meant to serve, the poor. In Nicaragua, for example, I calculate that less than 1 percent of the population could be said to be actively involved in base communities. Even in parishes using this pastoral methodology, only a relatively small number of people are willing to become involved, and as noted, only a minority of parishes opt for that method. Moreover, even though base communities are generally lay led, they require considerable input in the form of leadership training and encouragement.

By contrast, Pentecostal churches—and movements of Catholic charismatics—have been spreading rapidly among the poor. Partisans of liberation theology have been tempted to explain these as the result of well-funded evangelistic campaigns by the "sects," as they call them. In some instances, repressive armies have encouraged conservative evangelicals, while using violence and intimidation against base communities. Nevertheless, there is a growing recognition that the success of evangelicals is due to an inherent appeal. They are able to tap into people's feelings and yearnings; their leadership arises from among the people; and their approach seems to produce impressive effects, such as motivating problem drinkers to abstinence. Their household churches are closer than the distant parish church, and their music is catchy. Most important, all their members are eager to spread their good news and how it has changed their life. After an initial temptation to explain away Protestantism, I sense that some Catholics are now moving toward seeing it as an implicit indictment of Catholicism's pastoral shortcomings.

As long as Pope John Paul II is in office, it is unlikely that the Catholic Church will see the evangelical advance as calling into question the institutional arrangements of the Catholic Church, especially that of a celibate clergy, which remains distant from most poor Catholics. The Pope has also criticized efforts to bring Catholicism closer to popular culture. His position is that Latin America must return to the Catholicism that is already a part of its culture.

To the extent that the Catholic Church begins to take seriously competition from Protestants, it is likely to imitate some of their techniques. Toward that end, in coming years, one can foresee Catholic televangelists, campaigns in stadiums, and door-to-door visiting. How successful such efforts can be remains open to question. From the standpoint of liberation theology, an evangelization campaign designed to bring people back to Catholicism without a concern for justice is unfaithful to the Gospel—hence not evangelization at all.

As I have noted, liberation theology has already left its mark on the Latin-American churches, and indeed around the world. To what extent its impulse will be taken up by a new generation responding to the situation of the 1990s remains to be seen.

References

Abraham, K. C. *Third World Theologies: Commonalities and Divergences.* Maryknoll, NY: Orbis Books, 1990. ISBN 0-88344-681-2.

Adriance, Madeleine. *Opting for the Poor.* Kansas City, MO: Sheed and Ward, 1986.

Aristide, Jean-Bertrand. *In the Parish of the Poor: Writings from Haiti.* Maryknoll, NY: Orbis Books, 1990. ISBN 0-88344-682-0.

Assmann, Hugo. *Theology for a Nomad Church.* Maryknoll, NY: Orbis Books, 1976.

Azevedo, Marcello, S.J. *Basic Ecclesial Communities in Brazil: The Challenge of a New Way of Being Church.* Washington, DC: Georgetown University Press, 1987. ISBN 0-87840-430-9; 0-87840-448-1pa.

Barbé, Dominque. *Grace and Power: Base Communities and Nonviolence in Brazil.* Maryknoll, NY: Orbis Books, 1987. ISBN 0-88344-418-6pa.

Belli, Humberto. *Breaking Faith: The Sandinista Revolution and Its Impact on Freedom and Christian Faith in Nicaragua.* Garden City, MI: Puebla Institute, 1985.

Bermudez, Fernando. *Death and Resurrection in Guatemala.* Maryknoll, NY: Orbis Books, 1986. 77p.

Berryman, Phillip. *Liberation Theology: Essential Facts About the Revolutionary Movement in Latin America—and Beyond*. Philadelphia: Temple University Press, 1987. ISBN 0-87722-479-X (hardcover). New York: Pantheon, 1987.

Boff, Clodovis. *Feet-on-the-Ground Theology: A Brazilian Journey*. Maryknoll, NY: Orbis Books, 1987. ISBN 0-88344-579-4; 0-88344-554-9pa.

———, O.S.M. *Theology and Praxis: Epistemological Foundations*. Maryknoll, NY: Orbis Books, 1987. ISBN 0-88344-416-Xpa.

Boff, Leonardo. *Church: Charisma and Power: Liberation Theology and the Institutional Church*. New York: Crossroad, 1985. ISBN 0-8245-0590-5.

———. *Ecclesiogenesis: The Base Communities Reinvent the Church*. Maryknoll, NY: Orbis Books, 1986. ISBN 0-88344-214-0pa.

———. *Faith on the Edge: Religion and Marginalized Existence*. Maryknoll, NY: Orbis Books, 1991. ISBN 0-88344-742-8.

———. *Jesus Christ Liberator; A Critical Christology for Our Time*. Maryknoll, NY: Orbis Books, 1978. ISBN 0-88344-236-1pa.

———. *Liberating Grace*. Maryknoll, NY: Orbis Books, 1979. ISBN 0-88344-282-5.

———. *The Lord's Prayer: The Prayer of Integral Liberation*. Maryknoll, NY: Orbis Books, 1983. ISBN 0-88344-299-Xpa.

———, O.F.M. *The Maternal Face of God: The Feminine and Its Religious Expressions*. San Francisco: Harper & Row, 1987. ISBN 0-06-254159-5.

———. *Passion of Christ, Passion of the World: The Facts, Their Interpretation, and Their Meaning Yesterday and Today*. Maryknoll, NY: Orbis Books, 1987. ISBN 0-883440564-6; 0-88344-563-8pa.

———. *Trinity and Society*. Maryknoll, NY: Orbis Books, 1988.

———. *When Theology Listens to the Poor*. San Francisco: Harper & Row, 1988. ISBN 0-06-254162-5.

Boff, Leonardo, and Clodovis Boff. *Introducing Liberation Theology*. Maryknoll, NY: Orbis Books, 1987. ISBN 0-88344-575-1; 0-88344-550-6pa.

———. *Liberation Theology: From Dialogue to Confrontation*. San Francisco: Harper & Row, 1986. ISBN 0-86683-528-8.

———. *Salvation and Liberation*. Maryknoll, NY: Orbis Books, 1984. ISBN 0-88344-451-8pa.

Brett, Donna Whitson, and Edward T. Brett. *Murdered in Central America: The Stories of Eleven U.S. Missionaries*. Maryknoll, NY: Orbis Books, 1988.

Brockman, James R., S.J. *Romero: A Life*. Rev. ed. Maryknoll, NY: Orbis Books, 1989. ISBN 0-88344-652-9.

Brown, Robert McAfee. *Gustavo Gutierrez: An Introduction to Liberation Theology*. Maryknoll, NY: Orbis Books, 1990. ISBN 0-88344-597-2.

———. *Unexpected News: Reading the Bible with Third World Eyes*. Philadelphia: Westminster, 1984. ISBN 0-664-24552-8pa.

Cabestrero, Teofilo. *Ministers of God, Ministers of the People*. Maryknoll, NY: Orbis Books, 1983.

———. *Revolutionaries for the Gospel*. Maryknoll, NY: Orbis Books, 1986. ISBN 0-88344-406-2pa.

Cadorette, Curt. *From the Heart of the People: The Theology of Gustavo Gutiérrez*. Oak Park, IL: Meyer-Stone, 1988. ISBN 0-940989-27-1; 0-940989-18-2pa.

Carney, Padre J. Guadalupe. *To Be a Revolutionary: An Autobiography*. San Francisco: Harper & Row, 1985. ISBN 0-06-061319-X.

Carrigan, Ana. *Salvador Witness: The Life and Calling of Jean Donavan*. New York: Simon & Schuster, 1984.

Cleary, Edward L., O.P. *Born of the Poor: The Latin American Church Since Medellín*. Notre Dame, IN: University of Notre Dame Press, 1990. ISBN 0-268-00683-0.

———. *Crisis and Change: The Church in Latin America Today*. Maryknoll, NY: Orbis Books, 1985. ISBN 0-88344-149-7pa.

Comblin, Jose. *The Holy Spirit & Liberation*. Translated by Paul Burns. Maryknoll, NY: Orbis Books, 1988.

———. *Retrieving the Human*. Maryknoll, NY: Orbis Books, 1990.

Costas, Orlando. *Christ Outside the Gate*. Maryknoll, NY: Orbis Books, 1982.

Cox, Harvey. *The Silencing of Leonardo Boff: The Vatican and the Future of World Christianity*. Oak Park, IL: Meyer-Stone, 1988. ISBN 0-940989-35-2pa.

Croatto, J. Severino. *Biblical Hermeneutics: Toward a Theory of Reading as the Production of Meaning*. Maryknoll, NY: Orbis Books, 1987. ISBN 0-88344-583-2; 0-88344-582-4pa.

——. *Exodus: A Hermeneutics of Freedom*. Maryknoll, NY: Orbis Books, 1981. ISBN 0-88344-111-Xpa.

Dodson, Michael, and Laura Nuzzi O'Shaughnessy. *Nicaragua's Other Revolution: Religious Faith and Political Struggle*. Chapel Hill: University of North Carolina Press, 1990.

Dussel, Enrique. *Ethics and Community*. Maryknoll, NY: Orbis Books, 1988. ISBN 0-88344-619-7; 0-88344-618-9pa.

——. *History and Theology of Liberation*. Maryknoll, NY: Orbis Books, 1976.

Eagleson, John, and Philip Sharper, eds. *Puebla and Beyond: Documentation and Commentary*. Maryknoll, NY: Orbis Books, 1979.

El Rescate. *The Jesuit Assassinations: The Writings of Ellacuría Marín-Baró and Segundo Montes, with a Chronology of the Investigation*. Kansas City, MO: Sheed & Ward, 1990. ISBN 1-55612-409-0pa.

Ellacuria, Ignacio. *The Mission of Christ and His Church*. Maryknoll, NY: Orbis Books, 1976. ISBN 0-88344-1403; 0-88344-1411pa.

Ellis, Marc H., and Otto Maduro. *Expanding the View: Gustavo Gutiérrez and the Future of Liberation Theology*. Maryknoll, NY: Orbis Books, 1990. ISBN 0-88344-690-1.

——, eds. *The Future of Liberation Theology: Essays in Honor of Gustavo Gutiérrez*. Maryknoll, NY: Orbis Books, 1989. ISBN 0-88344-421-6.

Fabella, Virginia, M. M., and Mercy Amba Oduyoye. *With Passion and Compassion: Third World Women Doing Theology*. Maryknoll, NY: Orbis Books, 1988. ISBN 0-88344-623-6.

Fabella, Virginia, and Sergio Torres. *Doing Theology in a Divided World*. Maryknoll, NY: Orbis Books, 1985. ISBN 0-88344-197-7pa.

——. *Irruption of the Third World: Challenge to Theology*. Maryknoll, NY: Orbis Books, 1983. ISBN 0-88344-216-7pa.

Feiner, Johannes, and Magnus Löhrer, eds. *Mysterium Salutis: Manual de Teologlu Como Historia de la Salvación*. Madrid: Ediciónes Cristianded, 1970.

Galdamez, Pablo. *Faith of a People*. Maryknoll, NY: Orbis Books, 1986.

Gebara, Ivone, and Maria Clara Binyemer. *Mary, Mother of God, Mother of the Poor*. Maryknoll, NY: Orbis Books, 1989.

Gibellini, Rosino, ed. *Frontiers of Theology in Latin America*. Maryknoll, NY: Orbis Books, 1979. ISBN 0-88344-144-6pa.

Golden, Renny. *The Hour of the Poor, The Hour of Women: Salvadoran Women Tell Their Stories*. New York: Crossroad/Continuum, 1991. ISBN 0-8245-1088-7.

Goodpasture, H. McKennie, ed. *Cross and Sword: An Eyewitness History of Christianity in Latin America*. Maryknoll, NY: Orbis Books, 1989. ISBN 0-88344-590-5; 0-88344-591-3pa.

Gundry, Stanley N., and Alan F. Johnson, eds. *Tensions in Contemporary Theology*. Grand Rapids, MI: Baker Book House, 1983. ISBN 0-8010-3796-4.

Gutiérrez, Gustavo. *On Job: God-Talk and the Suffering of the Innocent*. Maryknoll, NY: Orbis Books, 1987. ISBN 0-88344-577-8; 0-88344-552-2pa.

———. *The Power of the Poor in History*. Maryknoll, NY: Orbis Books, 1983.

———. *A Theology of Liberation: History, Politics and Salvation*. rev. ed. Maryknoll, NY: Orbis Books, 1988. ISBN 0-88344-543-3; 0-88344-542-5pa.

———. *The Truth Shall Make You Free: Confrontations*. Maryknoll, NY: Orbis Books, 1990. ISBN 0-88344-679-0; 0-88344-663-4pa.

———. *We Drink From Our Own Wells: The Spiritual Journey of a People*. Maryknoll, NY: Orbis Books, 1984. ISBN 0-88344-707-Xpa.

Haight, Roger, S.J. *An Alternative Vision: An Interpretation of Liberation Theology*. New York: Paulist Press, 1985. ISBN 0-8091-2679-6.

Hassett, John, and Hugh Lacey. *Towards a Society That Serves Its People: The Intellectual Contribution of El Salvadors Murdered Jesuits*. Washington, DC: Georgetown University Press, 1991.

Hennelly, Alfred T., ed. *Liberation Theology: A Documentary History*. Maryknoll, NY: Orbis Books, 1990. ISBN 0-88344-592-1; 0-88344-593-Xpa.

———. *Theologies in Conflict: The Challenge of Juan Luis Segundo*. Maryknoll, NY: Orbis Books, 1979. ISBN 0-88344-287-6.

Hinkelammert, Franz J. *The Ideological Weapons of Death: A Theological Critique of Capitalism*. Maryknoll, NY: Orbis Books, 1986. ISBN 0-88344-260-4pa.

Hoonaert, Eduardo. *The Memory of the Christian People*. Maryknoll, NY: Orbis Books, 1988.

Keogh, Dermot, ed. *Church and Politics in Latin America*. London: Macmillan, 1990. ISBN 0-333-44534-1.

Kirkpatrick, Dow, ed. *Faith Born in the Struggle for Life: A Re-Reading of Protestant Faith in Latin America Today*. Grand Rapids, MI: William B. Eerdmans, 1988. ISBN 0-8028-0355-5.

Kita, Bernice. *What Prize Awaits Us: Letters from Guatemala*. Maryknoll, NY: Orbis Books, 1988. ISBN -0-88344-273-6pa.

Lernoux, Penny. *Cry of the People: The Struggle for Human Rights in Latin America—The Catholic Church in Conflict with U.S. Policy*. New York: Penguin, 1982. ISBN 0-14-00-6047-2.

————. *People of God: The Struggle for World Catholicism*. New York: Viking, 1989. ISBN 0-670-81529-2.

Levine, Daniel H., ed. *Religion and Political Conflict in Latin America*. Chapel Hill: University of North Carolina Press, 1986. ISBN 0-8079-1689-2; 0-8078-4150-1pa.

————. *Religion and Politics in Latin America: The Catholic Church in Venezuela and Colombia*. Princeton, NJ: Princeton University Press, 1981. ISBN 0-691-07624-3; 0-691-02200-3pa.

Lopez Vigil, Maria. *Don Lito of El Salvador*. Maryknoll, NY: Orbis Books, 1990. ISBN 0-88344-669-3.

Mahan, Brian, and L. Dale Richesin, eds. *The Challenge of Liberation Theology: A First World Response*. Maryknoll, NY: Orbis Books, 1981. ISBN 0-88344-092Xpa.

Mainwaring, Scott. *The Catholic Church and Power in Brazil, 1916–1985*. Stanford, CA: Stanford University Press, 1986.

Mainwaring, Scott, and Alexander Wilde, eds. *The Progressive Church in Latin America*. Notre Dame, IN: University of Notre Dame Press, 1989. ISBN 0-268-01573-2.

Martin, David. *Tongues of Fire: The Explosion of Protestantism in Latin America*. Foreword by Peter L. Berger. Oxford: Basil Blackwell, 1990. ISBN 0-631-17186-X.

McCann, Dennis P. *Christian Realism and Liberation Theology: Practical Theologies in Creative Conflict*. Maryknoll, NY: Orbis Books, 1981. ISBN 0-88344-086-5pa.

McGovern, Arthur F. *Liberation Theology and Its Critics: Toward an Assessment*. Maryknoll, NY: Orbis Books, 1989. ISBN 0-88344-595-6.

Mesters, Carlos. *Defenseless Flower: A New Reading of the Bible*. Maryknoll, NY: Orbis Books, 1989. ISBN 0-88344-596-4.

Mignone, Emilio F. *Witness to the Truth: The Complicity of Church and Dictatorship in Argentina, 1976–1983*. Maryknoll, NY: Orbis Books, 1986. ISBN 088344-630-8; 0-88344-629-4pa.

Miranda, José Porfirio. *Marx and the Bible: A Critique of the Philosophy of Oppression*. Maryknoll, NY: Orbis Books, 1974. ISBN 0-88344-306-6; 0-88344-307-4pa.

Moser, Antonio, and Bernardino Leers. *Moral Theology*. Maryknoll, NY: Orbis Books, 1990.

Mulligan, Joseph. *The Nicaraguan Church and the Revolution*. Kansas City, MO: Sheed & Ward, 1991.

Muñoz, Ronaldo. *The God of Christians*. Maryknoll, NY: Orbis Books, 1990. ISBN 0-88344-696-0; 0-88344-695-2pa.

Nessan, Craig L. *Orthopraxis or Heresy: The North American Theological Response to Latin American Liberation Theology*. Atlanta, GA: Scholars Press, 1989. ISBN 1-55540-298-4; 1-55540-299-2pa.

Novak, Michael, ed. *Liberation Theology and the Liberal Society*. Washington DC: American Enterprise Institute for Public Policy Research, 1987. ISBN-08447-2263-4; 0-8447-2264-2pa.

———. *Will It Liberate? Questions About Liberation Theology*. New York: Paulist Press, 1986. ISBN 0-8091-0385-0.

Nuñez, Emilio. *Liberation Theology*. Chicago: Moody Press, 1985. ISBN 0-8024-4893-3.

Pixley, George V., and Clodovis Boff. *The Bible, the Church, and the Poor*. ISBN 0-88344-614-6; 0-88344-599-9pa.

Randall, Margaret. *Christians in the Nicaraguan Revolution*. Translated by Mariana Valverde. Vancouver: New Star Books, 1983. ISBN 0-919573-15-0pa.

Richard, Pablo. *Death of Christendoms, Birth of the Church—Historical Analysis and Theological Interpretation of the Church in Latin America*. Maryknoll, NY: Orbis Books, 1987.

———, ed. *The Idols of Death and the God of Life*. Maryknoll, NY: Orbis Books, 1983.

Romero, Oscar. *The Violence of Love: The Pastoral Wisdom of Archbishop Oscar Romero*. Edited and translated by James R. Brockman, S.J., foreword by Henri J. M. Nouwen. San Francisco: Harper & Row, 1988. ISBN 0-06-254821-2; 0-06-254848-4pa.

Rubenstein, Richard L., and John K. Roth, eds. *The Politics of Latin American Liberation Theology: The Challenge to U.S. Public Policy*. Washington, DC: Washington Institute Press, 1988. ISBN 0-88702-039-9; 0-88702-040-2pa.

Schall, James V., S.J. *Liberation Theology in Latin America*. San Francisco: Ignatius Press, 1982.

Segundo, Juan Luis. *The Christ of the Ignatian Exercises*. (Jesus of Nazareth Yesterday and Today, 4). Maryknoll, NY: Orbis Books, 1987. ISBN-88344-570-0; 0-88344-569-7pa.

———. *An Evolutionary Approach to Jesus of Nazareth*. (Jesus of Nazareth Yesterday and Today, 5). Maryknoll, NY: Orbis Books, 1988. ISBN 0-88344-588-3pa.

———. *Faith and Ideologies*. (Jesus of Nazareth Yesterday and Today, 1). Maryknoll, NY: Orbis Books, 1984. ISBN 088344-127-6pa.

———. "The Future of Christianity in Latin America." In *Liberation Theology: A Documentary History,* edited by Alfred T. Hennelly. Maryknoll, NY: Orbis Books, 1990. ISBN 0-88344-592-1; 0-88344-593-Xpa.

———, S.J. *The Hidden Motives of Pastoral Action: Latin American Reflections*. Maryknoll, NY: Orbis Books, 1978. ISBN 0-88344-185-3; 0-88344-186-1pa.

———. *The Historical Jesus of the Synoptics*. (Jesus of Nazareth Yesterday and Today, 2). Maryknoll, NY: Orbis Books, 1985. ISBN 0-88344-220-5pa.

———. *The Humanist Christology of Paul*. (Jesus of Nazareth Yesterday and Today, 3). Maryknoll, NY: Orbis Books, 1986. ISBN 0-88344-221-3pa.

———. *The Liberation of Theology*. Maryknoll, NY: Orbis Books, 1976.

———, S.J. *Theology and the Church: A Response to Cardinal Ratzinger and a Warning to the Whole Church*. Minneapolis, MN: Winston Press, 1985. ISBN 0-86683-491-5.

Shaull, Richard. *Heralds of a New Reformation: The Poor of South and North America*. Maryknoll, NY: Orbis Books, 1984. ISBN 0-88344-345-7pa.

Sigmund, Paul E. *Liberation Theology at the Crossroads: Democracy or Revolution?* New York: Oxford University Press, 1990. ISBN 0-19-506064-4.

Smith, Christian. *The Emergency of Liberation Theology: Radical Religion and Social Movement Theory*. Chicago: University of Chicago Press, 1991. ISBN 0-226-76409-5; 0-226-76410-9pa.

Sobrino, Jon. *Archbishop Romero: Memories and Reflections*. Maryknoll, NY: Orbis Books, 1990. ISBN 0-88344-667-7.

——, S.J. *Christology at the Crossroads: A Latin American Approach*. Maryknoll, NY: Orbis Books, 1978. ISBN 0-88344-076-8pa.

——, et al. *Companions of Jesus: The Jesuit Martyrs of El Salvador*. Maryknoll, NY: Orbis Books, 1990. ISBN 088-344-699-5.

——. *Jesus in Latin America*. Maryknoll, NY: Orbis Books, 1987. ISBN 0-88344-412-7pa.

——. *Spirituality of Liberation: Toward Political Holiness*. Maryknoll, NY: Orbis Books, 1988. ISBN 0-88344-617-0; 0-88344-616-2pa.

——. *The True Church and the Poor*. Maryknoll, NY: Orbis Books, 1984. ISBN 0-88344-513-1.

Sobrino, Jon, S.J., and Juan Hernandez Pico, S.J. *Theology of Christian Solidarity*. Maryknoll, NY: Orbis Books, 1985. ISBN 088344-452-6pa.

Stoll, David. *Is Latin America Turning Protestant? The Politics of Evangelical Growth*. Berkeley: University of California Press, 1990. ISBN 0-520-06499-2.

Tamez, Elsa. *Against Machismo*. Oak Park, IL: Meyer-Stone, 1987. ISBN 0940989-13-1; 0-940989-12-3.

Thistlethwaite, Susan Brooks, and Mary Potter Engel, eds. *Lift Every Voice: Constructing Christian Theologies from the Underside*. San Francisco: Harper & Row, 1990. ISBN 0-06-067992-1.

Torres, Sergio, and John Eagleson. *The Challenge of Basic Christian Communities*. Maryknoll, NY: Orbis Books, 1981. ISBN 0-88344-503-4pa.

——, eds. *Theology in the Americas*. Maryknoll, NY: Orbis Books, 1976. ISBN 0-88344-479-8; 0-88344-476-3pa.

Trigo, Pedro. *Creation and History*. Maryknoll, NY: Orbis Books, 1991. ISBN 0-88344-737-1.

Williams, Philip J. *The Catholic Church and Politics in Nicaragua and Costa Rica*. London: Macmillan, 1989.

Witliet, Theo. *A Place in the Sun: Liberation Theology in the Third World*. Maryknoll, NY: Orbis Books, 1985. ISBN 0-88344-404-6pa.

Wright, Scott, et al., eds. *El Salvador: A Spring Whose Waters Never Run Dry*. Washington, DC: EIPCA, 1990. ISBN 0-918-346-09-6.

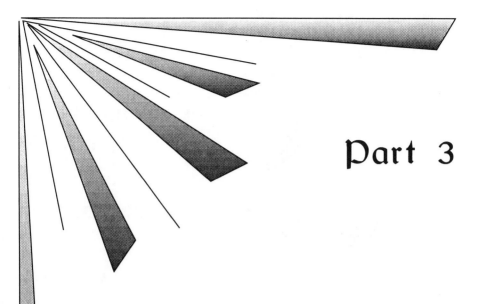

Part 3

The Literature
of Teaching
the Faiths

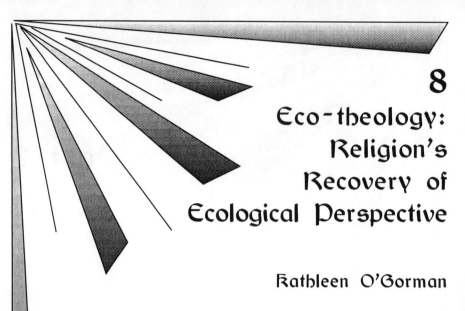

8
Eco-theology: Religion's Recovery of Ecological Perspective

Kathleen O'Gorman

Introduction

In 1992, John Cobb wrote, "A profound shift has come about since 1970, a shift to taking nature as a context of Christian theology. . . . This is a change worth celebrating."[1] This essay both elucidates and shares Cobb's enthusiasm for theology's renewed interest in the natural world. One indication of this development is the number of books taking on an ecological perspective and bringing a religious focus to the subject. Even a casual perusal of religious publishing houses' promotional materials indicates the extent to which the environmental movement has caught the attention of a growing number of theologians and spiritual traditions. Indeed, the steadily increasing interest in ecological matters and perspectives reflected in so much contemporary theological and spiritual literature suggests that a new genre in religious literature has made its appearance, rooted in a new field of specialization within the context of theological research and education.

Those outside the academy, with little access to the latest scholarly publications, are often left in the dark regarding such new developments in theology. This is as true for those committed to the environmental movement as it is for those who serve as institutional spokespersons for particular religious traditions. Neither environmental activists nor congregational leaders seem to realize the extent to which theologians (and scientists) are devoting interest and energy to the religious significance and meaning of the natural world. It is, therefore, both timely and appropriate that a book exploring contemporary developments in theology would include a chapter on this emerging field, which has yet to be given a name, but that might appropriately be called "ecotheology" or "religious ecology."

My interest in the subject grew out of my attraction to and involvement in the environmental movement over the past ten years. Within that context, I began to discern some voices out of my past, out of my Catholic culture and schooling—experiences of reading about St. Francis of Assisi befriending a wolf as a child; taking a fancy to images on classroom walls of Jesus holding lambs in his arms; reading Teilhard in the 1960s; and being reminded at worship that all creation gives God praise. These inclinations and sensibilities have intensified as they have been informed and inspired by a host of proponents of the environmental cause. They have also prompted my belief that this cultural ecological awakening comes from an affirmation of the spiritual significance and origins of the natural world. In retrospect, it seems that my religious tradition was provoking (however indirectly) my commitment to the ecological movement as it, in turn, renewed my interest in my religious heritage. I began to search out this connection and found others within my faith tradition who had not only discovered my newfound connection, but had written about it for decades.

This essay is animated by the hope of stimulating broader interest in the research and writing that assigns religious meaning and significance to the natural world. Much of the bibliographic material comes out of theology, and thus makes explicit the spiritual dimension of the larger-life community to which we humans belong. However notable and important the contribution and influence of this literature, it nonetheless finds an able and enthusiastic partner in the writing coming out of contemporary science. So important and compelling is the religious character of the scientific perspective, that I set it first in the review of the literature.

Because Thomas Berry represents a bridge between science and religion, I will begin with a discussion of his work. Berry offers a persuasive and informed articulation and justification of the religious significance of the natural world. Within this context, I will turn to the cutting edge of theology—the "new science"—the convergence of perspectives from evolutionary biology, chaos theory, and quantum physics. Those who have achieved a different view of reality have become the heralds of a new cosmology, whose inclusive and dynamic vision of life cannot be contained, much less appreciated, within the smaller, anthropocentric projections of the past three centuries. From these beginnings (or endings), which might be described as theologies of science, I will review some key texts that are trans-religious or explicitly religious in some universal sense in their scope, language, and message; books that defy easy categorization, for they are not only inter-religious, but are often interdisciplinary. These pioneering works neither assume nor promote the values, visions, perspectives, or interests of a particular religion; rather, they converge on a piece of common ground in which the natural world takes on spiritual significance.

Their perspectives transcend the boundaries of particular religions and specific fields of study, and address foundational dimensions of the subject, such as the emergence of a systemic worldview and an inclusive cosmology.

After sampling the intensifying dialogue between "new" science (science that is open to religious interpretations) and "new" theology (theology that is open to scientific insights and discoveries), I will take up a narrower focus, reviewing contemporary works with a distinctively Christian orientation. This section begins with an acknowledgment of the Christian tradition's debt to natural theology and goes on to trace present-day developments along traditional lines of specialization: Scripture, ecclesiology, morality, and spirituality. The essay closes with some "extracurricular" nonliterary resources that address the problematic relationship between Christian faith and reverence for creation.

Some illustrations of this work-in-progress might help describe the theological revision that is the subject of the chapter. Within Christian contexts, for example, Scripture scholars are rethinking and reinterpreting the meaning of covenant in the Old Testament after rediscovering the relevance of the Noachic (interestingly enough, the earliest) Covenant. Celtic and mystic forms of spirituality have been brought out of the storage bin, dusted off, and made available to those for whom the natural world is, as Thomas Berry so poignantly states, the primary mode of divine presence. Moral theologians are reconstructing and extending the meaning of peace and justice to include all forms of life on the planet, and rethinking traditional understandings of stewardship, love of neighbor, and natural law.

For the most part, the resources included in the essay are drawn from works at hand. The review is in no way an exhaustive introduction to an established field of inquiry; nor does this essay seek to present a comprehensive listing of theological books with an ecological focus. Rather, it is intended to provide access to a developing field of theological scholarship, and to indicate something of the breadth, scope, depth, and excitement that can be found in an investigation of its literature. For those who wish to read more about what I refer to as ecotheology, a topical bibliography on the subject is included after the essay.

Looking Back from Where We Are

When pressed to locate the ecological awakening of contemporary theology, many would point to the 1960s, when people first saw a photograph of the earth from space, or the early 1970s, which ushered in a new phase of the environmental movement. The organized efforts of various groups to put an end to our planet-devastating behaviors and activities have borne fruit in a new awareness of the fragility and sacredness of life, an awareness that has not been lost in theological circles. In a recent lecture at Tulane University, theologian Elizabeth Dodson Gray attributed much of the impetus for this reformed behavior to feminist, particularly ecofeminist, theology. Critiquing the system of patriarchy that, in her perspective, has emphasized the importance of ranking and controlling reality and intellect and spirit, Dodson Gray points to the emergence of a new paradigm that challenges us to appreciate our connectedness and interdependence on the lifeforms we had previously considered means toward our human ends, rather than ends in themselves. She sums up the situation in which we find ourselves as a fork in the road that leads in two directions—the more alienating and familiar *patriarchal* path, and the less-traveled, alternative, emergent *ecozoic*[2] path. Dodson Gray argues vigorously the merits, indeed the necessity, of choosing the latter path. The rationale she offers for this choice was constructed out of a variety of sources— from science, particularly biology and physics; feminist philosophy and theology; systems theory; and social science. Her connections evoked a few of my own associations—that photograph of the earth from space, and a PBS program in which the astronauts who had landed on the moon some twenty-three years ago were asked how that event had changed their lives. Most spoke of a conversion experience and a change in the direction of their lives—the choice of the ecozoic path.

Rewriting the Cosmic Story

Few have labored longer or with greater intensity to argue the merits and necessity of choosing the ecozoic path than Thomas Berry, whose *The Dream of the Earth*[3] is generally regarded as a primer in religious ecology. This remarkable work, the synthesis of a lifetime of research and reflection on the earth's story, is gleaned from Berry's experience as an historian and student of Chinese and Native American cultures, from scientific research, and from a theological education that bears the influence of Catholic roots, particularly the imprint of St. Thomas Aquinas and Pierre Teilhard de Chardin. Like these earlier synthesizers, Berry has rendered theology credible to the scientific community. He earned this credibility by first learning what science had to teach him (and he found that there was much to learn), and by using this knowledge to construct his vision, his theology. What's more, Berry, who refers to himself as "geologian," has constructed a new language to accommodate and communicate his inclusive theology of the earth.

Born in Greensboro, North Carolina in 1914, Berry was ordained a Passionist priest in 1942. After spending ten years in a Passionist monastery, he became a professor of Chinese and Native American history and an avid student of Native American culture. More recently, he founded and directed the Center for Religious Research on the Hudson River. During these years, he chronicled his research and reflections in *The Riverside Papers*, which he reworks and expands in *The Dream of the Earth*, and further reworks and expands in *The Universe Story* (1992),[4] which he coauthors with physicist Brian Swimme. Berry's use of science in his research and writing about the earth attracted the attention of Brian Swimme, who left a university teaching position to study with Berry at his center. Swimme's *The*

Universe Is a Green Dragon,[5] inspired and informed by this educational experience, relates his synthesis of theological and scientific understanding of the origin and significance of the universe. The most recent fruit of their collaboration, *The Universe Story*, recounts the "unfolding of the cosmos," from its "flaring forth" some 15 billion years ago to the present time of crisis. One cannot read this epic narrative and not wonder about the validity of traditional beliefs that made humankind the ultimate end of creation, when we do not even show up until the eighth chapter. Such is Berry's ability to affect a perspective transformation.

In his earlier work, Berry calls for an end to the pervasive illiteracy about the natural world that characterizes so much of Western society. In his view, such an inability to see, to name, and to understand the natural world has precipitated the crisis in which we find ourselves. Berry insists we have to reinvent ourselves, the human, if we and the planet are to survive. An oft-quoted proverb that sums up his sense of the problem is, "The pathos of the human is identical to the pathos of the planet. You can't have healthy humans on a sick planet."[6] He warns that the future, indeed the very survival of the human, is tied to the survival of the planet, and the planet is in peril because humans have lost sight of their interdependence and interconnectedness with this larger reality. This short-sightedness, or what Berry describes as a distorted mode of consciousness, is rooted in an anthropocentric worldview, a preoccupation with the viability of the human species, with little or no concern for the larger life community upon which human life depends for its continued existence.

Berry maintains that this distorted consciousness has dominated human attitudes and behaviors for the past twenty centuries, culminating in the narcissistic obsession with progress that has gripped us since the Industrial Age. He locates partial responsibility for its origins and long-term influence in Western religions, particularly in Christian preoccupation with a written Scripture, a transcendent personal deity, and an emphasis on Redemption rather than creation.

Berry criticizes the arrogance that prompts humans to assume and believe that their story is *the* story, that history is equivalent to *human* history, and says that, as a consequence, we have failed to learn and appreciate the larger story of which we are, at best, the latest chapter. He argues that this anthropocentric orientation needs to be transformed into a new biocentric mode of consciousness that recognizes the planet as the ultimate point of reference and acknowledges the interconnectedness and interdependence of every form of life. Once achieved, such a consciousness will enable humankind, the species characterized by its capacity to reflect on the meaning of the universe, to assume its appropriate responsibility to nurture and foster the well-being of all.

What sets Berry's work apart from other seminal thinkers and social critics is not only the inclusivity that characterizes his vision, but also the breadth of his scholarship and research. While others focus (and limit) their investigations on one or another aspect of social or environmental issues (i.e., the flagging economy, erosion of topsoil, rising crime statistics, the disappearance of ancient forests, the lack of adequate health care), Berry's analysis takes on the whole (i.e., the plight of the planet within the universe). He lays out the crisis confronting the planet and all its inhabitants in scientific, sociological, psychological, philosophical, and theological perspectives, making it possible for each to hear the message in the language that is the most familiar. What's more, Berry's inclusive language makes sense to specialists *within* each discipline as well. An example of this can be drawn from the way he talks about the religious dimensions of the crisis and the story. He writes in such a way that Buddhists, Native Americans, Christians, and Jews can hear the message through their own particular religious dialects.

Berry's genius lies not only in dreaming an inclusive vision, but in spelling out steps we can take to implement what he calls a "biocentric frame of reference." One concrete suggestion pertains to rethinking and reconstructing education. Berry proposes a radical curriculum revision in *The Dream of the Earth*, a revision that puts the earth's story at the center of learning. His approach would challenge each discipline to ground itself in a biocentric orientation so that economics would include the earth's interests in its cost accounting; medicine would include the earth's natural remedies within its healing protocols and prescriptions; law would take seriously the principles ordering other forms of life; history would realize that it has left out most of the story; music would incorporate the song of the birds; and theology would recognize the natural world as "the primary revelation of the divine."[7] Such a model seems not only plausible, but would seem to offer a breath of fresh air to curriculum specialists.

To sum up Berry's significance, no theologian or scientist, in my judgment, has offered a more comprehensive and informed understanding of the earth and its religious meaning and significance for its human creatures than has Thomas Berry.

The Intensifying Dialogue That Is the "New Science" and the "New Theology"

Not too long ago, to understand the meaning and message of the natural world, one was forced to choose between science and theology. One was either persuaded by religion's appeal to the authority of Scripture and the commentaries that explicated its teaching, or one believed the more cautious but confident conclusions of the scientific enterprise. Recently, however, a number of scientists and theologians are overcoming their wariness and distrust of one another, and having discovered something complementary in their purposes and perspectives, are forming partnerships in the interpretive task. This convergence of interest, investigation, and concern for the natural world, and the consequence on it of numerous influences and events, owes some debt to a recognition of the limitations of a single perspective (either that of science or religion), and to a heightened interest in the larger-life community generated by the environmental movement. The agents or mediators of the convergence warrant further elaboration.

What I refer to as "new science" is a metaphor for the evolving life-investigating model that owes its development to the genius of intellectual observers such as Albert Einstein, Niels Bohr, Paul Dirac, and Werner Heisenberg. Often identified by the term "quantum," the new science is oriented toward and informed by evolutionary development, chaos theory, organic-systemic relations, dynamic processes, particle physics, and microbiology and sociobiology. John Polkinghorne, a quantum physicist, affirms the relevance of theology to the scientific enterprise in these words:

> I find myself in sympathy with Bernard Lonergan when he says: "since we define being by its relation to intelligence, necessarily our ultimate is not being but intelligence."[8] Lonergan was talking about God conceived as the unrestricted act of understanding. The unpicturable and Unpicturable have something in common."[9]

The emergence of a "new theology," a more empirically-oriented religious discipline that seeks collaboration with other modes of inquiry and interpretation, forms a corollary to the new science. It might best be described as a revision and extension of the nexus comprised of process, practical, and liberation theologies and hermeneutics and critical theory, which engages in a more empirical, inductive approach to articulate divine presence and activity. New theology calls the attention and expertise of theologians focused in the human sciences to a recognition of the contribution science offers to an understanding of the natural world. In their book *Cosmology and Theology*, David Tracy and Nicholas Lash sum up the openness in this way:

> The shift in both content and the self-understanding of the methods of science has occasioned . . . a new intellectual situation where the relationship of science and theology seems at once more promising and more difficult. . . . It is more promising because the collapse of earlier mechanistic, materialist, and positivist models has freed science itself to a sense of the ultimate mystery of reality and to a chastened but real willingness to dialogue with any plausible philosophical and theological cosmological hypothesis. . . . It is equally important to recall, of course, that theological self-understanding and theological content have undergone analogous paradigm-shifts in the same period. . . . And theologians . . . have learned their own form of chastened methodological and material modesty.[10]

Paul Davies, a professor of mathematical physics, confirms the present reconciliation between science and theology in these words:

There has been an enormous resurgence of interest in what might be crudely described as the science-religion interface. This has taken two distinct forms. First, a greatly increased dialogue between scientists, philosophers, and theologians about the concept of creation and related issues. Second, a growing fashion for mystical thinking and Eastern philosophy, which some commentators have claimed makes deep and meaningful contact with fundamental physics.[11]

The following works represent significant contributions to the contemporary dialogue between theology and science. The authors are thoughtful and, for the most part, interdisciplinary scientists who might also be described as the pioneering theologians of the ecozoic era. That they show up at all in this chapter would have come as a surprise to me at its early stages of development. The process of tracking the literature led me unexpectedly to its source in science. One might say that I backed into science from my reading of ecological theologians, and discovered a new breed of theological partners preparing a path to the twenty-first century. These are a sampling of the literature that is currently available on the subject.

Resources in the New Science and the New Theology

Birch, Charles, and John B. Cobb, Jr. *The Liberation of Life: From the Cell to the Community*. New York: Cambridge University Press, 1981.

Birch, a biologist, and Cobb, a theologian, collaborate on this effort to liberate their readers' thinking about life. In their view, the liberation of human thinking about life will enable us and the rest of our earthly companions to live more freely. The first part of the book is an introduction to an evolutionary model of biology. Cobb integrates this biological understanding with process theology, with an acknowledged debt to Alfred North Whitehead. They conclude their synthesis with an analysis of specific forms of ecological oppression, such as the market economy and our taxing transportation system, and offer their recommendations for lessening our destructive impact on the earth. Readers might also want to consult Cobb's *Is It Too Late? A Theology of Ecology* (Beverly Hills, CA: Bruce, 1972).

Chopra, Depak. *Ageless Body, Timeless Mind*. New York: Harmony Books, 1993.

Chopra, a physician who trained in the West, brings his Indian heritage and tradition to his practice of medicine. In this book, he explores the mind-body connection as it relates to and affects the process of aging. Addressed to a lay readership in search of alternatives to technological medicine and a greater sense of control of their own lives, Chopra brings the new science to wholeness and healing, drawing upon cellular biology and microbiology, quantum physics, depth psychology, Eastern philosophy, and ancient Ayurvedic Wisdom. As in previous works, Chopra emphasizes the role of awareness in transcending limitations and obstacles to our understanding and well-being.

Davies, Paul. *The Cosmic Blueprint.* New York: Simon & Schuster, 1988.
 Davies attempts to give a responsible scientific accounting for the origins and continuing existence of the universe.

———. *The Mind of God: The Scientific Basis for a Rational World.* New York: Simon & Schuster, 1992.
 In his latest book, addressed to a broad and general readership, Davies describes developments "at the frontiers of science, some of which have led to interesting and exciting ideas about God, creation, and the nature of reality" (p. 16). One of the more exciting ideas Davies explores is the understanding of God as "changed by his creation, and by his own creative action, which includes an element of openness or freedom" (p. 183).

Drees, Willem B. *Beyond the Big Bang: Quantum Cosmologies and God.* LaSalle, IL: Open Court, 1990.
 A scientist-theologian with degrees in both physics and theology, Drees calls theology to task for its inadequate and uninformed responses to the contributions of modern science. He then sets out to construct a model of theological reflection and inquiry that, while respecting the distinctive uniqueness of both disciplines, perceives the shared mission of both, and relates them in what he terms "constructive consonance" (p. 12).

Henderson, Charles P., Jr. *God and Science: The Death and Rebirth of Theism.* Atlanta, GA: John Knox, 1986.
 This work is another effort to bridge the divide between theology and science. Henderson, a Presbyterian clergyman, writes "in the conviction that the stalemate between science and religion can be broken and our situation of conflict can be resolved, if scientists and religious leaders alike become aware of the similar crosscurrents in their respective domains" (p. 5). He continues, "This book takes the reader on an intellectual pilgrimage through doubt to faith, through science to religion, through the unrelenting rigor of skepticism to the threshhold of what may be a profound religious awakening" (p. 7). Henderson's approach to this goal involves reviewing the challenge of modern scientists and philosophers such as Einstein, Freud, and Marx. He then introduces modern theologians, Teilhard and Tillich, whose works wrestled with, if not met, the challenge.

Jastrow, R. *God and the New Astronomers.* New York: Warner Books, 1980.
 An exploration of the effects of theology as it encounters and responds to the new cosmology.

Kaiser, Christopher. *Creation and the History of Science*. Grand Rapids, MI: William B. Eerdmans, 1991.

Kaiser traces the relationship between theology and science from the early church's encounter with Greco-Roman science, through the Medieval, Renaissance, Reformation, and Modern periods, into the present interactions of new science with new theology.

Klaaren, Eugene M. *Religious Origins of Modern Science*. Grand Rapids, MI: William B. Eerdmans, 1977.

Klaaren seeks "to make a modest contribution to a fuller explanation of the new science by showing its roots in religious presuppositions" (p. 3). Rejecting the judgment that science is free of religious presuppositions and assumptions, Klaaren explores the depth and influence of its roots in Western Christian theology.

Mahin, Mark. *The New Scientific Case for God's Existence*. Boston: Mindlifter Press, 1985.

Through investigations into the origins and evolution of the universe, probability theory, and causality, Mahin reasons his way to the existence of God.

Oates, David. *Earth Rising: Ecological Belief in an Age of Science*. Corvallis: Oregon State University Press, 1968.

In addition to providing a basic introduction to a system's view of the universe, Oates describes his own spiritual awakening to the mysteries of the natural world.

Paul, Iain. *Science, Theology and Einstein*. New York: Oxford University Press, 1982.

Trained as a theologian and a scientist, Paul affirms the value of both forms of inquiry, and writes his book in an effort to heal the divisions between theology and science. His particular contribution to this challenging task is to "translate" Einstein's scientific epistemology and metaphysics into language for philosophers and theologians, and to introduce them to Einstein's religious views.

Peacocke, Arthur. *Creation and the World of Science: 1979*. Oxford, England: Clarendon Press, 1979.

In this early volume, which is a collection of published lectures delivered at Oxford University, Peacocke argues persuasively that the sciences can enrich our understanding of God. The opening discussions give an account of the uneasy relationship that has existed between science and theology for centuries, and indicates that an end to the long alienation is in sight. Peacocke summarizes the recent developments in science that point it in new directions. Those developments—evolutionary biology, chaos theory, relations between and among particular sciences, sociobiology, ecology, and futurology—reflect and affect revolutionary changes in our understanding of the earth, God, ourselves, and the cosmos. They provide new data for theological reflection. Peacocke relates, yet distinguishes, both types of inquiry:

> The viewpoint adopted in these lectures is that in both the scientific and theological enterprises the basic stance, the working assumption, is that of a sceptical and qualified realism—the belief that they are processes of finding out the "way things are." This belief is justified, in the case of science, by its success in prediction and control. In the case of theology, it is justified by providing resources which give moral purpose, meaning and intelligibility to the individual plotting his path through life. (Pp. 40–41)

In a somewhat stronger statement about the relevance of scientific knowledge for theology, he asserts:

> Any theological account of God's relation to the world is operating in an intellectual vacuum, not to say cultural ghetto, if it fails to relate its affirmations to the answers to these questions the natural sciences have been able to develop. . . . These [theological] questions . . . cannot be asked at all without directing them to the world as we best know and understand it, that is, through the sciences. (P. 47)

————. *God and the New Biology.* San Francisco: Harper & Row, 1986.
  Peacocke, a prominent physical biochemist and Anglican theologian, asserts that the "new biology" offers dramatic new insights into our understanding of ourselves, our planet, and God. True to his scientific tradition, Peacocke reiterates his belief that "our explicit concepts of God must be seen as the best knowledge of the world available to us" (p. xvii). In his view, "The investigations of the ecological sciences could provide us, if they were pursued energetically enough, with the knowledge that would make possible any implementation of this theologically informed view of nature as creation and of man's role in it as co-creator—a propitious marriage of theology and science" (p. 107). Unfortunately, Peacocke's most recent publication, *Theology for a Scientific Age* (Minneapolis, MN: Augsburg Fortress, 1993), was not released in time to be included into his discussion.

————, ed. *The Sciences and Theology in the Twentieth Century.* Notre Dame, IN: University of Notre Dame Press, 1981.
  This is a collection of the thinking of fifteen scholars in theology, philosophy, the sciences, and sociology, which came out of the Oxford International Symposium in September 1979. In his opening remarks, Peacocke, who chaired the conference, speaks of the variegated and numerous ways that science and religion relate and interact in the modern world, and states his intention to map these relations and interactions. Points that Peacocke identifies for his respondents include:

the natural world, humanity and God, epistemology, and sociological critique.

Sheldrake, Rupert. *The Rebirth of Nature: The Greening of Science and God*. New York: Bantam Books, 1991.

Sheldrake investigates the historical evolution of our understanding of nature from its prehistoric associations with fertility, power, and maternity to its modern associations with machines, conquests, and resources. In his opinion, we are gripped by a schizophrenia in which our intuition tells us nature is living subject, and our mindset tells us that nature is objective matter. After explaining the origins of this condition, Sheldrake shows "how science itself has begun to transcend the mechanistic world view" (p. 5). For

> science, like religion, is pervaded by a strong sense of a fundamental unity. This intuition underlay Einstein's search for a unified field theory and currently inspires attempts to conceive of the primal field of the cosmos and the primal source of energy. Here science meets theology; for if fields and energy have a common source that transcends both, we find ourselves back in the field of creative trinities. And as theology meets science, a new evolutionary conception of the creative trinity is coming into being; theology itself is evolving. (P. 201)

Sheldrake quotes Alfred North Whitehead's earlier observation of a creative trinity: "Biology is the study of the larger organisms, whereas physics is the study of the smaller organisms."[12] And in light of modern cosmology, physics is also the study of the all-embracing cosmic organism, and of the galactic, stellar, and planetary organisms that have evolved within it.[13]

Wiester, John. *The Genesis Connection*. Nashville, TN: Thomas Nelson, 1983.

Wiester begins his book with an account of his conversion from agnosticism to Christianity, and his subsequent search for connections between his new-found faith and his training in and practice of geology. After relating his experience and intention, he charts the story of the origin and evolution of the universe based on the latest available scientific evidence, and draws interesting corollaries between the scientific data and the book of Genesis. The book is similar to an earlier version of Berry's *The Universe Story*[14] in its aim and substance.

Theology and Ecology

In the preceding section, contemporary scientific works were introduced that take theology seriously, and indeed make theological connections and implications explicit. I turn now to the work of theologians who approach their task from an inclusive cosmological or ecological perspective. Influenced by the values, interests, and orientations of movements such as process philosophy, existentialism, Marxist analysis, feminist critique, and liberation theology, these theologians embrace an even more ambitious project. They seek to overcome the rift that has alienated religion from science for some 400 years, and extend the horizon of theology beyond the boundaries of humankind to embrace the whole of the natural world. One of the most respected proponents of this view, Jürgen Moltmann, sums up the matter as follows:

> Today theology and science . . . have become companions in tribulation, under the pressure of the ecological crisis and the search for the new direction which both must work for, if human beings and nature are to survive at all on this earth. It is only slowly that theologians are beginning to see that their continual attempts to draw dividing lines between theology and the sciences are no longer necessary, because science's earlier unquestioning faith in itself has disappeared. . . . In a global situation where it is a case of "one world or none," science and theology cannot afford to divide up the one, single reality.[15]

Whereas in the past, science was seen as the adversary (i.e., the "spirit of darkness"), Moltmann asserts that in our time, humankind's ignorance and exploitation of the natural world is the adversary that must be overcome. However, rather than radical revisions of the theological record, these ecologically-informed theologians go about their tasks in continuity with those who have preceded them, recovering and reclaiming the inclusive vision of life that lies in most religious traditions. Some of the most persuasive of these theologians are introduced in this section.

Resources on Theology and Ecology

Barbour, Ian G. *Religion in an Age of Science.* London: SCM Press, 1990.
    Barbour rejects the mechanistic model of the universe and presents his version of the evolutionary paradigm, describing the world as a community of interdependent beings.

Barnes, Michael, ed. *An Ecology of the Spirit: Religious Reflection and Environmental Consciousness.* Lanham, MD: University Press of America, 1993.
    Barnes undertakes a literary project similar in goal and structure to this volume, but which restricts its focus to ecotheology. He invites a number of distinguished theologians to explore connections between the earth and religion, focusing on specific issues such as the indifference of church, ecofeminism, church history, spirituality, morality, Eastern religions, and symbols.

Hendry, George. *Theology of Nature*. Philadelphia: Fortress Press, 1980.

If science and theology had not parted ways in recent centuries, there would be no environmental crisis in our times. So states Hendry, professor of theology at Princeton, in this soft critique of the attitudes of both disciplines. He particularly chides theology for ignoring science's knowledge of the natural world, and after offering some likely explanation for this response, suggests that:

> If all reference to a transcendent Creator is excluded, or "bracketed out" from the concept of nature, the exclusion may be methodological, not ontological: i.e., it may be intended not as a denial of the existence of God, but as an objection to the introduction of God into scientific inquiry as an explanatory principle or hypothesis. (P. 196)

Jaki, Stanley L. *Cosmos and Creator*. Chicago: Regnery Gateway, 1980.

Jaki, a Hungarian-born, Benedictine priest with doctorates in theology and physics, argues that new science enables Christians to recover a belief in the doctrine of creation.

———. *God and the Cosmologists*. Washington, DC: Regnery Gateway, 1989.

This critique of modern scientific cosmology is based on Jaki's conviction that it is founded on faulty philosophy and arrogant science. Jaki reaffirms traditional Roman Catholic teachings that the meaning, origin, and destiny of the universe can be discerned through the use of reason.

Johnson, Elizabeth A. *Women, Earth, and Creator Spirit*. Mahwah, NJ: Paulist Press, 1993.

Like most ecologically-sensitive theologians, Johnson lays out her understanding of the problem of human-earth relations. She then makes connections between the marginalization and exploitation of women and nature, grounding her theological response in a systemic worldview, earlier women's wisdom traditions, and an image of the ultimate life-giver as Creator Spirit.

McDaniel, Jay B. *Earth, Sky, Gods, and Mortals*. Mystic, CT: Twenty-Third, 1990.

McDaniel, Associate Professor of Religion at Hendrix College, writes, "This book attempts to articulate one version of an ecological Christianity that is open to all horizons of human life, open to other religions, and infused with a desire to affirm our inseparability from the natural world" (p. ix). In this reviewer's opinion, the author accomplishes his ambitious goal. He begins by distinguishing an ecological understanding of life from the mechanistic view that has held sway for 300 years. Within this new understanding, McDaniel describes an ecological spirituality, a "spirituality of mortals," which is open to and nurtured by animals, earth, sky, art, poetry, plants, other religious traditions and their gods, people, and various spiritual paths. Such openness, in his perspective, is a consequence of faith, which surrenders its need and search for absolutes, trusting rather in the "mystery that cannot itself be absolutized" (p. 39).

McFague, Sallie. *Models of God: Theology for an Ecological, Nuclear Age.* Philadelphia: Fortress Press, 1987.

Drawing upon her previous work in "metaphorical theology," McFague proposes the models of mother, lover, and friend to represent God. While these models do little to break with the anthropocentrism of the more dominant patriarchal symbols that have held sway over the centuries, the lengthy reflections that support McFague's preferences include many references to the "world as God's body" (p. xiii). Quite often, this metaphor is used to describe the godly character of other species in the larger-life community. She also suggests that we choose new metaphors to describe ourselves in relationship to the natural world:

> We need to imagine new models for the relationship between ourselves and our earth. We can no longer see ourselves as names of and rulers over nature but must think of ourselves as gardeners, caretakers, mothers and fathers, stewards, trustees, lovers, priests, co-creators, and friends of a world that, while giving us life and sustenance, also depends increasingly on us in order to continue both for itself and for us. (P. 13)

Her ecological emphasis is most evident in this passage: "When the world is viewed as God's body, that body includes more than just Christians and more than just human beings" (p. 71). McFague has recently completed *The Body of God* (Minneapolis, MN: Augsburg Fortress, 1993).

Miller, Randolph C., ed. *Empirical Theology: A Handbook.* Birmingham, AL: Religious Education Press, 1992.

Empirical theology is a distinctively American theological orientation, the practice of which is based on observation, experience, reason, testing and analysis, and making new connections. Miller describes it as "an open-ended theology, based on a naturalistic view of the world" (p. 5). Twelve scholars pool their theological experiences in this volume. Contributions include essays on the history and major themes of empirical theology, its relation to science and classical theology, and more specialized treatments of God, Jesus, church, and creation.

Moltmann, Jürgen. *God in Creation: A New Theology of Creation and the Spirit of God.* San Francisco: Harper & Row, 1895.

Moltmann, professor of systematic theology at the University of Tubingen in Germany, writes in the context of liberal Protestant theology, which retreated from its social mission of the transformation of the world and returned to an emphasis on the primacy of faith in Christ. In Moltmann's view, it may have been permissible for theology to withdraw from the public arena after the catastrophic events of the first half of the twentieth century; however, the crisis confronting us today no longer allows that option. Moltmann sums up the challenge confronting theology today as follows: "The salutory 'christological concentration' in Protestant theology then, must be matched today by an extension of theology's horizon to cosmic breadth, so that it takes in the whole of God's creation" (p. xii).

God in Creation is the elaboration of Moltmann's theological revision. He begins by explaining his rationale for an ecologically centered theology. He then proceeds to offer a detailed and in-depth analysis of the environmental crisis. On that foundation, he builds his formidable theology of nature. This book not only presents theology at the cutting edge of the environmental crisis, it offers a credible and respected account of theology's development through the twentieth century. Because of his standing within the theological community, Moltmann's works are both credible and authoritative.

Christianity and Ecology

Thomas Berry calls Christianity to an appreciation of the perspective science lends to our understanding of the universe. He maintains that, for the most part, Christians have resisted the revelations of science and failed to acknowledge their religious value and contribution to the story of the universe. While this critical observation seems to represent a legitimate lacuna within Christianity, it is inaccurate as a generalization. Theologians across denominations, influenced, if not inspired, by the environmental movement, are earnestly undertaking a hermeneutics of retrieval.[16]

The word recovery in the title of this chapter functions as a reminder that while there is a lot of new thinking going on about the religious nature of the physical world, there is also much to be retrieved from earlier and less accessible Christian perspectives. One of the more persistent and influential forgotten traditions of Christianity's recent past, natural theology, might well be regarded as a precursor to contemporary ecotheology. Conrad Cherry's Nature and Religious Imaginations[17] traces the development of natural theology through the eighteenth and nineteenth centuries in the United States. He explores the contributions of its primary spokespersons: Jonathan Edwards, Samuel Hopkins, William Ellory Channing, and Horace Bushnell. Jonathan Edwards's religious vision was "pervaded by images of relationship and open interchange among the parts of the Universe."[18] Cherry finds that, for Hopkins, "Physical nature is a set of instructions about God as moral Governor,"[19] and that Channing believed that "nature's chief spiritual function is its mirroring of innate human virtues which every person is called to perfect."[20] Finally, Bushnell warned against the indiscriminate use of the land, and stressed that "each person should be sensitive to how his creative acts contribute to the whole of God's system of nature and supernature. Those acts should be creative rather than destructive in design."[21] The prophetic nature of Bushell's vision rings clear in the following quotation:

> It is not absurd to imagine the human race, at some future time, when the population and the works of industry are vastly increased, kindling so many fires, by putting wood and coal in contact with fire, as to burn up or fatally vitiate the world's atmosphere. That the condition of nature will, in fact, be so far changed by human agency, is probably not to be feared.[22]

Bushnell would probably not be so optimistic today. Instead, he would lament the destructive behaviors of what he regarded as the most intelligent species in creation, and remind us of nature's revelatory purpose. In sum, he would be concerned that the natural world would no longer provide such clear and direct access to the Godhead.

Contemporary theologians, like Jürgen Moltmann, while acknowledging the influence of natural theology traditions, have affirmed and reworked the theological-ecological relationship. Moltmann distinguishes the former from the latter as follows:

> Every natural theology proceeds from the self-evidence of nature as God's creation. On the other hand, every theology of nature [Moltmann's way of describing the Enterprise] interprets nature in the light of the self-revelation of the creative God. So what is the relation between natural theology and the theology of nature? By asking this question we are turning the traditional interest in natural theology upside down: the aim of our investigation is not what nature can contribute to our knowledge of God, but what the concept of God contributes to our knowledge of nature. By reversing the question put to the natural theology in this way, we are also compelled to define revealed theology differently, where this has a bearing on nature.[23]

With this insightful distinction, Moltmann lays the foundation for the construction of a theology of nature. In his view, our understanding of God has implications for understanding creation. He calls upon the Christian theological community to undertake the task of making clear these implications for our time. The following literature takes on that challenge.

Resources on Christianity and Ecology

Austin, Richard Cartwright. *Beauty of the Lord*. Atlanta, GA: John Knox, 1988.

The second of a series on environmental theology, *Beauty of the Lord* is a Christian environmental handbook written to explain the theology of ecological relationships. Drawing heavily upon natural theology as interpreted by Jonathan Edwards, Austin defines a spiritual and physical bond that provides a better understanding of the Christian experience of nature.

Birch, Charles, William Eakin, and Jay B. McDaniel, eds. *Liberating Life: Contemporary Approaches to Ecological Theology*. Maryknoll, NY: Orbis Books, 1990.

This is a collection of fifteen essays sketching a vision of ecological theology that was presented at a 1988 conference sponsored by the World Council of Churches in Annecy, France. The unifying theme of the works is that liberation theology offers a starting point for theological reflection on the spiritual significance of the planet and our moral responsibility for its survival and well-being. The contributors, some of the most committed and respected ecological theologians, approach the task from several perspectives: ecotheology's roots within the Christian tradition, its implications for morality and spirituality, its relevance and relation to Third-World realities, and its challenge to and for the church. Overall, the book makes a nice introductory text to environmental theology's cutting edge.

Bowman, Douglas. *Beyond the Modern Mind: The Spiritual and Ethical Challenge of the Environmental Crisis*. New York: Pilgrim Press, 1990.

"It is my intention to set you loose for new forms of Christian thinking and living appropriate for this time of environmental crisis" (p. xiii). With this introduction, Bowman sets out to relate the postmodern vision of reality, as derived from the new science, to Christian spirituality and ethical decision-making. The text, with study questions at the end of each chapter, would work well in adult education programs in church or school settings.

Bradley, Ian. *God Is Green*. New York: Doubleday, 1992.

In this book, Bradley, a minister in the Church of Scotland and frequent contributor to the *London Times*,

> seeks to show that the Christian faith is intrinsically Green, that the Good News of the Gospel promises liberation and fulfillment for the whole of creation and that Christians have a positive and distinctive contribution to make to the salvation of our threatened planet and the preservation of the natural environment. (P. 1)

He begins this project by acknowledging the legitimacy of the critique Lynn White inveighed against Christianity for its indifference to, and indeed, implication in, the plunder of the planet.[24] This open acknowledgment of White's charge leads him to an examination of

Christian teachings in a search for the theological misunderstanding that prompted the church's failure to promote reverence and responsibility for the natural world. Three doctrinal emphases are identified as problematic in this regard: the belief that nature exists for human utility and pleasure; the association of God with transcendence; and the identification of the physical realm with evil, temporality, and darkness. Bradley then sets to work to construct a balanced and green response to these distorted emphases, a response grounded in Scripture, Christology, and human responsibility for life. The book is a lucidly written, well-argued, and balanced introduction to the integration of ecological issues and perspectives with mainstream Christian teaching.

Derrick, Christopher. *The Delicate Creation: Towards a Theology of the Environment*. Old Greenwich, CT: Devin-Adair, 1972.

Derrick begins his book with a wholehearted acknowledgment of the mounting environmental crisis, affirming the perspectives of researchers such as Lynn White and Rene Dubos, who initiated and acted as lively contributors to the conversation in the 1970s. White, in particular, has had much of the responsibility for the problem at the door of Christianity, citing its emphasis on overcoming the evil of this world and achieving salvation in the next. Derrick, who asserts that the environmental crisis is a religious crisis, takes White's challenge seriously enough to focus his inquiry on the Christian connection. What he uncovers is a residual influence of Manichaeansim, a fourth-century heresy that promoted contempt for the natural world. In his words, "We have collectively misused a good world: almost inevitably, where this principle is denied or forgotten, people will drift or plunge into the idea that we have been trapped in a bad one" (p. 98). Derrick insists that the heresy is an aberration of an authentic Christian spirituality, and urges church leaders to assert the goodness of creation and to promote the cultivation of what he calls a "cosmic piety," characterized by a collective humility and a practical asceticism. In his view, the environmental crisis demands such conversion. The work is a helpful resource for examining the Christian (and non-Christian) context as both contributor and critic to the mindset that has allowed or promoted the destruction of the planet. This work represents a giant step forward in constructing a theology of the environment.

Dunn, Stephen, and Anne Lonergan, eds. *Befriending the Earth: A Theology of Reconciliation Between Humans and the Earth*. Mystic, CT: Twenty-Third, 1991.

A series of conversations between Thomas Berry and Thomas Clarke, S.J., this book grew out of a symposium held at the Holy Cross Center for Ecology and Spirituality, Port Burwell, Ontario. Jesuit Thomas Clarke comes to the dialogue with a commitment to and expertise in liberation theology, with its strong social justice orientation; Berry comes with his inclusive biocentric view of the universe. Both are Roman Catholic priests, who, while thoroughly immersed in the Christian tradition, recognize the necessity for its ongoing revision and transformation. The topics that are addressed in their dialogue include: revelation, creation, the Trinity, the transcendent God, science, Teilhard, sacred community, spiritual discipline, ritual, Christology, sacrifice, grace, and the ecozoic age. In addition to being an interesting approach to religious ecology, the book offers a basic introduction to Berry's work.

Edwards, Denis. *Jesus and the Cosmos*. Mahwah, NJ: Paulist Press, 1991.

According to Edwards, science has presented us with a new cosmology; the ecological movement presents us with a crisis of the greatest magnitude; and contemporary historical criticism has opened up new perspectives on Scripture, Jesus, and the church. This book represents Edwards's response to these transformations of understanding. Edwards, an Anglican clergyman from Australia, begins his text with a parable about the fragility and pathos of the planet. After evoking the reader's sensitivities, he goes on "to tell the story of the universe in the way that reflects the mainstream of modern science [which he asserts] will provide a perspective for contemporary theological reflection" (p. 11). Most of this slim volume is devoted to this task, drawing heavily on the thought of Karl Rahner, which Edwards finds particularly helpful because of its evolutionary orientation; his theological reflection is likewise indebted to Rahner's Christology. Overall, Edwards offers a unique contribution to the developing synthesis between faith and science, which serves as an excellent introduction to ecotheology from a Christian perspective.

Fritsch, Albert, S.J. *Eco-Church*. San Jose, CA: Resource, 1992.

A creative and engaging guide for use with congregations who want to examine the use of the earth's resources in personal and family contexts and, in particular, within the community of church. The guide also offers concrete suggestions for personal and communal practice of authentic Christian stewardship that can extend itself to awaken the civic community. *Eco-Church* is highly recommended for educating the local church in the theory and practice of religious ecology.

Haught, John. *The Promise of Nature: Ecology and Cosmic Purpose*. Mahwah, NJ: Paulist Press, 1993.

According to Haught, professor of theology and Chairman of the Theology Department at Georgetown, Christianity (as other religions) has something important to contribute to the ecological agenda. In this volume, he develops his ecological theology, affirming the importance of scientific insights, and critiques earlier Christian interpretations of the natural world. The text gives an indication of theology's awakening and the religious dimension of the ecological crisis.

Joranson, Philip N., and Ken Butigan, eds. *Cry of the Environment: Rebuilding the Christian Creation Tradition*. Santa Fe, NM: Bear, 1984. (Currently out of print.)

This treasury of resources explores the Judeo-Christian's culpability and contributions in its teachings about creation. The collection provides an excellent introduction to the range of insights and research currently underway to infuse creation-centered perspectives into the tradition. The edited volume contains articles by scientists exploring evolution and physics, and articles by a number of theologians who bring a creation-consciousness to their specialized interests in spirituality, morality, and systematics. The volume also contains concrete suggestions for educating in this perspective.

Linzey, Andrew. *Christianity and the Rights of Animals*. New York: Crossroad, 1989.

As the title implies, *Christianity and the Rights of Animals* represents a Christian response to the animal rights movement. What makes the book even more significant is that Linzey builds a case for animals based on Christian foundations. Those who seek a theological rationale for their advocacy or work on behalf of animals will find this book an inspiring and helpful resource.

Linzey, Andrew, and Tom Regan, eds. *Animals and Christianity: A Book of Readings*. New York: Crossroad, 1988.

Linzey, a theologian, and Regan, a philosopher, assemble this collection that samples the teachings of the Christian tradition with regard to the existence and significance of animals. A first set of articles takes up the question of human attitudes toward animals. Commentaries of Aquinas and Calvin offer the more familiar "utilitarian" viewpoint, while the less familiar voices from the traditional, John Burnaby, Paulos Mar Gregorios, and Vladimer Lossky promote a more egalitarian vision.

Part 2 examines animal suffering and brings two viewpoints to bear on the subject: animal pain is of no consequence to the Creator (and thus to us); God does not want animals to suffer and expects humankind to respond to their needs with compassion. Part 3 raises the question of animal redemption, reviewing the stances of St. Augustine, Bishop Butler, St. Irenaeus, St. John of the Cross, Calvin Tillich, C. S. Lewis, and John Wesley on that issue. Part 4 considers our human responsibilities toward animals, and refers to the writings of Albert Schweitzer, Karl Barthly, St. Thomas Aquinas, Linzey, Regan, and Stephen Clark. The collection concludes with a discussion of issues and questions related to vivisection, fur-trapping, hunting, and factory farming.

Scripture

Resources on Scripture

Achtemeier, Elizabeth. *Nature, God and Pulpit*. Grand Rapids, MI: William B. Eerdmans, 1992.

Achtemeier, adjunct professor of Bible and homiletics at Union Theological Seminary, Virginia, sets out to "present the biblical witness concerning God and the natural world in a way that will furnish preachers with content for sermons on the subject" (p. ix). After sketching out some of the broad strokes of our present environmental crisis, and some of the insights arising from scientific research, Achtemeier teaches her readers how to use the Bible in relating to God's creation.

Anderson, Bernhard. *Creation and the Old Testament*. Philadelphia: Fortress Press, 1984.

————. *Creation Versus Chaos: The Reinterpretation of Mythical Symbolism in the Bible*. New York: Association Press, 1967.

In these works, Anderson, a distinguished Scripture scholar, lays bare the biblical roots of the creation tradition. He traces its development through Genesis, Job, Proverbs, the Psalms, and into New Testament literature. One of the most interesting persuasive contributions relates to his work on significance and primacy of the Noathic covenant.

Braten, Susan Power. *Christianity, Wilderness, and Wildlife*. London: Associated University Press, 1993.

In Braten's view, the Bible portrays the natural environment as responsive to God's will, a participant in the covenants and holy history. She seeks to explore this theme in her book, stating that its primary purpose is to trace the recurrence of key wilderness motifs through the Bible and note the development of new themes and new variants (p. 20). Specific themes and variants include the spirituality of the desert fathers, Celtic monastics, and Franciscans.

Westermann, Claus. *Creation*. Translated by John J. Scullion, S.J. Philadelphia: Fortress Press, 1971.

The fact that the astronauts were drawn to the creation narratives suggests to Westermann, a distinguished Old Testament scholar, that the spirit of these Scriptural texts is not lost on those with a scientific disposition. He notes, however, that this understanding is a recent development. Indeed, it is a consequence of a scientific exegesis that acknowledges the truth, though not the facts, found in the Book of Genesis. Westermann's own exegesis seeks to revise these narratives from a theological perspective in light of a modern understanding of mythology.

Church

I cannot resist beginning this section with Simone Weil's prophetic remark, "How can the church call itself Catholic if the universe itself is left out?"[25] Whether or not Simone's comment awakened some in the church to a recognition of its Protestant members would probably be immaterial to her; indeed, she would welcome the numerous contributions of committed Christian women and men animated by an inclusive vision of faith and life.

Dowd, Michael. *EarthSpirit: A Handbook for Nurturing an Ecological Christianity*. Mystic, CT: Twenty-Third, 1991.

Dowd introduces grassroots Christian communities to the theological significance of the environmental movement. The book serves as a primer in the emerging worldview, sketching out the problems confronting our earth because of human ignorance and indifference. Within this context, Dowd recasts the meaning and practice of Christian faith. Because he does not assume familiarity with the subject, and eases the reader into a basic understanding of its implications for Christian living, the book could serve as an effective resource for teens and adults in parish programs. In addition, his questions at the end of each chapter and suggestions for further reading lend practical value to the text.

McDonagh, Sean. *The Greening of the Church*. New York: Orbis Books, 1990.

McDonagh, an Irish missionary to the Philippines, makes connections between the poverty and oppression of the human community in which he ministered and the plight of the larger-life community that is similarly oppressed and impoverished. McDonagh's understanding of what is happening to the rain forests and other ecosystems is as informed and sophisticated as his understanding of the social context of the Philippines, and of the faith that animates his work there. His books, including *To Care for the Earth* (Santa Fe, NM: Bear, 1986), reflect the wholistic perspective of an ecologically sensitive theologian for whom "everything is connected to everything else" (p. 89).

Creation Theology

Matthew Fox is the founding director of the Institute in Culture and Creation Spirituality at Holy Name College in Oakland, California. A former Dominican priest, theologian, and educator, Fox is a prolific writer, persuasive speaker, and primary interpreter of Christianity's creation tradition. He rediscovered and actively promotes creation spirituality. Some of his most important works are listed below.

Resources on Creation Theology

Fox, Matthew. *The Coming of the Cosmic Christ*. San Francisco: Harper & Row, 1988.

While New Testament scholars have sought the historical Jesus, Fox reflects on the meaning of Jesus in an evolutionary perspective, and sketches this vision using christological events and symbols. He thus affirms the relevance and significance of Jesus for the next millennium.

———. *Creation Spirituality*. San Francisco: Harper & Row, 1991.

In this recently-published primer written during his period of Vatican-ordered public silence, Fox describes creation spirituality as an ancient yet new phenomenon, a movement that unifies and influences the Christian tradition. He structures his interpretation of the subject around two major themes: the cultivation and celebration of awe through experiences of mysticism, ecumenism, art, ritual, renunciation, and community; and the pursuit and celebration of liberation through confrontation, understanding, and conversion.

———. *Original Blessing*. Santa Fe, NM: Bear, 1983.

Fox introduces his popular book with a suggestion that humanity needs a new religious paradigm, and that creation spirituality seems a promising alternative to more traditional models. In this handbook, Fox constructs his critique of Christianity's fall-and-redemption preoccupation, and counters this emphasis with an alternative vision of life as a blessing and gift. In his words:

> The universe itself, blessed and graced, is the proper starting point for spirituality. Original blessing is prior to any sin, original or less than original . . . the time has come to let anthropocentrism go, and with it to let the preoccupation with human sinfulness give way to attention to divine grace. (P. 26)

He develops his theological vision in a thematic description of creation spirituality's key elements and emphases.

———. *A Spirituality Named Compassion*. San Francisco: Harper & Row, 1979, 1990.

Compassion is what Fox believes is most lacking in our world today. Drawing upon the collective wisdom of nature and the world's great religious traditions, this volume undertakes an inquiry into the meaning and practice of compassion in a cosmic context. Long on analysis, while short on solutions, this second work of Fox's trilogy probes such negative influences as sexual mystification, manipulation of life, fear of creativity, mechanistic worldview, economic exploitation, and unjust social structures.

Eco-Morality

Resources on Eco-Morality

Cobb, John B., Jr. *Sustainability: Economics, Ecology, and Justice*. Maryknoll, NY: Orbis Books, 1992.

True to his process-philosophy training and orientation, Cobb grounds his study in what he calls a new realism, an experience of finitude and limitation with regard to development and natural resources.

Whereas most discussions of the problems and excesses of the free enterprise system focus on its deleterious effects on human societies, Cobb's analysis extends to the larger-life community. Within this social, economic, and ecological matrix, he sets the vision and mission of the Gospel, and spells out its implications for promoting a livable, sustainable society that is just for all creation. Cobb's inclusivity makes this analysis valuable, pertinent, and unique.

Conlon, James. *Geo-Justice*. Canada: Wood Lakes Books, 1990.
      "Geo-justice re-visions justice-making" (p. 17). Conlon offers a book of reflections on the centrality of justice in contemporary interpretations of Christian morality. Throughout these reflections, Conlon weaves together an understanding of justice in personal, social, and ecological perspectives.

Merchant, Carolyn. *Radical Ecology*. New York: Routledge, 1992.
      A good introduction to the work of ecofeminism, deep ecology, and green politics, with a strong moral emphasis. The work includes a chapter on spiritual ecology.

Miller, Harlan B., and William H. Williams, eds. *Ethics and Animals*.
      Clifton, NJ: Humana Press, 1983.
      The editors write, "The social history of the last two centuries can be seen in part as a continuing struggle to enlarge the boundaries of moral community" (p. 5). They present a series of essays that trace the struggle for liberation, noting the linkages between various groups engaged in it.

Regan, Tom. *All That Dwell Herein*. Berkeley: University of California
      Press, 1982.

——. *Animal Rights and Human Obligations*. Englewood Cliffs,
      NJ: Prentice-Hall, 1976.
      Tom Regan is a philosopher who expands the principles of moral philosophy to include the natural world, particularly animals. Though his works are not explicitly theological, their moral sensitivity and challenge have clear implications for religious living.

——. *The Thee Generation: Reflections on the Coming Revolution*.
      Philadelphia: Temple University Press, 1991.
      Regan asserts that the humanistic tradition of the West is bankrupt as a moral guide because of its anthropocentrism (i.e., an exclusive focus on human life). In this series of essays addressed to a diverse audience, Regan refines his moral philosophy, inspired by signs of and hope for the emergence of the "thee generation," a community characterized by an expansive ethic of compassion and service.

Robb, Carol S., and Carl J. Casebolt, eds. *Covenant for a New Creation:*
      Ethics, Religion, and Public Policy. Maryknoll, NY: Orbis Books, 1991.
      The editors' originating impulse for the volume was the desire to build on the work of Phil Joranson and Ken Butigan in *Cry of the*

Environment (Santa Fe, NM: Bear, 1984). While the revision accomplishes this goal, it does so with an emphasis on social ethics. Three themes organize the text and invite the commentaries of fifteen theologians of various specializations—new models of ownership, revisioning relationship with the rest of nature, and reconstructing justice for environmental ethics. Robb states, "Each section contains perspectives relevant to covenantal responsibility to transform politics, economics, culture, and religious beliefs. No less a project [in her perspective] is required to heal the earth" (p. 21).

Educational Resources

Videocassettes

Animals, Nature, and Religion, produced and narrated by Dr. Michael W. Fox, 1987. 35 min. [c/o The Humane Society of the United States, 2100 L Street, N.W. Washington, DC 20037; (202) 452-1100], VHS.

An introduction to the new cosmology and, in particular, to the human-animal relationship implied in this vision, Fox's video examines the plight of animals, and relates it to the teachings of abuse and exploitation to the religious traditions of East and West. The video would be especially pertinent for introducing the cosmologies and moral teachings of world religions.

We Are All Noah. Produced and narrated by Tom Regan, 1986. [c/o PETA—People for the Ethical Treatment of Animals, P.O. Box 42516, Washington, DC 20015; (301) 770-PETA]

Representatives of Judaism and Christianity identify specific issues of animal cruelty and exploitation, and bring their religious traditions to bear in response to these problems. The video is a persuasive appeal to put an end to the suffering and exploitation of animals.

Newsletters and Journals

Earthkeeping News: A Newsletter of the North American Conference on Christianity and Ecology. [1522 Grand Avenue #4C, Saint Paul, MN 55105]

Realistic Living: A Journal of Ecological Ethics, Feminist Ethics, Christian Ethics. [P.O. Box 140826, Dallas, TX 752140]

SpiritEarth: A Center for Spirituality in the Ecological Age. [Box 830, 20 Glen Street, Dover, MA 02030-0830]

A Summation

Before becoming acquainted with the new science, I would have used the word *conclusion* as a final heading for wrapping up the subject. Now, given a processive view of an ever-evolving and changing world, the word *conclusion* seems inappropriate, inaccurate, inconsistent, even anacronistic. In the company of new science and religious ecology, interpretations, investigations, reviews, and research are rarely, if ever, finally conclusive; they are, rather, discontinued, interrupted, shut down for a bit. Perhaps it is this apprehension and realization that makes it so difficult for me to take leave of the subject. I keep seeing and finding more books, more connections, and more categories that relate to it.

Even as I bring the essay to a close, a colleague lends me a copy of a book titled *Leadership and the New Science*,[26] which opens up a new cycle of reflections and connections between our knowledge of the natural world via the new science and the professions. The author, Margaret Wheatley, explores this relationship as an organizational consultant. She begins, "This is a book about the early stirrings of new ways of thinking about organizations . . . it does not lend itself to definitive conclusions."[27] Her work, in its spirit and content, brought to mind *Systemic Religious Education*,[28] a book in my own field that makes the theoretical connection between religious education and the new science, but falls short of spelling out its implications for practice. Perhaps that is where this chapter has led me to begin anew—an appropriate place to pass the ball to another colleague.

Notes

1. John Cobb, *Sustainability: Economics, Ecology, and Justice* (Maryknoll, NY: Orbis Books, 1992), 82.

2. Thomas Berry, *The Dream of the Earth* (San Francisco: Sierra, 1988), 81.

3. Berry's name for the age or era into which we are moving. The Ecozoic period will be characterized by restoring the balance between human-earth relations. Berry elaborates on this topic in *The Dream of the Earth*.

4. Thomas Berry and Brian Swimme, *The Universe Story* (San Francisco: Harper & Row, 1992).

5. Brian Swimme, *The Universe Is a Green Dragon* (Santa Fe, NM: Bear, 1984).

6. Quoted from Berry's 1990 lecture at Loyola University, "The Earth's Story: The Crisis Moment."

7. Thomas Berry, "Classical Western Spirituality and the American Experience," in *Riverdale Papers*, 17.

8. Bernard Lonergan, *Insight* (London: Darton, Longmann and Todd, 1957), 677.

9. *Physics, Philosophy and Theology: A Common Quest for Understanding*, edited by Robert J. Russell, William R. Stoeger, and George V. Coyne. Vatican Observatory: University of Notre Dame Press, 1988.

10. David Tracy and Nicholas Lash, *Cosmology and Theology* (New York: Seabury, 1983), 88.

11. Paul Davies, *The Mind of God: The Scientific Basis for a Rational World* (New York: Simon & Schuster, 1992), 14.

12. Alfred North Whitehead, *Science and the Modern World* (New York: Macmillan, 1925), 101.

13. Ibid., 101–2.

14. Berry and Swimme, *The Universe Story*.

15. Jürgen Moltmann, *God in Creation: A New Theology of Creation and the Spirit of God* (San Francisco: Harper & Row, 1985), 34.

16. I am indebted to my colleague, Bernard Lee, for this and other contributions to the chapter.

17. Conrad Cherry, *Nature and Religious Imagination* (Philadelphia: Fortress Press, 1980).

18. Ibid., 66.

19. Ibid., 79.

20. Ibid., 138.

21. Ibid., 207.

22. Horace Bushnell, *Nature and Supernatural* (New York: Charles Scribner's Sons, 1877), 45–46.

23. Moltmann, *God in Creation*, 53.

24. Lynn White, "The Historical Roots of Our Ecological Crisis," *Science* 155 (10 March 1967): 1203–7.

25. Quoted from Ian Bradley, *God Is Green* (New York: Doubleday, 1992), x.

26. Margaret Wheatley, *Leadership and the New Science* (San Francisco: Berrett-Koehler, 1992).

27. Ibid., xii.

28. Timothy Lines, *Systemic Religious Education* (Birmingham, AL: Religious Education Press, 1987).

Resources for Further Reading by Subject

New Science—New Theology

Capra, Franz. *The Tao of Physics*. London: Collins, Fontana, 1976.

Griffin, David, ed. *The Reenchantment of Science*. Albany: State University of New York Press, 1988.

Harris, Errol E. *Cosmos and Theos: Ethical and Theological Implications of the Anthropic Cosmological Principle*. Atlantic Highlands, NJ: Humanities Press, 1992.

Haught, John F. *The Cosmic Adventure: Science, Religion and the Quest for Purpose*. New York: Paulist Press, 1984.

Hawking, Stephen W. *A Brief History of Time*. New York: Bantam, 1988.

Hitchcock, John L. *Atoms, Snowflakes and God: The Convergence of Science and Religion*. Wheaton, IL: Theosophical, 1986.

Hyers, Conrad. *The Meaning of Creation: Genesis and Modern Science*. Atlanta, GA: John Knox, 1984.

LeShan, Lawrence. *The Medium, the Mystic, and the Physicist*. New York: Ballantine Books, 1974.

Morowitz, Harold. *Cosmic Joy and Local Pain: Musings of a Mystic Scientist*. New York: Charles Scribner's Sons, 1987.

Rifkin, Jeremy, and T. Howard. *The Emerging Order: God in the Age of Scarcity*. New York: G. P. Putnam's Sons, 1979.

Sagan, Carl. *Cosmos*. New York: Random House, 1980.

Sexson, Lynda. *Ordinarily Sacred*. New York: Crossroad, 1982.

Templeton, John M. *The Humble Approach: Scientists Discover God*. New York: Seabury, 1981.

Templeton, John M., and Robert L. Hermann. *The God Who Would Be Known: Revelations of the Divine in Contemporary Science*. San Francisco: Harper & Row, 1989.

Theology and Ecology

Gilkey, Langdon. *Nature, Reality, and the Sacred: The Nexus of Science and Religion*. Minneapolis, MN: Augsburg Fortress, 1993.

Hargrove, Eugene, ed. *Religion and Environmental Crisis*. Athens, GA: University of Georgia Press, 1986.

Hefner, Philip. *The Human Factor: Evolution, Culture, and Religion.* Minneapolis, MN: Augsburg Fortress, 1993.

Christianity and Ecology

Breslin, Nancy. *A Wood Stork Named Warren, a Fable of Nature and God*. St. Petersburg Beach, FL: Prokaryote Press, 1992.

Gray, Elizabeth Dodson. *Green Paradise Lost*. Wellesley, MA: Roundtable Press, 1979.

Kitchen, Clarissa. *The Ecology Hymnal: New Words for Old Tunes.* Austin, TX: Sharing, 1974.

Overman, Richard H. *Evolution and the Christian Doctrine of Creation: A Whiteheadian Interpretation*. Philadelphia: Westminster, 1967.

Palmer, Martin. *Genesis or Nemesis: Belief, Meaning, and Ecology.* London: Dryad Press, 1988.

Santmire, H. Paul. *The Travail of Nature: The Ambiguous Ecological Promise of Christian Theology*. Minneapolis, MN: Augsburg Fortress, 1993.

Scripture

Brueggemann, Walter. *The Land: Place As Gift, Promise and Challenge in Biblical Faith*. Philadelphia: Fortress Press, 1977.

Frye, Roland M. *Is God a Creationist? The Religious Case Against Creation-Science*. New York: Charles Scribner's Sons, 1983.

Spirituality

Anderson, Lorraine, ed. *Sisters of the Earth*. New York: Vintage Books, 1991.

Armstrong, Edward. *Saint Francis: Nature Mystic*. Berkeley: University of California Press, 1973.

Armstrong, Regis, and Ignatius Brady, trans. *Francis and Clare: The Complete Works*. New York: Paulist Press, 1982.

Austin, Richard C. *Baptized into Wilderness: A Christian Perspective on John Muir*. Atlanta, GA: John Knox, 1987.

Bamford, Christopher, and William P. Marsh. *Celtic Christianity, Ecology, and Holiness*. Great Barrington, MA: Landisfarne, 1987.

Boone, J. Allen. *Kinship with All Life*. New York: Harper & Row, 1954.

Cummings, Charles. *Eco-Spirituality: Toward a Reverent Life*. Mahwah, NJ: Paulist Press, 1991.

Doyle, Bredan. *Meditations with Julian of Norwich*. Santa Fe, NM: Bear, 1983.

Fox, Matthew. *Breakthrough: Meister Eckhart's Creation Spirituality in New Translation*. Garden City, NY: Doubleday, Image, 1980.

Hausman, Gerald, ed. *Meditations with Animals: A Native American Beastiary*. Santa Fe, NM: Bear, 1986.

Heidtke, John. *Getting Down to Earth: A Call to Environment Action*. Mahwah, NJ: Paulist Press, 1993.

King, Ursula. *The Spirit of the Earth: Reflections on Teilhard de Chardin and Global Spirituality*. New York: Paragon House, 1989.

Kitchen, Clarissa. *The Ecology Hymnal: New Words for Old Tunes*. Austin, TX: Sharing, 1974.

Lonning, Per. *Creation—An Ecumenical Challenge?* Macon, GA: Mercer University Press, 1989.

MacNickle, Sister Mary Donatus. *Beasts and Birds in the Lives of Early Irish Saints*. Philadelphia: University of Pennsylvania Press, 1934.

Mauser, Ulrich. *Christ in the Wilderness*. Naperville, IL: Alec R. Allenson, 1963.

Granberg-Michaelson, Wesley. *A Wordly Spirituality: The Call to Take Care of the Earth*. San Francisco: Harper & Row, 1984.

Uhlein, Gabriele. *Meditations with Hildegard of Bingen*. Santa Fe, NM: Bear, 1982.

Wilkerson, Loren, ed. *Earthkeeping: Christian Stewardship of Natural Resources*. Grand Rapids, MI: William B. Eerdmans, 1980.

Woodruff, Sue. *Meditations with Mechtild of Magdeburg*. Santa Fe, NM: Bear, 1982.

Moral Philosophy

Carson, Gerald. *Men, Beasts and Gods: A History of Cruelty and Kindness to Animals*. New York: Charles Scribner's Sons, 1972.

Fox, Michael W. *Returning to Eden: Animal Rights and Human Responsibility*. Malabar, FL: Robert E. Krieger, 1986.

Morris, R., and Michael W. Fox, eds. *On the Fifth Day*. Washington, DC: Acropolis Books, 1978.

Rodd, Rosemary. *Biology, Ethics, and Animals*. Oxford: Clarendon Press, 1990.

Seed, John, et al., eds. *Thinking Like a Mountain*. Philadelphia: New Society, 1988.

Singer, Peter. *Animal-Liberation: A New Ethic for Our Treatment of Animals*. London: Jonathan Cape, 1976.

Creation Theology

Balasuriya, Tissa. *Planetary Theology*. Maryknoll, NY: Orbis Books, 1984.

Daly, Gabriel. *Creation and Redemption*. Wilmington, DE: Michael Glazier, 1990.

De Lubac, Henri. *A Brief Catechesis on Nature and Grace*. San Francisco: Ignatius Press, 1984.

Fritsch, Albert, S.J. *Renew the Face of the Earth*. Chicago: Loyola University Press, 1987.

Gilkey, Langdon. *Maker of Heaven and Earth*. Lanham, NY: University Press of America, 1985.

Hart, John. *The Spirit of the Earth*. New York: Paulist Press, 1984.

Hayes, Edward, ed. *Prayers for a Planetary Pilgrim*. Easton, KS: Forest of Peace Books, 1989.

Hayes, Zachary, O.F.M. *What Are They Saying About Creation?* New York: Paulist Press, 1980.

Murphy, Charles M. *At Home on the Earth*. New York: Crossroad, 1989.

9

Religious Education: Contemporary Theory and Practice

Kathleen O'Gorman

Introduction

The inclusion of religious education as a relevant topic for a volume exploring contemporary theological literature might come as a surprise to some readers. What, they might ask, is the rationale for including a chapter about the practice of indoctrinating well-intentioned members of a congregation in a religious tradition's beliefs and values in a survey of contemporary theological texts? This chapter focuses on making an adequate response to that query. Moreover, it attempts to convey something of the richness of the thinking going on in religious education circles, the diversity of perspectives that converge in the field, and the rigor of current efforts to revise and reconstruct its meaning for our times.

Given the richness and breadth of the topic, a first consideration in preparing a survey of the literature of religious education is the choice of perspective. It seems most appropriate for this volume to offer a wide-angle lens on the subject. Such an effort to render an inclusive interpretation of religious education, however, might be likened to the challenge Inuit folk would experience if asked to say a few words about snow. Because of the Inuit's recognition of snow's multiple forms, such an overview might seem impossible. A similar difficulty confronts anyone who attempts to write a responsible account of developments within the field of religious education. Like "snow" to the Inuit, the label "religious education" is an abstraction representing a subset of specific and particular forms.

Reducing either term to only one of these forms is comparable to describing life on the planet through the perspective and experience of a single species. Understanding them requires attention to their multiple forms; discussing them demands a knowledge of the names of these distinctive expressions; and describing them assumes precision in the use of language.

Viewed in this perspective, religious education can be described as a generic summation of formal and informal activities that engage individuals and groups, intentionally and unintentionally, in the pursuit of spiritual ends. Particular forms of religious education include (but are not limited to): teaching from a religious perspective, teaching about religion, teaching to promote affiliation with a religion, educating in faith, conducting a retreat experience, preaching a sermon, developing curricula on a religious theme, promoting religious values as a history teacher, facilitating the search for meaning, and administering an educational program within a religious organization. Each form has an integrity of its own, a unique emphasis and purpose; each has its own role to carry out within the larger rubric that goes by the name "religious education."

The above analogy can be pressed further to make the point that Inuits rarely speak in generalities when referring to snow. Anthropologists tell us that Inuits have approximately 100 specific words for snow. While our taxonomy of terms for religious education is less impressive numerically and differs from one religion to another, a specificity in its terminology has also developed over its centuries-old practice. Christian denominations, for example, use a variety of names to identify their educational activities. While Protestants practice Christian education, Sunday School, and Bible School, Roman Catholics refer to their educational efforts as religious instruction, catechesis, and Confraternity of Christian Doctrine (CCD). Such diversity should not be construed as a preference for a specific model of religious education. More often than not, the denominational name is either assumed to be synonymous with the more inclusive meaning of religious education, or a reduction of its meaning to one form of practice.

One cannot fully appreciate contemporary insights into the scope and significance of religious education without understanding the larger context from which it emerged in this century, and to which it remains indebted for its identity and mission. The chapter will begin with a prologue that lays out the larger scenario within which religious education moved to the center of the stage. It then surveys some of the influential texts that articulate contemporary views of professionals in the field. Criteria for their selection are based on three factors: first, the works reviewed in the chapter reflect a Christian theory and practice of religious education; second, the literature has been published within the past twenty years; and third, the resources discussed are restricted to books.

Another set of influences at work in the chapter relates to the agenda, experience, and perspective of the author. The works selected, and the interpretations derived from them, represent the view of one professional religious educator who has worked in both religious and secular contexts for some twenty-five years. While this experience lends confidence and a degree of competence to the project, it also bears the limitations imprinted by personal history, social location, formal education, and religious formation. The selection of only Christian authors[1] and omission of those from other religious traditions is but one indication of these influences.

Education in a Systemic Perspective

There is an array of educational forms practiced in our society. Besides schooling (which might be designated as its principle form), education goes on in homes, gymnasiums, and twelve-step programs; in television studios and on radio talk shows; in voluntary associations, the arts, literary societies, and the military service; in the workplace and marketplace; in national parks; at museums; in libraries; and in religious institutions. This awareness of educational diversity is a consequence of the more comprehensive understanding of education that has emerged in recent decades. Such is the major contribution of Lawrence Cremin, whose "latitudinarian" description of educational forms and contexts identifies and traces the educational activity of social institutions through three centuries. Cremin's three-volume series *American Education* (1970, 1980, 1988) chronicles the educational legacy of a large cross-section of cultural institutions in the United States, and ranks among the most respected contributions to such an evolutionary and systemic understanding of education. His inclusive vision is reflected and expressed most succinctly in his oft-cited definition of education as "the deliberate, systematic, and sustained effort to transmit, evoke, or acquire knowledge, attitudes, values, skills, or sensibilities, as well as any outcomes of that effort."[2]

Cremin's historical and philosophical contributions have left an indelible mark on contemporary educational theory and practice, and brought new credibility and relevance to "extracurricular" contexts in which teaching and learning are promoted and carried out. Thus, he both affirms and legitimates education sponsored by religious institutions. It is this contribution that makes Cremin's work relevant reading in religious education. While there are numerous historical works that offer such comprehensive descriptions of education as it is practiced in a variety of contexts, few are as respected as the following.

Resources on Education in a Systematic Perspective

Cremin, Lawrence. *American Education: The Colonial Experience.* New York: Harper & Row, 1970.

Cremin states, "This first [volume] begins with the transit of civilization from Old World to New carrying the story through the completion of independence and the efforts of Jefferson's generation to create an education truly 'adapted to the genius of the American people' " (p. xii).

——. *American Education: The Metropolitan Experience*. New York: Harper & Row, 1988.

This "third volume will consider a more recent experience of metropolitan America, stressing on the one hand the radical changes in the architecture of education wrought by the evolution of the new media of communication and on the other hand the essential changes in the nature of education wrought by the emergence of America as a world metropolis, or exporter of culture" (pp. xii–xiii).

Cremin's work was influenced by John Dewey, who put life at the center of the curriculum, the development of social competencies in the classroom, and the reconstruction of experience at the heart of education.

——. *American Education: The National Experience*. New York: Harper & Row, 1980.

This volume deals with "the educational endeavors of the young nation, starting with the multifarious schemes of Noah Webster and concluding with the august formulations of William Torrey Harris" (p. xii).

Dewey, John. *Democracy and Education*. New York: Macmillan, 1961.

——. *Experience and Education*. New York: Macmillan, 1963.

Because Dewey's philosophy of education laid the foundation for the development of the field of religious education, and continues to inform the work of professionals in the field, it seems appropriate to include a sampling of his prolific work in this survey.

Although Dewey's educational contributions focused primarily on children, his philosophy gave impetus to the formalization of educational opportunities for adults as well. These opportunities multiplied as advocates of lifelong learning urged adults to pursue continuing education.

Knowles, Malcolm. *The Modern Practice of Adult Education*. New York: Association, 1971.

The field of adult education emerged in the early decades of the twentieth century and gained momentum through the writings of Malcolm Knowles, particularly *The Modern Practice of Adult Education*.

The Religious Character of Education

The descriptor *religious* might suggest a form of education that is authorized and sponsored by religion. This explicit connection broke down at the end of the nineteenth century, however, as the meaning of *religious* was distinguished from "membership in organized religion." Developments leading to the Social Gospel Movement, the liberalization of Christian theology, and the rise of progressive education broke through more traditional distinctions of *sacred* and secular, leading to a reconstruction of the meaning of terms like *spiritual* and *religious*. Rather than pointing to the explicitly sacred dimension of experience, words such as *religious* expanded their capacity to describe any dimension of life that prompted attention and response to the transcendent.

At the turn of the century, a new appreciation of the inherent religious nature of education led religious educators to take a new look at, and draw upon, the work of philosophers like Alfred North Whitehead and John Dewey. Whitehead's assertion that education is potentially a religious activity, inspiring responses of duty and reverence,[3] gave articulation to new depths of meaning. John Dewey's philosophy, calling educators to focus on the learner, to be responsive to life experience, to practice holistic education, to empower students for an active role in society, to lead children to discover their world, and to encourage questioning and searching added a prophetic dimension to their role. Contemporary writers continue, explicitly and implicitly, to give visibility and attention to the religious dimension of education. Some of the more familiar works follow.

Resources on the Religious Character of Education

Freire, Paulo. *Pedagogy of the Oppressed*. New York: Continuum, 1983.
    An educator respected throughout the world, Freire offers a critical assessment of traditional education's complicity in the oppression of the poor in Third-World countries. The vision of education he presents in *Pedagogy* finds expression in a praxis-model that seeks to promote freedom, agency, and social transformation, and influenced liberation theology, contributing its mission to confront exploitation and oppression throughout Third-World countries. It has likewise challenged and revitalized the theory and practice of education in "developed" societies, as the realities of poverty, oppression, and exploitation become more visible and palpable realities.

Greene, Maxine. *Landscapes of Learning*. New York: Teachers College Press, 1978.
    In this collection of essays, Greene identifies and analyzes the oppressive forces at work in U.S. society. Influenced by Dewey and Freire, she calls education to its emancipatory role—"one that will free persons to understand the ways in which each of them reaches out from his or her location to constitute a common . . . world" (p. 7).

Harris, Maria. *Teaching and Religious Imagination: An Essay in the Theology of Teaching*. San Francisco: Harper & Row, 1987.
    Harris has focused on imagination as an essential, yet overlooked resource for teaching in many of her publications. In this book, she probes religion and imagination to uncover "the dreams and the hopes, the vision and the grandeur that lie at the core of teaching" (p. xi).

Moran, Gabriel. *No Ladder to the Sky: Education and Morality*. San Francisco: Harper & Row, 1987.
    In characteristic style, Moran engages in a dialectical analysis of traditional interpretations of education and morality derived from unexamined assumptions. He begins his analysis by asserting that he is not writing about moral education, but rather about the interactive

relationship between the educational and the moral, in which the moral is mediated through educational experience. Moran's precision and creativity in his use of language influences his selection of three metaphors (conquest, enlightenment, and growth) that relate contemporary moral questions to the wisdom in religious tradition.

Palmer, Parker. *To Know As We Are Known: A Spirituality of Education*. San Francisco: Harper & Row, 1983.
  Palmer's subtitle is an apt description of his book. Rejecting the notion of "knowing" tied to the acquisition of empirical data and the pursuit of objectivity, Palmer articulates a spirituality of education informed by a person-centered and holistic epistemology.

Phenix, Philip. *Education and the Worship of God*. Philadelphia: Westminster, 1966.
  In Phenix's perspective, religion is a comprehensive orientation to life, overcoming the artificial distinctions of sacred and secular, and education is a primary means of understanding the depths of meaning in any and every experience. In this book, Phenix explores the dynamic and coextensive relationship between faith and learning, and the role education can play in disclosing and directing responses to the Holy.

Emergence of Religious Education

The reconstruction of education that would later be characterized as "progressive" found affirmation in the ascendancy of liberal Protestant theology. Out of this context, the expanded meanings of religions and education fused in a movement that laid a unique claim to religious and educational traditions. The movement took its first steps in 1903, when hundreds of educators from secular and religious contexts gathered in New York City to found the Religious Education Association. The event marked the emergence of a conscious, unified, and purposeful resolve to forge an interactive partnership between religion and education directed

> to inspire the educational forces of our country with the religious ideal; to inspire the religious forces of our country with the educational ideal; and to keep before the public mind the ideal of Religious Education, and the sense of its need and value.[4]

There is a subtle reminder in the vision expressed in this statement of mission that all religions have a vested interest in education and that education necessarily includes religious dimensions. It calls religious bodies to respect the tradition of education and view it as a means of promoting their ends, and conversely calls the field of education to respect the contributions of religious traditions that foster learning. The partnership was secured by summoning members of both religious and educational contexts to found a new profession, religious education.

Transcending the boundaries of sacred and secular, this new rubric opened up possibilities and challenges for the scope, meaning, and practice of the field.

Some of the more significant possibilities and challenges are worthy of mention. The name underscores the common interest that all religions have in education. It implies that all religions are of value, affirms a colleagueship between those who work in secular and religious contexts, and gives additional leverage to educators in religious institutions by emphasizing their role as educators, and giving them new access to the larger tradition. This was especially significant given the influence of theology and the church on Christian education.

The founding of the REA, and the movement that is a cause and consequence of the event, set the stage for the development of contemporary literature of the field.

Resources on the Emergence of Religious Education

Schmidt, Stephen. *A History of the Religious Education Association*. Birmingham, AL: Religious Education Press, 1983.

In this work, commissioned by the REA, Schmidt introduces the key figures who have shaped its mission for eighty years, and analyzes their influence on the mission, priorities, and developing agenda of the REA.

Foundational Works in Religious Education

Although the vision of the architects of the religious education movement has yet to be realized, it continues to prod professionals in the field to take a deeper and broader view of their task. Contemporary religious education theorists continue to grapple with questions about the nature and purpose of the field, as those before them have throughout its eighty-year history. Questions persist about the location of religious education within the larger context of education, its identity and boundaries, the relevance and meaning of its purpose, and its viability and status as a profession. Scholars in the field continue to discern and describe what is unique and specific about the practice of religious education, to give definition to the field, and to develop a consistent language that clarifies its mission in our world. The depth of this inquiry makes for stimulating and informative reading. A sampling of the more substantive of these works follows.

Resources on Religious Education

Boys, Mary. *Educating in Faith: Maps and Visions*. San Francisco: Harper & Row, 1988.

Boys creates a map of the field of Christian religious education, sorting through its primary territories (evangelism, catechetics, Christian and Catholic education) and identifying the contributions of significant historical religious educators (Sara Little, Randolph C. Miller, Gabriel Moran, Ellis Nelson, and others). Boys concludes with her own vision of what it means to educate religiously. In her words, Boys acts as a cartographer mapping the field, and as a teacher of the art of cartography to assist others in setting forth their own understanding of the field.

Gangel, Kenneth O., and Warren S. Benson. *Christian Education: Its History and Philosophy.* Chicago: Moody Press, 1983. (Currently out of print.)

Writing from an evangelical perspective, Gangel and Benson present a historical overview of Western philosophy, and trace its influence on Christian religious education. The authors detail formative influences in the field, but provide less information about its present realities and future direction.

Groome, Thomas. *Christian Religious Education.* San Francisco: Harper & Row, 1980.

Groome's book is an account of his own experience as a religious educator and the critical reflection that transformed his approach. He begins with a reflection on his practice, raising foundational questions and uncovering his own assumptions about his work. He then responds to these questions, informed by contemporary resources in developmental theory, the social sciences, theology, philosophy, and education. Having established his framework, Groome crafts an approach that all religious educators might find helpful, a model that he calls "shared praxis." The book is a lucid, comprehensive, substantive, and well-organized contribution to the field.

Lee, James Michael. *The Content of Religious Instruction.* Birmingham, AL: Religious Education Press, 1985.

——. *The Flow of Religious Instruction.* Birmingham, AL: Religious Education Press, 1973.

——. *The Shape of Religious Instruction.* Dayton, OH: Pflaum/ Standard, 1971.

While James Michael Lee is something of a rebel in religious education circles, he is a proponent of the need for an adequate theoretical foundation for the enterprise. His trilogy marks a significant departure from other foundational works in the field. Instead of taking theology as his beginning point, Lee construct his "macrotheory" on a scientific base, arguing the merits of his social-science approach to the task. In his view, an empirical orientation, focused on religious "teaching and learning" activities, provides a more explicit, predictable, and measurable model of religious education. A clue to this orientation can be found in his emphasis on religious instruction, a form of religious education compatible with social science methodology that allows for "truly effective and integrative teaching practices and religious curricula" (quoted from the book jacket of *The Content of Religious Instruction*). Lee's influence on the field is also a consequence of his company, Religious Education Press, the only publisher of academic texts on religious education. For a listing of publications, write to: REP, 5316 Meadow Brook Road, Birmingham, AL 35242.

Lines, Timothy. *Systemic Religious Education*. Birmingham, AL: Religious Education Press, 1987.

Timothy Lines undertakes an ambitious project in this book. Rejecting traditional interpretations of theology, philosophy, and education as adequate foundations for a theory of religious education, the author grounds his vision in a systemic worldview, and uses an open system to describe religion, education, and religious education. This foundation, he asserts, is sufficiently inclusive, dynamic, and comprehensive to disclose the full-range of possibilities required for a relevant reconstruction of the enterprise. The work renders a two-fold service to the field: it offers a comprehensive and substantive introduction to the emerging worldview, with its ties to science, cybernetics, and systems theory; and it presents a compelling vision that gives the field new challenge and credibility.

Miller, Randolph Crump. *The Theory of Christian Education Practice*. Birmingham, AL: Religious Education Press, 1980.

Considered "after Coe, the most influential Protestant theorist of this century,"[5] Miller has long and persuasively argued that theology is the foundation on which to build a theory of religious education. In this book, he explores the meaning and implications of process theology for accomplishing this task. Readers might want to review an earlier work, *The Clue to Christian Education* (New York: Charles Scribner's Sons, 1952), in which Miller argues the merits of the socialization model for religious education. Such an approach posits that the community teaches through its lifestyle, values, and activities; and the religious educator functions as a facilitator, catalyst, orchestrator of experiences that hone and shape the religious identity of the congregation.

Moran, Gabriel. *Religious Education As a Second Language*. Birmingham, AL: Religious Education Press, 1989.

Judged by many to be one of the most sophisticated writers in the field, Gabriel Moran has worked for thirty years to articulate a definitive theory of religious education. Given his influence and stature, and the fact that many of his earlier works are out of print (*Interplay* [Winona, MN: St. Mary's Press, 1981] and *Religious Education Development* [Minneapolis, MN: Winston Press, 1983]), it seems appropriate to insert a brief summation of Moran's contributions before taking up his latest book.

Moran's former works cover an array of topics, including developmental theory, morality, adult education, and gender issues in religious education. Each work demonstrates how Moran uses his expertise in critical analysis to strengthen the foundations of religious education. Much of this is diagnostic, characterized by critical perspective, rigorous analysis, and a dialectical approach that challenges religious educators to examine their assumptions and to be more precise in identifying and describing them. Anyone at all familiar with Moran's work recognizes at least five recurring themes in his writing.

The first of these relates to the world's urgent need for religious education. Moran believes that much of our social and environmental disorder stems from inadequate education in religious matters. A second theme that runs throughout Moran's works is his belief that religion plays an influential and important role in individual and social life. This conviction leads him to a more circumscribed vision of religious education. Unlike Timothy Lines, Moran fixes the boundaries of the field at the borders of religious institutions. In his view, religions are the appropriate agents of such education, and those who carry out the task share a common mission. Moran argues that individuals and groups need to be grounded in a particular faith tradition, and that an important task of religious education is facilitating this process. He calls religious educators from all traditions to a shared sense of purpose in the following goal statement: "The aim of religious education is a greater appreciation of one's own religious life and less misunderstanding of other people's" (*Interplay*, p. 51).

A third focus of Moran's analysis is the dialectical relationship that needs to be promoted between the religious and the educational, a relationship in which each affirms and critiques the other. A fourth concern relates to the blurring of distinctions between the various forms that religious education takes in practice. Like Cremin, Moran emphasizes the pluriform practice of education. Despite his preference for schooling, he respects the educational significance of institutions such as family, community, work, and leisure. A fifth critical issue that Moran raises pertains to the need for practitioners in every religion to develop a precise and common language that specifies and unifies their unique educational activity. In his view, the lack of a uniform language weakens the effectiveness and relevance of the field, and erodes its credibility as a profession.

In *Religious Education As a Second Language*, Moran takes up the search for this language, one that is adequately specific and inclusive. He argues that specificity is necessary to distinguish the identity and purpose of religious education from the broader spectrum of "secular" educational activities. He goes on to say that the language must also be inclusive enough to transcend denominational dialects. In a style that has become characteristic of his approach to this task, Moran presses the dialectic from both ends to sift out a language that expresses the uniqueness of religious education and unites the efforts of all those who practice their profession in religious contexts.

O'Hare, Padraic, ed. *Foundations of Religious Education*. Ramsey, NJ: Paulist Press, 1978.

This volume is a collection of papers presented at a Boston College Symposium on an "Intra-Catholic Dialogue" on the Foundations of Religious Education in 1977. Four distinguished Roman Catholic theorists, Thomas Groome, James Michael Lee, Bernard Marthaler, and Gabriel Moran, offer their perspectives on the nature and purpose of religious education to promote conceptual clarity, which leads to effective and faithful practice.

————. *Tradition and Transformation in Religious Education*. Birmingham, AL: Religious Education Press, 1979.

O'Hare invites four professors of religious education to respond to the question, "How can religious education faithfully teach biblical and ecclesial truths, while at the same time transforming the world and reforming the church?"

Smart, James D. *The Teaching Ministry of the Church*. Philadelphia: Westminster, 1971.

Smart takes an ecumenical approach to Christian religious education, urging churches to base their approach on a shared theological vision rather than on the particular theological emphases of their denomination. He argues that Scripture represents the common ground for constructing a unified curriculum and practice.

Westerhoff, John. *Who Are We: The Quest for a Religious Education*. Birmingham, AL: Religious Education Press, 1978.

Westerhoff initiated work on this volume to commemorate the seventy-fifth anniversary of the Religious Education Association. Its theme, expressed in the subtitle, revisits foundational questions about the identity and mission of the field. Contributors include some of the founders of the field, such as George Albert Coe and William Clayton Bower, and contemporary guides, such as Gabriel Moran, C. Ellis Nelson, and Randolph Crump Miller.

Wilhoit, Jim. *Christian Education: The Search for Meaning*. Grand Rapids, MI: Baker, 1991.

An evangelical perspective on foundational questions about religious education.

Descriptive Surveys of Christian Religious Education

The inclusion of the word *Christian* lends a more restricted and precise meaning to religious education. This next section identifies some key texts that work from a Christian orientation. These works also take a more "latitudinal" approach in analyzing and describing the field in its Christian expression.

Resources on Christian Religious Education

Boylan, Anne M. *Sunday School*. New Haven: Yale University Press, 1988.

Boylan presents an historical account of how nineteenth-century institution-building correlated with economic and social changes in the

United States and England. She stresses that this building of institutions served as the political, economic, and religious backbone of this country. Boylan examines in depth the development of one such institution, the Sunday School, in five Protestant denominations. She reviews the origins of Sunday School, and its responsiveness to the changing educational and spiritual needs of children and adults.

Durka, Gloria, and Joanmarie Smith, eds. *Emerging Issues in Religious Education*. Mahwah, NJ: Paulist Press, 1976.
This work applies "models theory" to religious education. The editors invite fifteen experts in theology, liturgy, Scripture, education, and developmental psychology to propose, refine, construct, and evaluate traditional and new models that explicate the meaning of religious education.

Lynn, Robert, and Elliot Wright. *The Big, Little School*. Birmingham, AL: Religious Education Press, 1980.
This highly respected work traces the history of the Sunday School Movement from its British origins through its centuries of practice in the United States. In addition to its research value, the book offers insight into Christian education as it is understood and practiced today in Protestant denominations.

Mayr, Marlene, ed. *Does the Church Really Want Religious Education?* Birmingham, AL: Religious Education Press, 1988.
Mayr's inquiry arises from her perception that the church does not take religious education seriously. She solicits responses to her challenging question from ten professionals representing a cross-section of Christian denominations.

————. *Modern Masters of Religious Education*. Birmingham, AL: Religious Education Press, 1983.
Mayr invites twelve leading theorists in Christian religious education to tell their stories and to share how their personal experience shaped their beliefs about the field. In her introductory remarks, she reviews the criteria for her selection process: an explicitly Christian orientation; ten years of leadership in the post-World War II field; innovative, pioneering contributions to the field; and influence within the larger church institution. The work not only presents a fairly comprehensive introduction to the primary architects of the field; it "presents a rich and intimate tapestry of twentieth-century American Christianity as seen from the inside" (p. 2)—in other words, from its educational interests and agendas.

Moore, Mary Elizabeth. *Education for Continuity and Change*. Nashville, TN: Abingdon Press, 1983.
Influenced by process theology and philosophy, Moore believes that change is a fundamental dynamic to any tradition. Her process of "traditioning" leads her to seek and construct a new model of Christian religious education that affirms and draws from its roots in its response to the demands and realities of the present.

Seymour, Jack, and Donald Miller. *Contemporary Approaches to Christian Education*. Nashville, TN: Abingdon Press, 1982.

This descriptive work surveys the breadth of Christian contexts in which religious education is carried out. Using a wide-angle view, the authors identify and describe five models that represent distinctive understandings and approaches that Christians bring to their practice of religious education. These models are identified as religious instruction, faith community (socialization), spriritual development, interpretation, and liberation. The book is essential reading for anyone seeking background in the Christian tradition.

Specialized Literature in the Field

As religious education becomes respected as a field and established as a profession, distinct areas of specialization are beginning to appear. Specialized areas include: religious education for specific age groups such as senior citizens or early childhood; vocational interests such as faith development and its bearing on healthcare and the marketplace; moral responsibility and career choice; and family accountability. Other forms of specialization can be found in professional titles that include youth minister, spiritual director, coordinators of volunteer services, and leaders of worship.

Resources for the Religious Educator

Barber, Lucie W. *Teaching Christian Values*. Birmingham, AL: Religious Education Press, 1984.

Barber believes that values education will become increasingly relevant to the curriculum in religious education. She outlines four sections describing Christian values: interpreting the meaning of Christian values, approaches to teaching these values, the relationship of developmental theories in values education, and discussion of seven Christian values. Barber feels that her numerous graduate studies offer an important perspective that complement and assist the efforts of theologically-trained religious educators.

Bickimer, David Arthur. *Leadership in Religious Education: A Prehensive Model*. Birmingham, AL: Religious Education Press, 1992.

This text helps religious education administrators assess the quality and effectiveness of their leadership. Bickimer's choice of the term *prehensive* reflects his reliance on the philosophy of Alfred North Whitehead for his vision of leadership. Rather than emphasizing logic and sensory acumen, Bickimer stresses the necessity of grasping the whole picture. Intuition plays an important role in his model of leadership. While Bickimer's Christocentric focus may obscure the book's relevance for non-Christian religious educators, the wide-ranging scope of leadership issues that it addresses makes the book interesting reading for any administrator.

Giltner, Fern, ed. *Women's Issues in Religious Education.* Birmingham, AL: Religious Education Press, 1985.

Eight women from various denominations and institutions reflect on the influence and contributions of their sisters to the field of religious education, and share their concerns about the need for new models of leadership, curriculum, and relationships.

Lines, Timothy Arthur. *Functional Images of the Religious Educator.* Birmingham, AL: Religious Education Press, 1992.

Lines describes the multiple roles that are subsumed in the title "religious educator" through a set of images that reflect and direct the practitioner's personal and professional self-understanding. Some of these images include: parent, coach, critic, storyteller, artist, revolutionary, therapist, and minister.

Resources on Religious Education and Society

Boys, Mary C., ed. *Education for Citizenship and Discipleship.* New York: Pilgrim Press, 1989.

This book is the result of a three-year study to better understand the relationship between church and education in the United States. Boys engages an interdisciplinary, ecumenical group of six educators in a discussion ranging from how to interpret Christianity today to how to better educate for the future. Boys provides six essays of religious educators on how to love God and neighbor.

Evans, Alice, and Robert Evans. *Pedagogies for the Non-Poor.* Maryknoll, NY: Orbis Books, 1987.

A contribution to the struggle to apply the liberating and transforming educational methods of Paulo Freire to those who practice religious education in white, middle-class contexts. Eight case studies are presented, followed by commentaries, teaching guides, discussion questions, and lists of resources.

Hauerwas, Stanley, and John Westerhoff, eds. *Schooling Christians: "Holy Experiments" in American Education.* Grand Rapids, MI: William B. Eerdmans, 1992.

The volume consists of a series of reflections on the most effective and appropriate methods for the schooling of Christians in a liberal society. Arguing that a socialization approach to Christian education is inadequate if it does not promote a critical awareness of "whatever is false, dehumanizing, and contrary to Gospel practices," contributors explore "an alternative way of envisioning life in the U.S. and the ways Christian churches, families, and agencies of education might live faithfully in relationship to the social order" (p. viii).

McClelland, V. Alan, ed. *Christian Education in a Pluralist Society.* London: Routledge, 1988.

McClelland collects a series of essays that explore the overall influence of the church on the practice of education in England, providing specific information on the church's educational involvement in social contexts such as family, state schools, and church schools. He also discusses the church's educational influence in Northern Ireland, Scotland, and Wales.

Moore, Allen J., ed. *Religious Education As Social Transformation.* Birmingham, AL: Religious Education Press, 1989.

Moore attempts to reconstruct a social theory of religious education based on the vision of George Albert Coe and his successor, Harrison Elliott.[6] He identifies contemporary issues such as sex and race discrimination, ecological exploitation, economic injustice, and nuclear devastation that religious education needs to address and influence. Each chapter describes a particular social problem and "attempts to move the reader . . . to a new social vision and to explore how religious education can participate in the work of social transformation" (p. 4).

Plantinga, Theodore. *Public Knowledge and Christian Education.* Lewiston, NY: Edwin Mellen Press, 1988.

Contemporary epistemology calls for a resolution of the split between theory and practice in education. Plantinga applies this insight and challenge to Christian education.

Seymour, Jack, Robert O'Gorman, and Charles Foster. *The Church in the Education of the Public.* Nashville, TN: Abingdon Press, 1984.

The authors respond to their perception of an internally absorbed church with a domesticated educational practice by reasserting the original vision of the religious education movement. This vision calls for a redefinition of the church's role in society as a transformative public mission, with its educational efforts focused on "the mediation of a religious perspective on all matters affecting our personal and corporate welfare" (p. 153).

Slater, Nelle G., ed. *Tensions Between Citizenship and Discipleship.* New York: Pilgrim Press, 1989.

United in an effort to discern how Christian education might contribute more faithfully and effectively to a viable future, an eleven-member group of educators reflect on church life and education in the United States.

Resources on Religious Education Across the Life-Span

Durka, Gloria, and Joanmarie Smith, eds. *Family Ministry.* Minneapolis, MN: Winston Press, 1980.

The editors believe that the church and religious educators need to acknowledge the role and influence of family in the development of persons, church, and society. This book explores a model of family ministry responsive to this insight, a model grounded in a dynamic and authentic faith community.

Foltz, Nancy T., ed. *Handbook of Adult Religious Education*. Birmingham, AL: Religious Education Press, 1986.

Foltz invited experts in the field of adult education to assist in developing a theoretical framework for practicing adult religious education. The volume begins with a discussion of the meaning and basic principles of religious education with adults. A second section weaves the insights of developmental theory into these reflections. A third section takes up particular adult experiential situations, and offers suggestions for responding to these from a faith perspective.

Knox, Alan. *Helping Adults Learn*. San Francisco: Jossey-Bass, 1986.

This substantive work serves as a comprehensive guide to all aspects of planning, implementing, and conducting programs for adult learners. The book is a reference and a practical resource that is clearly written and well organized.

Leslie, Karen. *Faith and Little Children*. Mystic, CT: Twenty-Third, 1990.

Leslie urges preschool teachers to use the resource of parents in nurturing the faith of small children. After laying out the educational philosophy that supports this approach, Leslie suggests topics and activities that are appropriate for use in home and church.

McKenzie, Leon. *The Religious Education of Adults*. Birmingham, AL: Religious Education Press, 1982.

McKenzie begins with a critical examination and assessment of current church practice, and presents an alternative educational model informed by contemporary theory of adult education, adult development, and theology. In addition to its solid theoretical foundations, McKenzie's book is a valuable practical resource for implementing programs with adults.

Parks, Sharon. *The Critical Years: The Young Adult Search for a Faith to Live By*. San Francisco: Harper & Row, 1986.

Arguing that interpreters of faith development have paid little attention to young adults, Parks attempts to fill the void, drawing from her own experience in higher education. Parks calls for an holistic approach to the religious education of college students, emphasizing the role of imagination and symbols as primary resources of religious development.

Ratcliff, Donald, ed. *Handbook of Children's Religious Education*. Birmingham, AL: Religious Education Press, 1992.

This is a well-researched, tightly organized, comprehensive guide to the religious education of school-aged children. The first two chapters relate to the cognitive, social, and physical development of children, and perspectives on faith development from Jim Fowler and Fritz Oser. Chapter 3 explores how children conceptualize religious meanings and symbols. Chapter 4 considers moral development and affectivity. Later chapters discuss socializing the child in the group's religious identity, pertinent topics such as discipline and play, and specific educational methods that work well with children.

————. *Handbook of Preschool Religious Education*. Birmingham, AL:
Religious Education Press, 1988.

A well-researched and comprehensive guide to the religious education of children between three and six years of age, this handbook
draws upon the expertise of fifteen specialists to assist preschool
teachers and administrators. The handbook first takes up a discussion
of the mental, social, and physical development of preschoolers and
then presents a review of the research on religious development,
particularly moral and faith development. A third section considers
socialization approaches to the religious education of young children,
appropriate and effective teaching and evaluative methodologies for
use with this group, and special topics such as the significance of play
and creativity.

Robbins, Duffy. *The Ministry of Nuture*. Grand Rapids, MI: Zondervan,
1990.

This is a handbook to assist youth ministers in promoting "lived"
faith and authentic discipleship.

Vogel, Linda Jane. *The Religious Education of Older Adults*. Birmingham, AL: Religious Education Press, 1984.

In this book, Vogel presents her interpretation of a holistic approach
to lifelong learning, emphasizing the importance of promoting reflection
rather than imparting instruction. Vogel integrates insights from psychology, sociology, theology, and adult education into her educational
philosophy. Her work also contains practical suggestions for educating
seniors in Christian contexts.

White, James W. *Intergenerational Religious Education*. Birmingham,
AL: Religious Education Press, 1988.

White begins his book with a rationale for practicing intergenerational religious education. He demonstrates the need for such a model
through a contemporary analysis of social life that reveals changing
family structures, rigid patterns of age-separation, and an overempha-
sis on individualism resulting in experiences of isolation and insula-
tion. He further justifies intergenerational religious education by
pointing to biblical and ecclesial authorities as well as the social
sciences and developmental psychology. On these foundations, he constructs a total intergenerational parish program with detailed attention to goal-setting, curriculum, and evaluation.

Resources on Religious Education and Developmental Psychology

Aden, Leroy, David G. Brenner, and J. Harold Ellend, eds. *Christian
Perspectives on Human Development*. Grand Rapids, MI: Baker,
1992.

A handbook delineating developmental theory's relevance to spiritual development.

Berryman, Jerome. *Godly Play: A Way of Religious Education*. San Francisco: Harper & Row, 1991.

Berryman describes "godly play" as growth-enhancing experiences that enable us "to make discoveries about a whole web of relationships—with self, others, nature, and God—to nourish us all our life" (p. 12). He describes religious education as structured experiences that promote creative processes of communication in these four contexts.

Fowler, James. *Stages of Faith*. New York: Harper & Row, 1981.

Building upon the work of Erikson, Piaget, and other developmental psychologists, Fowler, a Methodist clergyman and professor of theology at Emory University, sets out to learn if and how persons grow in their faith. This book describes Fowler's understanding of faith, and the research showing that faith develops in stages throughout the life cycle. Of particular significance to religious educators, Fowler's contributions to the understanding of the developmental nature of faith have forged new connections with other disciplines, infused empirical research methods and perspectives into the field, effected a greater credibility within its ranks, and freshened the theological base on which it rests. Indeed, Fowler's influence can be seen somewhere in most of the contemporary literature coming out of the field. His most recent book, *Becoming Adult, Becoming Christian* (San Francisco: Harper, 1984), relates his model of faith development to the vocation of Christian discipleship.

Fowler, James, Karl Ernst Nipkow, and Friedrich Schweitzer, eds. *Stages of Faith and Religious Development: Implications for Church, Education, and Society*. New York: Crossroad, 1991.

Fowler, Nipkow, and Schweitzer facilitate a critical conversation about the developmental nature of faith with colleagues Sharon Parks, Gabriel Moran, John Hull, and Gloria Durka. Further insights into the editors' views of the processive nature of faith are presented as each responds to the hard questions posed by critical thinkers in the field.

Gilligan, Carol. *In a Different Voice: Psychological Theory and Women's Development*. Cambridge, MA: Harvard University Press, 1982.

Gilligan critiques Lawrence Kohlberg's theory of moral development. Her own research in moral development involved women and abortion. She found a pattern of responses that led her to conclude that, unlike Kohlberg's subjects, women base their moral decisions on the ethic of care and responsibility. This research has obvious implications for the practice of religious education.

Peatling, John. *Religious Education in a Psychological Key*. Birmingham, AL: Religious Education Press, 1981.

Peatling, whose work reflects Kurt Lewin's principles of topological psychology, blends the psychology of religion with basic psychological principles to develop a well-rounded religious education program. He defines context, procedure, and subject as the framework of Christian religious education, and states that, while educators have good intentions, the research is often inadequate.

Resources on Religious Education and Technology

Redell, Kenneth B. *The Role of Computers in Religious Education.* Nashville, TN: Abingdon Press, 1986.

In his study of the use of computers in religious education, Kenneth Redell presents the pros and cons of such technology. He suggests the type of computers to purchase and the most appropriate software to use in church contexts. He explains how computers can be used effectively in church administration and education, and warns of the disadvantages of computerizing religious education. Finally, he raises the obvious question: "Is the value of computer-assisted education consistent with the goals of religious education?"

Sarno, Ronald A. *Using Media in Religious Education.* Birmingham, AL: Religious Education Press, 1987.

Sarno tells how Jesus, by using a variety of teaching techniques (words, deeds, and examples), was the model of an effective communicator. Sarno's research provides a link between the traditional methods of teaching and modern media used in education today. This book provides a variety of effective educational media techniques to enhance Christian religious education, and stresses the importance of moral and ethical evaluation of movies and television programs used in this context.

Resources on Religious Education and the Local Church

Byrne, H. W. *Improving Church Education.* Birmingham, AL: Religious Education Press, 1979.

The author calls on diocesan offices of religious education to consider how they might more effectively assist parish religious educators. He urges these offices to educate themselves in the theory and practice of supervision and evaluation so they can apply this expertise in the service of education at the grassroots level.

Dalglish, William A. *Models for Catechetical Ministry in the Rural Parish.* Washington, DC: National Conference of Diocesan Directors of Religious Education, 1982.

While some may feel rural communities are impoverished by lack of professional leadership, Dalglish states that the ministry of catechesis is alive and well in rural parishes. He believes opportunities for educational ministry in these areas is limited only by the creativity of the religious educators at work there. Dalglish provides models of religious education programs to meet the needs in rural settings, but he states that the uniqueness of each rural parish requires a unique responsiveness in programs of religious education.

Foltz, Nancy T., ed. *Religious Education in the Small Membership Church*. Birmingham, AL: Religious Education Press, 1990.
Foltz wrote this book to encourage those who serve in small membership churches to recognize the educational implications of their ministry.

Rogers, Donald B., ed. *Urban Church Education*. Birmingham, AL: Religious Education Press, 1989.
Rogers selected expert contributors who present a variety of teaching models based on practical and effective religious education programs in urban settings.

Resources on Religious Education and Church Life

Barker, Kenneth. *Religious Education, Catechesis, and Freedom*. Birmingham, AL: Religious Education Press, 1981.
Barker engages in a critical analysis of the Christian (and particularly the Catholic) tradition of education with an eye to its understanding of, and concern for, the human struggle for emancipation. Specifically, he seeks "to disclose the various ways theorists propose freedom as a goal of religious education, to examine the reasons for the differences, and to ascertain if these differences are irreconcilable" (p. 12).

Browning, Robert, and Roy Reed. *The Sacraments in Religious Education and Liturgy*. Birmingham, AL: Religious Education Press, 1985.

———. *The Sacraments in Religious Education and Liturgy: An Ecumenical Model*. Birmingham, AL: Religious Education Press, 1990.
In their first volume, Browning and Reed, Methodist clergymen and seminary professors, assert that the sacramental experience can become the core of religious education and liturgy. In their view, such an approach would enhance the effectiveness of education and worship within the Christian community. The revised volume provides an introduction to contemporary sacramental theology in an ecumenical perspective, explores the human experience from which Sacraments take their meaning, and puts this into dialogue with Christian education and liturgy.

Hunter, David. *Christian Education As Engagement*. New York: Seabury, 1963.
In an introduction to the theological and educational rationale for the "new curriculum" within the Episcopal Church, Hunter contrasts the traditional child-centered model, that ministers to congregations where they are, with an adult-centered model that prepares them for the future, contrasting an education that transmits a message with one that inspires action.

Moynahan, Michael. *Once upon a Miracle: Drama for Worship and Religious Education*. Mahwah, NJ: Paulist Press, 1993.
The latest of several volumes that use drama and other artforms for religious education.

Schipani, Daniel S. *Religious Education Encounters Liberation Theology*. Birmingham, AL: Religious Education Press, 1988.

Schipani relies on the teachings of Paulo Freire who inspired liberation theologians with his philosophy of religious education. Schipani concentrated on Latin America as the focus of his work because of his origins, and because of the acceptance and development of liberation theology in that part of the world.

Authoritative Resources for Christian Education

Warren, Michael. *Sourcebook for Modern Catechetics*. Winona, MN: St. Mary's Press, 1983.

The appearance of the word *catechetics* in the title of this book gives clear indication that it is intended for Catholic readership. Warren solicits and presents suggestions for implementing the theology born of the Second Vatican Council in the practice of catechetics.

Wilhoit, Jim, and Leland Ryken. *Effective Bible Teaching*. Grand Rapids, MI: Baker, 1988.

Wilhoit and Ryken define effective instructive procedures for teaching the Bible. Their particular emphasis lies in their attention to contemporary scholarly approaches in Scriptural hermeneutics.

Reference Works

Cully, Iris, and Kendig Cully, ed. *Encyclopedia of Religious Education*. San Francisco: Harper & Row, 1990.

More than 200 experts in the field of religious education have contributed to this one-volume resource that contains 600 articles pertaining to every aspect of the field, from action-reflection to Zionism. This reference offers easy access to subjects of particular interest, and an indication of the scope and substance of the field.

Journals

Living Light. [c/o Department of Education, USCC, 3211 Fourth Street N.E., Washington, D.C. 20017] Quarterly.

An official publication of the Department of Education of the United States Catholic Conference, *Living Light* is intended to inform catechists and religious educators of developments in the field, and to promote a wider dialogue about issues and trends that bear on its future.

Religious Education. Journal of the Religious Education Association and the Association of Professors and Researchers in Religious Education. [409 Prospect St., New Haven, CT 065511-2177] Quarterly.

The premier journal for the field, *Religious Education* is the best way to gain access to the thinking of scholars in this profession, and to learn about current issues and developments.

Emerging Specializations

Given the varied forms and purposes within the field of religious education and the ongoing evolution of its theory and practice, it seems both appropriate and necessary to project some possibilities for future developments. These are a few categories, specialized emphases, and predictions that I discern on the horizon.

Religious educators may be drawn into public education as "secular" institutions recognize the importance of teaching students "about" religion. A new interest in the subject seems to be brewing within the broader culture. Whether the interest arises from a newfound fascination with religious phenomena or from contemporary assessments of its social effects and influence (for better or worse), religion has been and remains an integral part of culture and life.

Within educating institutions there is a renewed interest in relating subject matter and methods of inquiry. Interdisciplinary education makes room for religious perspectives in literature, science, philosophy, social studies, history, math, law, and medicine. The proliferation of new interdisciplinary programs in women's, environmental, and "American" studies holds concrete opportunities for religious educators who seek a more dialogical context in which to practice. As in the public schools, doing interdisciplinary religious education demands an ability to separate personal religious beliefs and affiliations from the professional responsibility to promote an understanding of, and respect for, the many traditions found in the world.

More collaboration is seen among groups that Gabriel Moran describes as interreligious (or ecumenical), intergenerational (or mixing age groups), and international (or multicultural). An illustration of these developments can be drawn from the graduate program in which I teach. What once was a rather homogenous student body of Caucasian, Roman Catholic members of religious orders of (primarily) women has become a more diversified group of students. I now find myself among a heterogeneous mix of believers and nonbelievers, from the local community in New Orleans to Ireland and South Africa, mostly Roman Catholic, but also Episcopalian, Unitarian-Universalist, Baptist, and members of the Church of Christ. Men are as likely as women to enroll. The demographics are indeed changing in graduate religious education programs, and this both reflects and affects what is happening at the grassroots.

Finally, and probably least visible within explicitly religious (i.e., congregational) contexts is a need for a more inclusive practice of religious education, what I term *interspecies* or *interplanetary* education.

Some movement in this direction can be observed in the integration of ecological perspectives and sensitivities into the vision and practice of religious education. From Thomas Berry's prophetic call for a radical reconstruction of the curriculum[7] to more modest efforts to speak more inclusively about creation, it is clear that the environmental movement's influence presents a new challenge to the field of religious education.

Conclusion

World-renowned theologian Fr. Hans Küng, during a lecture given at Loyola University in 1990 in New Orleans, made the statement, "There will be no world peace until there is religious peace." His remark was based on his belief that religion plays a major role in international relations, and that more often than not, it plays the role of agitator. Küng went on to say, "There will be no religious peace until religions learn how to be self-critical." Both of these remarks imply that religion's contributions to world affairs leaves much to be desired. They also point out that religions must practice and foster tolerance and understanding, an appreciation of plurality and diversity, and the recognition of personal and communal shortsightedness. While Küng does not lay these responsibilities at the door of religious education, his message seems to sum up the vision articulated in the more substantive literature of the field. Küng's challenge to religions has already been taken seriously by those who view education as the means to becoming self-critical, and religious traditions as contexts for promoting and practicing it.

This review of selected literature that reflects and shapes contemporary understanding of religious education has served its purpose if it evokes any or all of these responses in its readers: 1) a heightened understanding of the field, and an appreciation for the wide diversity of views, allowing for an intentional inclusivity of religious traditions and an openness to new possibilities in both theory and practice; 2) an increased respect for the scholarly nature of the literature, and for the wealth of perspectives that articulate the scope and substance of the field; 3) a renewed interest in the vision that religious education brings to the world; and 4) a shared commitment to collaborate in carrying out its mission.

Notes

1. Selectivity is also expressed in the choice of Christian authors whose works have been given a fuller treatment in the chapter. These authors tend to work from the liberal end of the theological spectrum. A more comprehensive account of the theory and practice of Christian religious education would give more attention to works representative of an evangelical and fundamentalist orientation.

2. Lawrence Cremin, *Traditions of American Education* (New York: Basic Books, 1977), 134.

3. Alfred North Whitehead, *The Aims of Education* (New York: Free Press, 1957), 14.

4. Quoted from a publicity brochure distributed by the Religious Education Association. Copies can be obtained by writing to REA, 1409 Prospect Street, New Haven, CT 06510.

5. Thomas Groome, *Christian Religious Education* (San Francisco: Harper & Row, 1980), 147.

6. Dr. George A. Coe, the founding father of the field of religious education, maintained that the aim of the enterprise was the transformation of society (read "U.S. Society") into the "Democracy of God." He insisted that the primary mission of religious education was tied to the establishment of God's reign or the coming of the Kingdom. This vision is the subject of his classic text *A Social Theory of Religious Education* (1919; reprint 1969 [New York: Arno Press and the New York Times, 1969]). Harrison Elliott was a later proponent of Coe's philosophy. See his *Can Religious Education Be Christian?* (New York: Macmillan, 1953). Elliott reasserted the social mission of religious education at a time when there was a heavy emphasis on the more explicitly "spiritual" purpose expressed in the theological language of faith in Jesus Christ.

7. See Berry's chapter 8, calling for and proposing of a model of radical curriculum revision in higher education in *The Dream of the Earth* (San Francisco: Sierra Club Books, 1988).

10
Devotional Classics for Church Libraries

The Rev. William M. Yount

The Meaning of a Christian Classic

There are many types of Christian devotional literature. Devotional calendars such as those of Oswald Chambers or John Bailey's *Diary of Prayer* provide daily readings of Scripture, prayer, and inspiration. There are contemporary literary classics as represented preeminently by C. S. Lewis in his *Mere Christianity*. Although more theological and even apologetic in nature, such works have been greatly appreciated by many for their inspirational value. Another genre is that of Christian fantasy literature, again represented by C. S. Lewis in his *Chronicles of Narnia*, or the work of J. R. R. Tolkien. There are others that are more deeply theological such as J. I. Packer's *Knowing God*. This book, by an orthodox Anglican scholar, provides both depth of theological insight and practical application. Indeed, these and others might well be termed "contemporary classics." But the focus of this bibliographical essay is upon those works that have demonstrated themselves to be monuments of Christianity by their approval over the span of generations.

To call any work, whether a piece of visual art, music, or especially literature, a "classic" is to speak of its timeless appeal. There is in the classic an objective quality that transcends the limits of time and place and, to a great extent, culture. In this sense, it is genuinely universal. Such a work earns the honor of being called classic because it reflects the deepest emotions and aspirations shared by all. Indeed, people turn to the classics because this genre of literature represents the human situation in all its vagaries and inconsistencies.

Thus, the classics are products of the human spirit that instruct, encourage, and bring perspective to what it means to live life properly and to its fullest.

It should not be surprising that the history of Christianity is characterized by a literature rich in its universality. This is not to say that the Christian tradition does not have its share of popular "successful living," "positive-thinking," and "prosperity-through-peace" books. Just look at the bookstore shelves today! But the Christian tradition has provided many worthwhile books with permanent value. The problems to which they speak, the emotions they display, the truths they discover and seek to share are those common to Christians throughout the generations. They quicken the mind, inspire the spirit, and lift the soul. This is, after all, the purpose of devotional literature.

Devotional literature is not a substitute for the Bible, but the Bible does authorize Christians to encourage each other. And this encouragement has taken many forms. There is, for example, the literature of self-revelation, such as St. Augustine's *Confessions*, or the *Journals* of John Wesley and John Woolman. Sometimes the literature of devotion is more directly instructional, giving rules and examples for Christian living. Such is the style of Thomas à Kempis in his *Imitation of Christ*, William Law's *A Serious Call to a Devout and Holy Life*, and Jeremy Taylor's *Holy Living*. Sometimes Christian writers are not intentionally "devotional" at all, but purely theological or even polemical as is the *Apologia* of John Henry Cardinal Newman. However, because these writers plumb the depths of understanding and soar to heights of praise, they have been read over and over again. Or these devotional classics may even be documents that have defined and influenced Christian thought in such a way that, as Ferm (1959) says, their work occupies a "conspicuous place" in the history of the discipline. Such works are Martin Luther's *On Christian Liberty* and John Calvin's *Institutes of the Christian Religion*. Thus, some books are worth reading not only because of their literary merit or emotional appeal, but quite simply, because they must be continually read if those truths that define the Christian faith are to be preserved and maintained.

The purpose of this essay is to review the bibliographical and interpretative resources on the classics of Christian devotional literature. The first part of this work is a bibliographic survey of books or collections of articles that provide scholarly interpretations of the most significant works of Christian literature. Collections, anthologies, and devotional books in series are also surveyed as are a number of recent bibliographical guides. The second part of this study consists of a brief introduction to ten of the most significant works of classical Christian devotion, selected on the basis of their inclusion in almost every bibliography of religious literature. Each introduction includes a brief biographical sketch of the author; the historical setting and occasion of the work; a general overview of the contents, structure, and literary style; and areas of possible criticism. As many can testify, there can be no substitute for the personal reading and enjoyment of each of these great works. The purpose of the survey is merely to introduce the work and hopefully whet the appetite of prospective readers. As John T.

McNeil expressed it, "Great books, even the greatest, would be neglected by many of those who ought to read them if they were not from time to time brought to notice in slighter and more ephemeral ones" (1947, vii). So, it is hoped that this review of the literature will encourage the reader to discover the greatness of the classics of Christian devotion.

Bibliographical Essays

Scholarly Essays and Interpretations

Among the most helpful resources for a scholarly introduction to the classics of Christian literature are anthologies of critical and interpretative essays. As would be expected in resources on the classics of Christian devotion, there is overlap in the selections of each of these guides. But each is also unique enough to allow a significant contribution to the understanding of the works selected. These scholarly interpreters tend more toward the theological classics, perhaps reflecting their interest in the substantive content of the literary piece and its significance to the development of Christian thought. These also serve as an indication of which works the most learned scholars of this century have considered most deserving of the title "classic." It is interesting also to observe that these scholarly essays were originally written between the years 1945 and 1955, perhaps reflecting a time when the Christian classics enjoyed a greater appreciation than they do in our increasingly secular and global society. It is, however, precisely in these monuments of Christian devotion that there might again be found fulfillment for our deepest needs.

Brown, Juanita., ed. *An Introduction to Five Spiritual Classics*. New York: Woman's Division of Christian Service, Board of Missions of The Methodist Church, c.1955.
  This collection of essays, edited by Juanita Brown for the Woman's Division of Christian Service of the Board of Missions of The Methodist Church, is probably less well known than others of this literary genre. This delightful book was originally planned as an introduction and study guide for the Methodist Woman's study groups, but it is of permanent value for a far wider audience. This 194-page exposition still yields meaningful insights into the greatest of the devotional classics. Included are expository essays by five women: Louise Killingsworth discusses the *Confessions* of St. Augustine; Florence Hooper writes on Thomas à Kempis's *The Imitation of Christ*; Lillian Warrick Pope contributes a chapter on Nicholas Herman's (Brother Lawrence) *The Practice of the Presence of God*; Pearle Tibbetts treats William Law's *A Serious Call to a Devout and Holy Life*; and Helen Patten Hanson discusses Thomas R. Kelly's *A Testament of Devotion*. A biographical sketch of each of the contributing authors is included, as is a fine bibliography, "Books About the Classics and Their Authors."

Martin, Hugh. *Great Christian Books.* c.1945; reprint, Freeport, NY: Books for Libraries, 1971.

This series of interpretative essays, only 128 pages long, considers such theologians as St. Augustine, Samuel Rutherfurd, Brother Lawrence, John Bunyan, William Law, William Carey, and Robert Browning. Martin's own introductory essay, "The Power of the Book," is itself a genuine contribution to the literature of understanding the nature and value of the classics. The author's analysis draws extended selections from each of the subjects considered; in this respect, the work approaches an interpretative anthology. The book includes bibliographical notes and an index.

McNeil, John T. *Books of Faith and Power.* New York: Harper & Brothers, c.1947.

Renowned church historian and Calvin scholar John T. McNeil first presented this material as a series of lectures on the "Protestant Classics" at the Jewish Theological Seminary in New York in 1945. The lectures were later published as *Books of Faith and Power.* The work consists of six essays that include a brief sketch of the author's life, a digest of the literary piece, and interpretative commentary. The essays are on the following works: Martin Luther's *On Christian Liberty,* John Calvin's *Institutes of the Christian Religion,* Richard Hooker's *The Laws of Ecclesiastical Polity,* John Bunyan's *The Pilgrim's Progress,* William Law's *A Serious Call to a Devout and Holy Life,* and John Wesley's *Journal.* These classics writes McNiel, "justly claim a prominent place among those which express basic elements of the Christian tradition" (vii).

Peer, Allison E. *Behind That Wall: An Introduction to Some Classics of the Interior Life.* London: S. C. M. Press, 1947.

The serious student of the classics also will find this work interesting. Peer provides fourteen expositions of Medieval monastic and mystic authors, and three Anglican writers. The chief focus is a literary analysis of the works cited. These include works of St. Augustine, St. Bernard, Ramon Lull, Jan van Ruysbroeck, St. Ignatius of Loyola, St. Peter of Alcantara, St. Teresa of Jesus, St. John of the Cross, St. Francis of Sales, Jeremy Taylor, Henry Vaughan, and Thomas Traherne. Bibliographies and an index are included.

Sperry, Willard L., ed. *Classics of Religious Devotion.* Boston: Beacon Press, 1950.

This is one of the finest anthologies of scholarly essays on the classics of religious literature. As the title indicates, the scope of its six essays go beyond the Christian faith. Sperry himself contributed an analysis of Thomas à Kempis's *Imitation of Christ.* He enlisted a cadre of other Harvard Professors to lend their wisdom in helping the reader understand many of the great literary divines. John Wild, professor of philosophy, contributed a piece on St. Augustine's *Confessions*; one of the most insightful interpretations of Bunyan's *Pilgrim's Progress* was written by Perry Miller, the renowned professor of American literature;

and Henry J. Cadbury, Hollis professor of Divinity, wrote an article on John Woolman's *Journal*. Other contributors are Frederick M. Eliot, on Albert Schweitzer's *Out of My Life and Thought*; and Berly D. Cohon, with an exposition of Moses Maimonides's *Guide for the Perplexed*.

Devotional Anthologies

Connell, J. M. *A Book of Devotional Readings from the Literature of Christendom*. London: Longmans, Green, 1913.

Among the older anthologies, this book contains quotations from 114 authors in a chronological arrangement. It also contains some material from authors outside the Christian tradition.

Ferm, Vergilius. *Classics of Protestantism*. New York: Philosophical Library, c.1959.

The scope of this collection of selections from a number of devotional and theological sources is limited to classics in Protestant history, but it includes extended selections from seventeen devotional and theological treatises. This anthology begins with the anonymous *Theologica Germanica*, first written about 1350, and published by Martin Luther in 1516 and again in 1518. Thoroughly representing the gamut of Protestantism, however, Ferm's anthology continues with selections from the Reformed thought of Martin Luther and John Calvin, the Pietism of William Law, the Methodism of John Wesley, Schleiermacher's and Ritschl's brands of classical liberalism, Kierkegaard's Christian existentialism, William Ralph Inge's mysticism, and Karl Barth's Neoorthodoxy, among others. With only brief introductions to each selection, the chief value of this collection is its inclusion of those works that the editor sees as "conspicuous in Protestant history" (p. 2).

Harkness, Georgia, comp. *A Devotional Treasury from the Early Church*. Nashville, TN: Abingdon, 1968.

According to Harkness, the purpose of this collection is to make available some excerpts from the rich treasure of Christian devotion found in the writings that have been preserved for us from the earliest days of the Christian church. Restricted to works through the second century, Harkness selects devotional writings "which lie just beyond the close of the biblical canon," and in some cases, from those books that "came very near being included in the Bible," yet remain largely unfamiliar (p. 12). Harkness's introduction includes five ways in which these devotional materials may be used in personal and public worship.

Kepler, Thomas Samuel. *An Anthology of Devotional Literature*. 1947; reprint, Grand Rapids, MI: Baker, 1977.

In developing his *Devotional Resource Guide* (1986), Joseph D. Allison indicates his indebtedness to this massive volume, which he says "might be more accurately called a reference book than an anthology" (p. 53).

Kepler was himself a serious student of the Christian classics, having written more than a score of books on the subject, including individual works on Martin Luther (1952), the *Theologica Germanica* (1952), John Woolman (1954), and Evelyn Underhill (1962). He is also the author of a *Bibliography on Mysticism* (1957).

———. *Bibliography on Mysticism*. Boston: General Theological Library Bulletin, vol. 49, no. 2, February 1957.

———. *The Evelyn Underhill Reader*. New York: Abingdon Press, 1962.

———. *The Journal of John Woolman*. Edited with an introduction by Thomas S. Kepler. Cleveland, OH: World, 1954.

More, Paul Elmer, and Frank Leslie Cross, comps. *Anglicanism*. 1935; reprint, London: SPCK, 1962.
First published in 1935, the purpose of this anthology of seventeenth-century Anglican Literature is to illustrate the theology of Anglicanism from its literary sources.

Scott, Robert, and George Gilmore, eds. *Selections from the World's Devotional Classics*. 10 vols. New York: Funk & Wagnalls, 1916.
This ten-volume set is the most extensive anthology of devotional literature up to early in this century. This set of pocket-sized books is arranged chronologically, and represents sixty-four of the most outstanding Christian writers from the second through the nineteenth centuries. A brief biographical sketch of each author is given. Another special feature is a list of authors and sources of prayers.

Stuber, Stanley Irving, ed. *The Christian Reader: Inspirational and Devotional Classics*. New York: Association Press, 1952.
This collection includes selections from thirty-three Christian divines, with selections from Jesus and St. Paul to Tolstoy and Rauschenbusch. It is arranged chronologically, with brief biographical surveys.

William, Michael. *Anthology of Classic Christian Literature*. 1933; reprint, New York: Tudor, 1937.
This work, perhaps the best (though older) one-volume work of its kind, provides an excellent sample of the most distinguished literature of this genre. It also contains an extended introduction to Christian classics.

Devotional Manuals

Bouquet, A. C., comp. *A Lectionary of Christian Prose from the II to XX Century*. London: Longmans, Green, 1939.
This manual consists of devotional selections covering the second to the twentieth centuries. It is valuable for use in both private and public worship.

Inge, William Ralph. *Freedom, Love and Truth: An Anthology of the Christian Life.* London: Longmans, Green, 1936.

This is one of the first of a number of devotional manuals arranged topically. Drawing from mystical and Anglican traditions, Inge collects devotional reflections under such headings as "The Necessity of Religion," "Thoughts About God," "Jesus Christ," "The Fruits of the Spirit," "The Inner Life," "Life's Pilgrimage," "The Journey's End," and "Worship." Especially helpful for the student of devotional literature is the author's introductory survey of the impact of Christianity on society throughout the ages. Also interesting is his presentation of the criteria for his selection from various Christian writers. A work of almost 350 pages, an index of its 122 cited authors is also included.

Neufelder, Jerome M., and Mary C. Coelho, eds. *Writings on Spiritual Direction: By Great Christian Masters.* New York: Seabury, 1982.

This more recent publication includes an extended bibliography of individual devotional works and an index.

Potts, J. Manning, comp. *Listening to the Saints: A Collection of Meditations from the Devotional Masters.* Nashville, TN: Upper Room, 1962.

This book is divided into sixteen sections covering the traditional theological groupings such as "God," "Jesus Christ," "Man and Sin," "The Grace of God," and others. The thought of most of the great devotional writers is represented. The reader will find this book especially useful not only for its topical arrangement, but also because it contains a section on "Devotional Suggestions," in which many of the saints of old give guidance in the practice of devotional reading.

Devotional and Theological Books on the Life of Christ

Bibliographical Guides of Wilbur M. Smith

Dr. Wilbur M. Smith is recognized as one of twentieth-century America's greatest Evangelical scholars. For many years, Dr. Smith was editor of *Peloubet's Selected Notes* (for Sunday Schools), and was also a renowned Bible conference speaker. Smith was professor of English Bible at the Moody Bible Institute (1937–1947) and Fuller Theological Seminary (1947–1963), and was Professor Emeritus at Trinity Evangelical Divinity School until his death in 1976. His many years of service as pastor, teacher, apologist, and author are documented in his autobiography, *Before I Forget* (1971).

Among Dr. Smith's talents is a vast knowledge of the whole field of bibliography, especially Christian bibliography. His autobiography is full of references to unusual and little-known scholarly Christian books. He also has whole chapters on his work as a bibliographer and about the many books in his personal library, which numbered more than 25,000 volumes! One of Smith's bibliographies that is particularly helpful for the present topic is "Suggestions for Readings in the Great Christian Classics," which appears in his *A Treasury of Books for Bible*

Study (1960). In this essay, Smith evidences a broad grasp of the books dealing with the influence of Christianity upon both world and Western literature. In one section of this work, he presents a bibliographic survey of some outstanding guides to devotional literature. Although this piece is somewhat dated, it does list some of the most significant older works in the field.

Another quite remarkable feature of this bibliographic essay is Smith's compilation of a list of authors and literature for further reference. This list includes 180 authors, spanning six time periods from the early church fathers to the mid-twentieth century. In developing this list, Smith writes:

> During the sixteenth, seventeenth and eighteenth centuries, the larger number of the more influential writers were not only devout Christians, but wrote extensively on Christian themes. This has not been true since at least the dawn of the nineteenth century. As Gilbert Highet has said, "Christianity has been hated and despised by many of the most ardent lovers of the classics during the nineteenth century." Early in 1951, the *New York Times* published an article on "The One Hundred Greatest Books of the Last One Hundred Years, 1851–1951." A careful study of this list will reveal that not ten of these authors were Christians, and the majority were actually enemies of the Christian faith. (1960, p. 279)

Smith also includes a list of literature for further research on the Christian authors he has listed, as well as literature on hymnody and prayer books. Indeed, the scope of this entire essay is perhaps broader than that envisioned in the present work, but it is one in which the serious reader may find a number of additional avenues to pursue.

This does not exhaust the contribution by Wilbur Smith to guidance in reading the classics of Christian literature. In "Ten of the Greatest Christian Books: A Suggested List" (*Alliance Weekly* 1950), Dr. Smith presents a survey and evaluation of those books he considers to have been the most valuable through the ages. This list favors books of a more genuinely theological nature. His selections are also unique in that he includes a number of the most significant theological treatises and devotional works on the life of Christ. Smith writes:

> More books have been written regarding the life, and work, and character of Christ than have been written about any eight other individuals together in the history of the world. There must be at least 50,000 volumes written concerning the Lord Jesus. (P. 581)

And it should be remembered that Smith's estimate was made in 1950. Much more has been added to this body of literature since that time. But the early date of Smith's survey of this literature does not diminish its enduring value. Indeed, some of these works are still considered classics, not only because of their inspirational value, but because of their definitive interpretations of the nature of Christ's person and work. Because of his distinguished scholarship in this field, Smith's estimates of these books are worth extensive citation. All of these classical works on the life of Christ have appeared in numerous editions.

Edersheim, Alfred. *The Life & Times of Jesus the Messiah*. Rev. ed.
  (illus.) New York: A.D.F. Randolph, [1883]; reprint, Peabody, MA:
  Hendrickson, 1993.
    This work has gone through at least eight editions. Edersheim was
a nineteenth-century Jewish-Christian. He studied theology at the
Universities of Edinburgh and Berlin. At the age of twenty-one, he was
ordained to the Presbyterian ministry. In 1875, he became a clergyman
of the Church of England, lecturing at Oxford from 1884 to 1889. "In
some ways," writes Smith of this epochal work, "this book will probably
never be surpassed."

> It is especially valuable in showing how Jewish customs of
> Christ's day, and contemporary Hebrew literature, illumi-
> nate the acts of our Lord and many of the teachings which
> were uttered by His holy lips. (1950, p. 581)

Krummacher, Friedrich Wilhelm. *The Suffering Savior: Meditations
  on the Last Days of Christ*. Translated by Samuel Jackson. Boston:
  Gould and Lincoln, [1854/1855]; reprint, Chicago: Moody Press,
  1947.
    This work has been reprinted many times. This is probably the most
thorough study of the death of Christ ever written. It originally appeared
in German in 1854, but has appeared in many English editions. Indeed,
Dr. Smith himself edited the version that appeared in the Wycliffe
Series of Christian Classics published by Moody Press. Smith writes:

> It is generally acknowledged that Krummacher was the
> greatest of all preachers on continental Europe in the middle
> of the nineteenth century. This volume will send one to his
> knees. There is nothing to compare with it in our language—
> covering every aspect of the death of Christ as set forth in
> the Gospels. (1950, pp. 581-82)

Lange, John Peter. *The Life and Times of the Lord Jesus Christ*. 4 vols.
  Edinburgh, Scotland, 1872.
    Probably the most monumental documentation of the life of Christ,
the last two volumes were edited by New Testament scholar Marcus
Dods. Smith praises these volumes:

> These volumes are by one of the outstanding conservative
> theologians and New Testament scholars of the last half
> century in Germany. . . . The work is profound, theological,
> reverent, tremendously suggestive, exhaustive, occasionally

perhaps a little tedious, but never failing to move and inspire the careful reader. Indeed, [this is] so much so that one cannot read more than twenty or thirty pages of the work at a time. I have found, in referring to this work during the years, that comparatively few people in our country know of it, which leads me to lay added stress upon its greatness. I do not know anything to compare with it in this particular field. (1950, p. 581)

Liddon, Henry Parry. *The Divinity of Our Lord and Savior Jesus Christ: Eight Lectures Preached Before the University of Oxford in the Year 1866, on the Foundation of the Late Rev. John Bampton.* London: Rivingtons, 1867; reprint, Minneapolis, MN: Klock and Klock, 1978.

This work has gone through more than eighteen editions. Smith writes that this essential work, comprised of the Bampton Foundation lectures for 1866, "is without doubt the greatest single volume ever written in any language on the deity of the Lord Jesus Christ" (1950, p. 566). He also writes:

Liddon knew all the arguments that had ever been raised against Christ's deity. He passed by the trivial ones, but he devoted his great mind and burning heart to the great questions, and his book has restored faith and confidence in thousands of lives in the years that have passed since the book was first issued. (1950, p. 566)

Morgan, George Campbell. *The Crises of the Christ.* Old Tappen, NJ: F. H. Revell, 1903; reprint, 1989.

This classic has also gone through at least eight editions. Another of the landmark books on the life of Christ, this was written by one of the greatest preachers of the twentieth century. In this brilliant work, Morgan dares to bring perceptive synthesis to diverse portions of Scripture. His observations illuminate the transition, or that which Morgan calls the "crisis" events in the life of the Lord. The grand and lofty discernments of this book will enrich the meaningfulness of Christ's life for minister and layperson alike.

Two other important works mentioned by Smith are *The Lord's Prayer for Believers: Thoughts on St. John XVII*, by Marcus Rainsford, 5th ed. (London: Thynne and Jarvis, [1900]), and Alexander Whyte's now classic six-volume *Bible Characters* (Edinburgh: Oliphant, Anderson and Ferrier, [1902]; reprint, Grand Rapids, MI: Zondervan, 1967).

Smith also recommends these important books on the life and work of Christ: George Smeaton's *The Doctrine of the Atonement as Taught by Christ Himself* (Edinburgh: Tand T. Clark, 1868; reprint, Grand Rapids, MI: Zondervan, 1953), and *The Apostle's Doctrine of the Atonement* (Edinburgh: Tand T. Clark, 1870; reprint, Carlisle, PA: Banner of Truth Trust, 1991); and James Stalker's brief outline on *The Life of Jesus Christ* (Edinburgh: T. and T. Clark, 1879; reprint, Zondervan, 1983), and *The Trial and Death of Jesus Christ: A Devotional History of Our Lord's Passion* (New York: Hodder and Stoughton, 1894; reprint, Zondervan, 1970), both of which are suited for laypersons, the former being useful as a study guide.

There are other theological treatises by the early church fathers on the nature and work of Christ that have already found a permanent place in the history of Christian literature. These are important for both their conclusive formulation of orthodox doctrine, and also for their inspirational character. Among these should be mentioned St. Athanasius's *The Incarnation of the Word of God* (325 A.D.), and St. Anselm's *Why God Became Man* (1098 A.D.). The standard texts of the church fathers is J. P. Migne's *Patrologiae Cursus Completus, Series Latina* (Paris, 1844–1855 [221 vols.]), and *Patrologiae Cerus Completus, Series Graeca* (Paris, 1857–1866 [161 vols.]). The most available English translations are found in Philip Schaff and Henry Wace's *A Select Library of Nicene and Post-Nicene Fathers of the Christian Church* (Buffalo, NY: T. and T. Clark, 1886–1900 [28 vols.]; reprint, Grand Rapids, MI: William B. Eerdmans, 1952–1957 [14 vols.]). Many individual works of the church fathers also have been reprinted. For further information and standard translations, see Johannes Quasten's *Patrology* (Westminster, MD: Newman Press, 1950–1986 [9 vols.]). The layperson should not be intimidated by the classical theological treatises of the church fathers, and certainly every minister should read them instead of reading about them. The reader will often find the works of the church fathers less tedious, more theologically understandable, and even more practical than most of the books concerning the atoning work of Christ that are on the shelves today.

Some Standard Bibliographical Guides

Cave, Alfred, comp. *An Introduction to Theology: Its Principles, Its Branches, Its Results, and Its Literature.* Edinburgh: T. & T. Clark, 1896.

This bibliography comes from an era when theological literature was much better defined. The serious student should become familiar with this work for its comprehensive overview of the nature and literature of theology. There are only a few pages devoted to devotional books, but those works listed are the most significant up through the late nineteenth century.

Clarke, Jack A., ed. *The Reader's Advisor: A Layman's Guide to Literature.* 12th ed. 3 vols. New York: R. R. Bowker, 1977.

This is a standard reference guide to all areas of literature. Especially helpful for devotional literature are the sections (in volume 3), "Prayer Books" and "Religious and Contemplative Anthologies." The latter contains brief annotations on twenty-eight contemporary (c.1940–1970) collections of chiefly religious verse and prayers. Also of help is the section titled "Religious Leaders, Reformers and Thinkers," which surveys "standard classical works of inspiration." It contains annotated entries to fifty-eight specific classical and contemporary religious thinkers, including brief biographical sketches and important books about each author. Especially significant is the listing of standard editions of classical devotional texts. This reference guide should always be a first source for the serious inquirer.

Hurst, John Fletch. *Literature of Theology: A Classified Bibliography of Theological and General Religious Literature.* 1986; reprint, Boston: Milford House, 1972.
   Among the bibliographic guides most familiar to the theological librarian is this standard of the late nineteenth century. Based on his earlier *Bibliotheca Theologica* (1882), this work was "designed to be a systematic and exhaustive bibliography of the best and most desirable books in theology and general religious literature published in Great Britain, the United States, and the Dominion of Canada" (p. v). It is indispensable for the historical study of all types of devotional literature before the twentieth century. Of special interest are the sections "Devotional Works," "Religious Poetry," "Practical Religion," and "Prayer." The work includes author-subject indexes, and an alphabetical list of personalities in a "Bibliography of Religious Biography." This monumental work consists of more than 12,000 titles listed in 757 pages.

Some Recent Bibliographical Guides

In the past few decades, a number of general bibliographic guides for the Christian reader have appeared. Most of them have come from the evangelical presses, and they often include brief essays on the value of reading great Christian books. They also usually include lists of suggested Christian devotionals or Christian classics.

Allison, Joseph D. *The Devotional Resource Guide.* Nashville, TN: Thomas Nelson, 1986.
   This work, one of the most recent bibliographic guides, lists scores of individual titles under ten different rubrics: devotional classics, inspirational books, daily devotions, inspirational poetry, Christian fiction and allegories, books of prayer, Christian biographies and auto-biographies, journals and journal-keeping, discipleship resources, and family worship resources. Almost all citations have brief annotations, and there is an informative essay introducing each of the literary devotional motifs.

Batson, Beatrice. *A Reader's Guide to Religious Literature.* Chicago: Moody Press, 1968.
   One of the best general introductions to the history of classical devotional literature, this work is 174 pages in length, and surveys the history of religious literature from the Middle Ages and Renaissance

(St. Augustine and Dante) to the twentieth century (T. S. Eliot, C. S. Lewis, Charles Williams, Dorothy Sayers, and J. R. R. Tolkien). This work also provides brief historical sketches of the authors cited, a summary of their works, an index, and an extensive bibliography.

Branson, Mark Lau, comp. *The Reader's Guide to the Best Evangelical Books.* San Francisco: Harper & Row, 1982.

Branson, the editor of the *TFS Bulletin* (Theological Student's Fellowship), has compiled this guide on the Christian life, including entries on such topics as discipleship, spirituality, biography and testimony. Another section is titled "Inspirational and Gift Books." Annotations are uneven; some are quite extensive while others are very brief. An interesting special feature of this guide is a listing of the favorite books of fifty-four leaders of the contemporary church, who identify the five most influential books in their personal lives and a second five books most important in their professional lives.

Ferguson, Sinclair B. *Read Any Good Books?* Carlisle, PA: Banner of Truth Trust, 1992.

This booklet, an extended essay on the value of reading good books, is one of the most recent in this genre of guides for the Christian reader. A brief list of books published by the Banner of Truth Trust, which specializes in books of a distinctively reformed theological perspective, is appended.

Grier, W. J., comp. *The Best Books: A Guide to Christian Literature.* London: Banner of Truth Trust, 1968.

The section titled "Spiritual Classics and Titles by Some Leading Christian Authors" contains thirty-eight annotated entries of devotional classics in the Puritan tradition. A special feature is "Books for Boys and Girls," which includes Bible stories, biographies of great Christian leaders, and missionary stories.

Hinson, E. Glenn. *The Doubleday Devotional Classics.* Garden City, NY: Doubleday, 1978.

Hinson's *Seekers After Mature Faith* (1968) was the basis for this more expanded three-volume set, "which comes close to translating the genre of devotional literature into a modern phenomenon" (Boyd 1978, p. 1108). These volumes comprise nine titles, including: Richard Baxter's *The Saint's Everlasting Rest*; John Bunyan's *Grace Abounding* and *Pilgrim's Progress*; *The Journal of George Fox*, also by Bunyan; David Brainerd's *Diary*; John Woolman's *Journal*; Soren Kierkegaard's *Purity of Heart*; Thomas Kelly's *A Testament of Devotion*; and Douglas Steere's *On Listening to Another*. Hinson's introduction to each work includes a biographical sketch of the author and textual notes.

———. *Seekers After Mature Faith.* Waco, TX: Word Books, 1968.

This book, the product of a course taught by Dr. Hinson at the Southern Baptist Theological Seminary in Louisville, Kentucky, is one of the best general introductions to the history of classical devotional literature, with more emphasis on the period of the church fathers and Medieval classics than the work of Batson (1968). Included in this survey of the twentieth century ("The Age of Revolution," as Hinson calls it) are Soren Kierkegaard; the Jesuit Pierre Teilhard de Chardin; and the resistors to Nazism, Dietrich Bonhoeffer and Father Alfred Delp. Hinson also includes a helpful introductory chapter on the nature and use of the classics in a "Secular Age." Historical sketches of the authors cited, a summary of their works, an index, and an extensive bibliography are included for the reader's convenience.

Merchant, Harish D., ed. *Encounter With Books: A Guide to Christian Reading.* Downers Grove, IL: InterVarsity, 1974.
     A section on the Christian life includes the topics "Biography, Journals and Autobiography," "Christian Classics," and "Hymns and Psalms." It also includes a list of sixty-seven contributors and thirty-two books that made a significant impact on the life and thought of the editor.

Schneider, Louis, and Sanford M. Dornbush. *Popular Religion: Inspirational Books in America.* Chicago: University of Chicago Press, 1958.
     This less comprehensive guide to classical and devotional literature surveys forty-six "best-sellers" of popular religious devotion.

Walls, F. A. *A Guide to Christian Reading.* 3d. ed. London: InterVarsity Fellowship, 1962.
     This guide lists standard texts and editions of thirty classics of Christian devotion, and contains a section on "A Treasury of Devotional Literature." The sections on "Puritan and Evangelical Fathers" and "Sanctification" are unique lists of representative Puritan authors.

Books in Series

     Roman Catholic devotional literature is largely represented by the contemplative and mystical literature of the early and Medieval church. There are a few series of books that have made a definite contribution to extending the outreach of this portion of the classical devotional literature.

Baillie, John, John T. McNeil, and Henry P. Van Dusen, eds. The Library of Christian Classics series. Philadelphia: Westminster, 1953–1966.
     Although monasticism and mysticism have been the source of most Catholic devotion, these areas have not been overlooked by Protestants. As stated in the general preface to this series, the Christian literary heritage is one "that must be reclaimed by each generation" (p. 9). Edited under the distinguished scholarship of John Baillie, John T. McNeil, and Henry P. Van Dusen, this series presents in twenty-six

volumes selections from "the most indispensable Christian treatises written prior to the end of the sixteenth century" (vol. I, p. 9).

Of particular interest to those seeking devotional literature is volume 7, *Western Asceticism*, edited with an introduction by Owen Chadwick. With selections from "The Sayings of the Fathers," "The Conferences of Cassian," and "The Rule of Saint Benedict," the reader is introduced to some of the most representative writings on the contemplative life. A companion volume (8) is *Late Medieval Mysticism*, edited and introduced by Ray C. Petry. With selections from St. Bernard of Clairvaux, St. Francis of Assisi, St. Bonaventure, Ramon Lull, Meister Eckhart, Richard Rolle, Henry Suso, St. Catherine of Siena, Jan Van Ruysbroeck, the *Theologica Germanica*, Nicholas of Cusa, and Catherine of Genoa, this work represents the wellspring of Christian mysticism. Other volumes in this series present primary works of St. Augustine, St. Anselm, Aquinas, Luther, Calvin, and others who shaped Christian thought and modeled devotion from the second through the sixteenth centuries.

The Classics of Western Spirituality series. Ramsey, NJ: Paulist Press,
   1978.

This is the one greatest series of devotional writings ever published. There are to date seventy-four volumes in this series. It provides the most in-depth and scholarly panorama of Western mysticism ever attempted. The series includes the original writings of universally acknowledged teachers within the Catholic, Protestant, Eastern Orthodox, Jewish, Islamic, and American Indian traditions. Each volume in the series is selected, translated, and introduced by an internationally recognized scholar. Included are works from St. Athanasius, St. Augustine of Hippo, St. Bernard of Clairvaux, St. Bonaventure, Meister Eckhart, Martin Luther, Jeremy Taylor, John Wesley and Charles Wesley, and William Law, to name only a few.

Sources of American Spirituality series. Ramsey, NJ: Paulist Press,
   1985.

Another series-in-progress, this one focuses on the sermons, essays, meditative poetry, correspondence, and other devotional writings of Americans. In addition to important writings of the Roman Catholic Church, the various traditions of Protestantism are also well represented with the sermons and devotional writings of such theologians and church leaders as Charles Hodge, Horace Bushnell, and William Ellery Channing.

Twentieth Century Encyclopedia of Catholicism series. New York:
   Hawthorn Books, 1958–1971.

This magnificent series surveys the entire compass of Catholic theology. Each volume covers some special topic of theology, worship, liturgy, or Catholic perspective on the contemporary arts, culture, society, and world religion. Many of these works are translations from the French or German that have never before appeared in English. The series consists of 150 volumes, the last two of which are detailed topical and Scriptural indexes of the entire set. Each of the individual volumes has an extended bibliography on its topic. For those seeking information on the classics of Christian devotion, a number of the following volumes in this series will be especially useful:

Cognet, Louis. *Post-Reformation Spirituality*. Vol. 41. 1959. Translated from the French.

Daujat, Jean, trans. *Prayer*. Vol. 37. 1964. Translated from the French.

Fulbert, Cayrbe. *Spiritual Writers of the Early Church*. Translated by W. Webster Wilson. Vol. 39. 1959.

Graef, Hilda. *Devotion to Our Lady*. Vol. 45. 1963.

Knowles, M. D. *The Nature of Mysticism*. Vol. 38. 1966.

Lhermitte, Jaques Jean. *True and False Possession*. Vol. 43. Edited by Daniel-Rops; translated by from the French by Hepburne-Scott. 1963.

Sheppard, Lancelot. *Spiritual Writers of Modern Times*. Vol. 42. 1967.

Sitwell, Gerard. *Spiritual Writers of the Middle Ages*. Vol. 40. 1961.

Svenens, Leon Jose. *Mary the Mother of God*. Vol. 44. Translated from the French by Brenell. 1959.

Volumes 117–119 of this series deal with contemporary Christian writers and literature, and might also prove to be helpful guides to more recent devotional literature.

Publishers of Devotional Literature

Some small religious presses have filled a vital niche by providing reprints of the devotional classics in series of more affordable paper editions. Among these are the Paraclete Living Library, in Orleans, Massachusetts. The evangelical presses such as Moody, Eerdmans, Kregel, and Baker have provided similar reprint series. Baker, for example, has provided a whole series of classical reprints in its Summit Books series, and more recently in its Direction paperback books.

Within the last decade, there also has been a revival of interest in Puritan authors, and a corresponding flood of reprints of the works of seventeenth-century divines. The Puritan writings are known for their depth of theological insight and their relation to the practical disciplines of life. These presses are making a contribution in preserving and disseminating this devotional-literary heritage. Among these are:

A Press
P. O. Box 8796
Greenville, SC 29604

Banner of Truth Trust
P. O. Box 621
Carlisle, PA 17013

Soli Deo Gloria
Suite 2311, Clark Building
717 Liberty Avenue
Pittsburgh, PA 15222

Sprinkle Publications
P. O. Box 1094
Harrisonburg, VA 22801

A Survey of Ten Classics
of Christian Devotion

St. Augustine of Hippo, *Confessions* (A.D. 397)

St. Augustine, the Bishop of Hippo, is one of the most significant figures of the early church. As both a philosopher and theologian, he played a vital role in shaping the formative theology of the early church as it came into contact with the intellectual and religious currents of classical culture. Augustine possessed one of the most fertile minds in the early church. As a polemicist, apologist, and theologian, he is revered by both Roman Catholics and Protestants alike. Among the most significant of his many writings is *Concerning the Trinity*, as well as those for which he is more familiarly known, *The City of God* and his famous *Confessions*. The latter work is included in almost every list of great Christian classics. It is his spiritual autobiography, presented as a series of reminiscences and confessions or prayers of thanks to God for the grace experienced throughout his life. It is through the *Confessions* that much of the life story of Augustine is known.

Augustine was born in 354 in Tagaste in North Africa of a pagan father and a devoutly Christian mother. Augustine was educated at Carthage, a cosmopolitan city of North Africa. In 373 he was inspired by Cicero's *Hortensius* to pursue divine wisdom. Although he was familiar with the Bible, he was not as yet fully open to its claim upon his life.

Augustine sought meaning first in Manichaeism, an Eastern dualistic religion. But he became disillusioned when, after nine years, its ascetic teachings only frustrated his search for personal moral rectitude.

Augustine turned next to the skeptics or "academics," but despaired at their moral relativism and the uncertainty of discovering truth. Augustine's search continued, but this time he found more satisfaction in the doctrines of neoplatonism. These doctrines made him more receptive to the Gospel when he heard it from the lips of the great orator of Milan, Saint Ambrose.

In the Gospel of Christ, St. Augustine found both an intellectual understanding of the problem and solution to the origin of evil, and a personal remedy to the problem of sin that had preoccupied his life. After his conversion to Christianity in the year 385, Augustine retired to Cassiciacum to reflect on the full implication of his "beatific vision." In 388 he returned to North Africa, where he established a monastic order. In 396, he was appointed Bishop of Hippo, where he spent the remainder of his life as a pastor, theologian, and apologist for the Christian faith until his death in 430.

Among Augustine's many writings, *Confessions* stands as a unique tract of autobiographic devotion. It was written between the years 397 and 400, just a few years after Augustine's appointment as Bishop of Hippo. In it, he describes the events of the first thirty-five years of his life. Augustine traces his spiritual pilgrimage from the lusts of his youthfulness, through overcoming the intellectual limitations of skepticism, his moral conflicts with Manichaean dualism, and the theological dilemmas of neoplatonism. At the end of his journey, he found in the God of the Scriptures the *summum bonum*, or highest good for which one can live.

A spiritual autobiography, Augustine's *Confessions* is one of the earliest examples of reflective introspection as a literary style. His confessions are a recognition of his own finiteness and sinfulness as cast against the majesty and graciousness of God. The *Confessions* is a magnificent display of personal devotion, and seems to be self-consciously designed to first pull the reader into Augustine's spiritual despair, and then elevate the reader with him to the heights of experience of the divine majesty.

Thomas à Kempis, *Imitation of Christ* (1480)

The *Imitation of Christ* has been published in nearly 3,000 editions, and in nearly every language into which Christianity has been introduced. But there are very few important commentaries on, or books about, this great classic of Christian devotion. This lack of criticism prompted Willard L. Sperry to remark that no classic in the world "has remained so free of the need of critical aids to its interpretation" (1950, p. 43).

Tradition has assigned the *Imitation* to the pen of Thomas Hammerken, who was born in the town of Kempen, near Dusseldorf, Germany, circa 1380. Thomas was said to have been a shy, dreamy lad who grew into a retiring young man of mystical inclination. After an early education under the Brethren of the Common Life at their school in Devanter, Holland, Thomas entered into the Augustinian Order at the monastery of Mount Saint Agnes near Zwolle, Holland. There he served for some seventy years; he died there in 1471 at the age of ninety-one.

The *Imitation of Christ* is probably the most famous among the medieval ascetic and monastic writings. In spite of its simplicity and timeless appeal, the origin of the *Imitation of Christ* has been problematic over the centuries. It makes no direct statement of its authorship. But the conclusion of one of its most important manuscripts declares that it was "finished and completed in the year of Our Lord 1441 by the hands of Brother Thomas à Kempis near Zwolle." But there are at least twenty-two handwritten editions of the work dated before that particular manuscript. Some have also suggested a distinctive difference between the style of the *Imitation* and other known works of Thomas à Kempis. This has occasioned speculation that it might actually have been the work of some other medieval religious writer, such as John Gersen or Saint Bernard.

The *Imitation of Christ* has been, next to the Bible itself, the chief work of devotion for many Christians throughout the centuries.

A more stern title, *Contemptus Mundi* (contempt of the world), was given to the *Imitation of Christ* in an earlier age. Its dominant theme is not "imitation," but closeness, intimacy, and communion. It is an appeal to a life of tranquillity, with injunctions to worldly detachment and self-sacrifice. The work presents an argument for benevolent living and spiritual discipline.

The *Imitation* is composed of four short books or sections. The title of the work is derived from the heading of the first book, "Of the Imitation of Christ and Contempt of All the Vanities of the World." Some editions bear the subtitle "The Ecclesiastical Music," quite appropriately because of the natural rhythm to which the reading of the text lends itself. The first book was written for the ordinary Christian.

Book two is titled "Concerning Inward Things." The title "Jesus" is used extensively in this portion of the work. Its emphasis is the intimate fellowship the Christian should have with Christ.

Book three is titled "Of Inward Consolation"; its theme is that of watching and waiting for the coming of Jesus. Much of this portion of the work takes the form of a series of dialogues between the Lover and the Beloved, and is reminiscent of the theme and style of the Song of Songs of the Old Testament.

The fourth book is about Holy Communion. It could be called a manual of self-examination. It is a fit instrument to aid the participant in following the injunction of the Apostle Paul, "Let every man examine himself."

Austere and simple in style, the *Imitation* has been criticized by some as being self-effacing to a psychopathological degree. Rather, it reflects the complete otherworldliness of the medieval intellect. And although it is notably unscholarly and unacademic, these are the very qualities that have also given it great appeal to the religious spirit.

The *Imitation* is not profoundly original, but is clearly a mosaic of early Christian and medieval devotion. It characteristically draws directly from the biblical text, and such other early classics as the devotional writings of Saint Augustine and the mysticism of St. Bernard of Clairvaux.

With tact and insight into human behavior, the author attempts to lead the reader to greater heights of personal endeavor. The enduring popularity of the *Imitation* is undoubtedly due to its deep roots in Scripture. The language and teaching of the Bible are reflected throughout. This, in no small measure, is a result of the fact that the author was himself a copyist and thoroughly imbued with the very words of the Vulgate Bible, which he meticulously transcribed for fifteen years from 1425 to 1440. Thus, perhaps it should be seen as quite providential that Thomas à Kempis was engaged in this occupation just before the invention of printing. The *Imitation* also appeals to simple and humble folk. While it does not despise or ridicule learning, it is not wrapped in academic garb. It avoids every trace of technical theology and dogmatic formulation.

The *Imitation* has been severely criticized for creating a caricature of Christianity. Those who see it as such find it a manual of slavish devotion, Gnostic otherworldliness, and isolationism. The sympathetic reader, however, will understand the *Imitation* to be a simple polemic against self-satisfaction, and a genuine affirmation of the value of Christian refection. It calls the reader not to "isolationism," but to solitude, to reaffirm one's utter dependence upon God. Its injunctions serve as a gentle reminder that salvation is ultimately a very private and personal matter.

Martin Luther, *On Christian Liberty* (1520)

The great Protestant Reformer, Martin Luther, was born in Eisleben, Germany in 1483. He studied law at the University of Leipzig, but after surviving a fearful thunderstorm, Luther took a holy vow and joined the order of the Augustinian Hermits in 1505. Luther was ordained in 1507 and was sent to the University of Wittenberg to teach theology. By 1519, Luther came to the exegetical insight that Christ himself, not the Catholic hierarchy, was the "righteousness" needed by people, and the grace provided by God.

The crisis that precipitated the Protestant Reformation in 1517 was Luther's posting his famous ninety-five theses on the door of the Wittenberg church. Among other protests, he assailed the practice of selling indulgences for the alleged release of souls from Purgatory. When Luther's attack on the papal doctrine reduced church revenues, the Archbishop of Mainz appealed to Rome. The controversy came to a head in 1519, when Luther met with the great papal polemicist John Eck at Leipzig to debate the issues at hand. In confrontation with Eck, Luther denied the twin principles of ecclesiastical authority: the supremacy of the Pope, and the infallibility of church councils. Although threatened with excommunication, Luther again refused to recant, even when called before the Imperial Diet of Charles V at Worms in 1521. It was here that he made a solemn pronouncement:

> Unless I am convicted by the testimony of Scripture or by clear reason . . . I am bound by the Scriptures I have quoted, and my conscience is captive to the Word of God. I cannot and will not retract anything, since it is neither safe nor right to go against conscience. Here I stand. I can do no other. May God help me. (*Luther's Works*, Volume 1, pp. 112–13)

Now declared an outlaw, Luther was sheltered by his loyal patron Frederick, the Duke of Saxony, at his castle at Wartburg. While in self-imposed exile, and in just a matter of months, Luther translated the New Testament into the vernacular to make it directly available to the German people. In 1522, Luther again emerged, this time to correct the excesses of radical reformers. By this time the Reformed theology was well rooted, and it remained for Luther to introduce reforms in worship, preaching, and Christian education.

In 1530, Luther approved the first Protestant creed, the *Augsburg Confession*, which was drafted by his colleague Philip Melanchton. In 1537, he wrote the *Schmalkald Articles,* which, along with the *Augsburg Confession*, became the doctrinal foundation for the church of the Lutheran tradition.

Luther's treatise *On Christian Liberty* was written in the fall of 1520 in the midst of the controversy he had created. This treatise was the last of four early documents that identify the fundamental issues of the Reformation. The first of these was a *Treatise on Good Works*, published in June of 1520. It was intended to correct the misimpression that Luther's emphasis on faith diminished the need for good works. The next two works were quite controversial and polemic in tone: *Address to the Christian Nobility of the German Nation*, published in August 1520, and *The Babylonian Captivity of the Church*, published in October 1520. These two works questioned the exclusive ecclesiastical authority of the Pope, repudiated the theology of four of the seven Sacraments, and affirmed the doctrine of the "priesthood of all believers."

Unlike the three previous treatises, *On Christian Liberty* does not smack of the spirit of polemic or controversy. In temperate words, it reveals the spiritual pilgrimage of its author. The work provides evidence of Luther's appreciation of both St. Bernard of Clairvaux and of the *Theololgica Germanica*. But in spite of their ascetic appeal, Luther's profound sense of spiritual emptiness persisted, until ultimately satisfied by his exegetical insight into the true meaning of St. Paul's letter to the Romans. As expressed in the theme verse (Romans 1:17), Luther came to see that the Gospel, in its very essence, is "the righteousness of God" revealed in Jesus Christ, and that "the justified man" is he who lives by this faith. "At last," Luther wrote, "I perceived that the justice of God is that by which the just man lives, that is to say faith. . . . Thereupon I felt as if born again. . . . The righteousness that is in us is from God by faith" (p. xii, p. 25).

Reminiscent of St. Augustine, Luther provides a personal confession of the grace of God in his life. The "liberty" of which Luther wrote was not that of political freedom, nor even of freedom of the will, about which he would later debate with the humanist Erasmus. His view of Christian liberty was thoroughly soteriological—a freedom from the struggle to please God by one's own righteousness. In this sense, Luther proclaimed the essence of the Protestant faith, and *On Christian Liberty* may indeed be considered the first devotional classic representative of the Protestant tradition.

Luther's work anticipates misunderstanding. Relying on a proper understanding of the relationship between the law and the Gospel in the believer's life, Luther makes it abundantly clear that salvation by faith alone, without works of the law, is no permit to lawlessness. Even as the Apostle Paul had anticipated the same objection (Romans 6:1–11), so does Luther. Because the Christian is "dead" to the law as a means of salvation, he is correspondingly "free" of its enslavement to duty. But he who does receive God's gift of righteousness by faith is for the first time made morally alive, so that he *can* live after the pattern of Christ's example.

A second misunderstanding of Luther is one that he could not anticipate because of his time in history. The essence of this criticism is that the Reformer did not see civil liberty as a corollary of the same liberty of conscience by which he proclaimed freedom from ecclesiastical authority. Indeed, because of his high regard for the civil magistrate as God's earthly sword, Luther has been seen by some as the historical, if not the intellectual base, of political totalitarianism. Particularly since World War II, there has been a theory of historical interpretation that has represented Luther's writings as the type of Teutonic authoritarianism evidenced in Nietzsche and Hitler. Indeed, Luther probably did not see the Gospel as a guarantor of political liberty. But the critic should be reminded that, as surely as Luther resisted the legitimacy of any moral lawlessness, so did he also assail *any* authority, ecclesiastical or political, that would seek to usurp the authority of the word of Christ.

John Calvin, *Institutes of the Christian Religion* (1536)

John Calvin, the patriarch of the Reformed branch of Protestantism, was born in 1509 in Noyon, France. At the urging of his father, he studied law at the universities of Orleans and Bourges. In 1531, he moved to Paris, where he came under the influence of the humanist scholars and began the study of classical literature. His earliest scholarly work was not in Biblical exposition, but philosophy. He wrote a *Commentary on Seneca's Treatise on Clemency* (1532), revealing some appreciation of the stoic philosophy of natural and civil law.

In 1533, Calvin fled Paris to escape persecution after his friend and associate, Nicholas Cop, publicly challenged the traditional theology of the Sorbonne professors.

Calvin was converted to Christianity between 1533 and 1534. He had already been exposed to the teachings of Martin Luther, but the probable influence of the humanist biblical scholar Jacques Lefevre cannot be underestimated. Some years later, Calvin reflected upon his conversion: "God subdued and brought my heart to docility. It was more hardened against such matters than was to be expected in such a young man."

After leaving Paris, Calvin returned briefly to his birthplace at Noyon, but, by 1535, he was situated in Basel, Switzerland. By this time, he fully identified with the Reformation, as is evidenced by the preface he wrote to a French translation of the Bible published that same year.

While in Basel, Calvin also began to formulate his theology. In 1536, he published the first edition of what was to become the monumental *Institutes of the Christian Religion*. It was dedicated to Francis I, King of France, as a brief exposition of the Reformed faith, and as a defense for those suffering severe persecution in France. Although a brief tract in its first edition, the work developed into the most comprehensive and systematic treatise of the Reformed Protestant faith ever written.

In 1537, William Farel, the Reformer of Geneva, persuaded Calvin to join him to consolidate the Protestant advances there. Both were expelled, however, when the citizenry resisted their imposition of a conservative confession and austere morality.

Calvin then moved to Strasbourg, where he met the leader of that city's Reform movement, Martin Bucer. Under Bucer's influence, Calvin published a commentary on the Apostle Paul's Letter to the Romans, and then a series of Biblical expositions. While at Strasbourg, Calvin also served as pastor to a congregation of French refugees.

Calvin was called back to Geneva in 1541, but much resistance to his movement continued. Although his image was marred by his condemnation and burning of the antitrinitarian Michael Servetus, Calvin proved to be a strong leader. After a few years of his preaching and teaching, Calvin's authority was less disputed. He gained an international reputation and was admired by many as the leader of a Christian republic. Students from throughout Europe came to study under him at the renowned Academy at Geneva.

If Martin Luther was the greatest personal force behind the Reformation, Calvin was the greatest systematizer of the Reformed theology. By 1559, Calvin's *Institutes* had gone through at least ten editions, and was five times the length of the first edition. The *Institutes* have long been recognized as the classic statement of the Reformed faith. It is arranged into four major books; following the outline of theology as traditionally presented in the Apostle's Creed. Thus, the first book is on the knowledge of God the Creator. Its central focus is creation, the attributes of God, and His relationship to the created order. The second book, on the knowledge of God the Redeemer in Christ, deals with the divine nature of Christ; His prophetic, priestly, and kingly offices; and the theology of the atonement. The third book, on the mode of obtaining the grace of Christ and the benefits it confers, deals with the doctrines of salvation in its application to the Christian in justification and its evidence in sanctification, the Christian's life of prayer, and the hope of resurrection. The fourth book concerns the means by which God attracts us into fellowship with Christ and keeps us in Him. This final book concerns the nature of the church, the Sacraments, and civil government.

Calvin's background in the tradition of classical rhetoric is clearly reflected in the literary style of the *Institutes*. His passages are sometimes extended and repetitious, and in controversial sections, he is often caustic and sarcastic. And although thoroughly familiar with the history and issues of philosophy, Calvin is never speculative. He accepts unashamedly the mysteries of Scripture without exalting reason over revelation. Yet he does not disregard the need for reasonableness.

Calvin and his *Institutes* have often suffered from critics who have fixed upon the most forbidding and controversial portions of his work. Calvin's theology is organized around the themes of God's sovereignty in election and predestination. But Calvin's theology of salvation cannot be fully appreciated except in contrast to the total moral helplessness of humans. For Calvin, God extended mercy to a rebellious humankind, and to that extent, this mercy is an evidence of His sovereign grace.

John Bunyan, *Pilgrim's Progress* (1678)

Next to the Bible itself, and Thomas à Kempis's *Imitation of Christ*, John Bunyan's *Pilgrim's Progress* has been widely recognized as the third best-selling work of devotional literature. John Bunyan was an unlettered man of modest means and of humble disposition. That is why he was able to speak so easily to the heart of the common man.

In addition to *Pilgrim's Progress*, Bunyan was author of a number of other works of Puritan devotion, including his own spiritual autobiography, *Grace Abounding*. Born in 1628 in Elstow, Bedfordshire, the son of a tinker, Bunyan had a sensitive nature. He testified of the "fearful dreams" and "dreadful visions" he had even as a child.

In 1644, the adolescent Bunyan served in Oliver Cromwell's army. In 1649, Bunyan married his first wife, whose name is unknown, who was presumably the model for "Christiana," the heroine in the second part of *Pilgrim's Progress,* which was published in 1684.

A significant influence on Bunyan's life were two works of devotion that he received from his first wife's father. These were Arthur Dent's *The Plain Man's Pathway to Heaven* (1601), and Lewis Bayly's *The Practice of Piety* (1624). These works awakened him to the spiritual dimensions of life, and marked the beginning of his own spiritual pilgrimage. Another influence on Bunyan's spiritual development was John Gifford, minister of the Bedford church near his hometown. Gifford counseled Bunyan through continued bouts of depression and doubts about the possibility of his salvation. Through his diligent study of the Scripture, however, Bunyan became fully persuaded of God's saving grace in Jesus Christ.

In 1653, about two years after his conversion, Bunyan felt called to preach. He left the tinker's shop he had inherited from his father to follow his new calling. Bunyan joined the Bedford church, where his ministry was gladly received. The Restoration of the Monarchy in 1660, however, brought severe restrictions to Puritan religious practices. Despite this, Bunyan persisted in his ministry, and as a consequence, spent twelve years, from 1660 to 1672, in the Bedford prison. By the end of this imprisonment, Bunyan had written nine books, including *Grace Abounding*. In 1672, under Charles II's Act of Toleration, Bunyan was released from prison and returned to the Bedford church. Bunyan was again imprisoned for a short time in 1675, but upon release, he continued his preaching and writing. He expanded his autobiography into six editions before his death in 1688. The greatest of Bunyan's eighty works is, of course, his famous *Pilgrim's Progress*.

Pilgrim's Progress consists of two separate tales, written at different times. The first, written while Bunyan was still in prison, was published in 1678. The second, the story of the pilgrimage of its central character, "Christian," appeared in 1684. The value of this work as a classic of Christian devotion is in its direct presentation of the common person's religious struggles. Of special appeal is the simple language and familiar types, which spoke to those attempting to live a sincere Christian life in an environment superficially steeped in Puritan Christian values.

The theme is brought to life in the literary device of "Christian," who undertakes a spiritual pilgrimage. The idea of pilgrimage was not unfamiliar. Even if they did not read, people were familiar with Chaucer's *Canterbury Tales*. These also brought to life the experiences of real-life pilgrims on their "Canterburys."

What distinguishes *Pilgrim's Progress* from other devotional classics is its unique use of allegory as a literary style. A contemporary reader would not have to know history or philosophy to identify, for example, the frivolity of the famous Strawbridge Fair at Cambridge with Bunyan's "Vanity Fair." The same may be said of many of Bunyan's images, as vivid to today's pilgrims as they were to his contemporary readers. Who has not himself seemingly been trapped in the Slough of Despond, or Doubting Castle, or come near to the Valley of the Shadow of Death? Or who has not been encouraged on life's way by Mr. Faithful, reviled by Lord Hategood, or subverted by Mr. Talkative? And does not the answer to these questions reveal the universality and timelessness of not only the images, but also of the message they bear?

Pilgrim's Progress is not merely religious, but also deeply theological. As Perry Miller points out in his insightful essay, this great literary work can be most fully appreciated when understood in the historical context in which it was created (1950, pp. 74–76). In this sense, it is an example *par excellence* of the theological tensions with which the Puritans had to struggle, that is, the need of a sense of personal perseverance within a theological framework of absolute predestination. But even wrestling with theological issues, Bunyan reflects a universal theme: the life of every Christian is a struggle for spiritual survival, but through God's grace he can persevere to the Celestial City at the end of his journey.

Jeremy Taylor, *The Rule and Exercise of Holy Living* (1650) and *Holy Dying* (1651)

To call someone "holy" today is at least condescending, if not demeaning. But there was a time when this appellation was not a mark of ridicule, but of honor and strength of character. This was true when Jeremy Taylor wrote his inspiring pair of devotional classics, *Holy Living* (1650) and *Holy Dying* (1651).

Jeremy Taylor was born in 1613 in Cambridge, England. He was one of the first to be educated at the Perse School, Cambridge, which has since become world renowned. Taylor also studied at Gonville and Caius College, and was ordained to the Anglican priesthood at the early age of twenty. He continued as a Fellow of All Souls, at Oxford, where he came under the influence of Archbishop William Laud. Probably through Laud's influence, Taylor was later appointed Royal Chaplain.

Taylor also served as Rector at Uppingham, Rutland (1638), and Overstone, Northampton (1643). In 1645, he became principal of a school at Newton Hall, Carmarthenshire, and chaplain to the Earl of Carbery. This was the most fruitful period of his literary life. In addition to a *Discourse on the Liberty of Prophesying* (1647), a plea for religious toleration, and his *Great Exemplar* (1649), a study of the life of Christ, Taylor produced numerous other books, tracts, sermons, and poems. But it is the twin titles *Holy Living* and *Holy Dying* that won his place in the history of Christian devotional literature.

After the Restoration of 1660, Taylor was made Bishop of the Irish diocese of Down and Conner, and administrator of the dioceses of Dromore, where he directed the building of the famous cathedral. Taylor died in 1667 in Lisburn, Ireland.

Taylor's *Holy Living* was published in 1650 after the condemnation of Archbishop Laud in 1644, shortly following the execution of Charles I. Thus, it appeared amidst the turmoil of Cromwell's Civil War, which divided the church as well. *Holy Living* appeared during that period when even the *Book of Common Prayer* was placed under ban. Thus, Taylor's *Holy Living* may well have been a substitute for the *Book of Common Prayer* until it was returned in a new edition in 1662. The language in *Holy Living* is grand and magnificent. Especially noteworthy are Taylor's prayers, which are simple and restrained, but rich in depth of thought and reflection.

Holy Living is broad in scope, but practical in the application of theology to the routine of life. The first section of the book is "Instruments of Holy Living," in which Taylor presents a careful consideration of the stewardship of time, purity of motive, and especially "the practice of the presence of God." The latter phrase was popularized by the French monastic Brother Lawrence, who was a contemporary of Taylor. But Taylor's understanding of "the presence of God" was not as vivid as those living pictures of Brother Lawrence's life. It is more abstract and theological. Thus, he speaks of God as "wholly in every place," yet "included in no place"; and as "filling heaven and earth with His present power, and with His never absent nature."

The main body of the work covers such topics as "Christian Sobriety," "Christian Justice," and "Christian Religion." The latter refers to the "inner" life of faith, hope, and love; "external" acts of devotion consist of hearing God's word in preaching, prayer, fasting, giving in stewardship, and observance of the Lord's Day. Taylor's overall theme is that the Christian life requires self-sacrifice and self-discipline, but is obtainable by the grace of God through the Holy Spirit. If any criticism is to be leveled at Taylor's work, it is perhaps in his Pelagian theological tendencies that, as Hinson said in speaking of his sequel work, *Holy*

Dying, "placed a sort of pharisaical burden" on the shoulders of his parishioners (1968, p. 178).

William Law, *A Serious Call to a Devout and Holy Life* (1728)

William Law was one of the most powerful influences on eighteenth-century England. His was not the power of politics, however, nor even that of the expanding economic might that characterized England during the latter era of the eighteenth century. Rather, Law's was a profoundly moral influence. And Law is all the more significant because his moral influence came at a time of genuine spiritual need. The growing influence of deism and rationalism dulled the spirit of the English people. Christianity was widely professed, but seldom practiced. God had become an impertinence. So William Law's *A Serious Call to a Devout and Holy Life* (1728) appealed to moral renewal and Christian commitment. This work has been recognized by Martin as the "first impulse" of the Great Revival of the eighteenth century (1971, p. 81).

William Law was born in 1686 in Northamptonshire, England. The son of a grocer, he entered Emmanuel College, Cambridge, as a fellow in 1705. Beginning in 1711, he served the Church of England for two years as Curate at Hastingfield. But with the accession of George I, Law could not in conscience continue in the Anglican Church under allegiance to the Stuart Monarchy. In 1716, Law joined the ranks of the Nonjuring party, which he saw as being the genuine Church of England.

In the early 1720s, Law became chaplain-tutor to the household of Edward Gibbon, grandfather of the famous historian of the same name, who later referred to Law as "the much honored friend and spiritual director of the whole family" (1907, p. 17). After ten year's service to the Gibbon family, Law retired to his family estate in King's Cliffe. Here, with his aged aunt, he managed a school for the Christian education of young women. Law maintained a secluded life in King's Cliffe, devoting himself to literary work until his death in 1761.

Law was a high-churchman with strong mystical tendencies. He made no secret of his regret at the passing of the age of monasticism. His self-denial of an ecclesiastical calling under the Hanoverian Monarchy was fortunate, for it permitted him a condition of detachment in which to cultivate a personal piety, while providing an opportunity for its literary expression. The Christian church thus benefits from his quiet labors as evidenced by the profound influence of *A Serious Call to a Devout and Holy Life*.

Law was not an evangelical-revivalist. His calling and ministry was almost exclusively to the people of higher social and economic classes. The first part of *A Serious Call* is directed to men of means. His presumed audience was businessmen and tradesmen, but especially the leisured class, those who were "free from the necessity of labor or employments." Law emphasized the proper use of time and money as a stewardship to the Lord, reminding that "to whom much is given, much will be required." (Luke 12:48)

The second part of *A Serious Call* is a discourse on prayer, the "noblest exercise of the soul." He models prayers and gives rules on how to address God. Law advises a regular and disciplined program of prayer each day.

Law makes effective use of character portrayals. In this, he is reminiscent of Bunyan. And there is some speculation about the extent to which Law's literary portrayals reflected actual persons. Edward Gibbon, the historian, claimed that Law was actually describing his two aunts in his characters Flavia and Miranda. Law presented the former as outwardly religious, but inwardly vain and presumptuous. She was given to fine clothes, worldly amusements, and gossip. Miranda, however, was a model of self-sacrifice for others and personal Christian devotion.

The power of William Law's literary work, especially his *Serious Call*, is seen in the profound influence it had upon John Wesley and the Methodist movement, for whom it became the basis of their "rules for living." Many others give testimony of its impact upon their lives, including Gibbon. The extent of Law's influence can also be measured by the testimony of Samuel Johnson, as recorded by Boswell:

> I became a sort of lax talker against religion, for I did not think much against it; and this lasted 'till I went to Oxford where it would not be suffered. When at Oxford I took up Law's *Serious Call to a Holy Life*, expecting to find it a dull book (as such books generally are) and perhaps to laugh at it. But I found Law quite an overmatch for me; and this was the first occasion of my thinking in earnest of religion, after I became capable of rational inquiry. (P. 29)

To the names of those upon whom Law exerted a tremendous influence may also be added Henry Vann, the evangelical Anglican; Thomas Scott, the famous biblical commentator; John Henry Newman; Alexander White; and undoubtedly many others.

The literature is full of criticisms of Law's devotional writing. It is seen by many to be too austere and ascetic. Its emphasis on self-denial and humility seem too idealistic and overly demanding. For some, it is also said to have too little evangelical zeal. For others, it has too little theological depth. And for many, it is simply too long. But it must be remembered that Law is setting forth an ideal—for he saw within each individual two men: one of sin, selfishness, covetousness; the other, that which we would like to be. It is the latter that Law holds out to us as an example.

A Serious Call presents a very practical guide to the Christian life. In an age of how-to and successful-living books, William Law presents a meaningful dose of genuine Christian devotion.

John Wesley, *Journal* (1740–1784)

Perhaps more than any other force during the eighteenth century, the evangelism of John Wesley and Charles Wesley served to overcome the intellectual and moral decay of deism, to enliven the religious formalism of the English church, and to bring a genuine evangelical revival to the British. The Great Evangelical Revival, as it was known, began in the 1730s. The Calvinist Jonathan Edwards was the leading figure of revival in America; George Whitefield was the great evangelistic preacher in England. But it was left to the Methodists, as they came to be called, to make new converts and create with them an evangelical church. This task fell to the great leaders of Methodism, John Wesley and Charles Wesley. Charles is remembered for the many majestic hymns he created. John was the preacher, pastor, and administrator of the newly-organized Methodist Societies.

John Wesley was born in 1703, four years before his brother Charles. Both were born in Epworth, Lincolnshire, to a staunch Anglican pastor, the Reverend Samuel Wesley, and his wife, Susanna, who like their father, exercised a remarkable influence on the boys' early spiritual development.

In 1713, John Wesley was admitted to the Charterhouse School, London; he entered Christ College, Oxford, in 1720. He was ordained a deacon in 1725, and served with his father as curate for two years. In the year of his ordination, Wesley began reading the devotional books of Thomas à Kempis, Jeremy Taylor, and especially William Law's *Serious Call*. Through these, he developed a sublime view of God's law and resolved to keep it, believing in this way to find salvation. In 1729, he returned as a Fellow to Oxford, where the Holy Club was formed; it was called "Methodist" because of the methodical religious habits of its members.

In 1736, the Wesley brothers sailed to colonial Georgia on behalf of the Society for the Propagation of the Gospel. However, John Wesley's chief motive in traveling to America was, as he reveals in his *Journal* (October 14, 1735), "the hope of saving my own soul. I hope to earn the sense of the Gospel by preaching it to the heathen" (p. 16). This was quite an admission for one who had been a "son of the parsonage," and active in ministry all of his life! But it was on this journey that the Wesleys met some Moravian brethren, and were impressed with the impact of the Gospel upon their lives—especially the peace which the Moravians exhibited while the Wesleys were gripped with fear during the stormy voyage.

After his return to England a year later, John came under the influence of another Moravian, Peter Boehler. John Wesley's remarkable conversion took place while attending a Moravian meeting at Aldersgate Street in London. It was after hearing a passage from Martin Luther's preface to "Romans" that John felt his heart "strangely warmed." This was a turning point in his life. And, indeed, it could be said to be a turning point in the spiritual life of his country, too. Wesley would later write that the experience at Altersgate was of more importance to England than all the victories of Pitt.

Being loosed from spiritual bondage, Wesley also set himself free of the confines of the parish ministry. In 1739, with missionary vision and zeal, he began his legendary itinerant ministry. Riding horseback, he traveled an estimated 8,000 miles each. His circuit ministry converted multitudes, and established his "Methodist" societies across the country, preparing it for the bleaker days of the Industrial Revolution that lay ahead. Indeed, Rev. Hughes, in his introduction to the *Journal*, says that Wesley was the first preacher since the days of the Franciscan friars in the Middle Ages to reach the working class. His itineraries were designed to bring him into contact with the industrious, self-supporting working man.

The Evangelical Revival and the establishment of Methodism encouraged the sending of missionaries to the British colonies, the publication and dissemination of Christian literature, the establishment of Sunday schools, and a renewed sense of Christian responsibility to the issues of slavery, labor exploitation, poverty, and the other ills of an increasingly urban and industrial society.

John Wesley's *Journal* is a personal record of his many miles of travel and preaching the Gospel. He acknowledges his indebtedness to Jeremy Taylor, who in his *Rules for Holy Living* admonishes his readers to write down and account for the way they spend their lives. And this Wesley did. After a brief note on the origin of the Holy Clubs, or Methodist societies, the *Journal* opens on October 14, 1735 with a note regarding his plans to travel to America. It covers fifty-six years to the last entry on October 24, 1790, only a few months before Wesley's death in 1791. In its original form, the *Journal* consisted of twenty-six unprinted volumes. The edited *Journal* was issued in twenty-one installments from 1740 to 1789, comprising four volumes.

The *Journal* records a wide variety of experiences, and touches upon topics as diverse as war, books, medicine, the parapsychological, and even Wesley's opinions of such personalities as Mary Queen of the Scots. At the same time, Wesley also reveals the intimate details of his spiritual struggles and personal life. And although he did not have their theological precision or keenness of expression, Wesley did stand against the stern soteriological determinism as taught by St. Augustine and Calvin.

Augustine Birrell, in his introductory "Appreciation" to the *Journal*, presents perhaps the most sensitive report of the literary character of the *Journal*: "Wesley himself is no alarmist, no sentimentalist, he never gushes, seldom exaggerates, and always writes on an easy level." Birrell also says there is no other literary work from this period that gives such a vivid account of eighteenth-century England. Indeed, it is his opinion that the *Journal* is an incalculably more varied and complete account of the people of England during this period than even Boswell's famous *Life of Johnson* (1791).

John Woolman, *Journal* (1774)

John Woolman is among the few Americans who contributed to the body of classic devotional literature. As a Quaker, it was not unusual for John Woolman to keep a personal diary of religious experience. But Woolman was not typical. He earned a place in American religious history as a pioneer of social justice. And his *Journal* has earned a place in American literary history as a record of the development of an American social conscience.

John Woolman was born in 1720 on a small farm in Northampton, New Jersey. He worked as a shopkeeper and as a tailor. Having only a moderate education himself, he also taught school and later published a primer. Woolman was married and had one child.

Much of Woolman's career, especially the latter years of his life, was spent traveling the Eastern coast to visit and testify at the Meetings of the Friends. In 1772, Woolman traveled to England. But after visiting there for six months with the Quakers, he contracted smallpox, which was fatal.

Although self-educated, Woolman was well read, and his *Journal* reflects a clear and careful mode of expression. The chief value of a diary is that the author records self-revelation of character. Woolman's *Journal* demonstrates that, although he was thoroughly imbued with the Quaker way of life, he was not sectarian in spirit. He writes, "I found no narrowness respecting sects and opinions, but believed that sincere, upright-hearted people in every society who truly love God were accepted of him" (Kepler, xvii).

The *Journal* sets Woolman apart as a man not only of charity, but also of compassion. He records his feelings on a journey to visit the Native Americans across the Delaware River in the wilds of unsettled Pennsylvania:

> The 12th, and first of the week, being a rainy day, we continued in our tent; and here I was led to think on the nature of the exercise which hath attended me. Love was the first motive, and thence a concern arose to spend some time with the Indians, that I might feel and understand their life, and the spirit they live in, if in any degree helped forward by my following the leadings of Truth amongst them. (Sperry 1950, p. 93)

Woolman extended his compassion, not only toward American Indians, but especially toward black slaves in America. He repeatedly relates experiences in which conscience forced him to quietly yet firmly oppose the accepted social practices of his day. When, for example, he was a guest in a home where a slave served, he would politely pay the slave for his services. He would often deprive himself of products such as sugar, that might have been produced by slave labor. It was this quiet resistance by Woolman, not by protests, sit-ins, or demonstrations, that persuaded his fellow Quakers to also oppose slavery. Woolman possessed an optimistic view of the possibilities of men in service to each other, rather than in slavery to one another. Indeed, as Cadbury points out, a small group of Quakers in 1688 were the first of any religious group in America to formally protest black slavery. And by 1788, not a single American Quaker was a slave owner (Sperry 1950, p. 97).

There is little to criticize in Woolman's work, although some might object that Woolman is too mystical to be taken seriously, at least from a theological point of view. And, indeed, these tendencies are there. But Henry J. Cadbury, in his sympathetic essay, rejects the notion that Woolman was a mystic. Even from his youth, Woolman's "visions" were most often reflections on the truth of Scripture in times of solitude. And it is this solitude that, says Cadbury, seems to be "a kind of moral pressure on man's conscience" (Sperry 1950, p. 97).

The lessons from John Woolman are clear: there may always be attitudes in our society that are taken for granted, but such attitudes cannot stand up under the scrutiny of a sanctified conscience.

John Henry Cardinal Newman, *Apologia Pro Vita Sua* (1864)

Early in the nineteenth century, a movement arose from within the Anglican Church of England that stressed the unity of the church universal under Apostolic succession. "Tractarians," as these conservators of the church were known, originated in a group of Fellows of the Oriel College, Oxford. It was because of their academic positions that the reforming activities of this group was known as the Oxford Movement.

The Oxford divines had high regard for the tradition of the church, elevating its authority as a united and historical witness of the Christian faith. They denigrated the evangelical Reformers' emphasis upon the primary authority of Scripture, seeing in this authority shades of the subjective individualism of private judgment. Also inspired by the Romantic spirit of the era, the Oxford theologians had a sacramental view of nature, and an exalted view of the church visible. The leaders of this reform movement were John Keble, E. S. Pusey, Hurrell Froude, Robert Wilburforce, and most preeminently, John Henry Newman.

John Henry Newman was born in 1801, the son of an evangelical London banker. In 1816, he entered Trinity College, Oxford, and in 1822, was elected a Fellow of Oriel College. It was at this time that Newman's view of the church began to change, largely because of his friend and colleague Hurrell Froude, who favored the glory of the Roman Catholic Church over the liturgical dogma of the Reformers. From 1832 to 1833, Newman and Froude toured the Mediterranean, but during a stop in Rome, Newman was convinced of the idolatry of the ancient church. It was during his return voyage to Oxford that he wrote the timeless hymn, "Lead, Kindly Light."

Upon his return to England, Newman became a luminary of the Oxford movement, and its attempt at reviving the beauty and simplicity of the Catholic Church. His passion for the traditional can be seen in his *Parochial and Plain Sermons* (1868). In a series of pamphlets, *Tracts for the Times* (1834-1841), Newman is very critical of both the Anglican liturgy and theology. In these famous apologetic tracts, Newman defended the notion that the Anglican Church stood a glorious middle ground between the Roman Catholic and Reformed traditions. But though he struggled to remain loyal, Newman felt increasingly alienated from the Anglican Church. In 1841, however, when he wrote *Tract 90* to argue that the Thirty-Nine Articles could be interpreted from either a Reformed or Catholic perspective, he created such a furor that the Bishop of Oxford silenced him. This led to him turning completely to the Roman Catholic Church, to which he was ordained in 1845. He immediately wrote *Essay on the Development of Christian Doctrine*.

In 1854, Newman was appointed Rector of the Catholic University at Dublin, where he remained for four years. Although the university fell upon hard times, Newman continued to deliver the lectures that became his work, *The Ideal of a University*, regarded as a definitive statement of the nature of a liberal education.

In 1864, Newman responded to an attack leveled against him by Charles Kingsley. His response, the *Apologia Pro Vita Sua,* developed into his own spiritual autobiography, and is now generally regarded as the greatest classic of devotional literature of the nineteenth century. In 1870, Newman wrote another theological classic, *Grammar of Assent*. Newman was elevated to the position of Cardinal eleven years before his death (in 1890).

The *Apolgia Pro Vita Sua* (1864), Newman's autobiography, might be called "A Defense of My Life." A number of the chapters are devoted to analysis of, and response to, Kingsley's accusation that Newman taught that truth is not a virtue. In addition to replying as a spiritual and, indeed, an intellectual biography, Newman divides each section into a history of his religious opinions through four eras of his life. In *Apologia*, Newman reveals the philosophical assumptions that were the foundations of his intellectual development. Although he reveals mystical tendencies, he rejects completely the role of intellectual skepticism.

Newman also reveals the circumstances surrounding his intellectual conversion in 1816 when he entered Oxford, and he recounts the influence of his Oxford colleagues in shaping his theology. Like so many others whose lives had been radically changed, he cites the impression made upon him by William Law's *Serious Call*. He also reveals his inner struggles while a vicar of the Anglican Church, and traces systematically the issues and events that led to his conversion to Catholicism.

Resources on the Reading of Classical and Devotional Literature

Baldwin, Barry. "Reading Christian Literature: Historical Profits and Literary Pleasures." *Patristic and Byzantine Review* 9 (1990): 135–48.

Benedict, Philip. "Print and the Experience of Ritual: Huguenot Books of Preparation for the Lord's Supper." In *Le Livre Religieux et Ses Pratiques*, edited by H. Beodeker et al. Göttingen, Vandemhoeck and Ruprecht, 1991.

Bielby, M. R. "Works of Devotion as Literature." *London Quarterly and Holborn Review* 180 (October 1955): 260–64.

Boyd, Malcolm. "Interior and Exterior Pilgrimages." *Christian Century* 95 (15 November 1978): 1106–1109.

Brown, Raymond E. "Medieval Spirituality." *Baptist Quarterly* 27 (January 1978): 194–211.

Brumm, Ursula. "Faith and Imagery in Puritan Meditation Literature." In *Religion and Philosophy in the USA*, Vol. 1., edited by P. Freese: 61–75. 2 vols. Proceedings of the German-American Conference at Paderborn, July 29–August, 1986.

Casteel, John L. "Bibliography for Ministers: The Life of Prayer and Devotion." *Union Seminary Quarterly Review* 14 (March 1959): 37–41.

Chinnici, Joseph P. "Organization of the Spiritual Life: American Catholic Devotional Works, 1791–1866." *Theological Studies* 40 (June 1979): 229–55.

Cunningham, Lawrence S. "The Classics of Western Spirituality: Some Recent Volumes." *Religious Studies Review* 12 (April 1986): 104–111.

Eliot, T. S. "Religion and Literature." In *The Christian Imagination*, edited by L. Ryken. Grand Rapids, MI: Baker, 1981.

"Focus on Resources: Liturgy an Devotion." *Review of Books and Religion* 10, no. 4 (Fall 1982): 4.

Hansen, C. D. "Reading for Your Ministry." *Christianity Today* 26 (5 March 1982): 90–91.

Holmer, Paul L. "Uses of Devotional Literature." *Journal of Bible and Religion* 22 (April 1954): 99–103.

Howe, Rex. "Spirituality in the Modern World: Modern Spiritual Reading." *Expository Times* 89 (May 1978): 228–230.

Huston, James M. "A Guide to Devotional Reading." *Crux* 22 (November 1986): 2–15.

Lagorio, Valerie M. "Variations on the Theme of God's Motherhood in Medieval English Mystical and Devotional Writings." *Studia Mystica* 8 (Summer 1985): 15–37.

Lapsley, James Norvell, Jr. "The Devotional Life and Mental Health: An Exploration of Relationships." Ph.D. diss., University of Chicago, 1962.

Lewis, Clive Staples. "On the Reading of Old Books." *Epiphany* 1 (Fall 1980): 102–6.

Lovelace, Richard C. "The Anatomy of Puritan Piety: English Puritan Devotional Literature." in *Christian Spirituality: Post-Reformation and Modern,* edited by L. Dupre. New York: Crossroad, 1989.

Low, Anthony. "Interrelationships Between Religion and Poetry: Recent Studies of the Early 17th Century English Poets." *Religion and Literature* 17 (Summer 1985): 55–60.

Marty, Martin E. "My Choice of Books: Martin Marty Sifts the Books That Have Had a Lasting Effect." *Leadership* 4 (Winter 1983): 95.

Montgomery, John Warwick. "Can We Recover the Devotional Life?" *Christianity Today* 5 (25 September 1961): 3–6.

———. "100 Select Devotional Books." *Christianity Today* 5 (25 September 1961): 6–8.

Mudge, James. "Books of the Inner Life." *Methodist Quarterly Review* 64 (April 1915): 229–44.

Noll, Mark A. "A Precarious Balance: Two Hundred Years of Presbyterian Devotional Literature." *American Presbyterians* 68 (Fall 1990): 207–19.

———. "The Language(s) of Zion: Presbyterian Devotional Literature in the Twentieth Century." In *The Confessional Mosaic: Presbyterians and the Twentieth-Century Theology,* edited by M. Coalter et al. Louisville, KY: Westminster, 1990.

Owst, G. R. "Sermon As Literature." *London Quarterly and Holborn Review* 180 (October 1955): 250–54.

Quayle, William Alfred. "The Literature of Devotion." *Methodist Review* 86 (January 1904): 36–50.

Richardson, Cyril Charles. "Christian Classics in Translation." *Union Seminary Quarterly Review* 15 (March 1960): 251–54.

Smith, Wilbur M. "Suggestions for Reading in the Great Christian Classics." In *A Treasury of Books for Bible Study*. Natick, MA: W. A. Wilde, 1960.

———. "Ten of the Greatest Christian Books: A Suggested List; Part One." *The Alliance Weekly* 85 (2 September 1950): 547–48.

———. "Ten of the Greatest Christian Books: A Suggested List; Part Two." *The Alliance Weekly* 85 (9 September 1950): 565–66.

———. "Ten of the Greatest Christian Books: A Suggested List; Part Three." *The Alliance Weekly* 85 (16 September 1950): 581–82.

Stanwood, P. G. "Seventeenth-Century English Literature and Contemporary Criticism." *Anglican Theological Review* 62 (October 1980): 395–410.

Stoeffler, F. Ernest. "Mysticism in the German Devotional Literature of Colonial Pennsylvania." Ph.D. diss., Temple University, 1972.

Stone, Frank F. "Seventeenth-Century Devotional Literature in the Anglican Church." Ph.D. diss., Hartford Seminary Foundation, 1950.

Stormon, E. J. "The English Mystics." in *Christian Spiritual Theology on Ecumenical Reflection*, ed. Noel Ryan. 161-172. East Malvern, VC: Dove Communications, 1976.

Tischler, Nancy M. "The Christian Reader." In *The Christian Imagination*, edited by L. Ryken. Grand Rapids, MI: Baker, 1981.

Tracy, David W. "On Thinking with the Classics." *Criterion* 22 (Autumn 1983): 9–10.

Tsirpanlis, Constantine N. "The Saints' Message for Today." *Orthodox Thought and Life: A Journal Devoted to Popular Orthodox Enlightenment and Eastern Christian Spirituality* (1986). Kingston, NY: Hellenism in America, 1984.

Wakefield, Gordon S. "Spirituality in the Modern World: Classics of the Spiritual Life and Their Use Today." *Expository Times* 89 (June 1978): 260–64.

Walker, C. R. "Devotional Literature." *Scottish Journal of Theology* 3 (1950): 149-61.

Journals

For those interested in a more intensive study, there are a number of journals dealing with particular aspects of classical and contemporary devotional literature.

Bibliographia Internationalis Spiritualitatis. Edited by the Pontifical Institute of Spirituality. Milan: Editrice Ancora, 1966- .
"A comprehensive classified bibliography of monographic and journal literature on spirituality."—John Bollier.

Christianity & Literature. Baylor University, Waco, Texas. 1973- .
As the title indicates, serious articles on all aspects of the relationship between Christianity and classical or contemporary literature.

References

Allison, Joseph D. *The Devotional Resource Guide.* Nashville, TN: Thomas Nelson, 1986.

St. Anselm. *Why God Became Man.* Translated by Joseph M. Colleran. [1098 A.D.] Albany, NY: Magi Books, 1982.

St. Athanasius. *The Incarnation of the Word of God.* 325 A.D.

Boswell, James. *The Life of Samuel Johnson.* Vol. 1. (Mowberry Morris edition). London: Macmillan, 1912.

Brown, Juanita, ed. *An Introduction to Five Spiritual Classics.* New York: Woman's Division of Christian Service, Board of Missions of the Methodist Church, c.1955.

Ferm, Vergilius. *Classics of Protestantism.* New York: Philosophical Library, c.1959.

Gibbon, Edward. *The Autobiographies of Edward Gibbon.* London: J. Murray, 1896.

Luther, Martin. *Luther's Works.* 55 vols. St. Louis, MO: Concordia, 1958–1986.

Martin, Hugh. *Great Christian Books.* c.1945; reprint, Freeport, NY: Books for Libraries, 1971.

McNeil, John T. *Books of Faith and Power.* New York: Harper & Brothers, c.1947.

Migne, J. P. *Patrologiae Cursus Completus, Series Latina* (Paris, 1844-1855). 221 vols.

———. *Patrologiae Cerus Completus, Series Graeca* (Paris, 1857-1866). 161 vols.

Schaff, Philip, and Henry Wace. *A Select Library of Nicene and Post-Nicene Fathers of the Christian Church.* (Buffalo, NY: T. and T. Clark, 1886-1900. 28 vols. reprinted, Grand Rapids, MI: William B. Eerdmans, 1952-1957. 14 vols.).

Quasten, Johannes. *Patrology.* (Westminster, MD: Newman Press, 1950-1986. 9 vols.).

Smith, Wilbur M. *Before I Forget.* Chicago: Moody Press, 1971.

———. "Suggestions for Readings in the Great Christian Classics." In *A Treasury of Books for Bible Study.* Natick, MA: W. A. Wilde, 1960.

———. "Ten of the Greatest Christian Books: A Suggested List; Part One." *The Alliance Weekly* 85 (2 September 1950): 547–48.

———. "Ten of the Greatest Christian Books: A Suggested List; Part Two." *The Alliance Weekly* 85 (9 September 1950): 565–66.

———. "Ten of the Greatest Christian Books: A Suggested List; Part Three." *The Alliance Weekly* 85 (16 September 1950): 581–82.

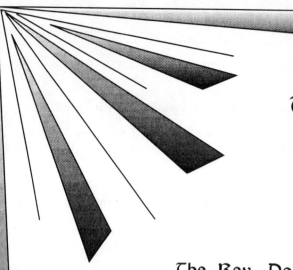

11
The Gift of Long Life: Aging and Religion

The Rev. Dora Elaine Tiller

Introduction

If we could gather all the people who have lived to be sixty-five years or older in all of history, *one half of them would be living today!* This amazing fact was pointed out in a speech given by Father Charles Fahey of the Fordham University Third Age Center. It vividly illustrates the enormous extension of life expectancy that we are seeing in the twentieth century. With the conquest of many diseases, better nutrition, improved sanitation, and more effective health care, the potential exists for many more of us to live to an older age than at any other time in history. Indeed, the fastest growing segment of our population is persons over eighty-five years of age.

Consider these facts:

- In 1993, one of every eight persons in the U.S. was sixty-five years or older, representing 12.7 percent of the U.S. population.

- In 1993, approximately 5,500 persons celebrated their sixty-fifth birthday every day, while each day there were only 4,090 deaths of persons age sixty-five or older; thus, each day, the net increase of people sixty-five or older in the U.S. was 1,410.

- In 1970, there were one-third more teenagers in the U.S. than persons sixty-five or older; in 1990, there are one-third more people over sixty-five than there are teenagers.

- The average person reaching sixty-five today can expect to live approximately 17.5 years more.

- In the next thirty years, according to Census Bureau estimates, the under-fifty population will grow by only 1 percent, while the over-fifty population will grow by 74 percent. (U.S. Senate Special Committee on Aging 1987-88; AARP 1994)

Some call this older adult population the "Third Age." The National Benevolent Association put out a film in 1975 called *The Third Age: The New Generation*. The film is about older persons involved in volunteer work. It is a positive, upbeat, realistic look at retirement, saying that it is not a time for the rocking chair, but a time for growth, developing new potentials and dreams, and using the accumulated wisdom of a lifetime. The film celebrates the too often untapped resources of older persons.

The term Third Age was coined by the French for the period of life after schooling (the First Age), and after parenting and the world of work (the Second Age). The Third Age is a time when we are no longer defined by being parents, or by the career we pursued. In the Third Age we have the opportunity to seek an identity that comes from inside ourselves rather than from what we do. "Being" becomes as important as "doing." Internal issues and concerns become a priority. Because a person's faith is so integral to these issues of self, it becomes imperative for religious congregations to develop ministries with, by, and for older persons. It also behooves religious congregations to understand aging and older persons.

As a nation, as individuals, and as religious bodies, we are growing older. When we combine living to an older age with more and more people choosing to accept early retirement, we find that many will have twenty, thirty and more years of retirement to live out in productive ways. The retirement years are not years away *from* something, they are years to *become* something new. As author-lecturer, Eda LeShan says,

> self-discovery starts at birth and should never end. It ought to range from the first discovery of one's toes and the excitement of recognizing an image in the mirror as one's own, all the way to figuring out what a whole lifetime has been all about. The people who are still alive at the time of their death are the ones who wake up each morning wondering what new thing they will learn about themselves. (*It's Better to Be Over the Hill Than Under It*, p. 179)

Our religious institutions can enable older persons to continue to grow and learn, to become something new, for as long as they live.

This chapter reviews a variety of books and videos to help you, as a person in a religious congregation, to begin to develop a program with, for, and by senior adults in your congregation and community that takes their interests, needs, strengths, and accumulated wisdom into consideration. These resources are organized in areas of interest to anyone working with senior adults in religious institutions. Obviously, this will not be an exhaustive list of the books and videos on the market. Rather, the hope of this author is to provide resources for clergy and laypersons wanting to include aging issues and concerns in the programs of the congregation such as sermons and educational events. Also, to help those responsible for developing programs with senior adults themselves, and for those who want to learn more about aging.

Understanding Aging Issues

The first step in helping people of any age understand their aging process is to get an immersion in the literature of the field. Preferably, this immersion will enable readers to look at their own aging and to integrate these experiences into themselves. One of the reasons that we are age denying is that we have not integrated our aging into ourselves. If we are afraid of our aging, then we will certainly deny others' aging. When we deny aging in this way, we discount older persons in our congregations and communities. We try to ignore their presence and so deny their personhood and their importance as creatures of God. We take part in a U.S. culture that, unlike some other cultures, does not respect aging or the contributions of its aging members—a culture that remains youth-oriented and age-denying.

When we deny our aging and the aging of others, we become depressed. It takes enormous amounts of energy to deny something that surrounds us and is within us. Whole congregations are depressed because of this age-denying syndrome. To begin to let the light shine into this darkness, one can begin with this great book on aging:

Nouwen, H. J., and W. J. Gaffney. *Aging: The Fulfillment of Life.* Garden City, NY: Image Books/Doubleday, 1976. 160p. $5.95pa. LC 74-1773. ISBN 0-385-00918-6.

This book is written in a poetic, contemplative style that draws the reader of any age into the writers' perspective on the interdependence of all ages—the interconnectedness of all persons. The authors begin by saying,

> This is a book about aging. It is a book for all of us, since we all age and so fulfill the cycle of our lives. This is what the large wagon wheel reclining against the old birch in the white snow teaches us by its simple beauty. No one of its spokes is more important than the others, but together they make the circle full and reveal the hub as the core of its strength. (p.13)

The sense of wholeness of this book is enhanced by the use of photographs throughout, beginning with a picture of an old wagon wheel.

The theological underpinnings of this book are an awareness of the interconnectedness of all of God's creation. It is in this wholeness, this togetherness of the ages, that we find healing. Nouwen and Gaffney encourage us to break through the stereotypes of our society to see the real persons who are older with all of their weaknesses, their humor, their wisdom, their hopes, their longings, and their fears. In this way, they bring wholeness to those of us who are younger, just as younger persons bring wholeness to those who are older. In the wisdom of God, the generations need each other for completeness and fulfillment.

These authors challenge us to open ourselves to our aging process and the aging of others.

> There is the temptation to make aging into the problem of the elderly and to deny our basic human solidarity in this most human process. Maybe we have been trying hard to silence the voices of those who remind us of our own destiny and have become our sharpest critics by their very presence. Thus our first and most important task is to help the elderly become our teachers again and to restore the broken connections among the generations. (p. 17)

Reading this beautifully written book would be a good first step for an individual or small group to begin to accept their aging, and thus begin to also accept the aging of others. As Nouwen and Gaffney say, "to care one must offer one's own vulnerable self to others as a source of healing. To care for the aging, therefore, means first of all to enter into close contact with your own aging self." (p. 97)

This inspirational book brings new perspectives to aging. The authors believe that "aging is not a reason for despair but a basis for hope, not a slow decaying but a gradual maturing, not a fate to be undergone but a chance to be embraced." (p. 20) This book can enable the reader to look at older persons and themselves in a new way, and be more open to being cared for and more open to caring for others. The fact that life ends, rather than being a reason for despair, is a reason to rejoice in its preciousness, and to savor each moment and each day. Reading this book can be a transforming experience if the reader is open.

Another wonderful book on aging that persons of all ages can enjoy and learn from is

Tournier, Paul. *Learn to Grow Old.* San Francisco: Harper & Row, 1972. 248p. $8.95pa. LC 83-10770. ISBN 0-06-068361-9.

Paul Tournier's life and writings effectively combine the insights of modern psychotherapy and Christian faith. Tournier quotes Denis de Rougemont,

> Man has two aims in life, the first is the natural aim of the procreation of descendants and the care required for the

preservation of his young, involving the acquisition of wealth and social status. When this aim has been satisfied, another phase begins, the goal of which is culture. (p. 10)

Tournier then goes on to say that there are two great turning points in life: the passage from childhood to adulthood, and that from adulthood to old age. He says that the first turning point is an advance to maturity, and the second turning point is an advance into fulfillment. Tournier then asks why we are so afraid of this second turning point, trying to keep it at a distance and separate from ourselves. He says that to refuse to grow old is as foolish as to refuse to leave behind one's childhood. Through the rest of the book, Tournier explores the ways we, as individuals and as a society, keep ourselves from the fulfillment of old age, and then explores ways that we can prepare and plan for growing older throughout life. Tournier sees growing old as a process that goes on throughout all of life, if it is accomplished successfully and with grace.

Tournier has much to offer to those of us in faith communities that want to work with older persons. He says that the well-being of the aged is partly dependent on the attitude of those around them. If we deny their aging, then we insist that they also deny it. When this becomes impossible, they either leave the community or withdraw emotionally into themselves. "On the other hand," he says, "there is plenty of evidence of the spectacular transformation that can take place in old people once they feel themselves to be accepted as valued members of a friendly community."(p. 37) The church can be the community that rejects aging and drives the elderly to withdrawal and depression, or it can be a community that accepts the gifts older persons have to offer. The most exciting part of working with churches in developing senior adult ministries is to watch this transformation take place in individuals and their community of faith.

Another important statement by Tournier that we in faith communities must take seriously is: "It is not just a matter of consoling and entertaining the old by offering them some leisure occupation. It is that society desperately needs the services which the old are better qualified than the young to provide." (p. 123) It is not a matter of doing things to, or for, our elderly population, of feeding them pablum, but it is instead a matter of working with them to develop senior adult ministries that feed the souls of older persons. Tournier sees our goal as enabling a fruitful old age, which he defines as being "open to the world, attentive to people, an old age that is ardent as well as serene, an old age which goes on fighting, and with passion; differently from youth, of course, but fighting nevertheless, for all life is a struggle."(p. 131)

After reading the above introductory materials to aging, if laypersons or clergy want to continue to read in this field to begin to think of developing ministries with older persons, the next book to turn to might be:

Taylor, Blaine. *The Church's Ministry with Older Adults.* Nashville, TN: Abingdon Press, 1984. 143p. $10.95pa. LC 86-22142. ISBN 0-687-08382-6.

Rev. Taylor wrote this book after thirteen years in a large urban church, where over half the active members were over sixty-five years old. He writes, "Already close to 30 percent of the active members of Christian churches in the United States are over sixty-five; however, many churches concentrate their ministries on other age groups." (p. 11). Many congregations in the United States are 80 or 90 percent older persons. Yet when you ask what their hopes, dreams, or goals for the congregation are, they will say, "To have youth groups or to attract younger people." I hear this repeatedly and marvel that we aspire to ministry with persons who are not in our pews, at the expense of those who are and who need ministry for themselves, and to provide ministry for others. This book describes the pilgrimage of a pastor and his congregation as they took seriously the persons in the pews—what their needs were and what their strengths were. "This is a handbook for pastors and churches trying to better serve those over sixty-five years of age." (p. 11) It is not a how-to book, but rather a "toolbox of suggestions, illustrations, and program hints designed for clergy and lay people committed to ministry with America's fastest growing population group." (p. 11)

Blaine Taylor's book is one by a pastor listening and learning from his older congregation, and developing ministries that relate both to their needs and their gifts. He says

> I knew the church should minister to them [older persons], but I did not see them as people who were fully alive and active in all areas of life. In just a few months I discovered how wrong I had been. As I visited with those over sixty-five in their homes and at church, I discovered, with quite some surprise, that they were just like other people. . . . They didn't want to be ministered *to*; they wanted to *minister.* (p. 19)

The book continues in this way as Rev. Taylor tells of learning from the older persons in his congregation. It offers an interesting new perspective on the wealth of resources to be tapped in our older congregations—riches and resources so often ignored.

Another book that should be mentioned, and which is very worthwhile for a good summary of the theories of aging that have been developed over the years is

Hightower, James E., Jr., ed. *Caring for Folks from Birth to Death.* Nashville, TN: Broadman Press, 1985. 163p. $6.95pa. LC 84-20005. ISBN 0-8054-2415-6.

Chapter 6, contributed by Albert L. Meiburg, is called "Senior Adulthood: Twilight or Dawn?" This chapter reviews the different theories of the developmental tasks of aging, and then discusses pastoral care issues of older persons in the light of these tasks. It is an informative chapter and well worth the time to digest.

Stafford, Tim. *As Our Years Increase—Loving, Caring, Preparing: A Guide*. Grand Rapids, MI: Pyranee Books/Zondervan, 1989. 251p. $14.95pa. LC 88-13766. ISBN 0-310-32840-3.

Tim Stafford presents much practical information in this book organized around seven days of growing older as a play on the seven days of creation. This book goes beyond practical information to probing the ultimate questions like: "What is aging for?" "What is the meaning of aging?" and "Why is aging part of God's plan?" In this book, Stafford answers these questions from his Christian perspective. He encourages the reader to develop a better image of old age—one that does not ignore the difficulties of growing older, but one that is not immobilized by the fear of growing older. He finds the positives of growing older as well as the difficulties.

Resources on Understanding Aging Issues

The following is a list of some other books on understanding aging, with very brief descriptions:

Clements, William M., ed. *Ministry with the Aging: Designs, Challenges, Foundations*. New York: Harper & Row, 1981. 274p. $9.95. LC 80-7739. ISBN 0-06-061496-X.

A comprehensive book that covers aging, beginning with the biblical foundations of ministry with the aging to some specific models of senior adult ministries. This book is academically geared and may be difficult reading for laypersons. It will certainly be helpful to professional church staff.

Erikson, Erik H., Joan M. Erikson, and Helen Q. Kivnick. *Vital Involvement in Old Age: The Experience of Old Age in Our Time*. New York: W. W. Norton, 1989. 352p. $10.70pa. LC 86-16380. ISBN 0-393-30509-0.

This book uses as its basis Erik Erikson's eight stages of psychological development throughout the life cycle. Many octogenarians were interviewed over a period of years, and the majority of the book interprets their life experiences. It presents these people as persons who have been reworking and integrating their experiences while remaining involved in the present.

Jacobs, Arthur T., ed. *Judaism, the Synagogue, and the Aging: A Sabbath Study Session*. New York: Union of American Hebrew Congregations, 1962. 60p. Price not reported.

This booklet is a collection of thirteen short lectures given at a symposium on the concerns and issues of an aging society and aging congregations. These lectures include such topics as the religious foundations of being involved with older persons, health services, housing, income maintenance, and the meaningful use of time. Even though this symposium took place in 1962, it remains worthwhile reading, and continues to sound a call to the religious person to take seriously the needs of the elderly.

Butler, R. N. *Why Survive? Being Old in America.* New York: Harper & Row, 1985. 510p. $10.95pa. ISBN 0-06-131997-X.

This is a classic book written about older persons' experiences in America in the early 1970s. Butler introduces the ideas of ageism, the devaluing of older persons in our society, and the negative stereotypes of older persons that we live by. The roles that religious institutions and religion play in the lives of older persons are interwoven throughout the book. Also introduced in this book are Butler's ideas of life review and reminiscence, and are discussed in a later section of this chapter.

Neugarten, Bernice L., ed. *Middle Age and Aging: A Reader in Social Psychology.* Chicago: The University of Chicago Press, 1968. $20.00pa. LC 68-55150. ISBN 0-226-57382-6.

This is another classic work of studies by pioneers in the field of gerontology. It is an academic work, so it may not be accessible to all laypersons, but for others it will be very helpful. There is a chapter specifically on religion and old age contributed by David Moberg.

Audiovisual Resources on Understanding Aging Issues

Besides books, there are other educational resources for yourself and others about aging issues and concerns. Following are videos and films that can be used for educational events in your congregation. See the "Resources" section of this chapter for ordering information. Some of these resources may also be available through the audiovideo department within your faith group. Write and order a catalog from that department.

All Your Parts Don't Wear Out at the Same Time. Produced by Alfred Shands, 1979. 16mm, 1/2" VHS, color, 28 min. $35 rental. junior high through adults. Order from Mass Media Ministries.

A delightful, insightful film that shows older persons taking risks and continuing to grow. In the film you meet members of a drama group called "Senior Players," who present humorous skits taken from their lives. This is a fun film that teaches us about the ingredient of laughing at ourselves and risking, in order to continue growth throughout the life cycle.

Annie and the Old One. Produced by BFA Educational Media, 1976, VHS, 16mm, color, 24 min. $20 rental. Children of all ages can learn from it. Order from EcuFilm.

Annie's grandmother teaches her about life and death, and about how her grandmother's wisdom will live on through her.

Because Somebody Cares. Produced by Terra Nova Films, 1982. 16mm, color, 27 min. $35 rental. Adults. Order from EcuFilm.
This film portrays persons involved in a volunteer ministry with isolated older persons. This is a ministry of young and old that maintains the dignity and individuality of the frail older persons that receive visits.

Close Harmony. Produced by Learning Corporation of America, 1981. 16mm, color, 30 min. $25 rental. Children through adults. Order from EcuFilm.
Wonderful film about a Jewish community center in Brooklyn, New York, where senior adults became pen pals with children from a Quaker elementary school. The movie shows what they learned from each other and they gave a joint choral concert. Gives interesting insights into the way children perceive older persons.

A Good Old Age. Produced by United Methodist Communications, 1989. 1/2" VHS, color, 23 min. $18 rental. Adults. Order from EcuFilm.
Interesting older persons share the rewards, problems, pains, fears, and joys of aging. They discuss health, accepting change, new opportunities they have to be helpful to others, learning, and growing.

Hello in There. Produced by Franciscan Communications, 1978. 1/2" VHS, color, 21 min. $12.50 rental. Youth through adults. Order from American Baptist Films/Video.
A touching story about an elderly, lonely woman living in a sterile retirement home, who fills her days in meaningless ways. She is eventually befriended by a customer-relations worker in a department store, and they both gain from the relationship they build.

Independence and 76. Produced by Family Films, 1981. 16mm, color, 30 min. $35 rental. Adults. Order from American Baptist Films/Video.
This is a specifically Christian film about a seventy-six-year-old widower searching for independence from his affluent adult son in whose home he lives. The widower meets an elderly woman, Aggie, who teaches him about inner peace and freedom found in the relationship with God through Christ. Aggie, who has little worldly wealth, is a very wealthy woman spiritually, and is willing to share her wealth with her newfound friend.

Journey Together. Produced by Guenette-Asselin Productions, 1978. 16mm, color, 22 min. $25 rental. Junior high through adults. Order from American Baptist Films/Video.
This film is about the relationship between a teenager struggling with adolescent difficulties and a lonely older woman struggling with

issues of poverty. The teenager mobilizes her friends to help secure help for older persons on fixed incomes. Helpful in creating intergenerational discussions.

Minnie Remembers. Produced by United Methodist Communications, 1976. 1/2" VHS, color, 5 min. $12.50 rental. Youth through adults. Order from EcuFilm.

This short film, adapted from a poem by Donna Swanson, is a good discussion-starter about aging and issues of loneliness and isolation. This is a sad and disconcerting film, in which viewers feel Minnie's mortality and loneliness, bringing their own loneliness and mortality into focus.

The Shopping Bag Lady. Produced by Learning Corporation of America, 1975. 16mm, color, 21 min. $20 rental. Youth. Order from EcuFilm.

Teen-aged Emily becomes acquainted with an elderly street woman, and discovers in the old woman the young girl she used to be. Emily begins to confront her immortality through her newfound friend. Emily grows through this experience to develop new compassion and tolerance for her family members and others. Helpful in creating intergenerational discussions.

The Third Age: The New Generation Produced by National Benevolent Association, 1975. 16mm, color, 15 min. $10.50 rental. Adults. Order from EcuFilm.

A positive, upbeat, realistic view of older persons, and the growth that can take place in the Third Age. A variety of older volunteers are interviewed about their lives. This is a celebrative film of the resources and wisdom of older persons.

To a Good Long Life. Produced by BFA Educational Media, 1976. 16mm, color, 22 min. $22 rental. Youth through adults. Order from EcuFilm.

This film shows young persons the positive as well as the negative aspects of aging. This is a documentary about three elderly people who lead vigorous and interesting lives, and handle their difficulties creatively. These older persons are models for people of all ages.

Aging Me . . . Aging You . . . The Journey of a Lifetime. Produced by Office on Older Adult Ministry, Congregational Ministries Division, Presbyterian Church (USA), 1994. 1/2" VHS. 33 min. $19.95 purchase. Youth through adults. Order from Distribution Management Services.

A video and study guide that offers the audience a realistic glimpse into the journey of aging—a journey from birth to death. Follow up video to be available May 1995.

Volunteer to Live. Produced by CBS-TV, 1976. 16mm, 1/2" VHS, color, 30 min. $20 rental. Adults. Order from EcuFilm.

This is a documentary about the development and functioning of the Shepherd Center in Kansas City. The Shepherd Center is an interfaith program, where older persons help themselves by sharing their time and talents, enriching their lives and the lives of those in their community. This presents a good model of interfaith senior adult ministry run for, with, and by senior adults.

A Week Full of Saturdays. Produced by Film Makers Library, 1979. 16mm, color, 20 min. $22 rental. Adults. Order from American Baptist Films/Video.

This film interviews persons from a variety of backgrounds and interests, and depicts in each interview the need for pre-retirement planning to meet personal goals, and to assure satisfying retirement years.

Spiritual Growth and Aging

This section will review books on the topic that we in the church should be most involved with and concerned about—spiritual growth and development in the senior adult years. Other topics related to aging are also important, but there are secular organizations concerned about health care and caregiving. Only the church, though, works with senior adults in their continued spiritual development. No matter what age we are, we continue to have the possibility of spiritual growth and faith development. However, like any other growth, it takes work, time, energy, and thoughtfulness. One of the ways the church can be supportive of older persons is to continue to encourage and challenge growth in relationship to God and other persons.

Resources on Spiritual Growth and Aging

Aleshire, Daniel O. *Faithcare: Ministering to All God's People Through the Ages of Life.* Philadelphia: Westminster, 1988. 179p. $12.95pa. LC 87-30880. ISBN 0-664-24054-2.

This book addresses how to enable faith development throughout each age of life. The final chapter speaks specifically to the growth of faith in the older years. Aleshire writes that growth comes in the older years when the "experiences of life intersect with the work of grace."(p. 169) He continues, "The experience of life influences the faith that adults fashion, and that faith redefines the experiences of life."(p. 165) Aleshire helps us to see that adult growth never ends if we continue to take the events and experiences of life and interpret them in the light of our faith. By being aware of this integration of experience, we continue to grow and develop in our faith as well as in our understanding of life. This book is useful for pastors and laypersons, encouraging readers to think about how faith changes and develops throughout life, and how the church can encourage and support this process.

Fischer, Kathleen. *Winter Grace: Spirituality for the Later Years.* Mahwah, NJ: Paulist Press, 1985. 170p. $8.95pa. LC 84-61975. ISBN 0-8091-2675-3.

This book should be read by anyone in the church who plans to work with older persons. Dr. Fischer is a theologian and a counselor who combines these disciplines in her writing. She describes spirituality not as a separate compartment of our life, but as the deepest dimension of all experience. She says that all life is of spiritual concern. Thus, questions of meaning in retirement, of housing in our later years, the loss of a spouse, making new friends, and developing new interests, are all spiritual concerns. She writes, "spirituality involves the entire human person in all of his or her relationships."(p. 9) Dr. Fischer is not talking about religious involvement, or church involvement in the later years. He is talking about that faith which informs the real life questions each person faces, the relationship to God that informs all other relationships.

This author believes that our spiritual life incorporates the rest of life—the physical, the psychological, the social, and the economical. Thus, the spiritual informs all parts of the aging process. Fischer goes on to describe how the experiences of aging: love and sexuality, humor and hope, loss, dependence and independence, memories, losing a spouse, dying, and resurrection, can be transformed by our spiritual life. Fischer has a delightful way of intertwining biblical models in her writing to illustrate her points. Losses that accompany aging can be transformed by our spiritual life into new understandings and new perspectives. Aging can be "winter grace" if we continue in our later years to develop our spirituality. This author provides readers with ways to do this through two kinds of prayer, deepening relationships, and exploring biblical personalities for models of living.

Maves, Paul B. *Faith for the Older Years: Making the Most of Life's Second Half.* Minneapolis, MN: Augsburg Fortress, 1986. 189p. $10.95pa. LC 85-30716. ISBN 0-8066-2195-8.

This is a personal testimony of the author's faith search for personal answers to the ultimate questions of life, death, pain, suffering, and aging. He asks the eternal "why" questions, and answers them from his life experience as a pastor, counselor, and researcher in the field of aging for forty years. This book blends the author's theoretical understanding of aging, his theological understanding of aging, and his personal aging process for more than seventy years. He says that the book is an attempt to respond to questions put to him over the years, and also an attempt to clarify his faith and to chart his course through time more faithfully. It is this latter motivation that comes through in the book. Reading this book is like being on Paul Mave's faith journey with him, a journey of questioning and exploring and building a deeper faith in the process.

This book is a positive view of the older years precisely because of the author's faith perspective. He writes

> The last one-third of life can be as satisfying, as meaningful, and as fulfilling as any other period of life, in spite of any pain or loss we may sustain. As the consummation and completion of life, the last one-third ought to be more meaningful than any other period of life. In making this affirmation let me lay to rest some of the stereotypes held by so many. (p. 14)

He then goes on to deal with the stereotypes of aging, such as aging as a disease and as a time of disability. He then writes

> life itself is a gift. The years of old age given to us in this century are a bonus for us to use. . . . We are called to be stewards of this time and our talents. . . . Life does not end at 40, or at 55, or at 65, or even 75. Possibility does not cease at any of these ages either. (p. 26)

Paul Mave's book can have a profound effect on our personal faith journey of aging as we are enabled to look at the doors open to creativity and growth as we take charge of our aging.

Missinne, Leo E. *Reflections on Aging: A Spiritual Guide.* Liguori, MO: Liguori, 1990. 112p. $3.95pa. LC 89-64247. ISBN 0-89243-319-1.

This is a small, large-print, very readable book with much depth, and it would make an excellent resource for a small group study, or as a personal meditation, devotional booklet. However, one would gain more from the book if it was discussed as well as reflected upon. Father Missinne writes, "we'll realize that neither friends nor guides can find the meaning of life and suffering for us; we have to discover it for ourselves" (p. 7), and the rest of his book is an exploration of this meaning. He states further that, "only *you* can respond to the events of your life, give meaning to them, and take responsibility for your own answers."(p. 9) Missinne's writing reflects his personal journey to find meaning in life, death, and suffering, and challenges readers to ask similar questions and to go on their own personal journey in search of personal answers.

Missinne suggests that we need to explore our underlying values, and that the way to do this is through dialogue, nondirective dialogue. We discover the meaning of life by talking and by formulating our thinking into words. To do this, we need someone to listen to us. Then we also need to help others by listening to them.

Missinne divides contemporary Christian spirituality into four styles, all of which lead outward into the world. Missinne's understanding of spirituality is one that goes beyond a personal relationship to God, in that it leads us back into the world to relate to others. Working for peace and justice and to feed the poor are part of our spirituality as much as meditation and prayer. This is an interesting book, well worth the time to read and digest.

Morgan, Richard L. *No Wrinkles on the Soul: A Book of Readings for Older Adults.* Nashville, TN: Upper Room Books, 1990. 158p. $8.95pa. LC 89-51765. ISBN 0-8358-0610-3.
This is a book of 62 devotionals, each containing a Bible verse, a reading to reflect upon, a meditation, and a prayer. The writer is a retired Presbyterian minister who works with older adults as an enabler for the Older Adult Ministry in North Carolina. The meditations are grouped in the following subsections: "Life Begins Every Day," "Tasks of Aging, Old-Age Vulnerabilities," "No Use Denying It," "Keeping the Spirit Renewed," and "Ultimate Thoughts."

Patterson, Leroy. *The Best Is Yet to Be.* Wheaton, IL: Tyndale House, 1986. 220p. $5.95pa. LC 85-52011. ISBN 0-8423-0183-6.
This is a book of 85 devotions for older adults. Each contains a scripture, a meditation, and a prayer. Written by a retired chaplain of Wheaton College, this book is written from personal experiences of growing older. The devotionals are grouped around the topics of attitudes, lifestyle, relationships, renewal, opportunities, hope, and changes. Useful for both personal devotions and small group devotions.

Sapp, Stephen. *Full of Years: Aging and the Elderly in the Bible and Today.* Nashville, TN: Abingdon Press, 1987. 208p. $8.95pa. LC 87-1840. ISBN 0-687-13710-1.
This book, written by an Associate Professor of Religious Studies at the University of Miami (Coral Gables, Florida), begins by talking about the demographic changes that are taking place in our world, and how we need to prepare to deal with these changes over the next few years. Sapp goes to the Bible, both the Hebrew writings and the Christian writings, to find directions for issues of aging today. After finding guidance in the Scriptures, Sapp applies it in the final two chapters on attitudes toward the aging and obligations toward the aging. This book will be helpful to pastors and layleaders alike who are working with older persons in congregations.

Stagg, Frank. *The Bible Speaks on Aging.* Nashville, TN: Broadman Press, 1981. 192p. $8.95pa. LC 81-66092. ISBN 0-8054-5292-3.
This book is a special gift from a retired professor of New Testament at The Southern Baptist Seminary in Louisville, Kentucky. The author writes, "This book grew out of a fresh study of the Bible, with a careful working through it from Genesis through Revelation, putting to it the various questions bearing on age, aging, and ageism."(p. 6) And a fresh study he produced! This is a book that pastors and laypersons alike will turn to time after time for information on the

Bible and aging. Dr. Stagg discusses biblical characters that are models of how to age and how not to age.

Caregiving and Aging

Another area that continues to affect our society and our congregations, elderly and young alike, is caregiving. In this section, we will look at books and other resources for persons giving care to older adults. Many different segments of our population provide this care, including health professionals and social workers. However, the major portion of this care, approximately 85 percent, is provided by family members, especially by adult children and spouses. The majority of caregivers, approximately 75 percent, are females living with care recipients. Opposed to the myth that modern day families do not care for their elderly members is the reality of statistics that show that we do. Indeed, it seems that caring for a relative is so common place that it should be regarded as a normative life event, just as expected as becoming married, working, raising children, or retiring. These and other statistics on caregiving can be found in a 1988 national survey of caregivers conducted for the American Association of Retired Persons, and the Travelers Companies Foundation called *The National Survey of Caregivers: Final Report*. Many good books have been published to help caregivers.

Deane, Barbara. *Caring for Your Aging Parent: When Love Is not Enough*. Colorado Springs, CO: NavPress, 1989. 276p. $9.95pa. LC 89-62760. ISBN 0-89109-578-0.
    This is written from a Christian perspective by a woman who cared for her mother in her home for eight years, and co-founded a support group for caregivers called Christian Caregivers. This book gives practical advice and provides support that will enable a caregiver to set limits, and learn how to be a care manager rather than attempt to provide all the care alone. This book has an excellent chapter on self-preservation during caregiving.

Edinberg, Mark A. *Talking with Your Aging Parents*. Boston: Shambhala, 1988. 220p. $9.95pa. LC 86-29826. ISBN 0-87773-390-2; 0-87773-440-2pa.
    This is a book written for adult children to encourage positive communication with older parents about difficult topics such as alternative housing, legal and financial matters, death and dying, confusion, nursing homes and long term care, and much more. This book is full of valuable information. It is written by a clinical psychologist who specializes in counseling older persons and their families.

Gillies, John. *A Guide to Caring for and Coping with Aging Parents*. Nashville, TN: Thomas Nelson, 1981. 208p. $5.95pa. LC 81-1138. ISBN 0-8407-5772-7.

This is another book written from the perspective of a man who provided care for his parents, and it is full of concrete information about alternative housing, adult daycare, nursing homes, transferring from wheelchair to car, bathing and showering, incontinence, and more. There is a chapter titled "The Religious Community's Ministry to the Aging," which includes what churches are doing and what is not being done. This chapter would be helpful to laypersons and pastoral staff alike.

Hauk, Gary. *Building Bonds Between Adults and Their Aging Parents.* Nashville, TN: Convention Press, 1987. 159p. $4.25pa.

Written for families before family caregiving begins, this book enables adult children and older parents to talk about important issues, to bond on deeper levels, and to prepare and plan for the future. As the author states, the goals of this book are:

- to help aging parents and adult children better understand each other,

- to look at possible changing roles,

- to define and express needs,

- to cope with adjustments,

- to look at potential problems,

- to choose workable solutions,

- to better understand how to grow old, and

- to establish and use biblical-based guidelines for building and maintaining healthy and meaningful relationships. (p. 17)

Throughout this book are exercises, learning activities and questions that enable the reader to grow in personal understanding, and in relationship with family members. This book could be used as a study aid within a family, in a Sunday School class, or in other small church groups. It is also a good resource to enable older persons to ask themselves some hard questions such as "What do you expect from your adult children in the way of care when you become frailer?" and "Have you talked with your adult children about their expectations of their role in helping you as you become frailer?" This is a book that combines personal stories from the author's life, as well as more intellectual sources. It is a book that would enable readers to grow in relationships within their family.

Horne, Jo. *Caregiving: Helping an Aging Loved One.* Washington, DC: published for the American Association of Retired Persons by Scott, Foresman, 1985. 319p. $13.95pa. LC 85-18343. ISBN 0-673-24822-4.

This is another comprehensive book, giving hands-on, concrete information for caregivers, such as basic nursing techniques, caring for the mentally impaired, setting ground rules for the primary caregiver, and other help for caregivers. It also has a chapter on political advocacy around caregiving issues—needed changes, and how to be part of bringing about these changes. This book also does a good job of giving information and understanding of specific diseases and mental impairments. This is a very practical and down-to-earth book that a person contemplating becoming a caregiver, or who is involved in caregiving, would find helpful.

Manning, Doug. *When Love Gets Tough: The Nursing Home Decision.* Hereford, TX: In-Sight Books, 1988, 12th rev. ed. 91p. $4.50pa.
    This is a very useful book for persons who are having to make tough choices between what Manning calls "distasteful" options. In this book, he discusses his personal decision-making, and the issues of guilt that surround the nursing home decision. The first chapter in the book is "Love Is Doing What People Need—Not What They Want," and each of the chapters that follow reflect the pain and struggle of making these difficult choices with or for a loved one.
    Mishkin, Barbara. *A Matter of Choice: Planning Ahead for Health Care Decisions.* Washington, DC: American Assoc. of Retired Persons, 87pp. Order from Program Resources Dept., AARP, 601 E. Street NW, Washington, DC 20049. Order # PF 3861 (1289): D12776. U.S. Senate Special Committee on Aging. Distributed by the American Association of Retired Persons. The booklet is free of charge. This booklet is essential reading for anyone planning seminars or other educational events in this area of legal decisions. It explains in great detail about advanced directives, as well as about guardianship, patient consent, and family consent laws on a state-by-state basis. It also contains samples of advanced directive documents.

Pierskalla, Carol Spargo, and Jane Dewey Heald. *Help for Families of the Aging.* 2d rev. ed. Swarthmore, PA: Support Source, 1988. Leader's manual, 224p.$39.95 (spiralbound); participant's workbook, 80p. $11.95 (spiralbound). ISBN 0-9619558-0-5; 0-9619558-1-3.
    The leader's manual is written for an eight-week seminar, and provides the tools for an inexperienced group leader to facilitate healthy decision-making, problem-solving, and communication on the part of participant caregivers. The group leader would not need to be a professional, but would need the ability to listen carefully and to accept others' pain.
    The participant's workbook is integrated carefully with the leader manual so that participants have work to do with the group to enable more growth in opening up options for themselves in their caregiving. The goal of this seminar is to enable participants to be intentional in their caregiving and to set limits for themselves so that they can promote the most loving relationships possible. This seminar encourages caregivers to think through what they can and cannot provide to

their loved one, so that they do not exhaust themselves trying to provide everything. In this second edition of this manual is a new section on spiritual issues and caregiving that addresses passages from both the Hebrew and Christian Scriptures. This is a wonderful addition for persons in churches looking for materials for caregivers. As it says in the leader's manual, "Caregiving *is* a journey; it can turn out to be a pilgrimage"—a pilgrimage of self knowledge and growth. (p. 40)

Silverstone, Barbara, and Helen Kandel Hyman. *You and Your Aging Parent: The Modern Family's Guide to Emotional, Physical, and Financial Problems.* New York: Pantheon Books/Random House, 1982. 361p. $8.95pa. LC 81-47214. ISBN 0-394-52169-2; 0-394-74948-0pa.

This comprehensive, almost encyclopedic book on caregiving would be a good resource to use to answer specific questions as they arise. It covers the psychological and sociological dimensions of aging and caregiving, including marriage, sex, widowhood, disabilities, death, relationships, financial matters, family roles, family rivalry, community resources, and more. This revised and updated edition is a classic in this field.

Sommers, Tish, and Laurie Shields. *Women Take Care: The Consequences of Caregiving in Today's Society.* Gainesville, FL: Triad, 1987. 224p. $9.95pa. LC 87-25465. ISBN 0-937404-27-6.

This book is different from the other books listed here, in that it is written to describe who caregivers are and what the issues are for caregivers, to develop a public policy agenda. It does provide practical information, but goes way beyond this to outline suggestions for social change designed to free persons to make choices about caregiving without feeling guilty. The title *Woman Take Care* is both a statement and a warning, stating that women "must take care that more and more of us are not thrust unprepared into a task that is too much for us."(p. 198) This book also talks about how caregiving often leaves women drained both emotionally and financially. At the end of the book is a good listing of resources for caregivers, including equipment resources to national associations.

The Women's Initiative, AARP Health Advocacy Services, Travelers Foundation. *The National Survey of Caregivers: Final Report.* Washington, DC: AARP Program Department, 1988. 119pp. Free from AARP Fulfillment, 601 E. Street NW, Washington, DC 20049.

Audiovisual Resources on Caregiving and Aging

Best Wishes Edith and Harry. Produced by Ruth Stiehl and Vicki Schmall, Oregon State University Extension Service, 1984. Slide tape show, 1/2" VHS, color, 18 min. $25 to rent slide show with workshop guide or $30 for video and guide. Adults.

This slideshow is part of a whole workshop encouraging the older adult and family members to look ahead and plan for their aging. This particular slideshow is about not putting off decisions until there is a crisis. No particular answers are provided, but the workshop encourages persons to seek alternatives, and then to make decisions. It encourages the family to talk together and work together at problem-solving.

The Dollmaker. Produced by Ruth Stiehl and Vicki Schmall, Oregon State University Extension Service, 1987. Slide tape show, 1/2" VHS, color, 17 min., $25 to rent slide show with workshop guide or $30 for video and guide. Adults.

This slideshow is part of a workshop on the need to prepare and support family caregivers for aging relatives. It depicts the emotional and physical stress that caring for relatives puts on family caregivers. It shows how a primary caregiver can become the victim of the disease even more than the person receiving the care. This is a powerful slideshow that enables persons to talk about caregiving issues and hopefully plan for support and self-care.

In Your Hands: The Tools for Preserving Personal Autonomy. Produced by the American Bar Association's Commission on Legal Problems of the Elderly, 1987. 1/2" VHS, color, 16 min., $18 to rent video includes 50 workbooks for participants. Adults.

This video, narrated by Helen Hayes, is very informative. It discusses advance decision-making tools for financial matters and on health-related matters. The legal tools for financial matters covered are durable power of attorney and trusts. The legal tools for health care covered are medical power of attorney and living wills. This is a good introductory video to use before having a lawyer speak to a group about advanced directives.

A Matter of Life and Death. Produced by West End Video Productions for Older Women's League, 1987. 1/2" VHS, color, 20 min., $25 to purchase (no rental) includes a leader's guide. Adults.

This video is about planning for health care decisions at the end of life. It comes with a leader's guide for a workshop on the same topic. The video introduces the audience to the need for making advance directives and decisions for their future health care now, in case there comes a time when they are no longer able to make those decisions. It encourages people to plan, and informs them of possible advance directives such as the living will and the durable power of attorney.

My Mother, My Father. Produced by Terra Nova Films, 1984. 16mm, 1/2" VHS, color, 33 min. $55 to rent includes a guidebook. Adults.

This is a documentary that shares the lives of four families caregiving for an elderly family member. It shows the stresses, the joys, the conflicts, the emotions, the struggles, and the celebrations of caregiving from a variety of different family settings. There are no easy answers offered in the video, but rather an honest, direct, and compelling view into the needs of four families, as they plan and make decisions about caregiving concerns. It is a good way to initiate discussion around issues that are often hard to raise.

260 Primrose Lane. Produced by Ruth Stiehl and Vicki Schmall, Oregon State University Extension Service, 1987. Slide tape show, 1/2" VHS, color, 18 min. $25 to rent slide show with workshop guide or $30 for video and guide. Adults.
This slide show is part of a workshop on exploring alternative living-arrangement decisions in later life. The video shows three persons who have chosen different living arrangements, and what the decisions have meant for each one of them.

Memories and Remembering

In this section, we will look at some literature on the importance of memory in the later years. These books use the terms "life review" and "reminiscence." "Life review" generally means a systematic, chronological telling of our life story, while "reminiscence" is a more spontaneous telling of life stories. From the literature it is clear that telling our life story is important, allowing us to integrate our experiences into ourselves and accept them, including things that we are proud of and things that we are not. Memories are the gateway to our past. Memories are fun. Locked inside each of us is a lifetime of good times and bad times and in-between times that are worth remembering, learning from, and sharing.

This became personally clear to me when I took an eight-week course at the Jewish Community Center on writing our own stories. I was the only person in the class under sixty-five years of age, and I was forty-five at the time. It was a marvelous experience, not only because of the chance to write my own personal stories, but also because of the gift I received from the others in the class, that of hearing their stories read aloud. We shared many tears and much laughter in the course of those eight weeks.

Sharing personal life stories is also an incredible way to begin to come to an in-depth understanding of other persons, as well as to build bonds between people. The church would do well to encourage storytelling in the congregation, to build a stronger sense of understanding and community among members—personal story sharing enables deeper stronger relationships to develop.

Resources on Memories and Remembering

Boyle, Sarah-Patton. *The Desert Blooms: A Personal Adventure in Growing Old Creatively.* Nashville, TN: Abingdon Press, 1983. 207p. $7.95pa. LC 83-8800. ISBN 0-687-10484-X.
This book describes the author's adventure of growing older, and the growth that took place during years of change.

Dewey, Kirk. *Stories: God's Hand in My Life*. Swarthmore, PA: Support
Source, 1990. 207p. $10.95pa. LC 89-91377. ISBN 0-9619558-2-1.

As one reads this Protestant minister's stories of his life and faith,
one can hardly keep from the challenge he poses to reflect on one's own
life journey. Our thanks to Rev. Dewey's daughter, who commissioned,
edited, and published this book. This book also provides a very positive
model of aging—one man's adventure with life and with growing older.

Geissler, Eugene S. *The Best Is Yet to Be: Life's Meaning in the Aging
Years*. Notre Dame, IN: Ave Maria Press, 1988. lllp. $3.95pa. LC
87-72783. ISBN 0-87793-376-6.

This is a personal look at the author's experiences of growing older,
and the growth and change that took place in his life.

Hateley, B. J. *Telling Your Story, Exploring Your Faith: Writing Your
Life Story for Personal Insight and Spiritual Growth*. St. Louis:
CBP Press, 1985. 117p. $8.95pa. LC 85-13307. ISBN 0-8272-3626-3.

This book can be used for individual work in exploring one's
personal life story to bring about spiritual growth and development, or
it could be used in small groups interested in this area of exploration.
This book is a wealth of materials and exercises. It is not formatted
session by session, so it will take more time on the part of a group leader
to develop sessions for a group. This book works around themes of our
lives—family, work, health, money, death, moral development, and so
on. This book also encourages journaling or writing about one's life.
Anyone interested in analyzing how their faith has shaped their lives,
how God has worked in their lives, and in finding spiritual meaning in
life's everyday experiences would find this a helpful book. It is a helpful
guide for persons on a quest for spiritual understanding of their lives.

Hickman, Martha Whitmore. *Fullness of Time: Short Stories of Women
and Aging*. Nashville, TN: Upper Room Books, 1990. 125p.
$7.95pa. LC 90-70326. ISBN 0-8358-0620-0.

This is a book of short stories about aging and women.

Horlick, Reuben, Lee E. Sharff, and A. R. Suritz. *My Personal Memory
Book*. Washington, DC: Lee, 1976. 108p. $4.95pa. LC 76-026744.

This is a resource for people who want to record their memories to
leave for their families. It asks readers questions about specific periods
of their lives to make writing their personal history easier. There are
quotations from a variety of persons on most pages.

Levy, Judith. *Grandfather Remembers: Memories for My Grandchild*.
New York: Harper & Row, 1986. 64p. $14.95. LC 85-45645. ISBN
0-06-015561-2.

This beautifully illustrated books offers guidance for those who
want to write their life stories to give to their families.

Maclay, Elise. *Green Winter: Celebrations of Old Age*. New York: Reader's Digest Press/McGraw-Hill Books, 1977. 137p. $8.95. LC 76-54239. ISBN 0-07-044617-2.

This is a book of poems, or "word portraits," of older persons. The author creates these word portraits from the heart as she watches and listens to older persons. These are not interviews with or reports on older persons, but insightful glimpses into the depths of people's lives.

Maxwell, Cassandre. *A Legacy for My Loved Ones*. Old Tappan, NJ: Fleming H. Revell, 1984. 94p. $12.95. ISBN 0-8007-1374-5.

This is another title showing readers how to record their life stories for their loved ones. Beautifully illustrated, *A Legacy for My Loved Ones*, has both Hebrew and Christian Scriptures quoted on most pages.

"A Modern Will: Jerusalem, 1963." In *Jewish Reflections on Death*, ed. Jack Riemer. New York: Schocken Books/Pantheon Books/Random House, 1974. 192p. $5.95pa. LC 74-18242. ISBN 0-8052-0516-0.

The modern will is different from a traditional will, one that divides property. Instead, it is a will to leave to each person in the family special gifts of love.

Mulhall, Daniel, and Karen Rowe. *A Time For...: A Six Session, Small Group Discussion Process with Older Adults*. Los Angeles: Franciscan Communications, 1988. 83p. $15.00pa.

This book gives a process that incorporates Scripture readings and thematic life review, giving a variety of exercises from which to choose. The sessions can be shortened or lengthened as needed. This is not a book of Scripture study, rather it encourages people to reflect on their life journeys and connect them with stories from Scripture. Each of the six sessions has step-by-step instructions, but are also very adaptable to different situations. Journaling for individual participants is encouraged. There are many recommended activities for each session, but there is the flexibility for the group leader to use different materials if it seems more appropriate.

"Reminiscence: Reaching Back and Moving Forward." Washington, DC: American Association of Retired Persons, 1989. 4p. free. Order #D13186, Order from Program Resources Dept., AARP. Order from Program Resources Dept., AARP, 601 E. Street NW, Washington, DC 20049.

Reminiscence: Finding Meaning in Memories, Resource Materials. Washington, DC: American Association of Retired Persons, 1989. 71p. $1.00pa. Order #D13405. Order from Program Resources Dept., AARP.

This is a booklet of short articles on what memories mean to us and the usefulness of remembering. One of the articles, by James E. Birren, discusses how autobiography gives meaning to our lives by letting us understand the past. Also included are articles by Dr. Robert Butler, who is one of the grandfathers in the field of aging and in the development of life review specifically. There are articles on life review as a method of pastoral counseling, on the use of sharing life stories as a way to interact with persons in nursing homes, and personal storytelling as a way of encouraging the grieving process. There are also helpful hints on visitation with elderly persons who are grieving, who have hearing problems, or who are depressed. This booklet has a wealth of material and reading of use to people working in congregations with older persons.

Scott-Maxwell, Florida. *The Measure of My Days*. New York: Penguin, 1968. $6.95pa. LC 78-27682. ISBN 0-14-005164-3.

This book is a personal journal kept by a remarkable woman of eighty-two years of age.

Manuals and How-To Books for Creating Senior Adult Ministry

This chapter would not be complete without mention of denominational books on enabling laypersons and clergy to develop senior adult ministries in their congregations and communities. The following are some of these books:

Armstrong, Julie, Lorraine D. Chiaventone, James A. McDaniel, and Thomas B. Robb, eds. *Older Adult Ministry: A Resource for Program Development*. Atlanta, GA: Presbyterian, 1987. 228p. $5.95pa. ISBN 21785429.

This manual is the product of a joint venture of three denominations— United Church of Christ, Presbyterian, U.S.A., and Episcopal Society for Ministry on Aging.

Bergmann, Mark, and Elmer Otte. *Engaging the Aging in Ministry*. St. Louis: Concordia, 1981. 80p. Price not reported. LC 81-314. ISBN 0-570-03833-2.

Custer, Chester E., ed. *The Gift of Maturity*. Nashville, TN: Discipleship Resources, 1986. 37p. $3.50pa. #4310C.

Gentzler, Richard H., Jr. *Designing a Ministry By, With, and For Older Adults*. Nashville, TN: Office of Older Adult Ministries, United Methodist Church, 1993. 58p. $7.95pa.

Kerr, Horace L. *How to Minister to Senior Adults in Your Church*. Nashville, TN: Broadman Press, 1980. 139p. $9.95. LC 77-80944. ISBN 0-8054-3222-1.

Laurello, Bartholomeo J. *Ministering to the Aging: Every Christian's Call*. New York: Paulist Press, 1979. 89p. $2.45pa. LC 79-90992. ISBN 0-8091-2268-5.

Maves, Paul. *Older Volunteers in the Church and Community: A Manual for Ministry*. Valley Forge, PA: Judson Press, 1981. 93p. $6.95pa. LC 80-28093. ISBN 0-8170-0889-6.

Mundahl, Thomas T., and Omar G. Otterness. *Manual for Ministry with Older Persons*. Minneapolis, MN: Augsburg Fortress, 1987. 64p. $6.50pa. #23-62173.

That Thy Days May Be Long in the Good Land: A Guide to Aging Programs for Synagogues. Washington, DC: Synagogue Council of America, 1975. 93p. $1.50pa. Prepared by the Institute for Jewish Policy Planning and Research, and the National Council on the Aging under an AOA Grant.

Weisman, Celia B. *The Future Is Now: A Manual for Older Adult Programs in Jewish Communal Service Agencies*. New York: National Jewish Welfare Board and the Brookdale Foundation, 1976. 176p. Price not reported.

Future Issues in Aging

The growing number of older persons in our society is raising important public policy issues. For example, there have been proposals of limiting health care according to age. Intergenerational equity has become an issue. However, when we make public policy decisions, do we make them only on the basis of who is more powerful in terms of numbers of voters; or do we make them on some moral, ethical basis of what is right for all ages? Is it okay to spend thousands and thousands of dollars keeping an elderly person with very little hope for any quality of life alive, while other persons do not have enough to eat? These are the issues of the future, and the future is here! Religious congregations and persons need to be involved in the public debate that goes on around these concerns, and to bring ethical thought to these issues.

Most hospitals have ethics committees that help make decisions about who gets what forms of health care. Now there is a move to enable the development of these kinds of ethics committees in nursing homes as well. As persons of faith from religious institutions, we should encourage the development of these ethics committees and have a willingness to serve on them.

Resources on Future Issues in Aging

Callahan, Daniel. *Setting Limits: Medical Goals in an Aging Society.*
New York: Simon & Schuster, 1987. 256p. $18.95. LC 87-13029.
ISBN 0-671-22477-8.

Written by the director and co-founder of The Hastings Center, a
renowned center for the study of medical ethics, this is a very controversial book, and one that is guaranteed to challenge your thinking.
Callahan examines the goals of medicine in an aging society, and asks
the hard questions about when we should say no to further treatment,
and fits these kinds of questions into the context of what is good for all
persons, all ages, and all generations.

Ethics Committee Program Kit. Includes a 30-min. video showing an
ethics committee at work, a facilitator's manual, and a participant's
guidebook. $20.00. Order from AARP A/V Programs, Program
Resources Dept./ER.

Longman, Phillip. *Born to Pay: The New Politics of Aging in America.*
Boston: Houghton Mifflin, 1987. 308p. $17.95. ISBN 0-395-383692.

This is a helpful book on thinking through intergenerational equity
issues, and a call to older persons to become statesmen and states-
women to make public policy that provides justice for all persons and
all ages.

Rivlin, Alice M., and Joshua M. Wiener. *Caring for the Disabled
Elderly: Who Will Pay?* Washington, DC: The Brookings Institute,
1988. 318p. $12.95pa. LC 88-10528. ISBN 0-8157-7497-4.

This is a study on long-term care and home care costs, and how
they are currently paid. It is technical reading, but well worth looking
through. It analyzes and makes recommendations for the expansion of
both private long-term care insurance and public insurance programs.

Snyder, Graydon F. *Tough Choices: Health Care Decisions and the
Faith Community.* Elgin, IL: Brethren Press, 1988. 129p. $6.95pa.
ISBN 0-87178-558-7.

This is a very readable, easy to understand, well-written book on
medical ethics and the Christian faith, and would be a good study book
for a small group of senior adults.

Resources

AARP A/V Programs
Program Resources Dept./ER
P.O. Box 19269, Station R
Washington, DC 20036

American Baptist Films/Video
P.O. Box 851
Valley Forge, PA 19482-0851
(215) 768-2306

Distribution Management Service
100 Witherspoon St.
Louisville, KY 40202-1396

EcuFilm
810 Twelfth Ave. South
Nashville, TN 37203
(800) 251-4091

Mass Media Ministries
2116 North Charles Street
Baltimore, MD 21218
(301) 727-3270

Program Resources Dept.
AARP
601 E. Street, N.W.
Washington, DC 20049

References

U.S. Senate Special Committee on Aging. *Aging America: Trends and Projections, 1987-88 Edition*. Order from American Association of Retired Persons Fulfillment, 601 E Street, N.W., Washington, D.C. 20049.

"A Profile of Older Americans," 1994. Order from American Association of Retired Persons Fulfillment, 601 E Street, N.W., Washington, D.C. 20049.

12
Church Libraries: Their History, Organization, and Development

Joyce L. White

Introduction

The term "church library" as used in this essay refers to a library located in a building of a church or parish. It does not include libraries in church-related institutions such as colleges, parochial schools, or seminaries. Their purpose is to support the general education of their particular denomination, including books for both adults and children. Church libraries, though, have the more specific focus of providing books on spiritual growth, church history, liturgy, doctrines, customs, and ecclesiastical arts that are unlikely to be available from the local public library.

Church libraries are on the rise in this country, and the demand for literature on the subject has also grown. Basically, the literature of church libraries falls into two categories: 1) studies on church libraries covering such topics as their history, their development, and the place of church libraries in the larger library field; and 2) literature designed to aid nonprofessional volunteers in the establishment and operation of the library in their own parish church. This article is focused primarily on the latter type of material—manuals and guides about how to start a church library and how to make it function. It is a review of most of the handbooks that are available for the volunteer church librarian, as listed in the current volumes of *Books in Print*.[1]

The material covered in this chapter is arranged according to the process of establishing and running a church library. The general organization is as follows:

General references about church libraries

Organizations that support church librarians

Manuals for administering a church library

Articles on organizing a church library

Manuals dealing with financial and physical issues

Manuals about staffing volunteers in the library and providing reference service

Guides on how to select books and how to prepare them for lending

Books on using audiovisual aids and computers in church libraries

Manuals on promoting the church library

Manuals about archives in the church library

Periodical resources available to help volunteer church librarians in running a library

Growth of church libraries in the twentieth century and their role in the future

General References About Church Libraries

The only title currently available that covers the field of church libraries in general is titled simply *Church and Synagogue Libraries*, by John Harvey (1980). It is a pioneer volume and an important resource describing the state of church-library development, the demography of church libraries, and providing some indications for the future of "one of the library world's newest, largest, and least known fields" (press release). Harvey estimated that there were about 40,000 church libraries in the United States in 1980.

A review of literature on the church library [literature] between 1950 and 1970 was published in "Church Libraries," by Joyce White (1970). This article is of interest to the volunteer librarian who wants to know how and why libraries in local churches developed. It includes a bibliography of published manuals, periodical articles, unpublished studies and theses, a list of organizations and associations that support libraries in their own denominations, and periodicals published by them for the benefit of the volunteer church librarian.

Organizations That Support Church Librarians

Today, most churches have some organized support for their own parish or church libraries. The best known of these denominational library associations are the Parish Libraries Section of the Catholic Library Association, the Lutheran Church Library Association, and the Church Library Department of the Southern Baptist Convention Sunday School Board. All three have published a regular periodical with guidance, tips, and book reviews for more than twenty years. *The Catholic Library World* carries a regular column or page specifically for parish libraries. *Lutheran Libraries* and *The Church Media Magazine* are devoted entirely to church library issues. All are available by subscription.

The Church and Synagogue Library Association (CSLA), an ecumenical, non-denominational organization, was established in 1967 for the benefit of other church librarians. An in-depth article titled "The Church and Synagogue Library Association," by Ruth Smith (1970), was published in the *Encyclopedia of Library and Information Science*. Ruth Smith later authored a piece titled "The Church and Synagogue Library Association: A 10 Year History," which was distributed to the members at the Annual Meeting celebrating the first decade of the association.

CSLA has focused on the publication of manuals and bibliographies designed to aid volunteer church librarians. *Church and Synagogue Libraries,* a substantial periodical that is indexed annually, is published bimonthly. It is available with membership in the association, or separately by subscription.

After deciding to establish a library in one's local church or parish, an immediate question arises: "How do we start?" The first suggestion is to join one of the church-library associations just described. The cost of membership is small, and the benefits of a support group are great. All of these organizations hold local and national workshops and conferences where a volunteer librarian can meet other volunteers with similar questions, and learn hands-on skills. In addition, a periodical will arrive at your library on a regular basis with additional information for operating the library, and reviews of books appropriate for the parish library.

Administering the Library

A number of guides, manuals, and bibliographies are available to provide assistance for the establishment, administration, and operation of a church library. Most have been produced by members of church-library associations established during the twentieth century for the benefit of volunteer librarians.

An outstanding resource is *The Church Librarian's Handbook*, 2d ed., by Betty McMichael (1989). It is a complete guide for the library and resource center in Christian education, including new filing rules compatible with computer data, and current information on sources for computer software for church libraries.

The Key to a Successful Church Library (1982)—a book that is active and serves the needs of the congregation—was first written in 1958 by Erwin E. John, based on his uncharted experience in beginning a church library. The book includes what to do and how to do it—starting a library, convincing the appropriate people of the need for a library, where it should be located, budgeting, accounting, book selection, cataloguing, classification, doing displays, and promoting the library. This work has been revised several times, bringing the total copies to more than 22,000. Tried, true, and still in print, this book is highly recommended.

How to Administer and Promote a Church Media Library, by Jacqulyn Anderson and Dick Ham (1991) is also a good all-purpose manual. It includes advice on organization, staffing, layout, location, book selection, cataloging, and promoting use of the library. Another excellent handbook for the administrator of a church library is *Setting Up a Library: How to Begin or Begin Again*, by Ruth S. Smith (1994). Now in its third edition as CSLA Guide 1, this book not only includes all the standard information about administration, but also guidance for the reorganization of a defunct library, with advice on weeding the collection and building a new spirit of volunteer cooperation.

A good standard work still in print is *The Church Library Workbook: How to Start and Maintain the Church Library*, by Francine Walls (1980). As do most administrative and organizational manuals, this one points out the need to develop a plan of action, enlist support, and secure needed funds to see that the library is maintained. *Maintaining the Congregational Library*, by Dorothy Rodda (1985) is written for the library administrator who needs the skills mentioned previously for a library already organized and running. Last, but by no means least, is a work that has stayed in print for a decade, *Running a Library: Managing the Congregation's Library with Care, Confidence, and Common Sense*, by Ruth Smith (1982). This book, written by one of the most ardent authors in the field, is for the potential volunteer insecure about taking on responsibility of a library and needing a boost of self-confidence to get started.

Standards for Church and Synagogue Libraries (1993) is an essential work for the administrator. Doing library tasks in conformity with standard library practices will make all the difference in the look and efficiency of the library. This manual covers the basics of standard cataloging, which classification system is best for the size of your collection, the standard procedure for ordering books, and the standards for shelf size, in the event that you are having shelving made to order for your library.

In addition to general manuals of operation, several manuals on specific tasks and issues have been published during the past twenty years. These topics include, for example, finance and budget, furnishings and equipment, and training volunteers. Manuals that are devoted to only one routine are also beneficial. They often give greater detail and include illustrations, and it is convenient to have separate guides to give to volunteers who are doing different tasks.

A *Policy and Procedure Manual for Church and Synagogue Libraries*, by George Ruoss (1980) is a good model to use for developing such a manual for your own library.

Organizing the Library

In his book *Advice On Establishing a Library*, Gabriel Naude, a French librarian of the seventeenth century, stated that a room full of books is no more a library than a pile of building materials is a house.[2] Without question, the first task for the volunteer church librarian, too, is organization.

Two periodical articles are clear on the subject: "Organization Is the Key," by Mary Hartman (1988), and "How to Organize a Parish Library," by Irene Pompea (1982). Two equally good manuals for the beginner are *Church Library Organization and Development*, by Anne Dennis (1988), and *How to Organize Your Church Library and Resource Center*, by Mary Hammack (1985).

Financing and Physical Issues for the Library

A, B, C's of Financing Church and Synagogue Libraries, by Claudia Hannaford (1985) was published as CSLA Guide 13. It is clearly written, with effective illustrations, by an author who has both accounting and church-library experience. Hannaford points out the importance of getting the library onto the church budget, and presents good ideas for independent fund-raising. Highly recommended, even for experienced church librarians.

Most general manuals on establishing church libraries devote a chapter to space, location, essential furniture, and equipment. But if you are looking for something specific, *How to Plan Media Library Space and Furnishings*, by Glynn Hill (1983) gives comprehensive coverage to the topic. Obviously, this is a book one needs at the beginning of the process of establishing a library. It helps the reader determine size and location of the library, the shapes and sizes of tables and chairs, and provides guidelines for building bookshelves, including facilities for organizing audiovisual materials. Also, *The Church Library: An Outline of Procedure*, by Callie Milliken (1986) is a valuable manual (with a particularly useful chapter on computer use and layout, by Kent Landrum) for the church library fortunate enough to have its own computer.

Volunteer Staffing for the Library

According to information from surveys done over the past twenty years, virtually 95 percent of all church libraries are run by volunteers. This situation is clearly described in "Volunteers—The Heart of the Parish Library," by Charles Dollen (1976). Another useful article is "A Parish Library Is Only As Good As Its Librarian," by Rod Brownfield (1983). Additionally, the CSLA Guide by Lorraine Burson, titled *Recruiting and Training Volunteers for Church and Synagogue Libraries* (1990), and "The Church Librarian: An Essential Volunteer, Too," by Claudia Hannaford (1984) are extremely useful. These resources suggest ways to accomplish the difficult and important task of recruiting volunteers. Burton points out that some people like to be asked to work in the library, while others respond better to a notice in the church leaflet on Sundays or through the church newsletter. Also, unlike employed staff, volunteers who are displeased about even simple things can be quick to quit. Therefore, patience is important for one volunteer to have for another when supervising tasks and responsibilities.

Providing Reference Service

Actual reference use of a church library is sometimes inadequately represented by the statistics that reflect the circulation of books. Therefore, it is well to highlight for volunteers the theme of two articles that appeared in *Catholic Library World*: "Parish Librarians Are Information Providers" (1984), and "Parish Librarians Are Educators" (1984), both by Mary Hartman. A guide published by the Church and Synagogue Library Association titled *Providing Reference Service in Church and Synagogue Libraries*, by Jennifer Pritchett (1987) is an excellent handbook for training volunteers, and a useful guide for selecting essential reference books for the collection.

Selecting Books for the Library

Another basic reference tool for the volunteer church librarian is *Church and Synagogue Library Resources*, by Rachel Kohl and Dorothy Rodda (1984), a CSLA guide now in its 4th edition. It includes addresses of supply houses, publishers, specialized organizations, and some bibliographies of standard reference books for almost any collection. A companion publication is *A Basic Book List for Church Libraries* (1991), now in its 3rd revised edition, compiled by Bernard Deitrick, the former book review editor of *Church and Synagogue Libraries*.

Subject Bibliographies

Several topical bibliographies on the market have become standards in their field. For example, *The Bible in Church and Synagogue Libraries*, by William Gentz (1989) was published as CSLA Guide 16. It presents a controlled selection of texts, commentaries, dictionaries, atlases, and other Bible-related books from which to build a Bible section in the library. *The Jewish Book of Books: A Reader's Guide to Judaism*, by Ruth Frank and W. Wollheim (1986) is the most practical and authoritative guide available to the best books on Judaism. It includes listings of Bibles, books about the Bible, books on Jewish life and customs, secular history, archeology, Jewish thought, reference books, and children's books.

For the ecumenical section of the library, *Know Your Neighbor's Faith*, by Bernard Dietrick (1983) is essential. This annotated bibliography consists of books whose authors are presenting an introduction to their own churches for the benefit of non-members.

Helping Children Through Books: A Selected Booklist, by Patricia Pearl (1990) is the newest revision of a very popular title providing bibliotherapy for children coping with social situations such as divorce, death, grief, or terminal illness. Another excellent annotated bibliography of juvenile books on religious subjects in general, also in a new edition, is *Religious Books for Children*, by Patricia Dole (1993), compiled by the same person, but now with a new name. A new, timely bibliography is *Books for Teens: Stressing the Higher Values*, by Edith Tyson (1993). It is a useful selection tool for young people from grades seven through twelve. Fictional titles are included in such genres as biblical, contemporary, fantasy, science fiction, historical, and short stories.

Another specialized manual is *Developing a Church Music Library*, by Jacqulyn Anderson and Dick Ham (1989). It is useful for organizing either a separate music collection or the music section of the church library. An article by Martha Powell, "Twenty-Five Books on Hymns for the Church Library" (1983), is an annotated bibliography that could be copied and referred to from time to time when building the music section. But if you are overwhelmed with selecting books, find the article by Lorraine Burson (1990) titled "Book Selection; A Growing Headache" for help. It's guaranteed to bring relief.

Using Audiovisual Aids and Computers

During the 1970s, audiovisual materials became popular, particularly as instructional aids in curriculum planning. The library, being closely linked to the educational program, was the obvious place for the collection of this new material. However, because the format of audiovisual materials was distinctly different from books, some librarians felt that they should have a home of their own. The issue is addressed in the articles "Diocesan A-V Library: To Be or Not To Be," by Mary

Hartman (1985), and "Parish Video Libraries," by Angela Zukowski (1990). Some libraries with print and nonprint materials changed their name to "resource" or "media" center to emphasize their inclusion of audiovisual materials.

Margaret Korty was among the leaders in helping church librarians tackle a new media. She produced one of the first manuals in 1977, *Audio Visual Materials in the Church Library: How to Select, Catalog, Process, Store, Circulate and Promote*. It is now revised and updated (1992).

Making use of the teaching advantages of audiovisual aids, Jacqulyn Anderson, Head of the Church Library Department of the Southern Baptist Sunday School Board, developed a useful set of 4 audio cassettes with worksheets, titled *Media Library Techniques* (rev. 1986). The cassettes are a vocal guide literally telling the church librarian, step by step, how to handle and organize audiovisual materials.

Undoubtedly, the most obvious trend in the past ten years is the ubiquitous computer. As computers come into popular use in the church office, they naturally became incorporated into the library. Michele Blackman undertook an exploratory survey of 122 churches based on replies from attendees at the national CSLA conference in 1985. Her result showed that, in forty cases, computers were used in the church office, but not in the church library. However, in six cases, although there was no computer in the church office, the church librarian was making use of one. Blackman also collected other statistical data about the libraries, such as size of the collections, budgets, classification schemes, and so on. The work "Computer Use in Congregational Libraries" was submitted as a thesis at the University of California in 1986.

Although many library processes are computer adaptable, by far the greatest library benefit is the production of catalog cards. The husband of a church librarian developed just such a program, so his wife would not have to type so much, but it was too good to keep in the family. Dale Pritchett and Jennifer Pritchett placed the program on the market under the name *Librarian's Helper: A Productivity Tool for Librarians,* Version 5 (1989). The program follows AACR II rules, and comes with a data file and manual. In addition to producing sets of catalog cards with standard layout, the program has the capacity to produce labels for the books, as well as customized bibliographies. Because it is designed for nonprofessional, volunteer librarians, absolutely no church library should be without the program.

Church-library association periodicals now carry many articles about the use of computers in church libraries. *Church and Synagogue Libraries, Lutheran Libraries*, and *The Church Media Magazine* all publish helpful articles on the subject for the volunteer church librarian. A particularly good article is "Computers and the Parish Library," by Mary Hartman (1987), which appeared in *Catholic Library World*.

Cataloging and Classifying Books

Two manuals by Dorothy Kersten, published in 1990, are *Classifying Library Materials for Church or Synagogue*, and *Subject Headings for Church or Synagogue Libraries*. Another useful title is *Cataloging Made Easy*, by Ruth Smith (1987). All three titles were issued as CSLA Guides. Together they form a complete set of technical processing manuals that include chapters dealing with audiovisual materials. Another essential resource is the *Dewey Decimal Classification: 200 Religion Class* (1989), published by Forest Press. This is the best scheme to use for classifying a church library because it is simple and familiar. Homemade schemes only run into trouble as libraries grow, and such schemes are almost always unclear to users of the library.

Promoting the Church Library

The need for promotion is probably more acute for church libraries than for any other type. Free space in the church building, and volunteer time to run the building, are justified only if they serve the library's function by attracting voluntary use. It is not surprising, therefore, that a very large proportion of literature about church libraries falls into this category. Essentially, the promotion literature is divided into two types: that which promotes the concept of a church library, exemplified by "Every Church Needs a Library and Here's Where To Get Help," by William Gentz (1978); and that which promotes the use of a library already established in the local church.

To help in the latter case, *Getting the Books off the Shelves*, by Ruth Smith (1991) has been a standard for more than a decade. Chapters include ideas for book parties, reading circles, displays on book trucks at coffee hour, special collections in classrooms to support a study topic, and, of course, use of bulletin boards. *Church Library Promotion: A Handbook of How-To's*, by Ginger Caughman (1990) also is a useful work, with substantial illustrations. A specific publication on bulletin boards, *Planning Bulletin Boards for Church and Synagogue Libraries*, by Janell Paris (1984) was issued as a CSLA Guide. The manual is well done, with lots of illustrations highlighting religious themes. *Promotion Planning*, by Claudia Hannaford and Ruth Smith (1982) is a revised edition of an earlier work. The ideas and techniques described in this book are timeless. It is highly recommended as a CSLA Guide—authored by two enthusiasts, both of whom have written independently on the subject. *Promotion Handbook for Church Media Libraries*, by Mancil Ezell and Charles Businaro (1983) also is an excellent work, with good illustrations and ideas.

In 1980, Angela E. Weyhautt studied "User Expectations of a Church Library" as the topic for her thesis at the University of Northern Illinois. Although it is unpublished, it is well worth writing to the University of Northern Illinois for a copy, because it is the only item of its kind available. Following the same idea, *How to Expand Media*

Library Service, by Keith Mee (1983) is aimed at promoting the library by meeting the needs of the people who use it.

Handling Archives in the Church Library

As a result of the national bicentennial in 1976, many churches began to take interest in their own history. Parishes and local churches were faced with the problem of where to put, and how to handle, old papers that for years had been packed in boxes in the church basement. The library seemed to be the obvious choice. Volunteer church librarians needed instruction about the care and housing of archives—dealing with papers and letters rather than books. Manuals and workshops were provided by church library associations and by the Religious Archives Section within the Society of American Archivists.

One highly recommended manual is *Religious Archives: An Introduction*, by August Suelflow (1980), a giant in the field of church archives. This manual is a timeless resource, one that will never become dated. It is useful for all levels of religious archive collections; simple enough for the local church, with enough expansion for a national depository. Another excellent handbook is *Archives in the Church and Synagogue Library*, by Evelyn Ling (1981). It was published as one in the series of the CSLA Guides. An unpublished thesis by Ronald Baker, "The Beulah Alliance Church Archives: A Model for the Arrangement and Description of Local Church Archives," (1986) is intended to be a pattern for archivists putting together a manual for use in their own church libraries. Copies can be obtained from the School of Library and Information Science at the University of Alberta.

As a result of interest in and support of church archives, many church libraries now proudly house a Heritage Collection.

Histories of Church Library Associations

Although the field of church libraries in the current sense is still very young, it has reached some standard milestones. The growth and continuity of voluntary associations such as the Lutheran Church Library Association, the Parish Libraries Section of the Catholic Library Association, and the Church and Synagogue Library Association demonstrate a strongly-grounded dedication to the concept of church libraries. All three of these associations have celebrated their twenty-fifth anniversaries.

The History of the Catholic Library Association: The First Sixty Years, by Jane Hindman (1982) covers the establishment and growth of the association from 1921 to 1981. Included in this period is the establishment in 1956 of the Parish Libraries Section.

The Church and Synagogue Library Association: A 10 Year History was written by Ruth Smith, first president of the Association, and distributed at the annual conference of the Association in 1977. In it, she recounts from personal experience the detailed background of

CSLA's establishment. Ten years later, Dorothy Rodda, Executive Secretary of the Association, updated the history with *The Church and Synagogue Library Association: A 20 Year History* (1987).

The 25th-Anniversary (1958–1983) issue of *Lutheran Libraries* (Summer 1983) carries a brief history of the Lutheran Church Library Association. In the article "He Had a Dream," Marian Johnson highlights the vision of Erwin E. John and his friends—to establish libraries in Lutheran churches.

The Church Library Department of the Southern Baptist Sunday School Board has supported the development of libraries in their churches through a paid staff at headquarters, and through publications for more than thirty years.

Periodicals for church-library volunteers issuing from all these associations result in a substantial number of newsletters, magazines, and journals. *Church and Synagogue Libraries, The Church Media Library Magazine, Lutheran Libraries,* and *Catholic Library World* (with its regular column of "Parish Libraries") also have histories of their own, covering more than two decades. These periodicals are well established and are received regularly by their subscribers.

Growth of Church Libraries

From 1970 to 1990, church-library literature has increased by 33 percent over the period from 1950 to 1970. Of fifty manuals now available for church librarians, half cover eight different specialized tasks and procedures. Likewise, papers and theses from academic institutions have doubled in number, and cover nine areas of specialized study. Periodical articles also show an increase. Articles on the subject of church libraries have appeared in fourteen professional library journals, as compared with only six during the previous twenty-year period. In addition, articles about church libraries have also appeared in several non-library oriented periodicals.

The fact that articles about church libraries have increased in professional library journals signals a growing trend of professional library recognition. Also indicative of this trend are sessions devoted to the subject of church libraries at state library associations.

The Role and Future of Church Libraries

Two concepts imbedded in literature about church libraries are the vision of church librarianship as a specialized ministry, and the church library as a specialized religious library to serve the whole community.

The idea of librarianship as a specialized ministry within the church is still in the infant stage. Nevertheless, there are people speculating on a structure that provides for an established volunteer position on the church or parish staff under the Director of Religious Education.

A few articles are stating that church libraries must begin to view themselves as special libraries within the total library world. They must not try to be (nor thought of as being) mini public libraries or major religious repositories. They must be focused on supporting the programs of their parent churches. They must also provide religious resources for their members that are unlikely to be available at the local public library.

However, working in concert with their public library, church libraries in a community could provide a substantial resource of religious books. The trend toward the separation of religion from publicly-funded institutions begun in America during the latter half of the twentieth century, continues to reduce religious literature in both school and public libraries. The role of the church library, therefore, becomes increasingly important, not only to members of the local church, but to the communities in which they are located.

Notes

1. "Libraries, Church," in *Books in Print: Subject Guide*, vol. 3 (New Providence, NJ: R. R. Bowker, 1993/94).

2. Gabriel Naude, *Advice on Establishing a Library* (Berkeley: University of California Press, 1950), 63.

References

Anderson, Jacqulyn, and Dick Ham. *Developing a Church Music Library.* Rev. ed. Nashville, TN: Convention Press, 1989.

———. *How to Administer and Promote a Church Media Library.* Nashville, TN: Broadman Press, 1985.

———. *Media Library Techniques: A Set of 4 Sound Cassettes With Worksheets.* Rev. ed. Nashville, TN: Broadman Press, 1986.

Baker, Ronald J. "Beulah Alliance Church Archives: A Model for the Arrangement and Description of Local Church Archives." Thesis, University of Alberta, Faculty of Library and Information Studies, 1986.

Blackman, Michelle R. "Computer Use in Congregational Libraries: An Exploratory Survey." Thesis, University of California at Los Angeles, Graduate School of Library and Information Science, 1986.

Brownfield, Rod. "A Parish Library Is Only As Good As Its Librarian." *Catholic Library World* 54 (April 1983): 373–76.

Burson, Lorraine E. "Book Selection; A Growing Headache." *Christian Education Today* 42 (Winter 1990): 12–14.

———. *Recruiting and Training Volunteers for Church and Synagogue Libraries*. (CSLA Guide 14). Bryn Mawr, PA: Church and Synagogue Library Association, 1986.

Caughman, Ginger. *Church Library Promotion: A Handbook of How-To's*. Portland, OR: Church and Synagogue Library Association, 1990.

Deitrick, Bernard E. *A Basic Book List for Church Libraries*. 3d rev. ed. Portland, OR: Church and Synagogue Library Association, 1991.

———. *Know Your Neighbor's Faith: An Annotated Bibliography*. Bryn Mawr, PA: Church and Synagogue Library Association, 1983.

Dennis, Anne W. *Church Library Organization and Development*. Independence, OH: A. W. Dennis, 1988.

Dewey Decimal Classification: 200 (Religion) Class. Albany, NY: Forest Press, 1989.

Dole, Patricia Pearl. *Religious Books for Children: An Annotated Bibliography*. Rev. ed. Portland, OR: Church and Synagogue Library Association, 1993.

Dollen, Charles. "Volunteers: The Heart of the Parish Library." *Catholic Library World* 48 (October 1976): 131.

Ezell, Mancil, and Charles Businaro. *Promotion Handbook for Church Media Libraries*. Nashville, TN: Convention Press, 1983.

Frank, Ruth S., and W. Wollheim. *The Book of Jewish Books: A Reader's Guide to Judaism*. San Francisco: Harper & Row, 1986.

Gentz, William H. *The Bible in Church and Synagogue Libraries*. (CSLA Guide 16). Portland, OR: Church and Synagogue Library Association, 1989.

———. "Every Church Needs a Library, and Here's Where to Get Help." *Living Church* 178 (May 1978).

Hammack, Mary L. *How to Organize Your Church Library and Resource Center*. Valley Forge, PA: Judson Press, 1985.

Hannaford, Claudia. *A, B, C's of Financing Church and Synagogue Libraries: Acquiring Funds, Budgeting, Cash Accounting*. (CSLA Guide 13). Portland, OR: Church and Synagogue Library Association, 1985.

———. "The Church Librarian: An Essential Volunteer." *Catholic Library World* 56 (December 1984): 217–22.

———. "The Church Librarian: An Essential Volunteer, Too." *Catholic Library World* 56 (1982): 217–22.

Hannaford, Claudia, and Ruth Smith. *Promotion Planning.* 2d ed. (CSLA Guide 2). Bryn Mawr, PA: Church and Synagogue Library Association, 1982.

Hartman, Mary L. "The Diocesan A-V Library: To Be or Not To Be." *Catholic Library World* 56 (March 1985): 319–20.

———. "Organization is the Key." *Catholic Library World* 59 (January/February 1988): 155.

———. "Parish Librarians Are Educators." *Catholic Library World* 56 (March 1984): 207–8.

———. "Parish Librarians Are Information Providers." *Catholic Library World* 55 (May/June 1984): 430.

———. "Why Your Parish Needs a Librarian." *Today's Parish* 14 (April/May 1982): 46.

Harvey, John F., ed. *Church and Synagogue Libraries.* Metuchen, NJ: Scarecrow Press, 1980.

Hill, Glynn T. *How to Plan Media Library Space and Furnishings.* Nashville, TN: Sunday School Board of the Southern Baptist Convention, 1983.

Hindman, Jane F. *History of the Catholic Library Association: The First Sixty Years, 1921–1981.* Haverford, PA: Catholic Library Association, 1982.

John, Erwin E. *The Key to a Successful Church Library.* Minneapolis, MN: Augsburg Fortress, 1982.

Johnson, Marion. "He Had a Dream." *Lutheran Libraries* 25, no. 3 (Summer 1983): 2–3.

Kersten, Dorothy B. *Classifying Church or Synagogue Library Materials.* Rev. ed. (CSLA Guide 7). Portland, OR: Church and Synagogue Library Association, 1990. 20p.

———. *Subject Headings for Church or Synagogue Libraries.* Rev. ed. (CSLA Guide 8). Portland, OR: Church and Synagogue Library Association, 1990.

Kohl, Rachel, and Dorothy Rodda, comps. *Church and Synagogue Library Resources.* 4th ed. Bryn Mawr, PA: Church and Synagogue Library Association, 1984.

Korty, Margaret. *Audio Visual Materials in the Church Library: How to Select, Catalog, Process, Store, Circulate and Promote*. Riverdale, MD: Church Library Council, 1977; rev. ed., 1992.

Ling, Evelyn R. *Archives in the Church or Synagogue Library*. (CSLA Guide 10). Bryn Mawr, PA: Church and Synagogue Library Association, 1981.

McMichael, Betty. *The Church Librarian's Handbook*. 2d ed. Grand Rapids, MI: Baker, 1989.

Mee, Keith. *How to Expand Media Library Services*. Nashville, TN: Sunday School Board of the Southern Baptist Convention, 1983.

Milliken, Callie Faye. *The Church Library: An Outline of Procedure*. Abilene, TX: Milliken, 1986.

Paris, Janell A. *Planning Bulletin Boards for Church and Synagogue Libraries*. (CSLA Guide 11). Bryn Mawr, PA: Church and Synagogue Library Association, 1984.

Pearl, Patricia. *Helping Children Through Books: A Selected Booklist*. Rev. ed. Portland, OR: Church and Synagogue Library Association, 1990.

Pompea, Irene. "How to Organize a Parish Library." *Today's Parish* 14 (April/May 1982): 44–45.

Powell, Martha C. "Twenty-Five Books on Hymns for the Church Library." *Hymn* 34 (April 1983): 85–88.

Pritchett, Jennifer. *Librarian's Helper: A Productivity Tool for Librarians*. Version 5. Metuchen, NJ: Scarecrow Press, 1989. 1 data file and manual.

———. *Providing Reference Service in Church and Synagogue Libraries*. (CSLA Guide 15). Bryn Mawr, PA: Church and Synagogue Library Association, 1987.

Rodda, Dorothy, comp. *Church and Synagogue Library Association: A 20 Year History*. Bryn Mawr, PA: Church and Synagogue Library Association, 1987.

Rodda, Dorothy. *Maintaining the Congregational Library*. (CSLA Guide). Bryn Mawr, PA: Church and Synagogue Library Association, 1985.

Ruoss, George Martin. *A Policy and Procedure Manual for Church and Synagogue Libraries*. (CSLA Guide 9). Bryn Mawr, PA: Church and Synagogue Library Association, 1980.

Smith, Ruth S. *Cataloging Made Easy: How to Organize Your Congregation's Library*. (CSLA Guide 5). Portland, OR: Church and Synagogue Library Association, 1987.

———. *Setting Up a Library: How to Begin or Begin Again*. (CSLA Guide 1). Bryn Mawr, PA: Church and Synagogue Library Association, 1994.

———. "Church and Synagogue Library Association." *Encyclopedia of Library and Information Science* 4: 674–81. New York: Marcel Dekker, 1970.

———. *Church and Synagogue Library Association: A 10 Year History*. Bryn Mawr, PA: Church and Synagogue Library Association, 1977.

———. *Getting the Books off the Shelves*. (CSLA Guide 12). 2d rev. ed. Portland, OR: Church and Synagogue Library Association, 1991.

———. *Running a Library; Managing the Congregation's Library with Care, Confidence, and Common Sense*. New York: Harper & Row, 1982.

———. *Standards for Church and Synagogue Libraries: Guidelines for Measuring Effectiveness and Progress*. (CSLA Guide 6). Portland, OR: Church and Synagogue Library Association, 1993.

Suelflow, August R. *Religious Archives: An Introduction*. Chicago: Society of American Archivists, 1980.

Tyson, Edith S. *Books for Teens: Stressing the Higher Values*. Portland, OR: Church and Synagogue Library Association, 1993.

Walls, Francine E. *Church Library Workbook: How to Start and Maintain the Church Library*. Winona Lake, IN: Light and Life Press, 1980.

Weyhautt, Angela E. "User Expectations of a Church Library." (Course 571: Paper 329). Northern Illinois University, Department of Library and Information Studies, 1980.

White, Joyce L. "Church Libraries." In *Encyclopedia of Library and Information Science*, edited by Allen Kent and Harold Lancour, vol. 4: 662–73. New York: Marcel Dekker, 1970.

Zukowski, Angela Ann, Sr. "Parish Video Libraries." *Catholic Library World* 61 (January/February 1990): 160–63.

Author/Title Index

455

Subject Index

A Press, 389
AACRII rules, 445
AARP. *See* American Association of
  Retired Persons
Abbasid caliphs, 144-46
Abbasid dynasty, 145
Abbasids, 151
Abbas I Shah, 149, 150
Abbas II Shah, 149, 150
Abdelmalik, 144
Abdul Baha, 156
Abdullah Malik ibn-Anas, 133, 140
Abortion, 189, 367
Abraham, 74, 133, 135
Abu Bakr, 133, 142, 143
Abu Jafer, 144
Abu Muslim Marwazi, 144
Abu Talib, 133
Abu-Hanifah, 141
Abuse
  by male clergy, 254
  sexual violence and, 253
  of women, 252
Academy of Geneva, 396
Acholi people, 24
Acosmic traditions, 13
Act of Toleration (1672), 397
Action
  audio resources on contemplation
    and, 109
  and contemplation, 105-7
  and prayer, 127
  resources on contemplation and,
    107-9
Action-reflection, 370
Activism, 106
Acts of the Apostles, 53
Aden Protectorate, 158
Adi Granth, 31, 32
Adult daycare, 427
Adult education, 358
Advaita Vedanta tradition, 21, 28
Advanced directive documents, 428
Africa, 14, 24-25, 264
  Islam in, xxiv
  Muslims in, 131, 132
  Shafiites in, 140
  voices of women from, 184-86

African American religious literature
  and history of African Ameri-
    can religious tradition, 254-67
  introduction to, 263
  outside main Christian tradition,
    273-74
  on Martin Luther King Jr., 271-73
  and spirituality in African tradi-
    tion, 270-71
African Methodist Episcopal Church,
  269
African traditions, 13, 23, 24-25
African-Americans
  spirituality of, xxv, xxvi. *See also*
    Blacks
Ageism, 250, 419
Aging, xxix, 325
Aging and religion
  audio visual resources on aging,
    419-22
  caregiving and aging, 426-31
  future issues in aging, 435-36
  introduction to, 412-14
  manuals and how-to books for
    senior adult ministry,
    434-35
  memories and remembering, 431-34
  resources on, 436-37
  spiritual growth and aging, 422-26
  understanding aging issues, 414-22
Aghlabid dynasty, 145
Ahad (the Unity), 142
Ahimsa, 30
Ahmad ibn-Hanbal, 140
Ahmadiyya Movement (Qadianism),
  xxiv-xxv, 152, 153-55, 156,
  157. *See also* Islam
Ahriman, 132
Ahura Mazda, 41
AIDS
  impact on women and persons of
    color, 256
A.I.M. *See* Alliance for International
  Monasticism
Akan of Ghana, 24
Akbar, Emperor, 148
al-Abbas, Abu, 144
al-Adawiyyah, Rabiah, 141
al-Amri, Uthman, 151